Brian Loesgen
Charles Young
Jan Eliasen
Scott Colestock
Anush Kumar
Jon Flanders

Microsoft® BizTalk® Server 2010

UNLEASHED

 800 East 96th Street, Indianapolis, Indiana 46240 USA

Microsoft® BizTalk® Server 2010 Unleashed

ISBN-13: 978-0-672-33118-3

ISBN-10: 0-672-33118-7

Library of Congress Cataloging-in-Publication data is on file

Printed in the United States of America

First Printing September 2011

Trademarks

All terms mentioned in this book that are known to be trademarks or service marks have been appropriately capitalized. Pearson Education, Inc. cannot attest to the accuracy of this information. Use of a term in this book should not be regarded as affecting the validity of any trademark or service mark.

Warning and Disclaimer

Every effort has been made to make this book as complete and as accurate as possible, but no warranty or fitness is implied. The information provided is on an "as is" basis. The author and the publisher shall have neither liability nor responsibility to any person or entity with respect to any loss or damages arising from the information contained in this book.

Bulk Sales

Pearson offers excellent discounts on this book when ordered in quantity for bulk purchases or special sales. For more information, please contact:

U.S. Corporate and Government Sales
1-800-382-3419
corpsales@pearsontechgroup.com

For sales outside of the U.S., please contact:

International Sales
+1-317-581-3793
international@pearsontechgroup.com

Editor-in-Chief
Greg Wiegand

Executive Editor
Neil Rowe

Development Editor
Mark Renfrow

Managing Editor
Kristy Hart

Project Editor
Andy Beaster

Copy Editor
Keith Cline

Indexer
Lisa Stumpf

Proofreader
Apostrophe Editing Services

Technical Editor
Gijsbert in 't Veld

Publishing Coordinator
Cindy Teeters

Book Designer
Gary Adair

Compositor
Gloria Schurick

Contents at a Glance

Table of Contents

About the Authors

Brian Loesgen is a Principal Architect Evangelist with Microsoft on the Azure ISV team. Based in San Diego, Brian is a six-time Microsoft MVP and has extensive experience in building sophisticated enterprise, ESB, and SOA solutions. Brian was a key architect/developer of the "Microsoft ESB Guidance," initially released by Microsoft October 2006. He is a coauthor of the *SOA Manifesto* and is a coauthor of eight books, including *SOA with .NET and Windows Azure*, and is the lead author of *BizTalk Server 2010 Unleashed*. He has written technical white papers for Intel, Microsoft, and others. Brian has spoken at numerous major technical conferences worldwide. Brian is a cofounder and past-president of the International .NET Association (ineta.org), and past-president of the San Diego .NET user group, where he continues to lead the Architecture SIG, and is a member of the editorial board for the *.NET Developer's Journal*. Brian has been blogging since 2003 at http://blog.BrianLoesgen.com, and you can find him on Twitter as @BrianLoesgen.

Charles Young, MVP, MCPD, is a principal consultant at Solidsoft, an independent integration specialist working with BizTalk Server and related technologies. He has been a professional developer for a quarter of a century, worked for several years as a technical trainer, and has more than a decade of experience as a consultant. Charles has worked extensively with BizTalk Server since joining Solidsoft in 2003. He architects, designs, and implements enterprise-level integration applications for public- and private-sector customers, delivers seminars and workshops, and maintains a blog site. In recent years he has specialized in the area of decision systems and business rule processing and is vice-chair of Rules Fest, an annual technical conference for developers and researchers involved in the implementation of reasoning systems.

Jan Eliasen, MVP, MCTS, has a Master of Science degree in Computer Science and has been in the IT industry since 2003, currently working at Logica as an IT architect, focusing on delivering solutions to customers that meet the customers' needs. He started working with BizTalk 2002 just after graduation in 2003 and has been working with BizTalk ever since. He has passed the exams in BizTalk 2000, 2004, 2006, 2006R2, and 2010 and is a five-time MVP in BizTalk Server. He is a well-known contributor on the online MSDN forums and a blogger at http://blogs.eliasen.dk/technical/. You can follow him on Twitter as @jan_eliasen.

Scott Colestock lives and works in Minnesota. He has consulted on BizTalk, WCF, CQRS architecture, Agile methods, and general performance engineering. Recently, he has focused deeply on mobile and SaaS architectures using Windows Azure. He is an MVP and frequent speaker at conference events.

Anush Kumar is the chief technology officer at S3Edge (www.s3edge.com), a software solutions company focused on Auto-ID technologies, which he helped cofound following a distinguished career at Microsoft that spanned closed to a decade of working on multiple incubations from concept to shipping. In his last avatar at Microsoft, Anush was BizTalk RFID's leading light from early incubation of the project to its recent productization efforts, and has been heavily involved in the design and architecture of the RFID product, with multiple patents to his name. His efforts have also resulted in the vibrant partner and customer ecosystem for the product, and he is a sought-after speaker and thought leader in this space.

Prior to RFID, Anush worked on the business rules engine for BizTalk Server 2004, technology that has been deployed by several enterprise customers to improve agility and increase efficiency of their business processes. In his spare time, Anush enjoys backpacking off the beaten track; volunteers for organizations focused on education; and is a huge fan of Malcolm Gladwell, Guy Kawasaki, cricket, cooking, bungee jumping, and of course, All Things RTVS™ (http://rtvs.wordpress.com), his blog that spans RFID, and more! Anush holds a Bachelor of Engineering degree in Computer Science from University of Madras and a Master degree in Engineering from Dartmouth College.

Jon Flanders is a member of the technical staff at MCW, where he focuses on connected systems technologies. Jon is most at home spelunking, trying to figure out how things work from the inside out. Jon is the author of *RESTful .NET* and *ASP Internals*, and was a coauthor of *Mastering Visual Studio.NET*. Jon's current major interest is helping people to understand the advantages of REST and how REST connects to products such as SharePoint 2010. You can read his blog at http://www.rest-ful.net/

Dedications

I would like to dedicate this to my family, and to all the friends I've made over the years in the BizTalk community. I also want to thank the members of the stellar author team for all the hard work and effort they put in to make this book happen, and the team at Sams Publishing for making it all possible in the first place.
—Brian Loesgen

To the four girls and one boy in my life who amaze me by their care and love for each other and for me.
—Charles Young

This book is dedicated to my loving and caring wife, Helle, and our two sons, Andreas and Emil. Thank you for all your support when I was writing this book.
—Jan Eliasen

Thank to my beautiful wife, Tracy, and our fantastic kids (Nathan, Grant, Grace, and Anna) for your patience during Saturday and late-night writing sessions.
—Scott Colestock

The book is dedicated to all the guys and gal at S3Edge: I salute the tireless dedication and passion that's made our little start-up so much more than a place to work. To Mom and Dad for putting up with me through all the years To my lovely wife, Melissa, thank you for always being there for me, darling, and letting me live my dream…. And finally to Ambuloo, your turn now, sis!
—Anush Kumar

Acknowledgments

My thanks to Johan Hedberg, a solution architect at Enfo Zystems, who helps run the fabulous BizTalk User Group in Sweden, and who thoroughly reviewed the rules processing content. His feedback was invaluable and much appreciated. My thanks, also, to Gijs in 't Veld at Covast who played such a crucial role in reviewing the book as a whole, to the team at Pearson, to my sister Dorothy who doesn't know what BizTalk Server is, but is first in line to buy a copy of the book, and to my colleagues at Solidsoft who always ensure I keep my feet firmly planted in the real world of EAI.

—Charles Young

First, I want to thank my wife, Helle, and my children, Andreas and Emil. Thank you, Helle, for allowing me to spend all that time writing this book, and thank you for forcing me to keep writing even when I was tired of writing. Andreas and Emil, I am sorry for all the time I could not spend with you. Thank you for putting up with me, though.

Second, a big thank-you to Microsoft MVP Randal van Splunteren, who did me a personal favor by reviewing my stuff so that it wasn't too bad when I handed it in for the official review. And getting to that, also a thank-you to Microsoft MVP Gijs in 't Veld for doing the official review. And from the reviewers to the publisher: Thanks to Brook Farling for looking me up to begin with; thanks to Neil Rowe for taking over from Brook; and a big thanks to all involved at Sams.

Third, a thanks must go to the other authors (Brian, Charles, Scott, Jon, and Anush) for joining this team and writing their stuff, and a thanks also goes to my boss, Michael Hermansen, and my employer, Logica, for allowing me to spend time on this project.

Finally, another very big thanks to my wife, Helle.

—Jan Eliasen

Though I was only responsible for the two chapters on RFID, this would not have been possible for a first-time author without a stellar support cast in the background, starting with Ram Venkatesh, my colleague at S3Edge and the primary inspiration behind nudging me down the "authoring" path. The RFID chapters would not have been possible without your selfless help and guidance. So, many thanks, my friend! A big thank-you to Clint Tennill from Xterprise, and Gijs for their time and effort to review and provide invaluable feedback. To Brian and the rest of the veteran authoring crew, thanks for the opportunity to be part of this; you guys totally rock! And finally to Mark, Andy, Neil, and the rest of the crew at Pearson, thanks for your tireless efforts in getting us to the finish line; you guys have been consummate professionals all through the process, and just great to work with.

—Anush

We Want to Hear from You!

As the reader of this book, *you* are our most important critic and commentator. We value your opinion and want to know what we're doing right, what we could do better, what areas you'd like to see us publish in, and any other words of wisdom you're willing to pass our way.

You can email or write me directly to let me know what you did or didn't like about this book—as well as what we can do to make our books stronger.

Please note that I cannot help you with technical problems related to the topic of this book, and that due to the high volume of mail I receive, I might not be able to reply to every message.

When you write, please be sure to include this book's title and author as well as your name and phone or email address. I will carefully review your comments and share them with the author and editors who worked on the book.

Email: feedback@samspublishing.com

Mail: Neil Rowe
         Executive Editor
         Sams Publishing
         800 East 96th Street
         Indianapolis, IN 46240 USA

Reader Services

Visit our website and register this book at informit.com/register for convenient access to any updates, downloads, or errata that might be available for this book.

Foreword

In 2010, we celebrated two significant milestones—it marked both the 10-year anniversary of BizTalk and the release of BizTalk Server 2010. Over the past decade, there have been seven releases of Microsoft's enterprise integration platform, and it's become the most broadly deployed integration middleware technology on the planet (with nearly 12,000 customers worldwide). A key reason for this impressive growth was due to the explosion of the industry use of web services over the past decade; BizTalk Server helped fill a critical need as our customers began to transition from the world of client-server systems to service-oriented architectures. BizTalk Server was commonly used by our customers to service-enable existing LOB systems and extend the value of existing IT assets into newer applications.

As we look forward to the next decade, it's clear that we're beginning a similar magnitude of platform shift as the industry moves toward cloud computing. Although many are still grappling with how to begin the journey to the cloud, it's a matter of when they move not if—the long-term economic benefits to move to a public cloud computing model are undeniable, providing both cost-savings and simultaneous benefits in terms of business agility and ability for innovation. However, for most customers this journey will be a measured one—moving to the public cloud on their own terms and timeframe, and occurring in parallel with the continuing need to evolve and support an existing portfolio of on-premises applications.

BizTalk Server will play a key role—again—in this next industry platform shift. Integration technologies can play a key role as the gateway to the cloud by future-proofing today's applications so that even as you move ahead to the next-generation cloud platforms you can still leverage the existing investments you've made over the years. BizTalk Server 2010 has built in the capability to easily and securely bridge your existing integration business logic with the world of Windows Azure (Microsoft's cloud OS)—which can accelerate hybrid on/off premises application scenarios that we believe are critical to adoption of cloud computing.

The importance and relevancy of integration for the decade ahead is now more important than ever before, and this book can help you start. In this book, you get a comprehensive overview of BizTalk Server 2010 and its latest and greatest new capabilities. The team of authors (Brian Loesgen, Jan Eliasen, Charles Young, Scott Colestock, Jon Flanders, Anush Kumar) collectively have a tremendous wealth of practical, hands-on experience from implementing real-world integration solutions, and this book can help you start—regardless of whether you are new to BizTalk Server, or if you're an experienced developer wanting to stay current on the latest new features.

Burley Kawasaki
Director of Product Management
Microsoft Corp.

PART I

The Basics

IN THIS PART

What Is BizTalk Server?

Microsoft BizTalk Server 2010 is Microsoft's seventh-generation integration server. The first incarnation was in 1999, when it was released to meet *enterprise application integration* (EAI) needs. There have been new releases on a fairly regular basis, roughly every 2 years. BizTalk Server 2004, the third release, was a rewrite, because the .NET Framework had appeared. As the platform has evolved, and as new standards such as the WS-* specifications have emerged, BizTalk Server has adopted them.

The reality is that as BizTalk Server, and the open standards it is based on, has matured, it has evolved into a comprehensive solution development environment and a powerful runtime host that runs the solutions. For any given problem, therefore, there is a good chance that there is more than one way to implement a solution using BizTalk Server, and some ways will be better than others.

A Brief History of Application Integration

To better understand BizTalk Server and its benefits, consider the evolutionary path that led to its design. In earlier times, organizations used just standalone applications. These isolated silos of information were created to address specific requirements such as accounting or resource management. They were self-contained, with no need to interact with other applications. Integration often involved redundant data entry ("swivel-chair" integration) or file dumps to transfer information from one system to another.

The barriers between applications were substantial, and seamless integration was rare and difficult to achieve.

As time passed, organizations bound their applications more tightly through point-to-point integrations (see Figure 1.1). Data could then flow more readily between applications. However, this type of integration could take significant time and effort to implement. Different teams of architects and developers needed to collaborate to establish technical contracts, thus comprising communication mechanisms, protocols, and shared data models.

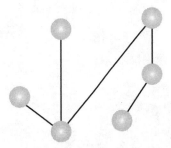

FIGURE 1.1   Single point-to-point integration.

Despite the overhead, point-to-point integrations became widespread. However, they had several disadvantages and were inherently brittle. If the contract for one system changed, each connected system had to change, as well. Point-to-point integrations became increasingly difficult to manage (see Figure 1.2) forcing organizations to devote precious IT resources to integration maintenance instead of to solving new and emerging business requirements. As the number of connections to a single point increased, versioning that point meant updating an increasing number of clients. Versioning and the ultimate decommissioning of systems were often not considered in the initial design, leading to increasing expense and risk over time.

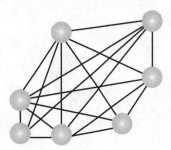

FIGURE 1.2   More complex point-to-point integration.

NOTE

Cloud computing styles enable deployment of individual services to cloud-based platforms such as Azure. They also enable a more distributed form of point-to-point integration with the same resulting complexity. Architects and developers with integration experience understand the weakness of the point-to-point model. However, a significant risk exists that past mistakes will be repeated. Fortunately, building blocks are available to help avoid these mistakes and foster good architecture and design.

Over time, point-to-point integration evolved into a hub-and-spoke model (see Figure 1.3), where messages are published to an intermediate hub service that forwards them to one or more message recipients (the spokes). The relationship between the publisher and recipients could now be defined by configuration or by publish-subscribe (pub-sub) rules. The pub-sub model enables applications to publish messages without regard to the recipients. Subscribers receive those messages without regard to the publisher.

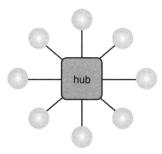

FIGURE 1.3   Hub-and-spoke integration.

Consider an online order-processing system that receives orders and publishes them to a hub service. A warehouse fulfillment system can subscribe to these orders and process them as they are received. The two applications now operate independently. They are loosely coupled and do not communicate with each other directly. All message interchange is via the central hub, and neither application needs to know about the other's existence. Now consider a sales-tracking *business intelligence* (BI) application. It can also subscribe to the same order messages and process them independently without knowledge of the other two applications.

In this model, contract information still needs to be shared. If the online order-processing application changes the structural definition of an order, some mechanism must be in place to ensure proper functioning of any subscribers. This could be handled by an appropriate versioning strategy. Depending on the implementation, contracts could be published in a central repository or via the hub, thus making it easier to maintain agreements made between publisher and subscriber organizations and teams.

BizTalk Server 2004 introduced a pub-sub model as part of a hybrid hub-bus architecture (see Figure 1.4) that combines the hub-and-spoke approach with a message bus topology. In this hub-bus model, functionality can be distributed across multiple machines. Each machine is a physical hub that shares a centralized message bus with no single point of failure. Configuration of the distributed system is centralized, as are capabilities such as capturing operational and business metrics. Conceptually, you can think of a BizTalk Server host as a logical hub. Individual BizTalk Server machines run a local instance of that host. These host instances collaborate using the message bus. The bus encompasses the centralized BizTalk Server Message Box (messaging data store) and the management database (configuration data store) together with the centralized operational and management capabilities and tools.

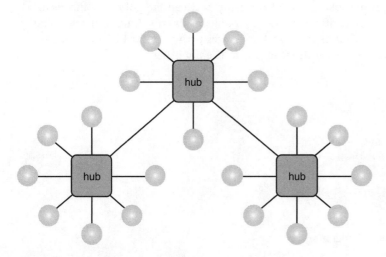

FIGURE 1.4   Hub-bus integration.

From the perspective of functional stratification, BizTalk Server can combine many host instances across multiple machines to provide functionality for receiving, processing, and relaying messages. As messages from an external source are received by a host instance, they are stored in the central Message Box. Other host instances subscribe to the messages and act on them. Several host instances may share a common subscription. In this case, a specific host instance is selected dynamically through a collaborative algorithm implemented by individual message agents running on each machine. After performing its work, the host instance can, if it wants, publish resulting messages to the Message Box for further routing. Alternatively, the host instance may relay messages to an external target.

Hub-bus architecture eliminates many of the limitations of earlier approaches. For example, it is highly scalable. You can increase the processing power of a hub by adding more machines or scale back by removing machines. You can partition processing by defining new hosts and assigning host instances to specific boxes. The centralized Message Box, configuration database, and *business activity monitoring* (BAM) tracking infrastructure are all implemented using SQL Server, a proven and highly scalable product that can be clustered and made highly available and fault tolerant.

This architecture does have certain limitations. For example, it is often not feasible to geo-distribute the hubs because they share a common back-end database and require low network latency. In addition, although the original BizTalk Server 2004 model provided foundational support for dynamic message routing, it lacked direct support for the patterns of runtime resolution of artifacts and policies that characterize evolving service bus designs. These patterns could be implemented only by building additional custom functionality on top of BizTalk Server. Later versions of BizTalk Server introduced the *Enterprise Service Bus Toolkit* ([ESB Toolkit], which started out in the first version as [ESB Guidance]) to address these requirements in a consistent manner and provide a common framework for exploiting BizTalk Server as a dynamic service bus platform.

BizTalk Server Capabilities

BizTalk Server provides a sophisticated, scalable model for enabling message exchange between different systems. However, by itself, the hub-bus model addresses only a subset of the concerns common to integration. BizTalk Server builds on this model to handle many different requirements. The following sections outline these requirements and describe how BizTalk Server addresses each one.

Adaptation

Different systems support different approaches to sending or receiving information. In some cases, the only supported integration route may be via file dumps or direct database access. Some systems support *File Transport Protocol* (FTP) or message queue protocols. Others implement web service interfaces using *Representational State Transfer* (REST) or *Simple Object Access Protocol* (SOAP). Although TCP/IP is the most commonly used (lower-level) transport protocol, some systems support proprietary or less-common protocols, which may be connection-oriented or connectionless. Some systems support transport-level encryption, bidirectional communication, and other capabilities.

BizTalk Server separates these concerns from its hub-bus model through the use of an adaptation layer. It provides a host environment for managing running instances of adapters together with a programmatic framework for creating adapters or extending existing adaptation functionality so that it can interact with BizTalk Server. In addition, BizTalk Server provides an extensive library of out-of-the-box adapters for different protocols, database systems, and third-party *enterprise resource planning* (ERP) and *customer relationship management* (CRM) systems such as SAP and Siebel, together with management and configuration capabilities. It also ships with Host Integration Server for integration with mainframe and midrange systems and DB2 using *Systems Network Architecture* (SNA), *Customer Information Control System* (CICS), *Advanced Program-to-Program Communication* (APPC), and IBM WebSphere MQ. Apart from these out-of-the-box adapters, Microsoft provides several "accelerators" that are vertical-specific solutions and include (among others) specific adapters. SWIFT is a good example here. In addition, many *independent software vendors* (ISVs) have developed and marketed specific adapters for BizTalk Server.

Adapters can be used to receive messages and to relay messages on to target systems. Through configuration, adapters are associated with BizTalk message ports. BizTalk Server implements "receive" and "send" ports and supports different message exchange patterns. Adapters are free to push (for example, *Hypertext Transfer Protocol* [HTTP]) or pull (for example, FTP, *Post Office Protocol 3* [POP3]) messages as required.

Mediation

One of the advantages of the BizTalk Server model is that it provides a natural location for message mediation. Mediation involves processing to decode and encode, validate, and enrich messages. In addition, mediation capabilities include the ability to transform messages into different formats, disassemble them into separate messages, or compose multiple messages together into single composite messages (so-called batches). BizTalk Server separates these concerns from adaptation and other capabilities by providing a common and extensible framework for extending message channels with "pipelines."

A major aspect of mediation is to associate useful metadata with each message for a variety of purposes. This metadata, called message context, is used principally to enable routing. Message context travels with each message as it passes over the BizTalk message bus. To achieve clean decoupling (and high performance), the subscription engine evaluates message context rather than message content. A common approach is to process messages in pipelines to copy relevant values from the content into the context to enable forms of content-based routing.

The ESB Toolkit adds additional functionality for mediation involving routing and policy resolution from central service directories and policy stores. The toolkit also enables service choreography by associating itineraries (also called routing slips) with individual messages.

Exception Handling

If all messages followed "happy" paths between different systems, integration would be simple and cheap. A core part of the value proposition of BizTalk Server is its capability to handle the "unhappy" paths where messages cannot flow as intended or desired. This might happen because external systems are unavailable, contracts are inadvertently broken, messages are invalid or malformed, they are delivered in an incorrect order, or for many other reasons.

There are many different aspects of exception handling within BizTalk Server. For example, it offers built-in support for automated retries when messages cannot be relayed to external systems. During message interchange, failed messages can be suspended, handed off to a secondary transport, or routed to an exception handler. When an individual message within a batch fails, BizTalk Server can be configured to either fail the entire batch or to handle the failed message separately.

All messages are persisted to the Message Box within a transaction. This provides the basic mechanism for suspending failed messages so that they can be resubmitted at a later date. Later versions of BizTalk Server also offer an error message portal as part of the ESB

Toolkit. As well as providing better visibility of failed messages and self-service subscription to error notifications, the portal provides capabilities for storing failed messages so that they can be viewed and edited before resubmission.

More advanced forms of exception handling and error recovery can be implemented using BizTalk Server's orchestration features. Orchestration provides a mechanism for implementing custom error-handling logic and implements a compensation mechanism based on an extended form of the Saga model supported in standards such as *Business Process Execution Language* (BPEL).

Orchestration and Choreography

Interchange between different systems and services must often be orchestrated to manage data flow, decision points, parallelism, exception handling, and other requirements. Orchestration services support these requirements. A BizTalk orchestration is a custom service that sits directly on the BizTalk message bus and uses the same subscription mechanisms used for message routing. Orchestrations can consume and publish messages freely and extend the built-in message-correlation features of the pub-sub mechanism with additional capabilities. Orchestrations support long-lived, recoverable business activities through asynchronous service interchange and can nest atomic transactions within these long-lived activities.

Orchestrations are commonly used to implement automated processes. These may represent specific business processes or may simply automate aspects of message interchange. A single parent orchestration can be decomposed into child orchestrations to foster better separation of concerns and reuse, and to enable certain advanced forms of message exchange. Different orchestrations can collaborate as peers on the single message bus. Orchestrations are created using graphical model-driven development techniques. They represent a superset of the BPEL standard and can enforce strict BPEL compliance.

Service choreography offers a complementary model to orchestration. It is a decentralized approach in which participating services agree on common interchange protocols. BizTalk Server enables choreography through the use of itineraries created and managed via the ESB Toolkit. Each itinerary represents a routing policy that can be externalized and managed through a central store. Itineraries are typically associated with individual messages as part of BizTalk mediation services and used within pipelines and orchestrations. They can also be created, retrieved, or consumed by non-BizTalk services (for example, web services) to enable broader collaboration models at the enterprise level.

Performance and Scalability

Organizations must often handle variable workloads without incurring significant additional costs and without the need for extensive reengineering of existing systems. Many techniques can be used to achieve scalability and provide sufficient performance. These include load balancing, data and process partitioning, distributed processing, and other approaches. BizTalk Server uses these techniques internally and also supports their use at the external level.

One of most problematic areas in integration involves the handling of performance mismatches. These typically occur when systems publish messages at a higher rate than they can be consumed. These mismatches might occur only intermittently but can cause havoc if not handled adequately. BizTalk Server provides a sophisticated approach to handling these types of mismatch. For example, it implements various internal algorithms that manage message and process throttling within configurable parameters. Together with its persistence, exception handling, and recovery facilities, these capabilities provide a robust platform for managing spate conditions, intermittent or slow network connections, and a variety of other problems. Internally, BizTalk Server manages its own resources carefully to ensure that it can continue to operate in the most optimal fashion possible regardless of external factors beyond its control. Most of the settings used for throttling, memory management, and throughput can be configured at the host instance level through BizTalk Server's Administration Console.

Sometimes, it is necessary to exchange large messages. BizTalk Server provides special handling for this purpose and can also manage transformation of large messages.

Security

Systems must often exchange sensitive data without compromising business interests or customer expectations. Solutions may use transport- or message-level security to protect messages or specific data values. They must ensure that sensitive data is decrypted only at the point of use. BizTalk Server's out-of-the-box adapters support transport-level security where appropriate. Message-level security is supported via the *Windows Communication Foundation* (WCF) adapters. WCF adapters can also be used to support federated authentication, where users authenticated by one organization can access services provided by another based on cross-organizational trust rather than the use of centralized user accounts.

Solution architectures often define trust boundaries to simplify the security model and minimize risk. BizTalk Server enables trust boundaries to be modeled using different logical hosts. External systems may implement their own authentication and authorization mechanisms. BizTalk Server must honor these security models even if they contradict the architectural trust boundaries. For this reason, it provides a single sign-on server to securely map security principals to the credentials required by target systems.

Insight

Integrated environments can be complex and difficult to understand and manage. Technical detail can make it difficult to verify that the overall solution meets business requirements. Organizations require insight into the status, topography, and behavior of their solutions. They need to monitor system performance and health, maintain audit trails of distributed business activities, and ensure commercial and regulatory compliance.

Tracking and monitoring provides the basis for analysis and insight. BizTalk Server provides tools for tracing message flows, drilling into the details of each interchange, and restarting failed interchanges. The BAM framework supports business perspectives and enables situational awareness by collecting and aggregating event data from distributed business activities. The *Business Rules Engine* (BRE) enables decision logic to be separated from processes and message flows so that it can be managed and changed independently. Rules are represented in ways that allow them to be traced back directly to business policies.

Electronic Data Interchange

Integration often involves the electronic interchange of data between different organizations. BizTalk Server provides extensive support for the most widely used *electronic data interchange* (EDI) standards, including EDIFACT, ANSI X12, and secure AS2 transmission over the Internet. It offers extensive and customizable support for standard EDI schemas and handles batching, acknowledgment, and other concerns. These features are combined with updated and improved trading partner management features that enable BizTalk Server 2010 to capture and model information about trading partners, business profiles, agreements, and protocols used extensively in *business-to-business* (B2B) communities.

RFID Event Handling

BizTalk Server provides a *radio frequency ID* (RFID) device-management and event-processing platform. This is a separate "edge" server, distinct from the hub-bus architecture used for message interchange and orchestration. As well as support for various RFID industry standards, the server provides an infrastructure for deployment, management, and monitoring of different categories of devices together with an event-processing framework designed for scalable and efficient event filtering and detection. It offers integration with other BizTalk features such as the rules engine and BAM. BizTalk Server 2010 also provides RFID Mobile for development of sensor application on handheld and mobile devices.

What Is a "Typical" BizTalk Solution?

Given the powerful set of capabilities BizTalk brings to the table, there actually is no "typical" solution. People who use BizTalk to meet the needs of EDI exchanges say that this is a typical solution, others who use it as a service composition tool or an enterprise service bus communications backbone say that is a typical solution.

A quick survey of the team involved in writing this book resulted in the following list of solutions it has implemented using BizTalk Server:

► Uniform processing of orders-to-cash scenarios in multiple formats with multiple customers

► Hosting composite services by invoking and orchestrating several (on-premise or cloud-based) services and exposing them as one uniform interface to the consuming entity

► EDI solutions, bridging trading partners in B2B exchanges

▶ A country-scale ESB, forming the backbone facilitating communications between government agencies and external parties

▶ Supply chain automation, using BizTalk RFID to streamline supply chain and materials management to reduce costs

▶ Robotics automation, sending product manufacturing instructions to shop floor assembly line robots

▶ Scan-to-workflow solutions

▶ Insurance portals with quotation/interview processing

▶ Pension fund switching and rebalancing based on inference over high-level policy statements

▶ Enabling faster payment processing for retail banks

▶ Point-of-sale integration for national store chains

▶ Handling citizens' change-of-circumstance event processing (birth, death, and so on) and distribution of event data to government agencies and organizations

▶ Integration of scheduling and estimation software and mobile devices with back-office systems for a national building maintenance company

▶ Processing of continental meteorological data gathered from thousands of automated stations

▶ Periodically sending out reminders to suppliers to make sure they deliver on time

▶ Handling process for starter/leaver employees

Integration is not specific to any vertical market. Organizations operating in entirely different areas of business and commerce face a common set of issues when attempting to integrate their systems effectively. BizTalk Server 2010 concentrates on addressing these common problems and has wide application across many different industries and agencies in both the public and private sectors.

BizTalk Server, WCF, and WF

The Microsoft .NET Framework implements two important technologies that mirror, to a degree, some of the central capabilities of BizTalk Server. *Windows Communication Foundation* (WCF) provides a foundational library that unifies service interchange across the Microsoft platform. It binds behavior to the communication channels between service endpoints and supports code-centric contract definition. The *Windows Workflow Foundation* (WF) enables developers to compose and host workflows using activity components. It offers a general-purpose, highly extensible framework for building workflow-centric functionality with optional persistence and other features.

WCF and WF are foundational class libraries. They are designed as a code platform on which developers can build individual services and entire frameworks and applications. Together with their core functionality, the .NET Framework provides a number of additional features and tools to aid rapid development and deployment of web services, workflow services, and other application types.

The similarities between WCF and WF and BizTalk Server sometimes serve to obscure the value proposition of the product. WF shares some similarity to BizTalk's orchestration capabilities, and WCF provides an architecture that is not dissimilar to BizTalk's adaptation and message pipeline infrastructure. With the advent of Windows Server AppFabric, the confusion has grown worse. AppFabric extends Windows Activation Service and *Internet Information Services* (IIS) to support hosting of WCF and WF services and offers a degree of recoverability for failed services. Microsoft also provides Windows Azure AppFabric as part of their cloud-based platform. This provides simple routing services and support for running off-premises WF Services.

These .NET Framework technologies do not compete with BizTalk Server. BizTalk Server 2010 is a licensed and supported enterprise-level product that combines many different technologies and tools within a unified platform for on-premises integration, message interchange, service orchestration, policy externalization, and automated business processing. It implements a sophisticated distributed host environment with single-point administration and handles a vast array of concerns that arise when integrating different systems. By contrast, WCF and WF are programmatic class libraries. They provide a rich framework for rapid development of custom business logic and service hosts. They do not, however, provide the rich tooling needed to tackle enterprise-level integration requirements and do not ship with enterprise-ready runtime environments.

WCF and WF are complementary to BizTalk Server 2010. They enable developers to construct discrete services. Those services can then be orchestrated by BizTalk Server and integrated with existing systems and applications using BizTalk Server's capabilities. In addition, BizTalk Server exploits WCF directly to extend its capabilities. Through its integrated WCF adapters, BizTalk Server can expose or consume web services using the WCF model. Existing WCF bindings can be exploited as the equivalent of adapters, and BizTalk Server 2010 even ships with the WCF Line-of-Business Adapter Pack. In the future, it is likely that BizTalk Server will be extended to embrace WF alongside its existing orchestration capabilities. It will also provide better facilities for integrating with services hosted in the cloud. Microsoft will introduce new cloud-based integration-as-a-service capabilities on the Windows Azure platform allowing seamless integration across both on-premises and off-premises platforms and systems.

The value of BizTalk Server 2010 lies in the way it combines many additional capabilities into a single coherent platform for enterprise-level integration. If Microsoft were to start building BizTalk Server from scratch today, it would doubtless base it from the ground up on WCF and WF. However, the resulting product would still greatly extend the core functionality provided within the .NET Framework. Without BizTalk Server, many aspects of real-world integration require costly and detailed development of custom logic together with additional capabilities that must be purchased or built separately. Over time, the relationship between BizTalk Server, WCF, and WF will grow ever stronger, enabling BizTalk Server to continue its evolution as the premier integration server for the .NET platform.

Summary

This chapter provided an overview BizTalk Server 2010 capabilities, the evolution of its architecture and design, and the kind of real-world (integration) problems and scenarios it addresses. BizTalk Server is a rich and mature enterprise-level integration server with extensive support for adaptation, mediation, orchestration, secure interchange, industry standards, EDI, trading partner management, tracking and tracing, business activity monitoring, decisioning, and event processing. It supports model-driven and contract-first development techniques and provides a flexible, scalable, and robust approach to distributed message interchange based on its innovative hub-bus architecture.

The BizTalk ESB Toolkit extends this model to support modern service bus patterns. BizTalk Server provides single-point administration of distributed host environments together with a comprehensive library of monitoring, management, and diagnostics tooling. It exploits WCF directly to provide first-class support for service-oriented designs and will evolve over time to embrace emerging cloud service technologies and platforms.

The rest of this book describes the capabilities of BizTalk Server 2010. Part I introduces the essential capabilities of the product. It describes each of the major BizTalk development artifacts (schemas, maps, orchestrations, and pipelines) in turn. It also introduces the native adapters that ship with the product. Part II moves on to advanced topics. It describes how BizTalk Server can exploit WCF and Windows Azure. It explains business activity monitoring and provides a comprehensive introduction to rules processing. It also describes how to build enterprise service buses with the ESB Toolkit. Part III explains how to deploy and administer BizTalk Server 2010 applications. Part IV introduces BizTalk RFID Server and RFID Mobile.

CHAPTER 2

Schemas

Schemas are an important part of a BizTalk solution for several reasons.

The schemas describe the structure of the messages that are to be sent back and forth between BizTalk and the system BizTalk is exchanging messages with. Naturally, this structure, also known as the contract, is essential because without a contract no verification of the transmitted messages can occur, which makes it impossible to guarantee a consistent and predictable system. If BizTalk cannot assume that the input is valid, it cannot guarantee the output is valid either. This is clearly not desirable. When the schema is agreed upon by both parties, it makes it easier for you to troubleshoot failed messages and to establish whether the sender is sending invalid messages or the receiver is wrongly rejecting a valid message. Also, a detailed and exact contract allows you to reject invalid incoming messages upon reception, giving developers the option to assume correctness for input for all other parts of a BizTalk solution.

Based on the schemas, BizTalk generates a message type. This message type is used extensively in subscriptions, making it invaluable for the MessageBox for deciding what orchestrations and send ports should receive a published message. For example, without the message type, it is impossible to have an orchestration that receives and handles only messages of type orders and nothing else because there is no way of knowing what messages are orders.

The schemas are used as input and output structures for maps, which are used in almost all BizTalk solutions. The output of a map is *Extensible Stylesheet Language Transformations* (XSLT), which is built upon the schemas for the source and destination messages. To keep your maps as simple as possible, it is vital that you rely on the structure of the input.

Because the schemas are so important in a BizTalk solution, they should not be taken lightly. Time spent getting the schemas as correct and as detailed as possible is well spent. If you do not spend enough time on the schemas, you will face difficulties verifying input and building transformations that handle invalid input.

Also, if you run into the need to have multiple versions of the same schema deployed at the same time, you need to version the schema, which can be cumbersome. Spending enough time on the schemas in the first place minimizes the risk of having to version your schema later on because of errors in the schema. Of course, changes may occur later on in any case, naturally, if business needs change. In this case, versioning might also be necessary.

In this chapter, schemas are discussed extensively. After a general introduction to BizTalk schemas, you learn how to leverage existing schemas rather than create your own. The chapter then describes ways you can generate a schema automatically to assist you in creating a schema, and then walks you through how to create an XML schema from scratch. You then learn how to create a schema for flat files, both using a wizard and creating from scratch. Then, after a short introduction to the *Electronic Data Interchange* (EDI) schemas that are supplied with BizTalk, you cover property promotion in BizTalk. The discussion then turns to ways to handle schemas that are not supported out-of-the-box in BizTalk and how to deal with versioning of schemas, where applicable. This chapter also covers built-in testing features and the built-in unit testing framework. As the chapter concludes, we cover testing schemas using pipeline tools and look at the schemas that have been developed to be used throughout this book.

BizTalk Schemas

BizTalk uses *XML Schema Definitions* (XSDs) to describe the messages that come into BizTalk and the ones BizTalk sends out. This section discusses XML schemas briefly and then describes some of the properties that are available for schemas in a BizTalk project.

XML Schema Definition

Basically, an XSD is an XML document that describes how other XML documents should look. Figure 2.1 shows a small example. The figure describes that XML documents that conform to this schema must have a root node called `Simple`, which is in the namespace `http://biztalkserver2010unleashed.com`. The root node must have an attribute called `MyAttribute` and an element called `MyElement`. An XML example that conforms to this schema, and can therefore be validated against the schema, is shown in Figure 2.2. Schemas are almost never as simple as the example shown here. Often, there are lots of elements and attributes in different hierarchies, and some are optional and others mandatory. Some are even mandatory given that their parent in the tree structure exists and so on. This book does not go into detail about all the possibilities with XSDs. You can find the formal definition of the XSD standard at http://www.w3.org/XML/Schema. This book does, however, discuss how you can create schemas using the BizTalk Schema Editor and how to leverage existing schemas in other formats than XSD and existing XML examples.

```xml
<?xml version="1.0" encoding="utf-16" ?>
<xs:schema xmlns="http://biztalkserver2010unleashed.com"
    xmlns:b="http://schemas.microsoft.com/BizTalk/2003"
    targetNamespace="http://biztalkserver2010unleashed.com"
    xmlns:xs="http://www.w3.org/2001/XMLSchema">
    <xs:element name="Simple">
        <xs:complexType>
            <xs:sequence>
                <xs:element name="MyElement" type="xs:string" />
            </xs:sequence>
            <xs:attribute name="MyAttribute" type="xs:string" />
        </xs:complexType>
    </xs:element>
</xs:schema>
```

FIGURE 2.1   Simple XSD schema.

```xml
<ns0:Simple MyAttribute="AttValue"
            xmlns:ns0="http://biztalkserver2010unleashed.com">
    <MyElement>ElementValue</MyElement>
</ns0:Simple>
```

FIGURE 2.2   Simple XML example.

Properties

When you add a schema to your BizTalk project in Visual Studio 2010, some properties can be set on the new project item (XSD), as shown in Figure 2.3.

FIGURE 2.3   Properties for XSD schemas.

The properties are fully described at http://msdn.microsoft.com/en-us/library/aa547891(BTS.70).aspx and briefly described in Table 2.1.

TABLE 2.1   Properties for XSD Schemas

Property Name	Description
Build Action	Describes the action the compiler will perform when compiling the project. A value of None means that the schema is not compiled at all. A value of BtsCompile means that the schema is compiled into the assembly.
Namespace	The .NET namespace the compiled schema will belong to. This is *not* to be confused for the target namespace of the schema, which is an XSD-specific property.
Type Name	The .NET type name of the class the schema will be compiled into.
Fully Qualified Name	This is a concatenation of the namespace and the type name. Together they form the .NET fully qualified name used to uniquely identify a type in .NET. You must make sure that no two types in your entire BizTalk environment have the same fully qualified name.
Generate Instance Output Type	A value of XML means that if you generate an instance based on a schema, the instance will be created as XML. A value of Native means that the instance will be created as the format the schema specifies, like a flat file. For schemas describing XML, the instance created both for XML and Native are the same. This is used for generating instances from schemas to be used in your test scenarios.
Input Instance Filename	The file specified in this property is used as input if you choose to validate an instance against the schema you are creating.
Output Instance Filename	The file specified in this property is used at the output filename, when generating an instance of a schema.
Validate Instance Input Type	A value of XML means that the input file specified in Input Instance Filename is an XML instance. A value of Native means that the input file is in native format, such as a flat file. This is used for testing instances against the schema.
File Name	The filename of the schema.
Full Path	The full path, including the filename, of the schema.
Default Property Schema Name	If you do not specify another property schema, when promoting a property from this schema, this property schema is used. We return to promoted properties later in this chapter.

Internal Schemas

When developing a BizTalk solution that integrates between systems, you might want to consider developing an internal schema format, also called a canonical data model, for BizTalk that can be used internally in BizTalk to not map directly between the formats used by the external systems you are integrating to.

To understand why, consider an alternative scenario where a customer sends you an order and you need to map this order to an order confirmation for the customer, an InfoPath form for a manager to approve, and an order format for your *enterprise resource planning* (ERP) system. Other systems might also need some message that has been mapped from the order, but these three will do.

If the customer wants to change his order format, you must change your schema for the order that you have received and change all three maps. Had you used an internal order schema that you could map the customer order into and used that as a base for the three maps, you would need to change only the schema and the map that maps into the internal schema.

It gets even worse if a business process is involved because if you do not map incoming orders from different customers into a common internal format, you need to have one orchestration per format defined that picks up the order and handles it.

Therefore, the best practice is to always maintain a set of internal schemas that are used inside BizTalk and your business process, which effectively decouples your business processes form any specific formats used by either trading partners or internal systems.

NOTE

Defining the internal schemas should be the first thing you do. You want them to reflect the business definition of what you are creating a schema for (for example, an order). In other words, you do not want to be biased from having looked at the schemas from trading partners or internal systems because you really want to be decoupled from those. You want schemas that can be used throughout time even if all other schemas change. This requires that the business define the data that should be in the schemas (and not a developer, who will probably merely create a union of the information from the different schemas involved from trading partners and internal systems).

If you are under pressure for time, do not have a business process defined, but are merely doing content-based routing, and if you need to map only an incoming order to the order format of your ERP system and not to other formats, it is tempting to skip the internal format because receiving an order and mapping it to the format of the receiving side involves creating three schemas and two maps rather than just two schemas and one map. Even in this case, though, consider creating an internal schema. If time really isn't available for doing the full-blown business definition of the schema, consider taking the schema that your ERP system uses and just changing the namespace and using that as an internal schema.

The schema is in this case easily created, and the map between the internal format and the format of the ERP system is also easily created. This way you still have a decoupling of your internal BizTalk workings and your ERP system, making it easier to change the ERP system later or perhaps introduce a business process, other mappings, and so on.

XML Schemas

As explained previously, BizTalk uses XSDs for describing messages that arrive at BizTalk and are sent from BizTalk. BizTalk uses XSDs for describing both XML documents, flat files, and other formats. This section covers schemas for XML documents: how to add existing ones, how to generate schemas, and how to manually create your own schemas.

Existing XSDs

Because BizTalk is fully XSD standard-compliant, you can take any valid existing XSD and include it in your existing project. You do so by choosing **Add**, **Existing Item** in Visual Studio 2010 (see Figure 2.4). A file picker then opens, enabling you to select the existing files you want to add.

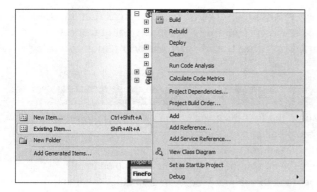

FIGURE 2.4   Add an existing schema to your project.

Adding an existing XSD has some obvious benefits over generating or creating a schema:

- ▶ It saves time.

- ▶ Receiving an XSD from a trading partner to use for message transmissions usually means that the trading partner knows what they are doing and have probably done this before, improving the chance of success.

A potential drawback of using an existing XSD provided by a trading partner is this: If they are not fully aware of how to create good XSDs, they might have created a collection of XSDs that are not reusing data types across schemas and perhaps do not use namespaces at all. For a BizTalk solution, namespaces should always be used for schemas because otherwise you can end up with schemas from multiple partners that have the same root node, like Order, but no namespace. If this happens, BizTalk cannot determine which schema to use at runtime.

When Visual Studio 2010 adds the existing XSD to your project, it gives it a type name and a .NET namespace, which is not to be mistaken for the target namespace of the schema, and those two combined provide the fully qualified .NET type name. You can see what Visual Studio 2010 has generated if you click the schema in the Solution Explorer and then look at its properties.

Generating an XSD

If no existing XSD can be used, you have three options to create one automatically. These three options are available from within Visual Studio 2010 when you right-click your project and choose **Add Generated Item**:

▶ **Document Type Definition:** You can generate an XSD based on a *Document Type Definition* (DTD). DTDs are rarely used nowadays, but they do exist on legacy systems.

▶ **XML Data Reduced:** The *XML Data Reduced* (XDR) schema format was created by Microsoft just before the XSD standard was published. Microsoft used this standard for BizTalk 2000 and 2002.

▶ **Well-Formed XML Instance:** You can generate a schema based on a well-formed XML instance. Often, if a trading partner does not have an XSD to give to you, they can provide an example of the XML they can generate.

No matter which of the three options you use, you must carefully go through the generated schema and make any needed changes. The Schema Generator makes assumptions wherever it cannot be sure about what to generate. If you are generating a schema based on an XML instance that has the value 1, for example, the generated schema will have the data type of that element to be `unsignedByte`, which often needs to be changed to another type (`int`, `integer`, or the like).

As mentioned earlier in this section, do not take schemas lightly. Spend time getting them right.

The first time you want to generate a schema, you will find that only generating a schema given an XDR schema is available. The other two options are marked as Not Loaded. To leverage the two other options, go to <InstallationFolder>\SDK\Utilities\Schema Generator and run the appropriate script. The InstallDTD.vbs is for enabling generating schemas based on a DTD, and the InstallWFX.vbs is for enabling generating schemas based on a well-formed XML example.

Creating an XSD

If you cannot get your hands on an existing XSD and you cannot generate one (or do not want to), you can create a schema manually using the BizTalk Schema Editor from within Visual Studio 2010. This section describes how to manually create a schema for XML documents. Creating schemas for flat files is described later.

Schema Editor

The BizTalk Schema Editor consists of three parts:

▶ The tree structure of the generated schema (left side of Figure 2.5), which visually shows you the structure of the generated schema.

▶ The XSD in text format (middle of Figure 2.5), which shows you a read-only view of the XSD as it would appear if you were to open it in a text editor. Although this is just read-only, it still gives developers who know about the XSD standard a way of seeing it all, and this way they can more easily find out what might be wrong with the schema.

▶ The properties of the selected item in the tree structure (lower right of Figure 2.5). The properties part lets you set individual properties of the selected item, such as the cardinality of the element, the data type, and so on.

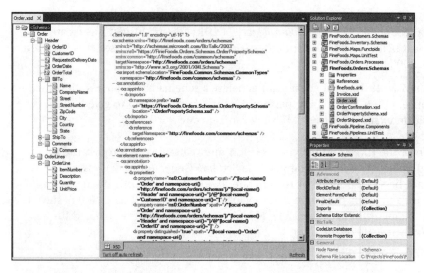

FIGURE 2.5   BizTalk Schema Editor.

Whenever you change the XSD in the tree structure by inserting, deleting, renaming, or moving elements around, the view of the XSD in the middle is automatically updated. For large schemas, this update can take awhile. Unfortunately, the schema view in the middle updates even if the change you made in the tree structure isn't even viewable in the current view in the middle, meaning that although the schema view is taking some time to update itself, you won't see any change in the *graphical user interface* (GUI) before you scroll to the appropriate node you have changed.

This is not always desirable and can be turned off. The reason this is not always desirable is that for large schemas this can cause you to have to wait awhile between making changes to the tree structure because when the automatic refresh of the view in the middle finishes, the entire UI is refreshed. So, if you insert a node and are in the middle of giving it a name, and the automatic refresh finishes, the entire UI refreshes, causing focus to leave the node you are editing, which can be rather annoying.

Schema Elements

A schema primarily consists of records, elements, and attributes. The three different possibilities are shown in Figure 2.6, where Header is a record, RequestedDeliveryDate is an element, and OrderID is an attribute.

FIGURE 2.6   Three types in a schema.

In XML, we do not normally distinguish between what is a record and what is an element because they are pretty much the same. In BizTalk, however, extra functionality is added (for instance, in maps, where certain logic applies to records but does not apply to elements or attributes).

If you are not certain what to choose, a rule of thumb is that if you need to group some values together, use a record. A record can have records, elements, and attributes inside it. If you need to store a value of some sort without having other records, elements, or attributes grouped below where you need the value, choose either an element or an attribute.

It usually doesn't matter whether you choose an element or an attribute, but there are a couple of things to consider when choosing:

- ▶ If you are creating a schema that must match some given XML that some system is producing, you need to choose elements and attributes that match the XML this system is generating.

- ▶ If this is not the case, consider three things:

  - ▶ **Personal Preference:** Lots of developers have some idea about whether they like attributes or elements better. These preferences are usually based on readability. Some developers think either attributes or elements are easier to read.

  - ▶ **File size:** Attributes take up only about half the size that elements do because elements need both a start and an end tag. Especially for large flat files that are converted into XML, this can be a big difference.

  - ▶ **Demotion:** Later in this chapter, the concept of property demotion is discussed. In essence, this is about getting values from the context of a message put into the content of the message when the message is to be sent out. Property demotion works only for elements and not for attributes.

Add New Schema

To create your schema, you first add a schema to your project. This is done like adding any other artifact to your project. You right-click your project and choose **Add**, **New Item**. The screen shown in Figure 2.7 then opens.

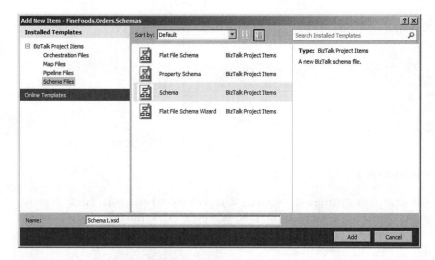

FIGURE 2.7   Adding a schema to your project.

As shown in Figure 2.7, after choosing **Schema Files**, you have four options. For this section of the book, we will use the **Schema** option. The **Flat File Schema**, **Flat File Schema Wizard**, and **Property Schema** options are described later.

After you add the schema to your project, it opens up automatically in BizTalk Schema Editor. The two things to change initially are as follows:

▶ Rename the root node of the schema.

▶ Change the target namespace of the schema.

In BizTalk, the name of the root node and the target namespace are used to construct the message type of a message. The message type is the concatenation of the target namespace of the root node, a hash sign (#), and the name of the root node. Table 2.2 gives examples of the message type given different root nodes.

TABLE 2.2   BizTalk Message Types

Root Node	Message Type
<root xmlns="http://mycomp.com/schema/v1.0">	http://mycomp.com/schema/v1.0#root
<ns:root xmlns:ns="http://mycomp.com/schema/v1.0">	http://mycomp.com/schema/v1.0#root
<root>	root

The reason for changing the name of the root node and the target namespace is that having two schemas deployed in your BizTalk installation with the same message type will cause you almost nothing but trouble. The reason for this is that when a message arrives at BizTalk, it checks the message type to make sure there is a schema deployed that matches the incoming message and possibly validates the message against the schema if this is configured. If two schemas are deployed with the same combination of root node and target namespace, at runtime BizTalk cannot determine which of the schemas to use. And if the schema cannot be unambiguously chosen, the .NET type of the schema that is used at runtime cannot be chosen. You will get an error at runtime if BizTalk receives a message for which there are two schemas deployed. To avoid this, as stated, change the root node, the target namespace, or (preferably) both.

Adding Elements to Your Schema

After changing the root node and the target namespace of the schema, which is optional but highly recommended, you can start building your schema. To insert new records, elements, and attributes in the schema, you can either use keyboard shortcuts or right-click an existing element in the schema and insert new elements.

If you right-click, you get the option to insert the following, as shown in Figure 2.8:

- **Child Record:** A record that is the child of the element you right-clicked.

- **Child Field Attribute:** An attribute that is a child of the record you right-clicked.

- **Child Field Element:** An element that is a child of the record you right-clicked.

- **Sibling Record:** A record that is the sibling of the element you right-clicked.

- **Sibling Field Attribute:** An attribute that is a sibling of the record you right-clicked.

- **Sibling Field Element:** An element that is a sibling of the record you right-clicked.

- **Sequence Group:** A sequence in which you can insert other elements that must then appear in the sequence given by the order they appear in, in the schema.

- **Choice Group:** A group of elements, of which only one should appear.

- **All Group:** A group of elements that can occur in any order. The All Group can be added to a record only and only if the Content Type property of the record is set to ComplexContent.

- **Attribute Group:** A group of attributes for a record.

- **Any Element:** An element placeholder that can contain any element with any content below it. Having an element like this will allow you to put anything in your XML at this point, but validation will not be possible, because the schema has no description of what might appear.

- **Any Attribute:** An attribute that can be any attribute.

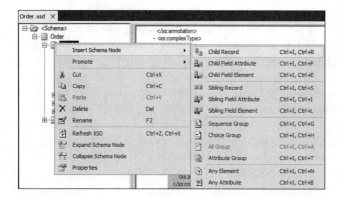

FIGURE 2.8   Options when right-clicking an element in a schema.

A child of an element is an element that is one level below the element you right-clicked. A sibling is on the same level as the element you right-clicked. To illustrate this, consider Figure 2.9, where the following is true:

▶ BillTo and Comments are child records to Header.

▶ OrderDate and OrderTotal are sibling elements.

▶ OrderID is a sibling attribute to Header.

▶ RequestedDeliveryDate is a child element of Header.

FIGURE 2.9   Description of children and siblings.

Other than right-clicking and inserting records, elements, and attributes, you can also use shortcuts. Figure 2.10 shows the shortcuts.

For a full description of all the keyboard shortcuts usable in BizTalk Schema Editor, and not just the ones for inserting elements, visit http://msdn.microsoft.com/en-us/library/aa559145(BTS.70).aspx.

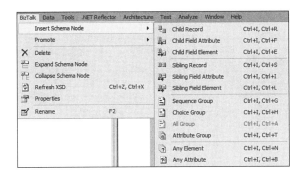

FIGURE 2.10   Keyboard shortcuts for inserting elements in a schema.

After inserting lots of elements in your schema, you might realize that some records, elements, or attributes have been placed wrong. For this, you can also drag and drop elements inside the Schema Editor. If you click an element and drag it, an arrow appears in the places where you can drop it. The arrow can be one of three:

▶ **Pointing straight up:** This means that if you drop the element you are dragging here, it will appear as a sibling of the element the arrow is located at, just above it.

▶ **Pointing straight down:** This means that if you drop the element you are dragging here, it will appear as a sibling of the element the arrow is located at, just below it.

▶ **Pointing down to the right:** This means that the element you are dragging will be inserted as a child of the element the arrow is located at. If this element already has children, the dragged element will appear as the last of the children.

As mentioned before, consider turning off the automatic refresh of the XSD view because it will slow down your experience, and perhaps even be annoying when inserting lots of elements in large schemas.

Properties of Nodes in the Schema

For records, elements, and attributes, a lot of properties can be set that describe the data type, the cardinality, and other properties. This book does not cover all possible properties but instead describes the ones most commonly used and therefore most important. For a full description of all the properties, visit http://msdn.microsoft.com/en-us/library/aa561245(BTS.70).aspx. Also, to fully understand many of the details, you should familiarize yourself with the XSD standard, which is described at http://www.w3.org/XML/Schema, and a walkthrough of the standard, which is published at http://www.w3schools.com/schema/schema_elements_ref.asp.

Properties for the Schema

This section describes the most important properties for the <Schema> node in the schema tree. These properties are not relevant for the schema itself but are more like metadata about the schema used by the BizTalk runtime to determine how to handle the documents that adhere to this schema. Systems other than BizTalk won't be able to read and

understand these properties because they are kept inside the XSD in BizTalk-specific annotations. They are listed in Table 2.3.

TABLE 2.3   Default Values Set on the Schema

Property	Description
Main Properties: These are the main properties and therefore the ones that are used the most.	
Target Namespace	The Target Namespace property specifies the target namespace of the schema. Although it can be blank, best practice is to have a namespace on your schema, and it should be something that is unique for your business. The namespace is a string, but usually looks like a URI. As mentioned earlier, the target namespace is important because it forms the message type of a message internally in BizTalk together with the name of the root node of the message.
Imports	The Imports property allows you to include and import other schemas into the current one, to utilize existing types defined in these other schemas. When clicking the Imports ellipsis, you will see the window as it appears in Figure 2.11. You can import schemas that have a different target namespace than the target namespace of your current schema and then use the types defined in the imported schema.
	You can include schemas that share the target namespace with your current schema or that have an empty target namespace and then use the types defined in the included schema either as is or create new types that derive from them.
	Finally, you can use XSD Redefine to do what you can do with an XSD Include, but with the XSD Redefine, you can also modify the types.
Envelope	The Envelope property specifies if this schema describes an envelope schema used to contain other messages. It is used at runtime by BizTalk in the disassembler components along with the Body XPath property of the root node, which is described in Table 2.5.
Promoted Properties	The Promoted Properties property is used to manage what content from a message should be placed in the context of the message when BizTalk receives the message. Promoted properties are explained later.
Internal Naming and Versioning: These properties are used mainly for business purposes to distinguish between schemas and versions of the same schema. These properties are not used by BizTalk but can be used for business purposes.	
Document Type	Can be Document (default) or Property. Indicates if this is a regular schema or a property schema. Property schemas are covered in the section about promoted properties, later in this chapter.
Document Version	Some version of the schema. This can be any versioning standard you want to use. It is not used by BizTalk.
Specification Name	Contains the name of your schema. This is not used by BizTalk but can be used for business purposes.

TABLE 2.3   Default Values Set on the Schema

Property	Description
Standard	Contains a specification of what standard this schema conforms to. This is not used by BizTalk but can be used for business purposes.
Standard Version	Allows to you add a versioning string to the standard name. This is not used by BizTalk but can be used for business purposes.

Miscellaneous: These properties are not used very much but are still important to know about.

Root Reference	If you create a schema that has more than one top-level record, you can use this property to specify which of the top-level nodes to consider the root node. Without this property set, BizTalk guesses, and when generating instances based on this schema, the chosen node acts as root node, which might not be what you want.
Schema Editor Extensions	Provides the means to choose which, if any, editor extensions should apply for the current schema. Editor extensions are described later in this chapter.

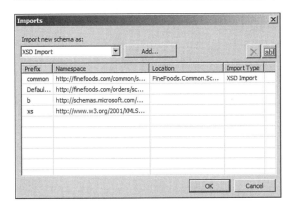

FIGURE 2.11   The Imports dialog box.

Undocumented Properties for the Schema   Other than the properties seen here, there are some properties that cannot be set using the Properties window for the schema. The most used is the `displayroot_reference` property.

Consider the schema shown in Figure 2.12. The screenshot is taken from within InfoPath and displays the schema for a simple form. An InfoPath form (the .XSN file) is just a cabinet file, so if you need BizTalk to understand and use the schema for the form, you can extract the XSD from the .XSN file by renaming the file to .CAB and opening it. The schema is usually called myschema.xsd, and it can then be added as an existing item to your BizTalk solution. If you do this and open the schema in BizTalk Schema Editor, the schema will look different from when opened inside InfoPath, as shown in Figure 2.13. This is because some schemas have lots of records, attributes, and elements defined at the root level and then reuse these elements in the actual root node. In some circumstances, when generating an instance of this schema the wrong node is chosen as the root node instead of myFields, which is the proper root node in this case. If this occurs, you can use the Root Reference property as described in Table 2.3 to let BizTalk Schema Editor know what the right node is to choose as root node. If you also want the schema to appear with the right node as the root node and ignore the rest of the nodes at the root level, you can use the displayroot_reference property. This property, as described, is not accessible in the Properties window. To change it, you must edit the schema in a text editor of your choice. It must be a text editor that can open and save files in Unicode, so Notepad will do. What is needed to insert is an attribute to the SchemaInfo element that is in the annotations. If the SchemaInfo element is not already present, you can make it appear, by explicitly setting the value of either the CodeList Database property of the schema or any of the properties that appear in the Reference group of properties. Figure 2.14 shows how to set the property.

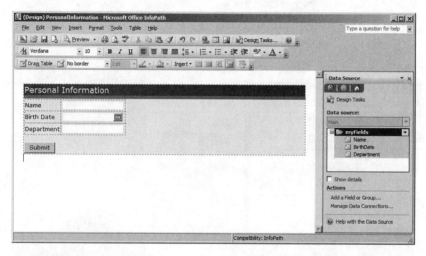

FIGURE 2.12   InfoPath form in Design mode.

FIGURE 2.13   Schema extracted from InfoPath form opened in BizTalk Schema Editor.

After you change this property, the schema shown in Figure 2.13 will look like the schema shown in Figure 2.15.

```
myschema.xsd - Notepad                                              _ |□| x|
File  Edit  Format  View  Help
<?xml version="1.0" encoding="utf-16"?>
<xsd:schema xmlns:my="http://schemas.microsoft.com/office/infopath/2003/myXSD/2010-07-
12T14:57:04" xmlns:xd="http://schemas.microsoft.com/office/infopath/2003"
xmlns:xsi="http://www.w3.org/2001/XMLSchema-instance"
xmlns:b="http://schemas.microsoft.com/BizTalk/2003"
targetNamespace="http://schemas.microsoft.com/office/infopath/2003/myXSD/2010-07-12T14:57:04"
xmlns:xsd="http://www.w3.org/2001/XMLSchema">
   <xsd:annotation>
      <xsd:appinfo>
         <schemaInfo root_reference="myFields" displayroot_reference="myFields"
xmlns="http://schemas.microsoft.com/BizTalk/2003" />
      </xsd:appinfo>
   </xsd:annotation>
   <xsd:attribute name="EmployeeName" type="xsd:string" />
   <xsd:element name="myFields">
      <xsd:complexType>
         <xsd:sequence>
            <xsd:element minOccurs="0" ref="my:BirthDate" />
            <xsd:element minOccurs="0" ref="my:Department" />
         </xsd:sequence>
         <xsd:attribute ref="my:EmployeeName" />
         <xsd:anyAttribute namespace="http://www.w3.org/XML/1998/namespace" processContents="lax" />
      </xsd:complexType>
   </xsd:element>
   <xsd:element name="BirthDate" nillable="true" type="xsd:date" />
   <xsd:element name="Department" type="xsd:string" />
</xsd:schema>
```

FIGURE 2.14   How to choose what node is displayed as root.

FIGURE 2.15   InfoPath schema opened in BizTalk Schema Editor after the
displayroot_reference property has been changed.

Properties Common for Records, Elements, and Attributes   This section deals with the most
important properties that are common for records, elements, and attributes.

TABLE 2.4   Most Important Properties That Are Common for Records, Elements, and Attributes

Property	Description
Base Data Type	If the type for the element in question should be derived from another type and either extended or restricted, the data type that is to be derived from should be given here. For strings, it is common to derive from xs:string and then define a maximum length, or write a regular expression or an enumeration that describes the allowed values.
Derived By	Specifies how the Base Data Type is derived from another type. Can be Restriction and Extension for records and can be Restriction, List, and Union for elements and attributes.
Instance XPath	This property specifies the exact XPath expression for the record, element, or attribute in question.
Notes	The Notes property can be used to insert notes about any record, element, or attribute. The notes are not used by BizTalk at all but serve as internal documentation for business purposes.

> **TIP**
>
> The value from the XPath property can be handy. XPath expressions can be trouble-some to get right, so this value is useful for getting the right XPath expression to use in orchestrations, maps, or anywhere else.

Properties for Records   This section describes the most important properties for records.

TABLE 2.5   Properties for Records

Property	Description
Body XPath	If this schema is an envelope schema, the Body XPath property is used to point to the parent of the records that will be debatched and submitted one at the time. This property is available only for records at root level and only if the Envelope property is set to True.
Content Type	Specifies whether the record is a simple type or a complex type. The simple types can contain values, whereas the complex types can only contain elements and attributes, but no values.
Data Structure Type	This field is used to determine the type of the structure of the record. If a new unique name is entered in this field, a new complex type is created that can be used elsewhere in the schema and in other schemas that include or import this schema. If no new name is entered, a structure type can be selected in the drop-down, either by selecting the type of the record or by choosing another record to refer to (<RecordName> (Reference)).
Group Order Type	Specifies if the group of elements below this record is a Sequence, a Choice, or an All group.
Max Occurs	Specifies the maximum number of times this record can occur. For an unlim-ited number of times, enter Unbounded. If you enter an asterisk (*), the Schema Editor translates that into Unbounded for you. The default value is 1, meaning that the record can occur a maximum number of 1 time.
Min Occurs	Specifies the minimum number of times the record must occur. The default value is 1. If the value is 0, the record is optional and does not have to appear in the XML.

Properties That Are Common for Elements and Attributes   This section describes the most important properties that are shared between the elements and the attributes.

TABLE 2.6   Properties That Are Shared Between Elements and Attributes

Property	Description
Data Type	The data type of the element.
Default Value	The default value of this node. For elements, the default value is used if the element in the instance file is empty. For attributes, the default value is used both if the attribute does not have a value and if the attribute is not present at all.

TABLE 2.6   Properties That Are Shared Between Elements and Attributes

Property	Description
Enumeration	If the node is derived by restriction, this property can contain a list of strings that are valid values for the node, effectively creating an enumeration of valid values.
Length	Specifies the exact length the value in the node must have. In effect, a value in the Length property is the same as setting both Minimum Length and Maximum Length to the same value. You cannot specify a value in this property and at the same time specify either Minimum Length or Maximum Length.
MaxFacet Type	Possible values are Inclusive and Exclusive. Only active when a value is set in the MaxFacet Value property. See detailed explanation of using facets in the description of the MinFacet Value and MaxFacet Value properties.
MaxFacet Value	Determines the value of the MaxInclusive or MaxExclusive facet, and which one is used is determined by the value of the MaxFacet Type property. This is used to apply validations to restrictions on the Base Data Type that is chosen. For instance, for a base data type of xs:int, the MaxFacet Type set to Inclusive and the MaxFacet Value set to 12, this means that the value in the node cannot be greater than 12.
Maximum Length	Specifies the allowed maximum length of the node.
MinFacet Type	Possible values are Inclusive and Exclusive. Only active when a value is set in the MinFacet Value property.
MinFacet Value	Determines the value of the MinInclusive or MinExclusive facet, and which one is used is determined by the value of the MinFacet Type property. This is used to apply validations to restrictions on the Base Data Type that is chosen. For instance, for a base data type of xs:int, the MinFacet Type set to Inclusive and the MinFacet Value set to 2, this means that the value in the node must be greater than or equal to 2.
Minimum Length	Specifies the allowed minimum length of the node.
Pattern	Specifies a regular expression that can be used when restricting the possible values of a node. This is useful for describing email addresses, phone numbers, social security numbers, and so on. For instance, a regular expression of [0-9]{8} is a regular expression that causes validation to make sure the element has a value that has exactly eight numbers between 0 and 9. For information on regular expressions, search the Internet.

Properties for Elements   This section describes the most important properties for elements.

TABLE 2.7   Properties for Elements

Property	Description
Max Occurs	Specifies the maximum number of times this element can occur. For an unlimited number of times, enter Unbounded. If you enter an asterisk (*), the Schema Editor translates that into Unbounded for you. The default value is 1, meaning that the element can occur a maximum number of 1 time.
Min Occurs	Specifies the minimum number of times the element must appear. The default value is 1. If the value is 0, the element is optional and does not have to appear in the XML.

Properties for Attributes   This section describes the most important properties for attributes.

TABLE 2.8   Properties for Attributes

Property	Description
Use Requirement	Used to specify whether the attribute is required. Valid values are Optional (the default), Prohibited, and Required. If a value of Optional is chosen, the attribute may or may not occur. Prohibited means that the element may not occur, and Required means that the attribute must occur in the instance. A value of Prohibited seems weird, because you could then just as well not have the attribute in the schema at all. It is useful, however, when using a type from another schema and wanting to prohibit the usage of a certain attribute that is in this type.

Enveloping

It is common to group several smaller messages into one bigger message and transmit this one message instead of transmitting all the small messages. This proves especially useful when dealing with scenarios where some company pays a service provider per message they transmit. In this case, wrapping all messages to a specific customer in one envelope minimizes expenses. This is basically the same as if a company needs to send four letters via postal mail to customer. The company might choose to put all four letters inside one envelope to cut back on expenses for envelopes and stamps.

BizTalk supports debatching of XML envelopes out of the box by leveraging the Envelope property described in Table 2.3 and the Body XPath property described in Table 2.5.

Consider the XML example shown in Listing 2.1. This is an example of an envelope with two separate documents inside it: an order and an invoice.

LISTING 2.1   Example of an XML Envelope

```
<ns0:MyEnvelopeRoot xmlns:ns0="http://mycompany.com/schemas/envelope">
      <MyEnvelopeHeader>
            <Sender>sender@sender.com</Sender>
            <Receiver>receiver@receiver.com</Receiver>
      </MyEnvelopeHeader>
      <Documents>
            <ns1:Order xmlns:ns1="http://mycompany.com/schemas/order">
                  <OrderHeader>Some values</OrderHeader>
            </ns1:Order>
            <ns2:Invoice xmlns:ns2="http://mycompany.com/schemas/invoice">
                  <OrderHeader>Some values</OrderHeader>
            </ns2:Invoice>
      </Documents>
</ns0:MyEnvelopeRoot>
```

To instruct BizTalk to get the documents out of the envelope, you need the following:

▶ A schema for the envelope. The root node must be `MyEnvelopeRoot`, and the target namespace must be http://mycompany.com/schemas/envelope. Also, the property Envelope must be set to True. Also, the Body XPath property must be set to point at the Documents record.

▶ A schema for both the order and the invoice. These schemas must be constructed to validate the XML you would get if you simply took out the order and invoice XML from the envelope and validated it against the schemas.

▶ A receive pipeline that utilizes the XML disassembler component.

At runtime, BizTalk looks at the incoming XML and finds the schema that matches it. The schema has the Envelope property set to True, so BizTalk looks at the Body XPath property to find the XPath that leads to the body of the message. In this case, the Body XPath points to the Documents record. BizTalk then takes all children of the Documents record and submits them individually for further processing.

Processing Instructions

Many XML documents have a processing instruction at the top, which is also called the XML declaration. It looks like this: '`<?xml version="1.0" encoding="utf-8" ?>`'. There can be many processing instructions in an XML document, though. Processing instructions are used to let the program that reads the XML know something about what to do with it.

The format of a processing instruction is always `<?NAME VALUE ?>`, where the `NAME` is the name of the processing instruction (that is, `xml` in the XML declaration). After the `NAME`, the value appears. Although this often times looks like it is XML attributes, it really isn't. In the XML declaration, it appears that there are two attributes: the version and the encoding attributes. The reality, however, is that the processing instruction has a name of xml and a value of 'version="1.0" encoding="utf-8"'.

Processing instructions are used heavily by InfoPath. All instances of an InfoPath form have processing instructions in them, which instructs the Explorer in Windows to open the XML documents in InfoPath, and which informs InfoPath about the location of the form, the version of the form, the existence of attached files, and other things. Listing 2.2 shows the processing instructions that can be found in an InfoPath form.

LISTING 2.2   Example InfoPath Processing Instructions

```
<?mso-infoPathSolution solutionVersion="1.0.0.4" productVersion="12.0.0"
    PIVersion="1.0.0.0" href="file:///C:\Projects\Forms\PersonalInformation.xsn"
    name="urn:schemas-microsoft-com:office:infopath:Personal-Information:-myXSD-
    2010-07-12T14-57-04" ?>
<?mso-application progid="InfoPath.Document" versionProgid="InfoPath.Document.2"?>
<?mso-infoPath-file-attachment-present?>
```

As shown in Listing 2.2, there are three processing instructions:

▶ **mso-infoPathSolution**: This processing instruction contains a lot of information InfoPath needs when opening the form, such as where to find the template for the file, the version number, which version of InfoPath has been used, and so on.

▶ **mso-application**: This instructs Explorer and other systems that need the information that this particular XML file is an InfoPath form. When reading this, systems may choose to handle the file differently than a normal XML file. For instance, Explorer shows an InfoPath icon rather than an XML icon and opens the XML file using InfoPath instead of the program you have associated with XML files.

▶ **mso-infoPath-file-attachment-present**: This instructs InfoPath and other systems that want to read the InfoPath form and that the form can contain attached files, which are base64 encoded and kept in an element in the resulting XML.

You can find more information about processing instructions at the W3 website (http://www.w3.org/TR/xml/#sec-pi).

Flat File Schemas

BizTalk uses XSDs for describing flat files and XML documents. At first glance, this might seem odd because XSDs are for describing XML. The trick is that all the information in the schema that is flat file-specific, like what delimiter to use in a delimited file or the length of the fields in a positional file and other such information, is kept in annotations in the schema. So, for instance, a record in a schema that describes a flat file that has its fields delimited by a comma is shown in Figure 2.16.

```
<xs:element maxOccurs="unbounded" name="OrderLine">
  <xs:annotation>
    <xs:appinfo>
      <b:recordInfo sequence_number="1" structure="delimited" preserve_delimiter_for_empty_data="true"
        suppress_trailing_delimiters="false" child_delimiter_type="char" child_delimiter="," child_order="infix" />
    </xs:appinfo>
  </xs:annotation>
  <xs:complexType>
    <xs:attribute name="ItemNumber" type="xs:string">
      <xs:annotation>
        <xs:appinfo>
          <b:fieldInfo sequence_number="1" justification="left" />
        </xs:appinfo>
      </xs:annotation>
    </xs:attribute>
    <xs:attribute name="Quantity" type="xs:string">
      <xs:annotation>
        <xs:appinfo>
          <b:fieldInfo sequence_number="2" justification="left" />
        </xs:appinfo>
      </xs:annotation>
    </xs:attribute>
  </xs:complexType>
</xs:element>
```

FIGURE 2.16   Example of a record in a flat file described in an XSD.

As shown in Figure 2.16, the OrderLine element is declared the normal XSD way. The information about the flat file structure, delimiter type, and so on is written in an element called xs:annotation. This element is meant for comments, and inside the xs:appinfo element BizTalk stores its information. For this, BizTalk defines a namespace alias b, which is a namespace alias for the flat file Schema Editor Extension that is defined earlier in the schema. A Schema Editor Extension is an extension for BizTalk Schema Editor, and it is used for letting a programmer define new properties that should be available for elements in the tree view. This is how we can describe flat files in our schemas. The Flat File Extension provides the BizTalk Schema Editor with information about what properties should be available when describing the flat file. Custom Schema Editor extensions are described briefly in a later section. If you want to switch between what Schema Editor extensions are available on a schema, click the **<Schema>** node in the tree view, and go to the **Schema Editor Extensions** property. Clicking the ellipsis for this brings you the screen shown in Figure 2.17.

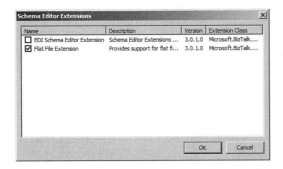

FIGURE 2.17   Schema Editor extensions that ship with BizTalk.

To create a flat file schema, you have three options, which all start with right-clicking your project and choosing **Add**, **New Item**, and then choosing **Schema**, as shown in Figure 2.7. The three options are as follows:

▶ **Flat File Schema:** This is for creating a flat file schema manually.

- ▶ **Flat File Schema Wizard:** This is for going through a wizard that will help you create a schema for a flat file.

- ▶ **Schema:** This creates a normal schema but you can then add the Flat File Extension to the schema manually. This basically corresponds to the first option, so this does not have a separate section in the book.

Just as with regular schemas, be aware that there are no two schemas with the same combination of target namespace and root node. This is not immediately clear because flat files do not have root nodes or target namespaces. The reason it is still important is that the flat files are transformed into XML by the flat file disassembler and the message type is promoted to be used for routing, correlation, choosing the correct map to execute, and so on. This makes it just as important to focus on the message type for flat files as for XML.

Flat files are mostly found when integrating to older legacy systems. Newer systems tend to use XML, and also EDI (be it EDIFACT, X12, HIPAA, or other) is widely used. The format of the flat files is often not well described because they can be formats that have been developed over the years, extended to meet specific needs several times during the life time of the system. This has the side effect that often it is difficult to find a decent description of the flat file format in question. Two systems exchange flat files; it goes well, but no one has sat down and formalized important issues like data types of elements, cardinalities of elements, which elements are required, which are optional, and such. As described at the beginning of this chapter, schemas are not to be taken lightly, so do take the time to write the definition of the document structure down, if it is not present. Do not rely on someone telling you that a particular record can only occur once in a message because she has only ever seen it appear once. You need specifics.

Add Existing Schemas

Just as with XML schemas, you can add an existing schema, if one can be provided from your trading partner. This has to be a schema created by BizTalk, however, because the only flat file schemas BizTalk can understand are the schemas it has created itself using the BizTalk-specific annotations.

Creating by Hand

Most experienced BizTalk developers will probably make use of the Flat File Schema Wizard to create the schema for flat files because using it can decrease development time significantly. But often when using the Flat File Schema Wizard, you will get stuck not knowing how to approach some specific structure in the flat file. This is because sometimes you need to wrap some records in another logical record for the schema to end up just right. Therefore, you should have some experience getting the schemas to work manually before using the Flat File Schema Wizard. The Flat File Schema Wizard is described in the next section. This section walks you through creating a flat file schema manually.

After adding a flat file schema to your project, you get a view that is similar to that of normal XSDs. This is because both schema types have records, elements, and attributes, which really are all the tree view cares about. The main difference is in the properties available for the elements in the tree view. Visual Studio 2010 has added the flat file extensions to the schema for you, so all the needed properties for flat files are already present. In this section, the creation of flat file schemas is discussed.

Basically, flat files consist of records, elements, and attributes just like normal XML schemas. The semantics are the same, as well. Records contain elements and attributes, which in turn contain values. Records, including the root node, are defined as either positional or delimited. If a record is defined as positional, all the children of this record have a fixed start position and length. If the record is defined as delimited, it means that there is some delimiter specified that is used to mark where the children start and end.

The most common case is that the root node is delimited by either Line Feed (LF) as in UNIX systems or by Carriage Return (CR)/Line Feed (LF) as is used on the Microsoft platform. Any delimiter is allowed, though. The reason the root node is almost always delimited is that a flat file almost always consists of lines that may be either delimited or positional, but hardly any flat file has the content in one big mess without line feeds. To know exactly what delimiter is used in your specific file, team up with your favorite hex editor. Plenty of free hex editors are available on the Internet.

Also, for creating schemas for flat files that are positional, you need some easy way of determining how long a given field is, if you do not have the specifications. Again, utilize your favorite text editor that has the option of showing you the line number and column number the cursor is placed at.

Defining Structure

When creating a schema for a flat file, it is important to get an overview of the flat file first, to determine a strategy for creating the flat file schema. Consider the flat file instance shown in Figure 2.18. First, it has seven lines in it, meaning that it is a delimited file on the root level. It consists of the following types of lines:

▶ A header, which is a positional record, which consists of the following fields:

  ▶ **Tag Identifier**, which is used to let any parser that must read this file know that this line is a header. The value of the tag identifier is H.

  ▶ **Order Date**, which takes up the first eight characters after the tag identifier. It is quite common for flat file to have a custom date format, and the format for the date in this field is yyyymmdd.

  ▶ **Customer Number**, which takes up the next 15 characters after the order date.

▶ An order header, which is a delimited record, using the comma as delimiter. It consists of the following fields:

  ▶ **Tag Identifier** (with the value 0)

  ▶ **Order Number**

  ▶ **Salesperson** (in charge of this order)

- ▶ An order line, which is a delimited record, using the comma as delimiter. It consists of the following fields:

    - ▶ **Tag Identifier** (with the value OL)

    - ▶ **Item number** (which in this case is an integer)

    - ▶ **Quantity** (which in this case is an integer)

    - ▶ **Item Price** (which in this case is a decimal)

All lines in the example end with CR/LF. When creating a schema for this kind of flat file, you usually create only two records below the root node, which might at first seem odd because there are three different types of records. The reason is that you will want to group an order into one record that will contain both the order header and the order lines. There are three reasons for wanting to group an order into one element:

- ▶ It provides a nice logical grouping, which is easier to understand.

- ▶ It will make it easier to map the file afterward because you will probably be mapping to or from a similar structure and hence the mapper will have a better chance of getting the map right.

- ▶ If you need to split the flat file or the generated XML when receiving the flat file into separate order messages, this is much easier.

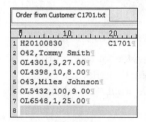

FIGURE 2.18   Flat file example with same delimiter for several records.

So, at the root level, you will have a schema that looks like Figure 2.19. The root node has been chosen to describe the customer number the schema is for and the type of message (for example, Order). In this scenario, the resulting root node in the XML from parsing the flat file will have one Header record and a number of Order records in it.

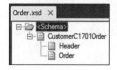

FIGURE 2.19   Root-level layout of flat file schema.

This is perfectly legal, but you usually want to group the orders inside a record, which in this case would be called Orders just to make it look nice (see Figure 2.20). Both are perfectly valid options, and it is up to you to choose which you find most intuitive to use.

FIGURE 2.20   Alternative root-level layout of flat file schema.

After deciding on the records needed at the root level, the records for the order header and order lines should be created (see Figure 2.21). Just as with the orders, you might want to group inside one Orders record that is on the same level as the header; you have the same option with the order lines to group them together in an OrderLines record.

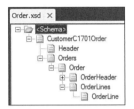

FIGURE 2.21   Flat file schema with all records defined.

For the Header record, the property Structure should be set to Positional because the fields below this record have fixed lengths. When you change the value of the Structure property, the Schema Editor presents you with a warning. This is because different properties are available for your record depending on the value of the Structure property; so when changing the value, some properties disappear. Only the Header record is positional in the example given in Figure 2.18, so the rest of the records should have the Structure property set to Delimited, which is also the default value.

Setting Delimiters
The tricky part of a flat file schema is almost always in the delimiters used because you sometimes have records that are delimited inside another record that is delimited. If they share the delimiter, you need to be careful how you handle this. Consider the flat file in Figure 2.18, which is a small example of a flat file order.

As you can probably see by now from Figure 2.21, getting the delimiters right is somewhat difficult. For setting the delimiter on a record, you have some decisions to make. First of all, what is the delimiter, and second, where does the delimiter appear relative to the child fields?

The record OrderHeader should have the Child Delimiter Type set to Character because a single character serves as the delimiter of the child fields of the OrderHeader record. The Child Delimiter property should be set to comma (,).

In Figure 2.18, for example, all records that contain other records have CR/LF as delimiter, which means that you can set the Child Delimiter Type of the root node, the Orders node, the Order node, and the OrderLines node to be Hexadecimal. The value Hexadecimal indicates that you need to specify a hexadecimal code that describes the delimiter because you cannot describe CR/LF as a character because it is not printable. For the Child Delimiter, therefore, specify 0x0d 0x0a, which is the hexadecimal code for CR/LF. After setting the correct delimiter, you need to decide where the delimiter appears relative to the children of the record you have set the delimiter on, and this is where it can get tricky. The property Child Order is used to tell the parser where the delimiter is placed relative to the children. The relevant values are as follows:

▶ **Infix:** This means that the delimiter appears in between the fields. There is no delimiter before the first field, and there is no delimiter after the last field.

▶ **Postfix:** This means that there is a delimiter in between all fields, like with the Infix value, but there is also a delimiter after the last field.

▶ **Prefix:** This means that there is a delimiter in between all fields, like with the Infix value, but there is also a delimiter before the first field.

The flat file shown in Figure 2.22 has three examples, and all three lines have the delimiter as a comma. The first line is Infix, the second is Postfix, and the third is Prefix. A value of Prefix is hardly ever used, but the Flat File Schema Wizard occasionally uses it.

```
     0          10          20
 1 This,is,the,first,line¶
 2 This,is,the,second,line,¶
 3 ,This,is,the,third,line¶
```

FIGURE 2.22   Three examples of the Child Order property.

The instance in Figure 2.18 has seven CR/LF inside it, which must be used to delimit records. The way to do this is to start from the root node. The root node has two records below it: the Header and the Orders records. There is no CR/LF before the Header record, so the Child Order cannot be Prefix. There is, however, an empty line at the end of the flat file, meaning that the last line with content is ended with a CR/LF. Now, this last CR/LF can be seen as both a CR/LF that ends the Orders record and as a CR/LF that ends the last OrderLine record. Again, both are valid, but usually a value of Infix is used because this will make it possible to treat all orders the same. Figure 2.23 depicts the instance with a square around the delimiter that has been dealt with by setting the Child Order to Infix on the root node. This leaves you with three delimiters for each order, which now must be addressed.

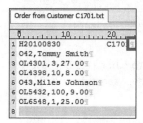

FIGURE 2.23   Visualization of what delimiters have been dealt with after setting Child Order on root node.

The Orders record that contains lots of orders should have its Child Order property set to Postfix. The main reason for this is that this will eat the last CR/LF for each order, which still leaves you with a symmetric view of the remaining delimiters. Figure 2.24 depicts what delimiters have been dealt with after setting the Child Order property on both the root node and the Orders record. The delimiters handled by setting the property on the Orders record are marked with a square in lines 4 and 7, and the delimiter that was handled by setting the Child Order property on the root node is marked with a square in line 1.

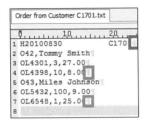

FIGURE 2.24   Visualization of what delimiters have been dealt with after setting Child Order on root and **Orders**.

The next record to deal with is the Order record. It has an OrderHeader and an OrderLines record beneath it. Because the Orders delimiter eats the delimiters in lines 4 and 7, you cannot set the Child Order to postfix on the Order record because there is no delimiter after the last record beneath it. So, you must set it to Infix, leaving the instance as shown in Figure 2.25. The new delimiters that are dealt with by setting the Child Order property on the Order record are marked with a square in lines 2 and 5.

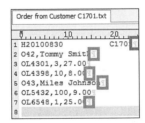

FIGURE 2.25   Visualization of the delimiters that are dealt with before setting the final Child Order property.

The only record left that hasn't got the Child Order specified is the OrderLines record. Because the only delimiter left in the instance that hasn't been dealt with is in between the OrderLine records, you must set the Group Order property to Infix, which will then take care of the remaining two delimiters in the instance.

Tag Identifiers

After setting the delimiters correctly, you need to set any tag identifiers that are applicable. Tag identifiers are used to let the parser know what type a given record is. In the example from Figure 2.18, the header has an identifier of H, the Order header has a tag identifier of O, and the order lines have a tag identifier of OL. These values should be set on the records in question. Note that the tag identifier 0 can be set on both the OrderHeader record and on the Order record. This is because the 0 starts both a new Order and a new OrderHeader. If OrderHeader could occur multiple times, you could not set the tag identifier on the Order record. Which one to choose is up to your personal preference. For this example, you can set the tag identifiers on Header, OrderHeader, and OrderLine (which is most intuitive). Note that on Header you can also specify a Tag Offset, which is the offset into the positional record where the tag identifier can be located. For delimited records, the tag identifier needs to be at the beginning of the record.

NOTE

Tag identifiers are quite important because they help the flat file parser in determining when records end and begin. One place where this really matters is on the root node. This is because a pipeline that handles an incoming message can at runtime determine which schema to use for parsing the incoming flat file. This works only if there is a tag identifier on the root node. So, if you need this, you would set the tag identifier of H on the root node rather than the Header record.

Also, for BizTalk to know when the Header ends and the Document begins when debatching, BizTalk relies heavily on tag identifiers. Debatching is described in a later section.

Cardinality

For each record, you also need to consider if the record is optional or required, which is determined by the Min Occurs property. A value of 0 means that the record does not have to appear, whereas a value of 1 or larger means that the record must appear the specified number of times.

In addition, you need to decide whether the record can occur only once or if it can appear multiple times. This is determined by the Max Occurs property. This property determines the maximum number of occurrences this record can have for each parent of the record. For instance, you can determine that an order can have a maximum of three order lines. This does not mean that the OrderLine record can occur only three times in the entire message, but it means that the OrderLine record can only occur a maximum of three times for each Order record.

Naturally, the Max Occurs property cannot have a value smaller than the Min Occurs property.

The default value for both Min Occurs and Max Occurs is 1, meaning that the record must appear and can only appear once.

For the flat file given in Figure 2.18, the Max Occurs should be changed to Unbounded on the Order and the OrderLine records. The rest should keep their default values. The word *unbounded* is specified in the XSD standard and must be set exactly like this. The Schema Editor provides a shortcut for this. If you type in an asterisk (*),the Schema Editor replaces that with Unbounded for you.

Value Fields

After getting the structure right, setting the delimiters, and setting the cardinality of the records, you need to add the fields that will contain the actual values. For the fields, you can choose between elements and attributes. For the most part, it doesn't matter which ones you choose. There are, however, two points to consider when choosing:

▶ Attributes take up only about half the space that elements take up. This is because an attribute called `OrderNumber` will only have the word `OrderNumber` once, whereas an element will have both a start tag and an end tag, meaning that the word `OrderNumber` will appear twice, as well as the opening and closing brackets for the tags. For large flat files that are converted into XML, this can become a bottleneck.

▶ Elements can occur multiple times, attributes cannot. This can come in handy if you have some value field that can occur multiple times.

Other than these two points, also keep in mind that element and attribute names should be as short as possible while still being names that describe the content (because of performance issues that might arise with large files).

After you have chosen whether to use elements, attributes, or a combination thereof, you can start adding the fields to the records.

For fields that are present in delimited records, the most important property to set is the Data Type.

For fields that are present in positional records, the three most important properties to set are as follows:

▶ **Data Type:** This is the data type of the field, like `xs:string`, `xs:boolean`, `xs:int`, and so on, where the `xs:` means that they are the data types you normally have available for XSDs.

▶ **Positional Length:** This specifies the length of the field.

▶ **Positional Offset:** This specifies the offset where this field begins relative to the end of the previous field. This allows you to skip data in a positional record because you can let a field start 10 characters later than the last field ended, effectively ignoring those 10 characters of data. This comes in handy if you are not interested in all the data in a flat file.

For the `Header` record, you need to add three fields:

▶ **Tag:** This field is, strictly speaking, not necessary. If you add it and give it a Positional Length of 1, it will contain the tag identifier `H`. The reasons for adding it are as follows:

  ▶ You might, although this rarely occurs, need it in your maps or in other functionality later on.

- ▶ It lets you keep the default value of the Positional Offset of the next record because this would otherwise have to have the Positional Offset set to the length of the tag identifier.

- ▶ **OrderDate:** This should have a Positional Length of 8. The Positional Offset should remain at the default value unless you decided not to have the first field defined, in which case you should enter a value of 1.

- ▶ **CustomerNumber:** This field should have a Positional Offset of 0 (the default value) and a Positional Length of 15. Notice that the string, although 15 characters long, has only 8 characters of data. The rest of the string is the Pad Character, which defaults to a space. For this instance, the data is right-justified, meaning that the pad characters, if any, are to the left of the data. You need to change the Justification property to **Right**.

Localization

Sometimes you need to handle localization issues like custom date formats, different separators between a number and the decimals, and so on.

At times, you will need to create schemas, which has a custom date format. If you specify the data type to be date, you will get into trouble because the date data type in XSDs requires the date to be in the format YYYY-MM-DD and then perhaps a Z for UTC or an offset like this: YYYY-MM-DD-06:00. The instance seen in Figure 2.18 has the date as YYYYMMDD without dashes. The normal way of handling this is to define the data type as a string, and then in your map use string manipulation to extract year, month, and date and put them back together to match the format required by the output. There is, however, a smarter way of doing this. Specify the data type as xs:date and then a new property appears called Custom Date/Time Format. In here, you can specify the format the date is in. Choose **yyyyMMdd** and the parser will automatically parse the date given this format and convert it to the proper XML date format for you when generating the XML.

Sometimes you will need to parse flat files that have decimal numbers with a comma between the number and its decimals rather than a period. This is achieved by setting the Culture property of the <Schema> node in the tree view. Set the property to a culture that matches your requirements.

Complex Schemas

The parser is optimized to be really fast, which also means that memory consumption by default is minimal. This, in turn, means that some flat files cannot be parsed before you tweak some settings first. Note that for normal flat file schemas you can leave these tweaks alone because they will parse just fine. If you get errors validating instances against your schemas, and you cannot determine any cause of this error, however, it might because your schema is so complex that the parser simply fails even though your schema is valid. In this case, you can tell the parser to be more thorough, which will of course mean larger memory consumption and will take more time to parse.

The two properties to tweak are Parser Optimization and Lookahead Depth. Both properties are found as properties of the <Schema> node in the tree view.

The value for Lookahead Depth determines how far ahead in the parse tree the parser should look for determining what token it is currently looking at. The default value is 3, which allows the parser to look at a token, look at the next token (which can be a delimiter), and at the next (which may then be a tag identifier). This is often far enough. If you get mysterious errors, you can tweak this value. A value of 0 means unlimited.

The value for Parser Optimization can be set to Speed (the default) or Complexity. With Speed, the parser parses top down, meaning that if a data is encountered it is assumed to belong to the next possible field in the schema. This can cause issues if this field is optional and the value actually belongs to a required field appearing after the optional field. With Complexity, the parser parses both top down and bottom up, trying to assign values to fields.

> **TIP**
>
> Consider always setting these properties to allow for complex schemas; that is, set Parser Optimization to **Complexity** and Lookahead Depth to **0** when you start creating your flat file schemas. This will make sure you are not wasting time looking at irrelevant errors when building the schema. When the schema is done, relax the settings, and if the schema still works, keep the values as optimized for speed as possible, while still parsing the instances. Implement unit testing of the schema with lots of instances to make sure you still have a valid schema after relaxing the settings.

Enveloping

Just as with XML, BizTalk has support for debatching incoming flat files that contain several documents that need to be handled individually. For flat files, there are no extra properties to set on any schemas to support this. What is needed is this:

- ▶ A schema (Header schema) that describes everything that may appear before the documents that are to be extracted

- ▶ A schema (Document schema) that describes the documents that are to be extracted

- ▶ A schema (Trailer schema) that describes what may come after the documents that are to be extracted

These schemas, of which the Header schema and Trailer schema are optional, are specified on the flat file disassembler component, and it will then automatically perform the debatching for you.

Flat File Schema Wizard

The previous section described how to create a flat file schema by hand. This section uses the same flat file instance and uses the Flat File Schema Wizard to create the same schema. The first subsection takes you through the wizard, and the second discusses changes that need to be done after the wizard has finished. Finally, a short description of how to go about testing the generated schema follows.

To revisit the flat file instance, see Figure 2.26, which is a copy of the flat file instance shown in Figure 2.18.

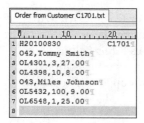

```
Order from Customer C1701.txt

 0        10        20
1 H20100830          C1701¶
2 O42,Tommy Smith¶
3 OL4301,3,27.00¶
4 OL4398,10,8.00¶
5 O43,Miles Johnson¶
6 OL5432,100,9.00¶
7 OL6548,1,25.00¶
8
```

FIGURE 2.26   Flat file example with the same delimiter for several records.

The Wizard

This section takes you through using the wizard step by step to generate a schema for the flat file instance shown in Figure 2.26.

1. Right-click your project and choose **Add**, **New Item**.

2. Choose Flat File Schema Wizard and provide a filename for the schema. You will now be seeing the wizard, as shown in Figure 2.27, which appears after you move on from the Welcome screen, which can be disabled from appearing anymore.

3. After the Welcome screen, the wizard needs an instance of a flat file on which to base the rest of the wizard. Browse to the appropriate flat file and enter values for Record Name and Target Namespace. The default values for the root node and target namespace are the exact same values as if you had just added a flat file schema to your project to build it manually. Change them appropriately and choose a code page for the input. Often, UTF-8 is fine, but when integrating with older legacy systems in countries that have special characters, some instances will be using old code pages. If you check the Count Positions in Bytes check box, this will cause both the wizard and the BizTalk runtime to count Positional Offset, Positional Length, and Tag Offset using bytes rather than characters. If selected, the wizard sets the property Count Positions in Bytes to Yes in the properties of the generated schema.

NOTE

You normally want to count the number of characters and not the number of bytes, because an encoding might use 1 byte for some characters and 2 or more bytes for other characters, but sometimes you will need to count using bytes when integrating to SAP or mainframe systems that count using bytes or when dealing with *multibyte character set* (MBCS or DBCS) data.

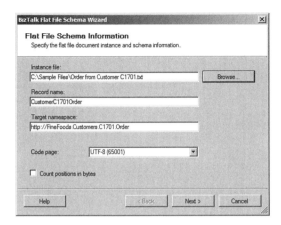

FIGURE 2.27   Flat File Schema Wizard, choosing instance and main properties.

4. When these fields are filled out, click **Next**, which brings you to the screen shown in Figure 2.28.

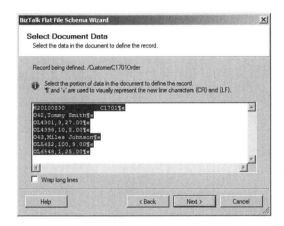

FIGURE 2.28   Flat File Schema Wizard, choosing relevant data.

5. In this screen, you need to choose the data that is relevant for the schema you are going to define. By default, all data is selected, because the wizard assumes you want to create a schema that describes the entire flat file. This is usually the case, but sometimes you want to generate a schema for just part of the flat file. For instance, if a flat file has a header record and lots of details records, you can create a schema that parses just one detail record and then use this schema in a receive pipeline to split up incoming messages into lots of messages that each conform to this schema. Click **Next**.

6. Now you get the screen shown in Figure 2.29. In this screen, you need to specify whether the root node is delimited or positional. This instance has a delimited root node, so choose **By Delimiter Symbol** and click **Next**, which brings you to the screen shown in Figure 2.30.

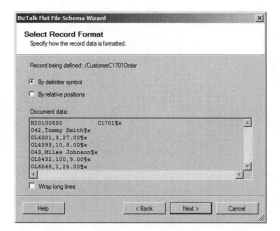

FIGURE 2.29   Flat File Schema Wizard, choosing the format of the root node.

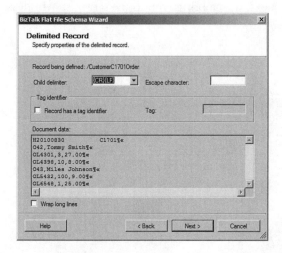

FIGURE 2.30   Flat File Schema Wizard, choosing the delimiter and tag identifier.

7. Here you need to specify what delimiter to use for the root node. CR/LF has been preselected for you, but you can change it if you want to. Also, if the record you are specifying has a tag identifier, you can add it here. For this scenario, do not choose a tag identifier because it will be put on the Header record instead, as with the manually created flat file. Click **Next** to go to the screen shown in Figure 2.31.

8. In this screen, you must specify the children of the record. The columns in this screen are Element Name, Element Type, Data Type, and Contents.

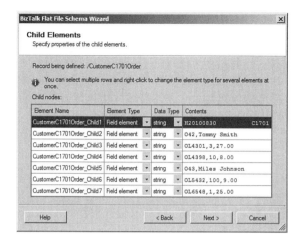

FIGURE 2.31   Flat File Schema Wizard, specifying child elements.

The wizard has one row in this table for each record it has found utilizing the delimiter chosen in Figure 2.30.

The Element Name column shows the name of the element as it will appear in the tree view once the schema is done, and which also will be the names of the relevant XML records, elements, and attributes in the instances after they are converted into XML. It is preferable to provide descriptive names here, but they can also be changed in the tree view at any time after the wizard has finished creating the schema.

The Element Type column can have five different values:

▶ **Field Element:** Used to create an element in the schema, which will then contain values.

▶ **Field Attribute:** Used to create an attribute in the schema, which will then contain values.

▶ **Record:** Used to create a record. If you choose this, the wizard later asks you to define this record, meaning that you have to specify delimiters and go through this exact same screen defining the children of this new record.

▶ **Repeating Record:** Used to define a record that can occur multiple times. As with Record, you are later be asked to define this record.

▶ **Ignore:** Used to tell the wizard to ignore a specific field that comes after a repeating record because the field is of the same type as the record that was repeating.

The Data Type column defines the data type of the row, provided the row is either a field element or a field attribute.

The Contents column shows the contents of the child, which can help you remember what the element should be called and defined as.

1. For this example, choose values as shown in Figure 2.32. This is where the tricky part comes in, which is also the reason you are encouraged to have experience in defining flat file schemas manually before attempting to use the Flat File Schema Wizard. Setting the first record to Header was expected, but then setting the second to Orders and ignoring the rest of the flat file seems odd. This is because of the limitations of the wizard. Later, when defining the Orders record, you will reevaluate what data belongs to that and then carry on defining it. Also, the Order isn't supposed to be reoccurring, but the wizard will not let you ignore the rest of the flat file if you choose Record instead. This will have to be fixed after the wizard has finished. Click **Next** to get to the screen shown in Figure 2.33.

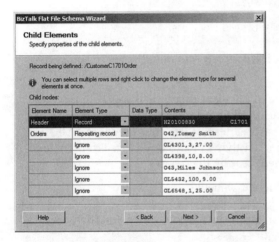

FIGURE 2.32   Flat File Schema Wizard, child elements specified.

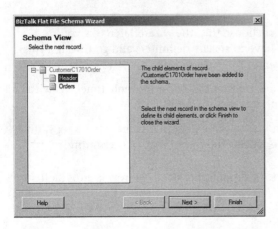

FIGURE 2.33   Flat File Schema Wizard, choosing the next record.

2. In this screen, you need to choose which of the records just defined in Figure 2.32 you want to define now. Choose **Header**, click **Next**, and you will get the screen shown in Figure 2.34.

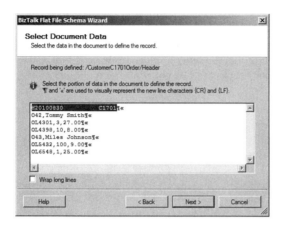

FIGURE 2.34   Flat File Schema Wizard, selecting data for **Header** record.

3. In this screen, you need to choose what part of the data from the input instance constitutes the Header record. The wizard has already chosen the first line of data for you, excluding the CR/LF because this not part of the Header record but rather the delimiter needed by the root node. Accept the proposal from the wizard, and click **Next** to start defining the content of the Header record.

4. In the next screen, choose **By Relative Positions** and click **Next**. The screen shown in Figure 2.35 will then appear.

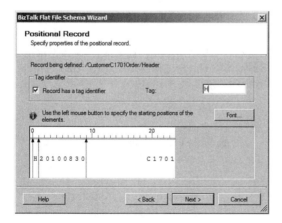

FIGURE 2.35   Flat File Schema Wizard, specifying positional fields.

5. This is where you define which fields exist in the positional record. The first thing to do is to define the tag identifier, if any. For the Header record, the tag identifier is H.

6. Then you define what fields exist by clicking inside the white box that shows the content of the record. When you click, you add a vertical line that divides the content into fields. For this scenario, click just right of the H, which is the tag identifier, and just right of the date, resulting in the screen shown in Figure 2.35. If you accidentally set a vertical line in the wrong place, you can click the line to make it disappear. After setting the field delimiters, click **Next** to get the screen shown in Figure 2.36.

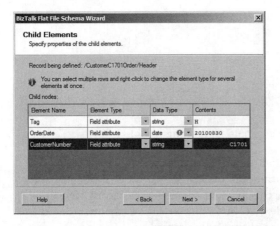

FIGURE 2.36   Flat File Schema Wizard, determining data types of **Header** record.

7. In this screen, you should set the data types and names of the fields that are in the Header record. Specify the fields as shown in Figure 2.36 and ignore the warning on the OrderDate field. The warning just wants to let you know that the data content in the instance does not match the xs:date data type, and therefore you need to change the Custom Date/Time Format property after the wizard has finished. Click **Next** and you get to the same screen as shown in Figure 2.33; only now the Header is grayed out, and you can only select Orders to specify that.

8. Choose **Orders** and click **Next**. You will see a screen similar to the screen in Figure 2.34, where only the second line is selected.

9. We want the root node to contain the Header and the Orders record, so the Orders record should cover all data in the instance that is not covered by the Header. Therefore, select the data as shown in Figure 2.37, and click **Next**.

10. As shown in Figure 2.36, there is a red exclamation mark on the date data type of the OrderDate field. The reason for this is that the data the wizard has determined is the value of the field does not match the data type of date. If you hover over the exclamation mark, you will get a message describing the error. In this case, it tells you that the data does not match the chosen data type and that you need to set the value of the Custom Date/Time Format of the field OrderDate after the wizard finishes.

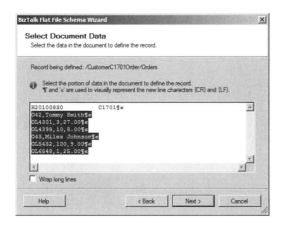

FIGURE 2.37 Flat File Schema Wizard, selecting data for **Orders** record.

11. On the next screen, choose **By Delimiter Symbol** and click **Next**.

12. Because the Orders record does not have a tag identifier (we are keeping that for the OrderHeader record) and the proposed delimiter has the right one, click **Next** again to get the screen shown in Figure 2.38.

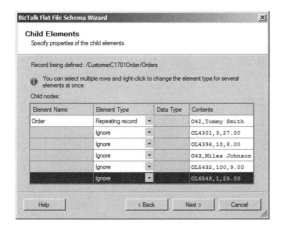

FIGURE 2.38 Flat File Schema Wizard, defining the records beneath **Orders**.

13. Because you need to define an Order record that will actually span multiple records, you need to define this one record and then ignore the rest. Set the values as shown in Figure 2.38, and click **Next**.

14. You can now select that you want to define the Order record. Select this and click **Next** to get to a screen where you need to select what data belongs to an Order record.

15. Choose as shown in Figure 2.39, and click **Next**.

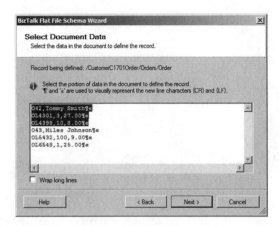

FIGURE 2.39   Flat File Schema Wizard, choosing data for the **Order** record.

16. On the next screen, choose **By Delimiter Symbol** and click **Next**.

17. Because the Order record does not have a tag identifier, accept the suggested delimiter and click **Next**.

18. In the next screen, define the records as shown in Figure 2.40, and click **Next**.

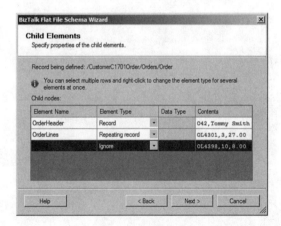

FIGURE 2.40   Flat File Schema Wizard, defining records beneath the **Order** record.

19. Choose to define the OrderHeader record and click **Next**.

20. The wizard will have selected the data it believes belongs to the OrderHeader record, and because the wizard is right, click **Next** again.

21. Then choose **By Delimiter Symbol** and click **Next**.

22. In the next screen, choose a comma as the delimiter, and let the tag identifier be 0. Then click **Next**.

23. Define the two fields as OrderNumber and SalesPerson, provide relevant data types, and click **Next**.

24. On the next screen, you need to choose **OrderLines** and click **Next** to define what is inside the OrderLines record.

25. On the next screen, choose what the OrderLines record contains. The OrderLines record contains all the orderlines, so choose them as shown in Figure 2.41, and click **Next**.

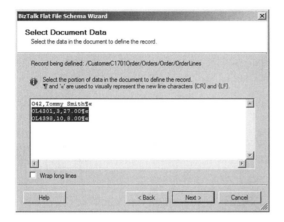

FIGURE 2.41   Flat File Schema Wizard, defining the content of the **OrderLines** record.

26. Then, choose **By Delimiter Symbol** and click **Next**.

27. Chose **{CR}{LF}** as delimiter and click **Next**.

28. Choose values as shown in Figure 2.42, and click **Next**.

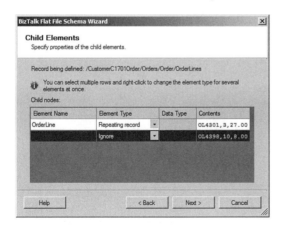

FIGURE 2.42   Flat File Schema Wizard, defining the records beneath the **OrderLines** record.

29. Click **Next** to start defining the OrderLine record, choose the data as shown in Figure 2.43, and then click **Next**.

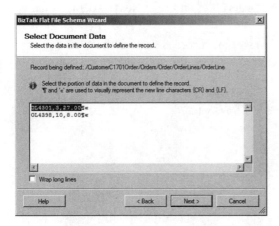

FIGURE 2.43   Flat File Schema Wizard, choosing data for the **OrderLine** record.

30. Choose **By Delimiter Symbol** and click **Next**.

31. Now choose the comma as delimiter and **OL** as tag identifier, and click **Next**.

32. Name the fields as shown in Figure 2.44, and click **Next**, and because you have now defined all the records in the flat file, you can click only **Finish**.

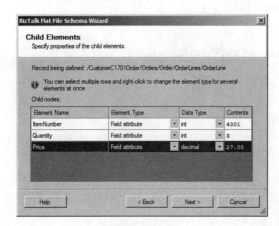

FIGURE 2.44   Flat File Schema Wizard, naming the children of the **OrderLine** record.

If you make a mistake at some point that you cannot undo because the wizard does not allow you to go back enough steps to undo it, you can still fix it using the wizard later on. You can usually go back in steps within the record you are defining. But once you have clicked **Next**, as shown in Figure 2.33, you have accepted the record you have just defined and cannot get back to it. If you have made an error, the way to fix it is to redefine that record. This is done in the tree view of the generated schema, where you can right-click a record and choose **Define Record from Flat File Instance**. If you do this, the wizard starts up again, asking you to specify an instance file, which is prefilled for you because the wizard wrote the instance filename into the <projectname>.btproj.user file in the EditorInputInstanceFilename element.

Changes After the Wizard

After completing the wizard, you will almost always need to make changes to the generated schema. The changes that are the most common include the following:

▶ **Cardinality:** When creating recurring records, the wizard sometimes inserts the actual number of records found in the instance as MinOccurs and MaxOccurs, which most of the time is not what you want and therefore quite silly.

▶ **Custom date and time formats:** As shown in Figure 2.36, you get a warning when you set a field to the type date if the value in the field does not match the xs:date data type usable in XSDs. In this case, you need to remember to set the value of the Custom Date/Time Format property.

▶ **Switching record to elements:** Because you cannot use the wizard to create recurring elements, you need to create a recurring record and have an element inside it. You might want to change that afterward.

Other than these, there might be other changes you want to implement. As with all wizards, check the output.

For the generated schema to work, the following things need to be changed:

▶ The Child Order property on the root node should be changed to Infix.

▶ The Max Occurs property on the Orders record should be reset to the default value.

▶ The Child Order property on the Order record should be changed to Infix

▶ The Child Order property on the OrderLines record should be changed to Infix.

▶ The Max Occurs property on the OrderLines record should be reset to the default value.

▶ The Custom Date/Time Format property of the OrderDate attribute should be set to yyyyMMdd.

Test the Generated Schema

After generating the schema and manually changing the needed properties, you should enable unit testing of the schema with as many flat file instances as you have, to make sure the schema is valid. Unit testing of schemas is described later in this chapter.

EDI Schemas

We have now discussed schemas that describe XML and flat files. For EDI purposes, BizTalk ships with 8,000+ schemas out of the box that you can use for your EDI solutions. Because there are so many schemas, they are zipped and not immediately available. To get to the schemas, go to the %Installation Folder%\XSD_Schemas\EDI folder, and execute the MicrosoftEdiXSDTemplates.exe file. Unless you change the folder for the unzipped files, they will be unzipped to the same folder. This will give you roughly 8,000 schemas for EANCOM, EDIFACT, HIPAA, and X12. You can use these schemas in your solutions by simply adding them as existing items to your projects.

Before you add any of these schemas to your projects, consider which trading partners you have and which schemas they use. You will probably find that a lot of companies do not use the exact standard schemas but some modified version to suit the exact business needs. You are free to change the schemas after you have added them to your projects, but as with normal schemas, be aware that you should not have two schemas deployed at the same time with the same combination of root node and target namespace (that is, the message type). More important, EDI schemas also rely heavily on annotations that contain specific EDI processing instructions. So, changing these schemas should be done carefully and by someone with knowledge of EDI document definitions and EDI implementation guidelines. To use the schemas in your project, right-click the project, and choose **Add, Existing Item**. Point out the schema you want to use and include it in your project. Remember to change the target namespace if you are planning to make changes to the schema to accommodate some specific partner version of the schema. If you need to use the exact standard schema, consider creating a project for the standard schemas alone, which you can then use in maps and orchestrations in other projects.

Messages That Are Not XML and Not Flat File

BizTalk has nice and rich featured support for XML, EDI, and flat files such as delimited files, positional files, and combinations thereof. Sometimes, however, you need to receive documents into BizTalk that BizTalk does not support out-of-the-box. This can be Excel spreadsheets, PDF files, Word documents, image files, and other types of documents. To get these documents through BizTalk, you have a few options, which are described in this section.

Pass-Through Pipeline

As a general rule, when a message arrives at BizTalk, BizTalk converts this message into XML in the receive pipeline. This is needed to do anything intelligent with the incoming message, such as look at the values inside it, transform it, route based on the message type, and so on.

If you do not need any of these, however, but just need to get the message in as is, you can use the PassThruReceive pipeline. Pipelines are discussed in Chapter 5, "Pipelines."

This pipeline does not attempt to parse or in any way understand what is in the received message. It merely passes it through to the MessageBox, where it will be submitted, and you then need to route it based on the limited knowledge you then have of the file, like received filename, time stamp, and so on.

Custom Disassembler

The component in BizTalk that does the transformation from the received format to XML is the disassembler component that is placed in the pipeline. In theory, any pipeline component at any stage in the pipeline can do anything with the received message, but the right place to do it is the disassembler stage in the pipeline. If the disassemblers that come out of the box cannot help, you can develop your own disassembler. Chapter 5 describes the pipeline components that come out of the box and how to develop your own custom pipeline component.

Custom Editor Extensions

As mentioned previously, editor extensions enable you to describe extra properties that should be available on records, elements, and attributes. So if you want to develop a generic component that parses some specific format you need to exchange documents in, or perhaps you want to develop a BizTalk accelerator that can be sold, you might want to consider developing your own Schema Editor extension.

This book does not cover how to develop a custom Schema Editor extension because this is out of scope. Instead, visit http://msdn.microsoft.com/en-us/library/aa560896(BTS.70).aspx, where you can find more information about this topic.

Third-Party Components

Sometimes it will take you so long to develop your own schemas or disassembler to parse messages that it is faster and cheaper to buy a component, adapter, or accelerator. Lots of add-ons on the market will help you with specific types of messages, like Excel spreadsheets, PDF files, Word documents, image files, vertical or country-specific EDI standards, and so on.

Property Promotion

There are plenty of reasons that you might need to access values from fields in messages in different stages of your business process, including the following:

> ▶ **Content-based routing:** Often you need to route incoming messages based on content of the messages, like total order amount, supplier ID, and so on.

> ▶ **Evaluating business rules based on content:** Often you need to make decisions based on the content of the message.

Property promotion in BizTalk is usually about taking values from incoming messages and moving them into the context of the message, so they are easily accessible and usable for routing. The context of a message is a set of metadata about a message that resides in the MessageBox with the message, allowing different parts of BizTalk to read in the small set of metadata, instead of the entire message, in case a value from the message is needed at runtime. Inside orchestrations, to get to values of messages, you have only three options: distinguished fields, promoted properties, and using XPath directly on the message. Distinguished fields and promoted properties are discussed in this section. The xpath function is described in Chapter 4, "Orchestrations."

Not all content in a message can be used as distinguished fields or promoted properties. Only fields that can occur only once in the message can be promoted to context as either distinguished fields or promoted properties. If you try to promote an element that can occur multiple times in the message, you will get the error shown in Figure 2.45. Visual Studio 2010 evaluates the path to the node from the root node, and if one of the nodes on the path to the node you want to promote has a maxOccurs that is not 1, you cannot promote this node.

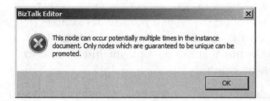

FIGURE 2.45   Error when promoting a value that can occur multiple times.

This can at times seem to be quite an obstacle, but when you think of it, it makes sense. If an element can occur multiple times, the disassembler component, which does the promoting, cannot choose which one to promote. Disassemblers are explained in detail in Chapter 5. Although this makes sense, sometimes you are sure that a given element will occur only once, even though the schema allows it to occur multiple times. In these cases, you might be tempted to try a small hack, like manually editing the XSD file to add the XPath to the element you know will occur just once. This will not work, however, because the compiler will just give you the error instead. Again, this might seem like an unnecessary obstacle, but it is done to help you. Consider, for instance, you have the XML shown in Figure 2.46.

As you can imagine, the OrderLine element is marked to be able to occur multiple times. Therefore, you cannot promote the Quantity element to either a distinguished field or a promoted property. Now, if you provide this XPath

```
/*[local-name()='Order' and namespace-
uri()='http://finefoods.com/orders/schemas']/*[local-name()='OrderLines' and
namespace-uri()='']/*[local-name()='OrderLine' and namespace-
uri()=''][ItemNumber='4301']/*[local-name()='Quantity' and namespace-
uri()='']/text()
```

```
<ns0:Order xmlns:ns0="http://finefoods.com/orders/schemas">
 - <Header OrderID="42" CustomerID="C1701">
     <RequestedDeliveryDate>2010-12-31</RequestedDeliveryDate>
     <OrderDate>2010-08-30</OrderDate>
     <OrderTotal>279.00</OrderTotal>
 + <BillTo>
 + <ShipTo>
 + <Comments>
   </Header>
 - <OrderLines>
   - <OrderLine>
       <ItemNumber>4301</ItemNumber>
       <Description>Black Truffle Oil (250ml)</Description>
       <Quantity>10</Quantity>
       <UnitPrice>27.00</UnitPrice>
     </OrderLine>
   - <OrderLine>
       <ItemNumber>5432</ItemNumber>
       <Description>Pure Tahitian Vanilla Extract</Description>
       <Quantity>1</Quantity>
       <UnitPrice>9.00</UnitPrice>
     </OrderLine>
   </OrderLines>
</ns0:Order>
```

FIGURE 2.46   XML example with reoccurring element.

Then you know that it will return the value 10 because this is the value in the Quantity element of the OrderLine element that has ItemNumber equal to 4301. But because this is only something you know and BizTalk does not know, the compiler will still not accept this because BizTalk will not be able to guarantee that that XPath expression always evaluates to just one value. One way to overcome this is to use a custom pipeline component that will evaluate the XPath expression and promote the value. This is only for promoted properties, though, because distinguished fields need to be defined within the window in which you usually define these to be useful inside an orchestration.

Distinguished Fields

Distinguished fields are fields from a message that have been marked as distinguished. Fields marked as distinguished can be used through dot notation in orchestrations and can be used to both access the value from this specific field and to set the value of this field. They are not written to the MessageBox Subscription tables for routing as the promoted properties are.

To mark a field as distinguished, you have two options:

▶ Click the **Promote Properties** property on the <Schema> node in the tree view.

▶ Right-click an element, and choose **Promote, Show Promotions**, as shown in Figure 2.47.

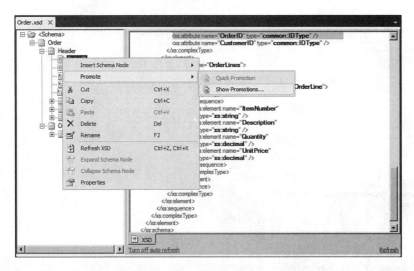

FIGURE 2.47   How to promote a field.

Both options get you to the window shown in Figure 2.48, where you choose which field in your schema you want to promote as distinguished. The field you right-clicked is preselected for you if you took that option. After promoting a field as a distinguished field, you can access it in an orchestration in an expression shape like this:

```
varStr = SimpleMessage.MyElement;
```

If MyElement had been inside a record in the schema called MyRecord, the dot notation would just go a level deeper like this:

```
varStr = SimpleMessage.MyRecord.MyElement;
```

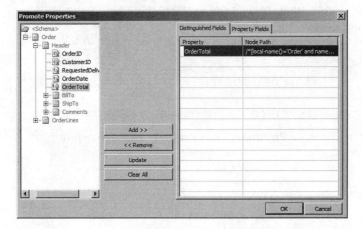

FIGURE 2.48   Promoting a distinguished field.

TIP

Note that when you use the dot notation to get to your distinguished field, none of the words used in the path to the field can be a reserved word. If `MyRecord` was a reserved word, the preceding statement would fail compilation. For a complete list of reserved words, refer to http://msdn.microsoft.com/en-us/library/aa547020(BTS.70).aspx. If you run into this issue, you need to either change the name of the element in question or use the `xpath` function inside your orchestration to get or set the value instead. The `xpath` function is described in Chapter 4.

For BizTalk to know what content to put into the context when a message arrives, the information is actually stored inside the schema, as shown in Figure 2.49. The relevant part of the schema is framed in red. When a message is received, the disassembler looks at the schema and makes sure that all properties defined therein are copied to the context.

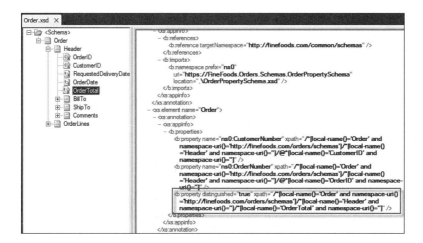

FIGURE 2.49   Schema view of distinguished field.

The main advantage of distinguished fields is that you can access values from the message in a fast, easy, and intuitive way.

Promoted Properties

Distinguished fields are an excellent and fast way of both accessing and writing values to and from messages inside an orchestration. Sometimes, however, you need to mark content in a message as something you would like to route based upon. This is what promoted properties are for. Also, distinguished fields contain content from messages that is put into the context of a message, whereas promoted properties can be both content that is put into the context of a message and it can be metadata, constants, and other that is put into the context. Whereas both distinguished fields and promoted properties can be accessed in your orchestration, only promoted properties can be used for routing, which includes correlation, as discussed further in Chapter 4. This is because only promoted properties are written to the MessageBox Subscription tables and from there used by the routing mechanism to determine which subscribers should get the message.

Promoted properties are promoted to the context in much the same way as distinguished fields. This means, for instance, that the promotion happens in the same screen as the screen where you promote distinguished fields. The main difference is that whereas distinguished fields are just to be marked as distinguished fields, promoted properties need a property in a property schema in order to be used.

A property schema is in many ways like a normal schema with some differences:

▶ Only elements are allowed.

▶ Only top-level elements are allowed, so no children.

▶ The schema is marked as a property schema by using the Document Type property of the <Schema> node in the tree view. This instructs BizTalk to treat the schema differently than other schemas.

Reasons for having a property schema include the following:

▶ BizTalk needs to know what properties are available at design time because you might want to use these properties for routing purposes (including correlation) in your orchestrations.

▶ When deployed, the administration console lists the properties found in the deployed property schemas when you specify filters on send ports.

▶ When deployed, the properties are entered into the MessageBox database so that the MessageBox knows which properties to match up between published messages and existing subscriptions.

Promoted properties actually come in two variants. Some are promoted into the context, and some are written into the context. Distinguished fields are also written to the context; contrary to the written promoted properties, however, distinguished fields are mapped to specific fields in the message itself. Promoted properties that are written to the context are still context. The BizTalk runtime has lots of written properties in the context, which are useful because they are metadata about a message and they are accessible in orchestrations and in custom pipeline components. Because they are not promoted, however, no routing can occur based on these and therefore no performance hit is taken because of them.

Property Demotion

Property demotion is the opposite of property promotion. It is about getting values from the context of a message into the content of the message. Just as the disassembler

2

pipeline component handles property promotion, the assembler pipeline component handles property demotion.

For the assembler to be able to demote a value from the context to an element in the content, there are three prerequisites:

▶ Demotion in the built-in assembler component is supported only for elements. Attributes do not work.

▶ Just as with promotion, you need to establish a reference between the two so that the assembler knows which promoted property to take the value from and which element in the content to put the value into. This is done by promoting the element to the specific promoted property that holds the value you want demoted.

▶ You need to create empty elements in the output message that the assembler can put the values into. The assembler will not demote anything if the element to put the value into is not present in the message, and it will not overwrite an existing value.

Two exceptions to these rules are as follows:

▶ Orchestrations can do their own demotion. This will allow demotion into attributes, and it will overwrite existing values. This is described more in Chapter 4.

▶ If no message type is present on the document going through the XML assembler when demoting, existing values in the elements are actually overwritten, which they are not normally.

Demotion is usually used to make sure that values from envelopes are available to put back into an outgoing message. If you receive an envelope that has a `CustomerID` in it and 200 orders, for example, and you need to split the orders up so that they can be handled one at a time, you can promote the value of the `CustomerID` as a `MessageContextPropertyBase` property, and in your send port you can demote the `CustomerID` into the outgoing messages if needed.

As mentioned, demoting into attributes is not possible using the built-in assembler components. You can, however, do it inside an orchestration. Orchestrations are described Chapter 4. The way it works is simple. You create a message inside your orchestration and assign the values needed to the correct promoted properties. If the message has empty elements for the values, the values from context are demoted into the message when the message is published into the MessageBox by the orchestration.

When to Use What

Distinguished fields and promoted properties both have upsides and downsides, so choosing correctly between them is important. This section describes the advantages and disadvantages of each (which generalizes into when to use what).

The advantages of distinguished fields over promoted properties are as follows:

- ▶ Distinguished fields have nice dot-notation style access in orchestrations, making it visible to the developer where in the message the value is kept.

- ▶ Promoted properties require a property schema to work, distinguished files do not.

- ▶ The MessageBox generates a large join in SQL Server each time a message is published, which basically is a join between the context of the message, the possible properties, and the properties of all subscriptions. This means that the number of promoted properties should be kept at a minimum, for the join to be as fast as possible. So, do not have any properties defined in property schemas that are not used.

- ▶ Distinguished fields are the only ones of the two that can be used to write values into content of a message. Changing the value of a promoted property changes only the value in the context. Demotion can help you get the value into content, but distinguished fields are much easier to use for this.

The advantages of promoted properties over distinguished fields are as follows:

- ▶ Promoted properties are the only ones that can be used for routing.

- ▶ Because correlation is a special form of routing, this also requires promoted properties.

- ▶ Distinguished fields are restricted to contain values that come from some element (that can only occur once) in the messages. Promoted properties, on the other hand, can contain data that is purely metadata about the message.

- ▶ Only promoted properties can be used for tracking purposes with the built-in tracking functionality.

Although it does not affect distinguished fields or promoted properties as such, let's take a quick look at the xpath function. The xpath function is described in Chapter 4. Basically, it is used to get a value from a message or set a value in a message based on an XPath expression. This sounds powerful, but whereas distinguished fields and promoted properties are both in the context of a message and is therefore fast to retrieve, the xpath function requires the orchestration engine to load the entire message into memory to evaluate the XPath expression. The xpath function is therefore much slower than the alternatives, and should be used only for getting and setting values of elements that are recurring where distinguished fields and promoted properties cannot help you. Also, hard-coding an XPath expression in your orchestration is error prone and requires manual updating if schemas change.

From this description, it should be clear that if your requirements are to either track some values or to use a value from a message and route the message based on this value, you need to use promoted properties.

If you need a value from a message inside an orchestration for anything not related to routing such as usage in a Decide shape or to put into another message, you should use a distinguished field because of the performance gain over promoted properties.

Should you need to access fields that are allowed to recur in your schema, you have two options:

▶ Write a pipeline component that takes the correct value and promotes it as a promoted property. Writing custom pipeline components is covered in Chapter 5.

▶ Use the xpath function to access the field. The xpath function is covered in Chapter 4.

Versioning of Schemas

As mentioned at the beginning of this chapter, schemas are very important, and you should not take them lightly, however tempting that can be at the time of development. As also mentioned previously, many things depend on schemas, like transformations, message types, and so on. Versioning of schemas is therefore particularly laborious because there are so many dependent artifacts.

Also as mentioned, having two schemas deployed at the same time that share a combination of root node and target namespace is not recommended and will most of the time bring you nothing but trouble. Under some circumstances, this will present a challenge when a schema is updated.

If a schema changes and the old version is needed at runtime by existing pipelines, maps, and orchestrations and you do not want to version the schema, you must undeploy all the assemblies that are in some way depending on the assembly that contains the updated schema. Otherwise, you need to version the schema.

Two scenarios need to be considered when deploying a new version of a schema, as described in the following subsections.

No Long-Running Transactions and a Short Downtime Acceptable

If you do not have any long-running transactions and can actually undeploy the assemblies and redeploy them with an acceptable amount of downtime, this is by far the easiest solution. You can do so as follows:

1. Update the schema with the changes that have been identified as the ones that need changing.

2. Replace the schema in any maps where it is used with the updated schema.

3. Rebuild the project with the schema and any dependent projects.

4. Export bindings either for the entire application or for the involved assemblies, one at a time.

5. Stop and un-enlist all relevant artifacts, such as receive locations, send ports, and orchestrations.

6. Redeploy the rebuild assemblies. Remember to overwrite the existing assemblies and to put the new versions in the *Global Assembly Cache* (GAC).

7. If needed, import the bindings that were exported earlier.

8. Restart your relevant host instances.

9. Start your application.

Long-Running Transactions or a Short Downtime Is Unacceptable

If you have long-running orchestrations that are dependent on your schema, you cannot update the schema without versioning it. This is because assemblies that contain the orchestrations cannot be undeployed before all running instances have finished running. Therefore, you must either terminate all running instances or stop receiving new messages until the running instances have finished running, which can take days, weeks, or even months. Both scenarios are clearly not acceptable.

If you do not have long-running orchestrations, you can stop your existing functionality so that no new messages are received, undeploy the existing assemblies, and then redeploy with the updated schema, as explained earlier. This won't take long if it has been tested on a test server first.

If downtime is not acceptable for *service level agreement* (SLA) or other reasons, you will not be able to do the upgrade without versioning the schema.

To version your schema, you need to change either the root node or the target namespace of the schema.

The reason that you need to change either the root node or the target namespace is, of course, that otherwise you will break the requirement to only have one schema deployed at the time with any given message type. Best practice is to change the target namespace and not the root node. There are two reasons for this:

▶ The target namespace is "just" a string. This means that you can put in any versioning scheme you like. So you could change http://mycompany.com/biztalk/schemas/order/v1.0 to http://mycompany.com/biztalk/schemas/order/v2.0 for an updated schema.

▶ After changing a schema, you need to reload the schema in any maps that uses the schema. Because maps by default have links saved in the .BTM file without concern for namespaces, you can reuse all the existing links in the map. Changing the root node, however, invalidates all links in your map that come from the source schema, and therefore you must redo all those links. As a workaround to this, though, you can manually edit the .BTM file in your favorite text editor and search and replace the name of the root node, but this is error prone and should be avoided.

The built-in pipeline disassemblers will use the algorithm found on the MSDN site at http://msdn.microsoft.com/en-us/library/aa559564(BTS.70).aspx to do schema resolution at runtime. The algorithm includes case where schemas in the same assembly as the pipeline are preferred to other schemas, and so on. You should familiarize yourself with this in case you ever need to version schemas.

Testing

Testing your developed functionality is not limited to code you write. It should be applied to all developed functionality, whenever available. With BizTalk come several ways of testing your schemas, from manual validation of schemas to automated unit testing.

Validate Schemas

When creating a schema, you can validate your schema to make sure you have not created something that is not valid. In general, the BizTalk Schema Editor does not allow you to generate something invalid. However, if you choose to either add an existing schema or change a schema manually using a text editor, at times it will happen anyway. It can also happen if you delete or rename an XSD file that is referenced from another schema. This includes both normal schemas and property schemas. Validation of a schema is done via the context menu of the XSD, as shown in Figure 2.50.

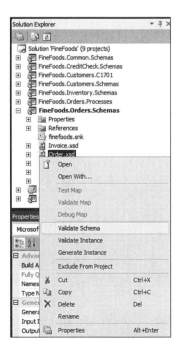

FIGURE 2.50   Validating a schema.

You can view the complete list of possible errors at http://msdn.microsoft.com/en-us/library/aa578513(BTS.70).aspx.

When you compile your project, all schemas are automatically validated first.

Validate Instances

If your schema validates, this means that syntactically it is valid. This does not, however, have anything to do with whether your XML instances will validate against the schema. There might still be wrong ordering, cardinalities, data types, naming of elements, and other issues with your schema. For this, there is the option to validate an instance. Validating an instance of a schema is useful in all cases.

If you have added an existing schema you received from a trading partner, you still need to make sure that the schema matches whatever the trading partner is sending or wants to receive. It is a possibility that the trading partner has made changes to their systems after creating the XSD and forgot to update it.

If you have generated a schema and adapted it to the correct data types, cardinalities, and so on, you want to make sure the schema is still validating the instances you will be receiving or generating the output that the trading partner wants to receive.

And finally, if you have created a schema from scratch, you most likely have an instance that you are using to build your schema from. In that case, continuously validating the instance gives you clues as to what parts of your schema still needs work.

To validate an instance, you must set two properties of the schema. Click the schema file in Solution Explorer to show the properties to change, as shown in Figure 2.51.

FIGURE 2.51   Properties on XSD needed to validate instance.

All the properties for XSD files are already explained in Table 2.1, to which you can refer. Basically, set the values of the Input Instance Filename to the file to use for validation and set the Validate Instance Input Type to either XML or Native depending on whether the instance is an XML document or some other format, like flat file, EDIFACT, or other.

Then, validate the instance using the context menu of the schema, as shown in Figure 2.52.

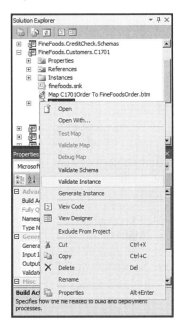

FIGURE 2.52   Validate instance of schema.

If the validation goes well, you will see an output in the output window like the one shown in Figure 2.53.

FIGURE 2.53   Success validating an instance.

If, on the other hand, something goes wrong during the validation, the output window will reflect this with a list of the errors, as shown in Figure 2.54.

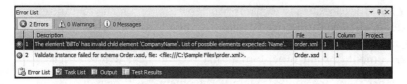

FIGURE 2.54   Errors when validating an instance.

In this example, the instance document was missing a required field called Name.

Generate Instances

When creating a schema from scratch, you will often want to be able to generate an instance of the schema you are creating. This is useful for several reasons:

▶ To validate visually whether the schema generates messages as you expect.

▶ For sending sample documents to trading partners, if the trading partner does not understand XSDs, but just wants an XML example to use as the basis for programming on his end.

▶ For generating a file that can be modified and later on used as test input for a map. Testing maps using test instances is described in Chapter 3, "Maps."

For generating an instance from a schema, two properties need to be set on the XSD. They are highlighted in Figure 2.55.

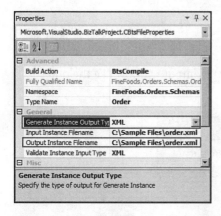

FIGURE 2.55   Properties for generating an instance from a schema.

All the properties for XSD files are already explained in Table 2.1, to which you can refer. Basically, set the values of the Output Instance Filename to the filename to be generated and set the Generate Instance Output Type to either XML or Native depending on whether the instance to be generated should be an XML document or some other format, like flat file, EDIFACT, or other. Note that even for non-XML formats you can still generate XML instances if you want. If the Output Instance Filename is not specified, a temporary filename is used.

After setting these properties, you can generate an instance using the context menu of the schema, as shown in Figure 2.56.

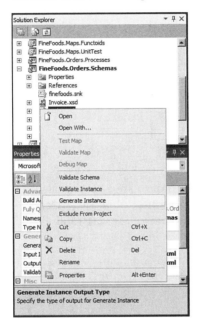

FIGURE 2.56   Generating an instance of a schema.

The output window will specify whether the instance generation was a success or a failure. In case of success, the path to the generated file is written in the output window, allowing you to Ctrl-click it to open it and view the result. Note that if you Ctrl-click it, it opens as read-only. If you need to open it for editing, mark the entire path to the file, and press **Ctrl+C**, **Ctrl+O**, **Ctrl+V**, **Enter** to copy the path, open a file, paste the filename, and open it.

Unit Testing of Schemas

In BizTalk 2009, unit testing of some of BizTalk's artifacts has been introduced. A BizTalk schema is one of the supported artifacts.

To enable the unit test, right-click the project that has your schema in it, and choose **Properties**. In the Properties window, go to Deployment and switch the Enable Unit Testing option to **True**, as shown in Figure 2.57.

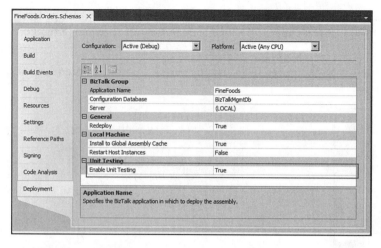

FIGURE 2.57   Enabling unit testing on a project.

After you enable unit testing on a project, all schemas in the project are now compiled with the `TestableSchemaBase` class as the base class rather than the normal `SchemaBase` class. The `TestableSchemaBase` class is in itself extending the `SchemaBase` class, adding a `ValidateInstance` method that can be used for unit testing purposes.

The unit test itself is written in a C# test project. To add a test to your solution, click **Test, New Test** in Visual Studio 2010. The screen that appears is shown in Figure 2.58.

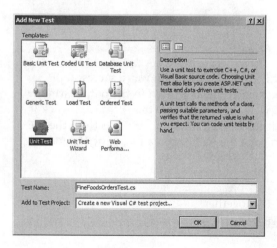

FIGURE 2.58   Adding a new test to your solution.

Only four of the alternatives in Figure 2.58 are relevant for you as a BizTalk developer: Basic Unit Test, Ordered Test, Unit Test, and Unit Test Wizard. The Ordered Test gives you a way of orchestrating your tests, deciding in what order they should be performed. The Unit Test option gives you a class to write your tests in, but some manual work needs to be done. The Unit Test Wizard helps you through some of the choices you must make.

The Basic Unit Test gives a version of the Unit Test, but without some of the comments and properties. For your first test project, name your file, choose **Unit Test**, and click **OK**. If you already have a test project, you can decide to add the file to an existing project by selecting it in the drop-down. If not, you are prompted to provide a name for the test project that is to be added to your solution.

The test project is created for you and includes a pretty empty class for your tests.

The class contains some definitions, methods, a constructor, and one method that is the one thing to focus on because this is the one you need to implement.

Before you change it, it looks like the method shown in Figure 2.59.

```
[TestMethod]
public void TestMethod1()
{
    //
    // TODO: Add test logic here
    //
}
```

FIGURE 2.59   Test method before implementation.

So, what you need to do in this method is to implement the unit test of the schemas you want to test in this test class. Remember that you can have as many test classes and test methods in each test class as you want.

To test a schema, you need to reference three different assemblies from your test project:

▶ The assembly that contains the schema. This assembly *must* have the Enable Unit Testing property set to True.

▶ The Microsoft.BizTalk.TestTools assembly. This is found in the .NET pane of the Add Reference screen.

▶ The Microsoft XLANG/s Base Types assembly. This is also found in the .NET pane of the Add Reference screen.

You can see the needed references in Figure 2.60. In the project, the XML instances that are to be used for the unit test can also be added. If you do this, consider marking their Build Action to None so that they are not compiled needlessly into the assembly. The instances are not required to be included in the project, but it gives you a nice way of having everything needed for the test grouped together. In Figure 2.61 you can see that there are two test instances, and the naming of the XML files indicates that one contains invalid data to also test a negative scenario.

After adding the project references, you need to implement the test method. Locate the method in the class file called TestMethod1, and change it to the code shown in Figure 2.61.

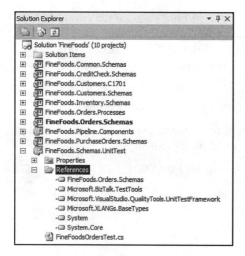

FIGURE 2.60   Needed project references for a unit test.

```
[TestMethod]
public void TestFineFoodsOrder()
{
    Order order = new Order();

    // Path to XML instances to test - relative to the testdir
    string valid = @"\..\..\FineFoods.Schemas.UnitTest\Instances\Order.xml";
    string invalid = @"\..\..\FineFoods.Schemas.UnitTest\Instances\InvalidOrder.xml";

    // Validating the valid instance against the schema.
    string complete = TestContext.TestDir + valid;
    Assert.IsTrue(order.ValidateInstance(complete, OutputInstanceType.XML));

    // Validating the invalid schema against the schema. Should fail.
    complete = TestContext.TestDir + invalid;
    Assert.IsFalse(order.ValidateInstance(complete, OutputInstanceType.XML));
}
```

FIGURE 2.61   Code to unit test a schema.

For the code to compile, the using statements shown in Figure 2.62 are needed.
BTSU.Domain.Schemas is the namespace of the project that contains the schema to be
tested. The Microsoft.BizTalk.TestTools.Schema namespace contains the
OutputInstanceType enumeration that is used to let the test runtime know whether the
test instance is XML or native format.

The first thing to do is to instantiate an instance of the schema you want to test. Then,
for each instance you want to test the schema against, call the ValidateInstance method
on the instance of the schema. Each call to ValidateInstance can occur inside a call to
Assert to make sure you get the desired output. In the code in Figure 2.61, two calls are
made to Assert. The first call is to make sure the validation of the valid instance goes
well, and the second is to make sure the validation of the invalid instance fails.

You should have as many instances as needed to make sure your schema can handle all
possible instances correctly. This means you should have plenty of instances that should
succeed in validation and you should have plenty of instances hat should fail validation.

```
using FineFoods.Orders.Schemas;
using Microsoft.BizTalk.TestTools.Schema;
```

FIGURE 2.62   Required **using** statements for a unit test.

You can find Microsoft's description of the unit test features at
http://msdn.microsoft.com/en-us/library/dd224279(BTS.70).aspx.

The built-in unit testing features do not, unfortunately, support validating an instance
against a schema that includes or imports other schemas. To do this, you can implement
a helper class that does the validation for you and assert on the return value of the
helper class.

In the example shown in Figure 2.63, two helper classes have been introduced. The first is
a class that basically just contains two properties used to contain the result of the validation. The class is shown in Figure 2.64. It has two properties, one for keeping the state of
the validation and one for keeping the actual error messages, if any, from the validation.
The other class performs the validation and is shown in Figure 2.65. Even with this helper
class, you cannot do everything. Only the built-in ValidateInstance method of the
TestableSchemaBase class has the capability to validate using the native format. These
helper classes will assist you only in validating XML against regular XSDs. The code
shown in Figure 2.65 is not entirely complete. Exceptions can be thrown from several
method calls, including the XmlSchemaSet.Add method call and the XmlReader.Create
method call. You should naturally catch these and handle them to have a robust helper
class to utilize in all your solutions.

```
[TestMethod]
public void TestFineFoodsOrder()
{
    Order order = new Order();
    SchemaValidator sv = new SchemaValidator();
    ValidationResult vr;

    // Path to XML instances to test - relative to the testdir
    string valid = @"\..\..\FineFoods.Schemas.UnitTest\Instances\Order.xml";
    string invalid = @"\..\..\FineFoods.Schemas.UnitTest\Instances\InvalidOrder.xml";

    // Validating the valid instance against the schema.
    string complete = TestContext.TestDir + valid;
    vr = sv.ValidateInstance(order, complete);
    Assert.IsTrue(vr.ValidInstance, vr.Errors);

    // Validating the invalid schema against the schema. Should fail.
    complete = TestContext.TestDir + invalid;
    vr = sv.ValidateInstance(order, complete);
    Assert.IsFalse(vr.ValidInstance, vr.Errors);
}
```

FIGURE 2.63   Unit test utilizing a helper class.

```
public class ValidationResult
{
    public string Errors { get; set; }
    public bool ValidInstance { get; set; }
}
```

FIGURE 2.64   Helper class for result of instance validation.

```
public class SchemaValidator
{
    ValidationResult vr;

    public ValidationResult ValidateInstance(TestableSchemaBase schema, string instance)
    {
        vr = new ValidationResult() { ValidInstance = true, Errors = String.Empty };
        var schemas = new XmlSchemaSet();
        schemas.Add(schema.Schema);

        var settings = new XmlReaderSettings()
        {
            Schemas = schemas,
            ValidationType = ValidationType.Schema
        };
        settings.ValidationEventHandler += settings_ValidationEventHandler;
        XmlReader reader = XmlReader.Create(instance, settings);
        try
        {
            while (reader.Read())
            {
            }
        }
        catch (XmlException xe)
        {
            vr.ValidInstance = false;
            vr.Errors += "\r\n\r\n" + xe.Message;
        }
        return vr;
    }

    void settings_ValidationEventHandler(object sender, ValidationEventArgs e)
    {
        vr.ValidInstance = false;
        vr.Errors += "\r\n\r\n" + e.Message;
    }
}
```

FIGURE 2.65   Helper class for unit test of schemas.

Testing Using Pipeline Tools

If you have created an envelope schema and document schemas to use for the debatched messages, you might want to test this setup without having to deploy it first. This is what the pipeline tools are for. The pipeline tools enable you to either run a given pipeline to see what happens when it executes or to emulate a pipeline, executing a specific pipeline component to see its output. This can prove very useful for testing your debatching capabilities and to make sure you get the right output.

There are six tools, and they can all be found at %Installation Folder%\SDK\Utilities\PipelineTools. Table 2.9 describes the tools. and You can also find more information about them at http://msdn.microsoft.com/en-us/library/aa547988(BTS.70).aspx, where you can see more about parameters and output of the tools.

TABLE 2.9   Pipeline Tools

Tool Name	Tool Description
DSDump.exe	Dumps in-memory representations of schemas to disk
FFAsm.exe	Runs the flat file assembler
FFDasm.exe	Runs the flat file disassembler
Pipeline.exe	Runs a pipeline
XMLAsm.exe	Runs the XML assembler
XMLDasm.exe	Runs the XML disassembler

If your schemas are to be used in custom pipeline components, the possibility exists to unit test these components using instances of your schemas (see Chapter 5).

Schemas for Scenario Used in This Book

Throughout this book, you will see screenshots and examples that use the same schemas. This section is divided into a subsection for each Visual Studio project that contains schemas, and the schemas are described in their respective subsections.

FineFoods.Common.Schemas

This project contains schemas that are common and can be reused from other projects. It does not contain anything specific to any trading partners, but only common types for the internal schemas at FineFoods.

The project contains a schema called CommonTypes.xsd, which simply defines some types that can be used throughout all the schemas that FineFoods leverages throughout their solution. The schema is shown in Figure 2.66, and the types declared are as follows:

- ▶ **ID:** Can be used for all ID fields, such as order numbers and customer numbers. Describes a string that must be at least 5 characters long and a maximum of 20 characters long and limited to a–z, A–Z, and 0–9 characters.

- ▶ **Email:** Can be used as the type for email fields. Describes a string that is restricted to a regular expression that will validate the value as an email address.

- ▶ **Address:** This type can be used to contain an address in other schemas. The type contains fields for name, street, ZIP code, and so on.

- ▶ **Contact:** This type can be used to contain contact information, such as name, phone, and email. The Email field leverages the Email type explained earlier, naturally.

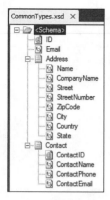

FIGURE 2.66   Schema view of CommonTypes.xsd.

FineFoods.CreditCheck.Schemas

This project contains one schema, CreditCheck.xsd, which is used to instantiate in orchestrations whenever a credit check needs to be done. An instance of this schema can then be used as a parameter to a call to a business rule, and it will contain the result of the credit check when the business rules finishes.

The schema is shown in Figure 2.67 and has just two fields:

▶ **CustomerNumber:** Must be set to the customer number of the customer to perform a credit check on

▶ **CreditOK:** A Boolean value that will contain True if the credit check went well and False otherwise

FIGURE 2.67   Schema view of CreditCheck.xsd.

FineFoods.Customers.C1701

This project contains all schemas relevant to customer number C1701. Currently, it contains only one schema, Order.xsd, which describes the order format this customer sends to FineFoods. The format is a flat file format, as was created both manually and by using the Flat File Schema Wizard earlier in this chapter.

The schema shown in Figure 2.68 is the schema created by the wizard.

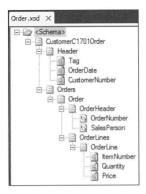

FIGURE 2.68   Schema view of Order.xsd from customer C1701.

The schema has a structure that allows for multiple orders in one file. Each order does not contain a lot of information but contains the most important information about an order, namely an order number and what items and quantity is required.

FineFoods.Customers.C1702

This project contains all schemas relevant to customer number C1702. Currently, it contains only one schema, Order.xsd, which describes the order XML format this customer sends to FineFoods.

The schema shown in Figure 2.69 is the schema created by the wizard.

FIGURE 2.69   Schema view of Order.xsd from customer C1702.

The schema has a structure that allows for multiple orders in one file. Each order does not contain a lot of information but contains the most important information about an order, namely an order number and what items and quantity is required.

FineFoods.Customers.Schemas

This project contains a schema that describes a customer, called Customer.xsd. The schema is shown in Figure 2.70 and consists of an ID of the customer and a list of contact persons.

FIGURE 2.70   Schema view of Customer.xsd.

FineFoods.Inventory.Schemas

This project contains schemas that are relevant for the inventory of FineFoods.

The first schema is called InventoryItem.xsd and is shown in Figure 2.71. The schema describes an item in the inventory and consists of an ID, a price, a description, and the quantity.

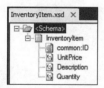

FIGURE 2.71   Schema view of InventoryItem.xsd.

The second schema is called ItemReceipt.xsd and is shown in Figure 2.72. The schema describes a receipt for an item that has been received.

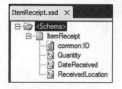

FIGURE 2.72   Schema view of ItemReceipt.xsd.

FineFoods.Orders.Schemas

This project contains schemas that are relevant to the process of receiving an order.

The first schema relevant to this is the order schema is shown in Figure 2.73. It consists of the following information:

- A `Header` record that contains the following information:

  - **OrderID:** The unique ID of this order

  - **CustomerID:** The unique ID of the customer who sent the order

  - **RequestedDeliveryDate:** The date the customer would like the ordered items to arrive

  - **OrderDate:** The date the order was sent

  - **OrderTotal:** The total order amount

  - **BillTo:** Information about the billing address of the order

  - **ShipTo:** Information about the shipping address of the order

  - **Comments:** Contains a list of comments about the order

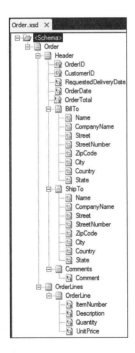

FIGURE 2.73   Schema view of Order.xsd.

- An `OrderLines` record that contains a number of `OrderLine` records with the following information:

  - **ItemNumber:** The item number of the item to purchase

  - **Description:** A description of the item

▶ **Quantity:** The quantity of the item that is to be purchased

▶ **UnitPrice:** The unit price of the item

The next schema in the project is the invoice, which is shown in Figure 2.74. The invoice consists of basically the same information as the order does with a few exceptions:

▶ An invoice number has been added to contain the unique number of this invoice.

▶ The `RequestedDeliveryDate`, `OrderDate`, and `OrderTotal` fields have been removed.

▶ The comments and the shipping address information have been removed.

▶ An `InvoiceDate` has been added to contain the date of the invoice, and an InvoiceTotal has been added to contain the total amount of the invoice.

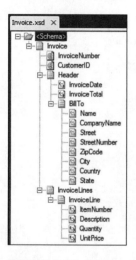

FIGURE 2.74   Schema view of Invoice.xsd.

The OrcerConfirmation.xsd, as shown in Figure 2.75, describes an order confirmation. It has only the most basic information needed for an order confirmation, such as an order ID and the relevant dates.

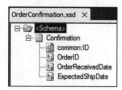

FIGURE 2.75   Schema view of OrderConfirmation.xsd.

To be able to correlate orders and information about an order having been shipped, a property schema has been created, which is shown Figure 2.76. The property schema consists of two properties: the customer number and the order number. This combination is assumed to be unique and can therefore be used to correlate the messages.

FIGURE 2.76   Schema view of OrderPropertySchema.

The OrderShipped.xsd, as shown in Figure 2.77, describes the format of the order shipped notification that can be sent to customers.

FIGURE 2.77   Schema view of OrderShipped.xsd.

FineFoods.PurchaseOrders.Schemas

Whereas the FineFoods.Orders.Schemas contains schemas relevant for receiving orders, this project contains schemas relevant for purchase orders to be sent to suppliers. The project contains one schema, which is shown Figure 2.78. The purchase order has the same fields as the order, with one addition: the information about the supplier the purchase order is going to.

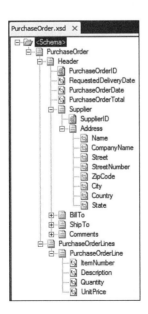

FIGURE 2.78   Schema view of PurchaseOrder.xsd.

Summary

Schemas are an important part of a BizTalk solution for several reasons:

- ▶ Verification of inbound and outbound messages
- ▶ Routing of messages based on message type and content of messages
- ▶ Transformations from one message type to another

Because the schemas are so important in a BizTalk solution, they should not be taken lightly. Time spent getting the schemas as correct and as detailed as possible is well spent. If you do not spend enough time on the schemas, you will face difficulties verifying input and building transformations that handle invalid input. Also, if you have an error in your schema that needs to be changed after you go into production, and the schema is in use, you will need to version your schemas, which can be cumbersome.

For both XML and flat file schemas, you can leverage existing schemas and create a schema manually. For XML schemas, you also have the option of generating a schema based on DTD, XDR, or well-formed XML; and for flat file schemas, you also have the option of using the Flat File Schema Wizard to create a schema. BizTalk also ships with 8,000+ schemas for all kinds of standard EDI messages and versions that can also be customized.

You can use promoted properties, which are defined in property schemas, and distinguished fields to take content of a message and put it into the context of the message, enabling routing and correlation based on those values and usage of the values in your business processes.

To test your schemas, you can use the built-in unit testing framework, which allows you to automate validation of as many instances as you have. For unit testing of schemas that include other schemas, you can write a helper class that enables this.

CHAPTER 3

Maps

As mentioned several times in Chapter 2, "Schemas," schemas are really important in your BizTalk solution. This is partly because they serve as the contract between systems and are therefore useful for determining which system is faulty. And it is partly because updating them is potentially particularly laborious because so many other artifacts depend on them.

One of the artifacts that depends heavily on schemas is a map. A map is a transformation from one *Extensible Markup Language* (XML) document into another XML document, and it is used in three places:

▶ To transform incoming trading-partner-specific or internal-system-specific messages into an internal XML format. This is achieved by setting the map on a receive port or on the receive side of a two-way port.

▶ To transform outgoing internal XML format messages into the trading-partner-specific or internal-system-specific formats they need to receive. This is achieved by setting the map on a send port or on the send side of a two-way port.

▶ To perform transformations needed inside business processes that do not involve receiving or sending messages to and from trading partners or internal systems.

Maps are developed inside Visual Studio 2010 using the BizTalk Mapper tool. This tool has a developer friendly interface, which allows you to have a tree structure view of both input and output schemas used by the map. When viewing these two tree structures, you can then use either direct links from nodes in the source schema to nodes in the destination schemas, or you can use functoids that perform some processing on its input and then generates output, which can be used either as input for other functoids or as a value that goes to a node in the destination schema.

Although maps are developed in a nice, user-friendly interface and stored as a BizTalk-specific XML format, they are compiled into *Extensible Stylesheet Language Transformations* (XSLT) when the Visual Studio 2010 project is compiled. In fact, you can even provide your own XSLT instead of using the Mapper if you are so inclined or if you need to do complex transformations that you cannot do with the Mapper. Only XSLT 1.0 is supported for this, though.

Incoming files are either arriving as *Extensible Markup Language* (XML) or converted into XML in the receive pipeline, which happens before the map on the receive port is executed. Also, on a send port, the map is performed before the send pipeline converts the outgoing XML into the format it should have when arriving at the destination. This makes it possible for the Mapper and the XSLT to work for all files BizTalk handles because the tree structure shown in the Mapper is a representation of how the XML will look like for the file and because the XSLT can only be performed and will always be performed on XML. This provides a nice and clean way of handling all files in BizTalk in the same way when it comes to transformations.

The Mapper

This section walks you through the main layout of the BizTalk Mapper and describes the main functions and features.

Developing a map is done inside Visual Studio 2010 just as with other BizTalk artifacts. Follow these steps to add a map to your project:

1. Right-click your project.
2. Choose **Add, New Item**.
3. Choose **Map** and provide a name for the map. This is illustrated in Figure 3.1.

Layout of Mapper

After adding the map to your project, it opens in the BizTalk Mapper tool, which is shown in Figure 3.2.

The Mapper consists of five parts:

▶ To the left a Toolbox contains functoids that you can use in your map. Functoids are explained in detail later. If the Toolbox is not present, you can enable it by choosing **View, Toolbox** or by pressing **Ctrl+Alt+X**.

▶ A Source Schema view, which displays a tree structure of the source schema for the map.

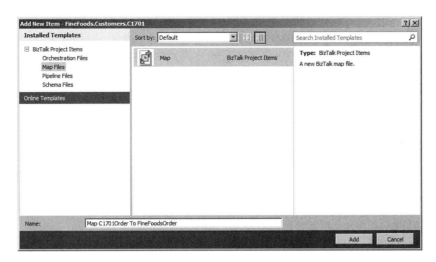

FIGURE 3.1   Add a new map to your project.

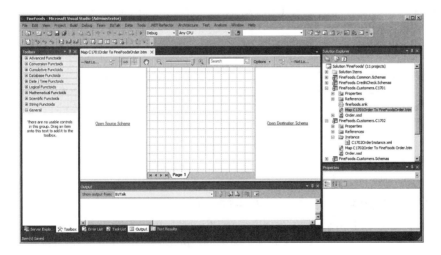

FIGURE 3.2   Overview of the BizTalk Mapper.

▶ The Mapper grid, which is where you place all functoids used by the map and also where lines between nodes in the source and destination schemas are shown. Above the Mapper grid there is a toolbar with some functionality that is described later.

▶ A Destination Schema view, which displays an inverted tree structure of the destination schema. An inverted tree structure means that it unfolds right to left rather than left to right, which is normal.

▶ The Properties window, which shows the properties that are available depending on what is the active part of the Mapper. For instance, it can show properties for a functoid in the map, a node in the source schema, or the map itself. If the Properties window is not present, you can always get to it by right-clicking the item for which you need the properties and choosing **Properties** or by clicking an item and pressing **F4**.

Initial Considerations

When developing a transformation, you usually assume that the input for the map is always valid given the schema for the source. This requires one of two things, however:

▶ Validation has been turned on in the receive pipeline, meaning that the pipeline used is either a custom pipeline with the XML validator component in it or validation has been enabled on the disassembler in use.

▶ You trust the sending system or trading partner to always send valid messages and therefore do not turn on validation. This can be done for performance reasons. The downside to this is, of course, that it can provide unpredictable results later on in the process and troubleshooting will be hard.

Either way, your business must decide what to do. Should validation be turned on so that errors are caught in the beginning of the process, or can it be turned off either because you trust the sender or because you decide to just deal with errors as they arise? As a developer of a transformation, you need to know the state of the incoming XML. If a map fails at some point, this can lead to unexpected behavior, like the following:

▶ Orchestrations can start failing and get suspended because the logic inside the orchestration is based on valid input.

▶ Incoming messages can get suspended if the map fails.

▶ If you validate your XML in a send pipeline and the map generated invalid XML according to the schema, the validation will fail, and the message will get suspended and not delivered to the recipient.

After this is dealt with, you can start looking at how to implement the map. Most of a map is usually straightforward, and you just specify which nodes in the source should be mapped to which nodes in the destination schema. For instance, the quantity on an order line is usually just mapped to the relevant quantity node in the destination schema that may have another name, namespace, or other. This works fine, as long as the cardinality and data type match between the source node and the destination node.

Special cases, however, must also be dealt with. Handling all the special cases can take a long time just to specify, and this time should be taken because you want to generate valid output. Determining how to handle these cases is usually not something a BizTalk developer can do alone because you need to specify what actions the business wants to perform in these cases. Therefore, this specification should be done in cooperation between a businessperson and a BizTalk developer. The most common special cases are described in the following paragraphs.

Different Data Types

If the source node and destination node have different data types, you might run into issues. Naturally, if you are mapping from one data type to another data type that has fewer restrictions, you are safe. If you are mapping form a node of type `decimal` to a node of type `string`, for example, you can just do the mapping because anything that can be in a node of type `decimal` can also be in a node of type `string`. The other way around, however, is not so easy. You have three options:

▶ Change the source schema either by changing the data type or by placing a restriction on the node that limits the possible values. You can use a regular expression to limit a string node to only contain numbers, for instance.

▶ Change the destination schema by changing the data type of the relevant node. Relaxing restrictions, however, can give you trouble later on in the business process.

▶ Handle the situation inside the map. After schemas are made and agreed upon with trading partners, they are not easy to change. So, you probably want to address this issue inside the map. You can use functoids, which are explained later, to deal with any inputs that are not numeric values.

Different Cardinality

If the source node is optional and the destination node is not, you have an issue. What you should do in case the input node is missing is a matter of discussion. Again, you have three options:

▶ Change the source schema by changing the optional node to be required.

▶ Change the destination schema by changing the relevant node to be optional.

▶ Handle the situation inside the map. You probably want to address this issue inside the map. You can use functoids to deal with the scenario where the source node is missing. This can either mean mapping a default value to the destination node or throwing an exception.

TIP

When developing a large solution that involves lots of trading partners, you will proba-bly find yourself numerous times in the situation where someone says that they know the schema doesn't reflect it but some field that is optional is always present, so you can assume that in your map.

Well, don't do it! If the node is always present, the schema should reflect this.

If the schema doesn't reflect it, then in case the incoming XML doesn't have the node present (regardless of the promises that have been made to you), something unpre-dictable will go wrong. Besides that, the Mapper actually includes some extra logic in the generated XSLT in case of mapping optional elements, which can be avoided if the schema is properly developed.

Creating a Simple Map

To start creating the map, you must choose which schema to use as the input for the map and which schema to use for the output. These are also known as the source and the desti-nation schemas of the map.

To choose the source schema, click **Open Source Schema** on the left side of the Mapper. Doing so opens a schema selector, as shown in Figure 3.3.

FIGURE 3.3   Choosing a schema to be used for the map.

In the schema selector, you can choose between schemas that exist in the current project or schemas that are in projects you have referenced from this project. You cannot add a reference from this window, so references must be added before choosing schemas in other projects. You choose a schema for the destinations schema by clicking **Open Destination Schema** and choosing a schema in the same way. If you choose a schema that has multiple root nodes, you get a screen where you need to choose which one of them to use as the root node for the schema you have chosen.

3

TIP

If you use a schema from a referenced project as either the source or the destination schema, and this schema uses types defined in yet another project, the schema shows up wrong in the Mapper view. No errors are provided until you test the map with the validation options turned on. These options are described later. There isn't even a compile-time error or an error when validating the map. So, when adding referenced to projects with schemas, remember to check whether the schema you will be using itself uses types defined in schemas in other projects, and add that reference, as well.

NOTE

Designing a map by adding a new map to your project and choosing the source and destination schemas only allows for one schema as input and one schema as output. At times, it is desirable to have one schema as input and multiple schemas as outputs, thereby creating multiple outputs or to have multiple schemas as input and combining them into one schema or even have multiple inputs and multiple outputs. This can be achieved by defining the map inside an orchestration, and this is therefore covered in Chapter 4, "Orchestrations." These maps can be called only from within orchestrations and not from receive ports or end ports.

After choosing the two schemas involved, you are ready to start designing your map. This is mainly done by dragging links between the source schema and the destination schema and possibly doing some work on the source values before they are put into the destination schema.

For values that just need to be copied from a source node to a destination node, you can simply drag a link between the nodes in question. Just click either the source or the destination node and hold down the left mouse button while you move the mouse to the other element. Then release it. Doing so instructs the Mapper that you want the values from the source node copied to the node in the destination schema when the map is executed.

TIP

If the cursor turns into a circle with a line through it, this means that you cannot create this link. This can happen, for instance, if you want to map something into a field in the destination schema, which might not occur, like an element that has maxOccurs at 0.

In between the source and destination schema is the Mapper grid. This grid is used to place functoids on, which perform some work on its input before its output is either used as input for another functoid or sent to the destination schema. Functoids are described later in this chapter. Figure 3.4 shows a simple map with a single line drawn and a single functoid on it. The functoid is an "Uppercase" functoid that converts the input it gets into uppercase and outputs that.

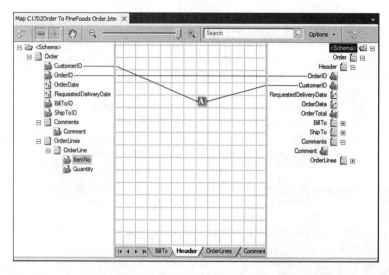

FIGURE 3.4   Simple map with one line drawn and one functoid used.

TIP

Be careful not to use too many functoids on the grid because this will seriously decrease readability. You can right-click the name of the map page (Default: Page 1) and choose **Add Page** to add another page. You can have up to 20 grid pages in your map. You can right-click a page name and choose **Rename Page** to rename it, and you can also choose **Reorder Pages** to change the order they appear in. Also, you can choose **Delete Page** if a page is no longer needed.

Pages are a great way of dividing your map into smaller, more manageable blocks. The functionality of the map is in no way influenced with how many pages you have and what functionality goes into what pages.

The map grid is actually larger than what you can see on your screen. If you move the mouse to the edge of the grid, the cursor changes to a large arrow, and you can then click to let the grid scroll so that you can see what is located in the direction the arrow points. You can also click the icon illustrating a hand in the toolbar at the top of the Mapper grid to get to the Panning mode, where you can click the grid and drag it around.

TIP

If you have so many functoids on one grid page that you need to scroll around to find the right place on the map grid, you can right-click the grid and choose **Grid Preview**. This will give you an opaque window providing easy access to choose which part of the map grid you want shown. After you've found the part of the grid you want to see in the map grid, just close down the opaque window.

If you need to move a functoid to another location on the grid, you need to first click it. When it is selected, you can drag it anywhere on the grid.

If you need to move a collection of functoids at the same time, you can click the grid and drag a rectangle to mark the functoids and links you want to move. After marking a rectangle on the grid, you can just click somewhere inside it and drag the entire rectangle to another location on the grid. Another option is to select multiple functoids/links by holding down **Ctrl** while clicking them. After they are selected, you can drag them to where you want them.

Sometimes you need to change one end of a link if, for instance, some destination node should have its value from another node than it does at the time. You can do this either by deleting the existing link and adding a new one or by clicking the link and then dragging one end of the link that has been changed to a small blue square to the new place. Changing the existing link instead of adding a new link has some advantages:

- ▶ All the properties you may have set on the link remain the same, so you do not have to set them again.

- ▶ If the link goes into a functoid, this will keep the order in which they are added. The order parameters are added to a functoid is important, so it is nice to not have to go in and change that order after deleting a link and adding a new one.

The window shown in Figure 3.4 has a toolbar at the top of the Mapper grid in the middle. This toolbar is new in the Mapper in BizTalk 2010 and contains some functionality that wasn't available in earlier versions of BizTalk.

One of the new features is the search bar. If you enter something in the search text box, the Mapper finds occurrences of this text within the map. The search feature can search in the source schema, the destination schema, and properties of the functoids such as name, label, comments, inputs, and scripts. You use the Options drop-down to the right of the search text box to enable and disable what the search will look at. Once a search is positive, you get three new buttons between the search text box and the Options drop-down. The three buttons enable you to find the next match going up, find the next match going down, or to clear the search. The search features are marked in Figure 3.5.

Another new option is the zoom feature. You get the option to zoom out, allowing you to locate the place on the grid you want to look at. For zooming, you can use the horizontal bar in the Mapper, as shown in Figure 3.6, or you can hold down the **Ctrl** key while using the scroll wheel on your mouse.

To let the map know that a value from one node in the source is to be mapped into a specific node in the destination schema, you drag a link between the two nodes. When you drag a link between two record nodes, you get a list of options:

- ▶ **Direct Link:** This creates a direct link between the two records. This helps the compiler know what levels of the source hierarchy correspond to what levels in the hierarchy of the destination schema.

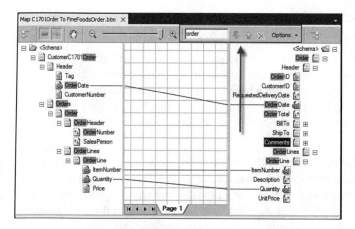

FIGURE 3.5   The search feature in a map.

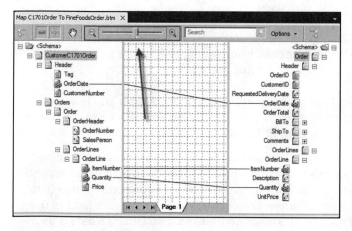

FIGURE 3.6   The zoom option in a map.

▶ **Link by Structure:** This lets the Mapper automatically create links between the child nodes of the two records you created the link between. The Mapper attempts to create the links based on the structure of the children.

▶ **Link by Name:** This lets the Mapper automatically create links between the child nodes of the two records you created the link between. The Mapper attempts to create the links based on the names of the children.

▶ **Mass Copy:** This adds a Mass Copy functoid that copies all subcontent of the record in the source to the record in the destination.

▶ **Cancel:** This cancels what you are doing.

This functionality is also new in BizTalk 2010. In earlier versions, there was a property on the map you could set before you dragged a link between two records.

Functoids and links can be moved between grid pages in two ways:

▶ After selecting one or more functoids/links, right-click them, and choose **Move to Page** or press **Ctrl+M Ctrl+M**. Doing so opens a small screen where you can choose between the existing pages or choose to create a new page to place the selected items on.

▶ Drag the selected items to the page tab of the page where you want them to appear. The page appears, and then you can place the items where you want them to be.

If you need a copy of a functoid, retaining all the properties of the functoid, you can also do this. Select a number of items and use the normal Windows shortcuts to copy, cut, and paste them. You can also right-click and choose **Copy**, **Cut**, or **Paste**. You can copy across grid pages, maps, and even maps in different instances of Visual Studio 2010. Some limitations apply to this, however, such as when links are copied and when not. For a full description, see refer to http://msdn.microsoft.com/en-us/library/ff629736(BTS.70).aspx.

For large schemas, it can be hard to keep track of which nodes are used in the map and in what context. To assist you, the Mapper has a feature called relevance tree view. This is a feature you can enable and disable on the source and destination schemas independently, and the feature is enabled or disabled using the highlighted button in Figure 3.7. As you can see, the relevance tree view is enabled for the destination schema and not for the source schema. The destination schema has some nodes coalesced to improve readability. This means that all the nodes in the Header record that are placed above the OrderDate node, which is the only node currently relevant for the map, are coalesced into one icon, showing that something is here but it is not relevant. You can click the icon to unfold the contents if you want. Records containing no nodes that are relevant for the map are not coalesced, but collapsed.

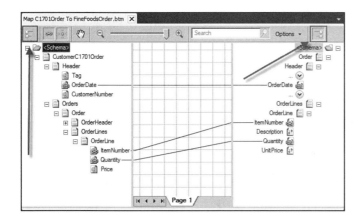

FIGURE 3.7   Relevance view.

If you have marked a field in the source schema and need to find the field in the destination schema to map it into, you can get some help from the Mapper, as well. This feature is called Indicate Matches. If you select a node in the source schema, you can either press **Shift+Space** to enable it, or you can right-click it and choose **Indicate Matches**. Figure 3.8 shows how the screen looks after enabling the Indicate Matches feature on the OrderDate node in the source schema. As you can see, the Mapper adds some potential links to the map, and the one the Mapper thinks is the most likely is highlighted and thus the currently chosen one. If none of the suggestions match, you can press the **Escape** key or click with the mouse anywhere that is not one of the suggested links. If one of the links the Mapper suggests is the one you want, you have two ways of actually adding the link to the map:

▶ Use the mouse to click the link you want added to the map. Note that you cannot click the node in the destination that the link points to; it has to be the link itself.

▶ Use the up- and down-arrow keys to switch between the suggested links, and press the **Enter** key when the right link is chosen and highlighted.

If the feature guesses right the first time, you can add the link simply by pressing **Shift+Space** and then **Enter**. And you did not have to find the right place in the destination schema yourself.

Unfortunately, functoids are not part of this feature, so if you want the source node to be mapped into a functoid, this feature provides no help. You will have to do that yourself.

After a link has been dragged, it shows up in the Mapper as one of three types of links:

▶ **A solid line:** This is used for links where both ends of the link are visible in the current view of the Mapper, meaning that none of the two ends are scrolled out of the view.

▶ **A dashed line that is a little grayed out:** This is used for links where only one of the ends is visible in the current Mapper view and the other end is scrolled out of view.

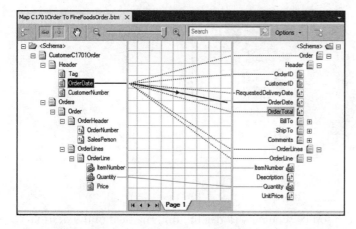

FIGURE 3.8 Illustration of the Indicate Matches feature.

▶ **A dotted line that is grayed out:** This is used for links where both ends are
scrolled out of view but the link still goes through the current view of grid.

Figure 3.9 shows the different types of links.

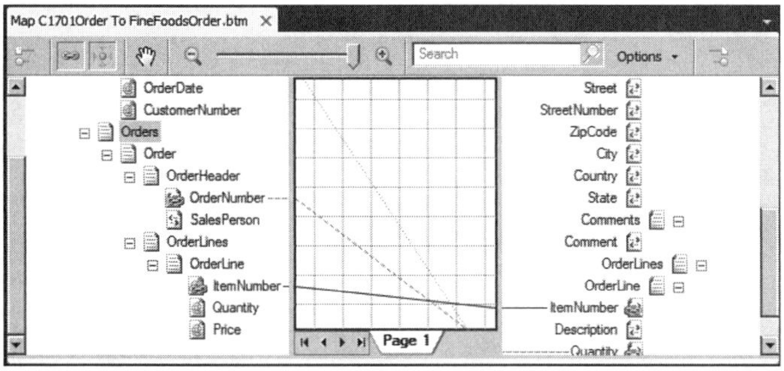

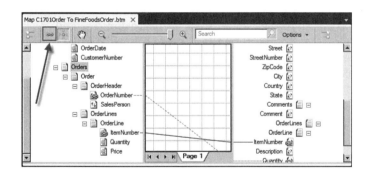

FIGURE 3.9   The three types of links in a map.

Because there may be a lot of links that are of the third type, where none of the ends of
the link is visible, you might want to choose to not have these links shown at all. To do
this, you can use a feature on the toolbar called Show All/Relevant Links. This is enabled
using a button, as shown in Figure 3.10.

FIGURE 3.10   Feature to show all or relevant links.

As you can see from Figure 3.10, one of links that was also present in Figure 3.9 is no
longer shown in the Mapper. The link still exists and is valid. If one or both of the ends of
the link come into view, the link reappears on the grid.

When a map gets filled up with functoids and links, it can get hard to keep track of which
links and functoids are connected. To help you with this, the Mapper automatically highlights relevant links and functoids for you, if you select a link, a functoid, or a node in
either the source or destination schema. For instance, take a look at Figure 3.11.

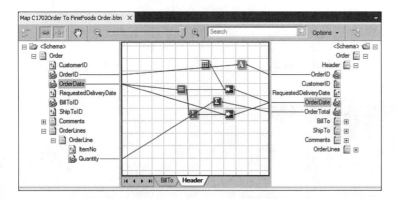

FIGURE 3.11   A map with lots of functoids.

Suppose you are troubleshooting to make sure the OrderDate in the destination schema is mapped correctly. If you click the OrderDate in the destination schema, you get the screen seen in Figure 3.12 instead. As you can see, the functoids and links that are relevant for mapping data into the OrderDate element have been highlighted and the rest of the links and functoids are now opaque, allowing you to focus on what is important. Had you clicked the link between the Equal functoid and the Value Mapping functoid, a subset of the links highlighted in Figure 3.12 would have been highlighted. If there are relevant links or functoids on another map page than the one currently shown, this is indicated by a small blue circle with an exclamation mark inside it to the left of the name of the page. Note also that the links have arrows on them, indicating the flow of data. This is also new in BizTalk 2010. In earlier versions of the Mapper, you could not have a functoid that gets its input from a functoid that was placed to the right of the first functoid on the grid. Now you can place your functoids where you want on the grid and the arrow will tell you which way the link goes. You cannot drag a link from a functoid to a functoid placed to the left of the first functoid, but after the link has been established, you can move the functoids around as you please.

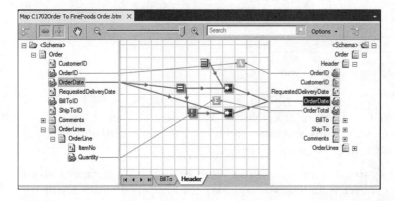

FIGURE 3.12   The links and functoids relevant for mapping into the **OrderDate** element.

Another feature is the Auto Scrolling feature. This feature, which is enabled and disabled using the button shown in Figure 3.13, allows the Mapper grid to autoscroll to find relevant functoids given something you have selected. If all the functoids had been out of sight in the Mapper grid and you then clicked the OrderDate in the destination schema with this feature enabled, the grid would autoscroll to the view shown in Figure 3.13. The Auto Scroll feature also applies to other parts of the map than clicking a node in a schema. If you click a functoid, for instance, the Mapper highlights relevant links and functoids that are connected to the selected functoid and uses the Auto Scroll feature to bring them into view, if enabled.

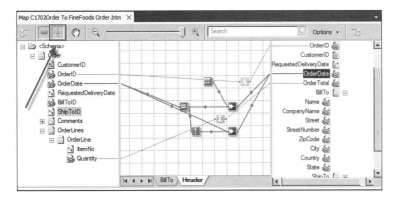

FIGURE 3.13   Example of using the Auto Scroll feature.

Sometimes you want insert a default value into a field in the destination schema. You can do this by clicking the field in question and in the properties for the field finding the property called Value and setting a value here. Other than setting a value, you can use the drop-down to select the <empty> option. This lets the Mapper create an empty field in the output. As explained in Chapter 4, it can be useful to have a way of setting values in messages outside a transformation. Also, empty elements are needed for property demotion, as explained in Chapter2, "Schemas."

If you choose to set a default value in a field in the destination schema in the map, you can no longer map any values to this node in the destination. If you open the *Extensible Markup Language Schema Definition* (XSD) and set a default value on the field in the schema itself instead of setting it in the Mapper, the Mapper uses this value, but you are allowed to map a value to the field, which overwrites the value set in the XSD. Unfortunately, there is no built-in support for using the default value from the XSD if the field that is mapped to a node is optional and not present in the source at runtime. You have to do this with an If-Then-Else sort of structure, as discussed later in this chapter.

If you choose to set a default value in a field in the source schema, this value is used only when generating instances for testing the map from within Visual Studio 2010. The value is not used at runtime when the map is deployed.

If you click the map grid, you can see the properties of the map in the Properties window. If this window is not present, you can right-click the grid and choose **Properties** or just click the grid and press **F4**. Table 3.1 describes the available properties for the map.

TABLE 3.1   Properties of the Map

Property Name	Description
General	
Ignore Namespaces for Links	Determines whether the map should be saved with information about the namespace of the nodes that are being linked.
Script Type Precedence	If a functoid that is used in the map can be both a referenced functoid or have (multiple) inline implementations, this property determines the order in which the implementations are to be preferred.
Source Schema	Read-only property that specifies the source schema to be used.
Target Schema	Read-only property that specifies the destination schema to be used.
Compiler	
Custom Extension XML	This property is used to point out a custom extension XML file that is used when providing your own XSLT instead of using the Mapper. This is explained more fully in the section "Custom XSLT."
Custom XSL Path	This property is used to point out a custom XSLT file that is used when providing your own XSLT instead of using the Mapper. This is explained more fully in the section "Custom XSLT."
Custom Header	
CDATA section elements	This property contains a whitespace-delimited list of element names that will have their values inside a CDATA construction to allow for otherwise-reserved characters. The whitespace can be a space or some other delimiter, but not, for instance, a comma.
Copy Processing Instructions (PIs)	Boolean value describing whether the map should copy any processing instructions from the source schema to the destination schema. Mostly used when transforming InfoPath documents.
Doctype public	Provides the value that will be written to the doctype-public attribute of the xsl:output element of the generated XSLT.
Doctype system	Provides the value that will be written to the doctype-system attribute of the xsl:output element of the generated XSLT.
Indent	Possible values are yes and no. If set to yes, the output of the map contains indentation to make the output more human-readable. Usually not needed, because systems often read the files and XML viewers show the XML nicely anyway.

TABLE 3.1   Properties of the Map

Property Name	Description
Media-Type	Used to specify the value of the media-type attribute of the `xsl:output` element in the generated XSLT. This determines the MIME type of the generated XML.
Method	Possible values are xml, html and text. The value specified goes into the method attribute of the `xsl:output` element in the generated XSLT.
Omit Xml Declaration	Can be true (default) or false. Is used as the value for the omit-xml-declaration attribute on the `xsl:output` element in the generated XSLT. Determines whether to omit the XML declaration at the top of the generated XML.
Standalone	Possible values are yes and no (default). Determines the value that is used in the standalone attribute of the `xsl:output` element in the generated XSLT.
Version	Specifies the value of the version attribute on the generated XML declaration, if any.
XSLT Encoding	This property contains a drop-down list of encodings. The chosen encoding is used to populate the encoding attribute of the `xsl:output` element. If you need another value than what is available, you can just enter it. The Mapper does not check the value, however, so check to make sure it is correct.

TIP

If you have a schema that has two elements on the same level of either the source or destination tree but with different namespaces, you need to set the **Ignore Namespaces for Links** to **False** because the Mapper cannot determine which of the nodes to use for the link when the map is opened up otherwise. The reason for the property to exist and not just default to "false" is that when the property is true, this allows you to change the namespace of your schemas without having to relink anything in the map. Also the .BTM file is easier to read when opened in a text editor like Notepad and it takes up less space.

NOTE

As explained later in this chapter, it is not possible to build a thread-safe referenced cumulative functoid. This means that if you are using any cumulative functoids, you should take care to have the Inline C# option or another appropriate inline option above the External Assembly option in the Script Type Precedence property.

NOTE

The CDATA Section Elements property is mapped directly to the `cdata-section-elements` attribute that can be present on the `xsl:output` element in XSLT and the use of this property can therefore be read about in an XSLT book. In short, any element with a name that appears in this list has its value wrapped inside a CDATA tag regardless of what level the element is on.

The only exceptions to this are elements with the same name, but in different namespaces, like elements that are of a type that comes from an imported schema. This also means that if you want those to have their content wrapped in a CDATA tag, you need to specify them as `ns0:elementname` in the CDATA Section Elements property. You can get he namespace prefix from the schema import dialog box where you imported the schema with the type you are referencing.

If you click a link in the map grid, you can see and change some properties of the link. If the Properties window is not present, you can right-click the link and choose **Properties** or click the link and press **F4**. Table 3.2 describes the properties for links.

TABLE 3.2   Properties for Links

Property Name	Description
General	
Label	In this property, you can specify a label that is used for this link.
Link Source	Read-only property that specifies the source of the link.
Link Target	Read-only property that specifies the target of the link.
Compiler	
Source Links	This property has three possible values: If you use the value Copy Text Value, the link copies the value from the source of the link to the destination of the link. If you choose Copy Name, the name of the source field is copied rather than its value. If you choose Copy Text and Sub Content Value, the source node and all its inner content is copied. This is like the `InnerText` property of a .NET `System.Xml.XmlNode`.
Target Links	This property determines the behavior of the link with regard to creating output nodes. Possible value are Flatten Links, Match Links Top Down, and Match Links Bottom Up. The value in this property allows the compiler to know how to match the source structure to the destination structure so that loops in the generated XSLT can be generated at the correct levels. Usually the default value is fine, but at times when you are mapping form recurring structures that are on different levels in the source and destination schemas, this can be useful.

Clicking the map file in Solution Explorer reveals some properties that you can set on the Visual Studio 2010 project item. Table 3.3 describes these properties.

TABLE 3.3   Properties for the Visual Studio 2010 Project Item

Property Name	Description
Advanced	
Build Action	This property determines what the compiler does with the .BTM file when building the project. A value of None instructs the compiler to ignore the file. A value of BtsCompile instructs the compiler to compile the map and include it in the assembly.
Fully Qualified Name	This is a read-only property displaying the fully qualified .NET name. It is a concatenation of the .NET namespace, a period, and the .NET type name.
Namespace	The .NET namespace this map belongs to. This has nothing to do with any namespaces used in schemas. As with normal code, the namespace is usually the same name as the project the file belongs to. Remember to change this if you move the .BTM file among projects.
Type Name	The .NET type name of the map. This corresponds to the class name of a class in a project. The type name is usually the same as the filename of the .BTM file.
Misc	
File Name	The filename of the map file. You can change this instead of renaming the file in Solution Explorer if you are so inclined.
Full Path	Read-only property containing the full path to the map file.
Test Map	
TestMap Input	Determines how Visual Studio 2010 can find a file to use as input when testing the map. A value of XML means that the file given in TestMap Input Instance is an XML file. A value of Native means that the file given in TestMap Input Instance is in the native format of the schema, which is in this case usually a flat file or an EDI schema, but it can also be XML. The last option is a value of Generated Instance, which lets Visual Studio 2010 generate an XML instance to be used for the test.
TestMap Input Instance	The full path to the file to be used for testing the map. This is used only if the TestMap Input property does not have a value of Generate Instance.
TestMap Output	Determines the format of the output from testing the map. Can be XML, which outputs the XML the map has produced, or Native, which translates the XML generated by the map into the destination format like EDI, flat file, or something else.

TABLE 3.3   Properties for the Visual Studio 2010 Project Item

Property Name	Description
TestMap Output Instance	The full path of where to place the output from testing the map. If not specified, the output is generated in your temp folder, and the output window provides a link to the specific file when testing the map.
Validate TestMap Input	Boolean value that determines whether the input for the map should be validated against the source schema before performing the map. If you know the instance to be valid, there is no need for validation, because this will only take time. On the other hand, making sure every time you test the map that the input is valid will confirm that you haven't accidentally changed the instance or the schema.
Validate TestMap Output	Boolean value that determines whether the output of the map should be validated against the destination schema. When developing your map, you will usually want to turn this off, to view the result of the partially complete map you have built. Then turn it on when you want to actually test the map in its entirety.

Functoids

BizTalk provides functoids to provide a way of performing some processing on the source values before it is copied to the destination. This processing can be anything from converting a string to uppercase over mathematical trigonometric functions to doing a database lookup.

The functoids are divided into categories, and the functoids in each category are described in the following sections. This chapter describes all the functoids. In the section "Advanced Maps," there are examples of advanced usage of the functoids.

After dragging a functoid to the grid, you can click it to see the properties of the functoid in the Properties window. If the Properties window is not present, you can right-click the functoid and choose **Properties**, or you can click the functoid and press **F4**. The Properties window contains the properties listed in Table 3.4.

TABLE 3.4   Functoid Properties

Property Name	Description
(Name)	The name of the functoid.
Comments	A text you can alter to contain some comments about this functoid.
Help	A textual description of the functoid that describes what the purpose of the functoid is.

TABLE 3.4   Functoid Properties

Property Name	Description
Input Parameters	Contains the text Configure Functoid Inputs. If you click in it, you get a button to the right of it with the ellipsis. If you click the ellipsis, you get to a window where you can add constant parameters to the functoid and change the order of the parameters. It usually also has text at the bottom that describes the parameters and what they are used for. After parameters are defined for the functoid, they are listed in this property rather than the text Configure Functoid Inputs.
Label	This is the only property you can edit. Here you can enter a friendly name for the functoid in question. This has no functional meaning, but it will perhaps ease the workload for a new developer taking over your map, and it can be used in utilities that do automatic documentation of your solutions.
Maximum Input Parameters	Describes what the maximum number of input parameters for this functoid is.
Minimum Input Parameters	Describes what the minimum number of input parameters for this functoid is.
Script	If the functoid is a Scripting functoid, which is explained later, you can click in this property and then click the ellipsis that appears to configure and edit the script the Scripting functoid should run when called.
Table Looping Grid	If the functoid is a Table Looping functoid, which is explained later, you can click this property and then the ellipsis that appears to configure the table looping grid.

TIP

Use labels on links extensively. When a link is an input to a functoid and you look at the functoid parameters, you can see something like Figure 3.14. If you label your links, however, the text in the label is shown rather than the default value, providing a much nicer interface to the parameter, enabling you to easily determine which parameter should come before which and so on. Figure 3.15 is the same as Figure 3.14, but with Comment from Source as the label on the link.

The screen for configuring the functoid parameters can be resized if necessary. Notice that when you drag a functoid to the grid, it has a yellow exclamation mark on it. This indicates, that the functoid is not fully configured, which at compile time would give you a warning or an error depending on the severity of the missing configuration. When you hover over a functoid that has the yellow exclamation mark on it, you get a tooltip describing what needs to be changed. Most of the time, you have missing input parameters or haven't connected the output of the functoid to anything.

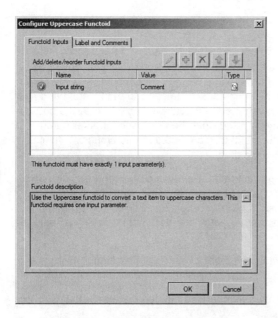

FIGURE 3.14   Parameters for a functoid without labels on the links.

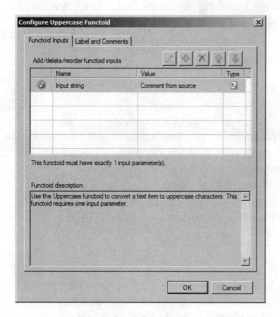

FIGURE 3.15   Parameters for a functoid, using labels on links.

String Functoids

The string functoids perform string manipulation on either an incoming value or a set of values. They all output a string, which can be used as the input for another functoid or sent directly to the destination schema. Table 3.5 lists the string functoids, their usage, and parameters.

TABLE 3.5   The String Functoids

Name	Description
Lowercase	This functoid takes in one parameter and returns the same string in lowercase.
Size	Returns an integer that equals the length of the input string. If the input string is null, a value of 0 is returned.
String Concatenate	This functoid takes in at least 1 string and a maximum of 100 strings. The strings are concatenated in the order they have been added as input to the functoid. The output is the concatenated string. Note this functoid cannot concatenate values in a reoccurring element in the source. You need a cumulative functoid for this, which is explained later.
String Extract	This functoid takes in three parameters and returns a substring of the first input. The second input determines the start position of the substring to be extracted and the third parameter determines the end position. Note that although the C# `String.Substring` method is actually used by the functoid, it wants the end position of the string to extract and not the length of the substring to extract. Also, contrary to the C# string methods, these parameters are 1 based and not 0 based, meaning that the first character of the input is a position 1.
String Find	This functoid takes in two parameters and returns the first found instance of the second parameter inside the first parameter. If the first parameter is `BizTalk` and the second parameter is `Talk`, the functoid returns the value 4. Note that this is also 1 based and not 0 based as is normally the case in C#.
String Left	This functoid takes in two parameters. The first is a string, and the second must be an int. The functoid returns the number of characters specified in the second parameter from the left of the string. If the second parameter is greater than the length of the string, the input string is returned.
String Left Trim	This functoid takes in a string and trims it from the left, effectively removing all characters from the beginning of the string until it reaches a nonwhitespace character. The characters that are defined as whitespace are the ones defined in C# as whitespace. These include spaces, carriage returns, line feeds, and others. Given null as input, the functoid returns the empty string.
String Right	This functoid does the same as the String Left functoid, only from the right rather than the left.

TABLE 3.5   The String Functoids

Name	Description
String Right Trim	This functoid takes in a string and trims it from the right. The functionality is the same as the String Trim Left functoid, only from the right rather than the left.
Uppercase	This functoid takes in one parameter and returns the same string in uppercase.

Mathematical Functoids

The mathematical functoids perform mathematical operations on their input and return an output that can be used as the input for another functoid or sent directly to the destination schema. Because the input parameters to a mathematical functoid are strings and a mathematical functoid returns a string, there are some methods used by the functoids to convert a string into a number to perform mathematical functions on the inputs. As a general rule, an input to a mathematical functoid that is not a number is ignored and if the parameter cannot be ignored, like either parameter in a division, an empty string is returned. Table 3.6 lists the mathematical functoids, their usage, and parameters.

TABLE 3.6   The Mathematical Functoids

Name	Description
Absolute Value	This functoid takes in one value and it returns the absolute value of the value. For a positive number, the absolute value is the same number. For a negative number, the absolute value is the number multiplied by -1.
Addition	This functoid takes in a minimum of 2 parameters and a maximum of 100 parameters. It sums the parameters and returns the result.
Division	This functoid takes in two parameters and returns the first parameter divided by the second parameter. If either parameter is not a number or if the second parameter is 0, the empty string is returned.
Integer	This functoid takes in one parameter and returns the integer part of the value, effectively removing the decimal point and all decimals. This differs from the Round functoid in that it will never round up (only down).
Maximum Value	This functoid takes in a minimum of 2 parameters and a maximum of 100 parameters. It returns the largest number found among the parameters.
Minimum Value	This functoid takes in a minimum of 2 parameters and a maximum of 100 parameters. It returns the smallest number found among the parameters.
Modulo	This functoid takes in two parameters. It returns the remainder from performing a division of the first parameter by the second parameter.
Multiplication	This functoid takes in a minimum of 2 parameters and a maximum of 100 parameters. It multiplies all the parameters and returns the result.

TABLE 3.6   The Mathematical Functoids

Name	Description
Round	This functoid takes one required parameter and one optional parameter. The first parameter is the value to round, and the second is the number of decimals to which the first parameter should be rounded off. If the second parameter is not present, the first parameter is rounded off to a whole number. Standard rounding rules apply.
Square Root	This functoid takes in one parameter and returns the square root of it.
Subtraction	This functoid takes in a minimum of 2 parameters and a maximum of 100 parameters. It subtracts all parameters that are not the first parameter from the first parameter and returns the result.

All the functoids return an empty value if a specified parameter is not a number. Optional parameters can be omitted, but if they are used, they must also be numbers or an empty string is returned.

Logical Functoids

The logical functoids perform logical operations on their input and returns a Boolean value that can be used later on as the input for another functoid or to instruct the compiler how to construct the generated XSLT. How the logical functoids aid the compiler in constructing the generated XSLT is discussed in the "Advanced Maps" section. Because the logical functoids are used for either input to other functoids or to instruct the compiler, you cannot get the output of a logical functoid into your destination schema. If you want to do so, you can add a C# scripting functoid (described later) with the code as shown in Listing 3.1 and place that in between the logical functoid and the destination node. Table 3.7 lists the logical functoids, their usage and parameters.

TABLE 3.7   The Logical Functoids

Name	Description
Equal	This functoid takes in two parameters and returns true if the parameters are equal to each other. If they are not equal, a value of false is returned.
Greater Than	This functoid takes in two parameters. It returns true if the first parameter is greater than the second parameter. Otherwise, it returns false.
Greater Than or Equal To	This functoid takes in two parameters. It returns true if the first parameter is greater than or equal to the second parameter. Otherwise, it returns false.
IsNil	This functoid takes in one parameter, which must be a node in the source schema and cannot be another functoid. The functoid returns true if the node in the source schema is set to nil, like this: `<myElement xsi:nil="true" />`

TABLE 3.7   The Logical Functoids

Name	Description
Less Than	This functoid takes in two parameters. It returns true if the first parameter is less than the second parameter. Otherwise, it returns false.
Less Than or Equal To	This functoid takes in two parameters. It returns true if the first parameter is less than or equal to the second parameter. Otherwise, it returns false.
Logical AND	This functoid takes in a minimum of 2 parameters and a maximum of 100 parameters. It returns the logical AND of all the inputs, meaning that if just one of the inputs is false, a value of false is returned. Otherwise, a value of true is returned.
Logical Date	This functoid takes in one parameter and returns a Boolean value depending on whether the input could be parsed as a .NET DateTime.
Logical Existence	This functoid takes in one parameter. If the parameter is another functoid, the input must be a Boolean, because the Logical Existence functoid doesn't do any conversion of the input into Boolean. The functoid just passes the value it receives on. If the input is a node in the source schema, however, the functoid returns true if the node is present in the source schema and false otherwise.
Logical NOT	This functoid takes in a Boolean value and returns the negation of it, meaning true becomes false and vice versa.
Logical Numeric	This functoid takes in one parameter and returns a Boolean value depending on whether the input could be parsed as a .NET double.
Logical OR	This functoid takes in a minimum of 2 parameters and a maximum of 100 parameters. It returns the logical OR of all the inputs, meaning that if just one of the inputs is true, a value of true is returned. Otherwise, a value of false is returned.
Logical String	This functoid takes in one parameter and returns true if the parameter is neither null nor the empty string. Otherwise, it returns false.
Not Equal	This functoid takes in two parameters and returns true if the parameters are not equal to each other. If the two values are equal, a value of false is returned.

LISTING 3.1   C# Code for Getting Output of a Logical Functoid into a Destination Node

```csharp
public string LogicalToString(string logical)
{
     return logical;

}
```

All the functoids that need to take a Boolean as input need to parse the input to make sure it is in fact a Boolean and not some random string. The algorithm for this is as follows:

1. The input is compared to the string `true` in a non-case-sensitive manner. If this succeeds, a value of `true` is returned, and processing stops.

2. The input is compared to the string `false` in a non-case-sensitive manner. If this succeeds, a value of `false` is returned, and processing stops.

3. The string is trimmed to remove leading and trailing whitespace.

4. The input is compared to the string `true` in a non-case-sensitive manner. If this succeeds, a value of `true` is returned, and processing stops.

5. The input is compared to the string "false" in a non-case-sensitive manner. If this succeeds, a value of `false` is returned, and processing stops.

6. The input is converted into a number. If this fails, a value of `false` is returned.

7. The number is greater than 0, a value of `true` is returned. Otherwise, a value of `false` is returned.

This algorithm is used by the Logical OR, Logical NOT, and Logical AND functoids to validate the input.

The Not Equal, Equal, Less Than or Equal To, Less Than, Greater Than or Equal To, and Greater Than functoids can all compare numbers to numbers and strings to strings.

Date/Time Functoids

The date/time functoids are a collection of functoids that deal with dates/times. Their output can be used as the input for another functoid or sent directly to the destination schema. Table 3.8 lists the date/time functoids, their usage, and parameters.

TABLE 3.8   The Date/Time Functoids

Name	Description
Add Days	This functoid takes two parameters and returns a new date as a result of adding the number of days specified in the second parameter to the date specified in the first parameter.
Date	This functoid takes no parameters and returns the current date.
Date and Time	This functoid takes no parameters and returns the current date and time.
Time	This functoid takes no parameters and returns the current time.

Conversion Functoids

The conversion functoids perform conversions on their input and return output that can be used as the input for another functoid or sent directly to the destination schema. Table 3.9 lists the conversion functoids, their usage, and parameters.

TABLE 3.9   The Conversion Functoids

Name	Description
ASCII to Character	This functoid takes in one parameter. If the parameter is a number less than 0 or greater than 127, an empty string is returned. Otherwise, the number is converted into the character that has this number in the ASCII table. 65 becomes A, for instance.
Character to ASCII	This functoid takes in one parameter. If the parameter is null or the empty string, an empty string is returned. If not, the first character of the string is converted into the ASCII representation. A becomes 65, for instance.
Hexadecimal	This functoid takes in one parameter. If the parameter is not a number, the empty string is returned. If the parameter is a number, the integer part of the number is converted to a hexadecimal value. The input is assumed to be a decimal value.
Octal	This functoid takes in one parameter. If the parameter is not a number, the empty string is returned. If the parameter is a number, the integer part of the number is converted to an octal value. The input is assumed to be a decimal value.

Scientific Functoids

The scientific functoids perform scientific mathematical operations on their input and return an output that can be used as the input for another functoid or sent directly to the destination schema. Table 3.10 lists the scientific functoids, their usage, and parameters.

TABLE 3.10   The Scientific Functoids

Name	Description
10^n	This functoid takes in one parameter. The functoid returns 10 lifted to the power of the parameter. For instance, a value of 2 results in 100, and a value of 5 results in 100000.
Arc Tangent	This functoid takes in one parameter. The functoid returns the result of performing the arc tangent function on the parameter.

TABLE 3.10   The Scientific Functoids

Name	Description
Base-Specified Logarithm	This functoid takes in two parameters. If either parameters is less than or equal to 0, an empty string is returned. Also, if the second parameter is 1, an empty string is returned. The functoid returns the base-specified logarithm function using the second parameter as base and performing the function on the first parameter. For instance, parameters 100 and 10 result in the value 2, and parameters 64 and 2 result in the value 6.
Common Logarithm	This functoid takes in one parameter. If the parameter is less than or equal to 0, an empty string is returned. Otherwise, the functoid returns the 10-based logarithm of the parameter. For instance, a value of 100 results in 2, and a value of 10000 results in 4.
Cosine	This functoid takes in one parameter. If the parameter is a number, the cosine function is called with the parameter as input, and the result of that is returned.
Natural Exponential Function	This functoid takes in one parameter. The functoid returns ℮ (The base for the natural logarithm) lifted to the power of the parameter. For instance, a value of 2 results in 7.389..., and a value of 3 results in 20.085....
Natural Logarithm	This functoid takes in one parameter. The functoid returns the natural logarithm of the parameter. The natural logarithm is the logarithm that is based on ℮.
Sine	This functoid takes in one parameter. If the parameter is a number, the sine function is called with the parameter as input, and the result of that is returned.
Tangent	This functoid takes in one parameter. The functoid returns the result of performing the tangens function on the input.
X^Y	This functoid takes in two parameters. The functoid returns the first parameter raised to the power of the second parameter.

For all the functoids you get an empty string as the result in case the input parameters could not be parsed as a number.

All trigonometric functoids like Sine, Cosine, Tangent, and Arc Tangent assume the input is in radians. This means that if you want to use any of these functoids on a value of 180° you need to convert the 180° into π first.

Cumulative Functoids

The cumulative functoids perform operations on reoccurring nodes in the source schema and output one value based on all the occurrences of the input node. The output can be used as the input for another functoid or sent directly to the destination schema. Table 3.11 lists the cumulative functoids, their usage, and parameters.

TABLE 3.11   The Cumulative Functoids

Name	Description
Cumulative Average	This functoid takes in all the occurrences of the input and outputs the average of the input values.
Cumulative Concatenate	This functoid concatenates the occurrences of the input into one string, which is then output.
Cumulative Maximum	This functoid takes in all the occurrences of the input and outputs the largest number found among the input values.
Cumulative Minimum	This functoid takes in all the occurrences of the input and outputs the smallest number found among the input values.
Cumulative Sum	This functoid takes in all the occurrences of the input and outputs the sum of the input values.

All the cumulative functoids take in two parameters. The first parameter is the value to be accumulated, and the second is a scoping parameter. The scoping parameter is used to generate the XSLT. If no value is passed on, a default value of 1000 is used in the XSLT. If a value is actually passed into the parameter, this is used as an indication of what level of scope to do the accumulation. A value of 0 means that all occurrences of the first parameter are accumulated and the functoid will therefore have only one output. A value of 1 means that the values are accumulated for each parent of the first parameter and an output is therefore generated for each parent. A value of 2 means that the values are accumulated for each grandparent of the first parameter and so on. Note that it is not the functoid that contains this logic. The generated XSLT will do all this for you, making sure that the functoid is called for each level of scoping needed.

NOTE

As explained later in this chapter, it is not possible to build a thread-safe referenced cumulative functoid. Therefore, if you are using any of the built-in cumulative functoids, take care to have the Inline C# option or another appropriate inline option above the External Assembly option in the Script Type Precedence property of the map.

Database Functoids

The database functoids can be split into two categories; Those that do database lookup and those that do cross referencing.

Database

The database functoids are used for looking up values in an ADO.NET-compliant database that can be used as the input for another functoid or sent directly to the destination schema. Table 3.12 lists the database functoids, their usage, and parameters.

TABLE 3.12   The Database Functoids

Name	Description
Database Lookup	This functoid takes in four parameters, which are all required. The first parameter (p1) is a lookup value, which could be some ID from the source message. The second parameter is a connection string that instructs the runtime where to do the lookup. The third parameter (p3) is the name of the table to do the lookup. The fourth parameter (p4) is the name of the column that is used to find the lookup value. BizTalk creates a query like this: SELECT * FROM p3 WHERE p4 = p1; and connects to the database, and thus selects all values from the row in the table specified that has the right lookup value in the column specified in the fourth parameter. This requires the column in the fourth parameter to be a unique key in the table. If it is not a key, the first row is returned. This functoid cannot be connected to an output node, because it outputs an entire row. Use the Value Extractor functoid, which is explained later, to extract a column value from this row.
Error Return	This functoid takes in one parameter, which is a Database Lookup functoid. The functoid outputs any error message that has arrived from performing the query against the database. If no errors occur, the functoid has an empty string as output.
Value Extractor	This functoid takes two parameters, which are both required. The first is a Database Lookup functoid. The second is the name of the column from the output row from the Database Lookup to extract. This effectively pulls out one specific value from a named column in the result set of the database query, and this value can then be output to the destination schema.

NOTE

Hard-coding the connection string inside your functoid is probably not what you want to do because it requires you to change it manually and recompile for each environment your map is deployed to. Rather, you should keep the connection string in some configuration storage and retrieve it at runtime. Options for this include *Single Sign-On* (SSO), a configuration file, a database, a .NET assembly, and others.

The preceding options are generic for all configuration options you might use throughout your solution, but one last option that is specific for the database lookup functoid exists. You can enter File Name=<PathToUDLFile> as the connection string. This requires, of course, that the file can be read at runtime by the host instance that is running. Parsing a UDL file is slow, so the options listed previously are recommended considering performance.

Cross Referencing

The cross-referencing functoids are used for looking up values in a database and using the values retrieved as the input for another functoid or sending it directly to the destination schema. This is used to map values that are specific to one system to the corresponding values from another system. For instance, you can use this setup to find your *enterprise resource planning* (ERP) system item number based on the item number your customer has supplied you with in the order you have received.

The cross-referencing functoids are restricted to and make use of the 9 xref_* tables that are present in the BizTalkMgmtDb database. Importing data into these tables is done via the BizTalk Server Cross Reference Import tool (btsxrefimport.exe), which you can find in the BizTalks installation folder. The utility takes in a parameter that specifies the filename of an XML file that basically contains references to eight other XML files, which contain the data that must be imported into the xref_* tables. When data is in the tables, the cross-referencing functoids can be used to look up values in the tables. For detailed information about the syntax of these XML files and how to import the data into the database tables, refer to http://msdn.microsoft.com/en-us/library/aa578674(BTS.70).aspx. Table 3.13 lists the cross-referencing functoids and their usage.

TABLE 3.13   The Cross-Referencing Functoids

Name	Description
Format Message	Returns a formatted and localized string using argument substitution and, potentially, ID and value cross referencing
Get Application ID	Retrieves an identifier for an application object
Get Application Value	Retrieves an application value
Get Common ID	Retrieves an identifier for a common object
Get Common Value	Retrieves a common value
Remove Application ID	Removes the identifier for an application object
Set Common ID	Sets and returns an identifier for a common object

You can see an example of the use of the cross-referencing functoids in the "Advanced Maps" section.

Advanced Functoids

The advanced functoids perform advanced operations on their input. Some of them return an output that can be used as the input for another functoid or sent directly to the destination schema. The use of others assists the compiler in creating the necessary XSLT. Table 3.14 lists the advanced functoids, their usage, and parameters.

TABLE 3.14 The Advanced Functoids

Name	Description
Assert	This functoid takes in three parameters. The first must be a Boolean value. If the map is compiled in Debug mode, an exception is thrown with the text from the second parameter if the first parameter is false. The third parameter is used as output. If the map is compiled in Release mode, the third parameter is always returned. This is useful for debugging your map, and just as with assertions in normal C# code, it allows you to make sure some conditions are always true.
Index	This functoid takes in a minimum of 1 parameter and a maximum of 100 parameters. The first parameter must be a node from the source schema. and the rest represent indexes in each level from the node that is the first parameter and back to the root node. The functoid returns the value in the node given by the first parameter and indexed by the values from the rest of the parameters. An example is provided in the "Advanced Maps" section.
Iteration	This functoid takes in one parameter, which must be a node in the source schema. The functoid returns the iteration of the node, meaning that it returns 1 for the first occurrence of the input node, 2 for the second occurrence, and so on.
Looping	This functoid takes in a minimum of 2 parameters and a maximum of 100 parameters. The input parameters must be nodes in the source schema and cannot be other functoids. The functoid has no functional purpose and therefore no output as such. You must connect the looping functoid to a record in the destination schema, and the map then generates one output record for each of the input records that correspond to the input parameters. An example of the Looping functoid is provided in the section "Advanced Maps" section.
Mass Copy	This functoid takes in one parameter, which must be a node from the source schema. The functoid must be connected to a node in the destination schema, and it copies recursively all the nodes below the source node to the destination node.
Nil Value	This functoid takes in one optional parameter. If specified, the parameter must be a Boolean. If not specified, a value of true is assumed. The functoid is connected to a node in the destination structure, and if a value of true is specified in the first parameter, the output node is created with a value of nil.
Record Count	This functoid takes in one parameter, which is a node from the source schema. The functoid returns the number of times the node appears in the input regardless of scope.

3

TABLE 3.14   The Advanced Functoids

Name	Description
Scripting	This functoid is used to execute some script. The functoid is configurable to either call a specific method in a .NET class in an assembly or to configure a script that is either Inline C#, Inline JScript .NET, Inline Visual Basic .NET, Inline XSLT, or Inline XSLT Call Template. The XSLT scripting options can be used to control creation of destination structure, because the XSLT has access to the entire source structure and the XSLT is inserted into the generated XSLT. The other script types can be used to perform operations on input values and they must output one value. The Scripting functoid is discussed in more detail in the "Advanced Maps" section. If you use a .NET language in your inline script, you have access to the .NET namespaces found at http://msdn.microsoft.com/en-us/library/aa561456(BTS.70).aspx.
Table Extractor	This functoid takes in two parameters. The first must be a Table Looping functoid, and the second is a number that indicates the column from the table to get the value from. The output from this functoid can then be sent to another functoid as input or directly to the destination schema. An example of the Table Extractor functoid is provided in the "Advanced Maps" section.
Table Looping	This functoid takes in a minimum of 3 parameters and a maximum of 100 parameters. The functoid builds a table in memory useful for creating records in the output that have some structure that is not present in the input. The first parameter is a scoping link from a node in the source schema. The second parameter is the number of columns that should be in the table, which corresponds to the number of fields to create in the output. The third parameter and all following parameters are values that can be used to build the table. An example of the Table Looping functoid is provided in the "Advanced Maps" section.
Value Mapping	This functoid takes in two parameters. The first must be a Boolean value, and the second parameter can be any value. The functoid outputs the second parameter if the first parameter was true. This functoid differs from the Value Mapping (Flattening) functoid in that this functoid does not attempt to flatten the input into the output.
Value Mapping (Flattening)	This functoid takes in two parameters. The first must be a Boolean value, and the second parameter can be any value. The functoid outputs the second parameter if the first parameter was true. This functoid differs from the Value Mapping functoid in that this functoid attempts to flatten the input into the output. This is useful when you have multiple Value Mapping functoids with outputs going to the same record, because otherwise two instances of the destination record will be created.

Third-Party Functoids

You can download several third-party functoids and use them in your solutions. Use your favorite search engine to locate them.

Advanced Maps

This section describes some advanced options for mapping and provides some more details on how mappings can be done. Specifically some scenarios of advanced usage of the functoids in combination are described.

Mapping Optional Fields

If the source document of a map has an optional field in it that you are mapping to a field in the destination schema, the XSLT actually handles this for you and creates the destination field only if the source field exists. This way you won't get an empty field in the output if the source field isn't there.

This is achieved by wrapping the creation of the destination field in an `if` statement, as shown in Figure 3.16.

```
<xsl:if test="OrderDate">
- <OrderDate>
    <xsl:value-of select="OrderDate/text()" />
  </OrderDate>
</xsl:if>
```

FIGURE 3.16   Resulting XSLT from mapping optional fields.

Had the `OrderDate` element in the source not been optional, the `OrderDate` field in the destination would always be created; and if the element at runtime had not been present, the output would have an empty element. The generated XSLT would be the same as shown in Figure 3.16 but without the enclosing `if` statement.

Note that if you try to map an optional field to a required field, you get a warning at compile time or when you validate the map.

Looping Functoid

The looping functoid can be used to give the compiler hints as to how to create the XSLT when you are mapping across different hierarchies in the source document. For example, consider the mapping in Figure 3.17.

The idea of the map is to create one `AddressInformation` record in the output for the `ShippingInformation` record in the source and one for the `BillingInformation` record.

The output, however, is shown in Figure 3.18.

This is clearly not the output you want, because the address information is mixed in one `AddressInformation` record. To fix this, you use the Looping functoid, as shown in Figure 3.19.

The output is now as expected, as shown in Figure 3.20.

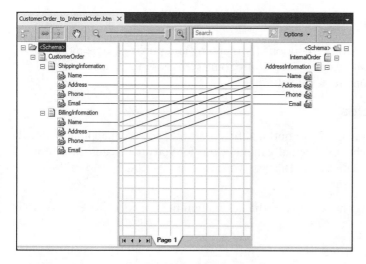

FIGURE 3.17   Mapping across hierarchies without Looping functoid.

FIGURE 3.18   The output of the map when the Looping functoid is not used.

Note that in this example the BillingInformation record is mapped to an AddressInformation record before the ShippingInformation. This is because the order you add the inputs to the Looping functoid matters. If you add the ShippingInformation to the Looping functoid before the BillingInformation, the ShippingInformation is mapped first.

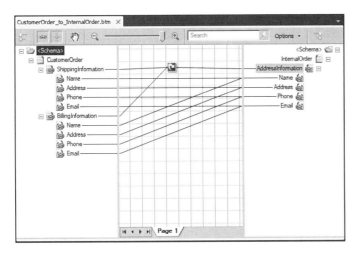

FIGURE 3.19   Mapping across hierarchies with Looping functoid.

FIGURE 3.20   The output of the map when the Looping functoid is used.

Index Functoid

The Index functoid provides a means to retrieve a specific value at a specific place in a hierarchy of fields.

If you have the XML shown in Figure 3.21 and you want to get the value `ItemNumber2` from the `ItemNumber` element in the second `OrderLine` in the first `Order` record, for example, you can use the Index functoid to do so.

This is done using the Index functoid as shown in Figure 3.22, with the parameters to the functoid being as shown in Figure 3.23.

```
CustomerOrderInstance.xml ×
⊟<ns0:CustomerOrder xmlns:ns0="http://Maps.CustomerOrder">
⊞   <ShippingInformation>...</ShippingInformation>
⊞   <BillingInformation>...</BillingInformation>
⊟   <Orders>
⊟     <Order>
⊟       <OrderLines>
⊟         <OrderLine>
             <ItemNumber>ItemNumber1</ItemNumber>
          </OrderLine>
⊟         <OrderLine>
             <ItemNumber>ItemNumber2</ItemNumber>
          </OrderLine>
        </OrderLines>
      </Order>
⊟     <Order>
⊟       <OrderLines>
⊟         <OrderLine>
             <ItemNumber>ItemNumber3</ItemNumber>
          </OrderLine>
⊟         <OrderLine>
             <ItemNumber>ItemNumber4</ItemNumber>
          </OrderLine>
        </OrderLines>
      </Order>
    </Orders>
  </ns0:CustomerOrder>
```

FIGURE 3.21   XML example of the Index functoid.

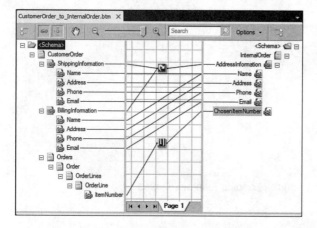

FIGURE 3.22   Using the Index functoid.

The parameters are first of all the field to get a value from and then the index of each parent level from that field and up. So, the parameters shown in Figure 3.23 are for the second OrderLine in the first OrderLines in the first Order record.

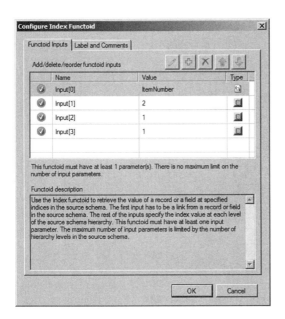

FIGURE 3.23   Parameters for the Index functoid.

Database Lookup

The Database Lookup functoids are used to look up values in a database if the data is not present in the source document of the map. This can be getting the price of an item or the address of a customer or anything else.

To explain the use of this functoid, consider the map depicted in Figure 3.24. You need to add the Database Lookup functoid first. This functoid takes four parameters:

► A lookup value. This is the value from the source document that you need to find information based on.

► A connection string to the database that holds the table you want to fetch information from.

► The name of the table you need to fetch information from. You can wrap the table name in square brackets ([and]) if you like (for instance, if spaces or reserved words are used in the table name).

► The column in the table that you want to match against the lookup value from the first parameter. This can also be wrapped in square brackets.

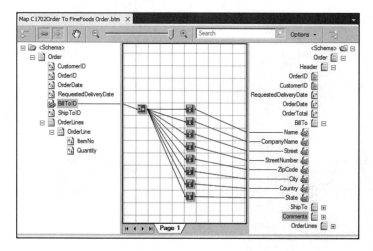

FIGURE 3.24   Using the Database Lookup functoid.

The functoid converts this into a SQL statement that looks like this:

```
SELECT * FROM <Param3> where <Param1> = <Param4>
```

In other words, it connects to the database using the connection string and then executes this SQL statement to get the row you need from the table you have specified.

> **TIP**
>
> If you are having trouble getting the connection string right, create an empty file on your desktop called conn.udl. Double-click it. A wizard will appear that helps you choose the provider, server, authorization scheme, and so on. When you have finished, save the work and open the .UDL file in a text editor to get the connection string.

The Database Lookup functoid returns only one row from the database. If the SQL statement returns more than one row, which is the case when the column specified in parameter four isn't a unique key in the table, the functoid just returns the first row from the data set returned by the SQL statement.

> **TIP**
>
> If you do not have one column that is unique, but need several, you can choose to use [Col1]+[Col2] as parameter four and then use a String Concatenate functoid to concatenate the fields from the source document that matches Col1 + Col2.

Because the Database Lookup functoid returns an entire row, you need to extract specific values from this row. In the example in Figure 3.24 there are eight Value Extractor functoids that will each extract a specific value from a column in the row.

A Value Extractor functoid takes in two parameters:

- The Database Lookup functoid that returns the row to extract a value from. Note that although the Database Lookup functoid is the only allowed input, the user interface allows you to use any Database functoid as the input for the Value Extractor functoid. This returns in runtime errors, however, so get this right at design time.

- The name of the column to extract. Note that this cannot be enclosed in square brackets (as you can with the table name and column name for the Database Lookup functoid, as discussed previously).

TIP

While developing a map that uses the Database Lookup functoid, you should add an Error Return functoid to your map. Let this functoid have the Database Lookup functoid as input, and let its output go to some element in the destination schema. This way, while developing and testing your map, you get any relevant error information that you can use to debug the connection. If you don't use the Error Return functoid, you will just have empty fields where the Value Extractor functoids should have put values.

Scripting Functoid

The Scripting functoid is used for two main things:

- To perform some task that the built-in functoids cannot do for you and which isn't needed often enough to justify developing a custom functoid. An example of this could be to generate a new *globally unique identifier* (GUID) or to do string replacement.

- To perform some task that the built-in functoids can do for you but that requires some combination of functoids that is too tedious to build. An example of this could be if-then-else functionality, which is described later in this section.

After dragging the Scripting functoid onto the map, you can double-click it to get to the functoid configuration window. Go to the Script Functoid Configuration pane, shown in Figure 3.25, where you can change the script.

In this screen, you may choose what language to use for your script. If you choose External Assembly, you can choose to call a public static method of a public class that is in a current assembly. The other five options allow for editing of the script to include in the map. For each, you can choose to import the script from an existing file by clicking the **Import from File** button. This is often a good idea because the editing window in the Script Functoid Configuration doesn't have IntelliSense, syntax highlighting, or even allow for the use of tabulators to indent code.

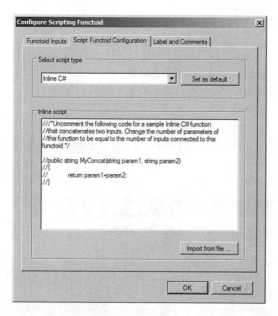

FIGURE 3.25   Scripting functoid.

The types of scripts that take parameters all take in strings. Therefore, you cannot send a node from the source document as a parameter and expect to treat it as an XmlNode. You only get the value of the node connected to the Scripting functoid.

Take care that the number of parameters your script takes matches the number of parameters you have provided to the functoid.

If you choose to leverage the power of one of the two XSLT scripting options and connect the Scripting functoid to a field in the destination schema, you take responsibility for creating the entire structure of the field you have connected the functoid to and any children of this field. The other four scripting types can output only a string, which is then copied to the field the Scripting functoid is connected to.

The XSLT scripting functoids are especially useful for performing tasks that deal with the source XML structure, because you have access to the entire source XML using XPath in the script, which you do not otherwise. Also, because you need to generate XML structures in the XSLT functoids, you have the possibility to create XML nodes for which there was no data support in the source XML. Assume, for instance, that you need to add an order line to all incoming orders that adds shipping expenses. You would need to copy all order lines from the incoming order to the destination document but also create a new order line to add to the existing ones. This is only doable in custom XSLT, be it either in a Scripting functoid or in a custom XSLT script that you use in your map instead of leveraging the Mapper.

Note that for XSLT you do not have access to all the nice features and functions of XSLT 2.0, because BizTalk only supports XSLT 1.0.

Functoid Combination

You can use the output from one functoid as the input for another functoid. This is useful for building functionality that doesn't exist in the built-in functoids.

If you want to make sure that a string in the input is trimmed for leading and trailing whitespace and also in uppercase, you need the functoids shown in Figure 3.26.

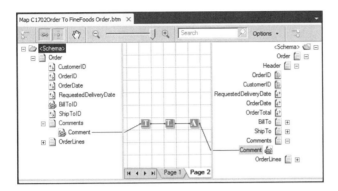

FIGURE 3.26   Functoid collection to trim input and convert it to uppercase.

Combination of Functoids for If-Then-Else

The built-in functoids provide you with two Value Mapping functoids that basically return their second parameter if the first parameter is true. This allows for an if-then solution, but there is no intuitive way of doing an if-then-else solution (that is, returning a third parameter if the first parameter is false). To build an if-then-else solution, you must use several functoids, as shown in Figure 3.27.

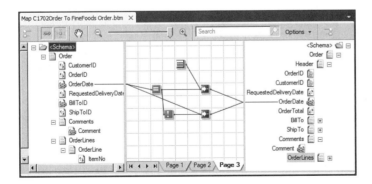

FIGURE 3.27   Performing the if-then-else logic.

The solution provided in Figure 3.27 is used to send the current date to the OrderDate field if the OrderDate provided in the input is empty. This is a case where the sender has a bug in his system that makes him send an empty element from time to time. The solution is to first use an Equal functoid to check whether the string equals the empty string and use the output of this comparison as the first input for a Value Mapping functoid that takes in the current date as the second input. So if the field is empty, the current date is mapped. The output of the Equal functoid is also used as input to a Logical Not functoid, which negates the input. This is then used to allow another Value Mapping functoid to output the value of the OrderDate in case the Equal functoid did not return true, meaning the string wasn't empty.

Create Separated List

Assume that the order from a customer can have many Comment fields, but the internal order format allows for only one Comment field. In this case, you might want to concatenate the Comment fields from the input into one string for the output and separate the comments by some separator. Figure 3.28 shows an example of how to do this.

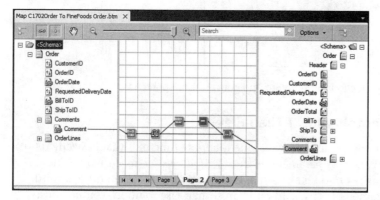

FIGURE 3.28   How to create a separated list of strings.

The functionality is built up using string functoids and one cumulative functoid. First, the input is concatenated with the separator. The output of this is sent to the Cumulative Concatenate functoid, which will then have the complete list as its output, with a separator at the end. This final separator is removed by using the String Extract functoid, which takes in the concatenated string as its first input. The second is the constant 1, and the third parameter is the length of the concatenated string minus 1.

Table Looping Functoid

The table looping functoid is useful to combine constants and fields from the source document into structures in the destination document. Let's revisit the challenge faced that was solved using the Looping functoid, as shown in Figure 3.19. Often, schemas that share a record for different addresses have a qualifier on the record, which contains information about what type of address the current record contains. So, the destination schema would probably be as shown in Figure 3.29.

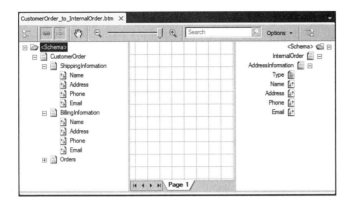

FIGURE 3.29   The map to implement before adding the Table Looping functoid.

The Table Looping functoid is used to build a table of information and then output each row in the table on at the time, thereby creating records in the destination schema. To implement the mapping in this example, first drag the functoid to the grid, and then drag a scoping record from the source to the functoid. In this case, that is the root node because that is the node that encompasses all the needed fields. The second parameter to the functoid must be a number indicating how many columns should be in the table. The third parameter and all the next parameters are values that can be used to build the table. As shown in Figure 3.30, all eight fields with information have been added as inputs to the functoid. Also, two constant strings have been added as parameters to the functoid (namely, the strings Bill and Ship). These two strings are the qualifiers used in this example, meaning that the AddressInformation record in the output that contains the shipping information must have a Type attribute with the value Ship and the other must have a Type attribute with the value Bill.

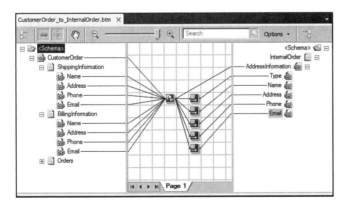

FIGURE 3.30   Using the Table Looping functoid.

To tell the compiler which record is to be created for each row in the table, you must drag the output of the Table Looping functoid to the record.

After doing this, you can start building the table, which is done either by double-clicking the functoid and then switching to the Table Looping Grid pane or by right-clicking the functoid and choosing **Configure Table Looping Grid**. This opens the table grid with as many columns as you have indicated by the second parameter to the functoid. You can now use the drop-down in each field to select which of all the parameters to the functoid to use for which columns in which rows of the table. The resulting table might look like Figure 3.31.

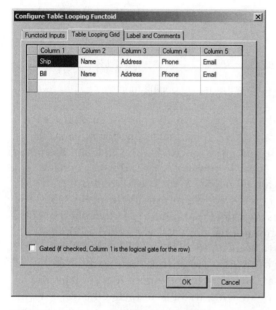

FIGURE 3.31   The table grid of the Table Looping functoid.

To determine which columns of the table go into which fields in the destination schema, you need to use the Table Extractor functoid. Add one of these, as shown in Figure 3.30, for each field to copy values into, and use the Table Looping functoid as the first input to each of them. The second parameter to each Table Extractor functoid must be the column number to extract. So, given the rows shown in Figure 3.31, let the first Table Extractor functoid have a second parameter of 1 and let its output go to the Type attribute of the AddressInformation record. Now configure the remaining four Table Extractor functoids to extract the correct column and map it to the correct field in the destination schema.

The resulting XML from testing the map should look as shown in Figure 3.32.

The grid configuration screen shown in Figure 3.31 has a check box at the bottom that can be checked to instruct the map that the data in the first column should act as a condition that specifies whether each row is created in the output. At runtime, the value of the first column is evaluated, and if data is found, the Value Extractor functoids associated with that row are called and the output record is created. If no data is found, the Value Extractor functoids are not called, and the record is therefore not created in the output. If the input for the first column is a Logical functoid rather than a field, the output record is created if the value from the Logical functoid is true (and not otherwise).

FIGURE 3.32   Result of using Table Looping functoid.

Conditional Creation of Output Nodes

You might sometimes want to implement conditional creation of output records. For instance, consider the opposite mapping of the one found in Figure 3.30. In this case, you will want to create a ShippingInformation record in case the Type attribute of the AddressInformation record has a value of Ship and similar with the billing information. This is achieved using logical functoids.

Logical functoids have a side effect to just being able to do logical operations. If you connect a logical functoid to an output record, the output record is only created if the functoid returns true. This means that the reverse mapping of the address information can be solved, as shown in Figure 3.33.

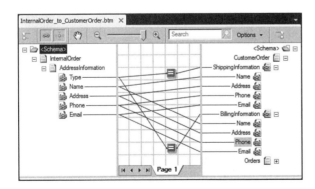

FIGURE 3.33   Conditional creation of records.

In this sample, the upper Equal functoid has a second parameter with a value of Ship, and the ShippingInformation record is therefore only created when the Type attribute has this value. The same applies for the BillingInformation, which is only created when the Type attribute has a value of Bill.

Custom XSLT

There are mappings that the Mapper cannot create for you using the built-in functoids. In that case, you have two options:

- ▶ Extend the map with Scripting functoids that perform the functionality you cannot accomplish with the built-in functoids.

- ▶ Create the map in the Mapper but don't use links or functoids. Instead, use a custom XSLT script for the functionality of the map.

Also, the XSLT generated by the Mapper is as good as it gets when things are automatically generated. If you know what you are doing, you can usually create yourself more efficient XSLT that performs better. If you have performance issues with your map, you might therefore also choose to write a custom XSLT script and bypass the Mapper.

If you choose the option of creating an entire XSLT script to use as the map, you need to use the Custom XSL Path and the Custom Extension XML properties of the map, as explained earlier. After creating your custom XSL and possibly a custom extension XML, you need to specify the path to the XSL and extension XML in the two properties. This effectively bypasses anything you might have done inside the Mapper.

> **TIP**
>
> As a starting point for your custom XSLT, you can get an XSLT with all the correct namespaces and definitions if you follow these steps: Add the map to your project and choose source and destination schemas. Then right-click the map in Solution Explorer and choose **Validate Map**. In the output window, you now get a link to the generated XSLT. Copy this file to your project and point your map to this file using the Custom XSL Path property. Edit the XSLT as needed.

The extension XML is some XML that is used to create a link between a namespace prefix that you can use in your custom XSLT and an external assembly that contains methods you want to call. Just as with the XSLT, you can get an example of a custom extension XML file when validating your map. You get an extension XML during this process only if you are actually calling an external assembly from the map you are validating.

Cross Referencing

Often you need to translate some numbering scheme into another during the execution of a map. An example of this is when mapping between customer order formats and your own format or between your own format and the format of your supplier. In this case, you might have an item number in your internal ERP system, and the customers and suppliers have their own numbers. The cross-referencing functoids help you achieve this. The setup is fairly simple: You create some XML files that contain the information about trading partners and the numbers that need to be translated and then you use an import tool to import this XML into the cross-referencing-specific tables (xref_*) in the BizTalkMgmtDb database. The functoids can then be used to extract values from the tables.

This section contains a simple example, covering the scenario of item numbers that need to be translated from the numbers the customer uses to the numbers FineFoods uses. This scenario leverages only half of the XML documents that can be used for other cross-referencing features. For a complete description of the other XML files, refer to http://msdn.microsoft.com/en-us/library/aa578674(BTS.70).aspx.

This scenario leverages five XML documents. The first one is just a container that contains links to the other four. The XML files can be seen in Listing 3.2, Listing 3.3, Listing 3.4, Listing 3.5, and Listing 3.6.

LISTING 3.2   Contents of Cross-Referencing Setup File

```xml
<?xml version="1.0" encoding="UTF-8"?>
<Setup-Files>
    <App_Type_file>C:\CrossReferencing\ListOfAppType.xml</App_Type_file>

<App_Instance_file>C:\CrossReferencing\ListOfAppInstance.xml</App_Instance_file>
    <IDXRef_file>C:\CrossReferencing\ListOfIDXRef.xml</IDXRef_file>
    <IDXRef_Data_file>C:\CrossReferencing\ListOfIDXRefData.xml</IDXRef_Data_file>
</Setup-Files>
```

Listing 3.2 shows the contents of the setup file, which is really just a collection of links to the XML documents that contain the actual data that should be imported. Other than the four shown references, four other XML documents can be specified:

- ▶ ValueXRef_file

- ▶ ValueXRef_Data_file

- ▶ Msg_Def_file

- ▶ Msg_Text_file

These are not covered in this simple scenario.

LISTING 3.3   Contents of App_Type_file

```xml
<?xml version="1.0" encoding="UTF-8"?>
<listOfAppType>
  <appType>
    <name>ERP</name>
  </appType>
</listOfAppType>
```

Listing 3.3 shows the contents of the App_Type_file XML document. It is basically a list of application types that can exist. You can use any string you want. For this scenario only the application type ERP is used.

LISTING 3.4   Contents of App_Instances_file

```
<?xml version="1.0" encoding="UTF-8"?>
<listOfAppInstance>
  <appInstance>
    <instance>ERP_C1702</instance>
    <type>ERP</type>
  </appInstance>
  <appInstance>
    <instance>ERP_Internal</instance>
    <type>ERP</type>
  </appInstance>
</listOfAppInstance>
```

Listing 3.4 shows the contents of the App_Instances_file XML document. It is a list of instances of the application types from the App_Type_file XML document. The XML in Listing 3.4 has two instances of the ERP type, namely the ERP system from the customer and the internal ERP system.

LISTING 3.5   Contents of IDXRef_file

```
<?xml version="1.0" encoding="UTF-8"?>
<listOfIDXRef>
  <idXRef>
    <name>ItemID</name>
  </idXRef>
</listOfIDXRef>
```

Listing 3.5 shows the contents of the IDXRef_file XML document. It is a list of types of IDs that need to be translated. In this scenario, we need to translate identifications of items, but this can be any string you specify.

LISTING 3.6   Contents of IDXRef_Data_file

```
<?xml version="1.0" encoding="UTF-8"?>
<listOfIDXRefData>
  <idXRef name="ItemID">
    <appInstance name="ERP_C1702">
      <appID commonID="ITEM1">123</appID>
      <appID commonID="ITEM2">456</appID>
      <appID commonID="ITEM3">789</appID>
```

```
    </appInstance>
    <appInstance name="ERP_Internal">
      <appID commonID="ITEM1">4301</appID>
      <appID commonID="ITEM2">4398</appID>
      <appID commonID="ITEM3">5432</appID>
    </appInstance>
  </idXRef>
</listOfIDXRefData>
```

Listing 3.6 shows the contents of the IDXRef_Data_file XML document. It is the actual values that can be translated. In this scenario, the value 123 as an item identification from customer C1702 is translated into 4301, which is the corresponding item identification in the internal ERP system.

The functoids used to do the translation are shown in Figure 3.34.

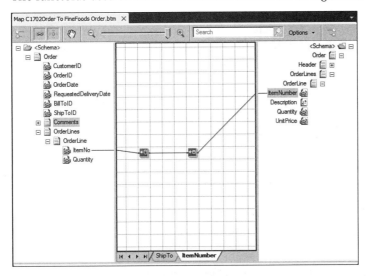

FIGURE 3.34   Using the cross-referencing functoids.

Figure 3.34 shows how to translate the item identification from the ItemNo field in the order from customer C1702 to the ItemNumber in the destination schema. The ItemNo field is mapped to a Get Common ID functoid, which has these three parameters:

▶ The constant string ItemID, which matches the type of ID to convert, as specified in the IDXRef_file XML document

▶ The constant string ERP_C1702, which matches the application instance of an ERP system, as found in the App_Instances_file XML document

▶ The ItemNo field

The functoid uses the value form the source to retrieve the common ID for this application-specific ID. For instance, a value in the source document of 123 returns a common ID of ITEM1. This value is then passed into a Get Application ID functoid, which also has three parameters. The first parameter is the same as for the Get Common ID functoid. The second is the constant string ERP_Internal, which tells the functoid to get the ID for this particular application instance. The third is the output of the Get Common ID functoid. For this scenario, the third parameter has a value of ITEM1, and the output of the functoid is the string 4301.

Building Custom Functoids

You can use the built-in functoids as building blocks to provide for most mapping needs you will encounter. Sometimes, however, you will need functionality that the built-in functoids cannot provide. Other times, you might find yourself building the same combination of functoids to solve a specific problem in your map over and over again, which is tiresome and which creates a mess in your map. To overcome this, you can develop your own functoids. Developing custom functoids is not nearly as scary as it sounds, and in fact you will probably find out that the most difficult part is to create an icon that is nice and descriptive of your functoid. This section describes how to develop a custom functoid.

Functoids are divided into two categories:

▶ The noncumulative, or "normal," ones, which expose one method that takes in some parameters or possibly no parameters and returns a string.

▶ The cumulative ones, which expose three methods, where the first is called to initialize the functoid; the second is then called for all inputs, and the third method is called to get the final value.

Also, functoids can be divided into two other types:

▶ The type that is compiled into an assembly and put into the Global Assembly Cache (GAC). It exposes one or more methods that are called at runtime to perform your functionality. This type is also known as a referenced functoid.

▶ The type that doesn't expose a method that is called at runtime, but instead outputs a script that is included in the map. This type is also known as an inline functoid.

You should consider developing an inline functoid when

▶ You have no worries about your code getting into the map as clear text (which allows others to read it and possibly modify it).

▶ Your functoid depends only on .NET namespaces that are available to maps. For a full list of these, refer to http://msdn.microsoft.com/en-us/library/aa561456(BTS.70).aspx.

▶ You do not want to have to maintain another assembly, remembering to add it to installation scripts, deploying it to all servers in your BizTalk group, and so on.

- ▶ You want to provide the developer that uses the functoid with the ability to debug the maps that use your functoid.

- ▶ You are developing more than one functoid, and they need to share variables.

You should consider developing a referenced functoid when

- ▶ You want to be able to put a new assembly in the GAC and restart host instances for it to work in all maps that use the functoid without any need to maps to be recompiled.

- ▶ You do not want your business logic code exposed in clear text for all to read and possibly modify.

- ▶ Your functoid depends on .NET namespaces that are not available to maps.

You do not have to choose either an inline functoid or a referenced functoid. As a matter of fact, you can develop your functoid to be both and let the developer of the map choose which implementation to use.

Initial Setup

No matter what type of functoid you want to create, you want to create a Visual Studio 2010 project for it. You do this by either right-clicking your solution and choosing **Add**, **New Project** or by creating a new project in a new solution if you do not have an existing solution you want to add the project to. You can have the project with your functoids in the same solution as your BizTalk projects and any other projects, if you like. The project should be a Class Library project, as shown in Figure 3.35.

FIGURE 3.35   Adding a new Class Library project to your Visual Studio 2010 solution.

After adding the project to your solution, you should either rename the automatically added class to a better name or delete it and add a new one. Also, you need to add a reference to the Microsoft.BizTalk.BaseFunctoids.dll, which you can find under <InstallationFolder>\Developer Tools. Finally, you need to add a string name to the assembly so that it can be GAC'ed after the functoid has been developed.

The Microsoft.BizTalk.BaseFunctoids namespace contains a BaseFunctoid class that must be the base class for all functoids. You must therefore let your class inherit from this and call the constructor of the base class. Listing 3.7 shows an example.

LISTING 3.7   Extending the Needed Base Class Required to Create a Custom Functoid

```
using Microsoft.BizTalk.BaseFunctoids;

namespace FineFoods.Map.Functoids
{
    public class StringReplace : BaseFunctoid
    {
        public StringReplace()
            : base()
        {
        }
    }
}
```

Inside the constructor, you need to set the value of some properties and call some methods on the base class. The steps you must go through for all functoids are described in this section, and the ones that are specific for either normal or cumulative functoids are described in the next sections:

1. Add a resources file to your project. To do so, right-click your project and choose **Add, New Item**. In the next screen, choose **Resources File**. Provide a descriptive filename that reflects whether the resources file is for one functoid only or for a collection of functoids that are in the same assembly. Figure 3.36 shows an example.

NOTE

For functoids, adding a resources file is not optional like it is for developing pipeline components, where it is still best practice to do so. The base class needs a resource file for the values for the functoid name, tooltip, description, and icon.

2. Add three string resources: one for the name of the functoid, one for the tooltip of the functoid, and one for the description of the functoid. Provide descriptive names of the resources. Figure 3.37 shows an example.

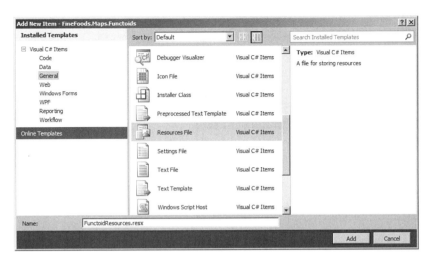

FIGURE 3.36   Adding a resources file to your project.

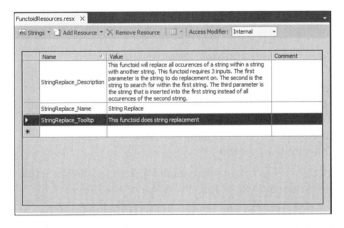

FIGURE 3.37   Adding resources for name, tooltip, and description..

3. Add an image resource of type `Bitmap` for the icon of the functoid. Provide a descriptive name of the resource. After adding it, you can edit the bitmap. Change it to be 16x16 pixels in the properties of the bitmap, and then release your inner artist. Figure 3.38 shows how to add the bitmap resource.

4. Assign a value to the `ID` property. The value must be an int, and it must be greater than 6000 because the first 6000 are reserved for internal BizTalk usage. Always keep track of all IDs you use in your organization to make sure you do not get an overlap. If you use third-party functoids, there is no way of knowing what other IDs are in use by these other than using reflector on the assemblies and looking at the source code.

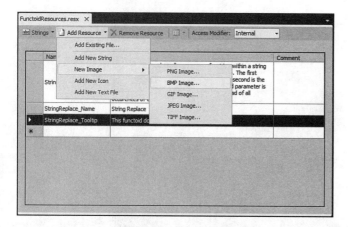

FIGURE 3.38   Adding a bitmap resource to serve as the icon for the functoid.

5. Call the SetupResourceAssembly method to let the base class know where to find the resources file that contains the resources for name, tooltip, description, and icon. The method takes two parameters. The first is the fully qualified .NET type name of the resources file. This is normally the name of the project concatenated with a period and the name of the resources file without extension. So if your project is called FineFoods.Maps.Functoids and your resources file is called FunctoidResources.resx, the fully qualified .NET type name of the resources file will be FineFoods.Map.Functoids.Resources. If in doubt, open <ResourceFile>.Designer.cs file, where <ResourceFile> is the name of your resources file without the .resx extension. In the designer file, you can see namespace and class name. Concatenate these with a period in between and you have the fully qualified name. The second is the executing assembly. Listing 3.8 shows an example.

6. Call the SetName method, which takes in one string parameter that defines the name of the resource that the base class should use to find the name of the functoid.

7. Call the SetTooltip method, which takes in one string parameter that defines the name of the resource that the base class should use to find the tooltip of the functoid.

8. Call the SetDescription method, which takes in one string parameter that defines the name of the resource that the base class should use to find the description of the functoid.

9. Call the SetBitmap method, which takes in one string parameter that defines the name of the resource that the base class should use to find the icon of the functoid.

10. Set the value of the Category property. This property is of the type FunctoidCategory, which is an enumeration, and it must be set to match the category this functoid should belong to. There are 25 different categories, of which only 7 are supposed to be used in custom functoids. These are Conversion, Cumulative, DateTime, Logical, Math, Scientific, and String.

   As you can probably imagine, these are used to let the Mapper Toolbox know in which group of functoids to show your custom functoid. Some of the categories are also used to let the Mapper know how to create the XSLT; that is, functoids in the category Logical are useful for determining when to create destination nodes. This is explained in more detail later.

11. Determine how many parameters your functoid should take in as a minimum and as a maximum. Call the `SetMinParams` and `SetMaxParams` with the correct values.

12. For each parameter, determine what the source of the input link for the parameter can be. For custom functoids, the parameters can often be links coming from anything that has a value. After determining what possible inputs the parameters can have, you must call `AddInputConnectionType` for each parameter in the order of the inputs to specify what possible inputs the parameters can have. The possible parameter values for the `AddInputConnectionType` method call are the values in the `ConnectionType` enumeration, and there is a value for each functoid category and also some other possible values like `All`, `AllExceptRecord`, `Element`, and so on. The `AllExceptRecord` is often used because this will allow all inputs that are not a record, and this can be useful because a record does not have a value, whereas others have a value.

13. Determine what the outgoing link from the functoid can be connected to. After determining this, set the appropriate value to the `OutputConnectionType` property, which is of type `ConnectionType` enumeration.

NOTE

The tooltip you add to your functoid is actually not used anywhere. Microsoft is aware of this and will look into it for future releases. This has two implications. The first implication is that you should still add the tooltip and provide valid values for it so that your functoid will look fine in the next versions, as well. The second implication is that you don't need to worry when you don't see the tooltip of your custom functoid anywhere.

For setting either the input connection type or the output connection type, you can set it to a combination of values, which gives you control of what possibilities you want to allow.

Listing 3.8 shows a functoid that does a string replacement on an incoming string. The functoid code is not complete, but contains the methods and properties that have been discussed up to now.

LISTING 3.8   Functoid That Does String Replacement

```
public class StringReplace : BaseFunctoid
{
    public StringReplace() : base()
    {
        ID = 8936;

        SetupResourceAssembly(GetType().Namespace + ".FunctoidResources",
```

```
                Assembly.GetExecutingAssembly());

        SetName("StringReplace_Name");
        SetTooltip("StringReplace_ToolTip");
        SetDescription("StringReplace_Description");
        SetBitmap("StringReplace_Icon");

        Category = FunctoidCategory.String;
        SetMinParams(3);
        SetMaxParams(3);

        AddInputConnectionType(ConnectionType.AllExceptRecord);
        AddInputConnectionType(ConnectionType.AllExceptRecord);
        AddInputConnectionType(ConnectionType.AllExceptRecord);

        OutputConnectionType = ConnectionType.AllExceptRecord;
    }
}
```

Normal Functoid

The functoid code in Listing 3.8 is not finished yet. It still has no implementation of the functionality it is supposed to do. As explained earlier, this can be achieved either as a referenced functoid or as an inline functoid and either as a normal functoid or as a cumulative functoid. Implementing it as both a referenced functoid and as an inline functoid is explored in this section.

Referenced Functoid

When implementing a functoid as a referenced functoid, you must provide the method that is to be called at runtime. Listing 3.9 shows a method that provides the string replacement functionality.

LISTING 3.9   A Method Performing String Replacement

```
public string Replace(string str, string search, string replace)
{
    if (String.IsNullOrEmpty(str))
        return String.Empty;
    if (String.IsNullOrEmpty(search))
        return str;
    return str.Replace(search, replace);
}
```

To instruct BizTalk what method to call at runtime, you must call the
SetExternalFunctionName method. This method has two overloads.

▶ The first takes in three parameters, where the first is the full name of the assembly,
the second is the class that contains the method, and the third is the name of the
method to call.

▶ The second takes in four parameters but is not intended to be used in custom code.

Listing 3.10 shows the added functionality to the functoid from Listing 3.8 that is needed
to make the functoid work.

LISTING 3.10   A Referenced Functoid That Does String Replacement

```
public class StringReplace : BaseFunctoid
{
    public StringReplace()
        : base()
    {
        // Functionality from Listing 3.8
        SetExternalFunctionName(GetType().Assembly.FullName,
            GetType().FullName,
            "Replace");
    }

    public string Replace(string str, string search, string replace)
    {
        if (String.IsNullOrEmpty(str))
            return String.Empty;
        if (String.IsNullOrEmpty(search))
            return str;
        return str.Replace(search, replace);
    }
}
```

The call the SetExternalFunctionName in Listing 3.10 is coded to have the method to call
inside the same class as the functoid itself. If this is not the case, you must change the
parameters to point to the correct assembly, class, and method.

TIP

If your functoid needs to check whether an input parameter is either a valid numeric value or a valid date, the `BaseFunctoid` class provides static methods you can use for this so you do not need to implement this yourself. You can just use `BaseFunctoid.IsNumeric(stringparameter)` to check for numeric values and `BaseFunctoid.IsDate(stringparameter)` to check for date values. Both methods return a Boolean, and the `IsNumeric` method can optionally have a ref parameter that will contain the converted value.

Inline Functoid

If you should choose to implement an inline functoid rather than a referenced functoid, you should not call the `SetExternalFunctionName` method, but instead some other methods and properties must be used.

The first is a method called `AddScriptTypeSupport`. It takes in one parameter, which is the `ScriptType` enumeration. You must send in the value that matches the script type you will be creating. For instance, you can send in a value of `ScriptType.CSharp` to tell the Mapper that the script is a C# script.

The second is a method called `SetScriptBuffer`, which is called to set the script that will be included in the map. It takes in two parameters and one optional parameter. The first parameter is the `ScriptType` for this script. The second parameter is the string that is the actual script. Most often, this parameter is a method call to a method that returns the string that contains the script and not a constant string itself, because that would be too big and confusing. The third and optional parameter is used for cumulative functoids, which are described in the next section.

The third method used for inline functoids is called `SetScriptGlobalBuffer`. This method is used to add some script that must be global for all your scripts. This can initialize a variable, for instance, which is needed for cumulative functoids or functoids that just need to know values from other scripts. Just as the `SetScriptBuffer` method, this method takes in the `ScriptType` of the script and a string that contains the script.

The fourth is a property called `RequiredGlobalHelperFunctions`. This is used to let the Mapper know whether some built-in helper functions are needed for the script to execute. This is to allow for the use of the built-in `IsNumeric` and `IsDate` methods that are easily accessible in a referenced functoid. Also, for inline functoids, you can make use of the `ValToBool` method, which tests whether your string is a Boolean value. This method is not accessible for referenced functoids.

NOTE

When developing custom inline functoids, you can add inline script for as many of the supported languages as you want. Just call `AddScriptTypeSupport` for the appropriate script type and call `SetScriptBuffer` to set the appropriate script. Which one is chosen by the map is dependent on the Script Type Precedence property you can set as a property on the map grid.

Listing 3.11 shows a method that generates the same method as shown in Listing 3.9, only for an inline functoid.

LISTING 3.11   An Inline Functoid That Does String Replacement

```
private string GetCSharpBuffer()
{
    StringBuilder sb = new StringBuilder();
    sb.Append("\n");
    sb.Append("public string Replace(string str, string search, string
    ➥replace)\n");
    sb.Append("{\n");
    sb.Append("\tif (String.IsNullOrEmpty(str))\n");
    sb.Append("\t\treturn String.Empty;\n");
    sb.Append("\tif (String.IsNullOrEmpty(search))\n");
    sb.Append("\t\treturn str;\n");
    sb.Append("\treturn str.Replace(search, replace);\n");
    sb.Append("}");
    return sb.ToString();
}
```

So, as you can see, for inline functoids, you must create a string that contains the exact same C# method you would have written if it were to be called in a referenced functoid. The new lines and tabulator characters are not needed, but are there to make the method look readable when viewing it inside the map after you have compiled it.

For inline functoids, you have the option of generating an inline script that takes in a variable number of inputs. This requires some other method calls and is described in the "Advanced Functoids" section.

TIP

The easiest way to create a method to be used in an inline functoid is to create the method as a normal method first and test your functoid as a referenced functoid. Once the functionality is as you want it to be, you can do a string replacement on the method, replacing all quotation marks with escaped quotation marks. Then you just cut and paste the lines from the method one at the time to a new method where you append to the StringBuilder and change the functoid to be an inline functoid instead.

The code for the inline functoid that does string replacement can be seen in Listing 3.12.

LISTING 3.12   An Inline Functoid That Does String Replacement

```
public class StringReplace : BaseFunctoid
{
    public StringReplace()
        : base()
    {
        // Functionality from Listing 3.8
        AddScriptTypeSupport(ScriptType.CSharp);
        SetScriptBuffer(ScriptType.CSharp, GetCSharpBuffer());
    }

    private string GetCSharpBuffer()
    {
        StringBuilder sb = new StringBuilder();
        // Code to build the method, as shown in Listing 3.11.
        return sb.ToString();
    }
}
```

Creating an inline C# functoid is most of the times the most appropriate over XSLT for three reasons:

▶ You get the .NET framework, which enables you to write your functionality with a minimum number of lines.

▶ XSLT has lots of quotation marks, which can get heavy to track when building a string. For information purposes, the code that is needed in an XSLT Call-Template functoid for string replacement is shown in Listing 3.13. The reason for this quite long code in XSLT is that the version of XSLT that BizTalk supports does not include a native Replace function, so you have to do it yourself. Imagining the code to build this as a string for an inline functoid is left to the reader.

▶ The real strength of XSLT functoids is that XSLT can access the entire structure of the source schema and it has the responsibility of creating the output structure. This means that the functoid will be hard wired to those two structures. Because the purpose of a custom functoid is to take some functionality that is often needed and wrap it in a common generic component, custom XSLT functoids actually go against this purpose.

LISTING 3.13   XSLT Example of Doing String Replacement

```
<xsl:template name="MyXsltReplaceTemplate">
  <xsl:param name="str" />
  <xsl:param name="search" />
  <xsl:param name="replace" />
  <xsl:element name="Field6">
```

```
    <xsl:call-template name="DoReplace">
      <xsl:with-param name="str" select="$str" />
      <xsl:with-param name="search" select="$search" />
      <xsl:with-param name="replace" select="$replace" />
    </xsl:call-template>
  </xsl:element>
</xsl:template>

<xsl:template name="DoReplace">
  <xsl:param name="str" />
  <xsl:param name="search" />
  <xsl:param name="replace" />
  <xsl:choose>
    <xsl:when test="contains($str, $search)">
      <xsl:value-of select="substring-before($str, $search)" />
      <xsl:value-of select="$replace" />
      <xsl:call-template name="DoReplace">
       <xsl:with-param name="str" select="substring-after($str, $search)" />
       <xsl:with-param name="search" select="$search" />
       <xsl:with-param name="replace" select="$replace" />
      </xsl:call-template>
    </xsl:when>
    <xsl:otherwise>
      <xsl:value-of select="$str" />
    </xsl:otherwise>
  </xsl:choose>
</xsl:template>
```

Cumulative Functoid

Cumulative functoids are useful for performing functionality on recurring elements. The built-in cumulative functoids provide functionality for finding the smallest number, greatest number, and so on of a reoccurring element.

If you want to develop a cumulative functoid yourself, you need to specify three methods rather than one. The first method initializes the functoid at runtime. The second is called for each occurrence of the recurring element, and the last is called at the end to retrieve the aggregated value that should be output in the end.

Thread Safety

For cumulative functoids, an issue of thread safety arises that is usually not present for normal functoids.

Normal functoids have just one method that is called, and unless you use some variable inside your method that is globally defined, you are usually safe. Cumulative functoids are different, though, because you need a global variable in your functoid to hold the state of your calculations across the initialization, multiple calls to the add method, and the final call to the get method.

You get some help in making your functoid thread safe, though. To all three methods, an index variable is sent as a parameter, which is unique for each instance of the functoid inside the map, which means that you can use it as an identifier into some data structure you must maintain with the calculations you perform. Listing 3.14 shows an example of how the XSLT looks when a cumulative functoid is used multiple times in a map. You can see that the first occurrence of the cumulative functoid uses an index of 0 and the second occurrence uses an index of 1.

LISTING 3.14   XSLT Generated When a Cumulative Functoid Is Used Two Times in One Map

```
<xsl:template match="/s0:InputRoot">
  <ns0:OutputRoot>
    <xsl:variable name="v1" select="userCSharp:Init(0)" />
    <xsl:for-each select="/s0:InputRoot/Field1">
      <xsl:variable name="v2" select="userCSharp:Add(0,string(./text()),"1000")" />
    </xsl:for-each>
    <xsl:variable name="v3" select="userCSharp:Get(0)" />
    <Feld1>
      <xsl:value-of select="$var:v3" />
    </Field1>
    <xsl:variable name="v4" select="userCSharp:Init(1)" />
    <xsl:for-each select="/s0:InputRoot/Field2">
      <xsl:variable name="v5" select="userCSharp:Add(1,string(./text()),"1000")" />
    </xsl:for-each>
    <xsl:variable name="v6" select="userCSharp:GetCumulativeMax(1)" />
    <Field2>
      <xsl:value-of select="$var:v6" />
    </Field2>
  </ns0:OutputRoot>
</xsl:template>
```

This way of using an index is the same both for a cumulative referenced functoid and a cumulative inline functoid. The scope parameter to the second method is not used and can therefore be ignored in your code.

Cumulative Referenced Functoids

For referenced functoids, the runtime engine doesn't necessarily instantiate an object of your functoid class for each map it executes, but rather reuses the existing object if present. Unfortunately, this means that your functoid can get an index of 0 as parameter to any one of the methods from multiple instances of the map at the same time without your code being able to distinguish them from each other. This, in turn, means that it is impossible to develop a custom referenced cumulative functoid that is thread-safe, and this should therefore be avoided.

If you want to develop a custom referenced cumulative functoid, you need to set the three methods that are to be used at runtime by the mapper. This is done via the `SetExternalFunctionName`, `SetExternalFunctionName2`, and `SetExternalFunctionName3` methods. They set the initialization method, the accumulation method, and the get method, respectively. Listing 3.15 shows an example of the code needed. The code is given in full except for the code already listed in Listing 3.8 because it will make it easier to understand the code in Listing 3.16, which shows how to build he same functionality for an inline functoid.

LISTING 3.15   Sample Code of a Custom Referenced Cumulative Functoid

```csharp
private Dictionary<int, string> myCumulativeArray = new Dictionary<int,string>();


public CummulativeComma() : base()
{
        // All the functoid setup code seen in Listing 3.8
        SetExternalFunctionName(GetType().Assembly.FullName, GetType().FullName,
"InitializeValue");
        SetExternalFunctionName2("AddValue");
        SetExternalFunctionName3("RetrieveFinalValue");
}

public string InitializeValue(int index)
{
    myCumulativeArray[index] = "";
    return "";
}

public string AddValue(int index, string value, string scope)
{
    string str = myCumulativeArray[index].ToString();
    str += value + ",";
    myCumulativeArray[index] = str;
    return "";
}

public string RetrieveFinalValue(int index)
{
    string str = myCumulativeArray[index].ToString();
    if (str.Length > 0)
        return str.Substring(0, str.Length - 1);
    else
        return "";
}
```

Cumulative Inline Functoids

Contrary to referenced cumulative functoids, you can develop a thread-safe inline cumulative functoid. This is because whereas the Mapper reuses the same object for referenced functoids, there is no object to reuse for an inline functoid because all the code is inline in the XSLT. Therefore, the data structure is not shared among multiple instances of the map, effectively making the index parameter, which is unique across multiple instances of the functoid in one map, enough to guarantee thread safety. This requires, naturally, that you develop the functoid using the index parameter to access a specific entry in the data structure.

Building a custom inline cumulative functoid basically requires the same three methods as for a referenced cumulative functoid. As with the referenced version, you need to initialize the needed data structure.

For setting the needed three methods that are used at runtime, you must call the SetScriptBuffer method three times, with a parameter indicating whether you are setting the initialization, adding, or retrieval method. For initializing the data structure, you must call the SetScriptGlobalBuffer method. Listing 3.16 shows sample code for a custom inline cumulative functoid, with the code from Listing 3.8 omitted.

LISTING 3.16   Inline Version of the Referenced Functoid from Listing 3.15

```
public CummulativeComma() : base()
{
  // All the functoid setup code seen in Listing 3.8
  SetScriptGlobalBuffer(ScriptType.CSharp, GetGlobalScript());
  SetScriptBuffer(ScriptType.CSharp, GetInitScript(), 0);
  SetScriptBuffer(ScriptType.CSharp, GetAggScript(), 1);
  SetScriptBuffer(ScriptType.CSharp, GetFinalValueScript(), 2);
}


private string GetFinalValueScript()
{
    StringBuilder sb = new StringBuilder();
    sb.Append("\npublic string RetrieveFinalValue(int index)\n");
    sb.Append("{\n");
    sb.Append("\tstring str = myCumulativeArray[index].ToString();");
    sb.Append("\tif (str.Length > 0)\n");
    sb.Append("\t\treturn str.Substring(0, str.Length - 1);\n");
    sb.Append("\telse\n");
    sb.Append("\t\treturn \"\";\n");
    sb.Append("}\n");
    return sb.ToString();
}
```

```
private string GetAggScript()
{
    StringBuilder sb = new StringBuilder();
    sb.Append("\npublic string AddValue(int index, string value, string
scope)\n");
    sb.Append("{\n");
    sb.Append("\tstring str = myCumulativeArray[index].ToString();");
    sb.Append("\tstr += value + \",\";\n");
    sb.Append("\tmyCumulativeArray[index] = str;\n");
    sb.Append("\treturn \"\";\n");
    sb.Append("}\n");
    return sb.ToString();
}

private string GetInitScript()
{
    StringBuilder sb = new StringBuilder();
    sb.Append("\npublic string InitializeValue(int index)\n");
    sb.Append("{\n");
    sb.Append("\tmyCumulativeArray[index] = \"\";\n");
    sb.Append("\treturn \"\";\n");
    sb.Append("}\n");
    return sb.ToString();
}

private string GetGlobalScript()
{
    return "private Dictionary<int, string> myCumulativeArray = new
Dictionary<int,string>();";
}
```

Developing Advanced Functoids

This section covers some advanced topics related to developing custom functoids.

Functoids with a Variable Number of Inputs

Sometimes you need to develop a functoid that should take in a variable number of parameters. For instance, the Addition functoid in the Math category takes in a variable number of parameters. Doing this is only supported for creating inline functoids and can therefore not be done with a custom referenced functoid.

To develop a custom inline functoid that takes a variable number of parameters, you must do this:

1. Set the property `HasVariableInputs` to true.
2. In the constructor, call `AddScriptTypeSupport` for each script type you support.
3. Override the `GetInlineScriptBuffer` method. Listing 3.17 shows an example. This method takes in three parameters:
   ▶ A script type determining the type of script to return.
   ▶ An integer determining the number of parameters your functoid will be getting.
   ▶ A function number for use with cumulative functoids. Values can be 0, 1 and 2, for initializing, accumulating, and retrieving functions, respectively.
4. Set the `RequiredGlobalHelperFunctions` to reflect any global helper methods you may need, such as the `IsDate`, `IsNumeric`, and so on.
5. Use `SetScriptGlobalBuffer` to declare any global variables you may need. For cumulative functoids, you need to initialize some data structure that is used across the calls to the three functions.

LISTING 3.17   Generating a Functoid That Takes in a Variable Number of Parameters

```
protected override string GetInlineScriptBuffer(ScriptType sT, int numPar, int
func)
{
    if(ScriptType.CSharp == scriptType)
    {
        StringBuilder builder = new StringBuilder();

        builder.Append("public string MyFunction(");

        for(int i=0; i<numParams; i++)
        {
            if(i > 0)
                builder.Append(", ");

            builder.Append("string param" + i.ToString());
        }
        builder.Append(")\n");
        // Method body; Do what you need with the parameters.
        builder.Append("{\n");
        builder.Append("}\n");

        return builder.ToString();
    }
    return string.Empty;
}
```

The code in Listing 3.17 assumes this is not a cumulative functoid and therefore ignores the func parameter. Had this been for a cumulative functoid, the method would have to return one of three functions, given the value of the func parameter. Also, the method shown in Listing 3.17 works only for C#. If the developer of the map requires something else, you must extend the method to also support that ScriptType and return valid methods for that.

Functoid Categories

When assigning a functoid category to your functoid, you get to choose between 25 different categories, of which only 7 are supposed to be used in custom functoids. These are Conversion, Cumulative, DateTime, Logical, Math, Scientific, and String.

Assigning one of these categories to your functoid has some effects:

▶ The category maps to one of the categories in the Mapper Toolbox in Visual Studio 2010, so choose a category that matches where you want the functoid to be placed.

▶ Some functoids have restrictions as to what types of input they can have. For instance, a Value Extractor must have a Database Lookup functoid as its first input. The Database Lookup is actually a functoid category in itself; it just belongs to the Database group in the Toolbox. This means that how your functoid will be used in a map may therefore also influence what category you want to choose for it.

▶ Some categories imply some semantics other than just the two preceding bullets. For instance, a Logical functoid, as explained earlier, when connected to an output record determines whether the record should be created. You can therefore not create a functoid that is in the Logical category and use it to map a value of true or false to a field.

You can see all the possible values for the functoid category when developing custom functoids on the MSDN site at http://msdn.microsoft.com/en-us/library/microsoft.biztalk.base-functoids.functoidcategory(BTS.70).aspx. Most of them are for internal use only, because they impose some semantics that you cannot control in your code.

Deployment of Custom Functoids

After developing a functoid, it must be deployed to be used. Deployment of a functoid can be divided into deployment on a development machine where a developer can then use the functoid in any maps created and deployment on a server that needs to be able to run the functoid at runtime.

For a server that needs to execute the functoid at runtime, the assembly containing the functoid must be put into the *Global Assembly Cache* (GAC) if the functoid is a referenced functoid. If the functoid is an inline functoid, no deployment is necessary.

For easy deployment, you can add the assembly with the functoid to your BizTalk application, which will deploy it along with the rest of the assemblies when the exported MSI package is installed on the server. To do this, follow these steps:

1. Open the BizTalk Server 2010 Administration Console.

2. Right-click your application and choose **Add**, **Resources**.

3. Click **Add**.

4. Browse your way to the assembly that contains the pipeline component and double-click it (or click it once and click **Open**).

5. In the File Type drop-down, choose **System.BizTalk:Assembly**.

6. Make sure the **Add to the Global Assembly Cache on MSI File Install (gacutil)** check box is checked.

7. Click **OK**.

The final screen should look like Figure 3.39

For deployment to a developer machine, the assembly must be copied into the <InstallationFolder>\Developer Tools\Mapper Extensions folder. After copying the assembly to this folder, you can add it to the Toolbox in Visual Studio 2010.

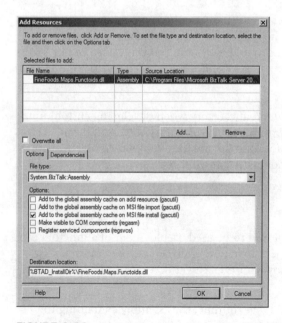

FIGURE 3.39   Adding an assembly to your BizTalk application to have it automatically deployed with the MSI file.

To deploy the assembly on a development machine for it to be used when developing maps, you should copy the assembly to the <InstallationFolder>\Developer Tools\Mapper Extensions folder. This is not strictly required, but it is the easiest way, because your functoid will then always be in the Toolbox, no matter how many times the Toolbox is reset. To add the component to the functoid Toolbox that is available at design time, follow these steps:

1. Open Visual Studio 2010

2. Go to **Tools**, **Choose Toolbox Items**, or right-click the Toolbox and choose **Choose Items**.

3. Go to the Functoids pane

4. If the functoid is present in the list, make sure it is checked.

5. If the functoid is not present in the list, click **Browse**, and browse your way to the assembly that contains the pipeline component.

If the functoid is placed in the <InstallationFolder>\Developer Tools\Mapper Extensions folder you can also right-click inside the Toolbox and choose **Reset Toolbox**. Be aware, though, that this completely resets the Toolbox, which might not be what you want.

Note that the Toolbox sometimes fails to update itself when new versions of a functoid are deployed. In this case, you can delete the following four files, which contain Visual Studio 2010s Toolbox setup:

- toolbox.tbd

- toolbox_reset.tbd

- toolboxIndex.tbd

- toolboxIndex_reset.tbd

On Windows Server 2008, using Visual Studio 2010, you can find these under C:\Users\<User>\AppData\Local\Microsoft\VisualStudio\10.0. For different operating systems or different installation options, you can search for them. They are hidden files, so you need to search for those. If you want to script the deletion of the files in a batch file, you can use the script shown in Listing 3.18 in a batch file.

LISTING 3.18   Script for Deleting Visual Studio 2010 Toolbox Items

```
@echo off
C:
cd "\Users\<User>\AppData\Local\Microsoft\Visual Studio\10.0"
del toolbox* /AH

pause
```

If you need to update a functoid that is also in the GAC, you must both update it in the GAC and in the <InstallationFolder>\Developer Tools\Mapper Extensions folder. This is because Visual Studio 2010 uses the version in the GAC if present and any updates in the file system are therefore not used.

Note that overriding the assembly that has been copied to the <InstallationFolder>\Developer Tools\Mapper Extensions folder is not always possible because it might be in use by Visual Studio 2010, BizTalk runtime, or some isolated host like *Internet Information Services* (IIS). In these cases, you need to restart whatever programs are locking the assembly before you can copy the new version.

If you are trying to add your functoid to the Toolbox and get an error doing this, the most common causes are as follows:

- ▶ Your resources are not set up correctly, so the name, tooltip, description, and icon cannot be correctly fetched and used by the Toolbox.

- ▶ Your class is not marked public.

- ▶ There is an older version of your component in the GAC that is not valid.

If you get a sharing violation when copying your newly compiled assembly to the <InstallationFolder>\Developer Tools\Mapper Extensions folder, you might consider writing a script that deploys the new component for you. The script should

- ▶ Restart IIS using `iisreset`. Only needed in your script if you have any receive functionality running in IIS like hosted WCF services, HTTP, SOAP, or others.

- ▶ Restart BizTalks Host instance. Only needed if the functoid has been used by BizTalks runtime. This can be done in a couple of ways:

    - ▶ By using `net stop BTSSvc$BizTalkServerApplication` and `net start BTSSvc$BizTalkServerApplication`.

    - ▶ By using PowerShell and doing `get-service BTS* ¦ foreach-object - process {restart-service $_.Name}`

    - ▶ By using WMI. For details about this, refer to http://msdn.microsoft.com/en-us/library/aa578621(BTS.10).aspx.

- ▶ Copy the DLL to the <InstallationFolder>\Developer Tools\Mapper Extensions folder.

- ▶ Use gacutil to add the new version to the GAC, like this: `"C:\Program Files\Microsoft SDKs\Windows\v6.0A\Bin\gacutil.exe" /if NewlyCompiled.DLL`

- ▶ Delete the Toolbox items, as described earlier, if you are having issues updating the toolbox.

Visual Studio 2010 should probably be closed first, as well. You can do this a bit faster if you test your functoid in a Visual Studio 2010 BizTalk project that is the only project in a test solution. This Visual Studio 2010 will be the only instance of Visual Studio 2010 that has a lock on the file, and it can be closed and reopened faster than your entire solution.

Debugging

When developing a custom functoid, at some point you will probably want to debug it to make sure not only that it provides you with the expected output under normal circumstances but also to test borderline cases where input might be missing or be in an unexpected format. For a functoid that is to be used throughout your company, it is essential that all other developers can trust on your functoid to behave as expected and give the expected output under all circumstances.

How to debug a custom functoid depends on whether you have developed a referenced or an inline functoid.

Common Debugging Options for Inline and Referenced Functoids

The first and obvious way of debugging your custom functoid is to use it in a map and then validate and test your map from within Visual Studio 2010, checking that no errors occur and manually inspecting the output to make sure it provides the expected result.

Whether you need to debug a custom referenced or a custom inline functoid, you can and should leverage the unit testing capabilities of BizTalk maps. This basically enables you to check all cases the functoid should be able to handle. Because unit testing of maps should be enabled for all maps even if no custom functoids are present, it is an obvious testing solution for your custom functoids, as well. Unit testing of maps are explained in the "Testing" section.

Debugging Referenced Functoids

Debugging a custom referenced functoid can be achieved in different ways. No matter which way you choose, the functoid must be compiled in Debug mode.

Separate Assembly   If the functionality the functoid is to perform is complex, you can write a separate assembly with the functionality and then a small console application that uses your assembly or do some standard unit tests on this to make sure the functionality is as expected. When satisfied with the results, you can wrap the functionality in a functoid either by copying the code or by referencing the unit-tested assembly.

Runtime Debugging   Another way of debugging your functoid is to deploy a map that uses the functoid and debug it when an instance is sent through BizTalk. Sometimes your functoid actually depends on the context it is executed in, and in this case, this is your only option of debugging it.

When debugging the functoid inside BizTalks runtime, make sure the latest compiled version is in the GAC and make sure your host instance has been restarted, so it hasn't cached a previous version. Inside Visual Studio 2010, set breakpoints in your code wherever you want the code to break and allow you to inspect values and step into code. When this it done, a few steps are needed to start debugging:

1. Inside Visual Studio 2010, go to **Debug, Attach to Process**.

2. Choose the BTSNTSvc.exe process.

3. If the BTSNTSvc.exe process is not available, check

   ▶ That the host instance is started

   ▶ That you have checked **Show Processes from All Users** and **Show Processes in All Sessions**

   If multiple instances of the BTSNTSvc.exe process are running, you can stop the host instance that will be executing the map and notice what PIDs are active and then start the host instance. The new PID will be the one to attach to. Another option is to attach to all the BTSNTSvc.exe processes.

4. Click **Attach**.

5. Send a message through BizTalk

This causes BizTalk to load the functoid at runtime, and your debugging session breaks the runtime when one of your breakpoints is hit, allowing you to step through the code to debug your component.

DebugView   A third way of debugging your custom referenced functoid is to leverage the System.Diagnostics namespace, which contains classes called Debug and Trace. In your code, you can insert statements that leverage these classes to write out either trace or debug statements, which are then viewable by tools like DebugView, which you can download from Microsoft's home page.

Listing 3.19 shows statements for leveraging the Debug and Trace.

LISTING 3.19   Leveraging the **Debug** and **Trace** Classes for Debugging

```
public string Replace(string str, string search, string replace)
{
    Trace.WriteLine("Replace method of \"String Replace\" functoid was
called.");
    Debug.WriteLine("Parameter str: " + str);
    Debug.WriteLine("Parameter search: " + search);
    Debug.WriteLine("Parameter replace: " + replace);

    if (String.IsNullOrEmpty(str))
    {
        Debug.WriteLine("First input was null or empty. Returning empty
string.");
        return String.Empty;
    }
    if (search == null)
    {
        Debug.WriteLine("Second parameter was null. Returning first
```

```
parameter.");
        return str;
    }
    Trace.WriteLine("Replace method of \"String Replace\" functoid has
ended.");
    str = str.Replace(search, replace);
    Trace.WriteLine("Replace method will return " + str);
    return str;
}
```

> **NOTE**
>
> When testing your map from within Visual Studio 2010, DebugView correctly shows any debug and trace statements you have in your code. When your map is executed at runtime by BizTalk, however, they are not. To rectify this, you must enable the **Capture, Capture Global Win32** option.

Debugging Inline Functoids

For inline functoids, you do not have the option of attaching to a process and setting breakpoints allowing you to step through your code because the code is inline in the map and doesn't use the assembly you compile.

Also, the option of using the `System.Diagnostics` namespace and leveraging the `Debug` and `Trace` classes will not work because the `System.Diagnostics` namespace is not one of the namespaces you can access from inline scripts.

When developing an inline functoid, it is impossible to know whether the script that is encoded in the string you output is actually a valid method that can compile. Therefore, it is often easiest to either develop your functoid as a referenced functoid or to develop the functionality needed in a separate assembly. Either way, you can debug that as mentioned earlier in the section about debugging custom referenced functoids, and once the functionality is as you want it to be, you can create a method that wraps the entire method in a string.

Testing of Maps

A map performs a transformation from one XML format into another. It is essential that the output generated is valid given the schema that describes the output, because otherwise you are sending invalid messages to trading partners and internal systems.

The Mapper helps you generate XSLT that generates valid XML, and it warns you about certain issues when validating the map or when compiling the project. Ultimately, however, it is the responsibility of the developer to make sure that the output generated by a map is valid.

This means that after developing your map you want to test it. Preferably, test all possible cases the map can get into at runtime. This section walks you through your options for testing your map.

Validating Maps

First of all, when developing a map, you should validate it. This is done by right-clicking the map file (.BTM) in Solution Explorer and choosing **Validate Map**. This will let Visual Studio 2010 go through the map and check for different kinds of syntactical errors such as functoids with the wrong number of inputs and other such things. If no errors occur, the map can be compiled and deployed.

The validation might be successful but with some warnings. If warnings occur, you must decide whether to ignore them because you know you have handled the issue the warning is about or whether you must do something about it. A warning that you will probably see many times is the "Warning btm1004: The destination node 'NameOfNode' has multiple inputs but none of its ancestors is connected to a looping functoid." Basically, this warning comes because you have multiple source nodes connected to the same output node. This can be by design if you are using multiple Value Mapping functoids to do conditional mapping of values into one node.

> **TIP**
>
> If you want to avoid the warning about multiple inputs to one destination node, you can use a String Concatenate functoid to concatenate the output of your multiple Value Mapping functoids and connect that to the output node.

Warnings are there for a reason, so take them seriously and deal with them all. As a general rule, BizTalk by default does not validate any messages sent out, meaning that your map really needs to be working well.

> **TIP**
>
> When you validate a map, the output window contains a link to the XSLT that is generated. This XSLT can be useful in determining why your map doesn't work. It can enlighten some of the logic used to build the XSLT and thereby help you build the map using the right functoids for the job.

Testing Maps

After validating your map, you can test it from within Visual Studio 2010. To test the map, you need to provide Visual Studio 2010 with a test instance. You can set some properties on a map file (.BTM) in Solution Explorer to facilitate this. Figure 3.40 shows these, and they are explained in Table 3.15.

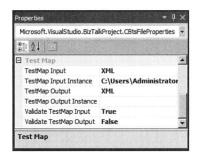

FIGURE 3.40   The properties you can set on a .BTM file in Solution Explorer.

TABLE 3.15   Properties on .BTM Files for Testing a Map

Property	Description
TestMap Input	Can be either Generate Instance, XML, or Native. If set to Generate Instance, Visual Studio 2010 generates an instance of the source schema for the map and uses that as test instance no matter what the other properties are set to. If set to XML, Visual Studio 2010 assumes that the instance you are providing for testing the map is in XML format. If set to Native, Visual Studio 2010 assumes that the instance you are providing is in the native format of the source schema. This allows you to use a flat file or EDI instance as a test instance. Visual Studio 2010 then first converts it into XML using the appropriate schema and editor extensions and uses the XML as input.
TestMap Input Instance	Full path to the file to use as test instance for the map. If the TestMap Input is set to Generate Instance, this property is ignored.
TestMap Output	Can be set to either XML or Native. Determines whether the output of testing the map should be in XML format or the format that is native for the destination schema in the map.
TestMap Output Instance	Full path to where Visual Studio 2010 should write the output of testing the map. If this is not specified, the output is written to a temporary file. The full path to the file that is generated is always written in the output window, giving you access to open it after the test is done.
Validate TestMap Input	If set to true, the instance that is either generated or read from a file is validated against the schema before the map is executed. If set to false, the map is executed without validation.
Validate TestMap Output	If set to true, the output of the map is validated against the schema for the output. If set to False, the output is not validated and written to a file as is.

When developing a map, it is useful to set the value of Validate TestMap Output to False until you are quite sure the map is working. This is because it allows you to test your map even though it isn't finished. This way you can build the part of the map that creates a part of the destination document and test that before starting on the rest of the map. When satisfied, you can enable the validation and make sure the validation succeeds.

After setting the properties as you want, you can test the map by right-clicking the .BTM file and choosing **Test Map**, as shown in Figure 3.41.

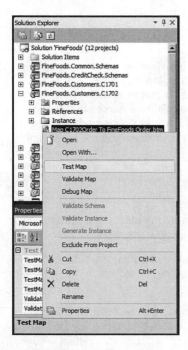

FIGURE 3.41   How to test your map.

After you choose the Test Map option, Visual Studio 2010 reads the properties on the .BTM file as specified in Table 3.15 and tests the map. If the test is successful, you get a link to the generated output in the output window. If the test fails, you receive a list of errors in the Error List window. A test is considered successful if no exceptions are thrown during execution and if input and output validation succeeds, if turned on. Exceptions can occur during execution if the Assert functoid is used or if a functoid actively throws an exception.

Debugging a Map

If your map does not provide you with the output you need and expect, some debugging might be in order. BizTalk supplies you with the option to debug your map line for line to see what happens.

Unfortunately, this functionality does not work for referenced functoids because the debugger cannot find the right external assemblies at runtime. If you want to debug your map and you are using functoids, it is therefore a good idea to make sure you are using the inline versions of all functoids, where possible. The functoids that are shipped with BizTalk, for instance, often have both an inline implementation and a referenced implementation. Which implementation to use when a functoid supports multiple implementations is controlled by the Script Type Precedence property of the Mapper grid. When you click the ellipsis for that property, you get a small window where you can set the script type precedence, as shown in Figure 3.42.

FIGURE 3.42   Setting the Script Type Precedence property.

Basically, you should get the External Assembly possibility moved to the bottom to make sure external assemblies are used as a last resort. If you trust that the inline versions of the functoids is equal to the version that is referenced, you can change the order back after debugging if you want to.

After setting the Script Type Precedence, you need to set the value of the TestMap Input Instance property to point to the instance you want to use as input when debugging the map. You can also specify the TestMap Output Instance if you would like to control the filename the output is written to.

After setting these properties, you can right-click your .BTM file in Solution Explorer and choose **Debug Map**. Visual Studio 2010 then generates the XSLT that is to be debugged and opens it with a breakpoint already set on the first line. Besides this pane, two other panes are also opened. The first contains the output, which lets you keep track of the output that is built while the map is being debugged, and the other is the input XML, which lets you see which fields in the input XML are currently used to build the output. You can drag the windows around so that you can see all three panes at the same time. Figure 3.43 illustrates this.

FIGURE 3.43   Debugging a map.

As you can see in Figure 3.43, three panes are open: the XSLT, the input XML, and the generated output. As you can also see at the bottom of the figure, you get the watches, as well, thus enabling you to keep track of the values of the variables and optionally change the values at debug time to test what will happen. Also, you can set breakpoints and use F5 (to run until next breakpoint), F10 (to step over the currently active line of code), and F11 (to step into the currently active line of code), as you are used to doing when debugging .NET code inside Visual Studio 2010.

Unit Testing

After a map is developed, validated, tested, and possibly debugged, you should enable unit testing of the map. As a matter of fact, many great people insist you should write your unit tests before even starting developing anything. This is called *test-driven development* (TDD). In either case, BizTalk ships with the option to do unit testing on your maps, which you should leverage, and this section describes this functionality.

The first thing to do is to enable unit testing on the project that contains a map you want to unit test. To do so, follow these steps:

1. Go to Solution Explorer.

2. Right-click the project that contains the map that is to be unit tested, and choose **Properties**.

3. Go to the Deployment pane and enable the **Enable Unit Testing** property, as shown in Figure 3.44.

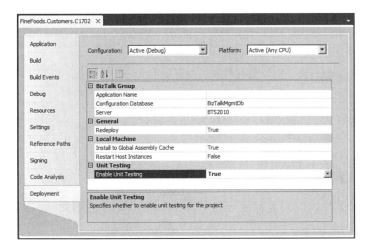

FIGURE 3.44   Enabling unit testing on project.

After enabling unit testing on the project, all maps in the project that are compiled will be inheriting from the `TestableMapBase` class in the `Microsoft.BizTalk.TestTools.Mapper` namespace instead of the normal `TransformBase` class in the `Microsoft.XLANGs.BaseTypes` namespace. The `TestableMapBase` class actually inherits from `TransformBase`, so nothing is lost. What is gained, however, are some methods and properties that can be leveraged for unit testing.

Next, you should add a test project to your solution. This is done by using the menu in Visual Studio 2010, where you can click **Test**, **New Test** to open the screen shown in Figure 3.45. In this screen, you can choose to either add the new test to an existing test project, if one is present in the solution, or create a new Visual C# test project. In addition, you can choose between four different tests:

▶ **Ordered Test:** This gives you a way of orchestrating your tests, deciding what order they should be performed in.

▶ **Unit Test:** This option gives you a class to write your tests in, but some manual work needs to be done like referencing the right assemblies and so on.

▶ **Basic Unit Test:** This option provides an even smaller and simpler version of a unit test class than the unit test. More to implement yourself.

▶ **Unit Test Wizard:** This helps you through some of the choices you must make, like what maps to test, and then generates the test class for you.

The other five options for adding a new test are not relevant for a BizTalk project.

For your first test project, name your file, choose **Unit Test**, and click **OK**. If you already have a test project, you can decide to add the file to an existing project by selecting it in the drop-down.

The test project is created for you, and it includes a pretty empty class for your tests. The class contains some definitions, methods, a constructor, and one method that is really the one thing to focus on, because this is the one you need to implement.

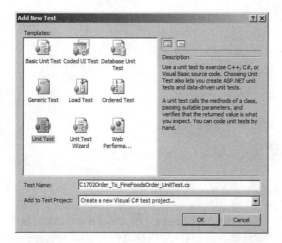

FIGURE 3.45   Adding a new test to your test project.

So, what you need to do in this method is to implement the unit test of the maps you want to test in this test class. Remember that you can have as many test classes and test methods in each test project as you want.

To test a map, you need to reference three different assemblies from your test project:

▶ **The assembly that contains the map:** This assembly *must* have the Enable Unit Testing property set to True.

▶ **The Microsoft.BizTalk.TestTools assembly:** This is found in the .NET pane of the Add Reference screen.

▶ **The Microsoft XLANG/s Base Types assembly:** This is also found in the .NET pane of the Add Reference screen.

In the project, the XML instances that are to be used for the unit test can also be added. If you do this, consider marking their Build Action property to None, so they are not compiled needlessly into the assembly. The instances are not required to be included in the project, but it gives you a nice way of having everything needed for the test grouped together.

After adding the project references, you need to implement the test method. Locate the method in the class file called TestMethod1, and change it to something like the code shown in Listing 3.20.

LISTING 3.20 Sample Test Method for Testing a Map

```
[TestMethod]
public void TestMapC17020rderToFineFoodsOrder()
{
    string INPUT = testContextInstance.TestDir + @"\..\Order.xml";
    string OUTPUT = testContextInstance.TestDir + @"\..\MappedOrder.xml";
    TestableMapBase map = new Order_to_InternalOrder();
    map.ValidateInput = true;
    map.ValidateOutput = true;
    map.TestMap(INPUT, InputInstanceType.Xml,
        OUTPUT, OutputInstanceType.XML);
    Assert.IsTrue(File.Exists(OUTPUT), "File does not exist");
    // Read in OUTPUT and check relevant values.
    // Compare file with expected output.
}
```

The two strings INPUT and OUTPUT are declared to contain the path to the input instance for the map and the path to the output file to write the output to. The functionality required basically instantiates the map as a TestableMapBase class, which contains the needed properties and methods for unit testing. Then the properties ValidateInput and ValidateOutput are set to true. These properties mean the same as the properties you can set on the .BTM file and will determine whether the TestMap method should validate the input and output against the respective schemas before and after the map is executed. Any failures in this validation results in the test failing. Both values are false by default.

For the code to compile, the using statements shown in Listing 3.21 are needed. The namespaces are as follows:

▶ Microsoft.VisualStudio.TestTools.UnitTesting: This is the namespace needed to use the TestClass and TestMethod attributes.

▶ FineFoods.Customers.FamilyRestaurant: This is the namespace the map is located in, providing you access to the Order_to_InternalOrder class that is the compiled map.

▶ Microsoft.BizTalk.TestTools.Mapper: This namespace contains the TestableMapBase class needed to call methods on the map object.

▶ Microsoft.BizTalk.TestTools.Schema: This namespace contains the two enumerations used for specifying the type of input and the type of the output for the TestMap method.

▶ System.IO: This is used to be able to access the File class that is used to check whether the output file exists in the assertion that is in the test method.

LISTING 3.21 **using** Statements Necessary for Code in Listing 3.20

```
using Microsoft.VisualStudio.TestTools.UnitTesting;
using FineFoods.Customers.C1702;
using Microsoft.BizTalk.TestTools.Mapper;
using System.IO;

using Microsoft.BizTalk.TestTools.Schema;
```

The code in Listing 3.20 shows just one assertion, which basically asserts that the output file is created. You might need other assertions, such as comparing the output to an instance of the expected output or reading in the output file and validating some of the actual values created.

You should have as many instances as needed to make sure your map can handle all possible instances correctly. This means you should have plenty of input instances and possibly plenty of samples of the output.

You can find Microsoft's description of the unit test features at http://msdn.microsoft.com/en-us/library/dd224279(BTS.70).aspx.

Summary

A map is a transformation from one XML format into another. It is important that maps generate valid output, because otherwise you can send invalid XML to customers, trading partners, internal systems, and others. Because the input to a map can be quite complicated XML with lots of optional fields and even fields that are not optional yet are still marked as such in the schema, developing a single map that deals with the possible inputs to the map can present a big challenge. Take care and study the input and output schemas and determine how to handle all special cases.

Maps are developed in the Mapper, which in turn is converted into XSLT, and you can even provide your own XSLT instead of that which is generated. BizTalk Server 2010 provides an all-new Mapper that helps developers get a good overview of the map to keep track of it and that helps developers change an existing map. The Mapper provides a nice and intuitive user interface for building your transformations. It provides functionality to both copy values directly from the source to the destination and also functoids that provide functionality that is performed on the source before it is mapped to the destination.

BizTalk ships with a lot of functoids that you can use as building blocks for the most common mapping challenges. If you run into either functionality that the built-in functoids cannot handle or a combination of functoids you use a lot and want to group together, you can build your own functoids. Custom functoids have access to the entire .NET framework for referenced functoids and a subset of the .NET framework for inline functoids, providing you with the power of expression you need to do almost anything.

CHAPTER 4

Orchestrations

In a BizTalk solution, you can get pretty far with schemas, maps, pipelines, and artifacts like receive ports, send ports, and so on. This is called a messaging-only solution. Sometimes, however, you either need to use a more complex process to be able to do things to incoming messages that you cannot do with a messaging-only solution, or sometimes you actually have a business-defined business process that you want to digitalize. This is what orchestrations can do for you.

A business process can be the process that takes place when a sales order arrives, such as receive order, send order confirmation, send sales order to *enterprise resource planning* (ERP) system, receive purchase orders from ERP system, send purchase orders to suppliers, receive order confirmations from supplier, and so on. It can also be something like a service aggregator orchestration, meaning that BizTalk can expose a service called CreateNewEmployee, which is called by some internal system, and BizTalk then in turn calls all the needed systems that need updating when a new employee is hired, such as creating the employee in the different internal systems, ordering some flowers for her, ordering a new laptop or desk, and stuff like that.

What is nice about letting BizTalk handle these business processes is that BizTalk first provides clever persistence out-of-the-box, meaning that even though the server running BizTalk crashes during the execution of a business process, nothing is lost, and when BizTalk is up and running again, it will just restarts the business process at the correct point. The only things that might be lost are the things that BizTalk has no control over. (For example, if you had called a .NET helper class that did something.) Using atomic transactions and .NET classes that can enlist in transactions can help you here. This is explained later. Second, BizTalk provides transactions inside the business process, enabling you to run transactions against the systems you talk to if the systems support this, but also provides mechanics to help you undo what has been done earlier in a business process if some business exception arises at some point later in the process.

Orchestrations do not have to be all-covering, but instead you can develop many small orchestrations and let one orchestration call the smaller ones. This provides you with the option to let multiple developers each work on their part of the business process at the same time, and it also modularizes the business process, allowing you to create reusable small orchestrations that can be used from multiple orchestrations.

Orchestration Designer

The development of orchestrations takes place inside Visual Studio 2010. You add a new orchestration to your project as follows:

1. Right-click your project in the Solution Explorer, and choose **Add**, **New Item**.

2. Optionally, choose **Orchestration Files** in the left window.

3. Choose **BizTalk Orchestration** in the right window.

4. Provide a name that describes the process the orchestration will implement and click **Add**. Figure 4.1 shows an example.

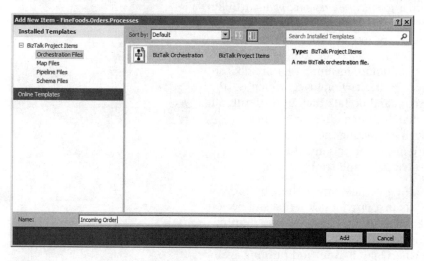

FIGURE 4.1   Adding an orchestration to your project.

After you add the orchestration to your project, it is automatically opened in the Orchestration Designer, as shown in Figure 4.2. The Orchestration Designer consists of a graphical view in the middle and two port surfaces on either side of the graphical view. To the left of the Orchestration Designer, you find a Toolbox with shapes you can use to build your business process. If the Toolbox is not visible, you can turn it on by using choosing **View**, **Toolbox** or by pressing **Ctrl+Alt+X**. The shapes are described in section "Shapes," later in this chapter. The port surfaces are for ports used for the business process to communicate with other systems and trading partners. A port can be placed on either side regardless of the type of the port. You just choose the side that gives you the best overview of your process.

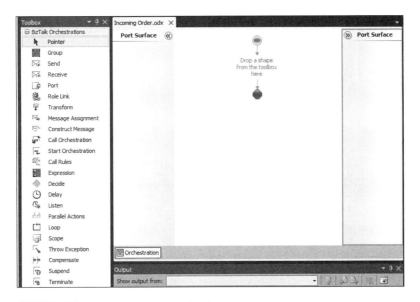

FIGURE 4.2   The Orchestration Designer.

To the right of the Orchestration Designer, you find the Orchestration View, which is placed alongside the Solution Explorer. The Orchestration View is shown in Figure 4.3. The Orchestration View is the place where the developer defines all the messages that are to flow through this orchestration, all variables used, all ports used, and so on. If the Orchestration View is not visible, you can enable it by choosing **View**, **Other Windows**, **Orchestration View**. The different parts of an orchestration are explained later in this chapter.

FIGURE 4.3   The Orchestration View.

If you click **Orchestration Properties** in Orchestration View or if you click inside the graphical view of your orchestration in Orchestration Designer, you get a set of properties you can set for the orchestration. These are illustrated in Figure 4.4.

FIGURE 4.4   Orchestration properties.

Table 4.1 describes the properties of an orchestration.

TABLE 4.1   Properties for Orchestrations

Property Name	Description
Description	Contains a text that describes the orchestration. This is not used at all, but serves only as information from one developer to another.
Module Exportable	Can be True or False. Mark this True if you want .NET types and orchestrations in this module to be exportable as *Business Process Execution Language* (BPEL). If you mark it True, you get two new properties called Module XML Target Namespace and Orchestration Exportable. Both are explained later in this table.
Module XML Target Namespace	This property is visible only if the Module Exportable is set to True. In that case, you must set this property to the wanted namespace of the BPEL module.
Namespace	This is the .NET namespace of the class file the orchestration is converted into at compile time.
Object Type	Always has a value of Orchestration Properties.
Orchestration Exportable	This property is visible only if the Module Exportable property is set to True. In that case, you must set this property True if this specific orchestration should be exportable to BPEL. Setting this property to True provides you with a new property called Orchestration XML Target Namespace, which is described next.

TABLE 4.1   Properties for Orchestrations

Property Name	Description
Orchestration XML Target Namespace	This property is visible only if the Orchestration Exportable property is set to True. In that case, you must set this property to the namespace you want this specific orchestration to have once it is exported to BPEL.
Report to Analyst	If you install *Orchestration Designer for Business Analysts* (ODBA) to your Visio, you can generate a Visio diagram based on an orchestration. Only the orchestrations marked as True in this property are visible to Visio.
Transaction Type	Can be set to None, Long Running, and Atomic. Allows you to specify what level of transaction is used for the orchestration. Transactions in orchestrations are explained later in this chapter.
Type Modifier	Some of the standard .NET type modifiers for classes. Can be set to Public, Private, and Internal. Useful for orchestrations designed to be called from other orchestrations. The default value is Internal. Set the type modifier according to how your orchestration will be used. Often a value of Private does just fine.
Typename	The .NET type name of the class that is generated at compile time.

TIP

Sometimes you need to copy an orchestration to another project or even to the same project to use it as a base for a new orchestration. If you do this, remember to change the value of the Typename property of the orchestration and possibly the Namespace property, as well. Otherwise, you get two classes with the same fully qualified .NET type name, which will fail when compiling. Neither property is changed automatically by Visual Studio 2010. This also goes for renaming the orchestration file. Remember to change the type name accordingly.

Defining Orchestrations

After adding an Orchestration to your project, you must begin building the orchestration, which basically means putting the right shapes in the right places of the Orchestration Designer and creating the needed artifacts such as messages, variables, ports, and so on. If the orchestration is a digital representation of a business process, a BizTalk developers should not undertake on their own but rather discuss the business process in question with a person from the business who knows about this particular business process. The business process must be described in a detailed way to correctly represent the business process, including the following:

▶ Determining the flow of the business process, including which systems to integrate with

▶ Determining the business rules that apply to the business process

▶ Determining what actions to take in case of failures

Defining the business process can be time-consuming, and often a perfectly clear description cannot be found, especially because the business rules needed to control the flow throughout the orchestration cannot be specified because they often depend on a subjective evaluation from a person. What you can do in this case is to specify as many rules and details as possible to cover as many scenarios as possible and then incorporate some human workflow where a manager must take some action to cover the rest of the scenarios.

Building Orchestrations

After the business process is specified, it must be implemented in an orchestration. The Orchestration Designer, as shown in Figure 4.2, is used for this. An orchestration begins its flow at the upper green circle and ends it at the red circle.

BPEL Compliancy

The Business Process Execution Language is a standard for describing business processes. BPEL is described at Wikipedia at http://en.wikipedia.org/wiki/ Business_Process_Execution_Language. BizTalk 2010 supports only version 1.1 of the standard and can both export orchestrations as BPEL and import BPEL.

Building and Exporting to BPEL

You can build your orchestrations in a way so that they are BPEL-compliant, and they can therefore be exported as BPEL to be imported in another system. To be BPEL compliant, you cannot use some of the building blocks of orchestrations. These are described at the MSDN site at http://msdn.microsoft.com/en-us/library/aa559882(BTS.70).aspx.

To export your orchestrations as BPEL, you must do two things. First, you must set BPEL Compliance, which is a property of the .BTPROJ file to True. This property is accessible in the Properties window if you click the project in Solution Explorer. Second, you must set four of the properties described in Table 4.1:

- ▶ Module Exportable

- ▶ Module XML Target Namespace

- ▶ Orchestration Exportable

- ▶ Orchestration XML Target Namespace

After setting these properties, you can right-click the .ODX file in Solution Explorer and choose **Export to BPEL**. Doing so exports a .WSDL file and a .BPEL file.

Importing BPEL   To import an existing BPEL flow, you need to add a new project to your solution and choose the **BizTalk Server BPEL Import Wizard** project type for the project. This will start a wizard, in which you can choose what BPEL flow to import and relevant .WSDL files and .XSD files.

Some restrictions apply to what can be imported. You can find these restrictions at http://msdn.microsoft.com/en-us/library/aa559576(BTS.70).aspx.

Building a Flow

You build the orchestration by dragging shapes from the Toolbox to the Orchestration Designer. The available shapes are described later in this chapter. You can drag a shape from the Toolbox to the Orchestration Designer and release it anywhere where you see a small green arrow when the mouse is hovering over it. This is usually between

▸ Two existing shapes or

▸ The green circle and a shape or

▸ A shape and the red circle

It can also be inside another shape, when nesting shapes within each other.

Another option for adding a shape to your Orchestration Designer is to right-click where you want to add the shape and choose **Insert Shape** and then choose the shape to be added. When you are dragging from the Toolbox, the green arrow appears only in places where you can legally drop the shape. For instance, the Compensate shape cannot be added outside an exception handler or a compensate block. The same goes for right-clicking a place in the Orchestration Designer to add a shape; only the allowed shapes are enabled in that dialog. There is a known bug that allows you to right-click and add a Call Rules shape only inside an atomic Scope shape. You can drag it from the Toolbox to wherever you want it, though.

The flow inside an orchestration can contain loops but cannot contain arbitrary links, like goto statements from programming languages. There are shapes that enable you to call or start other orchestrations, which are explained later, but inside a specific orchestration, you cannot jump arbitrarily around. An orchestration is a process and therefore any state transitions you need to be able to do must be a part of the model of the process you are implementing.

Callable Orchestrations

When defining business processes, you may end up with some common functionality that is used throughout many business processes or perhaps one business process gets so big that you want to split it up into smaller bits for readability and maintainability purposes. One orchestration is inside one file, which means that the entire orchestration must be checked out from source control if a developer is about to work on it. Therefore, you might also consider splitting one big orchestration up into several smaller callable orchestrations to allow multiple developers to work on the same business process at the same time.

If you create these bits of business process that are to be called from other business processes, you simply need to create your orchestration as a callable orchestration rather than a normal one. A callable orchestration is an orchestration that has parameters and not an activating Receive shape at the beginning. The Receive shape is one of the shapes you have available to build your orchestrations, and it is used to mark where a message is received by the orchestration. It is explained in more detail later. Note that a callable orchestration can have a Receive shape as the first shape; it just cannot be an activating Receive shape. You specify the parameters of an orchestration in the Orchestration View, as shown in Figure 4.5.

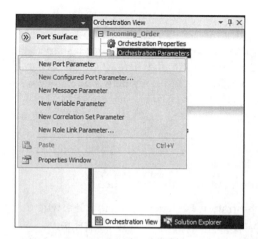

FIGURE 4.5   Adding parameters to an orchestration.

As you can see, you can send several types of parameters to an orchestration. The most commonly used are variables and messages. If your called orchestration needs to receive a message at some point, you also need to provide it with the correlation set to follow or you will get a compilation error just as you get with normal orchestrations that have a non-activateable Receive shape that doesn't follow a correlation set. Correlation sets are constructs that define some common set of properties that message that pertain to the same process must share. Correlation sets are explained in detail later in this chapter.

Large Orchestrations

If your orchestration gets big, there are a couple of tools to help you. First, you can switch to full screen by either pressing **Shift+Alt+Enter** or by choosing **View**, **Full Screen**. When in Full Screen mode, you have no access to the Toolbox, so you need to either right-click the Orchestration Designer to insert a shape or choose **BizTalk**, **Insert Shape** to do so. The menu option is available only in case you have selected a place to insert the shape first. You turn off Full Screen mode the same way you enabled it.

Besides Full Screen mode, you can also zoom. Zooming is either done by pressing **Ctrl** while using the wheel on your mouse or by choosing **BizTalk**, **Zoom** and then choosing an appropriate zoom level.

Expression Editor

The Orchestration Designer has an expression editor, which allows you to write code in the XLANG/s language and offers IntelliSense. The expression editor is used in many places to configure different shapes and artifacts. It will be mentioned explicitly in this chapter when the expression editor is used. Unlike in earlier versions of BizTalk, the expression editor can now be resized. You couldn't resize it earlier because if you are writing code in an expression editor that requires a larger expression editor than the default one you are most likely going down the wrong path because that much code does not belong inside the business process. Now you can resize it, but be aware that you do not start writing too much code in it. You do get long expressions at times, especially for using the xpath function explained later because an XPath expression used in the xpath function can get quite long.

xpath Function

Inside an expression editor, you might want to use the xpath function to either extract a value from a message or to set the value of a field in a new message being created. As mentioned in Chapter 2, "Schemas," the xpath function requires that the entire message be loaded into memory, which means that it performs much worse than using a distinguished field when retrieving a value from a message. Even though the xpath function doesn't perform very well, it is sometimes needed anyway, especially to reach the values of nodes in a message that can occur multiple times, because that is a (natural) limitation of both the promoted properties and the distinguished fields.

The xpath function is used as shown in Listing 4.1. The function takes in two parameters: the message part to perform the xpath function on and the XPath expression to use on the message. For messages that have just one part, you can provide the message as the first parameter. The two lines of code exemplify an important fact of the xpath function, namely that the result of the xpath function isn't always as expected at first. Behind the scenes, the call to the xpath function is translated into a method call to a .NET helper class, which evaluates the XPath expression and tries its best to convert the output from that into the type of the variable you are assigning it to. This means that the first line of code in the code listing returns the XmlNode that corresponds to the XPath, and the second returns the actual value of the same element. Instead of the string function inside the XPath expression, you can also use the number function, the count function, or one of the other possible functions.

LISTING 4.1   Example of Using the **xpath** Function

```
node = xpath(msgInput, "/*[local-name()='MyRoot' and namespace-
uri()='http://MyNS.MySchema']/*[local-name()='MyElement' and namespace-
uri()='']");


str = xpath(msgInput, "string(/*[local-name()='MyRoot' and namespace-
uri()='http://MyNS.MySchema']/*[local-name()='MyElement' and namespace-uri()=''])");
```

TIP

Getting your XPath expression right can be tricky if multiple namespaces are involved. Some are default namespaces in the *Extensible Markup Language* (XML) instance, and some have qualifiers, and so on. You can get a helping hand by opening up the schema for the message in the Schema Editor. If you click the element for which you need an XPath expression, you can find the Instance XPath property in the properties of that element. Copy this text to get a valid XPath expression. Remember to modify it, though, if you need, for instance, the third occurrence of the element or have some other requirement. Figure 4.6 shows where to find the value.

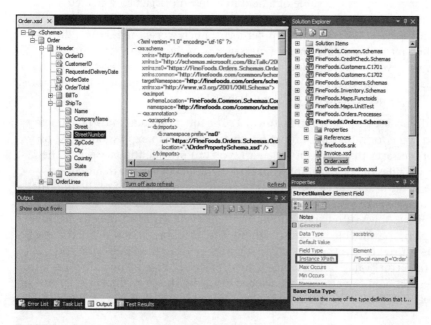

FIGURE 4.6   How to find the Instance XPath property of a node in your schema.

Messages

A message in an orchestration represents some information that must flow through the orchestration. A message can consist of multiple parts, of which one is defined as the body part. A lot of pipeline components deal only with the body part and leave the rest of the message parts alone, considering them to be some form of attachment to the body part.

Defining a Message

You define a message in you orchestration in the Orchestration View by right-clicking **Messages** and choosing **New Message**. After adding the new message, you can change its properties. First, you should change the identifier of the message. The identifier must be unique within the orchestration, meaning that you cannot have a variable or some other object within the same orchestration with the same name. Second, you must change the Message Type property. This property determines the type of the message, which can be one of the following four categories:

- ▶ **.NET Classes:** This can be either a standard .NET class or a .NET class you have created yourself. If chosen, you either use a class browser to locate the class you want to use or choose between the three most commonly used native .NET classes: `String`, `DateTime`, and `XmlDocument`.

- ▶ **Multi-part Message Types:** Below this option, you can find all the multipart message types that are defined in your orchestration, the option to create a new multipart message type, and the option to browse through the referenced assemblies to locate the multipart message type you want to use.

- ▶ **Schemas:** Perhaps the most commonly used type for a message inside an orchestration. Here you can choose what schema to use as the type for your message. You can choose between the schemas in your current project, to create a new schema in the current project, or to browse through the referenced projects to locate a schema from one of those assemblies.

- ▶ **Web Message Types:** The message types listed here are the ones that were created for you automatically when you added a reference to a web service to your project. You also have the option of browsing through referenced assemblies to locate generated web message types in those.

There is a special case of using a .NET class for your message. If you use the `System.Xml.XmlDocument` class, this actually enables you to deal with untyped messages and binary messages floating through your orchestration. This might seem silly, but defining a message of this class enables you to receive a binary message, like when you used the Passthru receive pipeline.

Restrictions on Message Types

No matter what type you choose for your message, it must be XML serializable because the messages need to be serialized when persisting the orchestration to the MessageBox. Persistence is discussed later in this chapter.

Messages inside an orchestration are immutable after they are created. The reason for this is that messages that are published to the MessageBox are then merely referenced from the orchestration instances, meaning that more than one orchestration can reference the same message. You can at any time, however, make a copy of a message and change that copy. This is done using the Construct Message shape, which is explained later in this chapter.

NOTE

There are situations that are often thought of as exceptions to the rule about messages being immutable.

First, messages can be altered inside the *Business Rules Engine* (BRE), which is the way you get the results of executing a policy back to the orchestration. In fact, in older versions of BizTalk, a call to the BRE was required to be inside an atomic scope, which guaranteed persistence after completion to persist the altered message. Note, however, that the BRE isn't actually changing the message, but rather it is creating a copy of the message with a new `MessageID` and returns this to the calling orchestration, keeping the original message intact.

Second, you can alter a message by sending it to an external assembly as a parameter and changing it in the external assembly. If you inspect this message after it has been altered, you can see the changes. The changes are, however, local to the orchestration because the actual message that is in the MessageBox hasn't been altered. If you alter a message like this and then send it out using a Send shape, you get the original message out because it is the message in the MessageBox that is sent out. Therefore, you shouldn't do this if at all possible because it is merely confusing and difficult to troubleshoot for developers not knowing what goes on behind the scenes. If at all possible, stick to the Construct Message shape and create new messages.

Multipart

A message in an orchestration can consist of multiple parts. This is useful for sending out emails that have attachments, for instance, and this is also the way a message is represented that encompasses the parameters a web service method accepts as input. If a web service method you must call takes in two parameters, a string and a Boolean, for example, this is represented as a multipart message with two parts: a string and a Boolean.

You create a multipart message type in Orchestration View, as shown in Figure 4.7.

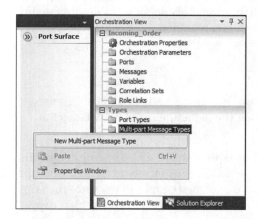

FIGURE 4.7   Adding a new multipart message type.

Other than using these for when a multipart message is actually needed, they can also be useful for adding a level of abstraction. If you have a Receive shape that is receiving a message of a specific type, and this Receive shape is connected to a port and you need to change the type of the message that is received, this is not immediately doable. The reason for this is that the operation on the port also has a reference to the type of message that can come through this operation, and if you change the type of the message these two are not in sync anymore. Therefore, you need to remove the link between the Receive shape and the port, change the type of the message, change the type of the operation, and then reconnect the two. If you instead used a multipart message type that has just the one part and let both the operation on the port and the message use this type, you can change the underlying types of the parts without interrupting anything. Using a multipart message to create this level of abstraction is considered a best practice unless you need to leverage *Windows Communication Foundation* (WCF), because WCF des not work with multipart messages.

Creating New Messages

You might at some point need to create a message inside your orchestration. As explained later, messages inside orchestration can be constructed only inside a Construct Message shape, and inside this shape you have the option of using a Transform shape, a Message Assignment shape, or a combination of the two to create the message. The usual ways of constructing a new message inside an orchestration are to either transform a message into a new one or to assign one message to another and then perhaps change the values of some of the fields using either distinguished fields or the xpath function. At times, however, you will need to create a new message that is either just some standard message or some message, whose values are in variables and are therefore not accessible in a map. At times, when you cannot use any of the normal approaches to creating a new message, you have some other options that are explained in this section.

XmlDocument   You can create a variable of type System.Xml.XmlDocument and then build your XML using this and assign it to your message afterward. Listing 4.2 shows an example of this.

LISTING 4.2   Using an **XmlDocument** Variable to Build a Message

```
xmldoc = new System.Xml.XmlDocument();
xmldoc.LoadXml(@"<myRoot><myElem>42</myElem></myRoot>");

msg = xmldoc;
```

If the property Use Default Constructor of the variable xmldoc is set to true, you might consider setting it to false or removing the first line of code, because otherwise you are initializing the object twice, which is not necessary.

The call to the LoadXml method on the xmldoc variable takes in a string that contains the XML to load. This string can be retrieved from a helper method, a resource, or some other source. Also, you can build the string beforehand by concatenating strings and variables. You can also use the XmlDocument class to build the XML instead of loading a string, leveraging the methods on the XmlDocument class. And finally, you could use the Load method rather than the LoadXml method and instead provide a stream, an XmlReader, or use one of the other overloads.

.NET Helper Class   If you want to separate out the functionality to build the XmlDocument, you can use a custom .NET helper class in two ways.

The first is to simply have a method in the .NET helper class that builds your XML using the .NET classes for this, and then returns an XmlDocument, which you can then assign to your message in your Message Assignment shape.

The second way is to create a class that corresponds to your *XML Schema Definition* (XSD) using the XSD.EXE tool. Then let your .NET helper class instantiate this class and return this object. The Orchestration Engine handles deserializing, serializing, and casting automatically for you.

Resources   Another option is to have XML files that have some specified structure compiled as resources into a .NET class and at runtime you can then retrieve one of them to assign it to a message.

Maps   Even though you do not have any message that actually has the information needed to create your new message, you can still use a map to create the new message. Just use any message as the input and then completely ignore the input inside the map. Inside the map, you can then either use a custom XSLT script that generates the output for you or you can use the functoids or set default values on appropriate nodes to build the output message. If you have variables in your orchestration that have values that need to go into the message, you can use a Message Assignment shape after the Transform shape but inside the same Construct Message shape to set these values.

Variables

Variables in orchestrations are almost just like you expect variables to be. The can have one of many types and contain some value that can be used throughout the orchestration. You define a variable in Orchestration View by right-clicking **Variables** and choosing **New Variable**. A new variable is then created for you, and you get the Properties window, where you can change the properties of the variable, which are listed in Table 4.2.

TABLE 4.2   Properties for Variables

Property Name	Description
Description	A textual description of the variable. Only serves as information to and from orchestration developers.
Identifier	The name of the variable.
Initial Value	If the Type is set to a value type, this property activates and you can enter a default value for the variable.
Object Type	Always has a value of Variable.
Report to Analyst	If you install *Orchestration Designer for Business Analysts* (ODBA) on top of Visio, you can generate a Visio diagram based on an orchestration. Only the variables marked as True in this property are visible to Visio.

TABLE 4.2   Properties for Variables

Property Name	Description
Type	The type of the variable. If you want to change this, you get a drop-down that contains the most common .NET value types and also the possibility to choose <.NET Class>. If you choose the <.NET Class>, you get to a browser of the namespaces and classes that are available. If you want an XmlDocument for instance, you can choose **System.Xml** on the left side of the class browser and then choose **XmlDocument** on the right side. This is shown in Figure 4.8.
Use Default Constructor	This property is available only if the Type property has been set to a class. If set to True, the object is called using the default constructor at the beginning of the orchestration. If set to False, the object is not initialized at all, and you will have to do that yourself. For example, if you declare a variable of the type System.Xml.XmlDocument and let this property be True, the variable is initialized as a new System.Xml.XmlDocument when the orchestration fires up. If you in an Expression shape also set the variable to be a new System.Xml.XmlDocument, the variable is initialized twice.

TIP

If a variable is set to have a .NET class as type, and if you need to pass in values to the constructor, always set the Use Default Constructor to False because there is no need to initialize the object using the default constructor first and then initialize it with another constructor later on. This can improve performance.

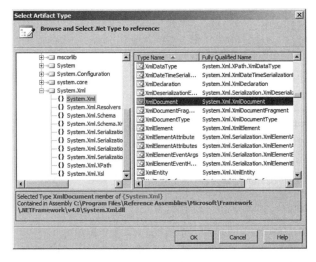

FIGURE 4.8   Choosing the right **System.Xml.XmlDocument** .NET class as type for a variable.

The type of any variable in an orchestration must be binary serializable. This is because BizTalk persists orchestrations at specific points in time to guarantee the sanity of the system in case of power failure or hardware failure and also to be able to take an orchestration that is waiting for input out of memory and later load it back in. Persistence is explained later in this chapter. The only place you can declare a variable to be of a nonserializable type is inside an atomic transaction. Transactions are also explained later in this chapter. The only exception to the requirement of types for variables having to be serializable is the System.Xml.XmlDocument class, because this is so widely used that it is treated as a special case. When you are serializing a variable of type System.Xml.XmlDocument or a derived class, the serialization process saves the type of the variable and the value of the OuterXml property, which can then later be used to instantiate a matching System.Xml.XmlDocument when deserializing.

Shapes

To build your business process, BizTalk provides you with a lot of shapes that are usable as building blocks. All shapes share three common properties:

- ▶ **Name:** Set this to the name of the shape. Avoid the default names, which are the type of shape concatenated with _X, where X is a number starting from 1.

- ▶ **Description:** Set this to contain a description of the shape. This is not used at compile time or runtime, but it is nice for other developers to see what your intention with a given shape is.

- ▶ **Report to Analyst:** If you install ODBA on top of Visio, you can generate a Visio diagram based on an orchestration. Only the shapes marked as True in this property are visible to Visio.

Unfortunately, there is no way of programming custom shapes to be used in your orchestrations, but the built-in ones are quite adequate for handling most business processes. The built-in shapes are described in this section.

As explained earlier, shapes can be added in several ways. After a shape has been placed on the Orchestration Designer, it has a red exclamation mark next to it, in case it has some required properties that have not been set. Clicking the red exclamation mark elicits an explanation of what property needs to be set. Clicking the explanation helps you set a proper value for the property in question. This can either be by allowing you to set the property immediately, as shown in Figure 4.9, or by creating a needed artifact for you, as shown in Figure 4.10 (or some other help). Another option is to click the explanation to open the expression editor, the configuration screen for the shape, or something else. In any case, it provides help as to what you need to configure.

To preserve the overview of the orchestration, you can collapse shapes. By clicking the minus sign just to the left of the shape icon, you will collapse a shape along with all its children and thus be able to concentrate on the visible shapes.

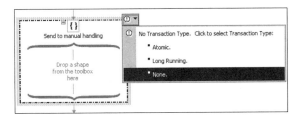

FIGURE 4.9   Setting the property to a value immediately using the red exclamation mark.

FIGURE 4.10   Creating an artifact using the red exclamation mark.

Scope

The Scope shape has three purposes:

▶ The first is to be a container for a transaction inside the orchestration. Transactions inside orchestrations are explained later in this chapter.

▶ The second purpose of the Scope shape is as the name implies: to be a scope, in which variables, messages, and correlation sets can be defined. Correlation sets are explained later in this chapter.

▶ The third is to provide exception handling, because an exception handler block can be added to the Scope shape. Exception handling is described later in this chapter.

Figure 4.11 shows an orchestration in which a Scope shape has been added. After you add a Scope shape, you get an item in the tree in Orchestration View that corresponds to this Scope shape, and you can then add variables, messages, and correlation sets like you can do globally for the orchestration in Orchestration View. When a scope ends at runtime, what is defined inside the scope is automatically out of scope and can be garbage collected. Therefore, you should define the variables, messages, and correlation sets globally only if they are needed in several scopes that are not nested within each other.

For some types of Scope shapes, you can add either an exception handler block or a compensating block by right-clicking the shape and selecting it. Figure 4.12 shows an example. The exception handler block is used to catch and handle exceptions in a try-catch manner that are thrown within the scope. The compensate block is used to override the default compensating algorithm used by an orchestration in case of errors. Exception handling in orchestrations is described in section "Exception Handling," and the compensating algorithm is discussed in section "Compensating."

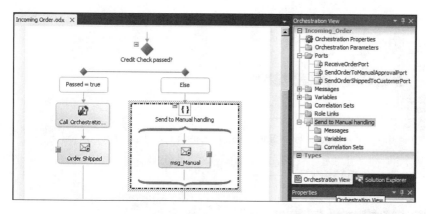

FIGURE 4.11   The Scope shape.

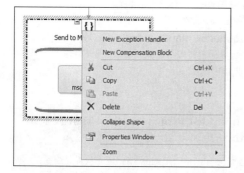

FIGURE 4.12   Adding either an exception handler block or a compensation block to a Scope shape.

Scopes can be synchronized by setting the Synchronized property to True on the Scope shape. Setting this property to True allows you to access the same piece of data in several branches of a Parallel Actions shape at the same time. The Parallel Actions shape allows you to define functionality that can run logically in parallel, like receiving two messages where you have no way to know which one arrives first. The shape is described in detail later in this chapter. Setting the property to True guarantees that only one branch uses the data at the same time. In fact, if you access the same data in two branches of a Parallel Actions shape, the compiler instructs you that the references in both branches must be inside a synchronized Scope shape.

Some rules apply to nesting scopes:

▶ Transactional/synchronized scopes cannot be nested inside synchronized scopes.

▶ Atomic transaction scopes cannot have any transactional scopes nested inside them. This follows from the first rule, because all atomic transaction scopes are also synchronized.

▶ Transactional scopes cannot be nested within nontransactional scopes or orchestrations.

- It appears that you can nest Scope shapes up to many levels deep. At some point, you will run into issues with the Orchestration Designer not being able to render them, though. If you run into this issue, rethink your design because this many nested Scope shapes is almost definitely a mistake in design.

- Call Orchestration shapes can be placed inside scopes, but the same rules apply, meaning that if the called orchestration is transactional it cannot be called from an atomic or synchronized scope.

- Start Orchestration shapes can be placed inside any scope, and no nesting restrictions apply. This is because the start orchestration basically starts up an orchestration that gets its own instance and runtime without knowing who started it.

NOTE

Name hiding is not allowed for BizTalk orchestrations, meaning that you cannot have a variable or message inside a Scope shape with the same name as an orchestration variable or message. You must have unique names. The compiler provides a compile time error if this happens so that you can detect it early.

Call Orchestration

This shape is used to call another orchestration from an orchestration. The orchestration that is to be called must have the type modifier set to an appropriate value to let others call it, meaning that if it is in another project/assembly, you must mark it as public.

When you double-click the **Call Orchestration** shape, you get a drop-down list of all the orchestrations that are either in the same project or in the referenced projects and that have the type modifier set appropriately. When you are choosing which orchestration to call, all the parameters the orchestration has defined appear in the Parameter Name column and you must choose the appropriate variables, messages, ports, and so on from the calling orchestration that are to be used as the parameters at runtime. This is shown in Figure 4.13. If only one possibility that matches the type of parameter is available in the calling orchestration, it is prefilled. If more than one option exists, one is chosen for you, but you get a drop-down to choose the correct parameter.

A call orchestration is a synchronous call, meaning that the calling orchestration waits for the orchestration to finish before it continues the flow after the Call Orchestration shape.

TIP

If you need to send constants in as parameters to another orchestration, you must declare variables to hold the values because constants cannot be specified in the screen where you configure the parameters for the called orchestration. You can add a Scope shape to contain the Call Orchestration shape and declare the needed variables in there and give them an initial value so that you don't have to add an Expression shape to initialize them.

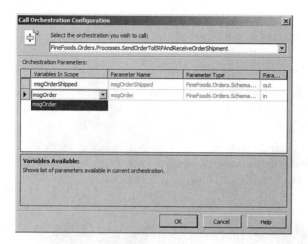

FIGURE 4.13   Configuring the Call Orchestration shape.

NOTE

Calling one orchestration from another is similar to calling one .NET method from another in normal .NET code. This means that the called orchestration executes within the host instance that hosts the calling orchestration no matter what host the called orchestration is associated with in the Administration Console.

Call Rules

The Call Rules shape is used to call a policy that is deployed to the BRE. If you add this shape to the orchestration and double-click it to configure it, you get a list to choose from of all the deployed policies. Figure 4.14 shows an example.

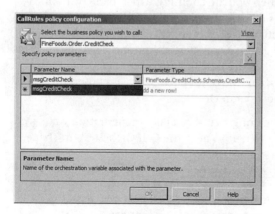

FIGURE 4.14   Configuring the Call Rules shape.

As you can see, a list of the deployed policies appears. Policies that are not deployed, but merely published, do not appear in the list. After you have chosen a policy, you can add parameters to be used when executing the policy in the parameter list below the list of policies. If you are not able to choose parameters for the policy, there are a couple of things to check:

- ▶ Check that you have a message/variable of the correct type in your orchestration.
- ▶ Check that the types of the XSD facts for the policy in Business Rules Composer match the fully qualified type name of the schemas used in the policy. This is explained in more detail in Chapter 10, "The Business Rules Framework."

Also, note that you cannot see a version number on the policy. This is because when a policy is executed from an orchestration, the newest policy is always executed. This is actually quite clever, because it means that someone can change the rules to have another implementation without affecting the orchestration at all, which again means no downtime, because rules can be updated without restarting any services. If you need to execute a specific version of a policy, you have to write code to do that.

Compensate

The Compensate shape can only be placed inside either an exception handler block or a compensate block that is associated with a Scope shape (see Figure 4.15).

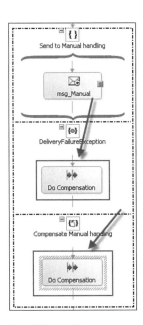

FIGURE 4.15   Where to place the Compensate shape.

Figure 4.16 shows the properties available to set on the Compensate shape.

FIGURE 4.16   Properties of the Compensate shape.

The only property you are required to change, which is also the only one worth mentioning, is the Compensation property. This property provides you with a drop-down of all the transactions that are available to compensate for.

The Compensate shape is used to instruct the engine which transaction to compensate for when doing exception handling. The possible transactions to choose in the drop-down are the current transaction and any immediate child transaction of the current transactions.

For more information about BizTalks compensation model, see the section "Compensation."

Construct Message

The Construct Message shape is used to indicate to the compiler that inside this shape a new message is constructed. Because messages inside an orchestration are immutable, you cannot change a message. You can, however, create a new message, and this must always be done inside a Construct Message shape.

A message can be constructed using two different shapes inside the Construct Message shape. These two shapes are as follows:

- **Transform:**The Transform shape executes a map to create some output messages.

- **Message Assignment:**The Message Assignment shape uses an expression editor to let the developer write code to create a new message.

These two shapes are the only two shapes that may appear inside a Construct Message shape, and they can appear multiple times inside the same Construct Message shape. Both are explained in their own sections.

Figure 4.17 shows the properties for the Construct Message shape.

As you can see, you can set the Report to Analyst, Name, and the Description properties as you can with all shapes.

Worth noticing is that the Messages Constructed is plural and in fact, as you can see from Figure 4.17, you can select a number of messages that are to be constructed. The messages you choose on the Construct Message must be constructed either by code in a Message

Assignment shape or as the output of a map that is called in a Transform shape. The compiler gives you an error if you do not construct the messages you have selected.

FIGURE 4.17   Properties of the Construct Message shape.

A common compile time error is the "Use of an Unconstructed Message" error, which arises if you try to use a message that hasn't been constructed in a Construct Message shape or received in a Receive shape before usage. This corresponds in .NET code to using an object that has been declared but not initialized.

TIP

If you have values in variables inside an orchestration that you would like to get into a new message, you can use either a Message Assignment or a Transform shape to construct the message with empty nodes for the nodes you need the values to go into. Then you can promote those nodes as distinguished fields and use those to put values into the nodes after constructing the message.

So, you can construct the same message or parts thereof in multiple shapes inside the same Construct Message shape.

Decide

The Decide shape is used to split the workflow into several branches, but only go down one branch, given some specific rules. When you add the Decide shape to your orchestration, it has two branches, but you can right-click it and choose **New Rule Branch**, as shown in Figure 4.18, to add another branch.

On all branches that are not the rightmost branch, you must either double-click the branch or right-click it and choose **Edit Boolean Expression**. Doing so opens the expression editor and enables you to set some Boolean expression that will determine whether the workflow should go down this branch.

At runtime, BizTalk tests the Boolean expression from left to the right. If a Boolean expression is true, that branch is executed, and the rest of the branches are ignored. If the Boolean expression is false, the next branch is tested. If BizTalk reaches the rightmost branch, this is executed because this is the branch that executes if all other branches do not execute.

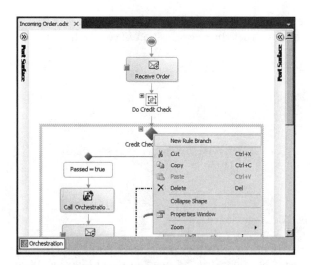

FIGURE 4.18   Decide shape and how to add a branch.

Delay

The Delay shape is used if you want to delay the execution of the orchestration for a specific length of time or until a specific time.

It is dragged to the orchestration, and when you double-click it or right-click it and choose **Edit Delay**, you get an expression editor, in which you must specify for how long time to sleep. Listing 4.3 and Listing 4.4 show two ways of instructing the orchestration to sleep for 42 days.

LISTING 4.3   Using a **DateTime** to Sleep for 42 days

```
System.DateTime.UtcNow.AddDays(42);
```

Obviously, you cannot have both statements in the expression for the Delay shape.

LISTING 4.4   Using a **TimeSpan** to Sleep for 42 Days

```
new System.TimeSpan(42,0,0,0);
```

As you can see from Listing 4.4, you can specify a TimeSpan for the length of time to wait. In Listing 4.4, the TimeSpan is set at 42 days. Other than a TimeSpan, you can also set a DateTime, and the Delay shape will then make the orchestration sleep until that specific time. The DateTime must be specified in UTC time. So, sleeping for 42 days can be achieved also by setting the value to the current UTC time and adding 42 days to that, as shown in Listing 4.3.

There will be no TimeoutException or any other exception. BizTalk just waits for the specified amount of time before continuing the execution. It is also important to note that it is not the orchestration thread that sleeps until the time to continue execution. Instead,

BizTalk handles this internally using a timer or something similar. The reason it isn't the thread that sleeps will become clear when you read about the Parallel Actions shape.

Delay shapes are most commonly used in conjunction with the Listen shape, which is explained later.

NOTE

As you can see in Listing 4.3 and Listing 4.4, the statement that is used in a Delay shape is ended with a semicolon (;). This is required when the Delay shape is used outside a Listen shape. If the Delay shape is used as the first shape in a Listen shape, you cannot have the semicolon at the end of the expression. The Listen shape is explained later.

Expression

The Expression shape is a shape that is basically an expression editor. You can use it to assign values to variables, read properties and distinguished fields from messages, call external assemblies, and more.

TIP

If you want to use the value of a promoted property of a message, you can access it using parenthesis, like this: MyMessage(Prop.Name). If the property does not exist because nothing has been promoted into it, however, you get an exception, and your orchestration is suspended. Therefore, you need to check whether it exists before you read it. Listing 4.5 shows how to use the exists operator for this.

LISTING 4.5   Using the **exists** Operator to Check the Existence of a Promoted Property

```
if (BTS.ReceivePortName exists MyMessage)
{
  PortName = MyMessage(BTS.ReceivePortName);
}
else
{
  PortName = "Not known";
}
```

TIP

The code in Listing 4.5 also shows that you can use the if statement to control what happens. Unfortunately, you lose IntelliSense if you do that, so consider writing the code somewhere else first and then copying and pasting it into the Expression shape.

Group

The Group shape serves as a grouping of other shapes. You can add the Group shape to the orchestration and then add all the shapes you want to this shape. The shape can then be collapsed to give the developer a higher-level view of the orchestration without having to know what is inside the Group shape. Figure 4.19 shows a Group shape with a number of shapes in it, and Figure 4.20 shows the same Group shape that has been collapsed.

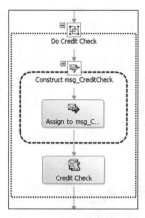

FIGURE 4.19   The Group shape with shapes inside it.

FIGURE 4.20   The Group shape after being collapsed.

The Group shape infers no functionality whatsoever on the orchestration. Its sole purpose is to group shapes together and be able to collapse it to provide a better overview of the process.

Parallel Actions

The Parallel Actions shape is used to execute several branches of the orchestration in parallel. When you add the Parallel Actions shape to the orchestration, you can add new branches to it, as shown in Figure 4.21.

In each branch, you can have as many shapes as you want to. The shapes after the Parallel Action shape are not executed until all branches of the Parallel Action shape have finished.

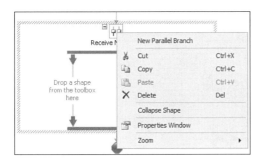

FIGURE 4.21   The Parallel Actions shape.

Having a Parallel Actions shape will not add threads to an orchestration. An orchestration is executed in one thread only. This means that when you think about the Parallel Actions shape you should not think of it in a developer sort of way, where you would expect multithreaded execution, but more in a business way, where several business activities might happen that are relevant to your business process, but you do not know the order in which they will happen. The most common usage is when the business process needs to receive a number of messages and you cannot determine at design time what order they will appear in. Scenarios could include the following:

▶ Your business process sends out a request for a quote to three different suppliers and must wait until the three quotes have been received before choosing which supplier to use. The three quotes can come back in any order, and therefore you can use the Parallel Actions shape to set up three simultaneous Receive shapes.

▶ A job applicant must send you her application, her resumé, and a copy of her diploma from the school she attended. Again, the documents can arrive in any order, and therefore handling this in a serial way will not suffice.

As a general rule, BizTalk executes the branches from left to right and executes each branch until a blocking shape occurs. Therefore, the leftmost branch is executed completely, and then the next branch, moving to the right, is executed, and so on. If a branch hits a Receive shape or a Delay shape, be it directly or through a Listen shape, the branch is blocked, pending the event that will unblock it, and the next branch is executed. When the event occurs that a blocked branch was waiting for, the branch is added to the execution queue again, and it is then executed once it is its turn. This is also the reason why the Delay shape does not utilize `Thread.Sleep` but instead handles the wait internally. If `Thread.Sleep` were used, the next branch could not be executed while another branch is waiting.

Listen

The Listen shape is a shape that can have as many branches as you want to. The first shape in each branch must be either a Receive shape or a Delay shape. Figure 4.22 shows an example.

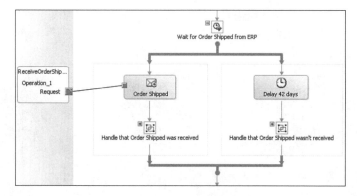

FIGURE 4.22   Example of the Listen shape.

As with the Decide shape and the Parallel Actions shape, you can add branches to the Listen shape by right-clicking the **Listen** shape and choosing **New Listen Branch**.

At runtime, BizTalk waits until either one of the Receive shapes receive the message it is waiting for or one of the Delay shapes times out. The branch that has the Receive shape that receives a message or a Delay shape that times out gets executed. The rest of the branches are ignored.

The most common usage of this is escalation, where you have sent out an order and are awaiting an order confirmation (for instance). If the order confirmation hasn't been received within some specified time interval, you might want to resend the order, email an account manager, or something else.

Loop

The Loop shape is used for creating a loop inside your orchestration. The Loop shape is shown in Figure 4.23 with a standard usage where some variables are initialized before the loop and the variables are updated at the end of each pass in the loop.

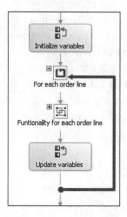

FIGURE 4.23   The Loop shape.

The Loop shape functions like a `While` statement in most programming languages. It evaluates a Boolean expression, and if the expression is evaluated to true, the functionality inside the loop is executed. When this is done, the expression is reevaluated and this continues until the expression is evaluated to false or some functionality inside the loop makes the flow jump out, such as an exception or the Terminate shape.

When you double-click the **Loop** shape or right-click it and choose **Edit Boolean Expression**, an expression editor opens, in which you must enter the Boolean expression that determines whether the loop should be executed. The Boolean expression cannot be ended with a semicolon.

The Loop shape is used for different things:

> **Looping around elements inside a message:** This is useful if, for instance, you need to do something particular for each order line in an order, or if debatching inside the receive pipeline isn't feasible for you.

> **Serial convoys:** These are used to receive a number of messages into one instance of an orchestration. The loop is then used to specify for how long this instance should receive messages or how many messages should be received or some other predicate.

> **Retries:** If you need a way of resending a message if an exception occurs, you can also use the Loop shape. Normal setups have retries specified on the send ports, but this merely takes care of technical issues. Retries inside the orchestration take care of how the business wants to react if the number of retries on the send port has been reached. A common scenario involves suspending the orchestration and then resuming it after things have been cleared with the trading partner in question.

> **Any other looping needs:** Any other looping needs you may have, like sending out a message to a trading partner until an answer is received and others.

When using loops, be careful what functionality you implement inside the loop. As explained later in the section "Persistence Points," the orchestration is at specific points persisted to the MessageBox. Because this is a time-consuming operation, whenever possible avoid having persistence points inside loops because they will occur multiple times if this is the case. This includes sending out messages, transactional Scope shapes, Start Orchestration shapes, and more.

Message Assignment

The Message Assignment shape can only occur inside a Construct Message shape. The Message Assignment shape is an instance of the expression editor, in which you can do almost everything you can do in an Expression shape. For instance, you cannot use the `if` statement. Inside a Message Assignment shape, you can also change the content and properties of the messages that are defined as the ones being constructed in the properties of the enclosing Construct Message shape. Listing 4.6 shows examples of what can be done in a Message Assignment shape.

The allowed statements include the following:

▶ Assigning the value of another message to a new message. See line 1 in Listing 4.6. This is used if you need to modify an existing message, which is not allowed. Create a copy and then alter the new message inside the Construct Message shape instead.

▶ Call an external class to create a new message to assign to your message. See line 2 in Listing 4.6.

▶ Assign a value to a specific part of a multipart message. See line 3 in Listing 4.6.

▶ Assign a value to a distinguished field in a message. See line 4 in Listing 4.6.

▶ Copy the promoted properties from one message to another. See line 5 in Listing 4.6. This is sometimes needed because assigning one message to another or creating a new message does not automatically copy or create any promoted properties for the new message, meaning that if some value was promoted earlier on and you need it to go along with the new message you must copy or create it manually.

▶ Assign a value to a specific promoted property of a message. See line 6 in Listing 4.6.

NOTE

If you are assigning a value to a distinguished field, you must make sure the fields actually exists in the message before you assign a value to it. If you assign a value to the distinguished field `MyMessage.MyField` where `MyField` is an element in the schema that has been promoted as a distinguished field, for instance, the element must be in the XML of `MyMessage` for the assignment to work.

LISTING 4.6   What Can Be Done in a Message Assignment Shape

```
NewMessage = OldMessage;
NewMessage = FineFoods.BizTalk.Helper.CreateNewMessage.Create();

AnotherNewMessage.Part1 = new System.Xml.XmlDocument();

NewMessage.Message = "My new message";

NewMessage(*) = OldMessage(*);


NewMessage(FILE.ReceivedFileName) = "MyNewFilename.xml";
```

A Message Assignment shape is also frequently used to assign values to a few distinguished fields in a message after the message has been created using a transformation. This is because the transformation engine does not have access to variables in the orchestration at the time of the transformation, and therefore the values must be inserted into the message afterward. In this case, let the map specify <empty> for the default value of the fields to assign values into, to make sure the node is created in the output. Chapter 3, "Maps," has a section describing default values of nodes in the destination schema.

Port

The Port shape is one of the two shapes that are not viewable on the Orchestration Designer surface, but rather in the port surface of the orchestration. To specify a port in your orchestration, you have three options:

- ▶ **Drag the Port shape to the port surface:** This starts a wizard that helps you define your new port. You can also drag it to the orchestration surface. This starts the same wizard.

- ▶ **Right-click the port surface and choose New Configured Port:** This starts the same wizard as when you drag the Port shape to the port surface.

- ▶ **Right-click the port surface and choose New Port:** This creates a port for you, but there is no wizard to guide you and you must use the properties of the port to define the port, including manually creating any needed port types before configuring the port.

Usually, the wizard is the way to go because it guides you pretty easily through the needed configuration steps, including creating a new port type for you, if you need it. The wizard guides you through the following steps:

1. On the Welcome screen, click **Next**.

2. On the next screen, enter a name for the port. The name should reflect the purpose of the port (for example, ReceiveOrderPort), and because the port will be compiled into a .NET type, the .NET naming restrictions apply, such as no spaces, special characters, and so on.

3. On the third screen, which is shown in Figure 4.24, you must choose an existing port type to use for the port or choose to create a new port type to use for the new port and the characteristics of the port type. A port type specifies some characteristics of a port that can be shared across multiple ports. This is useful so as to not fill your orchestrations up with ports that have the same values for lots of properties and also you use port types to specify the type of a port parameter in a callable orchestration, if a port is to be sent between orchestrations. If you choose to create a new port type for the port, you must specify the following:

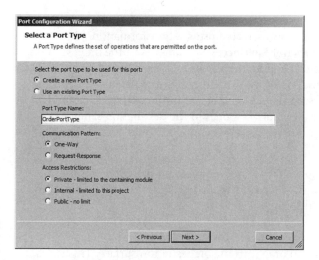

FIGURE 4.24   Screen three for configuring a new port.

▶ **Access Restrictions:** This specifies how visible the port type should be to other orchestrations. If set to Private, the port type is visible only to the orchestration it is specified in. If set to Internal, the port type is visible to all orchestrations in the same Visual Studio 2010 project. If set to Public, the port type is visible to all orchestrations that are either in the same project or reference the project the port type is defined in. In general, setting the value to Internal is good because you can then reuse port types across your orchestrations and they are not visible to other projects that may reference your project. A value of Public is required if you later on want to expose a port of this type as a web service or a WCF service.

▶ **Communication Pattern:** This determines whether the port type describes a port that is one-way or a request-response port. It does not determine if the ports that are of this type should be ports for receiving a message or sending a message, because this is a property on the port itself and not the port type. One-way port types are for asynchronous communication, whereas request-response port types are for synchronous communication.

▶ **Port Type Name:** This is the name you want to give the port type. As with the name of the port itself, this cannot contain spaces or any special characters. The name should reflect the type of message that will be sent through the ports of this type, but not the direction they are sent in (that is, if ports of this port type are for sending or receiving messages). This is because the port type doesn't know anything about this, as can be seen in the Communication Pattern property.

4. On the fourth screen, shown in Figure 4.25, you must specify properties for the port. These properties are as follows:

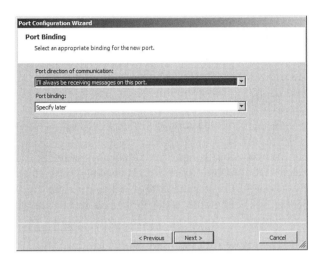

FIGURE 4.25 Screen four for configuring a new port.

▶ **Port Direction of Communication:** For a one-way port type, this must be set to either I'll Always Be Receiving Messages on This Port for a receive port or to I'll Always Be Sending Messages on This Port for a send port. For a request-response port type, you must choose between I'll Be Receiving a Request and Sending a Response for a port in which someone else will be calling your orchestration and I'll Be Sending a Request and Receiving a Response for a port where you will be calling another system.

▶ **Port Binding:** Several options are available, depending on whether the port type is a one-way port type or a request-response port type, and also depending on the direction of communication. Because these options are important, they are described later in this section.

5. On the Completing screen, click **Finish**.

There are four options for the port bindings, depending on whether you are specifying a port where you receive the first message or a port where you will be sending out the first message or receiving the first message.

In both cases, you have these options:

▶ **Specify Now:** If you choose this option, you get to configure the port right away, meaning that you get to choose adapter, location, pipeline, and so on. Upon deployment of the orchestration, a physical port is automatically created for you and bound to the logical port in the orchestration.

▶ **Specify Later:** This option allows you to specify that here a logical port will exist, but you won't specify anything about what adapter to use or what pipeline and so on. Logical ports specified as a Specify Later port must later be bound in the Administration Console to an actual physical port. Contrary to the Specify Now port binding, this allows the developer to develop the orchestration without regard to actual implementation of transport options.

▶ **Direct:** Direct bound receive ports are not bound to a physical port but instead have a filter on the Receive shape to determine what messages should be routed to this particular port. This allows for loose coupling. Direct bound send ports are not bound to a physical send port either. They basically just publish the message to the MessageBox and allow anyone with an appropriate subscription to pick it up.

For ports that send out the first message, there is a fourth option, namely a dynamic port. A dynamic send port is bound to a physical dynamic send port, which does not have any transport configuration set. The port must have its destination address set at runtime either from within the orchestration leveraging the dynamic send port or via setting the appropriate promoted properties in another place like a custom pipeline component.

Dynamic ports are useful for when you do not know at design time which location the message must be sent to. The downside is that at some point in time your business process must know the location to send the message to, so it can be set. This is usually achieved by either have the information in the message that arrives, like the email address of the receiver of an email, or by looking up the correct receiver in a database at runtime. The code to set the destination of a dynamic send port is like this, where `MyPort` is the name of the logical dynamic send port:

```
MyPort(Microsoft.XLANGs.BaseTypes.Address) = "mailto:my@email.com";
```

If you want to leverage a dynamic send port without an orchestration, you must set appropriate values to the `OutboundTransportType` and `OutboundTransportLocation` properties in the http://schemas.microsoft.com/BizTalk/2003/system-properties namespace. An alternative to using a dynamic send port that might suit you in some scenarios is to use role links, which are explained later in this chapter.

The Specify Now option should almost never be used, for several reasons:

▶ It requires that the developer must know details about what adapter and location to use for a specific integration.

▶ It provides a hard coupling between your business process and the details about some system to integrate with. Ideally, the business process is completely unaware of what systems it interacts with and how it interacts with them.

▶ Specify Now ports generate a physical port with a name that is long and confusing. You can change the name, but the next time you deploy your application it will be re-created.

Specify Later ports are probably the most common option. They allow the developer to basically say this: "Here is the business process, all developed and ready. Now someone should take care of defining where and how messages are to be transmitted." These types of ports provide a level of abstraction between the business process and the details about message transmitting that is essential to a good architecture of your solution.

The option that provides even looser coupling than the Specify Later ports is to use the Direct bound ports. These ports are not even connected to a physical port as the Specify Later ports are, but instead interact directly with the MessageBox by either publishing directly to the MessageBox or by setting up their own subscription on the MessageBox. Although this provides a flexible solution and loose coupling, great care must be taken especially in describing the filters on Receive shapes so as to not pick up messages you do not actually want to pick up. Filters on Receive shapes are described in the section about the Receive shape. The most common trap is a never-ending loop.

Consider this scenario: You have an orchestration that must handle all incoming orders. To accommodate this, you have a physical receive port that receives all incoming orders and maps them to your internal order format. The orchestration has a Direct bound port that receives all messages that are of your internal order type and processes them. At some point in time, the order must be sent to your ERP system, so the orchestration sends out the order, which is mapped to the format your ERP system uses in the send port.

This will end in an endless loop because each time your orchestration sends out the order to your ERP system, it is basically publishing the order to the MessageBox. Because your orchestration has a subscription that wants all orders that are published, it picks up the message it has just published itself and starts a new instance of the orchestration with this order. This continues forever. So, as you can see, great care must be taken to specify filters and thereby subscriptions so as to pick up the messages that are actually relevant to your business process.

Start Orchestration

The Start Orchestration shape is used to start up a new orchestration instance asynchronously. The orchestration that is to be started must have the type modifier set to an appropriate value to let others call it, meaning that if it is in another project/assembly, you have to mark it as public.

When you double-click the Start Orchestration shape, you get a window similar to the Call Orchestration shape. This means that you get a drop-down list of all the orchestrations that are either in the same project or in the referenced projects and that have the type modifier set appropriately. When you are choosing which orchestration to start, all the parameters the orchestration has defined appear in the column called Parameter Name, and you must choose the appropriate variables, messages, ports, and so on from the calling orchestration that are to be used as the parameters at runtime. If only one possibility that matches the type of parameter is available in the calling orchestration, it is prefilled. If more than one option exists, one is chosen for you, but you get a drop-down to choose the correct parameter.

Because the Start Orchestration shape merely starts up another orchestration, which has its own life, no out or ref parameters can be used. This is because both orchestrations do their own work and there is no way for the starting orchestration to know when the started orchestration will finish to get any results back. The starting orchestration may even have terminated.

A Start Orchestration is an asynchronous call, meaning that the calling orchestration simply starts up the started orchestration and then continues its work at the next shape after the Start Orchestration shape without caring for the life of the started orchestration.

TIP

Just as with the Call Orchestration shape, if you need to send constants in as parameters to another orchestration, you must declare variables to hold the values because constants cannot be specified in the screen where you configure the parameters for the started orchestration. You can add a Scope shape to contain the Start Orchestration shape and declare the needed variables in there and give them an initial value so that you don't have to add an Expression shape to initialize them.

NOTE

The started orchestration executes in a host instance of the host associated with it no matter what host instance the calling orchestration is executing in. This allows you to have some common functionality that can be leveraged from several orchestrations and the common functionality will then always execute with the host instance account associated with it and therefore always have the necessary rights to perform whatever is to be performed.

The way the Start Orchestration functionality works behind the scenes is that after an orchestration is enlisted, that is to be started from another orchestration, an activating subscription is created in the MessageBox. The subscription merely contains one property called ActivationServiceID. The subscription states that this property must have a value corresponding to the strong name of the orchestration that has the subscription. At runtime when an orchestration uses the Start Orchestration shape to start up another orchestration, all the parameters for the new orchestration are grouped as message parts in a new message, which has the ActivationServiceID property promoted and it is then published to the MessageBox. The orchestration with the right subscription is then fired up and provided the individual message parts from the published message as parameters.

> **TIP**
>
> The Start Orchestration is great for asynchronous processing of functionality, but using the Start Orchestration shape nonetheless still imposes a binding between the calling and the called orchestration. Consider using Direct bound ports instead to create fully loosely coupled functionality.

Receive

The Receive shape is used to indicate where in the business process a message is received into the business process. This can be the messages that fires up the business process, such as the reception of an order, or it can be the response from sending a query to a system or trading partner or something else that arrives.

The Receive shape is dragged onto the orchestration surface and configured using the properties in the properties window, as shown in Figure 4.26.

FIGURE 4.26   Properties for the Receive shape.

The properties of the Receive shape are described in Table 4.3 (except for the three general properties described earlier).

TABLE 4.3   Properties of the Receive Shape

Property Name	Description
Activate	This property can be set to either True or False. If set to True, this means that receiving a message to this Receive shape activates the orchestration and thereby fires up a new instance of the orchestration. If set to False, which is the default, the orchestration must be initialized in some other way, which can either be by calling it or starting it from another orchestration.

TABLE 4.3   Properties of the Receive Shape

Property Name	Description
Filter Expression	This property is available only if the Activate property is set to True. In this property, you can describe a filter that describes which messages this Receive shape wants to subscribe to. If the Receive shape is connected to a Direct bound port, which is described later, the filter makes up the entire subscription in the MessageBox. If the port is not Direct bound, the filter entered here is added to the filter that is created automatically when binding the logical port to a physical port.
Following Correlation Sets	This property is available only if the Activate property is set to False. In this property, you can specify what correlation set to follow in this port. When following a correlation set, the values needed to fulfill the correlation are added to the subscription that is created automatically. Correlation sets are explained later in this chapter.
Initializing Correlation Sets	This property is used to instruct the orchestration engine about any correlation sets that should be initialized upon reception of a message in this Receive shape.
Message	This property specifies the message that will be received in this Receive shape. This counts as a message construction, so the message can be used after the Receive shape, but as with all messages, it cannot be altered.
Operation	This property specifies the operation of a port that the Receive shape is connected to. Normally you do not change this value at all because it is set automatically when you connect a Receive shape with an operation on a port in the port surface.

Role Link

Role links are used to add a level of abstraction to your business process, allowing you to send and receive messages to and from a role, like a supplier instead of just sending out a messasge, and letting BizTalk choose which supplier and hence which send port to use at runtime.

Role links have roles that are either a provider or a consumer. The provider role is used for the role that provides a service and hence will be receiving the first message. The consumer role consumes a service and will therefore send the first message.

When using a consumer role, you must set some identifier on the role that the runtime engine can use to determine which trading partner you actually want the message to go to. This is done in an Expression shape with code like this:

```
ConfirmOrder(Microsoft.XLANGs.BaseTypes.DestinationParty) = new
Microsoft.XLANGs.BaseTypes.Party(Identifier, Qualifier);
```

The identifier and qualifier must then match an alias created for a partner in the Administration Console, and at runtime a send port that is connected to this party and enlisted in the correct role is used to send the message through. For instance, if it is an order coming from your ERP system, the supplier probably has a supplier ID, which can be output from the ERP system and at the same time used in an alias for the appropriate BizTalk party.

When you are using the provider role, the SourceParty property can be used to find out who sent the message. This is set in the ResolveParty stage of a receive pipeline, as described in Chapter 5, "Pipelines."

Role links are added to the port surface just like ports, and a wizard guides you through creating them. There are a few steps involved in creating a role link. First you should create a role link type. The wizard helps you do so, just like the Port Wizard helps you create a port type, but if you need a role link type with only one role you must delete one of the created roles. Therefore, it is usually easier to create the role link type manually by following these steps in Orchestration View:

1. Open **Types**, right-click **Role Link Types**, and choose **New Role Link Type**.

2. Provide an identifier for the role link type and optionally change the Type Modifier property and provide a description of it in the properties of the new role link type.

3. Open the created role link type and click the created role inside the role link type.

4. Provide a name for the role and optionally a description of it.

5. Right-click the role and choose **Add Port Type**. This opens the wizard for creating a port type.

6. Click **Next** and either use an existing port type or create a new port type using the wizard as you would normally do for port types. Notice, that the access restrictions of the port type you will be creating must encompass the type modifier of any role link types that use this port type.

7. After creating a port type, you can set the Message Type property of the operation in the port type or you can have it set automatically once a Send or Receive shape is connected to it.

8. If the role link type must be both a provider and a consumer, right-click the role link type and choose **New Role**. Then repeat steps 4–7 for the new role.

9. To add a role link of this new role link type to the port surface, either right-click a port surface or right-click **Role Links** in Orchestration View and choose **New Role Link**.

10. In the wizard, click **Next**, and then provide a name for the role link and click **Next**.

11. In the next screen, either create a new role link type or use an existing one. Creating a new role link type starts a wizard. Choose to use an existing role link type, choose the newly created role link type, and click **Next**.

12. Choose whether you will be a provider and therefore receive the first message, or a consumer, sending out the first message. Click **Finish**.

You can now connect Send or Receive shapes as needed to the roles inside the role link.

If you get an error during compile time about an uninitialized service link, this is because you haven't set the destination party of a consumer role before using it.

Send

The Send shape is used to send a message from the business process to some other system, which can be an internal system or a system at a trading partner. The Send shape must be connected to an operation on a port, just as a Receive shape must be. This is because it creates the connection that determines what port the message that is sent out should be sent through. Apart from the three standard properties (Name, Description, and Report to Analyst), the Send shape has the properties described in Table 4.4.

TABLE 4.4   Properties of the Send Shape

Property Name	Description
Following Correlation Sets	This property is used to determine what correlation sets to follow on this send. Correlation sets are explained later in this chapter.
Initializing Correlation Sets	This property is used to determine what correlation sets to initialize upon sending a message from this Send shape.
Message	This property is used to determine what message must be sent.
Operation	This property specifies what operation on what port to connect this Send shape to.

Connecting the Send shape to the operation of a port automatically sets the value of the Operation property of the Send shape.

Following a correlation set on a Send shape might seem odd, but it makes sense, because this is the way to promote properties in messages you have constructed and assigned values to the properties in Message Assignment shapes. If you do not follow or initialize a correlation set that is of a correlation type that contains these properties, they are merely written to the context and not promoted and hence cannot be used for routing later on.

Suspend

The Suspend shape is used if the programmer of an orchestration needs the orchestration to suspend in case some error condition has occurred. When an orchestration instance is suspended, it can be resumed only in the BizTalk Administration Console.

The suspension automatically incurs dehydration of the orchestration instance to the MessageBox, and when resumed, the orchestration instance is rehydrated and continues running from the last persisted point.

The Suspend shape has one property to be set called Error Message, which is a string that describes the error that has occurred that required a suspension of the orchestration instance. The message is viewable by the administrator when looking at the details of the suspended orchestration instance inside the Administration Console.

> **NOTE**
>
> If you are using the Suspend shape inside an orchestration that is called synchro-
> nously from another orchestration by using the Call Orchestration shape, the calling
> orchestration and any nested calling orchestrations are also suspended. This is
> because the nature of a synchronous call is to wait for the answer, so the calling
> orchestrations cannot continue anyway until the called orchestration finishes.

Terminate

The Terminate shape is used to terminate a running orchestration instance without letting
it run to a normal end of the processing. This is most often used as part of exception
handling if some exception occurs that cannot be dealt with inside the orchestration.
Termination inside a Parallel Actions shape terminates the orchestration instance immediately, without letting the other branches finish their processing.

The Terminate has one property to be set called Error Message, which is a string that
describes the error that has occurred that required termination of the orchestration
instance. The message is viewable by the administrator when looking at the details of the
terminated orchestration instance inside the Administration Console.

> **NOTE**
>
> If you are using the Terminate shape inside an orchestration that is called synchro-
> nously from another orchestration by using the Call Orchestration shape, the calling
> orchestration and any nested calling orchestrations are also terminated. This is
> because the nature of a synchronous call is to wait for the answer, so the calling
> orchestrations cannot continue anyway until the called orchestration finishes.

Throw Exception

The Throw Exception shape is added to the orchestration surface and used to throw an
exception at runtime in the processing of your business process if something excetional
has occurred.

Other than the three standard properties (Name, Description, and Report to Analyst), the
shape itself has a property used to specify the exception to throw, called Exception Object.
When changing this property, you get a drop-down list consisting of the string General
Exception along with all the variables in the current scope that have the class
System.Exception as base class. The option General Exception can be used only in an
exception handler block, because it simply translates into the C# throw, which just
rethrows an existing exception. If you choose a variable that is a derivation of
System.Exception, you must first instantiate it. If the Use Default Constructor property of
the variable is set to True, the object is automatically instantiated when the orchestration
starts up using the default constructor. Either way, you should instantiate the object in an
Expression shape before throwing it so that you can provide a descriptive error message.
This also means that the default instantiation of the object is a waste of time, and you
should therefore set the Use Default Constructor to False.

TIP

When used inside an exception handler block, remember to include the thrown exception as the inner exception of your own exception object to provide better error information for the poor guy who will be troubleshooting.

Transform

The Transform shape is used to perform a transformation of messages inside your business process. Performing a transformation inside an orchestration effectively creates one or more messages that are the output of the transformation. This means that a Transform shape must be located inside a Construct Message shape. As a matter of fact, when you drag a Transform shape onto the orchestration surface, it is automatically placed inside a Construct Message shape.

The Construct Message shape must be set up to describe which messages are constructed inside the shape. Setting up the Transform shape can be done in two ways; either by using the Properties window or by double-clicking the shape to get a screen to help you. If you double-click the shape, you get the screen shown in Figure 4.27.

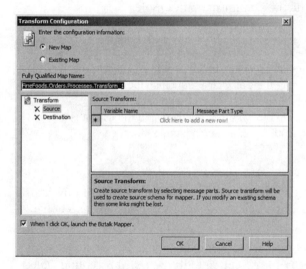

FIGURE 4.27   Configuring the Transform shape.

As you can see, your first choice is between whether to use an existing map located in either the project of the orchestration or in an assembly referenced from this project or whether to create a new map based on the choices you make in this screen.

If you choose to use an existing map, the text box for the fully qualified map name becomes a drop-down box, where you can choose between either <Select a Map File>, which is just a text placeholder and cannot really be chosen (you will get an error when you click OK), any of the maps in the existing project, or Select from Referenced Assembly, which opens an object browser that enables you to browse through the referenced assemblies to locate the map you want to use. After choosing the map to use, you must choose what messages will be the source for the map and what messages will be the destination of the map. This is done by selecting either Source or Destination on the left side of the screen and then in the drop-down on the right side choosing the appropriate messages. Notice that there is a red cross next to messages that do not have a type that matches the type of message the map uses and a green check mark next to the messages that have a matching type.

If you choose to create a new map, you must first provide a fully qualified map name for it. Everything after the last period you provide is the class name and also the name of the map file. Everything before the last period is the .NET namespace for the map. You should only change the values in the string provided to you after the last period to ensure that the map is in the same .NET namespace as the rest of the project. Later, when you click OK, the map is generated for you in your project, from which you can later move it to another project if you like. After naming the map, which can be renamed later on if you want, you must choose the messages to use as source and destination of the map that is to be created. You can choose any number of messages both as source and as destination messages. If you choose multiple messages for the source of the map, the map is created with a schema that includes each of the schemas for the selected messages as a child of the root node. Figure 4.28 shows an example of choosing multiple messages as the source.

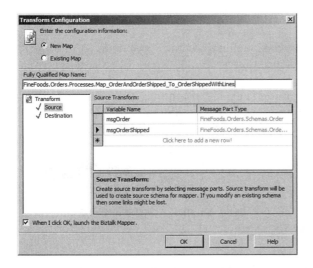

FIGURE 4.28   Choosing multiple messages as the source for a map.

As an example, if you have the schemas shown in Figure 4.29 and Figure 4.30 and create messages of these two schemas in your orchestrations and use both messages as source in a map, the source schema of the map will look as shown in Figure 4.31.

FIGURE 4.29   First input schema for map.

FIGURE 4.30   Second input schema for map.

FIGURE 4.31   Generated source schema for a map with multiple inputs.

As you can see, the two input schemas are wrapped in a common root node. At runtime, the orchestration engine generates an instance that wraps the two messages and uses this as input for the map. For destination schemas, the same applies. An intermediate schema is generated and used as the destination of the map, and at runtime, the orchestration engine extracts the destination messages from the generated output. This approach is especially clever if you need to either combine two or more messages into one or split a message into several messages.

TIP

Splitting of a message into several messages can be done by using multiple maps in different Transform shapes and does not have to be in one map. Doing it in one map, though, increases performance, because only one transformation has to be performed.

You can only create maps that have several source or destination schemas inside an orchestration. After creating them from within a Transform shape, they are added to your Visual Studio 2010 project and can be altered afterward.

Enabling the When I Click OK, Launch the BizTalk Mapper option in the screen opens the map in the Mapper tool when you click OK, both if you have chosen to use an existing map and if you have chosen to create a new map. If you have chosen to create a new map and do not enable this option, the map is simply created with source and destination schema with no links in it.

TIP

Transformations inside your business process should be minimized. For instance, try to prevent transforming anything into the format it must have when sending it to another system or trading partner. Maps on send ports are a better fit for these transformations. You want to keep your business process unaware and independent of specific formats used by other systems and trading partners. Inside a business process, you should only do business transformations on the internal schemas used by your business.

Delivery Notification and Handling Retries

When you let your orchestration send out a message, you can set some retry properties on the physical send port. These settings allow you to specify the number of times to retry and the interval between them. It can be desirable to get information in your orchestration as to whether the send of a message went well. For instance, you might want to update a database table with information about the status of the message or only send out another message if the first message was sent successfully.

The default behavior of the orchestration is that a Send shape has executed successfully if the message was published to the MessageBox without errors. The orchestration engine then gives the messaging engine the responsibility of actually sending out the message and continues the orchestration after the Send shape. The orchestration never knows whether anything went wrong with the actual transmission of the message.

If you want to get this information, you need to do two things:

▶ The logical send port in your orchestration must have its Delivery Notification property set to Transmitted.

▶ The Send shape must be enclosed in a scope. The scope must have an exception handler that catches the `Microsoft.XLANGs.BaseTypes.DeliveryFailureException`.

What happens is that when you set the Delivery Notification property to Transmitted, you are instructing the adapter to send back an ACK/NACK whether the transmission went well. The orchestration catches this ACK/NACK, and in case it was a NACK, the orchestration throws a `DeliveryFailureException`, which you must then catch. The ACK/NACK is not delivered to the orchestration until the end of the scope, so do not do anything after the Send shape inside the Scope shape that you only want done if the transmission went well.

> **TIP**
>
> If you search the Internet for information about this, you will find several posts that describe that the retry count of the physical send port must be zero for this to work. This is not true, however. The ACK/NACN is sent to the orchestration once the physical send port has exhausted its options, meaning that it will do its retries first and not until the send port gives up entirely will the ACK/NACK be sent.

Knowing what happened can prove useful if you need to hold off processing of the business process until the message has been successfully transmitted. In the exception handler, you can suspend the orchestration, and then after a BizTalk operator has fixed the issue with the message and resumed the suspended message instance and it has been successfully transmitted, the orchestration instance can be resumed and then continues its work.

Another option that might prove useful is to wrap the Scope shape in a Loop shape. This is especially useful if the issue with transmitting the message cannot be solved outside the business process. You can then wrap your Scope shape in a loop and keep a Boolean variable with a value determining whether the loop should be ended. This also allows you to simply keep looping even though the send port gives up. Note, however, that this requires that the suspended message instances that the physical send port could not deliver must be terminated and not resumed, because you will send multiple copies of the message otherwise.

Calling Pipelines

You have the option of calling a pipeline from within your orchestration. This is useful for several reasons:

- ▶ You have called an external assembly that has returned a string that you need to convert into XML and create a message from, just as if the string had been picked up by a receive location.

- ▶ You have a message that requires debatching inside the orchestration. Perhaps you have received an order, for example, and you need to perform something specific for each order line. This can also be achieved using the xpath function.

- ▶ You want to assemble multiple messages into one message.

The engine provides a class that lets you execute a pipeline. This class is called Microsoft.XLANGs.Pipeline.XLANGPipelineManager. It has two methods that are relevant:

- ▶ ExecuteReceivePipeline: This method executes a receive pipeline.

- ▶ ExecuteSendPipeline: This method executes a send pipeline.

To use the class, you need to reference Microsoft.XLANGs.Pipeline.dll, which you can find in the BizTalk installation folder.

Some limitations apply as to which pipelines you can call from within an orchestration and what is available to you in the pipeline. For a full description of this, refer to http://msdn.microsoft.com/en-us/library/aa562035(BTS.70).aspx.

Receive Pipelines

The ExecuteReceivePipeline method of the Microsoft.XLANGs.Pipeline.XLANGPipelineManager class takes in two parameters:

▶ A System.Type, which is the type of the pipeline to execute

▶ An XLANGMessage, which is the message to use as the input for the pipeline

As output the method returns an instance of the ReceivePipelineOutputMessages class. The output is not serializable, and therefore the call to this method needs to be done inside an atomic scope with a variable for the output declared locally.

The ReceivePipelineOutputMessages inherits from IEnumerator and as such it has a couple of methods that are relevant:

▶ MoveNext is the method that will move the IEnumerator internal cursor to the next element in the enumeration

▶ GetCurrent is the method to be used to get the current message from the enumeration.

Listing 4.7 provides a simple example of how to call a receive pipeline from within an orchestration.

LISTING 4.7   How to Call a Receive Pipeline from an Orchestration

```
pipeOut =
Microsoft.XLANGs.Pipeline.XLANGPipelineManager.ExecuteReceivePipeline(
    typeof(FineFoods.Pipelines.ReceivePipeline), msgInput);

pipeOut.MoveNext();

msgNew = null;



pipeOut.GetCurrent(msgNew);
```

Note that this needs to be done within a Message Assignment shape because you are constructing a new message. The code assumes that only one output is created. If the receive pipeline debatches msgInput into several message, you can use a Loop shape that has pipeOut.MoveNext() as the condition for the loop and inside the loop extract each message and do what you need to do with it.

> **NOTE**
>
> Because all this processing has to occur inside an atomic Scope shape, you will get no persistence points for the entire call to the receive pipeline and for the handling of all the output messages. You need to know and accept the consequences of this.
>
> First, because there is no persistence point, any messages you send out are not actually delivered to the physical send ports until the entire atomic transaction has committed.
>
> Second, if you call a .NET helper class for each message and at some point BizTalk crashes or an exception occurs, you are potentially in an inconsistent state because of what the .NET helper class has done. Consider creating your helper class as a transactional class to enlist in the atomic transaction.
>
> Third, you cannot do any request-response calls for each message like invoking a web service. This limitation is described later in this chapter, but in short, inside an atomic Scope shape you cannot have both the Send and corresponding Receive shape for a request-response port.

Send Pipelines

The `ExecuteSendPipeline` method of the `Microsoft.XLANGs.Pipeline.XLANGPipelineManager` class takes in three parameters:

- A `System.Type`, which is the type of the pipeline to execute
- A `SendPipelineInputMessages`, which is an enumeration of all the messages to send to the `Assemble` method one at the time
- An `XLANGMessage`, which is the message that is returned by the send pipeline

The method does not have any output but will change the third parameter to contain the result of executing the send pipeline.

Listing 4.8 provides a simple example of how to call a send pipeline from within an orchestration.

LISTING 4.8   How to Call a Send Pipeline from an Orchestration

```
inputMsgs = new Microsoft.XLANGs.Pipeline.SendPipelineInputMessages();


inputMsgs.Add(msg);

Microsoft.XLANGs.Pipeline.XLANGPipelineManager.ExecuteSendPipeline(
    typeof(FineFoods.Orders.Processes.SendPipeline), inputMsgs, msgOrderShipped);
```

Note that this needs to be done within a Message Assignment shape because you are constructing a new message; although, it doesn't seem like it. The sample code assumes that only one input is used. If the send pipeline needs several inputs to assemble them, you just need to call the `Add` method of the `SendPipelineInputMessages` class several times. You can use a Loop shape to loop around something and create all the messages that need to be assembled.

If you are leveraging the built-in XmlTransmit send pipeline, you should set the envelope schema name manually, as shown here:

```
MyMessage(XMLNORM.EnvelopeSpecName) = "FineFoods.Orders.Schemas.EnvSchema,
FineFoods.Orders.Schemas, Version=1.0.0.0, Culture=neutral,
PublicKeyToken=922354cb3fffba23";
```

This also applies to any other send pipelines you have created where the envelope schema needs to be specified at runtime. Alternatively, you can create a custom send pipeline, using the XML assembler component and set the envelope specification name at design time on the assembler component.

Web Services

This section deals with exposing and consuming web services, as this is a common requirement and it requires a bit more work than leveraging your normal adapters such as the FILE adapter, FTP adapter, or any of the others.

Exposing Web Services

If you want to expose a web service, you should run through the BizTalk WCF Service Publishing Wizard. This wizard guides you through choosing what you want to expose as a web service.

This section walks you through the wizard step by step.

1. To start the wizard, go to **Start**, **All Programs**, **Microsoft BizTalk Server 2010**, **BizTalk WCF Service Publishing Wizard**. This fires up a welcoming screen, on which you just click **Next**. Consider disabling the welcoming screen for the future by checking the check box at the bottom. You will now see the screen shown in Figure 4.32.

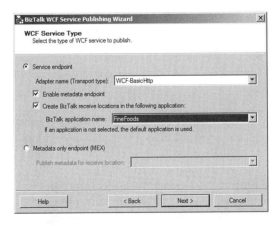

FIGURE 4.32   Choosing an endpoint type and adapter for the WCF Service Publishing Wizard.

2. Choose the **Service Endpoint** option, and choose which adapter to use. For a description of the adapters and for details about WCF and BizTalk, see other chapters in this book. Check **Enable Metadata Endpoint** if you want to expose the metadata about the service. If this is not checked, no one can automatically browse to http://yourserviceurl.com?wsdl to get the metadata and automatically generate the proxy classes that are needed to call the web service. Checking the **Create BizTalk Receive Locations in the Following Application** option lets the wizard create receive locations for you that match what you have chosen in the wizard. The receive locations can be renamed and reconfigured later if needed. If you choose the **Metadata Only Endpoint (MEX)** option, you get the option to publish a WCF service based on the current setup of a configured receive location. Click **Next** to open the screen shown in Figure 4.33.

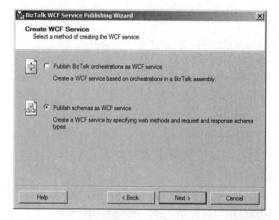

FIGURE 4.33   Choosing what to publish in the WCF Service Publishing Wizard.

TIP

Check the **Enable Metadata Endpoint** check box on development and test servers, but disable it on production servers. The information should not be needed on a production server because all development against your service should be done in a development or test environment.

---

3. In this screen, you need to choose if you will be exposing an orchestration as a web service or one or more schemas. Exposing an orchestration as a web service requires that the port type used for the port that is to be exposed from your orchestration is public. Exposing an orchestration should be avoided because this creates a service that has an interface that is the message type of the message your orchestration receives. This created a tight coupling of your exposed services and your internal business processes. A better option is to choose to expose one or more schemas, because this allows you to develop schemas to be used for the interface and then

map to and from these schemas in your two-way receive port. Click **Next** to get to the screen shown in Figure 4.34.

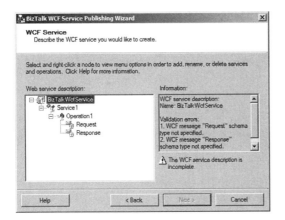

FIGURE 4.34   Defining names of service, operations and messages, and types of messages.

4. You can right-click any element in the tree view and choose to rename it. The service and the operation can also be deleted and replaced with something else. If you want a one-way web service, for instance, remove **Operation1**, right-click the service, and choose **Add Web Method**, **One-Way**. The name of the root node is used as the default name for the virtual directory that will be created for the web service in Internet Information Services (IIS). You should name your root node, service name, operation name, and message names appropriately. You also need to choose types for the messages. This is done by right-clicking either the **Request** or the **Response** and choosing **Select Schema Type**. This provides you with a file selector, where you need to find the assembly that contains the schema you want to use for that particular message, as shown in Figure 4.35.

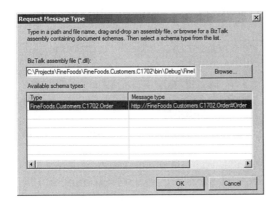

FIGURE 4.35   Selecting a type for a message in a published web service.

TIP

If the strong name of the assembly you point out matches an assembly that is in the *Global Assembly Cache* (GAC), the assembly in the GAC is used instead of the one you have chosen using the file explorer. This means that if you do any updates in your assembly, you need to add the new assembly to the GAC to get the wizard to use the updated assembly.

---

5. After naming all services, operations, and messages, you will have something similar to Figure 4.36.

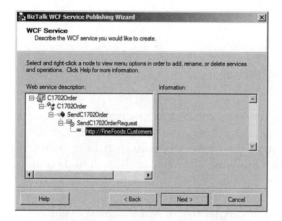

FIGURE 4.36   Configured web service before the actual deployment.

6. Clicking **Next** brings you to the screen where you need to set a target namespace for the web service itself. This does not influence the namespace of the XML you will be receiving in the end and therefore not the contract between you and the sending party. Figure 4.37 shows this screen.

7. Clicking **Next** takes you to the screen where you need to choose the location to deploy the web service to, as shown in Figure 4.38.

8. Web services published by BizTalk needs to run on a BizTalk Server. In Figure 4.38, the location is a virtual directory called C1702Order located at the root of the local-host website. If this is not the first time you are publishing a web service to this URL, the Overwrite Existing Location check box is enabled, allowing you to check it if you want the existing location to be overwritten. You also need to choose whether to allow anonymous access to the web service. If you do not allow anonymous access, integrated security is required for the web service. Clicking **Next** brings up the summary, as shown in Figure 4.39.

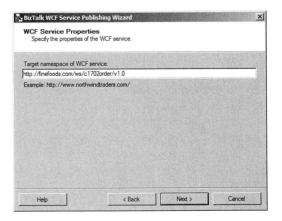

FIGURE 4.37   Setting the target namespace of a published web service.

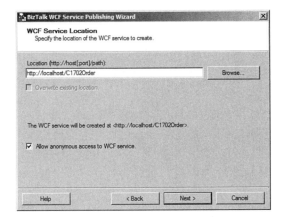

FIGURE 4.38   Choosing the location for the web service.

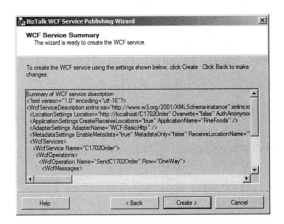

FIGURE 4.39   Summary of wizard configuration before actual publishing.

TIP

A command-line tool is available that can do the WCF publishing for you, which is very useful if you need to republish a web service in case of schema changes or other changes. You can find information about the command-line tool and a download link at the MSDN site at http://msdn.microsoft.com/en-us/library/bb245933(BTS.70).aspx. Note that the utility works for BizTalk 2010, although the download states it is for BizTalk 2006R2. The command-line tool takes in a lot of parameters, but the easiest way to republish a web service is to mark the summary XML and copy it to an XML file. This XML file contains all the information needed by the command-line tool to republish a web service.

---

9. Click **Create** and then click **Finish** to quite the wizard

After publishing of the web service, you need to make sure of two things:

- ▶ The IIS application pool your virtual directory is set to run under needs to run as a user that is a member of the BizTalk Isolated Host Users group.

- ▶ The host assigned to the receive location must be the one you actually want to use.

Consuming Web Services

To consume a web service from a BizTalk orchestration, you need to add the metadata about the web service to your BizTalk project. The metadata is mainly contained in the schemas that describe the messages that are sent to the web service and received from the web service.

To consume a web service, follow these steps:

1. Right-click the project that should have the metadata about the web service in it and choose **Add**, **Add Generated Items**. You will see the screen shown in Figure 4.40.

2. Choose the **Consume WCF Service** option and click **Add**. You will now see a welcome page. Optionally, check the **Do Not Show This Welcome Page Again** check box, and then click **Next** to get to the screen, as shown in Figure 4.41.

3. The Metadata File (WSDL and XSD) option allows you to use .WSDL files and .XSD files that you have locally on your server. It doesn't know anything about the location of the actual service or which binding is needed, though. The Metadata Exchange (MEX) Endpoint option allows you to get the binding information needed to create a send port that can call this web service and the needed schemas and so on. So for this example, choose that option. Then click **Next** to see the screen, as shown in Figure 4.42.

4. Enter the URL to the service endpoint, click **Get**, and if no errors occur, click **Next**.

5. On the next screen, you can change the .NET namespace of the artifacts that are added to your project if you want to. Click **Import** after you have decided whether you want to change the .NET namespace.

FIGURE 4.40   Add generated items to your BizTalk project.

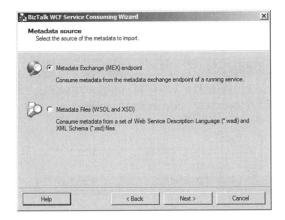

FIGURE 4.41   Choosing the source of metadata.

The wizard now generates some artifacts and puts them into your BizTalk project for you.

The following artifacts are added to the project:

- ▶ **Two XML binding files:** One is for the binding that is used by the service, and the other is for the WCF-Custom binding. You can import either one into your BizTalk application to create the necessary send port. Using the WCF-Custom binding gives you the best possibility of updating settings later on, whereas the other binding file has just what is needed to create the send port.

- ▶ **An orchestration file:** This basically just contains one or more port types and one or more message types, depending on the number of message types and port types are specified in the .WSDL file. These port types and message types can be used in your other orchestrations to call the service in question.

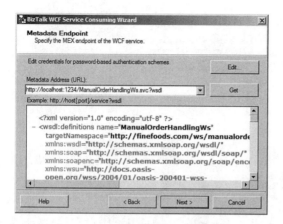

FIGURE 4.42   Specifying the metadata endpoint of the service to consume.

▸ **One or more .XSD files:** These describe the messages that are sent to and from the service operations. The XSDs are used as the base types of the message types and operations in the orchestration that is created.

TIP

You don't have to keep the generated orchestration. After the project is deployed, it will show up in the Administration Console and just disturb you. You can simply move the message types and port types from the orchestration to another orchestration that will actually use them.

TIP

Although using the generated port types and message types might seem easy and straightforward, this doesn't necessarily mean that it is a good idea. Should you choose to use these message types and port types, the business logic inside the orchestration will be strongly coupled to the service. In case of changes in the service, this means a redeployment of the entire orchestration and possibly versioning. Therefore, do what you would do with other integration scenarios, which is to use internal schemas and do any necessary mapping in the send port. You can still use the generated binding file to create the send port. Just remember to add the needed maps that map the service schemas to and from your internal schemas.

Dehydration and Rehydration

When lots of orchestration instances are executed at the same time, this takes up a lot of *central processing unit* (CPU), memory, and other resources. Performance can therefore take a hit. At any given time, some of the orchestration instances that are running are either delayed for a period of time or awaiting a message from another system, and they do not, therefore, need to be in memory but can be taken out of memory and brought back into memory when they should continue execution. Also, if too many instances are running at the same time and the engine determines that performance is decreasing, it might decide to take some instances out of memory even if they are actually ready to execute.

The process of taking an orchestration instance out of memory is called dehydration, and the process of loading an orchestration instance back into memory is called rehydration.

There are many situations in which the orchestration engine can choose to dehydrate a running orchestration instance, including the following:

▶ A Receive shape is waiting to receive a message. This can also happen in a Listen shape if the Receive shape is not activating.

▶ A Delay shape has been started up with a time span greater than some defined threshold.

Rehydration happens either if the engine determines enough memory is free for an orchestration instance that is ready to run or when the event a dehydrated instance is waiting for is fired. This can be a message arriving or a Delay shape timing out. Upon rehydration, the engine chooses a server with an appropriate host instance and rehydrates the orchestration to this server. This means that an orchestration instance can run on one server, get dehydrated, and then gets rehydrated on another server.

BizTalk uses several values in determining when to dehydrate a running orchestration instance. These values are set in the configuration file for the BizTalk process and can be found at <Installation Folder>\BTSNTSvc.exe.config. At runtime, the values are read and an algorithm is executed to determine whether any orchestration instances should be dehydrated. You can find the specifics about the values to set and the algorithm used at http://msdn.microsoft.com/en-us/library/aa995563(BTS.10).aspx.

Correlations

Correlations are used to associate a message that is published to the MessageBox with the correct instance of an orchestration. This is typically necessary when a message has been received from a trading partner or an internal IT system, but it can just as well be because another orchestration has published a message to the MessageBox that must be picked up by another orchestration.

Consider, for instance, that your ERP system sends out 100 orders to a number of suppliers. If this is handled by a business process, it fires up 100 orchestrations that send out the order to the supplier and then possibly wait for the order confirmation to arrive to escalate the matter if no order confirmation arrives within some specified time. Once an order confirmation is received in a receive port and published to the MessageBox, it is for only 1 of the 100 orchestrations, and the runtime must decide which 1 of the 100 orchestrations to send the order confirmation to. This is done using correlations.

Correlations basically consist of a correlation type and a correlation set, which is an instance of a correlation type. The correlation type is a set of promoted properties, which must constitute a key that is unique for the messages that are involved in receiving or sending messages to and from systems or trading partners where you need to correlate the messages back to the correct instance of an orchestration.

A correlation set is initialized on either a Receive shape or a Send shape. Upon initializing, the orchestration engine remembers the values that are in the promoted properties of the message that is either received or sent. When a Receive shape later on follows the same correlation set, the subscription that is created in the MessageBox has the correlation set appended to it, meaning that the promoted properties that are in the correlation type must have the values that were in the message that originally initialized the correlation set.

In the preceding example with the 100 orders, the order number could be used because it is present in the outgoing order to the suppliers and they will include the order number in the order confirmation.

> **NOTE**
>
> Because the correlation type consists of a set of promoted properties, each message that is involved in either a Send or Receive shape that uses the correlation set, *must* have the promoted properties promoted. This means that if the order number is to be used across an order and an order confirmation, both schemas must have the order number promoted to the *same* promoted property, which is then used in the correlation type.
>
> The only exception to this is the properties that are marked as MessageContextPropertyBase, in which case the messages do not have to have anything promoted to the properties, because the properties can have values that do not come from the message itself, like BTS.ReceivePortName and other pure context values.

The correlation type can consist of an arbitrary number of properties. So if your ERP system has an order number sequence for each supplier, you could let the correlation type consist of the order number and the supplier number.

> **NOTE**
>
> BizTalks documentation states that you can use a maximum of three properties in a correlation type. This is not true, as stated previously. What is true, however, is that a correlation set that is used in a convoy can only have three properties in it. Convoys are explained later in this chapter.
>
> This restriction comes from the fact that the MessageBox has specific tables that deal with convoys because there is a lot of extra logic around them, and these tables are hard-coded to contain only a maximum of three *globally unique identifiers* (GUIDs) that point to properties.

Inside an orchestration, all Receive shapes must either have the Activate property set to True or they must follow a correlation set that has already been initialized either in another Receive shape or a Send shape. If you do not make sure to adhere to this constraint, you will get an error about this at compile time. The reason for this constraint is fairly simple. If a Receive shape is not the one that will be firing up a new instance of an orchestration, it must make sure that it only receives messages that are for a specific instance of the orchestration at runtime. By specifying which correlation set to follow on a Receive shape, you are effectively doing two things:

▶ You tell the compiler that you have thought about this and that you guarantee it will work just fine at runtime.

▶ You tell how the runtime can be sure of which messages go into which orchestration instances.

At runtime, when an orchestration gets to a Receive shape that is following a correlation set, it creates an *instance subscription* in the MessageBox. An instance subscription is a subscription that is specific for an instance of the orchestration, and this means that the subscription that is created contains the predicates that are normally present for a subscription for a Receive shape, such as the `ReceivePortID` and the `MessageType`, but it also includes the properties that are in the correlation type that is used for the correlation set that is being followed.

Using this instance subscription the MessageBox can locate the correct instance of an orchestration that is waiting for the incoming message.

Correlation types and correlation sets are specified in Orchestration View, as shown in Figure 4.43. As you can see, correlation types, like all other types, are defined globally, whereas correlation sets can actually be defined either globally or within a scope. When defined inside a Scope shape, the correlation set is naturally not accessible outside the Scope shape.

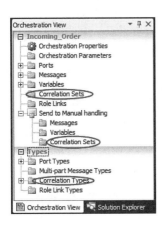

FIGURE 4.43   Where to define correlation types and correlation sets.

Because a correlation set is based on a correlation type, you must specify the correlation type first. This is done inside Orchestration View by right-clicking **Correlation Types** under Types and choosing **New Correlation Type**. When doing this, you get the screen shown in Figure 4.44, in which you must choose what properties are in this correlation type. You can change these later if you need to modify it.

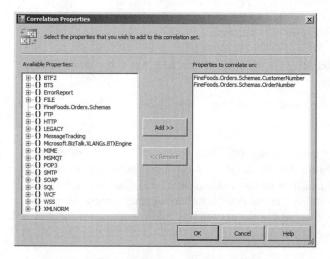

FIGURE 4.44   Choosing properties for new correlation type.

As you can see in Figure 4.44, you can add both properties that are from your own property schemas and properties that are from built-in property schemas. Therefore, you can correlate on the subject line of incoming emails, for instance, or any other promoted properties.

TIP

Because the correlation types are used to route messages to the right instance of an orchestration, the same restrictions apply to correlation types as for normal routing. This means that you can only use properties that are promoted as promoted properties and not properties that are merely written as promoted properties. For a further discussion on the difference between these, see Chapter 2.

After choosing the promoted properties for the correlation type, you can change some properties of the type. Table 4.5 describes these properties.

TABLE 4.5   Properties of a Correlation Type

Property Name	Description
Correlation Properties	This contains the promoted properties that are chosen for this correlation type. Click the ellipsis at the right to open the screen shown in Figure 4.44.
Description	Contains a textual description of this correlation type.

TABLE 4.5   Properties of a Correlation Type

Property Name	Description
Identifier	Contains a name for the correlation type.
Object Type	Always set to Correlation Type.
Report to Analyst	Determines whether this type should be visible in Visio when importing the orchestration to the ODBA.
Type Modifier	Standard .NET type modifier. Can be Public, Private, or Internal and determines the accessibility of the correlation type outside the orchestration.

TIP

The default value for the Type Modifier property is Internal, meaning that the correlation type can be used throughout the same project as it is defined in. This is actually necessary only if you have correlation sets of this type that you need to pass as parameters between orchestrations. Most of the time, therefore, you can change it to Private without losing any functionality.

When defining the correlation set, you right-click the **Correlation Sets** node in Orchestration View, either globally or inside a scope, and choose **New Correlation Set**. After that, you need to change two properties of the new correlation set:

▶ Set the Identifier name to something meaningful for the correlation set.

▶ Set the Correlation Type to be the correlation type to create this correlation set as an instance of.

If you want to, you can also set the Description property to be a proper description of the correlation set.

Note that you can define as many Correlation Types as you want to, and again as many correlation sets as you want to. During the execution of an orchestration, you might need to initialize several different correlation sets and to follow them later on. You can even initialize and follow several correlation sets on one Receive or Send shape.

TIP

Other than performing correlation, correlation sets actually also have another purpose. If you at some point in your orchestration assign a value to a promoted property of your message and this property is a `MessageContextPropertyBase` property, the property is actually not promoted but merely written to the context. To get the property promoted to be able to route based on it, you need to initialize a correlation set on the Send shape, which has the property in it.

Convoys

BizTalks orchestration provides special functionality for a couple of special cases called convoys. Convoys are needed when several messages need to be correlated into one orchestration instance and a race condition might arise because the messages can arrive at basically the same time, and only one of them can initialize the correlation set and the rest must follow it.

There are two types of convoys, parallel and sequential, and these are described in this section.

Parallel Convoys

Parallel convoys are used in orchestration when you need to receive a known number of messages as the first thing in your orchestration but you do not know the order in which they will arrive.

The way to implement a parallel convoy is to add a Parallel Actions shape at the beginning of your orchestrations and let this shape have as many branches as you will be receiving messages. Each branch must have a Receive shape as the first shape, and all the Receive shapes that are the first shapes in one of the branches must initialize the same set of correlation sets.

Figure 4.45 shows an example of a very simple parallel convoy.

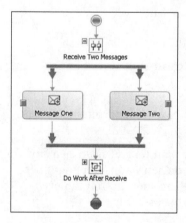

FIGURE 4.45   Simple example of parallel convoy.

What goes on behind the scenes is that once you deploy and enlist your orchestration, a subscription is created for you for each Receive shape, as you are used to. The difference between these subscriptions and the ones you normally see is that the subscriptions not only include the ReceivePortID and MessageType as usual. They also include the predicate that all the properties that form the correlation sets that are initialized in each of the Receive shapes must exist on the received messages.

At runtime, when a message arrives and a new orchestration instance fires up for this message, the other Receive shapes are automatically changed to be following the correlation set instead of initializing it. Also, if a message for another branch arrives, the engine first checks to see whether this message can be correlated into an existing orchestration instance giving the correlation sets. If it can, it is routed to the existing instance, and no new orchestration instance is fired up. If it cannot, however, a new orchestration instance is fired up to serve this incoming message. This all happens in the database, and it is not visible to you when you view the subscriptions in the Group Hub page.

Sequential Convoys

Sequential convoys are for handling incoming messages sequentially while correlating all related messages into one orchestration instance. The most common application of the sequential convoy is the aggregator pattern, in which you want to aggregate a number of messages into one message to send out a batch of messages instead of all the individual messages. This can save your company a lot of money if, for example, a *value-added network* (VAN) is used, which usually charges per message sent through it.

Sequential convoys are divided into uniform sequential convoys and nonuniform sequential convoys. A uniform sequential convoy is a sequential convoy that receives a number of messages that are of the same message type. This is among others used for the aggregator scenario. A nonuniform sequential convoy is a sequential convoy where you can receive a number of different message types into the same orchestration instance and you know the order in which they appear.

Figure 4.46 shows an example of a sequential convoy.

This example has an orchestration that is initialized upon reception of an order. The first Receive shape initializes a correlation set, which is based on the customer number found in the order. A limitation applies as to the number of promoted properties you can use in the correlation set, as discussed in the section about correlation sets. The next shape is an Expression shape, which initializes a Boolean variable to `True`, and this variable is used to indicate whether to keep looping or stop looping. Also inside the shape you can do what you need done with the first message, like initialize some variable that will contain the aggregated message, call an external assembly, or something else. After this Expression shape, there is a Loop shape, which will then continue looping until the Boolean variable is set to `False`. Another option is to let the Loop shape keep looping until a specific time or a specific number of times. Inside the loop, an Expression shape is used to determine for how long to wait for the next message to arrive and this value is then used in the Delay shape in the right-hand branch of the Listen shape that comes next. If you always want to loop say 10 times, you do not need the Expression shape, the Listen shape, and the Delay shape. Most of the time, however, you want a timeout, so you can handle it if an expected message never arrives or if you need to send your batch at least every hour or something like that. If the Delay shape fires before the Receive shape, an Expression shape is used to set the Boolean variable to `False`, effectively stopping the loop. If the Receive shape fires first, you must do whatever you need to do for each order that arrives (exemplified by a Group shape in Figure 4.46). When the loop finishes, you will probably want to send out the aggregated message if one has been created during the orchestration.

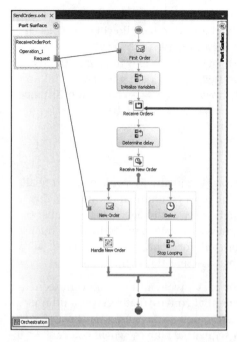

FIGURE 4.46   Example of sequential convoy.

Creating an aggregated message inside your orchestration can be achieved in a couple of ways:

▶ Maintain a variable of type System.Xml.XmlDocument that you build at runtime.

▶ Use a send pipeline with an appropriate assembler that you can call for each message and let the pipeline do the work.

▶ Create an external assembly that is used to hold the aggregated message.

Note that the restrictions about variables being binary serializable and messages being XML serializable still apply, so for all solutions you must consider the usage of these and use an appropriate scope set to have its transaction type to atomic if needed.

Sequential convoys require you to use the same port for all the Receive shapes that are involved in the convoy. It does not, however, require you to use the same operation on the port, so you still have the option of performing sequential convoys on different message types. For nonuniform sequential convoys, you just add operations as needed to your port type and then connect your Receive shapes to the appropriate operation.

Zombies

When using convoys, you might run into issues with the so-called zombie messages. A zombie message is a message that has arrived at BizTalk and has been routed to the orchestration instance that has a subscription for it, but the orchestration instance is running beyond the Receive shape or the orchestration has stopped executing before the message was delivered to the orchestration.

Consider the scenario in Figure 4.46. If a message arrives, which is queued up to be delivered to the New Order Receive shape just as the Delay shape times out, the orchestration instance continues down the rightmost branch, and the message that has been queued is not consumed by the orchestration instance.

Zombies do not occur for activating Receive shapes because these always create a new instance of your orchestration and therefore there is no orchestration instance that can move beyond the Receive shape while the message is queued up.

Convoy scenarios are more prone to zombies than when using normal orchestrations because parallel convoys are designed to deal with messages coming in, in any order, and one branch may terminate while the other is awaiting messages. Sequential convoys, on the other hand, usually have a loop that ends at some point causing messages that arrive from the point in time when the orchestration instance no longer consumes messages until the point in time when a new orchestration instance is fired up to become zombies.

To deal with zombie messages, you can write a *Windows Management Instrumentation* (WMI) script that listens to the event that is fired and then handles the situation. You may choose to send an email to an administrator, you may choose to save the message to disk and resubmit it, or any other solution that works in your business case.

Transactions

Orchestrations describe business processes. Most business processes can fail in some way or another. External assemblies may throw exceptions, external systems may be down for maintenance, network access may be broken, and other issues can occur. It is important to be able to deal with the issues that arise throughout a business process. The Scope shape provides access to an exception handler that can be used to deal with exceptions. Sometimes an exception handler isn't enough. Sometimes you want to consider a series of functionality as a transaction to deal with it at one time and to be able to get transactional behavior. This includes the ability to compensate for a transaction that has already committed.

Inside orchestrations, you have this option of using transactions to enclose functionality. In fact, you can mark your entire orchestration as a transaction if you want. Using transactions in an orchestration is done by placing a Scope shape on the orchestration and in the properties of the Scope shape choose the appropriate value for the Transaction Type property. The possible values are None, Atomic, and Long Running. The same property exists as a property on the orchestration itself. You can only set a scope to have a transaction type other than None if the orchestration itself is a long-running transaction. Atomic transactions cannot have nested transactions.

Transactional Scope shapes have three properties that nontransactional Scope shapes do not have, as described in Table 4.6.

TABLE 4.6   Properties for Scopes Marked as Either Atomic or Long Running

Property Name	Description
Compensation	Indicates the type of compensation that will occur for this transaction. The possible values are Default and Custom. Choosing Custom adds a compensate block to your Scope shape, and adding a compensate block to your Scope shape changes the property to Custom. Compensation is explained later in this section.
Timeout	Sets a timeout for the transaction. For a long-running transaction, this is the time before the TimeOutException is thrown, and for an atomic transaction, this is the time that must elapse before the transaction is considered to have failed, but only if it was engaged in a *Distributed Transaction Coordinator* (DTC) transaction with some other object.
Transaction Identifier	An identifier of the transaction. Primarily used in Compensate shapes to determine what transactions to compensate for.

Atomic

Scopes that have the transaction type set to Atomic are guaranteed by BizTalk to adhere to the ACID properties:

▶ **Atomic:** Everything inside the transactions is considered an atomic transaction and is guaranteed to happen or none of it will happen.

▶ **Consistent:** The system will be in a consistent state after the transaction if it was in a consistent state before the transaction. This requires the programmer to not do anything that will cause an inconsistent state, like withdraw money from one bank account and not deposit it to another account.

▶ **Isolated:** The transactions are isolated and will run as if no other transactions are running at the same time.

▶ **Durable:** After the transaction has committed, the changes are durable. This means that should anything go wrong, like a server crash, the state the orchestration was in just after the transaction committed is guaranteed to be persisted, and the orchestration can resume from that point.

Persistence of orchestrations is the process of taking an orchestration instance and persisting it to the MessageBox, allowing the orchestration engine to resume processing of the orchestration instance form this point in time in case failure occurs later. Persistence is described in a later section of this chapter. No persistence occurs inside an atomic transaction, which also means that inside a Scope shape that is marked as an atomic transaction you can define messages and variables of types that are not either binary serializable or XML serializable because they will never have to be serialized.

Scope shapes that are marked as atomic transactions have some properties that other Scope shapes do not, as described in Table 4.7.

TABLE 4.7   Properties for Scopes Marked as Atomic

Property Name	Description
Batch	The original meaning of this property was to indicate whether this atomic transaction should be processed in a batch. Doing this was supposed to allow instances of this transactions in different running orchestration instances to run simultaneously. This was supposed to improve performance, but at the risk of losing the Isolation property. Batching of atomic transactions, however, isn't supported, and the property is therefore deprecated and not actually used.
Isolation Level	Indicates the transaction isolation level. Possible values are Serializable (default), Read Committed, and Repeatable Read.
Retry	Boolean value that indicates whether this Scope shape can be retried. The logic around retrying atomic transactions is described later.

The most common usages of atomic transactions are as follows:

▶ Grouping several Send shapes, to avoid persisting the orchestration instance after each Send. Persistence is described later in this chapter.

▶ Leveraging classes that are not serializable for variables/messages.

▶ Using components that use COM+ transactions and enlist in transactions with the components.

The atomic transaction ensures that either everything that is to occur inside the transactions occurs or nothing occurs. This means that the transaction will hold state information of everything updated, including updated global variables, and only upon committing the transaction are these changes made visible to the world outside the transaction. The only exception to this relates to changes made by calls to external .NET assemblies. If you need your external assemblies to participate in the transaction, you need them to be COM+ objects derived from System.EnterpriseServices.ServicedComponents, and you need to make sure the isolation levels agree between transaction components. This is also the only scenario where the Timeout property of a Scope shape marked as an atomic transaction comes into place. If the atomic transaction participates in a DTC transaction with another ServicedComponent and the transaction takes longer than the timeout specified in the Timeout property, the transaction fails. If the transaction takes longer than the Timeout property specifies and no other components are ServicedComponents that participate in the transaction, the atomic transaction completes and commits normally.

If you are sending out messages inside your atomic transaction, the messages are actually not sent out until after the transaction commits. This is because it is impossible to automatically roll back the sending of a message to an external system. Messages are therefore sent to the MessageBox, but they are not released for routing until the transaction commits. Therefore, you cannot have a Receive shape that follows a correlation set that was initialized inside the same atomic transaction. The reason for this is that you would end up in a deadlock if you could. The instance subscription for the Receive shape would not be visible to the routing engine before the transaction was committed and the transaction wouldn't be able to commit until after a message has been received at the Receive shape. This also means that you cannot call a request-response port and get the result back inside the same atomic scope, because this is basically using correlation sets internally.

Setting the Retry property to True does not mean that the transaction will retry if it fails. A Scope marked as an atomic transaction only fails if either you throw a `Microsoft.XLANGs.BaseTypes.RetryTransactionException` explicitly or if a `Microsoft.XLANGs.BaseTypes.PersistenceException` occurs while the transaction is being committed. The `PersistenceException` is caused by database connectivity issues while committing and it also occurs if a component that was enlisted in the transaction fails upon committing. The `RetryTransactionException` is not thrown automatically but must be thrown by the code manually in case a retry is needed. An atomic transaction retries up to 21 times and the delay between retries is 2 seconds by default. If you are throwing a `RetryTransactionException` exception, you can set the value of the `DelayFor` property of the exception object to something other than 2 seconds if you determine that another delay is needed for some reason.

All other exceptions than the `RetryTransactionException` and the `PersistenceException` cause the orchestration to be suspended, and you can then resume it from the Administration Console.

> **NOTE**
>
> Using atomic scopes might seem like a good idea because you then get to use objects that are not serializable and you get some nice transactional behavior and more. Be aware, though, that atomic transactions also impose an overhead on your business logic, which includes a persistence point after committing that might not be necessary. So use the atomic transactions only when they are actually required.

> **TIP**
>
> Instead of using an atomic transaction to leverage a helper class you have built that is not binary serializable, consider marking your methods as static. Static methods can be used without transactions

Long Running

Atomic transactions are useful to guarantee execution of units of work atomically. For business processes that take a long time to finish, this is not very practical, however, because data would be locked for a long time. Business processes can take hours, days, and even months to complete. This is why long-running transactions are introduced. They guarantee consistency and durability but not atomicity and isolation. In other words, as long as you develop the business process in a suitable way, the state of your business will be consistent and the engine guarantees durability. (That is, changes made in transactions that are committed are guaranteed to be durable.) Long-running transactions do not guarantee isolation because the nature of them is to not lock data but to allow them to run for a long time. In the same way, atomicity is not guaranteed. Because these business processes potentially run for a long time, it is important that the orchestration engine can do persistence to guarantee a consistent state after a server crash, reboot, or other failures.

A long-running transaction does not require a commit after finishing. The transaction is considered committed once the last shape in the Scope shape has finished execution.

Long-running transactions provide you with a way of considering some units of work as a transaction and do compensation of this collection of units of work in case something goes wrong later in the entire business process, which can be months after the transactions have committed. Also, long-running transactions provide custom error handling and the ability to nest transactions, which cannot be done with atomic transactions.

Compensating Code

Long-running transactions have no automatic rollback, and although atomic transactions provide automatic rollback in case of failures, sometimes you need to undo what happened inside a transaction that has committed. This is called compensation. Compensation can take place only for transactional scopes and not for scopes that are not transactional.

As an example of the need for compensation, consider that you have received an incoming sales order and updated your ERP system appropriately. After some days, the person who sent you the order cancels the order, which basically requires that the ERP system should not have received the order and anything that has happened needs to be undone or at least compensated. In this case, you may want to delete the order from the ERP system or send an email to a manager and inform her of the situation or something else.

> **NOTE**
>
> What actions must be performed during compensation for a committed transaction must be decided on a business level. Too often, developers think that if they inserted a row in a database during the transaction, compensation is just to delete the row again and other situations like that.
>
> But there is no way of knowing what might have been done inside the ERP system once the order was received by the ERP system. Just deleting the order may not compensate for all that has been done. For instance, the ERP system might have created purchase orders that have been sent to suppliers based on the incoming sales order. Simply deleting the sales order or canceling it in the ERP system will not also compensate for sending out the created purchase orders.

In short, you need a businessperson who knows what happens in the business to decide what must be done to compensate for something that has happened. Often you are out of luck and will have to fall back to simply sending out an email to a manager who must deal with the situation manually, because compensation for the received sales order will require a service from the ERP system that can compensate. This requires that the ERP system on reception provide some ID to BizTalk that the ERP system can use later on to compensate.

Not many IT systems provide this level of support for compensation, which means that automatic compensation is difficult and often a person needs to manually update any involved systems. At any rate, a BizTalk developer cannot know what needs to be done to compensate for some specific system.

All transactions including orchestrations that are marked as a transaction have a default compensate block, which is executed only when called explicitly. The behavior of the default compensation block of a transaction is to call the compensate block for any nested committed transactions beginning with the last committed transaction and ending with the first committed transaction. Note that this is limited to one level, meaning that the default compensation behavior does not call the compensation block for the transactions that are nested within the immediate child transactions of the transaction that failed. This might sound quite confusing, so to visualize this, take a look at Figure 4.47.

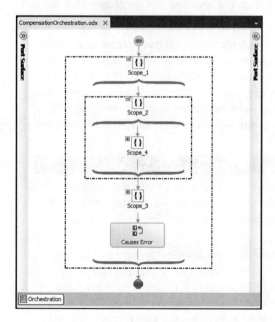

FIGURE 4.47   Illustration of default compensation behavior.

In Figure 4.47 all the Scope shapes are marked as long-running transactions, and neither of them have a custom compensation block.

The Expression shape at the end of Scope_1 causes an exception to be thrown, and after the exception is thrown, the following events take place:

1. Because no exception handler is present for Scope_1, the default exception handler kicks in, and this basically does the exact same thing as the default compensate block, which is to call the compensate block for any nested transactions that have committed backward, starting with the last committed transaction.

2. So in this example, after the exception is thrown, the default exception handler for Scope_1 calls the Compensate block for Scope_3 first.

3. Because Scope_3 only has the default compensate block, this is executed.

4. Because there are no nested transactions within Scope_3, the default compensate block for Scope_3 has no compensate blocks to call and therefore exits.

5. The exception handler for Scope_1 then calls the compensate block for Scope_2.

6. Because Scope_2 also only has the default compensate block, it will not actually do any compensation but merely call the compensate block for any nested transactions.

7. The compensate block for Scope_2 therefore calls the compensate block for Scope_4, which is the only nested transaction beneath Scope_2.

8. After completing the compensate block for Scope_4, which in this case does nothing because it is the default compensate block and there are no nested transactions, the exception handler for Scope_1 rethrows the exception and finishes. Rethrowing the exception is the default behavior of the default exception handler after the relevant compensate blocks have been called.

> **NOTE**
>
> Worth noticing explicitly and therefore mentioning again is that the default compensate blocks do not do any compensation at all. They only call the compensate block for nested transactions.

You can override the default compensate block of a transaction if you need behavior different from the default behavior (that is, if you actually need some compensation done). To override the default compensation behavior of a transactional Scope shape, you must either change the property called Compensation of the Scope to Custom or right-click the **Scope** shape and choose **New Compensation Block**. A transactional Scope shape can have only one compensate block, meaning that you can only add one, and when doing so you effectively override the default compensate block.

In Figure 4.48, you can see the same figure as shown in Figure 4.47, where Scope_2 has a custom compensate block because some compensation should be done for what has happened in Scope_2 in case of a failure. For this example, an Expression shape has been added to simulate that some compensation takes place.

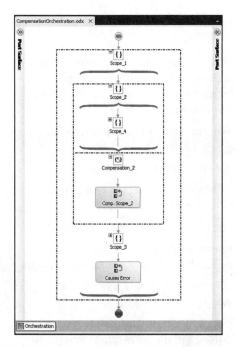

FIGURE 4.48   Adding a custom compensation block to a transactional Scope shape.

Worth noticing when adding a custom compensate block to a transactional scope is that once you do that, you take over the responsibility of compensating for the entire transaction, including compensation of the nested transactions, if needed.

In the example in Figure 4.48, compensation for Scope_4 will never occur because the only place this compensate block can be called is from either the compensate block or an exception handler of Scope_2, and because the compensate block of Scope_2 does not explicitly call the compensate block for Scope_4 and no exception handler is executed on Scope_2 to do default compensation, no one will call the compensate block for Scope_4. Therefore, be careful when adding a custom compensate block because you take over the responsibility of remembering to call the compensate block of all nested transactions, and if a transaction is added to an existing transaction later in the development process, you need to remember to add a call to the compensate block for this new transaction.

When using the Compensate shape inside either an exception handler or a compensate block, you can choose to compensate any of the immediate child transactions of the current transactions or the transaction itself. Choosing to compensate the current transaction, no matter if it is done from an exception handler or a compensate block, will always execute the default compensation block and not the custom compensate block, if added.

The reason for this is that when it is executed from within a custom compensate block, you are already compensating for the transaction, and in this case it merely provides you an easy way of making sure all nested transactions are also compensated without you doing it explicitly. If the custom compensate block could be called from within the same custom compensate block, that would lead to endless loops.

When executed from an exception handler, it makes sense because the transaction has not committed, and therefore real compensation cannot be done; and as explained in the "Exception Handling" section later in this chapter, you need to do compensation of whatever has occurred in the current transaction inside the exception handler instead.

TIP

XLANG/s has an operator that can be used to check whether a transaction succeeded. Using this operator, you can check at the end of a transaction for any nested transactions and whether they completed. The operator is called succeeded in lowercase and takes one parameter as input, which is the name of the transaction to check for. It returns a Boolean indicating if the transaction has committed. This operator can be used in a Decide shape to decide whether to throw an exception to mark the entire enclosing transaction as failed to do compensation or not. It can also be used in exception handlers and compensate blocks to decide which compensating actions to take.

When a compensate block is called, either using the Compensate shape to do so or when called by a default compensate block, the XLANG/s engine itself checks whether the transaction has committed using the succeeded operator before actually calling the compensate block for that transaction. Also, the engine makes sure that the compensate block of a transaction is called only once. Therefore, you do not need to worry about whether any given compensate block is executed twice, and you do not need to worry about whether a compensate block might be called without the transaction actually having completed and hence if compensation is actually needed.

NOTE

If you choose to use the succeeded operator in a Decide shape to choose whether to compensate for a given transaction and then use the Compensate shape to do the compensation, the succeeded operator is actually called twice because the Compensate shape does this as well before actually calling the compensation code. This is a small performance hit, and you might consider using an Expression shape rather than the Compensate shape and using the compensate operator to call the compensation block of the transaction explicitly. The compensate operator is used like this: compensate <TransactionIdentifier>(). Just as with the Compensate shape, this operator can only be used in Expression shapes that are either in an exception handler or a compensate block. Note that the compensate operator is not documented and therefore shouldn't be used unless it is really important.

Persistence Points

The orchestration engine persists running orchestrations to the MessageBox at strategic times for a couple of reasons:

▶ **Dehydration and rehydration:** As explained earlier in this chapter, dehydration and rehydration are used to pull running orchestration instances that don't need to be in memory right now out of the memory. This requires persistence for the orchestration instance to continue when rehydrated.

▶ **Controlled system shutdown:** If a server needs to be taken offline for maintenance or even decommissioned completely, all running instances on the server needs to be persisted to be able to run on another server later on or continue on the same server once it is back online.

▶ **Machine-agnostic execution and rehydration:** If a machine that is part of a BizTalk group is taken offline, crashes, or in other ways becomes unavailable, orchestration instances that were running on this server can continue running from the last persisted state on another server with an instance of the same host.

▶ **Compensation model:** The compensation model checks for the completion of transactions before compensating them in case this is needed. The persistence point at the end of a transactional scope is therefore necessary to guarantee a consistent state.

▶ **Recovery:** If your server recovers from a crash or sudden shutdown, the engine must be able to recover all the instances.

Persistence points persist the following information:

▶ The internal state of the engine, including its current progress

▶ The state of any .NET components that maintain state information and are being used by the orchestration

▶ Message and variable values

To support persistence and thus supporting the previously mentioned scenarios, the orchestration engine persists running orchestrations at the following points in time:

▶ The end of a transactional scope is reached.

▶ A debugging breakpoint is reached.

▶ A message is sent. The only exception to this is when a message is sent from within an atomic transaction scope.

▶ The orchestration starts another orchestration asynchronously, as with the Start Orchestration shape.

▶ The orchestration instance is suspended.

▶ When the orchestration engine is asked to shut down. This applies to the system shutdown in controlled condition and abnormal termination.

▶ The engine determines that the instance should be dehydrated.

▶ The orchestration instance is finished.

If a situation occurs where two persistence points are happening right after each other without anything happening in between, they are collapsed into one persistence point. If a Send shape is placed as the last shape of a Scope shape that is marked as a long-running transaction and the Scope shape is the last shape in the orchestration, for example, the Send shape incurs a persistence point, the end of the long-running transaction incurs a persistence point, and the end of the orchestration incurs a persistence point. These three are collapsed because there is no need for three persistence points. The only two exceptions for this are as follows:

▶ **An atomic scope as the last shape of an orchestration:** This is because the atomic scope must commit, which incurs a persistence point, and the long-running transaction that is the entire orchestration must also commit, which again incurs a persistence point.

▶ **A Parallel Actions shape at the end of an orchestration that has Send shapes at the end of a branch:** This is simply not done because at compile time it is not possible to say which of the branches will end last.

Upon persisting the state of a running orchestration to the MessageBox, the values of messages and variables are also persisted. This is done by serializing them and saving the persisted objects. This means that all object instances referred to either directly or indirectly through other objects must be marked as serializable for an orchestration to be persisted. The only two exceptions to this rule are objects declared within an atomic scope because no persistence occurs inside those and objects of type `System.Xml.XmlDocument` because this is treated as a special case because it is often needed.

Persistence is necessary for BizTalk to guarantee a healthy system at all times. Persistence points, however, take a lot of time because they require database access. Therefore, take care to design your orchestrations to have as few persistence points as possible.

> **TIP**
>
> You can minimize the number of persistence points by grouping Send shapes and Start Orchestration shapes in a Scope shape that is marked as an atomic transaction, because no persistence occurs in there.

Exception Handling

Just as with normal programming where you can run into exceptions at runtime that need to be dealt with, you can also run into exceptions in your orchestrations. Just as with normal programming, you need to deal with these exceptions, because if you do not, the orchestration will simply crash and get suspended. Exceptions can occur in multiple scenarios, such as timeouts for long-running transactions, external assemblies that you use throwing an exception, an adapter that cannot deliver a message, division by zero, deliberately throwing an exception using the Throw Exception shape, and lots of other situations.

Catching an exception can only occur in the context of a Scope shape, which in this case corresponds to the try construct of the C# programming language. All Scope shapes have a default exception handler, which is not visible in the Orchestration Designer. This default exception handler catches the general exception, which corresponds to the general catch construction in a C# program, where you do not specify the type of exception you want to catch.

The default exception handler merely calls the default compensate block of the current transaction and then rethrows the exception. Note that even if you have added a custom compensate block to the transaction, it is still the default compensate block that is called. This is because the transaction cannot have committed because the exception handler is executing, and because only committed transactions can be compensated, this is not an option. The default compensate block is executed to automatically compensate for any nested transactions that might have committed before the exception occurred.

> **NOTE**
>
> The only compensate blocks you can call from an exception handler are the compensate blocks of nested transactions (which is the custom compensate block if present or otherwise the default compensate block) and the default compensate block of the current transaction.
>
> This means that any compensation you want done for the functionality in the current transaction that was not wrapped in a nested transaction must be dealt with inside the exception handler itself. This includes if you want to compensate for the nested transactions in a different order than the default order.

You can add custom exception handlers to a Scope shape if you like. In fact, you can add as many as you like. Adding an exception handler is done by right-clicking a **Scope** shape and choosing **Add Exception Handler**. When added, you need to specify a couple of properties on the exception handler, namely the Exception Object Type property and possibly the Exception Object Name property. The exception object type is used to specify the class of exception that is to be caught and handled. The property provides you with two options: General Exception and <.NET Exception>. The General Exception is used to catch *any* exception that might arise, and therefore effectively overrides the default exception handler. If you choose the <.NET Exception> option, you get a class selector, where you can find the exact class of the exception you want to catch. If you choose to do this, you also need to set the Exception Object Name property to provide the exception object that is caught with a name, to which you can then refer inside the exception handler. As with normal C# programming, if you are in need of several exception handlers because you need to treat them differently, you must catch the exceptions in the order from the most specific exception to the least specific.

TIP

If you need to insert a new exception handler between two existing exception handlers or just to rearrange the existing ones, you can simply drag and drop the exception handlers to the place where you want them.

After you have dealt with an exception, consider rethrowing it, because in many cases you want the enclosing functionality to know about the exception, as well. For instance, consider Figure 4.49. In this figure, you see that an error occurs in Scope_3, which is dealt with in the exception handler for Scope_3. If the exception handler for Scope_3 does not rethrow the exception, no functionality will ever be called to compensate for Scope_2, if needed. Compensating Scope_2 would be the responsibility of an exception handler of Scope_1, which would catch the exception that is thrown in the exception handler for Scope_3.

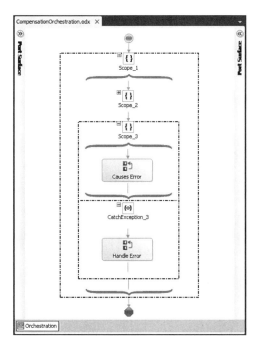

FIGURE 4.49   Inner exception handler that doesn't rethrow the exception that is caught.

Debugging

If your business process is not behaving as you expect it to do, you will find yourself in need of debugging it to pinpoint where things go wrong. Unfortunately, you cannot debug an orchestration like you can debug normal C# programs, by setting breakpoints and pressing F5 in Visual Studio 2010. Orchestrations can only be debugged when deployed to a BizTalk Server and when a message is actually sent through the orchestration.

That said, you have a couple of options available to you, as described in this section.

Send Out Messages

A commonly used debugging technique when developing orchestrations is to take messages that are used throughout the business process and write them out to a folder so that they can be manually inspected. The most common reasons for doing this are as follows:

▶ An XPath expression fails and you need the XML the XPath statement was executed upon to troubleshoot the XPath expression.

▶ A message that is the result of a transformation is not as expected, so the source message can be output to use it to test the map.

Debug and Trace

Inside an Expression shape, you have access to the `System.Diagnostics` .NET namespace, meaning that you can leverage the `Debug` and `Trace` classes to write out debug and trace information that you can then view using your favorite debug viewer.

Breakpoints in Orchestration Debugger

There is an unsupported way of setting breakpoints in the C# code that is generated at compile time and used to debug through your orchestration. Because it isn't supported, however, it is not described any further in this book.

This means that normally you cannot set breakpoints and debug your orchestration inside Visual Studio 2010. You can, however, set breakpoints on orchestration instances and attach to it to debug it. This is done inside the Group Hub page, where you can locate an instance of your orchestration (either a completed, terminated, suspended, or running one) and open it to set breakpoints. Note that to do this the orchestration needs to be tracked. Therefore, you need to have a host instance running, which is an instance of a host that has the Allow Host Tracking property enabled, and you also need to make sure that tracking of the specific orchestration is enabled. This is achieved in the Administration Console in the same place where you define the bindings for the orchestration. There is a Tracking pane, and in here you should make sure that at least the three properties beneath Track Events are enabled. They are enabled by default.

After setting breakpoints, you can initiate a new instance of your orchestration by sending a message through it. When the orchestration hits a breakpoint, it is suspended, and you can then open it and attach to it to see what is going on. The steps to do this are as follows:

1. Open BizTalk Server 2010 Administration Console.

2. Go to the Group Hub page.

3. Use the appropriate group to find an instance of your orchestration. This can be under Completed Instances, Terminated Instances, Suspended Service Instances, or any other group of instances.

4. Right-click an orchestration instance, and choose **Orchestration Debugger**, as shown in Figure 4.50.

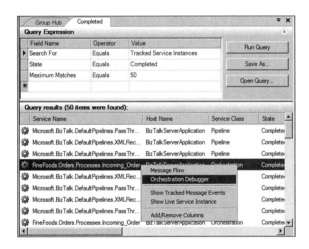

FIGURE 4.50   Choosing which orchestration to debug.

The Orchestration Debugger opens with an image of your orchestration in it, as shown in Figure 4.51. On the left side, you get the history of execution of shapes in the orchestration instance. A green arrow next to a shape means this is when the shape began, and a blue arrow means this is when the shape ended. As you can see in Figure 4.51, the Credit Check Passed? shape encompasses the Send to Folder shape, because the Decide shape does not finish until the chosen branch finishes. In this view, you can take a look at a previously finished orchestration instance and see which path through the orchestration was taken.

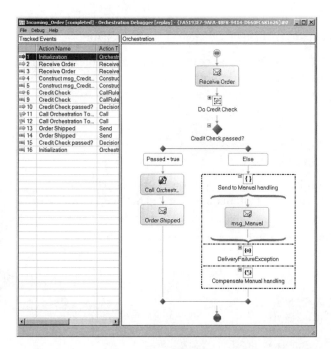

FIGURE 4.51   Orchestration Debugger.

5. Right-click any shape and choose **Set Breakpoint on Class**, as shown in Figure 4.52. Notice that this sets a breakpoint on the orchestration class, meaning that all orchestration instances of this orchestration will get suspended at the breakpoint from the moment you set it. This is mainly the reason why you should never debug orchestrations like this in a production environment. It is also possible to set breakpoints only for specific instances of an orchestration, which is explained later, but at least one class breakpoint must be set for the instance to get suspended.

6. After setting the breakpoint, you can close the Orchestration Debugger.

7. Send a new message through BizTalk.

8. Use the **Running Service Instances** query from Group Hub page to locate the orchestration instance that will have a status of In Breakpoint (Active).

9. Right-click the orchestration instance and choose **Orchestration Debugger**.

   The instance opens in the Orchestration Debugger, and as you can see in Figure 4.53, the left side shows you the shapes that have already executed and stops at the shape on which the class breakpoint has been set.

10. Choose **Debug**, **Attach** or click **Ctrl+A**. Doing so attaches the Orchestration Debugger to the instance and lets you view the values of messages, variables, and so on in a window just beneath the screen shown in Figure 4.53. This window is shown in Figure 4.54. Besides the window with the messages and variables opening up, the Orchestration Debugger also marks in yellow the current shape to be executed.

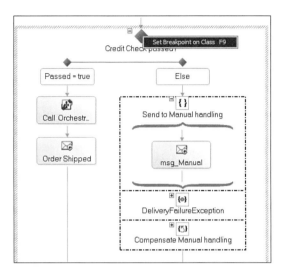

FIGURE 4.52   Setting a breakpoint on the class.

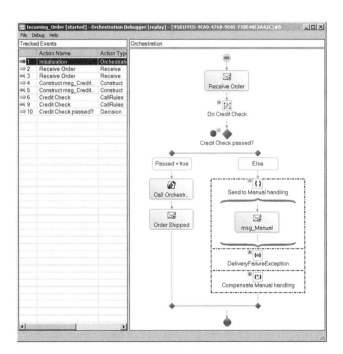

FIGURE 4.53   View of suspended orchestration instance that has hit a class breakpoint and then been opened in Orchestration Debugger.

Variable List				Variable Properties		
Name	**Value**	**Type**				
SendOrderShippedT...	{Port}	FineFood...		□ **Message Parts**		
ReceiveOrderPort	null	FineFood...		□ part		
SendOrderToManual...	{Port}	FineFood...			Part Name	part
msgOrder	{Message}	FineFood...			Part Properties	**(Collection)**
msgCreditCheck	{Message}	FineFood...			Part Size	1206
msgOrderShipped	null	FineFood...			Part Type	"FineFoods.Orders.Schemas.Order"
xmldoc	null	Microsoft...			Part Value	"<ns0:Order xmlns:ns0="http://finefood
				□ **Message Properties**		
				Context	**(Collection)**
				Name	msgOrder
				PartCount	1
				Scope	Incoming_Order
				Type	FineFoods.Orders.Schemas.Order
				Value	{Message}

FIGURE 4.54   View of messages, variables, and so on when attached to an orchestration instance.

After attaching to the orchestration instance, you can debug your orchestration. The screen with the messages and variables can be used to inspect these. For messages, when you click them, you get the right side, as shown in Figure 4.54. In this screen, you can also view the context of the message.

After inspecting the values of messages and variables, you then decide how to continue debugging. When debugging an orchestration, you cannot step over and step into as you can when debugging a normal .NET project. Once attached to an orchestration instance, a yellow marker is placed on the current shape of execution. If you need to continue from there, you can press **Ctrl+G** or choose **Continue** on the Debug menu. This will not just step to the next shape to be executed, but rather it allows the orchestration instance to continue until the next breakpoint that is set or until the end of the orchestration.

Once attached to an instance, you can set instance breakpoints rather than class breakpoints. You do this either by right-clicking a shape and choosing **Set Breakpoint on Instance** or by choosing a shape and pressing **F9**. These breakpoints are used throughout this specific orchestration instance and do not affect other instances in any way.

If your orchestration uses the Call Orchestration shape to call other orchestrations at runtime, you can right-click the entry in the Tracked Events list on the left side and choose **View Called Orchestration**, as shown in Figure 4.55, to inspect what path your instance took in this orchestration, set breakpoints in this orchestration, and so on. If you want to go back to the calling orchestration, use the **View Calling Orchestration** option on the Debug menu. If your orchestration, on the other hand, has used the Start Orchestration shape to start another orchestration asynchronously, you cannot do this. This orchestration instance will have its own entry in the Group Hub page, and you must locate it there and open it up in the Orchestration Debugger on its own.

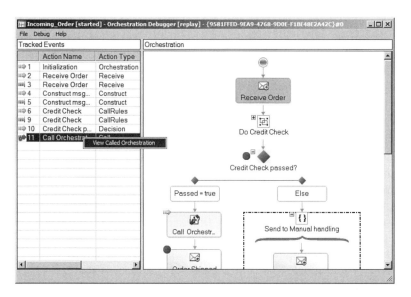

FIGURE 4.55   View a called orchestration in Orchestration Debugger.

At any time, if you are done debugging, you can choose to end the debugging session by using either the **Detach** option on the Debug menu or by pressing **Shift+F5**, as you would do in Visual Studio 2010. Note, however, that just because you detach from an orchestration instance will not make it run to its end. Any orchestration instances that are currently in a breakpoint must all be attached to manually, and then you must choose to continue the execution of the specific instance. Alternatively, the instances can be terminated from the Group Hub page.

Summary

Orchestrations are a representation of a business process that needs to be run under certain circumstances, like the reception of an order, the hiring of a new employee, or some other business process.

Orchestrations are artifacts in your BizTalk projects just like schemas, maps, and pipelines, and after they are added to your BizTalk project, you can design them in the Orchestration Designer. In the designer, you have a lot of shapes available that you can use to build the business process.

BizTalk introduces persistence points, which are points where running orchestrations are persisted to the MessageBox to make sure they can start up again in case of hardware failure, power failure, or some other unexpected crash. In addition, the persistence points provide scalability because they provide a way for BizTalk to move the execution of a running orchestration from one server in a BizTalk group to another.

Orchestrations can run for a long time, which BizTalk handles by introducing dehydration and rehydration. Dehydration is the process of taking a running orchestration and persisting it to the MessageBox to unload it from memory, allowing other instances to be loaded into memory and run. The engine chooses which orchestrations to dehydrate based on what it thinks will not do any work for some time. This can be if an orchestration instance is awaiting the reception of a message, is in a Delay shape, or something else. Rehydration is the opposite, namely the process of taking a dehydrated orchestration and loading it back into memory because it can now continue to run, which can occur if a Delay shape times out, a message is received, or some other event.

Orchestrations have the notion of transactions, which can be used in an orchestration if needed. There are two types of transactions: long-running and atomic. Atomic transactions comply with the ACID properties and automatically roll back any changes that occurred in them in case of failure. With long-running transactions, you might at some time encounter an exception that requires that previously committed transactions be reversed, and for this, exception handling (and specifically, compensation) is introduced, which enables you to write business logic that compensates for transactions that have already been committed, because these cannot be rolled back.

CHAPTER 5

Pipelines

Pipelines are either the piece of functionality that does everything needed on an incoming message before it is published to the MessageBox except mapping or the piece of functionality that does everything needed to a message after it is published to the MessageBox before it is sent to a trading partner or an internal system.

Pipelines are divided into receive pipelines and send pipelines. A receive pipeline is specified on a receive location, and a send pipeline is specified on a send port. A number of built-in pipelines ship with BizTalk. These pipelines are all you need for most of your solutions. If they do not suite your needs, you can create custom pipelines and determine what functionality should be in them in a drag-and-drop fashion. Pipelines consist of some stages that are executed in turn, and all stages can optionally contain pipeline components that do the actual processing. Most pipeline components have properties that can be set at design time, and the properties of the components that ship with BizTalk are discussed in this chapter.

This chapter first describes pipelines and the stages in them. It then describes the built-in pipelines that ship with BizTalk, and then the pipeline components that are available for custom pipelines. Next, it describes how to create custom pipelines and then how to develop custom pipeline components that can be used in custom pipelines. The last two sections contain information about testing pipelines and a summary of this chapter.

Stages in Pipelines

Pipelines consist of a number of stages that can in turn contain a number of pipeline components. For receive pipelines, the stages are as follows:

▶ Decode, where decompressing, decrypting, and other decoding functionality can take place.

▶ Disassemble, where incoming messages are converted into XML and metadata about the message is extracted. Also, this is where messages can be split into several messages (if, for example, you have received a batch of messages in one message).

▶ Validate, where validation of the incoming message can occur.

▶ ResolveParty, where BizTalk can determine which party sent the message.

For send pipelines, the stages are as follows:

▶ Pre-Assemble, where you can perform any functionality required by your business before the message is passed along in the pipeline.

▶ Assemble, where the XML representation of the message can be converted into the flat file format needed, and values from the context of a message can get copied into the message.

▶ Encode, where the message can get encrypted, compressed, or anything else needed before the actual transmission of the message.

The stages are executed one at a time by the BizTalk runtime. A stage has an execution mode attached to it, which is either FirstMatch or All. Stages that have FirstMatch execution mode ask the components one at a time until it finds one that accepts the input. After a component accepts the input, the other components in that stage are ignored. Stages that have an All execution mode execute all the specified components one at a time. The functionality for the FirstMatch is implemented by requiring that pipeline components that will be placed in a FirstMatch stage should implement the IProbeMessage interface. This interface allows BizTalk to ask the component whether it recognizes the message, and if so, the component is executed.

Pipeline components have an attribute on their .NET class that describes which stages of a pipeline the specific components can be placed in. It is therefore possible to develop a pipeline component that can be placed in any stage of any pipeline. This section describes the stages of the pipelines, focusing on the purpose of the stage and not what can actually be done in each stage. This means that although you can put components that do validation in the decode stage and so on, this is not the intention and is therefore not covered as such. Later in this chapter, we cover how to develop your own pipeline component and determine to which stages it can belong.

The stages of a pipeline function in a streaming manner, meaning that each pipeline component gets an object as input that has a stream inside it, which is the output from the previous pipeline component that was executed. When developing your own pipeline components, keep this streaming fashion in mind, whenever possible, to optimize performance and limit memory usage. When not using streaming mode, loading the entire message into memory may create a bottleneck (if, for example, messages are big or a lot of messages arrive at the same time).

Stages in a Receive Pipeline

A receive pipeline has four stages, as shown in Figure 5.1.

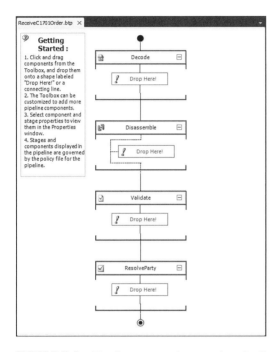

FIGURE 5.1   The four stages in a receive pipeline.

The four stages are Decode, Disassemble, Validate, and ResolveParty. The four stages are explained in detail in the following subsections.

Decode

The Decode stage can have up to 255 components specified in it, and it is an `All` execution mode pipeline stage.

This stage can contain functionality to decode the incoming message before further processing. This can be decrypting the message if it is encrypted, and it can be decoding it from MIME encoding or something similar. This stage is also often used for decompressing a message that has been compressed in some way.

Disassemble

The Disassemble stage can have up to 255 components specified in it, and it is the only `FirstMatch` execution mode pipeline stage that ships in-the-box with BizTalk.

This stage contains disassembler components, which usually have four important responsibilities:

▶ The disassembler must convert the incoming message to *Extensible Markup Language* (XML). Actually, a disassembler can choose not to do this. However, it is required for the rest of the built-in components to validate the message, perform transformations, leverage *business activity monitoring* (BAM) on the content of the message, use XPath to retrieve values inside the message, and generally use the message later in BizTalk. If a message is not converted into XML in the Disassemble stage in the receive pipeline, BizTalk can do nothing else with the message than moving it around (no transformations, no content-based routing, no property promotion, no correlation, no access to data inside the message at all, and so on). Some scenarios do not require anything other than the message being moved around unaltered, but for such use, BizTalk is usually overkill.

▶ The disassembler is responsible for promoting the message type of the message. The message type, as explained in Chapter 2, "Schemas," is a combination of the target namespace of the schema for the message and the root node of the generated XML. The message type is important for the further processing because business processes usually require a specific message type for them to handle a message and because any transformations require a match between the message type specified as the input for the map and the message type of the message.

▶ Any custom property promotion occurs in the disassembler, meaning that if the schema that matches the incoming message has either promoted properties or distinguished fields defined in it, the disassembler must promote or write these to the context so that they are available later during BizTalk's further processing of the message.

▶ Debatching of enveloped messages that have several individual messages inside them where the individual messages need to be dealt with separately. There is out-of-the-box support for debatching both XML and flat files.

Validate
The Validate stage can have up to 255 components specified in it, and it is an All execution mode pipeline stage.

This stage can contain components that validate the input. This can be the built-in component, described later, or custom components (if, for example, you need validation of a special kind, like validation of some non-XML format because you do not want to convert the message into XML when it is received). Later in this chapter, we cover how to develop custom components.

ResolveParty
The ResolveParty stage can have up to 255 components specified in it, and it is an All execution mode pipeline stage.

This stage is for components that determine the party that has sent the incoming message. Determining this is needed for routing based on sender rather than content of a message.

Stages in a Send Pipeline

A send pipeline has three stages, as shown in Figure 5.2.

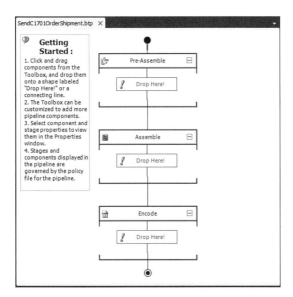

FIGURE 5.2   The three stages of a send pipeline.

The three stages are Pre-Assemble, Assemble, and Encode. The three stages are explained in detail in the following subsections.

Pre-Assemble

The Pre-Assemble stage can have up to 255 components specified in it, and it is an All execution mode pipeline stage.

This stage can contain pipeline components that manipulate the message before it is converted into the format needed by the assembler component.

Assemble

The Assemble stage can have only one component specified in it, and it is an All execution mode pipeline stage; although, that sounds like a contradiction. This is because if the execution mode had been specified as a FirstMatch, there would be an overhead of looking for the IProbeMessage interface and calling the Probe method.

This stage contains assemblers that have the responsibility of converting the XML into the format that should be sent out (XML, flat files, PDFs, and so on).

Just as the disassembler has the responsibility of doing property promotion on the incoming message, the assembler has the responsibility of performing demotion to copy values from context of the message into the message body. Also, whereas the disassembler must support debatching, the assembler supports batching of messages. For pipelines used in send ports, this supports only adding an envelope to an outgoing message, whereas calling a send pipeline from inside an orchestration can allow you to batch several messages into one message. This technique is explained more in Chapter 4, "Orchestrations."

Encode

The Encode stage can have up to 255 components specified in it, and it is an `All` execution mode pipeline stage.

This stage contains any components needed to encrypt, sign, encode, and compress the message (and so on) before it is handed to the adapter for transmission.

Built-In Pipelines

BizTalk ships with a number of built-in pipelines, which are described in this section. Because this book does not cover the *Electronic Document Interchange* (EDI) functionality of BizTalk, the EDI-specific pipelines are not discussed.

Receive Pipelines

This section describes the built-in receive pipelines.

PassThruReceive

The PassThruReceive pipeline is an empty receive pipeline, meaning that it does not have any components in any of the four stages of a receive pipeline. Therefore, it does not perform any actions on the incoming message, so the message is published into the MessageBox exactly as the adapter has handed it to the pipeline. This is useful for receiving binary files or other files that you need to basically just copy using BizTalk or for receiving files into a generic workflow that handles all files the same regardless of format.

XMLReceive

The XMLReceive pipeline is commonly used when receiving XML. This pipeline has the built-in XML disassembler component and the built-in party-resolution components added to the Disassemble and the ResolveParty stages.

When receiving XML in BizTalk, you will most likely always be using either the built-in XML receive pipeline or a custom pipeline that has the same base functionality and some more functionality added to it because without it you will have no message type to use for routing, property promotion, and so forth.

Also worth noticing is that the XMLReceive pipeline does not validate the input. This is because the XML disassembler component does not validate the input, and obviously neither does the party-resolution pipeline component. Validation is turned off by default for performance reasons. If you want to validate the input, you have three options:

▶ You can enable it on the XML disassembler per instance of the XMLReceive on the receive location.

- You can create a custom pipeline that uses the XML disassembler and enable validation on the disassembler.

- You can create a custom pipeline and use the XML validator component in it.

Send Pipelines

This section describes the built-in send pipelines.

PassThruSend

The PassThruSend pipeline is an empty send pipeline, meaning that it does not have any components in any of the three stages of a send pipeline. Therefore, it does not perform any actions on the outgoing message, which is therefore sent to the internal system or trading partner just as it was published into the MessageBox. The PassThruReceive pipeline is usually used only for handling messages that are binary, whereas the PassThruSend pipeline is commonly used for sending out XML messages because often there is no need to change the message going out if it is XML.

XMLTransmit

The XMLTransmit send pipeline has only one component in it, which is the XML assembler component, which is placed in the Assemble stage of the pipeline. The other two stages are empty. The XML assembler component is described in a later section. Note that for receiving XML you will almost always want to use the XMLReceive pipeline or a custom pipeline that has the XML disassembler on it, whereas when you are sending out XML, you will almost always not be using the XMLTransmit pipeline unless you need to use either enveloping or demotion, which will be relatively rare. The XMLTransmit pipeline does not validate the message that passes through it. Contrary to the XMLReceive pipeline, there isn't even a property you can change to enable it. To validate your message in a send pipeline, you therefore need to create a custom pipeline and use the XML validator component in this pipeline.

Built-In Pipeline Components

This section describes the pipeline components that ship with BizTalk. Because this book does not cover the EDI functionality of BizTalk, the EDI-specific pipeline components are not discussed.

If you need pipeline components that do decompressing, *Pretty Good Privacy* (PGP) decryption, Excel spreadsheet parsing, or some other functionality that is not covered by the built-in components, you can either develop your own custom pipeline component, as described in a later section, or search the Internet for an available third-party pipeline component.

Most pipeline components have properties that can be set at design time to instruct the component how to deal with input. However, there is also the possibility to change a property per instance of a pipeline, meaning that if you have one pipeline that does something generic and you have used this pipeline in a number of receive locations or send ports, you can specify other values for the properties that are only used for a specific instance of the pipeline. This is done in Administration Console by clicking the ellipsis to the right of the pipeline when editing your receive location or send port. Doing so brings up a property-editing window, where you can change the per-instance properties. Note that except for Boolean values, using this window does not provide the normal property editors like drop-downs and so on. You need to know the exact values you want to enter.

XML Components

This subsection to the "Built-In Pipeline Components" section describes the built-in pipeline components that can be used for handling XML. Some of the components can be placed only in a receive pipeline, some can be placed only in a send pipeline, and some can be placed in either a receive pipeline or a send pipeline.

XML Disassembler

The XML disassembler has three pipeline component categories attached to it: PipelineComponent, Streamer, and DisassemblingParser. This means that this component can be placed only in the Disassemble stage of a receive pipeline.

The XML disassembler has the responsibilities that any disassembler has (as described earlier), and it contains functionality to meet these requirements. The XML disassembler takes the incoming message and looks at the root node and the target namespace of the message. These two values are concatenated, and if the target namespace is not empty, the character # is put in between them. This forms the message type, which is in turn used to look up a schema that matches it. If no schema is found that matches the message type, a runtime error is thrown, and the message is then suspended unless the component explicitly allows unrecognized messages. If multiple schemas are found, a runtime error is also thrown, because BizTalk doesn't know which schema to use. After determining the message type and making sure a schema exists for the instance, some steps are taken to prepare the message for processing in the next pipeline components and preparing the message for routing. These steps are as follows:

1. Promotion of any promoted properties or writing of distinguished fields that are found in the schema to the context of the message.

2. Debatching of the message in case the schema found for the message is marked as an envelope. In this case, the internal messages are extracted according to the Body XPath property in the envelope schema. For each of these extracted messages, the same steps are performed recursively. If an extracted message is not an envelope, its message type is promoted, and the message is returned from the component for further processing.

Debatching incoming XML messages using the XML disassembler allows you to strip an envelope and publish each message from within the envelope individually. Sometimes, however, you need a different functionality. Consider the XML in Listing 5.1. If you need the employees debatched individually, you need to mark the schemas for CompanyInfo as an envelope schema and set the Body XPath property to point at CompanyInfo/Employees, which is the parent of the nodes you want debatched and published individually. This, however, given the XML from Listing 5.1, will result at runtime in one message containing the Year element to be published and two messages containing one Employee each to be published. Now, the two Employee messages are fine, but the Year message will almost certainly result in an error at some point because you probably do not have a schema for it and no subscription that will get the message after it is published to the MessageBox.

LISTING 5.1   XML Example of Debatching Issues

```
<CompanyInfo>
  <Employees>
    <Year>2010</Year>
    <Employee>
      <Name>John Johnson</Name>
      <Seniority>4</Seniority>
      <Salary>10000</Salary>
    </Employee>
    <Employee>
      <Name>Eric Smith</Name>
      <Seniority>10</Seniority>
      <Salary>20000</Salary>
    </Employee>
  </Employees>
</CompanyInfo>
```

Unfortunately, there is no nice solution to this. Your options are as follows:

▶ Write a custom pipeline component that removes the unwanted elements before the XML disassembler receives the message.

▶ Write your own disassembler that does what you want. Possibly write one that just wraps the XML disassembler and then discards the message it outputs if you do not want it.

▶ Create a schema for the messages that you do not need and create a send port that subscribes to them. In the send port, leverage either a consuming pipeline component or a consuming adapter that just deletes the message.

The component has the properties shown in Figure 5.3.

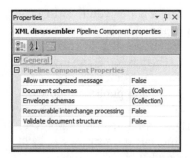

FIGURE 5.3   Properties of the XML disassembler pipeline component.

The Allow Unrecognized Message property lets you decide whether the component should allow messages that it does not recognize to pass through the component. This applies only to XML messages for which no schemas could be found and does not let you pass invalid XML messages or non-XML messages through BizTalk.

The Document Schemas property contains a collection of schemas that are the valid schemas to pass through this instance of the XML disassembler component. If any XML passes through that does not match the schemas given in this property, you get a runtime error unless it is an XML instance for which no schema is deployed and the Allow Unrecognized Message is set to True. If the collection is empty, all XML messages are allowed to pass through, given there is a schema deployed for it.

The Envelope Schemas property is a schema collection of valid schemas to apply as envelopes of the incoming message. If the collection is empty, the runtime finds the correct envelope schema automatically. There are two reasons for setting this property even though the component detects the envelope automatically otherwise. The first reason is performance. The correct schemas can be loaded without having to look at the incoming XML message. The other reason is to restrict what envelopes can be used for this particular receive pipeline. This can be used to help you make sure that a receive location picks up messages from only a specific trading partner, for instance. For more information about envelope schemas, see Chapter 2.

The Recoverable Interchange Processing property is used to let you decide whether to suspend an entire batch of messages if at least one debatched message fails in the disassembler or whether to allow the valid messages to be published and to suspend only the failed messages. Suppose you receive a message that has 200 orders in it, and one of them fails because it does not validate for some reason. If you set this property to True, the 199 good orders get published, and the failed order gets suspended. If this property is set to False, the entire batch of the 200 orders is suspended.

The Validate Document Structure property determines whether the disassembler should validate the structure of the incoming document. This property can be set to True only if you have specified schemas in the Document Schemas property. If not, you get a compile-time error.

XML Assembler

The XML assembler has three pipeline component categories attached to it: PipelineComponent, Streamer, and AssemblingSerializer. This means that this component can be placed only in the "Assemble" stage of a send pipeline.

An assembler generally has the responsibilities laid out in a previous section, and the XML assembler component naturally takes on these responsibilities.

One of the responsibilities for an assembler is to convert the output to the format required by the receiving party, which can involve converting into a positional flat file, an EDIFACT document, or others. The XML assembler can handle only XML and will therefore have XML as output.

Another responsibility of an assembler is property demotion on the outgoing message, which this component also does. Property demotion is explained in Chapter 2. Besides the responsibilities that all assemblers have, this component also performs some other standard functionality on XML that is about to be sent out through a send port. This functionality is controlled by the properties you specify on the component.

The component has the properties shown in Figure 5.4.

FIGURE 5.4   Properties of the XML assembler pipeline component.

The Add Processing Instructions property is used if you need to add processing instructions to the outgoing XML. Processing instructions for schemas are explained in Chapter 2. The property has three possible values: Append (default), Create New, and Ignore. When the value is set to Append, any processing instructions you enter in the Add Processing Instructions Text property are appended to any existing processing instructions in the XML. If you choose Create New, the existing processing instructions are deleted before the ones entered in the Add Processing Instructions Text property are added to the XML. And finally, if the value is Ignore, nothing is changed in the XML.

The Add Processing Instructions Text property contains the actual processing instructions you want added to your XML (if this is necessary). The compiler checks the string you entered to make sure it is valid. If you need more than one processing instruction, you can just concatenate them like this: "`<?MyFirstIP MyFirstValue ?><?MySecondIP MySecondValue ?>`".

The Add XML Declaration property determines whether the outgoing XML should have an XML declaration added to it. The XML declaration is really just a processing instruction, which looks something like this: '`<?xml version="1.0" encoding="utf-8" ?>`'. The version will always be `1.0`, but the value of `encoding` will match the charset that is determined by the property Target Charset.

The Document Schemas property contains a collection of schemas that are the valid schemas to pass through this instance of the XML assembler component. If any XML passes through that does not match the schemas given in this property, you get a runtime error. If the collection is empty, all XML messages are allowed to pass through.

The Envelope Schemas property is a schema collection of schemas to apply as envelopes of the outgoing message. If you add more than one envelope, they are nested in the outgoing XML. The order you add them to the collection is important because this reflects the hierarchy they are nested in.

The Preserve Byte Order Mark property lets you define whether you want the output to have a *Byte Order Mark* (BOM) or not in the output. The BOM is described at the Unicode website (http://unicode.org/faq/utf_bom.html). Basically, it is a set of bytes at the beginning of a message indicating what encoding should be used to read the message in question. If the first 3 bytes of a file are EF BB BF, for example, this means that the message is UTF-8 encoded. Older legacy systems can fail if a message contains a BOM, whereas newer systems appreciate it because it helps determine how to read the message.

The Processing Instruction Scope property can have two values: Document (default) and Envelope. The value determines whether the processing instructions should be added at document level or envelope level (if enveloping is used in this assembler instance).

The Target Charset property is used to determine what charset the XML should have when it comes out of the assembler component. At design time, it is a drop-down list of possible values. Setting the property on the pipeline component on a per-instance level gives you the opportunity to choose charsets that are not available in the drop-down at design time. The outgoing XML has a charset according to this algorithm:

1. The value of the `XMLNorm.TargetCharset` context property
2. The value specified at design time or as a per-instance property on the assembler component in the send port configuration
3. The value of the `XMLNorm.SourceCharset` context property
4. The default value, which is UTF-8

Flat Files

This section describes the built-in pipeline components that can be used for handling flat files in both send pipelines and receive pipelines.

Flat File Disassembler

The flat file disassembler has three pipeline component categories attached to it: PipelineComponent, Streamer, and DisassemblingParser. Therefore, this component can be placed only in the Disassemble stage of a receive pipeline.

This component is used for converting incoming flat files to XML and optionally debatches the incoming flat file into several XML files. The component understands the flat file extension annotations that are present in BizTalk flat file schemas and uses these to parse the flat file. The debatching functionality is achieved differently than the XML enveloping features leveraged by the XML disassembler. The XML disassembler relies on a property in a schema to tell it that the schema describes an envelope, whereas the flat file disassembler uses the schema that is to be used for parsing the incoming message. The flat file disassembler simply starts parsing the message, and if there is more in the flat file after the parser has read enough of the message to satisfy the schema, it assumes that more instances are in the message and starts over. So, if you receive a message with 200 orders in it, create a schema that can parse only 1 order; this makes the flat file disassembler parse 1 order, discover there is more data, and start over. It does this until it has read and parsed all 200 orders.

The component has the properties shown in Figure 5.5.

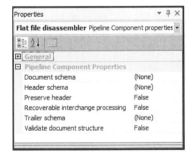

FIGURE 5.5   Properties of the flat file disassembler pipeline component.

The Document Schema property contains the single schema that describes the incoming messages after the header and trailer have been stripped from the message. If any message passes through that does not match this schema, you get a runtime error. If this property is empty, you get a compile-time error.

The Header Schema property is used to specify the schema that describes the header of the flat file that arrives. This means that a message that is an instance of the schema specified in this property should be prepended to the flat file that is received. Note that using Header Schema and Document Schema require a tag identifier in the document schema for the parser to know when the header has ended and when the document begins.

The Preserve Header property is used if you need the content of the header after the incoming message has been split up into messages according to the document schema and published to the MessageBox. Normally, information from the header is lost at that stage.

You can promote values from the header, and they then follow the message around, but you can also set this property to True. If you do this, the XML representation of the header is written to the context of each message that is published to the MessageBox. It is written to the `XMLNORM.FlatFileHeaderDocument` and can as such be accessed in an orchestration and in pipeline components using code.

The Recoverable Interchange Processing property is used to let you decide whether to suspend an entire batch of messages (if, for example, at least one of the debatched messages fails in the disassembler). If you do not want the entire batch suspended, set this to True, and this then allows the valid debatched messages to be published, and only the debatched messages that failed get suspended. Suppose you receive a message that has 200 orders in it, for example and 1 message fails because it does not validate for some reason. If you set this property to True, the 199 good orders get published, and the failed order get suspended. If this property is set to False, the entire batch of the 200 orders gets suspended.

The Trailer Schema property is used to specify the schema that describes the trailer of the flat file that arrives. Therefore, a message that is an instance of the schema specified in this property should be appended to the flat file that is received. Note that using a trailer schema requires a tag identifier in the trailer schema for the parser to know when the document has ended and when the trailer begins.

The Validate Document Structure property determines whether the disassembler should validate the structure of the incoming document. If this is turned off, the flat file is converted into XML, but no validation of the content is made, meaning that if a field that is marked as an integer contains letters, this will not be discovered. If it is turned on, the disassembler takes more time because the validation takes time.

Flat File Assembler

The flat file assembler has three pipeline component categories attached to it: PipelineComponent, Streamer, and AssemblingSerializer. Therefore, this component can be placed only in the Assemble stage of a send pipeline.

The component has the same responsibilities as all assemblers (and which were explained earlier in this chapter). This component is used to send out messages that are flat files, such as positional files, delimited files, or files that are a combination of the two. It takes the XML representation of a message as input and uses the schema for the message to find out how to build the flat file, which is then sent on through the pipeline for further processing and in the end delivered to the adapter for transportation.

The component has the properties shown in Figure 5.6.

The Document Schema property contains the schema that describes the valid messages to pass through this instance of the flat file assembler component. If any message passes through that does not match this schema, you get a runtime error. If the property is empty, the runtime discovers the correct schema itself. Note that whereas most pipeline components where you need to specify schemas have a property called Document Schemas (plural) for specifying a collection of schemas, this component has a Document Schema (singular) for specifying just one schema.

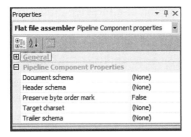

FIGURE 5.6   Properties of the flat file assembler pipeline component.

The Header Schema property is used to specify a single schema that describes the header of the flat file that is to be created. This means that a message that is an instance of the schema specified in this property is prepended to the flat file that will be generated by applying the matching schema to the XML. Because, at runtime, the XML instance that is the input to the flat file assembler is used to generate a flat file specified by the schema given in the Document Schema property, there is no runtime message to populate the fields that are present in the schema specified in the Header Schema property. Therefore, you have three options of getting values into the instance of the header schema:

▶ Write a value to the `XMLNORM.FlatFileHeaderDocument` property. This value is taken at runtime and matched with a schema and then converted to flat file and used as a header of the file. You can write a value to this property either by setting it in an orchestration using `"Message(XMLNORM.FlatFileHeaderDocument) = <an xml instance of the header schema>"` or you can write the value using a pipeline component using code like this: `outmsg.Context.Write("FlatFileHeaderDocument", "http://schemas.microsoft.com/BizTalk/2003/xmlnorm-properties", "<an xml instance of the header schema");`.

▶ Use property demotion, which is described in Chapter 2. This is not only useful for demoting values into the header schema specified on the pipeline. Because you can overwrite the value of the Header Schema property by setting the value of the `XMLNORM.HeaderSpecName` property, you can choose a header schema at runtime, and if you have promoted properties in this specific schema, they get demoted into the header. Setting the value of the `XMLNORM.FlatFileHeaderDocument` makes the assembler choose the schema that matches this XML as the header schema, thus overwriting the header schema you have either set at design time or set at runtime in the `XMLNORM.HeaderSpecName` property.

▶ If the header to be used as output is the same as the header that was taken from the input, you can set a property on the flat file disassembler called Preserve Header, which effectively writes the XML instance of the header to the context property mentioned previously, which allows the assembler to write the header to the outgoing file.

The Preserve Byte Order Mark property lets you define whether you want the output to have a *Byte Order Mark* (BOM) or not in the output. A BOM is described at http://unicode.

org/faq/utf_bom.html. Basically, it is a set of bytes at the beginning of a message indicating what encoding should be used to read the message in question. If the first 3 bytes of a file are EF BB BF, for example, this means that the message is UTF-8 encoded. Older legacy systems can fail if a message contains a BOM, whereas newer systems appreciate it because it helps determine how to read the message.

The Target Charset property is used to determine what charset the XML should have when it comes out of the assembler component. At design time, it is a drop-down list of possible values. The outgoing XML has a charset according to this algorithm:

1. The value of the XMLNorm.TargetCharset context property
2. The value specified at design time on the assembler component
3. The value of the XMLNorm.SourceCharset context property
4. The default value, which is UTF-8

The Trailer Schema property is used for specifying a schema that describes the trailer of a flat file (that is, some flat file content that is appended to the generated flat file). Just as with the Document Schema, this property is not a collection, but a single schema; and just as with the Header Schema, because there are no values at runtime, you need to use property demotion to get values into the fields in the instance of the trailer schema.

The properties Header Schema and Trailer Schema are rarely used on the flat file assembler, whereas they are often used on the flat file disassembler, which was discussed in the previous section. The reason it is rarely used is that because you cannot send three messages to the assembler at runtime, and you therefore need property demotion to get values into the header and trailer, it is easier to create one schema that encompasses both header, document, and trailer and use a map or message assignment in an orchestration to assign values to the fields in the header and trailer.

Encoding, Encrypting, and Signing

This section describes the built-in pipeline components that you can use to encode, encrypt, and sign messages in both send pipelines and receive pipelines. Encryption and signing of messages is important in scenarios where you need to transmit either sensitive information (encryption) or to be able to verify the sender of a message (signing).

MIME/SMIME Encoder

The MIME/SMIME encoder has two pipeline component categories attached to it: PipelineComponent and Encoder. Therefore, this component can be placed only in the Encode stage of a send pipeline.

MIME is an acronym for *Multipurpose Internet Mail Extensions* and is explained and defined in RFC1521. You can find its specification at http://tools.ietf.org/pdf/rfc1521.

The component is used for several things. First, it can be used to both sign and encrypt outgoing messages. Second, it can encode the outgoing messages using different encodings.

Note that this component cannot run in a 64-bit environment. This means that if this component is needed it has to run under a host instance that is running in 32-bit emulation mode. This is a property you can set on the host instance in the Administration Console.

The component has the properties shown in Figure 5.7.

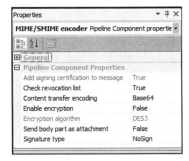

FIGURE 5.7   Properties of the MIME/SMIME encoder pipeline component.

The Add Signing Certification to Message property specifies whether the certificate used to sign the message should be included in the message. This property is accessible only if the Signature Type property has a value different from NoSign, meaning that you want the outgoing message signed.

The Check Revocation List property specifies whether to check with the *certificate revocation list* (CRL) to verify the certificate before using it. This decreases performance because it requires BizTalk to send a request to the server that hosts the CRL. If the server is down or otherwise unreachable, the message is suspended and must be resumed by an administrator.

The Content Transfer Encoding property specifies what encoding you want the message to have. Possible values are Base64 (default), QuotedPrintable, SevenBit, EightBit, Binary, and UUEncode.

The Enable Encryption property lets you decide whether to encrypt the outgoing message. If enabled, you then need to specify a value in the Encryption Algorithm property, which in turn specifies what encryption algorithm to use. Possible values are DES3 (default), DES, and RC2. If encryption is enabled on this component, the certificate specified on the send port that is using the pipeline is used for encrypting the message.

The Send Body Part as Attachment property specifies whether to send the body part of the BizTalk message going through the component as a MIME attachment.

The Signature Type property specifies how to sign the outgoing message. There are three possible values: NoSign (default), ClearSign, and BlobSign. If NoSign is chosen, no signing of the message occurs. If ClearSign is chosen, the certificate is appended to the message. This cannot be used when also encrypting the message. BlobSign appends the certificate to the message and also encodes the message. The certificate used for signing is the certificate associated with the BizTalk group, which you can change in the Administration Console.

MIME/SMIME Decoder

The MIME/SMIME decoder has two pipeline component categories attached to it:
PipelineComponent and Decoder. Therefore, this component can be placed only in the
Decode stage of a receive pipeline.

The MIME/SMIME decoder component can be leveraged to decode MIME/SMIME encoded
incoming messages. The component supports multipart messages, which may arrive
among others from the POP3 adapter, which actually uses the MIME/SMIME decoder
component internally. The component also handles decrypting of incoming messages that
are encrypted. For decrypting, the correct certificate must be installed in the certificate
store of the user running the host instance, and the thumbprint of the certificate must be
associated to the host, which can be done in the Administration Console. The component
also supports signature validation of the signature used to sign the message.

Note that this component cannot run in a 64bit environment. This means that if this
component is needed it has to run under a host instance that is running in 32-bit
emulation mode. This is a property you can set on the host instance in the
Administration Console.

The component has the properties shown in Figure 5.8.

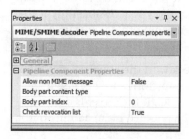

FIGURE 5.8   Properties of MIME/SMIME decoder pipeline component.

The Allow Non MIME Message property specifies whether to allow non-MIME/SMIME
encoded messages to pass through the pipeline component. This is useful for letting the
same receive location, and thus the same receive pipeline, receive messages that are
MIME/SMIME encoded and messages that are not.

The Body Part Content Type property specifies the content type of the body part, and the
Body Part Index property specifies a 1-based index determining which part is the body
part. This is useful if the message consists of several parts, to let the component know
which one of the parts is to be considered the body part of the message.

The Check Revocation List property specifies whether the CRL should be checked when
validating signatures on messages to check whether the signature has been revoked for
some reason. This might sound obvious that we want to check the revocation list, but
there is a trade-off because enabling this check decreases performance, and if the website
containing the revocation list is not responding for some reason, all messages that are
signed fail.

For decrypting messages, the certificate that is associated with the BizTalk group is used. You can change this in the properties of the group in the Administration Console. For checking a signature, BizTalk looks in the Local Machine certificate store of the server to find a matching certificate.

BizTalk Framework

This section describes the built-in pipeline components that you can use to handle the BizTalk Framework in both send pipelines and receive pipelines.

The *BizTalk Framework* (BTF) is a framework that extends *Simple Object Access Protocol* (SOAP) 1.1 and allows you to send messages wrapped in a SOAP envelope and allows for exactly once guaranteed delivery of messages. This framework is mainly used by BizTalk servers and can be used for exchanging messages with BizTalk versions all the way back to BizTalk 2000, which was the first release. The framework is not bound to BizTalk, though; it can be implemented in any system. You can find the details about the specification at www.microsoft.com/biztalk/techinfo/biztalkframework20.doc. A bug was corrected in BizTalk 2002 SP1, which means that BizTalk 2002 SP1 and later cannot use BTF2 to communicate with BizTalk 2000 or BizTalk 2002 unless they have the appropriate fix or service pack installed.

BTF2 is version 2 of the BizTalk Framework, which is designed to provide a means of doing reliable messaging. Messages sent via BTF2 have an envelope around them that describes the sender of the message, where a receipt for the message should be sent to, when the receipt must be received before, and so on. This enables you to confirm your message has arrived with the receiver.

BTF is almost exclusively used by BizTalk, and even among BizTalk installations it is almost exclusively used among older versions. You should therefore implement it only if you are integrating with another BizTalk server that uses it.

Listing 5.2 shows an example of a BizTalk Framework envelope. The <SOAP-ENV:Body> element contains the actual payload of the message.

LISTING 5.2   BizTalk Framework Envelope

```
<?xml version="1.0" encoding="utf-8"?>
<SOAP-ENV:Envelope xmlns:SOAP-
ENV="http://schemas.xmlsoap.org/soap/envelope/"
xmlns:xsi="http://www.w3.org/1999/XMLSchema-instance"
xmlns:biz="http://schemas.biztalk.org/btf-2-0/address/types">
      <SOAP-ENV:Header>
            <endpoints xmlns="http://schemas.biztalk.org/btf-2-
0/endpoints" SOAP-ENV:mustUnderstand="1">
                  <to>
                        <address
xsi:type="biz:MyToADdressType">MyToAddress</address>
                  </to>
```

```
                <from>
                        <address
xsi:type="biz:MyFromAddressType">MyFromAddress</address>
                        </from>
                </endpoints>
                <properties xmlns="http://schemas.biztalk.org/btf-2-
0/properties" SOAP-ENV:mustUnderstand="1">
                        <identity>uuid:1d65e8fc-16f9-4b56-82b7-
f07681887057</identity>
                        <sentAt>2009-11-14T14:33:44+00:00</sentAt>
                        <expiresAt>2009-11-15T15:03:44+00:00</expiresAt>
                        <topic>MyTopic</topic>
                </properties>
                <services xmlns="http://schemas.biztalk.org/btf-2-0/services"
SOAP-ENV:mustUnderstand="1">
                </services>
        </SOAP-ENV:Header>
        <SOAP-ENV:Body />
</SOAP-ENV:Envelope>
```

BizTalk Framework Assembler

The BizTalk Framework assembler has three pipeline component categories attached to it: PipelineComponent, Streamer, and AssemblingSerializer. Therefore, this component can be placed only in the Assemble stage of a send pipeline.

This component is used to send out messages in an envelope that conforms to the BTF2.

There is a small bit of magic going on in this component, as BizTalk needs some way to resend this message not only if the adapter fails to deliver the message but also if the receipt is not received within the specified number of minutes. This is achieved by setting some BTF-specific properties on the message that will let the runtime perform normal send-port retrying. After the retry interval has elapsed, the send port is executed, and the BizTalk Framework assembler checks to see whether a receipt has been received. If one hasn't been received, the message is re-sent. If one has been received, the message is just consumed by the assembler, meaning that it is not retransmitted or published to the MessageBox because it has been successfully transmitted.

The component has the properties shown in Figure 5.9.

The Add Processing Instructions property is used if you need to add processing instructions to the outgoing XML. Processing instructions for schemas are explained in Chapter 2. The property has three possible values: Append (default), Create New, and Ignore. When the value is set to Append, any processing instructions you enter in the Add Processing Instructions Text property are appended to any existing processing instructions in the XML. If you choose Create New, the existing processing instructions are deleted before the ones entered in the Add Processing Instructions Text property are added to the XML. And finally, if the value is Ignore, nothing is changed in the XML.

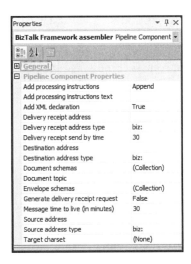

FIGURE 5.9   Properties of the BizTalk Framework assembler pipeline component.

The Add Processing Instructions Text property contains the actual processing instructions you want added to your XML if this is necessary. The compiler checks the string you entered to make sure it is valid. If you need more than one processing instruction, you can just concatenate them like this: `"<?MyFirstIP MyFirstValue ?><?MySecondIP MySecondValue ?>"`.

The Add XML Declaration property determines whether the outgoing XML should have an XML declaration added to it. The XML declaration is really just a processing instruction, which looks something like this: `'<?xml version="1.0" encoding="utf-8" ?>'`. The version is always `"1.0"`, but the value of encoding matches the charset that is determined by the property Target Charset.

The Delivery Receipt Address property specifies the address to which a delivery receipt should be sent, when the message is received at the receiver.

The Delivery Receipt Address Type property specifies the type of address the delivery receipt should be sent to. The type may be `http` or other protocol-specific strings. It can also be `biz:OrganizationName` to comply with older BizTalk versions that use organization names to determine where messages should go.

The Delivery Receipt Send by Time property specifies within how many minutes the receiver has to send the delivery receipt to the sender of the message. If the receipt is received after this time, it does not count as a receipt, because by then the message has either been re-sent or suspended depending on the configured number of retries.

The Destination Address property specifies the address of the destination of the message.

The Destination Address Type property specifies the type of address that is provided in the Destination Address property. This can be `biz:OrganizationName` to accommodate older versions of BizTalk, but it can also be `agr:duns_number` to specify a *Data Universal Numbering System* (DUNS) number; in fact, it can be anything the parties involved agree on.

The Document Schemas property contains a collection of schemas that are the valid schemas to pass through this instance of the XML assembler component. If any XML passes through that does not match the schemas given in this property, you get a runtime error. If the collection is empty, all XML messages are allowed to pass through.

The Document Topic property is a property that contains a value that describes the message that is to be sent. This can be any string, but it cannot be empty.

The Envelope Schemas property is a schema collection of schemas to apply as envelopes of the outgoing message. If you add more than one envelope, they are nested in the outgoing XML. The order you add them to the collection is important because this reflects the hierarchy they are nested in.

The Generate Delivery Receipt Request property is set to True if you want to receive a delivery receipt for the message from the receiver.

The Message Time to Live (in minutes) property specifies how many minutes the message is valid. If the receiver receives the message after this number of minutes have passed since the message was generated at the sender, the message is invalid and should not be processed.

The Source Address property specifies the address of the sender of the message. This can be any string, but must be a string that conforms to the type specified in the "Source Address Type property.

The Source Address Type property specifies the type of address that is provided in the Source Address property. This can be biz:OrganizationName to accommodate older versions of BizTalk, but it can also be agr:duns_number to specify a DUNS number; in fact, it can be anything the parties involved agree on.

The Target Charset property is used to determine what charset the XML should have when it comes out of the assembler component. It is a drop-down list of possible values. The outgoing XML has a charset according to this algorithm:

1. The value of the XMLNorm.TargetCharset context property
2. The value specified at design time on the assembler component
3. The value of the XMLNorm.SourceCharset context property
4. The default value, which is UTF-8

BizTalk Framework Disassembler

The BizTalk Framework disassembler has two pipeline component categories attached to it: PipelineComponent and DisassemblingParser. Therefore, this component can be placed only in the Disassemble stage of a receive pipeline.

Other than the responsibilities a disassembler always has, this component has two more:

▶ If the received message is a BTF receipt, the receipt is handled and consumed, meaning that no message is published to the MessageBox.

▶ The component takes an incoming document that is wrapped in a BTF2 envelope and removes the envelope and outputs the message inside for further processing by the pipeline before it gets published to the MessageBox. If the incoming message envelope contains information about a required delivery receipt, the disassembler generates a new message besides the message body, which is the receipt that must be sent to the sending party of the original message. This message is also returned from the component for further processing in the pipeline before getting published to the MessageBox.

The disassembler looks at the value of the identity element in the envelope to check whether a message has been received with the same identity earlier on. If yes, the messages is silently consumed because otherwise BizTalk would be dealing with the same message twice, and this is one of the main points of BTF2, namely exactly once delivery.

The component has the properties shown in Figure 5.10.

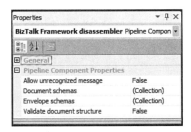

FIGURE 5.10   Properties of the BizTalk Framework disassembler pipeline component.

The Allow Unrecognized Message property lets you decide whether the component should allow messages that it does not recognize to pass through the component. This applies only to XML for which no schemas could be found. If set to False, it does not let you pass invalid instances through BizTalk.

The Document Schemas property is a collection of schemas that are the allowed schemas for the messages that are inside the BTF envelope.

The Envelope property contains a list of all the schemas that are allowed as envelope schemas inside the <SOAP-ENV:Body> element of the BTF envelope. After taking the payload out of the <SOAP-ENV:Body> element and checking it against the Document Schemas and Envelope Schemas properties, normal debatching, property promotion, and further processing occurs.

The Validate Document Structure property determines whether the disassembler should validate the structure of the incoming document. This property can only be set to True if you have specified schemas in the Document Schemas property. If not, you get a compile-time error.

Table 5.1 describes the runtime use of two of these properties, namely the Allow Unrecognized Message property and the Document Schemas property, because the usage is not quite clear. The table contains six unique scenarios, depicting the possible combinations of values of the two properties and a value indicating whether an error occurs at runtime.

TABLE 5.1   Description of When Messages Fail in the BTF Disassembler

Allow Unrecognized Message	Document Schemas	Instance	OK
True	<empty>	Schema1	True
True	<empty>	No schema	True
True	Schema1	Schema1	True
True	Schema1	Schema2	False
True	Schema1	No Schema	True
False	<empty>	Schema1	True
False	<empty>	No Schema	False
False	Schema1	Schema1	True
False	Schema1	Schema2	False
False	Schema1	No Schema	False

Possible values for the Allow Unrecognized Message column are True and False.

Possible values for the Document Schemas column are Schema1 and <empty>, where Schema1 is a schema that is deployed to BizTalk, and <empty> means that no schemas are selected.

Possible values for the Instance column are Schema1, Schema2, and No Schema, where Schema1 and Schema2 mean that an instance that conforms to either Schema1 or Schema2 is in the message, and a value of No Schema means that the instance is some XML for which no schema is deployed.

As you can see, if the pipeline component is set to allow unrecognized messages, and schemas are specified in the Document Schemas property, it will allow messages for which no schemas are deployed, but it will not allow for messages that have a schema deployed that is not specified in the Document Schemas property.

Validator and Party Resolution

This section describes the built-in pipeline components that can be used in both send pipelines and receive pipelines for party resolution and validation of messages.

XML Validator

The XML validator pipeline component has three pipeline component categories attached to it: PipelineComponent, Validate, and Any. The Any category means that in the pipeline designer you can add this component to any stage you like. Be aware, however, that adding it to the Disassemble stage of a receive pipeline or the Assemble stage of a send pipeline causes a runtime error because these two stages require components that implement either the IDisassemblerComponent interface or the IAssemblerComponent interface, and the XML validator component does not implement either of these. Also note that the component can only validate XML, so if you are receiving messages that are not XML, the component should not be placed before the disassembler in the receive pipeline because the message is not converted into XML before that. The same applies for send pipelines, where an assembler has generated a non-XML message. In this case, having the XML validator in a stage after the assembler in the send pipeline will fail. In both cases, you get a runtime error.

The component is used to validate the XML that comes into the component, and it can do so by using a collection of schemas you provide at design time or by finding the appropriate schema dynamically. If the component should locate the schema to be used dynamically, it uses the target namespace and root node of the XML, and therefore it does not rely on any pipeline component having promoted the message type to be used for this.

For both the flat file disassembler and the XML disassembler, you can turn on validation, so it might be somewhat difficult to see the advantage of the XML validator components as opposed to using the validation feature of the disassemblers. There are two main reasons for using the XML validator component:

▶ The XML validator component finds the schema to be used for validation dynamically, whereas the disassemblers need you to specify a schema in the properties. This is more flexible, allowing your pipeline to be used in more scenarios than only validating using the disassemblers.

▶ The XML validator does not do anything other than validation, so it can be useful to place it in a pipeline after a custom pipeline component to check that the output of the component is valid XML.

The XML validator component and the validation inside disassemblers are not different in any way.

Note that the component stops after finding just one error. This means that if incoming XML has several errors, you get a description of only the first found, and after fixing that, you might get another error.

The component has the properties shown in Figure 5.11.

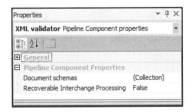

FIGURE 5.11 Properties of XML validator pipeline component.

The Document Schemas property contains a collection of schemas you choose. When schemas are chosen in this collection, these schemas are the only ones used for validation of the XML. If no schemas are chosen, the component tries to discover the schema in the list of currently deployed schemas at runtime, by using the target namespace and root node of the XML.

The Recoverable Interchange Processing property is used for deciding whether to suspend all messages from one interchange if just one message fails validation or whether to suspend only the failed messages and let the rest get published to the MessageBox. This is useful only for when the disassembler has debatched an incoming message into several messages. If this is not the case, there will be only one message coming to this component, and therefore this one message either gets suspended or published.

Party Resolution

The party-resolution pipeline component has two pipeline component categories attached to it: PipelineComponent and PartyResolver. This means that this component can be placed only in the ResolveParty stage of a receive pipeline.

The component is used to resolve which party has sent the received message. If successful, it populates the SourcePartyID property in the http://schemas.microsoft.com/BizTalk/ 2003/system-properties namespace and the PartyName in the http://schemas.microsoft. com/BizTalk/2003/messagetracking-properties namespace. These properties can then be used later.

The component has the properties shown in Figure 5.12.

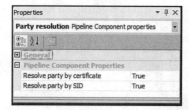

FIGURE 5.12   Properties of the party-resolution pipeline component.

The Resolve Party by Certificate property is used to let the component examine the certificate that was used to sign the message to determine the sending party.

The Resolve Party by SID party is used to let the component examine the Windows Security Identifier of the user who sent the message.

If both properties are set to True, the component first tries to use the certificate, and if that fails, it uses the SID.

Custom Pipelines

If the pipelines that come out-of-the-box cannot cover your needs, you can add custom pipelines to your project in Visual Studio 2010. Custom pipelines are added to your Visual Studio project just like other artifacts and compiled into an assembly that can be deployed to your BizTalk Server. Custom pipelines can leverage both the built-in pipeline components as well as custom pipeline components. When deployed, the custom pipelines can be used in Receive Locations and Send Ports just as the built-in pipelines.

Using the Built-In Pipeline Templates

To add one of the built-in send or receive pipelines, right-click your project and choose **Add**, **New Item**. This shows you the screen for adding new items, and you have two pipeline options, as shown in Figure 5.13. You can choose either a receive pipeline or a send pipeline. Remember to provide a better name for the pipeline than the generated receivepipeline1.btp or sendpipeline1.btp. You do not have to enter .btp because the wizard adds this for you automatically.

FIGURE 5.13   Add new pipeline to your project.

After adding a pipeline, you get to see the pipeline designer in Visual Studio 2010, where you can see the stages that are relevant for this particular type of pipeline. Figure 5.1 and Figure 5.2 show the view in Visual Studio 2010 you get after adding either a receive pipeline or a send pipeline. All available pipeline components are shown in the Visual Studio 2010 Toolbox, and you add a pipeline component to your pipeline by dragging it to the pipeline designer surface and dropping it where you want it to go. The arrow will be a circle with a line through it if you are trying to move the component to a place in the pipeline where the component does not belong.

Custom pipelines are needed for your solution whenever the built-in pipelines explained earlier do not meet your needs. This includes all scenarios where you need to receive or send non-XML messages, like flat files, and need to do anything other than move them around, in which case the pass-through pipelines can be used. Pipelines are compiled along with any other artifacts in your project and deployed with the project. After a pipeline is deployed, it can be used in receive locations (for receive pipelines) and send ports (for send pipelines) in the application to which it was deployed and in other applications that have a reference to the application to which the pipeline was deployed.

Creating Custom Pipeline Templates

You have the option to create your own pipeline templates if you want to do so. You can change the naming, order, and number of stages in pipelines. This is rarely used, but it can allow you to create a pipeline template that, for instance, has a Decompress stage rather than the Decode stage in the built-in receive pipeline template. This can allow you to make it easier for developers on your team to know what they need to put into a given stage of the receive pipeline.

To create a pipeline template, you need to create two files: a pipeline policy file and a BizTalk project item file.

Listing 5.3 shows an example of a pipeline policy file. In this pipeline policy file, which is a modified version of the existing BTSReceivePolicy.xml file, there are three stages: Decompress, Disassemble, and Validate. When creating a pipeline policy file, you can change only the following values:

- ► `FriendlyName` attribute of the Document root node. This specifies the name that appears in the Add New Item dialog box in Visual Studio 2010.

- ► `Name` attribute of the `Stage` element. This specifies the name of the stage that is shown in the pipeline designer.

- ► `minOccurs` attribute of the `Stage` element. This specifies the minimum number of components that should be in this stage, which allows you to force developers to use a stage.

- ► `maxOccurs` attribute of the `Stage` element. This specifies the maximum number of components that can be added to this stage. A value of –1 means that up to 255 components can be added to this stage.

- ► `execMethod` attribute of the `Stage` element. This can have three values:

  - ► `All`, meaning that all components in the stage are executed one at a time.

  - ► `FirstMatch`, meaning that the first component that returns true from the `Probe` method in the `IProbeMessage` interface gets the message and the rest do not get it.

▶ None. This is a valid value for the attribute, but setting it results in a compile-time error of any projects that use this particular new pipeline template.

LISTING 5.3   A Pipeline Policy File

```
<?xml version="1.0" encoding="utf-8"?>
<Document xmlns:xsd="http://www.w3.org/2001/XMLSchema"
xmlns:xsi="http://www.w3.org/2001/XMLSchema-instance" CategoryId =
"F66B9F5E-43FF-4f5f-BA46-885348AE1B4E" FriendlyName = "Decompress Receive">
  <Stages>
      <Stage _locAttrData="Name" _locID="1" Name = "Decompress" minOccurs =
"0" maxOccurs = "-1" stageId = "9d0e4103-4cce-4536-83fa-4a5040674ad6"
execMethod = "FirstMatch"></Stage>
      <Stage _locAttrData="Name" _locID="2" Name = "Disassemble" minOccurs
= "0" maxOccurs = "-1" stageId = "9d0e4105-4cce-4536-83fa-4a5040674ad6"
execMethod = "FirstMatch"></Stage>
      <Stage _locAttrData="Name" _locID="3" Name = "Validate" minOccurs =
"0" maxOccurs = "-1" stageId = "9d0e410d-4cce-4536-83fa-4a5040674ad6"
execMethod = "All"></Stage>
  </Stages>
</Document>
```

After the XML file is generated, it must be saved under <InstallationFolder>\Developer Tools\Pipeline Policy Files, where you will also find the pipeline policy files for BizTalk's internal send and receive pipelines. They are marked read-only for a reason.

After generating and saving the pipeline policy files, you need to create a file that lets Visual Studio 2010 show your component in the Add New Item dialog box. For this, you need to create another XML file. Listing 5.4 shows an example of this. It is a simple XML file that basically points to the pipeline policy file by filename.

LISTING 5.4   A BizTalk Project Item File

```
<?xml version="1.0" encoding="utf-16" ?>
<Document xmlns:xsd="http://www.w3.org/2001/XMLSchema"
xmlns:xsi=PolicyFilePath="Decompress Receive.xml" MajorVersion="1"
MinorVersion="0">
<Stages>
</Stages>
</Document>
```

After creating this XML file, save it in <InstallationFolder>\Developer Tools\BizTalkProjectItems as a pipeline file, meaning that the file extension needs to be .btp.

Based on the two files shown in Listing 5.3 and Listing 5.4, when you add a new item in Visual Studio 2010, the screen shown in Figure 5.14 opens.

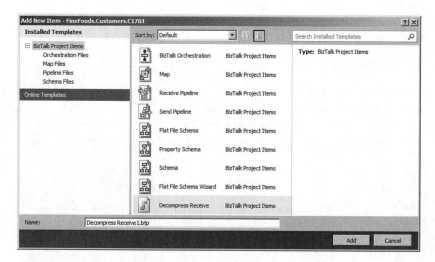

FIGURE 5.14   Add New Item dialog after creating a custom pipeline policy file.

When inserting a pipeline of this new type, the pipeline designer looks like Figure 5.15. Developers can now use this pipeline and add components to them, as specified in your custom pipeline policy file.

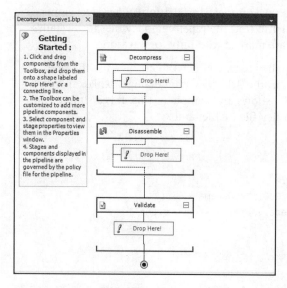

FIGURE 5.15   Pipeline designer with a new pipeline policy file.

Note that you cannot create new types of stages. The values for the `stageId` attributes on the `Stage` element in the pipeline policy file must correspond to the existing seven stage types. As a rule, therefore, it is easier to copy the existing receive or send pipeline policy file and use that as a starting point for your custom pipeline policy file.

Custom Pipeline Components

As you have seen, BizTalk ships with some useful pipeline components to build your own pipelines. In some cases, however, the built-in pipeline components cannot do what you need them to do, and in these cases, you might consider writing your own pipeline components.

To write your own pipeline component, create a project in Visual Studio 2010 that is a Class library project type, as shown in Figure 5.16. It is recommended to use C# as your programming language, for several reasons:

▶ Almost all examples (online, in books, in the SDK, and so on) are written in C#.

▶ When using the Expression shape in an orchestration, the language used is similar to the C# syntax.

▶ All generated code for compiled schemas, maps, orchestrations, and pipelines is in C#

You can choose VB.NET if you want to, but using C# makes it easier to understand the rest of the code out there and will probably be easier in the long run.

After adding the new project, add a signature to the assembly that will strong name it, to allow for the assembly to be put into the GAC. To do this, right-click the new project and choose **Properties**. Then go to the Signing tab, as shown in Figure 5.17. Here you check the **Sign the Assembly** check box. Click the arrow in the drop-down list, and if you have already created a strong key pair earlier, click **Browse** and select the key file. If you do not already have a key file that can be used, click **New**. A dialog box then asks for a name for

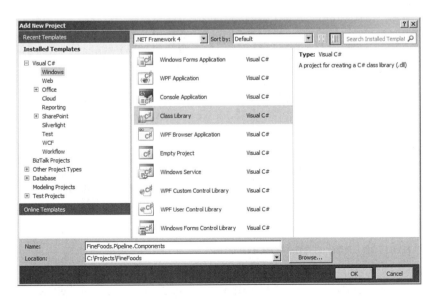

FIGURE 5.16   Add new class library to contain pipeline components.

the key file. Name the key file, and optionally provide a password for the key file allowing you to restrict who can sign assemblies with this particular key.

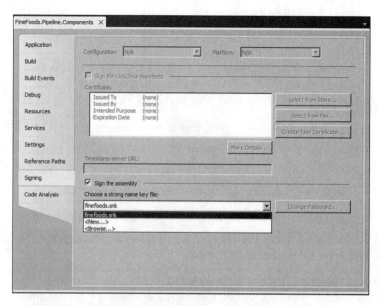

FIGURE 5.17   Adding a signature to the class library.

When you finish adding a signature to the assembly, close the Properties window.

To create classes that BizTalk recognizes as pipeline components, you need to implement some specific interfaces. These interfaces are specified in the `Microsoft.BizTalk.Pipeline` namespace. You therefore need to reference the assembly that contains this namespace and these interfaces. Right-click your project or on the References node in your project and click **Add Reference**. Go to the Browse pane and browse your way to <InstallationFolder>\Microsoft.BizTalk.Pipeline.dll and add this as a reference. Delete the Class1.cs file that was automatically created for you and instead add a new class to your project by right-clicking the project and choosing **Add, New Item**. Choose Class as the type and provide a name for your class, as shown in Figure 5.18.

You now have a class that is ready to be implemented. The next sections describe how to implement a custom pipeline component. The sections take you through all the aspects of developing a custom pipeline component, like the required interfaces and attributes and error handling, transactions, performance considerations, deployment, and debugging your component.

Resources, Attributes, and Constructors

Although not needed, you will most likely use a resources file to store your resources. These resources are the strings that are used at runtime to describe properties, as well as the icon showing up for your component in the Toolbox of Visual Studio 2010. If your class library will contain more than one pipeline component, you can create a folder inside your project and add the resources file there. To add a folder, follow these step:

1. Right-click your project and choose **Add**, **New Folder**.

2. You can name it Resources or any other name.

To add a resources file, follow these steps:

1. Right-click your project or the folder you have created, and choose **Add**, **New Item**, **Resources File**.

2. Provide it with a good name, perhaps as shown in Figure 5.19.

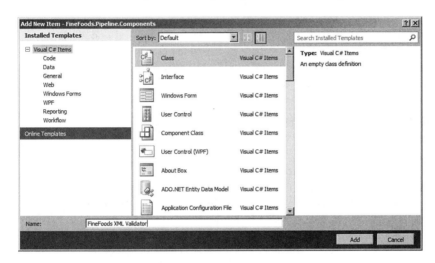

FIGURE 5.18   Adding a new class to your class library.

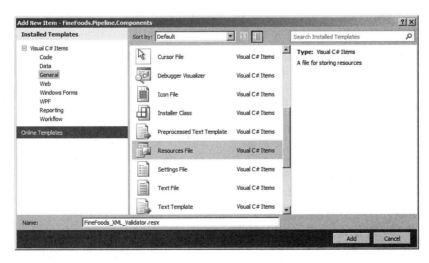

FIGURE 5.19   Adding a resources file to your project.

After adding this resources file, your project should look something like Figure 5.20.

FIGURE 5.20   Project after adding class and resources file.

Now you need to set up the code to use this resources file. You use the `ResourceManager` class from the `System.Resources` namespace to do so. Therefore, add using `System.Resources;` to your using statements at the top of your class, and add a static member and a static constructor to initialize it, as shown in Listing 5.5. The resource manager is declared static because it can then be used across all instances of the pipeline component. A static constructor is added to the pipeline component to initialize the resource manager.

The first parameter to the constructor of the `ResourceManager` class is a string defining the fully qualified name of the resources file. This can partly be found in the code and partly must be inferred. A fully qualified name consists of a namespace and a class name. The namespace of a file in your project is the default namespace of your project concatenated with the relative folder hierarchy the file is placed in. In this case, as you can see from Figure 5.20, the default namespace is `FineFoods.Pipeline.Components` because that is the name of the project. The resources file is placed in a folder called Resources, which is then also a part of the namespace of the resources file. Thus, full namespace of the resources file is `FineFoods.Pipeline.Components.Resources`. The class name is the same as the file-name without the extension, so the fully qualified name of the resources file is `FineFoods.Pipeline.Components.Resources.FineFoods_XML_Validator`.

The second parameter of the constructor of the `ResourceManager` class is the assembly currently executing.

Besides adding the resource manager to the class to deal with resources, you need to mark your class as `public` and to decorate it with some attributes telling the pipeline designer how the component can be used. As shown in Listing 5.5, three attributes have been added to this component.

The `Guid` attribute is in the `System.Runtime.InteropServices` namespace, so you should add that to your using statements. The GUID specified in this attribute must be unique for this class. To create a unique GUID, you can use guidgen.exe, which is located in the C:\Program Files(x86)\Microsoft SDKs\Windows\v7.0A\Bin folder (or similar for other versions of Windows). This utility generates a new and unique GUID for you.

The two `ComponentCategory` attributes tell the pipeline designer what sort of component this class is. There are 13 different values for the `ComponentCategory` attribute, as follows:

▶ `CategoryTypes.CATID_Any` Components in this category can be placed in any stage of any pipeline.

▶ `CategoryTypes.CATID_AssemblingSerializer` Components in this category can be placed in the Assemble stage of a send pipeline.

▶ `CategoryTypes.CATID_Decoder` Components in this category can be placed in the Decode stage of a receive pipeline.

▶ `CategoryTypes.CATID_DisassemblingParser` Components in this category can be placed in the Disassemble stage of a receive pipeline.

▶ `CategoryTypes.CATID_Encoder` Components in this category can be placed in the Encode stage of a send pipeline.

▶ `CategoryTypes.CATID_Parser` Not currently used.

▶ `CategoryTypes.CATID_PartyResolver` Components in this category can be placed in the ResolveParty stage of a receive pipeline.

▶ `CategoryTypes.CATID_PipelineComponent` This category does not affect which stages a component can be placed in, but merely serves as an indication for the pipeline designer that this is a pipeline component.

▶ `CategoryTypes.CATID_Receiver` Not currently used.

▶ `CategoryTypes.CATID_Serializer` Not currently used.

▶ `CategoryTypes.CATID_Streamer` Not currently used.

▶ `CategoryTypes.CATID_Transmitter` Not currently used.

▶ `CategoryTypes.CATID_Validate` Components in this category can be placed in the Validate stage of a receive pipeline.

All 13 values are public strings in the `CategoryTypes` class, and they each correspond to a unique GUID. So instead of using the `CategoryTypes.CATID_Any` parameter for the `ComponentCategory` attribute, you might as well have used the string `"9d0e4101-4cce-4536-83fa-4a5040674ad6"`. There are category types specific to all stages except the Pre-Assemble stage of a send pipeline. Five of the category types exist merely to provide some way of adding features in later versions and are not currently used. This means that you cannot, for instance, create a pipeline component and restrict it to exist only in send pipelines because no category type exists for this. For receive pipelines, you could add the four stage-specific category types to your component, but because there doesn't exist a category type for the Pre-Assemble stage, you need to use the Any category to write a component that can be placed in that stage, and using that category type will allow the component to be used in a receive pipeline, as well.

The most general of the categories will be the one determining what stages a component can be placed in. Therefore, a pipeline component that has the Any category assigned to it can be added to any stage no matter what other categories have been added to it.

LISTING 5.5   Class with Attributes and a **ResourceManager** for the Resources

```
[ComponentCategory(CategoryTypes.CATID_PipelineComponent)]
[ComponentCategory(CategoryTypes.CATID_Validate)]
[Guid("35FDAF6E-92E8-4779-8B85-025A948896E6")]
public class FineFoods_XML_Validator
{
    private static ResourceManager resManager;

    static FineFoods_XML_Validator()
    {
        resManager = new
ResourceManager("FineFoods.Pipeline.Components.Resources.FineFoods_XML_Valid
ator", Assembly.GetExecutingAssembly());
    }
}
```

After the `resManager` object has been initialized, resources can be retrieved in code by using `resManager.GetString("StringThatContainsTheNameOfTheResource");`.

To add a new resource to the file, open the resources file in Visual Studio 2010 and click **Add Resource**. You have the option to add existing files or new strings, images, icons, or text files, as shown in Figure 5.21.

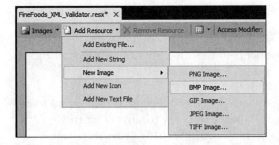

FIGURE 5.21   Adding a new resource to the resources file.

Interfaces

This section describes the interfaces you can and should implement when developing custom pipeline components.

All custom pipeline components must implement the following three interfaces:

- ▶ `IComponentUI`, which lets you specify an icon for the component and a method for validating any properties the user can set values in

- ▶ `IBaseComponent`, which basically lets you specify three properties that the pipeline designer uses to get a name, version, and description from your component to show in the designer

- ▶ IPersistPropertyBag, which lets you define methods used for persisting the properties set by the user and reading them at runtime

Other than these three interfaces, there are three more interfaces, of which all components must implement exactly one:

- ▶ IComponent, which is used for all components that are not assemblers or disassemblers. This interface specifies just one method to implement, and this is the method that will be doing all the work.

- ▶ IAssemblerComponent, which exposes two methods needed for an assembler component to run.

- ▶ IDisassemblerComponent, which exposes two methods needed for a disassembler component to run.

These are the needed interfaces. There is another interface that can be used if needed, but it is not required. This interface is called IProbeMessage, and it defines a single method that must return a Boolean value describing whether this component can accept the given message.

All the interfaces are in the Microsoft.BizTalk.Component.Interop namespace, so adding using Microsoft.BizTalk.Component.Interop; at the top of your class is probably a good idea to make the code more readable, although this is not required.

IComponentUI

The IComponentUI interface is shown in Listing 5.6. It has one property and one method that must be implemented.

The property is called Icon. This property returns the icon used in the Toolbox of Visual Studio 2010. First, add an icon to the resources file, and then return it from the Icon method. To add an icon to the resources file, open the resources file and click **Add Resource**, as shown in Figure 5.21. Choose **Add New Image**, **BMP Image**. Provide it with a name like **FineFoods_XML_Validator_Icon**, and an image editor will open with a sample icon ready for editing. Go to the properties of the image and change its height and width to **16**, and then edit the icon as appropriate and save it. You can create an image that is larger than 16x16 pixels, but you will probably not be happy with the way it will scale in the Toolbox.

LISTING 5.6   The **IComponentUI** Interface for Custom Pipeline Components

```
#region IComponentUI Members

public IntPtr Icon
{
    get { throw new NotImplementedException(); }
}
```

```
public IEnumerator Validate(object projectSystem)
{
    throw new NotImplementedException();
}
```

```
#endregion
```

Now, after adding the icon to the resources, you need to implement the Icon property. You need code that extracts the icon from the resources. Write code similar to the code in Listing 5.7, which basically just retrieves the image form the resource manager and returns it.

After implementing this property, implement the Validate method. This method is used to validate the properties your component exposes to the developer, to which she can assign values at design time. The types of the properties themselves, naturally, imply some validation on what values the developer can enter. However, if you need to validate, for instance, that if one property has a certain value then another property cannot be empty or similar, you need to do this validation in code. The method returns an enumerator that contains all the error messages, and at design time, the compilation fails if this enumerator has any error messages in it. If your component does not expose properties, or there is no need for any further validation, the method can just return null. This validation is only for design time using the pipeline designer, and the error messages are shown at compile time. The validation does not extend to the per-instance pipeline properties that you can set inside BizTalk Administration Console.

LISTING 5.7   Implementation of the **Icon** Property in the **IComponentUI** Interface

```
public IntPtr Icon
{
    get
    {
        return ResourceHandler.GetResourceBitmap(resManager,
"FineFoods_XML_Validator_Icon").GetHicon();
    }
}
```

Listing 5.8 shows sample code for the Validate method. It returns null because there are currently no properties exposed and therefore no validation needed. In the comments in the code, you can see an example of how to go about it if validation is needed.

LISTING 5.8   Implementation of the **Validate** Method in the **IComponentUI** Interface

```
public IEnumerator Validate(object projectSystem)
{
    // Do validation
    // ArrayList errorList = new ArrayList();
```

```
    // errorList.Add("\"Prop2\" cannot be empty if \"Prop1\" is set to
true");
    // return errorList.GetEnumerator();
    return null;
}
```

IBaseComponent

The IBaseComponent interface is shown in Listing 5.9. It has three properties that must be implemented.

The first property is called Description. It must return a string that contains a description of the component. This description is shown in the Properties window of the component.

The second property is called Name. It must return a name for the component. It is used in four places:

▶ As the name of the component in the Toolbox.

▶ As the name shown on the component in the pipeline designer if the component has been dragged to a stage.

▶ It is shown in the Properties window.

▶ As the name shown for the component in a given stage when setting per-instance properties on the pipeline in BizTalk Administration Console.

The third property is called Version. It must return a string that contains the version of the component. This is just a string, and you can write anything in here that you want. This does not interfere with the .NET assembly or file versioning and is merely for you to provide a version number to the developer.

LISTING 5.9   The **IBaseComponent** Interface for Custom Pipeline Components

```
#region IBaseComponent Members

public string Description
{
    get { throw new NotImplementedException(); }
}

public string Name
{
    get { throw new NotImplementedException(); }
}

public string Version
{
```

```
    get { throw new NotImplementedException(); }
}

#endregion
```

Implementing these can be as easy as just returning a string from each property, but just as with the icon, you should add these values to the resources file, as shown in Figure 5.22.

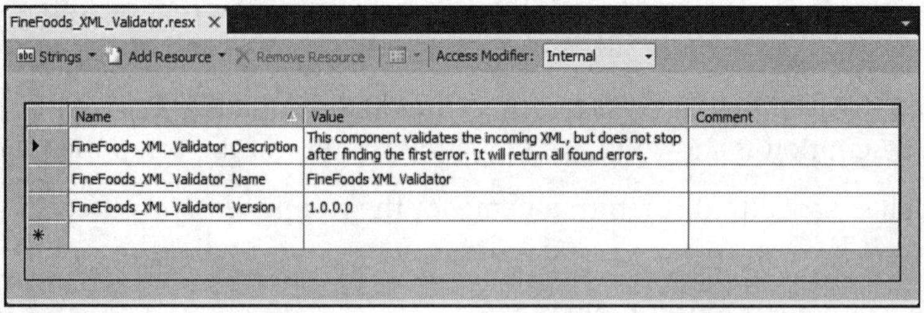

FIGURE 5.22   Adding three string resources to the resources file.

The resources must be of type string, and you can basically give them any name you want. The name of the resource is what you will be using in your code to get the values back out. After adding these three resources, you can implement the three properties in the IBaseComponent interface, as shown in Listing 5.10.

LISTING 5.10   Implementation of the **IBaseComponent** Interface for Custom Pipeline Components

```
#region IBaseComponent Members

public string Description
{
    get
    {
        return resManager.GetString("FineFoods_XML_Validator_Description");
    }
}

public string Name
{
    get
    {
        return resManager.GetString("FineFoods_XML_Validator_Name");
    }
}
```

```
public string Version
{
    get
    {
        return resManager.GetString("FineFoods_XML_Validator_Version");
    }
}

#endregion
```

IPersistPropertyBag

The IPersistPropertyBag interface is shown in Listing 5.11. It has four methods that must be implemented.

This interface is used to make sure that values entered, when designing a new pipeline, in the Properties window of the pipeline component and properties set as per-instance properties are stored in a property bag, allowing the runtime to read them back in and use them at runtime.

The first method you need to implement is called GetClassID. It does not return anything, but has an out parameter. In your method, you need to set the classID out parameter to a new GUID with a value that matches the GUID used as an attribute on the class. Listing 5.12 shows an implementation of this method.

The second method is called InitNew. It is used to initialize any objects needed by the component to use the persisted properties. For the most part, this method is not used, and in fact, it is not used in any of the built-in pipeline components. We won't use this component either, as shown in Listing 5.13.

The third method is called Load. It is used to read all properties from the property bag so that they are available at runtime. The method has two parameters: the property bag to read from and an integer that is the address of an error log. The integer that is the address of an error log can be ignored. It is a left over from older COM days, and is not used anymore. The method is called twice: once to load the properties set at design time and once to load the properties set as per-instance properties.

The fourth method is called Save. It is used to save the values for the properties entered by the developer into the property bag so that they can be read back at runtime using the Load method.

LISTING 5.11 The **IPersistPropertyBag** Interface for Custom Pipeline Components

```
#region IPersistPropertyBag Members

public void GetClassID(out Guid classID)
{
```

```
        throw new NotImplementedException();
}

public void InitNew()
{
        throw new NotImplementedException();
}

public void Load(IPropertyBag propertyBag, int errorLog)
{
        throw new NotImplementedException();
}

public void Save(IPropertyBag propertyBag, bool clearDirty, bool
saveAllProperties)
{
        throw new NotImplementedException();
}

#endregion
```

LISTING 5.12   Implementation of the **GetClassID** Method in the **IPersistPropertyBag**
Interface for Custom Pipeline Components

```
public void GetClassID(out Guid classID)
{
        classID = new Guid("35FDAF6E-92E8-4779-8B85-025A948896E6");
}
```

LISTING 5.13   Implementation of the **InitNew** Method in the **IPersistPropertyBag**
Interface for Custom Pipeline Components

```
public void InitNew()
{
}
```

Reading in a value from the property bag is as simple as a single line of code. However, single line of code can result in a couple of different exceptions that need to be caught and dealt with individually. This means that code to read one property will take up more than 10 lines of code. Therefore, it is usually helpful to have either a utility class with helper methods or just a helper method in the same class as the pipeline component that does this for you. The code for a helper method is shown in Listing 5.14. The value is read by using the Read method on the property bag. The method takes three parameters: the name of the property to read, an out parameter to store the value in, and an integer that specifies the address of an error log. As with the `Load` method of the `IPersistPropertyBag` interface, this is no longer used, and a value of `0` can be used.

LISTING 5.14   Implementation of a Helper Method to Read from a Property Bag

```csharp
public static object ReadPropertyBag(IPropertyBag pb, string propName)
{
    object val = null;
    try
    {
        pb.Read(propName, out val, 0);
    }
    catch (System.ArgumentException)
    {
        return val;
    }
    catch (System.Exception e)
    {
        throw new System.ApplicationException(e.Message);
    }
    return val;
}
```

Just as with reading a property from the property bag, it may be helpful to have a helper method to write to the property bag. Listing 5.15 shows such a helper method.

Suppose you have an enumeration in your code that looks like the one in Listing 5.16 and you want to have a property on your pipeline component that lets the designer choose the level of debug information your component should write. Also, suppose you have helper methods for reading and writing to the property bag and a property called `DebugLevel` in your pipeline component that is of the type `DebugLevels`. In this case, your code for the `Load` method could look like Listing 5.17, and your code for the `Save` method could look like Listing 5.18.

LISTING 5.15   Implementation of a Helper Method to Write to a Property Bag

```csharp
public static void WritePropertyBag(IPropertyBag pb, string propName, object
 val)
{
    try
    {
        pb.Write(propName, ref val);
    }
    catch (System.Exception e)
    {
        throw new System.ApplicationException(e.Message);
```

```
    }
}
```

LISTING 5.16 **DebugLevels** Enumeration

```
public enum DebugLevels
{
    None,
    Little,
    Normal,
    High,
    Verbose
}
```

LISTING 5.17   Implementation of the **Load** Method of the **IPersistPropertyBag** Interface
for a Custom Pipeline Component

```
public void Load(IPropertyBag propertyBag, int errorLog)
{
    object val = null;
    val = PropertyHelper.ReadPropertyBag(propertyBag, "DebugLevel");
    if ((val != null))
    {
        this.DebugLevel = ((DebugLevels)(val));
    }
}
```

LISTING 5.18   Implementation of the **Save** Method of the **IPersistPropertyBag** Interface
for a Custom Pipeline Component

```
public void Save(IPropertyBag propertyBag, bool clearDirty, bool saveAllProperties)
{
    PropertyHelper.WritePropertyBag(propertyBag, "DebugLevel", this.DebugLevel);
}
```

The Save method takes in two Boolean parameters called clearDirty and
saveAllProperties. These two parameters are not actually used. They are present because
the IPersistPropertyBag is actually a very old COM interface, which has these two parameters that other components can use. They are used to clear a component's dirty flag so
that other components know that the component is no longer dirty or to indicate
whether the component should save all properties or a subset of them respectively. For
implementations of a custom pipeline component, these are not needed and always have
the value true.

Note that to be consistent and make your code easy to read, understand, and modify, you will most probably want to use the same names for the properties in the property bag as you use for the properties in your pipeline component class. This is not mandatory, however. The code for the Load and Save methods could just as well have been as shown in Listing 5.19. The important thing is that you name the properties the same in both the Load and the Save methods.

LISTING 5.19   Implementation of **Load** and **Save** with Different Names for Properties in the Property Bag Than in the Pipeline Component Class

```
public void Load(IPropertyBag propertyBag, int errorLog)
{
    object val = null;
    val = PropertyHelper.ReadPropertyBag(propertyBag, "SomethingElse");
    if ((val != null))
    {
        this.DebugLevel = ((DebugLevels)(val));
    }
}

public void Save(IPropertyBag propertyBag, bool clearDirty, bool saveAllProperties)
{
    PropertyHelper.WritePropertyBag(propertyBag, "SomethingElse", this.DebugLevel);
}
```

IComponent

The IComponent interface is shown in Listing 5.20. It has one method that must be implemented.

The IComponent interface is used for all custom pipeline components that are not disassemblers or assemblers. The interface provides a single method, which is called at runtime. The method is called Execute. It has two parameters, which are the context of the pipeline executing the component and the input message to the component, as it is provided by the previous pipeline component or the adapter if your component is the first component to execute in the pipeline.

If you want to implement a consuming pipeline component (that is, a component that will consume any messages and not have any output), just return null from the Execute method. This can be useful when you want to have a send port that subscribes to some messages that you do not actually need in your business because if you do not subscribe to them, they all get suspended with errors.

LISTING 5.20   The **IComponent** Interface for Custom Pipeline Components

```
#region IComponent Members


public IBaseMessage Execute(IPipelineContext pContext, IBaseMessage pInMsg)
{
    throw new NotImplementedException();
}

#endregion
```

IAssemblerComponent

The IAssemblerComponent interface is shown in Listing 5.21. It has two methods that must be implemented.

The responsibility of an assembler component is to assemble a number of messages into one message and to convert it into the format the receiver wants to receive.

The first method of the interface is called AddDocument, and it is called once for all documents that this assembler must batch together.

The second method is called Assemble, and it is called after AddDocument has been called potentially multiple times. The method is called only once and must then return the batched message.

LISTING 5.21   The **IAssemblerComponent** Interface for Custom Pipeline Components

```
#region IAssemblerComponent Members


public void AddDocument(IPipelineContext pContext, IBaseMessage pInMsg)
{
    throw new NotImplementedException();
}

public IBaseMessage Assemble(IPipelineContext pContext)
{
    throw new NotImplementedException();
}

#endregion
```

For normal send pipeline execution in send ports, AddDocument is called only once because only one message is going through the pipeline. If possible, you should still take into account that someone might be using a send pipeline with your custom assembler component inside an orchestration and therefore might be calling AddDocument multiple times.

IDisassemblerComponent

The IDisassemblerComponent interface is shown in Listing 5.22. It has two methods that must be implemented.

The first method is called Disassemble. It is called with the input message to the pipeline component, and it is only called once.

The second method is called GetNext. It is called multiple times until it returns null. This allows the disassembler to debatch the incoming message and return any number of messages for further processing.

LISTING 5.22   The **IDisassemblerComponent** Interface for Custom Pipeline Components

```
#region IDisassemblerComponent Members


public void Disassemble(IPipelineContext pContext, IBaseMessage pInMsg)
{
    throw new NotImplementedException();
}

public IBaseMessage GetNext(IPipelineContext pContext)
{
    throw new NotImplementedException();
}


#endregion
```

The Disassemble method should split the incoming message into smaller messages if applicable and then keep each disassembled message in some data structure like the System.Collections.Queue (FIFO) or System.Collections.Stack (LIFO) that is easily accessible from the GetNext method when the disassembled messages must be returned.

IProbeMessage

The IProbeMessage interface is shown in Listing 5.23. It has one method that must be implemented.

This interface is used to let disassemblers do a quick evaluation of the input message before executing the Disassemble method on it. This facilitates the FirstMatch functionality of the Disassemble stage that lets you specify a number of disassemblers in the Disassemble stage. However, only the first that recognizes the input gets it, and the rest of the components are ignored.

The method to implement is called Probe. It has two parameters: the context of the pipeline executing the component and the input message to the component as provided by the previous pipeline component or the adapter if your component is the first component to execute in the pipeline.

The method returns a Boolean value indicating whether this component should handle the input. This means that before any processing is done inside the component, the Probe method is called, and the component is then executed only if the Probe method returns a value of True.

Implementing the IProbeMessage interface on a component that appears in a pipeline stage that has the execution mode All does not really make sense because the execution mode implies that all components must be executed. As would be expected in this case, the Probe method is not called at all. If you need to do probing on your component in these cases, you must call a probing method from within your Execute method yourself.

Out-of-the-box, the only stage in a pipeline that has an execution mode that is not All is the Disassemble stage of a receive pipeline, which has an execution mode of FirstMatch. For disassemblers, the Probe method is called if the disassembler component implements the IProbeMessage interface. If the component does not implement the IProbeMessage interface, it is assumed that the component should be executed.

Note that the IProbeMessage interface can be implemented on all pipeline components, but it is only used for disassemblers in the Disassemble stage of a receive pipeline. Even if you create your own pipeline policy file, as explained earlier, with a stage that is of type FirstMatch, like the Disassemble stage, it will not be used. Implementing it on components that are not disassemblers will therefore only add to the complexity of your class and not provide you with any advantages at runtime.

LISTING 5.23   **IProbeMessage** Interface for Custom Pipeline Components

```
#region IProbeMessage Members


public bool Probe(IPipelineContext pContext, IBaseMessage pInMsg)
{
    throw new NotImplementedException();
}


#endregion
```

The reason for providing disassemblers with this interface is to allow for fast detection of which of the components in the Disassemble stage should be executed. This also means that if you develop a custom disassembler and want to have multiple disassemblers in the same pipeline, you must implement this interface, and the Probe method should be really fast so that your component isn't a bottleneck.

This also applies to the Load method of the IPersistPropertyBag interface, because this is called before the Probe method so that the Probe method has the values of all the properties available for doing the probing.

Message and Context Interfaces

No matter what component you develop, you will most probably need to leverage the
IBaseMessage, IBaseMessagePart, and the IPipelineContext interfaces. This book does not
cover these interfaces in detail but does outline the most important properties and methods.

IPipelineContext

You can find the full specification of this interface at the MSDN site.

The IPipelineContext interface is used to access the context in which the pipeline
executes. Table 5.2 describes the most important properties and methods that are available to you.

TABLE 5.2   Most Important Members of the **IPipelineContext** Interface

Name	Type	Description
ComponentIndex	Property	Gets the index of this component within the stage it is placed in. If you have two disassemblers in the Disassemble stage, for instance, one will have ComponentIndex 0 and the other will have ComponentIndex 1.
PipelineID	Property	Gets the GUID that is associated with the current pipeline. This GUID is internal to the pipeline and usually not something you need to use.
PipelineName	Property	Gets the strong name of the pipeline class.
StageID	Property	Gets the GUID that is associated with this stage of the pipeline. This is the GUID you will find as the stageId attribute of the stage in the pipeline policy file.
StageIndex	Property	Returns the index of the stage the pipeline component is executing in. This is not the index relative to the number of possible stages, though. Instead, it is the index relative to the number of stages that have components in them.
GetDocumentSpecByName	Method	This method takes a string parameter that is the fully qualified name of the schema you want to look up and returns an IDocumentSpec instance of the schema. Throws an exception if the schema is not found.
GetDocumentSpecByType	Method	This method takes in a string parameter that is the message type of the schema you want to find. You can use the promoted property MessageType to dynamically determine which schema to look for. Throws an exception if the schema is not found.
GetMessageFactory	Method	Returns an instance of a class which implements the IBaseMessageFactory interface, which is explained later.

IBaseMessageFactory

You can find the full specification of this interface at the MSDN site.

The IBaseMessageFactory interface is used as a factory that can help you create new messages and message parts. It has four methods, which are explained in Table 5.3.

TABLE 5.3   Methods of the **IBaseMessageFactory** Interface

Name	Description
CreateMessage	Creates an object of a class that implements the IBaseMessage interface and returns its interface
CreateMessageContext	Creates an object of a class that implements the IBaseMessageContext and returns its interface
CreateMessagePart	Creates an object of a class that implements the IBaseMessagePart interface and returns its interface
CreatePropertyBag	Creates an object of a class that implements the IBasePropertyBag interface and returns its interface

IBaseMessage

You can find the full specification of this interface at the MSDN site.

The IBaseMessage interface is used to describe a message that comes through a pipeline. A message consists of a message context and a number of message parts, of which one is the main part, also called the body part. The interface for a message part is described in the next section. The most important properties and methods of the IBaseMessage interface are described in Table 5.4.

TABLE 5.4   Most Important Members of the **IBaseMessage** Interface

Name	Type	Description
Context	Property	You access the context of a message using the Context property, which returns an instance of a class that implements the IBaseMessageContext interface. This interface is described later. Using this property, you can read properties form the context of the message and you can write and promote properties to the context of the message.
GetPart	Method	You can access message parts by using the GetPart method, which takes in a string with the name of the part you want to get.
GetPartByIndex	Method	You can also access message parts by using the GetPartByIndex method, which takes an in parameter, which is an integer providing the index of the part you want to retrieve. The GetPartByIndex method also takes an out parameter that will contain the name of the part once the method exits.

TABLE 5.4   Most Important Members of the **IBaseMessage** Interface

Name	Type	Description
PartCount	Property	You can get the number of parts available from the PartCount property and use this to loop and get all parts, if needed.
BodyPart	Property	For quick access to the body part, which is often the only message part you want to handle, you can use the BodyPart property.
BodyPartName	Property	The BodyPartName property contains the name of the body part.

A message usually has only one part. The most common exceptions are as follows:

▶ Incoming email that either has multiple files attached or has one file attached and you need both the email body and the file attachment

▶ Outgoing email that has parts added for each file to attach

▶ Messages you have created yourself in a custom pipeline component where you have split a message into several parts for business reasons

▶ Multipart message created inside orchestrations when calling a web service operation that takes in multiple parameters

5

NOTE

When sending out a message that has multiple parts, make sure the adapter understands this. The FILE adapter, for instance, does not know what to do with multiple parts and will simply send the body part to the file and ignore the rest of the message parts without throwing an exception.

IBaseMessagePart
You can find the full specification of this interface at the MSDN site.

The IBaseMessagePart interface is used to describe a message part of a message that comes through a pipeline. The most important properties and methods of the IBaseMessagePart interface are explained in Table 5.5.

TABLE 5.5   Most Important Members of the **IBaseMessagePart** Interface

Name	Type	Description
PartProperties	Property	A message part can have its own context, which is accessible through the PartProperties property, which returns an instance of a class that implements the IBasePropertyBag interface.
Charset	Property	The Charset property is a string that can be used to determine/set the charset of the data in this message part.

TABLE 5.5   Most Important Members of the **IBaseMessagePart** Interface

Name	Type	Description
ContentType	Property	The ContentType property is a string that can be used to determine/set the content type of this message part.
Data	Property	The Data property returns to you a stream containing the data of this message part.
GetOriginalDataStream	Method	The GetOriginalDataStream method returns the original uncloned version of the part data stream. This often returns a stream with the same content as the Data property, but if another pipeline component has modified the content of the data stream, you can use this method to obtain the original stream. This is risky, though, because you might end up overwriting changes made by other components.

IBasePropertyBag

You can find the full specification of this interface at the MSDN site.

The IBasePropertyBag interface is used to contain a property bag, which in this case is associated with a message part. The interface has only one property and three methods, as explained in Table 5.6.

TABLE 5.6   Members of the **IBasePropertyBag** Interface

Name	Type	Description
CountProperties	Property	The CountProperties method returns the number of properties. This is useful for looping around all the properties.
ReadAt	Method	The ReadAt method takes in an index, which must be smaller than the value of CountProperties, and returns the value of the property at that index. It also has two out parameters, one for the name of the property that has just been read and one for the namespace.
Read	Method	The Read method takes in the name and namespace of a property and returns the value of the property.
Write	Method	The Write method takes in three parameters: the name, the namespace, and the value of a property. It writes these to the property bag. Properties on a message part cannot be promoted because they cannot be used by the runtime to route the message, because the routing engine wouldn't know which value to use if multiple parts have the same property promoted.

IBaseMessageContext

You can find the full specification of this interface at the MSDN site.

The IBaseMessageContext interface is used to contain the context that is associated with a message. The interface has the same property and the same three methods as the IBasePropertyBag interface, and they have the same functionality. Other than these, the IBaseMessageContext also has two important methods, as described in Table 5.7.

TABLE 5.7   Most Important Methods of the IBaseMessageContext Interface That Are Not in the **IBasePropertyBag** Interface

Name	Description
Promote	The Promote method takes in the same parameters as the Write method. The only difference is that the Promote method promotes properties, whereas the Write method only writes properties to the context.
IsPromoted	The IsPromoted method takes in a name and a namespace of a property and returns whether this property was promoted to the context. If the method returns false, the property was not promoted but written to the context of the message.

Miscellaneous Functionality

This section describe some miscellaneous functionality you can leverage in your pipeline components, such as enlisting in the transaction for the pipeline, error handling, wrapping built-in components, a resource tracker that helps you avoid garbage collection, and a helper class that assists you in copying the context between messages.

Transactions

At some point, you might want to write a component that is dependent on the successful execution of the entire pipeline. You might want to write a component that only outputs some information to a database if the received message is successfully persisted to the MessageBox (so, for instance, some information about the decoding of a message does not get written to the MessageBox if the message fails validation in a later stage).

To support this, you can enlist in the MS DTC transaction that the pipeline runs under. This transaction is initiated by the adapter if the adapter is a transactional adapter and by the *Endpoint Manager* (EPM) if the adapter is a nontransactional adapter.

Enlisting in this transaction makes sense only if your component is doing something that can also enlist in the transaction, like writing to a database. Enlisting into the transaction and then sending out an email through an SMTP server does not roll back the sending of that email unless the email client library you use can enlist in the transaction. If it cannot, the email is always sent, and there is no reason for enlisting in the transaction because nothing will be rolled back in case of failure later on.

Listing 5.24 shows an example of how to enlist in the transaction. For the code to compile and run, you must add a reference to the System.Transactions assembly.

LISTING 5.24   A Pipeline Component Enlisting in a Transaction

```
public IBaseMessage Execute(IPipelineContext pContext, IBaseMessage pInMsg)
{
    IPipelineContextEx pContextEx = pContext as IPipelineContextEx;
    if (pContextEx != null)
    {
        IDtcTransaction trans = pContextEx.GetTransaction() as
IDtcTransaction;
        if (trans != null)
        {
            // Do whatever you want to with the transaction.
            // For instance: Let a database connection enlist in it.
        }
        else
        {
            throw new Exception("GetTransaction didn't return a
transaction.");
        }

    }
    return pInMsg;
}
```

As you can see from the code, the transaction is not available from the pipeline context itself. The reason for the existence of the IPipelineContextEx interface is that the transaction was unavailable in BizTalk 2004, and to maintain backward compatibility, the IPipelineContext interface hasn't been changed. Instead, a new interface was added.

Besides getting a reference to the transaction and then using it to enlist database connections and other functionality in, you can also create a TransactionScope and perform your transactional code in there.

Wrapping a Built-In Component

You will sometimes want to perform what a built-in component does and then just a little bit more. This is most commonly seen when leveraging what the built-in disassemblers do, and then adding some logic on top of that. Suppose, for instance, that you are receiving a batch of orders from your *enterprise resource planning* (ERP) system and the XML disassembler splits this into as many orders as there are in the batch. What you really want, however, is to split the batch into one batch for any particular supplier. You can achieve this by writing a custom disassembler and then simply extending the built-in

XML disassembler and leveraging the functionality of this to do all the splitting and property promotion and so on and then adding your logic on top of that. Listing 5.25 shows an example.

LISTING 5.25   Leveraging Existing Pipeline Components and Adding Logic

```
public void Disassemble(IPipelineContext pContext, IBaseMessage pInMsg)
{
    var xmlDasm = new XmlDasmComp();
    xmlDasm.Disassemble(pContext, pInMsg);
    IBaseMessage newMsg;
    while ((newMsg = xmlDasm.GetNext(pContext)) != null)
    {
        string supID = (string)newMsg.Context.Read("SupplierID", "PropNamespace");
        if (hash.ContainsKey(supID))
        {
            ((Queue)hash[supID]).Enqueue(newMsg);
        }
        else
        {
            Queue q = new Queue();
            q.Enqueue(newMsg);
            hash.Add(supID, q);
        }
    }
}
```

The code in Listing 5.25 leverages the existing XML disassembler to split up the batch into several orders and promote the ID of the supplier from the order. After the batch is split into several orders, the GetNext method is called until there are no more orders, and then all orders for a specific supplier are queued up in one data structure. The responsibility of the GetNext method of your custom disassembler will be to take one entry in the Hashtable at a time and then consolidate all the IBaseMessage objects in the Queue object into one message, be it as a lot of message parts in one message or taking the XML from each individual order and putting an envelope around them or whatever you may want.

Error Handling
Handling errors in a custom pipeline component is not much different from handling them in other components you might write. In all situations where exceptions may arise, you need to consider whether to handle it in code or whether to throw an exception.

If a pipeline component throws an exception, it is always handled by BizTalk. BizTalk suspends the message in question and provides an error description.

Things to remember are as follows:

▶ Fail fast. The fail fast principle instructs you to fail the component instead of trying to return some default values or the like, which must be handled by the component that called your component. If something happens that you cannot handle, throw an exception and let the normal error handling internal to BizTalk do its thing instead of having your orchestrations handle that perhaps the output message is empty or something like that.

▶ Don't rethrow an exception, but throw a new exception instead that has the exception you caught as the inner exception. If an exception occurs, your component knows more about what happened than the component that will catch your exception does. Throwing a new exception gives you the possibility to add your own error message and at the same time keep the entire old exception as the inner exception

ResourceTracker

When writing a custom pipeline component, you will be using streams, stream readers, stream writers, and other types of objects that you do not always want garage collected just because they are no longer used. If an XmlTextReader is used to read a stream that you are also returning from your component, and the XmlTextReader is garbage collected, this also disposes the stream, which another pipeline component might still be reading. This will cause errors, as you can reasonably understand.

To avoid this, you get the ResourceTracker, which is basically just a collection of objects. So when using an object that contains a stream you do not want disposed, just add it to the ResourceTracker, and this way it will not be garbage collected until the EPM calls he DisposeAll method of the ResourceTracker to dispose all the objects that you wanted to not be garbage collected until the message is saved in the MessageBox.

Listing 5.26 contains an example of how to use the ResourceTracker.

LISTING 5.26   Using the **ResourceTracker**

```
public IBaseMessage Execute(IPipelineContext pContext, IBaseMessage pInMsg)
{
    XmlTextReader xtr = new XmlTextReader(new MemoryStream());
    // Do whatever you need with the XmlTextReader
    pContext.ResourceTracker.AddResource(xtr);
    return pInMsg;
}
```

PipelineUtil

When you use the `IBaseMessageFactory` to create new messages, which is often the case when programming a custom disassembler, you have the responsibility to copy over the properties in the context of the original message that are relevant to the newly created messages. You can find lots of examples online that explain how to loop through the context of a message and copy all the properties to another message, but the `PipelineUtil` class can also help you out. The two useful methods the `PipelineUtil` class exposes are described in Table 5.8.

TABLE 5.8   Useful Methods in the **PipelineUtil** Class

Name	Description
CloneMessageContext	This is a static method that takes in an `IBaseMessageContext` and simply clones it and returns the result.
ClonePropertyBag	This is a static method that takes in an `IBasePropertyBag` and simply clones it and returns the result.

Using the normal and recommended method of transferring context from one `IBaseMessage` to another, you get the code shown in Listing 5.27.

LISTING 5.27   Normal Code for Transferring Context from One Message to Another

```
public IBaseMessage Execute(IPipelineContext pContext, IBaseMessage pInMsg)
{
    IBaseMessage outMsg = pContext.GetMessageFactory().CreateMessage();
    // Generate data for message

    string m_name;
    string m_namespace;
    for (int i = 0; i < pInMsg.Context.CountProperties; i++)
    {
        object val = pInMsg.Context.ReadAt(i, out m_name, out m_namespace);
        if (pInMsg.Context.IsPromoted(m_name, m_namespace))
            outMsg.Context.Promote(m_name, m_namespace, val);
        else
            outMsg.Context.Write(m_name, m_namespace, val);
    }
    return outMsg;
}
```

If you choose to leverage `PipelineUtil` to help you, you get the code in Listing 5.28 instead.

LISTING 5.28   Leveraging **PipeineUtill** to Transfer Context Between Messages

```
public IBaseMessage Execute(IPipelineContext pContext, IBaseMessage pInMsg)
{
    IBaseMessage outMsg = pContext.GetMessageFactory().CreateMessage();
    // Generate data for message

    outMsg.Context = PipelineUtil.CloneMessageContext(pInMsg.Context);

    return outMsg;
}
```

> **NOTE**
>
> The documentation for both methods states that these methods are for internal use by BizTalk only and should not be used directly from your code. That said, they work just fine, with one little caveat: They clone the entire context. This means that if the source `IBaseMessageContext` has distinguished fields written to the context, these are copied to the new message, as well, which is almost always silly, because they are distinguished fields and should point via an XPath to an element in the message. Because this is a new message, however, this is no longer relevant.

Streaming

One of the most important things to remember when developing custom pipeline components is that basically everything happens in a streaming fashion. The EPM that orchestrates the pipeline needs to persist the message that comes from the last executed pipeline component to the MessageBox. The scenario is similar for both inbound and outbound scenarios.

The stream in the message part that you need to handle in your custom component should not be loaded fully into memory unless really necessary because this will increase the memory footprint of your component and increase the latency of the entire processing of an incoming message. When possible, deal with the stream you get as input, and merely do your thing while reading it and output your own stream.

To illustrate this, consider a scenario where a pipeline has three components. The first is the XML disassembler, the second is a custom XML validator you have written, and the third is the party-resolution component.

If your component reads the entire message into memory to process it, this is what happens:

1. Your component reads in the entire message in memory, does its processing, and creates a new message that is to be used as output.

2. The EPM uses the output from your component in the call to the Execute method of the party-resolution component.

3. The EPM publishes the output from the Execute method of the party-resolution component to the MessageBox.

The downsides to this approach are as follows:

▶ You are loading the entire message into memory. Depending on what approach you take, this can cause a memory consumption of more than three times the size of the message.

▶ The pipeline component after your component cannot start processing the output from your component until your component has completely finished processing the message. This increases latency.

If you develop your custom pipeline in a streaming fashion, what happens is that you implement a new class that inherits from the Stream class. In your pipeline component, you simply instantiate this new class and return an IBaseMessage that has the Data property on the BodyPart set to this instance of the new Stream class. The custom stream class should take in a Stream in the constructor and then keep this for future usage.

The main piece of functionality to write in the custom class is to override the Read method of the Stream base class and let this method do all the work. Whenever the Read method is called, your method should read from the source stream and perform any necessary processing and then return whatever should be returned. This can just be the read bytes, if you do not need to alter the contents of the message, or you can do any processing needed and then return the result.

Listing 5.29 shows an example of an Execute method of a decode component that uses a custom stream.

LISTING 5.29   An **Execute** Method Leveraging a Custom **Stream** Class

```
public IBaseMessage Execute(IPipelineContext pContext, IBaseMessage pInMsg)
{
    Stream inputStream = pInMsg.BodyPart.GetOriginalDataStream();
    XmlValidatorStream xvs = new XmlValidatorStream(inputStream);
    pInMsg.BodyPart.Data = xvs;
    pContext.ResourceTracker.AddResource(xvs);
    return pInMsg;
}
```

An example of the XmlValidatorStream class is shown in Listing 5.30.

LISTING 5.30   An Example of the **XmlValidatorStream** Class

```
public sealed class XmlValidatorStream : Stream, IDisposable
{
    Stream _input = null;
    public XmlValidatorStream(Stream inputStream)
    {
        _input = inputStream;
    }

    public override int Read(byte[] buffer, int offset, int count)
    {
        // Do what you need to return the next "count" number of bytes.
        // This can include reading from the _input Stream
        // Perhaps you need some data structure to buffer bytes in,
        // if you have read more than needs to be returned.
        return 0;
    }

    // The rest of the methods and properties of the Stream class
    // that need to be overridden and the Dispose method
    // should go here.
}
```

If the functionality of the custom stream class needs information provided in the properties of the pipeline component, provide them in the constructor of the custom Stream class.

The advantages of this approach are as follows:

▶ At any given time, your component uses only the memory needed to hold the bytes that are buffered because you had too many in the last call to your Read method and the bytes just read from the underlying Stream.

▶ Your component does not read anything form the underlying Stream before someone calls your Read method to get bytes from your Stream. This way, you process a small part of the message and immediately return the processed part, and the next component can execute simultaneously.

In other words, because you return an IBaseMessage that contains a Stream that will do your work, your method can return before anything is actually processed, and the Stream you return will do the work once it is required.

If all components in a pipeline do processing in a streaming fashion, all components work on the same message at the same time, and it can even start getting persisted to the MessageBox before it has been entirely read from the source by the adapter.

BizTalk provides a set of classes you can leverage that will help you do all this processing. The classes are found in Microsoft.BizTalk.Streaming.dll, which you can find in the installation folder for BizTalk. Table 5.9 describes some of the classes in this assembly.

TABLE 5.9   Classes That Help You Implement Streaming Pipeline Components

Class	Description
ReadOnlySeekableStream	This Stream class can be used to wrap another Stream to make it seekable. The first parameter to the constructor is always the source Stream that is to be wrapped. Besides this first parameter, there are two optional parameters. As the second parameter, you can use another Stream, which will be used for persistence inside the ReadOnlySeekableStream. By default, the class persists to the file system, but you can override this by using another Stream, like the MemoryStream or the VirtualStream explained later. The third parameter (which can also be parameter number two if no persistence Stream is used) is an integer providing the maximum buffer size for the class.
VirtualStream	Wrapping a stream in a VirtualStream class, you can set a threshold for how many bytes can be in memory at a time. If more bytes are read, these are written to the file system to be read back in later, and if fewer bytes are read, they are kept in a MemoryStream. This can help you maintain a maximum for the memory consumption of your component. As you can see, this can be used as the persistence Stream for the previously mentioned ReadOnlySeekableStream class, and it will let you decide how many bytes can stay in memory.

Properties

When programming a pipeline component, you might want to allow for the developer who will be using your component to specify values for some properties that are needed at runtime.

To provide a property for the user to set a value, you just need to create a public property on your class. The pipeline designer scans the class for properties, and all the properties that are found are shown in the Properties window. The Properties windows try to provide the best possible interface for the given property.

Property Editor

The pipeline designer tries to provide the best possible editor for any given property.

▶ If the property is of type bool, a drop-down is supplied, where the user can choose either True or False. The default value is False. If you need to allow for null values even for a Boolean, let your type be Boolean? (which instructs the property editor to allow three values in the drop-down: True, False, and blank). Blank will then be the default.

▶ If the property is of type string, a text box is provided with an initial value of an empty string.

▶ If the property is a decimal or an int, a text box is supplied with an initial of 0.

▶ If the property is of some enumeration, the possible values for the enumeration are supplied in a drop-down box for the developer to choose from.

If you want to allow for the developer to enter a list of schemas like the Document Schemas property of the XML validator, you should use the Microsoft.BizTalk. Component.Utilities.SchemaList class as the type of your property. And if you would like for the developer to choose just one schema like the Document Schema property of the flat file disassembler, use the Microsoft.BizTalk.Component.Utilities.SchemaWithNone class as the type of your property. You can find both classes in the Microsoft.BizTalk. Component.Utilities namespace, in the Microsoft.BizTalk.Component.Utilities.dll, which you can find in the GAC. To reference this assembly, copy the assembly from the GAC to a local folder and reference it from there. To copy the assembly from the GAC, open a command prompt and go to C:\Windows\assembly\GAC_MSIL\Microsoft.BizTalk. Component.Utilities\3.0.1.0__31bf3856ad364e35 folder and copy the DLL from there.

Second, you might want to hide some of the properties in your class, because you may have properties in your class that you use internally that you do not want the pipeline developer to see and change; in addition, the properties provided in the IComponentUI and IBaseComponent are often not relevant for the pipeline developer. Hiding properties is described later in this chapter.

Custom Property Name and Description

You might sometimes want to provide a different name in the Properties window of the pipeline designer than the actual name of the property in your class. Also, you might want to provide the developer with a description of the specific property. The BaseCustomTypeDescriptor class is a class that implements the ICustomTypeDescriptor interface. You can find it at Microsoft.biztalk.pipeline.components.dll. If you let your pipeline component class inherit form this class, you get the possibility to change these values.

To use the class as a base class for your own class, you need to change a couple of things. First, you must specify the class name as the base class before the interfaces. Also, you need to add a call to the constructor of the BaseCustomTypeDescriptor class in your own constructor. This constructor takes in a resource manager that is then used to retrieve needed texts. The code for this can look like that shown Listing 5.31, which you can compare to the code shown in Listing 5.4 to see the changes.

LISTING 5.31   Class Definition and Constructors After Introducing the Base **CustomTypeDescriptor** Class

```
[ComponentCategory(CategoryTypes.CATID_PipelineComponent)]
[ComponentCategory(CategoryTypes.CATID_Validate)]
[Guid("35FDAF6E-92E8-4779-8B85-025A948896E6")]
public class FineFoods_XML_Validator : BaseCustomTypeDescriptor,
IComponentUI,
    IBaseComponent, IPersistPropertyBag, IComponent
{
    private static ResourceManager resManager;

    static FineFoods_XML_Validator()
    {
        resManager = new ResourceManager("FineFoods.Pipeline.Components.Resources" +
            ".FineFoods_XML_Validator", Assembly.GetExecutingAssembly());
    }
    public FineFoods_XML_Validator() : base(resManager)
    {
    }
}
```

After utilizing the BaseCustomTypeDescriptor class, you get some attributes you can use to decorate the properties of your class.

The BtsPropertyName attribute allows you to specify a different name for the property in the Properties window than the name of the actual property in your class. As you might think, the parameter to the BtsPropertyName attribute is not the name you want displayed, but the name of the resource from the resources file that contains the name you want displayed. The base class uses the resource manager it was provided in the constructor to get the resource out of the resources file.

The BtsDescription attribute allows you to specify a different description for your property than the default, which is simply the name of the property. As with the BtsPropertyName attribute, this attribute takes a parameter that is the name of the resource in the resources file that contains the description you want shown.

Figure 5.23 depicts the default appearance of a property called DebugLevel in your custom pipeline component class. The property is of type DebugLevels, which is the enumeration shown in Listing 5.15. As you can see, the name of the property, as it is shown to the developer, is the same name as the property in the class, and the description of the property is useless.

FIGURE 5.23   The default appearance of a property called **DebugLevel** in your custom pipeline component class.

By entering two new values in your resources file, as shown in Figure 5.24, and by utilizing the two described attributes, BtsDescription and BtsPropertyName, you can get a much better look. Given the two resource strings and the updated code shown in Listing 5.32, you get the property shown in Figure 5.25 instead of the one shown in Figure 5.23.

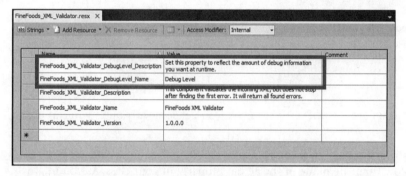

FIGURE 5.24   Two resources entered to provide name and description of property.

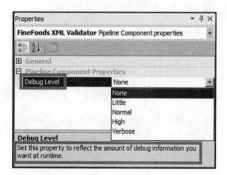

FIGURE 5.25   The **DebugLevel** property after utilizing the **BtsPropertyName** and **BtsDescription** attributes.

LISTING 5.32   Using the **BtsPropertyName** and **BtsDescription** Attributes

```
[BtsDescription("FineFoods_XML_Validator_DebugLevel_Description")]
[BtsPropertyName("FineFoods_XML_Validator_DebugLevel_Name")]
public DebugLevels DebugLevel { get; set; }
```

The BaseCustomTypeDescriptor class is in the Microsoft.BizTalk.Component namespace, which you can find in <InstallationFolder>\Pipeline Components\Microsoft.BizTalk.Pipeline.Components.dll, which you must reference to use the class.

Hiding Properties

After having implemented the Icon property in the IComponentUI interface and the Name, Version, and Description properties in the IBaseComponent interfaces and having deployed your component, you will find that the Properties windows of the component looks similar to what is shown in Figure 5.26.

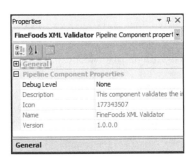

FIGURE 5.26   Default Properties window for a custom pipeline component.

If the component has other properties, these also appear, naturally. The issue here is that the values for the four properties appear in the lower half of the Properties window. They can stay there if you like, but because the properties have only a get and not a set implementation, they are read-only. If you want them to disappear from the lower half of the Properties window, you can decorate the properties with the Browsable(false) attribute. An example just for the Name property is provided in Listing 5.33.

LISTING 5.33   Decorating a Property with the **Browsable(false)** Attribute

```
[Browsable(false)]
public string Name
{
    get
    {
        return resManager.GetString("FineFoods_XML_Validator_Name");
    }
}
```

After setting this on all four properties (Name, Version, Description, and Icon), you will get a Properties window as shown in Figure 5.27 instead of the one shown in Figure 5.26.

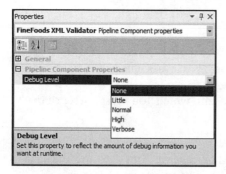

FIGURE 5.27   Properties window after adding the **Browsable(false)** attribute to the properties.

To use the Browsable attribute, you need a using System.ComponentModel; at the top of your class file. This results in a conflict, however, if you are implementing the IComponent interface, which is needed for all components that are not assemblers or disassemblers. This is because both the System.ComponentModel and the Microsoft.BizTalk.Component.Interop namespaces have a definition for IComponent, which will cause the compiler to give an error because it does not know which of the two interfaces you want to implement. There are three ways to fix this:

► Do not have a using System.ComponentModel; at the top of your class file, but instead write [System.ComponentModel.Browsable(false)] to decorate your properties.

► Do not implement the IComponent interface, but instead implement the Microsoft.BizTalk.Component.Interop.IComponent interface. That is, point to the explicit interface you want to implement.

► Add a namespace alias for the IComponent type that is ambiguous by writing using IComponent = Microsoft.BizTalk.Component.Interop.IComponent at the top of your class file. Of course, for readability you may choose to alias the other IComponent or to use another alias.

Each way is fine, but you need to choose one of them.

Really Fast Pipeline Component Implementation

All these interfaces and base classes and the methods and properties they bring with them might seem overwhelming at first, but there is no need to make things harder than they have to be. Listing 5.34 shows an example of a perfectly valid pipeline component that has next to no implementation:

▶ The Icon property returns an empty pointer, resulting in the pipeline designer using the default icon.

▶ The Name, Description, and Version properties just return strings without leveraging any resource manager.

▶ There is no constructor.

▶ There are no properties and therefore no implementation of the Load, Save, InitNew, and Validate methods.

Basically, all you need to change in this component is the implementation of the Execute method. This can be tricky enough, but hopefully this shows you that the interfaces need not scare you.

LISTING 5.34   Really Fast Implementation of a Custom Pipeline Component

```
[ComponentCategory(CategoryTypes.CATID_PipelineComponent)]
[ComponentCategory(CategoryTypes.CATID_Any)]
[Guid("3A732C33-B44B-4bf5-8B2E-26881C04725E")]
public class ReallyFastComponent: IPersistPropertyBag, IComponent,
IComponentUI, IBaseComponent
{
    public void GetClassID(out Guid classID)
    {
        classID = new Guid("3A732C33-B44B-4bf5-8B2E-26881C04725E");
    }

    public void InitNew() {}

    public void Load(IPropertyBag pb, int errorLog) {}

    public void Save(IPropertyBag pb, bool clearDirty, bool saveAllProps){}

    public IBaseMessage Execute(IPipelineContext pContext, IBaseMessage
pInMsg)
    {
        return pInMsg;
```

```
    }

    public IntPtr Icon { get { return new IntPtr(); } }

    public IEnumerator Validate(object projectSystem) { return null; }

    public string Description { get { return "My description"; } }

    public string Name { get { return "My name"; } }

    public string Version { get { return "My version"; } }
}
```

Deployment

After a new pipeline component has been developed, you need to deploy it. There are two ways to deploy a pipeline component, depending on whether you need to deploy it for runtime execution or for a developer to use when developing pipelines inside Visual Studio 2010.

For a server that needs to be able to execute pipelines that use the pipeline component, you need to put the assembly containing the pipeline component in the GAC of the server. This requires, naturally, that the assembly be signed using a strong key pair. If you do not want to bother remembering deploying the assembly to the GAC on each server, you can include it in the MSI package that is installed on the server. This is done by adding it to your application by following these steps on your development machine:

1. Open BizTalk Server 2010 Administration Console.
2. Right-click your application and choose **Add, Resources**.
3. Click **Add**.
4. Browse your way to the assembly that contains the pipeline component and either double-click it or click it once and click **Open**.
5. In the File Type drop-down, choose **System.BizTalk:Assembly**.
6. Make sure the **Add to the Global Assembly Cache on MSI File Install (gacutil)** check box is checked.
7. Click **OK**.

The resulting screen should look like Figure 5.28.

The next time you export an MSI file from the application this resource was just added to, it will be included in the MSI and installed in the GAC along with the other assemblies. An alternative to this is to include your assembly with the pipeline component in a custom MSI package. This is useful for developing and selling your pipeline components or when you need to distribute a new version to your servers.

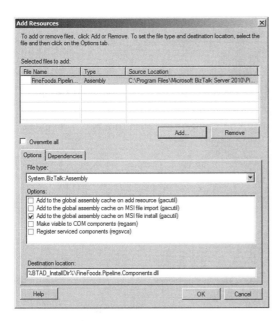

FIGURE 5.28   Adding the pipeline component assembly as a resource.

To deploy the assembly on a development machine for it to be used when developing pipelines, copy the assembly to the <InstallationFolder>\Pipeline Components folder. This is not strictly required, but it is the easiest way, because your pipeline component will then always be in the Toolbox, no matter how many times the Toolbox is reset. To add the component to the pipeline components Toolbox that is available at design time, follow these steps:

1. Open Visual Studio 2010.

2. Go to **Tools**, **Choose Toolbox Items** or right-click the Toolbox and choose **Choose Items**.

3. Go to the BizTalk Pipeline Components pane.

4. If the pipeline component is present in the list, make sure it is checked.

5. If the pipeline component is not present in the list, click **Browse** and browse your way to the assembly that contains the pipeline component.

If the pipeline component is placed in the <InstallationFolder>\Pipeline Components folder, you can also right-click inside the Toolbox and choose **Reset Toolbox**. Be aware, though, that this completely resets the Toolbox, which might not be what you want.

Note that the Toolbox sometimes fails to update itself when new versions of a pipeline component are deployed. In this case, you can delete the following four files, which contain Visual Studio 2010s Toolbox setup:

▶ toolbox.tbd

▶ toolbox_reset.tbd

- ▶ toolboxIndex.tbd

- ▶ toolboxIndex_reset.tbd

On Windows Server 2008, using Visual Studio 2010, they are found in C:\Users\<User>\AppData\Local\Microsoft\VisualStudio\10.0. (If you have a different OS or different installation options, you can search for them.) They are hidden files, so you need to search for those. If you want to script the deletion of the files in a batch file, you can use the script shown in Listing 5.35 in a batch file.

LISTING 5.35   Script for Deleting Visual Studio 2010 Toolbox Items

```
@echo off
C:
cd "\Users\<User>\AppData\Local\Microsoft\Visual Studio\10.0"
del toolbox* /AH
pause
```

If you need to update a pipeline component that is also in the GAC, you must both update it in the GAC and in the <InstallationFolder>\Pipeline Components folder. This is because Visual Studio 2010 and BizTalk use the version in the GAC if present, and any updates in the file system are therefore not used.

Note that overriding the assembly that has been copied to the <InstallationFolder>\ Pipeline Components folder is not always possible because it might be in use by Visual Studio 2010, BizTalk runtime, or some isolated host like *Internet Information Services* (IIS). In these cases, you need to restart whatever programs are locking the assembly before you can copy the new version.

If you are trying to add your pipeline component to the Toolbox and get an error doing this, the most common causes are as follows:

- ▶ There is a mandatory interface you have not implemented. The mandatory interfaces are as follows: IComponentUI, IBaseComponent, IPersistPropertyBag and one of IComponent, IAssemblerComponent, and IDisassemblerComponent. Remember, it is not enough to implement the methods and properties; the interface must be specified in the class header.

- ▶ You have forgotten to decorate the class with the ComponentCategory(CategoryTypes.CATID_PipelineComponent) attribute.

- ▶ Your class is not marked public.

- ▶ There is an older version of your component in the GAC that is not valid.

If you get a sharing violation when copying your newly compiled assembly to the <InstallationFolder>\Pipeline Components folder, you might consider writing a script that deploys the new component for you. The script should

▶ Restart IIS using `iisreset`. Only needed in your script if you have any receive functionality running in IIS like hosted *Windows Communication Foundation* (WCF) services, HTTP, SOAP or other.

▶ Restart BizTalks host instances. Only needed if the pipeline component has been used by BizTalks runtime. This can be done in a couple of ways:

   ▶ By using `net stop BTSSvc$BizTalkServerApplication` and `net start BTSSvc$BizTalkServerApplication`. Do this for each relevant host instance.

   ▶ By using PowerShell and doing `get-service BTS* ¦ foreach-object -process {restart-service $_.Name}`.

   ▶ By using WMI. For details about this, see http://msdn.microsoft.com/en-us/library/aa578621(BTS.10).aspx.

▶ Copy the DLL to the <InstallationFolder>\Pipeline Components folder.

▶ Use gacutil to add the new version to the GAC like this: "C:\Program Files\Microsoft SDKs\Windows\v6.0A\Bin\gacutil.exe" /if NewlyCompiled.DLL.

▶ Delete the Toolbox items, as described earlier, if you are having issues updating the Toolbox.

Probably Visual Studio 2010 needs to be closed first, as well. This can be done a bit faster if you test your pipeline component in a Visual Studio 2010 BizTalk project that is the only project in the solution. This Visual Studio 2010 will be the only instance of Visual Studio 2010 that has a lock on the file, and it can be closed and reopened faster than your entire solution, which might contain lots of projects.

Debugging

When developing a custom pipeline component, at some point you will want to debug it. Debugging a pipeline can be achieved in different ways. No matter which way you choose, the pipeline component must be compiled in Debug mode.

The most common way of debugging a custom pipeline component is to deploy a pipeline that uses the component and debug it when an instance is sent through BizTalk. The reason why this is the most common way is that this is the only way you can get a realistic context of execution. Often, your custom pipeline component will need to access the context of the message it will handle, which can include properties set by the adapter, other pipeline components, or other runtime functionality.

When debugging the pipeline component inside BizTalks runtime, make sure the latest compiled version is in the GAC, and make sure your host instance has been restarted so that it hasn't cached a previous version. Inside Visual Studio 2010, set breakpoints in your code wherever you want the code to break and allow you to inspect values and step into code. When this it done, a few steps are needed to start debugging:

1. Go to **Debug**, **Attach to Process**.

2. Choose the **BTSNTSvc.exe** process.

3. If the BTSNTSvc.exe process is not available, check

    ▸ That the host instance is started

    ▸ That you have checked Show Processes from All Users and Show Processes in All Sessions

4. If multiple instances of the BTSNTSvc.exe process are running, you can stop the host instance that will be executing the map and notice what PIDs are active and then start the host instance. The new PID is the one to attach to.

5. Click **Attach**.

6. Send a message through BizTalk.

This causes BizTalk to load the pipeline component at runtime, and your debugging session breaks the runtime when one of your breakpoints is hit, allowing you to step through the code to debug your component.

The second way of debugging your custom pipeline component is to leverage the pipeline.exe utility. The pipeline.exe utility is for testing pipelines, and it is discussed later in this chapter. To leverage it to debug a pipeline component, complete these steps:

1. Open the properties of your Visual Studio 2010 project.

2. Go to the Debug pane.

3. Select the **Start External Program** option.

4. In the text box for the external program, enter **<InstallationFolder>\ SDK\Utilities\PipelineTools\Pipeline.exe**, where you replace the <InstallationFolder> with the folder you have installed BizTalk to.

5. In the Command Line Arguments text box, enter **customPipeline.btp -d messageInstance.xml -c**. You need to replace `customPipeline.btp` with the full path to a pipeline that uses the pipeline component you want to debug, and you need to replace `messageInstance.xml` with the full path to an instance to test. The -c parameter makes the pipeline.exe tool write any output to the console so that no files are created.

6. Right-click your project and choose **Debug**, **Start New Instance**.

This executes pipeline.exe using a pipeline that uses your pipeline component, and this will enable you to debug it just like if you had attached to BizTalk's process.

> **NOTE**
>
> Pressing F5 to start the debugging process, which is common practice in .NET development, might not give the results you want, even if you have configured the project with the pipeline component as the startup project. This is because unless you have changed the default settings, pressing F5 compiles your entire solution and deploys all the BizTalk projects. Most of the time, building the entire solution is unnecessary and can take a lot of time.

The advantages of debugging by attaching to BizTalks processes are as follows:

▶ Your component is debugged in the exact environment it is also running in at runtime.

▶ You do not need to have a file ready for testing purposes but can wait for a file to arrive.

Following is the advantage of debugging by using pipeline.exe:

▶ You do not need to redeploy your custom pipeline component to debug changes made, which makes it a lot faster than attaching to BizTalk's process.

Pipeline Component Wizard

You can download a utility from http://btsplcw.codeplex.com/ and use it to create all the necessary piping needed for a pipeline component. The component is developed by Martijn Hoogendoorn and is freely available.

When you download it from Codeplex, you get the source code for the wizard. To use it, follow these steps:

1. Open the solution file.

2. Compile the entire solution.

3. If the setup project wasn't built, build it manually.

4. Exit Visual Studio 2010.

5. Go to the folder where the setup project placed its setup files after compiling.

6. Run the setup.exe file.

7. Go through the Setup Wizard.

8. Open Visual Studio 2010.

9. Open the solution you want to add a pipeline component project to.

10. Right-click the solution and choose **Add**, **New Project**.

11. Choose the **BizTalk Server Pipeline Component** project type, which is located at the same place as the other BizTalk project types.

12. Go through the wizard to describe your component, the properties, and so on.

13. After the wizard is done, implement the `Execute` method (for non-assemblers and non-disassemblers), the `AddDocument` and `Assemble` methods for assemblers, or the `Disassemble` and `GetNext` methods for disassemblers.

14. Feel free to change other stuff, if you want.

The wizard is easiest to use if you have tried creating a component manually first.

Testing

After developing a pipeline, test it to make sure that it behaves as you want it to in production. Debugging pipeline components was described earlier in this chapter, and this section deals with testing of pipelines.

There are two ways to test your pipelines, and these are described in this section.

Pipeline.exe

BizTalk ships with a command-line utility that you can use to execute a pipeline without having to deploy it first. The tool is called pipeline.exe, and it is located in <InstallationFolder>\SDK\Utilities\PipelineTools. This is the same tool that was used for debugging in one of the previous sections.

The utility has lots of parameters to help you perform the testing. For a full list of parameters, just execute pipeline.exe without any parameters. Figure 5.29 shows the pipeline.exe utility in use.

FIGURE 5.29   Using pipeline.exe to test a pipeline.

The parameters used in the example in Figure 5.29 are as follows:

▶ The pipeline to be tested.

▶ The instance to send through the pipeline.

▶ The schema that matches the instance. It must be deployed to BizTalk, so it is available at runtime.

▶ -p, which instructs pipeline.exe to write out information about the context of the message after pipeline processing has finished.

▶ -c, which instructs pipeline.exe to write the output to the console instead of to a file.

Unit Testing

BizTalk supports unit testing of pipelines. To perform unit testing, you must enable unit testing on the project that contains the pipeline you want to test. This is done in the properties of the project, as shown in Figure 5.30.

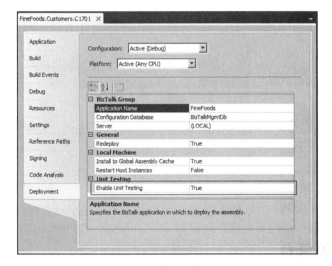

FIGURE 5.30   Enabling unit testing on the project that contains the pipeline that should be tested.

After you do this, Visual Studio 2010 lets all receive pipelines in the project derive from the abstract TestableReceivePipeline class in the Microsoft.BizTalk.TestTools.Pipeline namespace rather than the ReceivePipeline class of the ReceivePipeline class in the Microsoft.BizTalk.PipelineOM namespace. Similarly, all send pipelines will derive from TestableSendPipeline instead of SendPipeline.

TestableReceivePipeline and TestableSendPipeline have methods to support unit testing of the pipelines, which can then be used in your unit test project.

After enabling unit testing on the project, you need to add a test class to an existing project or create a new test project for your unit test. To do so, choose **Test**, **New Test** in the menu of Visual Studio 2010. When doing this, you get the screen shown in Figure 5.31.

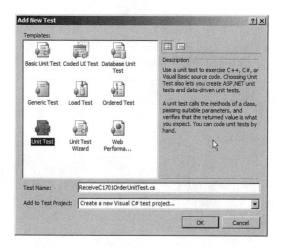

FIGURE 5.31   Adding a new test to a new test project.

In this screen, you can choose to either add the new test to an existing test project, if one is present in the solution, or create a new Visual C# test project. In addition, you can choose between four different tests:

▶ **Ordered Test:** This gives you a way of orchestrating your tests, deciding what order they should be performed in.

▶ **Unit Test:** This option gives you a class to write your tests in, but some manual work needs to be done referencing the right assemblies and so on.

▶ **Basic Unit Test:** This option provides an even smaller and simpler version of a unit test class than the unit test. This means you will have to implement more yourself.

▶ **Unit Test Wizard:** This helps you through some of the choices you must make, like what maps to test, and then generates the test class for you.

The other five options for adding a new test are not relevant for a BizTalk project.

For your first test project, name your file, choose **Unit Test**, and click **OK**. If you already have a test project, you can decide to add the file to an existing project by selecting it in the drop-down.

The test project is created for you, and it includes a pretty empty class for your tests. The class contains some definitions, methods, a constructor, and one method that is really the one thing to focus on because this is the one you need to implement.

So, what you need to do in this method is to implement the unit test of the pipelines you want to test in this test class. Remember that you can have as many test classes and test methods in each test project as you want.

To test a pipeline, you need to reference four different assemblies from your test project:

- ▶ **The assembly that contains the pipeline:** This assembly *must* have the Enable Unit Testing property set to True.

- ▶ **The Microsoft.BizTalk.TestTools assembly:** This is found in the .NET pane of the Add Reference screen.

- ▶ **The BizTalk Pipeline Interop assembly:** This is also found in the .NET pane of the Add Reference screen.

- ▶ **The Microsoft XLANG/s Base Types assembly:** This is also found in the .NET pane of the Add Reference screen.

In the generated class, change the code of the `TestMethod` to something similar to what shown in Listing 5.36.

LISTING 5.36   Example of a **TestMethod** That Performs a Unit Test of a Pipeline

```
[TestMethod()]
public void TestReceiveC1701Order()
{
    // Pipeline class derived from TestableReceivePipeline
    var target = new ReceiveC1701Order();

    // Collection of messages to test the flat file pipeline
    var documents = new StringCollection();
    string strSourceOrder_XML = testContextInstance.TestDir +
        @"\..\..\FineFoods.Customers.C1701\Instances\Order from Customer
C1701.txt";
    Assert.IsTrue(File.Exists(strSourceOrder_XML));
    documents.Add(strSourceOrder_XML);


    // No other parts than the body so an empty collection will be passed.
    var parts = new StringCollection();


    // Dictionary mapping the schema to the fully qualified .NET
    // type name of the XSD file.
    var schemas = new Dictionary<string, string>();
    string SchemaFile = testContextInstance.TestDir +
        @"\..\..\FineFoods.Customers.C1701\Order.xsd";
    Assert.IsTrue(File.Exists(SchemaFile));
    schemas.Add("FineFoods.Customers.C1701.Order", SchemaFile);
```

5

```
    // Test the execution of the pipeline using the inputs
    target.TestPipeline(documents, parts, schemas);


    // Outputs are generated in the "out" folder of the test directory.
    // Each output should be validated in some way.
    string[] strMessages = Directory.GetFiles(testContextInstance.TestDir +
        @"\out", "Message*.out");
    Assert.IsTrue(strMessages.Length > 0);
    Order Order_target = new Order();
    foreach (string outFile in strMessages)
    {
        Assert.IsTrue(Order_target.ValidateInstance(outFile,
            Microsoft.BizTalk.TestTools.Schema.OutputInstanceType.XML));
    }
}
```

As you can see at the bottom of Listing 5.36, this code validates the output from the pipeline against the schema it should conform to. Other assertions are also possible. Also note that the TestPipeline method outputs all files to the out folder of the test directory. Therefore, if you have more than one TestMethod in your TestClass, you will most likely want to clean up these output files after validating them. If you refrain from doing that, the files stay in the out folder next to any newer files generated in the next TestMethod, with no way of knowing which files are relevant. This can lead to errors and unit tests that fail but should not.

Summary

Pipelines are used in BizTalk to deal with messages that are either arriving at BizTalk or are being sent out.

A receive pipeline is specified on a receive location, and it has the responsibility of doing decryption, signature validation, conversion into XML, validation, and party resolution. Any steps can be skipped if they do not match the business requirements for receiving the documents this particular receive location has to live up to. Note that the conversion into XML is merely to create an XML representation of the message, which in the receive port can then be mapped into another format.

A send pipeline is specified on a send port, and it has the responsibilities of converting an XML message into the format required by the receiver, signing the message before transmission, and encrypting it, if needed. As with receive pipelines, any step can be skipped if it is not needed. Note that the conversion of the XML into another format is done after an optional transformation has been applied in the send port, so the conversion merely takes an XML representation of a message and converts it into the format specified by the schema, which could be a positional flat file or something else. This is the format that will actually be transmitted to the receiver.

BizTalk ships with some built-in pipelines that you can use in most scenarios that involve either receiving or transmitting XML or receiving or transmitting an unmodified message. If your business needs are not covered by these pipelines, you can add custom pipelines, which can leverage the pipeline components that ship with BizTalk. Some of these components are also used in the out-of-the-box pipelines.

If you need a pipeline component that does something that none of the out-of-the-box pipeline components do, you can program your own custom pipeline component to do the job. This could, for instance, be for altering a message, for decompressing a message, or something else.

For debugging and testing pipelines, BizTalk ships with a unit test framework that you can use to confirm that a pipeline acts as expected.

5

Adapters

by Charles Young

Integration requires the effective exchange of information between different systems. BizTalk Server 2010 plays a central role in enabling the integration of different systems across distributed environments and heterogeneous platforms. However, BizTalk Server is a distinct technology and platform in its own right. You need to adapt message exchange between BizTalk Server and an unbounded set of applications, services, and systems. BizTalk Server's adapter framework meets this need and offers a wide range of prebuilt adapters out-of-the-box. This chapter explores the adapter framework and the role and function of adapters. It also describes how adapters are registered and configured.

"Native" adapters are integrated directly into BizTalk Server, and most native adapters are preregistered on each BizTalk Server group. This chapter describes the characteristics and use of each of the native adapters. This includes seven native *Windows Communication Foundation* (WCF) adapters. Five of these WCF adapters use system-defined WCF bindings to enable *Simple Object Access Protocol* (SOAP)-based interchange between services across a variety of transport protocols. The other two enable any bindings, including custom bindings, to be exploited by BizTalk Server.

BizTalk Adapters

From a BizTalk perspective, an adapter is a component that handles communication and transmission of messages between BizTalk Server and external systems, services, and technologies. Adapters play a central role in BizTalk Server and represent the core integration capabilities of the system.

It is natural to consider BizTalk Server's messaging ports to be the central artifacts that contain adapters. However, a more accurate representation is to consider adapters as the central artifacts. BizTalk Server provides supplementary messaging infrastructure, configurable through ports, to support and facilitate hosted instances of adapters. BizTalk manages hosting on behalf of an adapter and implements additional message mediation and routing services. Adapters exploit this messaging infrastructure by communicating with BizTalk Server via an *application programming interface* (API) provided by proxy code instantiated in the same host process. *Independent software vendors* (ISVs) can exploit this model by integrating existing adapter technologies directly with BizTalk Server, enabling BizTalk Server to manage the hosting of their adaptation services.

Adapters are varied in their function, complexity, and features. They range from the simplest of components designed to deliver or transmit messages using basic mechanisms (for example, reading and writing to files) to sophisticated adaptation technologies and platforms that provide tooling, configuration, and metadata management for a wide range of purposes. Adapters may act as bridges between different technologies and platforms. They may provide gateway services to manage interchange between different organizations. They may implement general purpose protocol adaptation services to enable loose coupling between diverse systems, or they may rely on system-specific metadata to facilitate integration between BizTalk Server and specific applications or services.

The following sections describe the categorization of BizTalk adapters.

Native Adapters

Native adapters are distinguished from other adapters by being integrated directly into BizTalk Server and preregistered with the product. The precise nature of integration varies from adapter to adapter. You can usefully think of the native adapters as a base library that ships with the product, and which covers perhaps 80% or more of real-world adaptation needs. Most native adapters are transport adapters. They handle well-known transport protocols and delivery mechanisms and are not specific to any given system or application. However, Microsoft includes a native application adapter for Windows SharePoint integration.

> **NOTE**
>
> The native SQL Server adapter included in previous versions of BizTalk Server is no longer supported for general use. Use the WCF-based adapter that ships as part of the BizTalk Adapter Pack. Also, the SOAP adapter, although still supported, is now deprecated. Use the WCF adapters in preference to the SOAP adapter.

The native adapters include a library of WCF adapters for several of the system-provided WCF bindings. There are also two custom WCF adapters that enable the use of other bindings. The WCF adapters play an increasingly important role in BizTalk development and bridge between the BizTalk-specific adapter model and a newer WCF-based adapter model implemented in the WCF *line-of-business* (LoB) adapter *software development kit* (SDK).

Line-of-Business Adapters

BizTalk Server 2010 ships with a library of LoB adapters. These are specific to third-party technologies, including Oracle PeopleSoft, JD Edwards, Tibco Rendezvous, and IBM WebSphere. LoB adapters extend the reach of BizTalk Server to a number of widely used enterprise applications.

BizTalk Adapter Pack

The BizTalk Adapter Pack comprises a growing library of WCF-based adapters that ship under the BizTalk name. They can be exploited by BizTalk Server using its native WCF adaptation features or used outside of BizTalk Server as an extended set of WCF bindings. The adapter pack is included under the BizTalk Server license.

The BizTalk Adapter Pack provides LoB support for SAP, Siebel eBusiness, and the Oracle E-Business suite. In addition, the adapter pack provides adapters for SQL Server and Oracle databases.

The SAP, Siebel, and Oracle database adapters replace older BizTalk LoB adapters. The SQL Server adapter replaces an older native SQL Server native adapter. When migrating existing applications to BizTalk Server 2010, you might need to change your applications to use the new WCF-based adapters.

Host Adapters

BizTalk Server 2010 includes the BizTalk *Host Integration Server* (HIS). Previously sold as a separate integration server, HIS is now included under the BizTalk license. HIS includes a companion product called the *BizTalk Adapters for Host Systems* (BAHS). This is a pack of BizTalk adapters that supports host application and file integration for CICS, IMS, DFSMS DFM, and AS/400. BAHS also provides adapters for WebSphere MQ and DB2.

Third-Party and Custom Adapters

The BizTalk adapter model is extensible and documented. It can be used to build additional adapters for the widest possible range of adaptation needs. Over the years, a significant ecosystem of third-party adapters has evolved. Many of these represent integration of existing ISV adaptation technologies with BizTalk Server. Others have been developed to support specific technologies and applications.

Developers can build their own adapters. For the most part, BizTalk developers should find that BizTalk Server already offers the adaptation facilities they require. Where this is not the case, it may be more cost-effective to purchase a third-party adapter (for example, for integration with cloud services). Building custom adapters can be a significant undertaking and should not be embarked upon without careful thought.

For an example of a custom BizTalk adapter, see the Microsoft TCP/IP BizTalk adapter at http://btstcpip.codeplex.com/. This is an open source adapter maintained by Microsoft. It was originally designed to prove the ability to support duplex communication over TCP/IP in a healthcare context. It does, however, support a full range of message interchange patterns.

Additional Microsoft Adapters

Microsoft provides a number of additional adapters as part of other licensed products. For example, it provides BizTalk accelerators for healthcare, finance, and electronic business. Some of these include additional adapters such as the `InterAct` and `FileAct` adapters included with the SWIFT accelerator and the MLLP adapter included with the HL7 accelerator. Microsoft Dynamics AX provides a BizTalk adapter for use in building enterprise resource planning (ERP) solutions.

The Role of WCF Adapters

As you have seen, BizTalk Server 2010 provides native adapter support for a number of system-provided WCF bindings. Two additional "custom" native adapters are provided to handle other WCF bindings.

The WCF LoB adapter SDK enables ISVs and developers to exploit the WCF binding model to implement adapter functionality that can be exploited across the Microsoft platform. Be careful to distinguish between the native BizTalk WCF adapters (integrated BizTalk adapters that support WCF) and adapters created with the WCF LoB adapter SDK. The native WCF adapters are used to bridge between BizTalk Server and standard WCF bindings. They can also handle custom bindings, including bindings defined by WCF LoB adapters. WCF LoB adapters, including those provided in the BizTalk Adapter Pack, are not tied to BizTalk Server. They can be exploited more widely in distributed and service-orientated environments.

This distinction can seem a little confusing at first, but represents Microsoft's intention to move to an increasingly WCF-centric world when handling message transportation, delivery, and adaptation. Over time, you can expect the BizTalk Adapter Pack to grow as new WCF LoB adapters are added. Older BizTalk LoB adapters will, over time, be deprecated in favor of newer WCF-based adapters.

For an example of WCF adapters built with the WCF LoB adapter SDK, including source code, see the BizTalk Azure Adapters SDK 1.0 CTP at http://btsazureadapters.codeplex. com/releases/view/30117. You can download the WCF LoB adapter SDK from www. microsoft.com/biztalk/technologies/wcflobadaptersdk.mspx.

Adapter Characteristics

BizTalk Server adapters exploit and implement a set of defined programmatic interfaces that enable them to integrate tightly with BizTalk's message transport infrastructure. They exhibit a range of characteristics, as described in this section.

Direction

Most BizTalk adapters comprise two distinct adaptation handlers for use on either the receive or send side of BizTalk Server. Some adapters, however, support only the receive side or the send side.

On the receive side, adapters are used to deliver incoming messages to BizTalk channels associated with receive ports. Their handlers are configured as part of a receive location, together with the pipeline used to manage message processing within the channel. A single BizTalk receive port can handle messages delivered from multiple receive locations. Each receive location can exploit a different adapter.

On the send side, adapters are used to communicate outgoing messages to external systems and endpoints. Send handlers are associated directly with a send port. Send ports provide no direct analogy to receive locations. However, they do support primary and backup transports. Backup transports can be configured for automatic use when the primary transport fails to successfully relay messages, and the backup transport can be configured to use a different adapter to the primary transport.

Push and Pull

On the receive side, adapters may support push or pull models. For example, the WCF-WSHttp adapter enables external service consumers to push data to BizTalk Server via a well-defined service endpoint consisting of an address, a binding to a specific set of protocols and behaviors, and a contract that is described and published using additional metadata (for example, WSDL). The MQ Series adapter, by contrast, pulls data from external message queues through a polling mechanism. Some adapters, such as the SQL Server adapter, support both push and pull models.

Most adapters use a push model on the send side. Send ports push messages to external endpoints and destinations. However, is in entirely possible for an adapter to support models in which external systems pull data from BizTalk Server.

Message Interchange Pattern

Although each adapter supports one or both directions (receive or send), they also support specific message interchange patterns for each direction. BizTalk Server supports configuration of one-way and two-way patterns for each direction, giving a total of four basic interchange patterns:

- ▶ **One-way receive:** Used to support in-coming messages chiefly in "fire-and-forget" scenarios and for simple file-based transfer.

- ▶ **One-way send:** Used to support out-going messages chiefly in fire-and-forget scenarios and for simple file-based transfer.

- ▶ **Request-response:** Used to support request-response patterns on inbound messages. Internally, BizTalk Server uses correlation mechanisms to route response messages back to the external sender via the messaging infrastructure and receive location.

This pattern generally implies a synchronous-over-asynchronous approach in which senders may be blocked while waiting for a response message to be returned.

▶ **Solicit response:** Used to support solicit-response interchange on outbound messages relayed to an external system by a send port. The send adapter waits for an expected response message, which, on receipt, is submitted to BizTalk Server's messaging infrastructure to be processed and routed.

Although BizTalk Server offers explicit support only for these four patterns described, it can support additional patterns and variations, such as multiresponse interchange, loopbacks, and duplex communication. However, some additional coding may be required to implement these additional patterns of interchange.

Hosting

BizTalk Server instantiates and initializes adapters at runtime and communicates with BizTalk Server through an in-memory API. It provides a host environment in which adapters run. Hosting is configured using the BizTalk Server Administration Console. Each adapter type must be associated with one or more BizTalk hosts before instances of that adapter type can be created. Each association defines a direction (receive or send). Any one host can be used in both directions.

On the receive side, some adapters support in-process (regular) hosts. Instances of these adapters run in-process to the BizTalk Server service (BTSNTSvc.exe). Other adapters support isolated hosts. An isolated host defines host processes that run as worker processes under *Internet Information Services* (IIS). Send adapters always run in-process to the BizTalk Server service.

Each receive location and send port is associated with a specific BizTalk host via an adapter handler. The handler associates the adapter with the same host to allow it to be instantiated in the same host instances as the receive location or send port. The Administration Console reports any missing associations.

Configuration

Adapters support configuration via the BizTalk Server Administration Console. Configuration is handled at two levels. Some adapters support global configuration at the handler level. Each handler associates an adapter to a BizTalk host. Adapters also support local configuration of handlers at the level of individual receive locations and send ports. Local configuration can either supplement or override global handler configuration, as required. Each adapter is free to exploit these configuration capabilities in accordance with its requirements.

BizTalk Server stores all configuration data centrally in the *Single Sign-On* (SSO) database. This might appear a strange decision at first sight. However, the SSO database is ideal for this purpose. Adapter configuration may contain sensitive information such as user identities and passwords. SSO makes it easy to store such data securely. Because of its role in storing adapter configuration, SSO must always be installed to enable BizTalk Server to function.

NOTE

Microsoft provides the SSO Configuration Application MMC snap-in to allow developers to exploit the same SSO store for any other custom configuration purposes. See www.microsoft.com/downloads/details.aspx?displaylang=en&FamilyID=94e07de1-1d33-4245-b430-9216979cd587.

Batches

On the receive side, adapters handle messages as part of a BizTalk message batch. Each batch may contain one or more messages. Message batching may be a hidden aspect of adapter design but is often configurable. (For example, see batching configuration for the File adapter.) BizTalk developers often need to understand the implications of batching. A batch may contain multiple messages of different types. The batch is always processed as a single transactional unit. For example, if one message within a receive batch fails for any reason, BizTalk's default behavior is to fail the entire batch of messages. Alternatively, BizTalk can be configured to route individual failed messages separately from other messages. In this case, all messages, including failed messages, are published to the BizTalk Message Box as part of a single transaction. This is called recoverable interchange processing. If a message with 100 orders is received and a small number of messages fail, all other orders are processed correctly with minimal impact on the business.

CASE HISTORY

Batch-based processing can affect ordered delivery of messages if not properly handled by an adapter. Internally, receive adapters submit message batches to the messaging infrastructure in an asynchronous fashion. In one real-world scenario, a third-party adapter was configured to poll an external system and submit a large number of messages representing data records. The messages were read from the external system in order. However, the adapter had an undocumented behavior. It polled records in batches of 50 messages at a time. Within each batch, the order of the messages was fully maintained. However, the adapter provided no way to control the batch size or the order in which each separate batch was delivered to the messaging infrastructure and committed to the Message Box. Even with the use of BizTalk's ordered delivery features, and even despite the ordering of messages within any one batch, entire batches of messages were published out of order when the system operated under load. Because the use of the adapter was necessary to the application, the only viable solution was to introduce an additional staging database, use it to reestablish total ordering, and then publish records to the Message Box in a controlled fashion.

Adapters often support batching on the send side. However, this is not mandatory. If an adapter supports batching on the send side, it can choose to provide visibility of batches to the BizTalk Server messaging engine, enabling BizTalk Server to manage transactional control more effectively and optimize batch-level processing.

Transactions

BizTalk Server uses transactions internally to manage message batch processing. In addition, it provides extensive support for enlistment into distributed (two-phase commit) transactions to support integration and messaging requirements when communicating with external systems.

On the receive side, adapters hand messages off to the BizTalk messaging infrastructure in an asynchronous fashion. BizTalk Server processes the messages in each batch in a single internal transaction. Adapters can optionally receive a callback to be notified when the messaging infrastructure has successfully committed or rolled back a batch of messages. Adapters can use this mechanism to synchronize internal batch processing transactions with external distributed transactions. This internal indirection enables adapters freedom in deciding how to handle failed batches and how to work with external transactional resource managers.

On the send side, the BizTalk messaging engine inspects the capabilities of an adapter and either performs direct transmission of each message or hands off batches of messages to the adapter. The adapter can process each message or batch in a synchronous or asynchronous fashion. Adapters can create or enlist into distributed transactions to communicate data robustly to external transactional systems. After transmission, the adapter obtains a new batch object from BizTalk Server and uses it to communicate the results of transmission back to the messaging engine. The engine uses this data to delete successfully transmitted messages or suspend unsuccessful messages. Again, the internal indirection provided by BizTalk Server allows the adapter freedom to decide how to handle the outcome of transactional processing.

Message Context

Adapters submit messages to BizTalk Server and can attach additional metadata properties to each message as message context. Message context plays a central role in BizTalk Server. Contextual properties flow through BizTalk Server with each message and are used to enable message routing, identify message types, correlate messages, and so on. Adapters can add properties as needed to each message and can mark properties as promoted to make them visible to the subscription engine. Further properties may be added downstream by BizTalk Server and by pipeline components in the message channel.

Metadata Harvesting

Some adapters provide design-time support for obtaining metadata required to enable interchange. Design-time tooling is used to generate metadata for consumption in BizTalk applications. Typically, this involves the automated creation of *XML Schema* (XSD) schemas to represent message types and may also involve generation of additional BizTalk artifacts. The way this is done is specific to each adapter. However, adapters that provide design-time metadata harvesting capabilities generally elect to support a wizard *user interface* (UI) provided as part of BizTalk Server's development tooling. This is the Add Adapter

Metadata Wizard. It is invoked within Visual Studio by right-clicking a BizTalk project, selecting **Add**, and then selecting **Add Generated Items**. Select **Add Adapter Metadata** to launch the wizard.

Registering Adapters

Adapters are configured via the BizTalk management console. BizTalk Server manages hosting on behalf of adapters and provides a common infrastructure to manage adapter configuration. Of course, there is nothing preventing ISVs implementing their own configuration mechanisms. In some cases it might be necessary to use additional tools outside of the BizTalk Administration Console. However, adapters are generally written to exploit the facilities provided by BizTalk Server. This is certainly the case for all adapters provided with the product.

Before an adapter can be hosted by BizTalk Server, it must be registered with a specific BizTalk group in BizTalk's administration database. The native adapters are already registered, but other adapters may need to be registered manually. This only applies to adapters built using the BizTalk adapter framework. It does not apply to WCF-based adapters such as those contained within the BizTalk Adapter Pack. WCF-based adapters are exploited via BizTalk's native WCF adapters.

Registration is a two-step process. Adapters are first registered in the local Windows Registry of each BizTalk Server and then subsequently with a specific BizTalk group to which each server belongs. This second level of registration is stored in the central BizTalk management database. Local registration is generally carried out automatically as part of the installation routine used to install the adapter on each box. If this is not the case, refer to any relevant installation documentation for the given adapter.

To register an adapter in the central BizTalk management database, first run the BizTalk Administration Console on one of the BizTalk Server boxes on which the adapter has already been installed. Open a BizTalk group in the Administration Console and expand **Platform Settings**. Then expand the **Adapters** node. A list of all currently registered adapters will display. The list contains the native adapters. If the adapter is not already registered, right-click the **Adapters** node and select **New**. Alternatively, you can select **Adapters**, **New** from the Actions pane on the right side of the management console.

BizTalk Server displays the Adapter Properties dialog box, as shown in Figure 6.1. Enter a name for the adapter and select the adapter from the drop-down list. This list should contain any locally registered adapters that are not yet registered with the BizTalk management database. You can optionally add a description. It is necessary to perform this step on only a single BizTalk Server. The registration is created centrally for all servers in the BizTalk group.

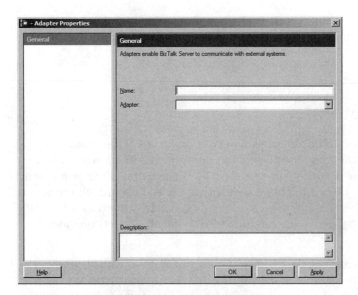

FIGURE 6.1   The Adapter Properties dialog.

Creating Adapter Handlers

Having registered an adapter with BizTalk Server, the next stage is to configure its handler code. Each adapter can register different .NET classes or COM components to handle inbound (receive) and outbound (send) messages. Before BizTalk can host adapter code, at least one of these classes or components must be associated with a BizTalk host.

A BizTalk host is a logic definition of a host process. Hosts are configured as 32-bit or 64-bit processes together with various parameters that manage thread pooling, authentication requirements, timeouts, Message Box polling intervals, and a wide variety of throttling parameters. Each host is associated with one or more physical servers within a BizTalk group. This association controls the instantiation of Windows processes at runtime. If a host is associated with two servers, each server runs an instance of the host process.

> **NOTE**
>
> Not all adapters support 64-bit processing. Specifically, the native FTP and POP3 adapters can run only in 32-bit hosts. This restriction also applies to the deprecated native SQL Server adapter. You must create hosts and configure them for 32-bit only execution to host these adapters. Many third-party adapters also support 32-bit execution only. When migrating existing BizTalk applications from 32 bit to 64 bit, you might need to redesign the hosting environment to accommodate these restrictions.

Adapter handlers bind handler code to BizTalk hosts. These bindings are created using the BizTalk Administration Console. To create an adapter handler, right-click a registered adapter and select **New**. Alternatively, click **Selected Item**, **New** in the Actions pane on the right side of the management console. Then select either **Send Handler** or **Receive Handler**. These options are presented according to which .NET classes or COM components have been registered by the adapter. Some adapters support both handler types, whereas others offer only one.

The BizTalk Administration Console displays the Adapter Handler Properties dialog box. An example is shown in Figure 6.2.

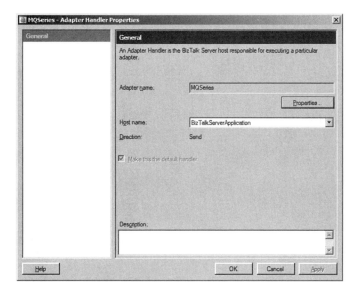

FIGURE 6.2   The Adapter Handler Properties dialog.

Select the hostname from the drop-down list. You can bind the same handler code to multiple hosts to create handlers that run in different processes. You can bind handler code for different adapters to the same host to run multiple adapter handlers of different types within a single process on each BizTalk Server.

If you create multiple send handlers for any one adapter, you can designate one of the handlers as the default. Default handlers are used by dynamic send ports. Each dynamic send port transmits outbound messages using a dynamically selected adapter handler. At runtime, BizTalk inspects properties in the outbound message context to decide which adapter handler to use. Multiple send handlers for any one adapter are hosted in different processes. BizTalk needs to select one of these processes to transmit the message and uses the one marked as the default.

Adapters may support configuration at the handler level. These configuration settings apply to all runtime instances of the handler. Property values at this level are often used as default values, which may be overridden at the port level. Click the **Properties** button to display property pages for the selected handler.

Many adapters elect to display properties using a simple list of properties in a Properties dialog provided by BizTalk Server. Properties can be displayed in groups. They are ordered alphabetically in each group rather than by function. The list is entirely customizable and can be extended with custom property editors and converters. Each adapter provides property schemas for receive and send handlers. These schemas are used to generate the user interface. Figure 6.3 shows an example of the Properties page in the FTP Transport Properties dialog box.

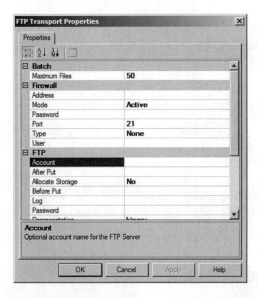

FIGURE 6.3   Adapter property list and handler level.

Alternatively, adapters can provide their own custom Properties page, which displays within the console. Figure 6.4 shows an example of a custom Properties page for the native HTTP adapter.

Adapter properties often include sensitive data such as user passwords. A well-designed adapter ensures that passwords never display in plain text on the screen and that they are stored securely. As discussed earlier, BizTalk adapters use the SSO database to hold their configuration data in a secure manner. This is the case for all the adapters that ship with the product, and most third-party adapters follow the same approach.

When BizTalk Server is first configured, a number of receive and send handlers are automatically generated for the native adapters. Each of these is bound to a default host also generated during configuration. In development environments and simple BizTalk Server production environments, it might not be necessary to create new handlers or remove generated handlers. Administrators may need to configure adapters only at the port level. This is described in the next section.

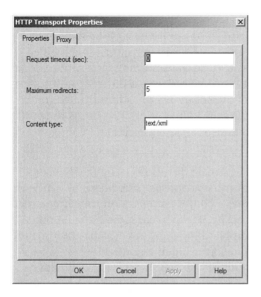

FIGURE 6.4   Custom adapter Properties page at handler level.

Any one adapter can be associated with a given BizTalk host by, at most, a single adapter handler. If you need to configure multiple instances of an adapter to run on a single box, you must create multiple hosts to support this.

Sometimes it is necessary to delete adapter handlers. For example, when removing the definition of a host, you need to remove all adapter handlers for that host before the host itself can be deleted.

Port-Level Configuration

Having registered adapters and created adapter handlers, the next step is to bind adapters to message channels at the port level. BizTalk Server's messaging ports are configuration artifacts that bind BizTalk adapter handlers to message channels to publish messages to the BizTalk Message Box (receive ports) or transmit messages to external systems via subscription rules (send ports). A BizTalk message channel comprises an adapter handler, a pipeline that manages processing and mediation requirements on behalf of the handler, and optional maps defined at the port level. Ports can be associated with multiple channels. In a two-way port, channels are defined in pairs to handle messages in both directions.

On the receive side, you define receive locations to bind adapter handlers to pipelines and ports. The chief purpose of receive locations is to publish BizTalk Server endpoints while hiding internal details of the ports to which they are bound. When creating a receive location, the administrator first selects an adapter type. This limits the receive location to using receive handlers for that given adapter. The administrator then selects and configures the handler, binding it to a pipeline. For two-way ports, the handler is bound to two pipelines. The selection of a handler decides which host is used to run the selected pipelines and any optional maps defined on the port.

On the send side, each static send port is bound to, at most, two BizTalk send handlers. The primary transport defines which handler is used to transmit messages to some external system or endpoint. You can also optionally define a backup transport using a different handler. This backup handler, if configured, is used to transmit messages in the case of failure of the primary transport. The handler can be associated with a different host to the handler used as the primary transport. As with receive locations, the administrator configures primary and backup transports by first selecting an adapter type. This limits the port to send handlers defined for that adapter. The administrator then selects and configures the handler.

Dynamic send ports are not bound to any specific handler. Instead, a designated default handler is selected dynamically at runtime based on the adapter type required to handle a given external address communicated to the port as a context property on the outbound message. There is no mechanism for defining a backup transport for dynamic send ports. Instead, developers can create their own exception handling logic in an orchestration and use this to retry sending of messages on a dynamic port using different addresses. In this way, developers can implement logic to specify multiple backup transports for dynamic send ports.

Static send ports are always bound to either one or two specified handlers. Receive ports can be bound to more than one handler by defining multiple receive location for the port. At runtime, dynamic send ports are bound temporarily to a single handler selected on the basis of values held in the context of outbound messages.

Configuring Receive Locations

To configure handlers on a receive location, expand a given BizTalk application in the BizTalk Administration Console, and click the **Receive Location** folder. A list of all current receive locations displays in the pane on the right. You might need to create new receive locations before configuring a handler. You must associate each receive location with a receive port.

To select an adapter handler for a given receive location and bind it to the message channel, double-click the receive location, right-click it, and select **Properties**, or select it and click **Selected Item**, **Properties** in the Actions pane on the right side of the console window. This displays the Receive Location Properties dialog box, as shown in Figure 6.5.

First select the required adapter type in the Transport section of the dialog box. This limits the contents of the Receive Handler drop-down list box to those hosts for which receive handlers exist that are bound to the given adapter type. Alternatively, you can select the host first in the Receive Handler drop-down box. This limits the Type drop-down box to display only those adapters associated with receive handlers defined for the given host.

You can configure the handler at the port level by clicking the **Configure** button. Port-level configuration defines a URI for the receive location. In many cases, this URI will be a URL for an endpoint published by BizTalk Server. An adapter may define additional properties, and some of these properties may override properties set at the handler level.

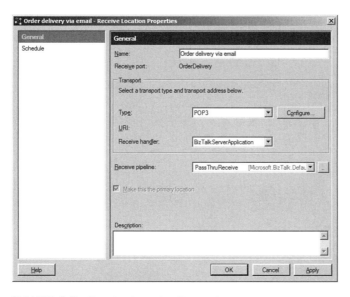

FIGURE 6.5   Receive Location Properties dialog.

Many adapters elect to display properties using a simple Properties dialog provided by
BizTalk. As with configuration at the handler level, the list is entirely customizable and
can be extended with custom property editors and converters. An example of the POP3
Transport Properties dialog box is in Figure 6.6.

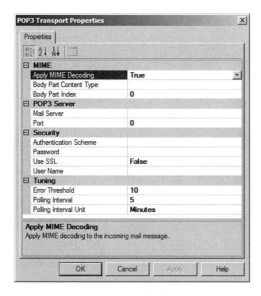

FIGURE 6.6   Adapter property list and port level.

Alternatively, adapters can provide their own custom Properties page that will display within the console. Figure 6.7 shows the tabbed Properties page for the native WCF-Custom adapter.

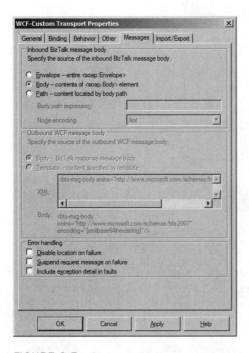

FIGURE 6.7   Custom adapter property page at port level.

To bind the selected handler to a message channel, select the appropriate pipeline from the Receive Pipeline drop-down box. You may need to create and deploy custom pipelines to support this. For two-way ports, you configure two pipelines.

Configuring Send Ports

To provide transport configuration on a send port, expand a given BizTalk application in the BizTalk Administration Console, and click the **Send Port** folder. A list of all current send ports will display in the pane on the right. You might need to create a new send port before configuring a handler.

To select a handler for a given send port and bind it to a message channel, double-click the send port, select **Properties** from the pop-up menu, or select it and click **Selected Item, Properties** in the Actions pane on the right side of the console window. This displays the Send Port Properties dialog box, as shown in Figure 6.8.

The hander is configured in a nearly identical fashion to receive locations. Select the required adapter type and host in the Transport section of the dialog box. Provide transport configuration for the send handler by clicking the **Configure** button. Transport configuration is required to define a URI for the external endpoint to which messages will be transmitted. This URI may be a URL.

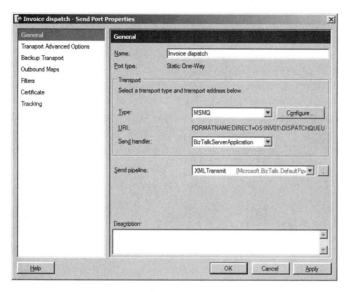

FIGURE 6.8   Send Port Properties dialog.

An adapter may define additional port-level properties, and some of these properties may override properties set at the handler level. As you have seen previously, adapters may elect to display properties using the Properties dialog provided by BizTalk Server or via a custom transport Properties page.

To bind the selected handler to a message channel, select the appropriate pipeline from the Send Pipeline drop-down box. You might need to create and deploy custom pipelines to support this. For two-way ports, you must configure two pipelines.

To define a backup transport, select **Backup Transport** on the left side of the Send Port Properties dialog shown in Figure 6.9. This displays the Backup Transport options, enabling a second adapter handler to be selected and configured. The options also enable configuration of retry options for the backup transport.

Dynamic Send Ports

The Send Port Properties dialog box for dynamic send ports does not provide the Transport sections shown in Figure 6.9. Instead, the handler is bound to the message channel at runtime for each outbound message based on inspection of the OutboundTransportLocation and optional OutboundTransportType properties in the message context. Dynamic send ports automatically select the default handler for the given adapter type and may use additional message context properties to provide additional handler configuration. A single send port can therefore transmit different outbound messages through different adapter instances running in different hosts.

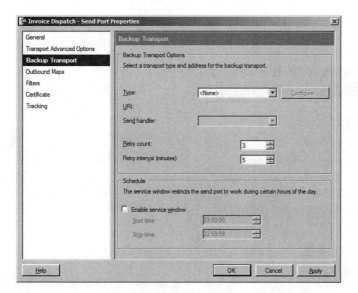

FIGURE 6.9   Send Port Properties dialog: Backup Transport.

To facilitate the selection of handlers by dynamic send ports, each adapter registers one or more aliases with the BizTalk management database. These aliases are typically used as schemas in URLs provided to the port at runtime. For example, the native File adapter registers the single FILE alias. The native HTTP adapter registers the HTTP and HTTPS aliases. Some adapters define aliases that are not used as URL schemas. For example, the native Windows SharePoint Services adapter registers the WSS alias. However, URLs will use HTTP or HTTPS as schemas.

Adapters often use URL schemas specified in the OutboundTransportLocation message property to select adapter handlers at runtime. Sometimes, however, the same URL schema may be applicable to multiple adapters or the transport location value may not be a URL. In these cases, the adapter-specific alias can be provided separately using the optional OutboundTransportType message context property.

When developing orchestrations, you define the values of the OutboundTransportLocation and OutboundTransportType message properties indirectly by assigning values to two port properties on an orchestration send port. Use Microsoft.XLANGs.BaseTypes.Address to set the value of the OutboundTransportLocation property and optionally use Microsoft.XLANGs.BaseTypes.TransportType to set the value of the OutboundTransportType property. For example, in XLANG/s, you might write code similar to the following:

```
POPort(Microsoft.XLANGs.BaseTypes.Address) =
               "http://contoso.com/orders/submit.srv";
POPort(Microsoft.XLANGs.BaseTypes.TransportType) = "HTTP";
```

Sometimes, the registered aliases for a given adapter may not be clearly documented. In this case, you can easily determine the aliases by connecting to the BizTalk management database using Microsoft SQL Server Management Studio and inspecting the content of the adm_AdapterAlias table. You may need to first look up the adapter ID value in the adm_Adapter table.

Adapter Properties

Adapters generally provide property schemas. These schemas are installed into BizTalk Server to support handler configuration. They are used like any other property schemas in BizTalk Server. Properties can be added to message context anywhere within a message flow. They can be promoted and distinguished in the normal way and accessed within pipeline components and orchestrations.

On the receive side, adapter properties are generally used by adapters to map adapter-specific or transport-related metadata into the context of BizTalk messages created by the adapter. Adapters use properties to deliver richer messages to BizTalk Server that contain both content and metadata. You can route on this metadata or exploit it within pipeline components and orchestrations.

On the send side, adapter-defined message properties are generally used as a mechanism to control handler configuration. They are often vital when using dynamic send ports. You saw earlier that handlers are selected using values of the OutboundTransportLocation and OutboundTransportType properties, but additional adapter-defined properties are often necessary to configure the selected handler appropriately. On static ports, adapter properties may be used to override static configuration, or they may themselves be overridden by property values configured at the handler or port levels. BizTalk Server affords adapters a great deal of freedom in choosing how they define and use adapter properties. Always refer to the appropriate product documentation for a specific adapter to discover the properties they define and the way those properties are used.

Deploying Bindings

You have seen, step by step, how to register adapters, define adapter handlers, and bind those handlers to BizTalk message channels. Developers and administrators often face an additional step of reproducing bindings, in part or in full, in different environments. For example, when migrating BizTalk applications from the development to a test environment, or deploying a fully tested application to the production environment, it is often necessary to reproduce a set of bindings in the target environment. These bindings might need to be amended. For example, adapters often use different URLs in the target environment to those used in the source environment.

To facilitate repeatable and controlled deployment of binding information, BizTalk Server allows port configuration metadata, including transport configuration and pipeline selection, to be exported directly to XML binding files. These binding files can be stored, managed, and amended for use when migrating applications between different environments. The XML files can be verbose, but they represent a straightforward serialization of port configuration data to a readily understandable format.

To export bindings, right-click a BizTalk application in the BizTalk Server Administration Console and select **Export**. Then select **Bindings** to display the Export Bindings dialog box shown in Figure 6.10. Alternatively, you can right-click the **Applications** folder and select **Export**, **Bindings** to export bindings for all applications in the BizTalk group. In this case, the Export All Bindings from the Current Application option in the Export Bindings dialog box is not available.

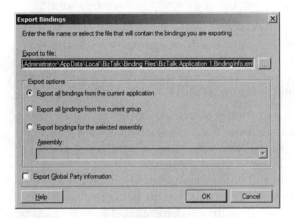

FIGURE 6.10   Export Bindings dialog.

The dialog box provides a number of options. You can export bindings for a single BizTalk application or for all applications in a BizTalk Server group. You can also export bindings for a single assembly created using BizTalk Server's development tools. By default, bindings are saved at a well-defined location in the local application data area of the user's profile.

Exported bindings do not convey the information required to define hosts, register adapters, or create adapter handlers. All this must be done separately. This level of configuration can be done manually or in a scripted fashion, for example, by scripting *Windows Management Instrumentation* (WMI) or by developing a PowerShell script, perhaps using the PowerShell Provider for BizTalk at http://psbiztalk.codeplex.com/. Binding files reference specific adapter handlers that must be configured in the target environment before bindings can be imported. If the target environment is configured differently to the source environment, edit the bindings file accordingly. Adapter handlers are exported with additional metadata about BizTalk hosts such their trust model. You must ensure that these settings in the binding file correctly match the configuration of hosts in the target environment.

Binding files, for obvious security reasons, do not contain passwords by default. Generally, they hold the masked characters used to in the property editor to indicate where passwords are used. You can edit binding files to contain passwords in plain text if you want, but give careful thought to ensuring that these passwords are kept private.

To import a binding file, right-click a BizTalk application in the BizTalk Server Administration Console, and select **Import**. Then select **Bindings**. Navigate to, and select, your binding file, and click **Open**. The bindings are imported for the target application. Alternatively, you can right-click the **Applications** folder and select **Import**, **Bindings** to export bindings for all applications described in the binding file.

Native Adapters

The remaining sections of this chapter explore the native adapters that ship with BizTalk Server 2010. The main source for detailed information for native BizTalk adapters is the MSDN Library help for BizTalk Server 2010. Developers should refer to this online source as their main reference. This chapter provides an overview only.

Microsoft's documentation categorizes each native adapter in terms of its transaction support, message interchange pattern support, ordered delivery capability, enablement for SSO, and the required host type. A useful summary table is provided in the product documentation.

File Adapter

The File adapter is illustrated in Figure 6.11. It supports one-way receiving and sending of files between BizTalk Server and local folders or network shares on NTFS file systems. Developers often use it during initial prototyping as a simple way to feed messages to BizTalk Server or dump messages to disk. In production environments it plays an important part in enabling integration with legacy systems that depend on simple file transfer.

Robust Interchange

One of the main challenges for the File adapter is to handle message transfer between folders and the Message Box in a robust fashion. Beginning with Windows Vista and Windows Server 2008, Microsoft introduced new transactional features for NTFS. However, the File adapter does not take advantage of these capabilities. Instead, it implements its own file-deletion and optional renaming mechanisms, which it links to internal BizTalk transactions.

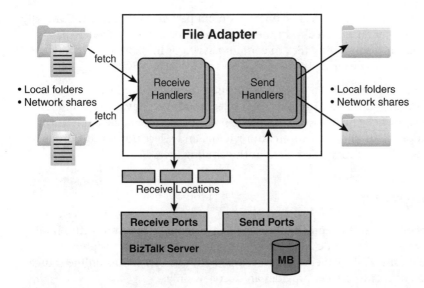

FIGURE 6.11   File adapter.

Receive handlers submit batches of files to BizTalk Server. By default, each batch contains the contents of up to 20 files to a maximum batch size of 100 KB. These limits are configurable. Each file in a batch is automatically deleted from disk when BizTalk Server successfully persists all the messages to the Message Box and commits its internal transaction. If one or more messages fail and are suspended, the handler deletes those messages from disk. If, for some, reason, BizTalk Server is unable to persist the contents of one or more files, the transaction is rolled back and the files are not deleted from disk.

Send handlers adopt a slightly different approach. If the Message Box contains multiple messages that match the port's subscription, the handler receives up to 20 files at a time in a batch. This limit is not configurable. The messages are removed from the queues. If one or more files cannot be written to disk, they are resubmitted to the Message Box to be retried according to the send port transport configuration.

Polling Locked Files

Receive handlers respond to Windows file change notifications for the configured file or share. When a notification occurs, the handler will read only unlocked, non-read only, nonsystem files from disk. Sometimes, it may receive a notification for a file that is still locked by a different process. In this case, the handler will enter a polling mode in which it will make continued attempts to read the file. The polling interval is configurable. If the handler is unable to connect to the folder, it will perform retries according to its Network Failure settings. If, having read a file and persisted it to the Message Box, the handler is unable to delete the file from disk, it will repeatedly retry deletion according to the Removing of files configuration settings. In this case, the Retry interval setting specified an initial interval, which is doubled between each retry until the Maximum retry interval is reached.

File Renaming

Sometimes, these simple mechanisms may not be sufficiently robust. If a receive handler is stopped while BizTalk Server is writing a batch of files to the Message Box, duplicate messages may be resubmitted when the location is restarted. The handler supports an optional file renaming mechanism to combat this. Before any file content is written to the Message Box, BizTalk Server can optionally rename files by adding a .BTS-WIP extension. The handler never rereads files with this extension. If the batch interchange fails to be persisted, the handler automatically removes the extension so that the files can be resubmitted.

A similar optional renaming approach is available on send handlers in scenarios where some process reads files dumped by BizTalk Server. The process may try to read files that are still locked by the adapter, for example, when BizTalk Server is handling large messages. The handler can be configured to temporarily name open files using the .BTS_WIP extension and rename the files only to their final name when completely written. This depends on the ability to configure the downstream process to ignore these temporary files.

Reliable Messaging Issues

The File adapter can operate in a reasonably robust manner. However, you might still encounter problems with reliable messaging. For example, there is no duplicate detection. If the same inbound file is delivered twice to a folder with sufficient delay to ensure that the first file has already been read and deleted before the second file arrives, the second duplicate file is persisted to the BizTalk Message Box. The receive handler has no built-in mechanism to ensure guaranteed one-time delivery. Similarly, the receive handler does not support ordered delivery. Although inbound messages are generally ordered according to their file time, this is undocumented behavior and should never be depended on.

Path and File Names

The file adapter works with local folders and remote shares. For shares, specify locations using UNC (\\<servername>\<sharename>\...). Mapped drives are specific to a given user's profile and should be avoided. If they are defined under an interactive user session (for example, while logged on as an administrator), they are generally not available to the handler at runtime because the handler normally runs under a different account.

Path names must always be absolute. Do not use relative paths. There are a number of well-documented additional constraints. When defining paths for a receive location, you also define a filename mask. This is used to filter inbound files using DOS-like wildcard characters and file extensions. The receive handler compares only the first three characters of file extensions to the mask, for example, a mask set to *.xslx retrieves *.xsl files, as well. You can define only a single mask per receive location.

Security

The host account must be configured with the necessary permissions to folders and shares for the File adapter to work correctly. On the receive side, this includes permissions to list folders, read data, and delete files. On the send side, the list of required permissions is more extensive because the send handler must be able to create files and open existing files to append new data. Microsoft's documentation provides a full definition of the permissions required. In development, it is common practice to simply set full permissions to everyone on file drop folders. This is not recommended for test or production environments. Instead, provide the minimal set of permissions required.

Additional Send Handler Issues

The send handler support facilities for controlling the name of outbound files using a number of predefined macros. Macros support dates and times, message IDs, party identifiers, and source filenames. See the product documentation for more information.

When writing files, you can control the copy mode so that message content is appended to any existing file of the same name or used to create a new file. When creating new files, the handler can be configured to either overwrite existing files or to fail if an existing file is encountered.

The send handler provides support for system-level disk-write caching. By default, caching is not used. Enabling caching can increase performance at the risk of losing message content if the BizTalk Server box fails.

FTP Adapter

The FTP adapter is illustrated in Figure 6.12. It supports one-way receiving and sending of files between BizTalk Server and FTP servers. It is not, itself, an FTP server. When submitting messages from an external system via FTP, the system first submits the messages to an FTP server. BizTalk Server then uses the BizTalk FTP adapter to pull these messages from the server using the FTP protocol. The FTP receive handler is configured to poll FTP servers for files.

The FTP adapter has been enhanced in BizTalk Server 2010 to support *File Transfer Protocol over Secure Sockets Layer* (FTPS). This much-requested feature allows FTP interchange to occur over secure communication channels using SSL.

You can configure the FTP adapter at either the handler level or the port level. Any configuration at the port level overrides configuration at the handler level.

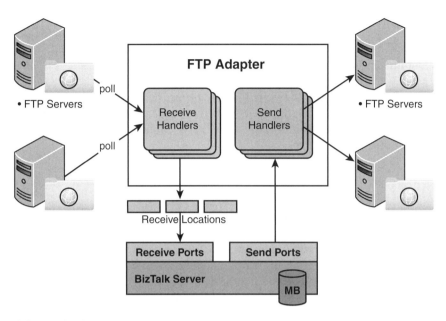

FIGURE 6.12   FTP adapter.

FTP Issues

It could be argued that, as a messaging protocol, FTP is characterized more by what it lacks than what it provides. The FTP protocol does not specify rules for file locking or reliable message delivery. It does not support ordered delivery. It offers no retry management or scheduling facilities. It cannot be used to secure messages, does not protect from a number of attacks, cannot explicitly handle Unicode encodings, does not verify clients, and so on. However, it is widely used as a simple mechanism for transferring files between machines. Different FTP servers exhibit a variety of additional characteristics beyond those specified by the protocol. For example, some servers implement forms of internal file locking, whereas others do not. Carefully consider these issues before using FTP in a BizTalk application.

Because of security concerns, the FTP adapter is not registered with BizTalk Server out-of-the-box. You must register the adapter manually and create adapter handlers before you can use it. FTP servers are generally placed behind firewalls, and the adapter implements explicit support for configuring connections via SOCKS4 and SOCKS5 firewalls. The adapter supports both active (where the adapter specifies a port to which the proxy connects) or passive (where the adapter connects to a port specified by the proxy) modes. In addition, consider using the adapter in conjunction with SSL to provide transport-level encryption between the firewall and the adapter.

If you must communicate with an FTP server behind a firewall using some different type of proxy, you might need to configure the adapter to connect to the firewall using the FTP properties rather than the firewall properties, and then use raw FTP commands (USER and PASS) to connect to the FTP server.

Handling Duplicate Messages

FTP provides no mechanism for reliably informing a BizTalk receive handler when a message has been fully received. In addition, FTP servers may allow further content to be written to files as they are being transmitted to BizTalk Server. If the transfer fails, or is partially completed, it is possible that the same file may be transmitted again to BizTalk Server. This problem is compounded by the use of multiple host instances. If you configure multiple host instances to read files from the same server endpoint, you are likely to encounter delivery of duplicate messages.

For any one host, each host instance runs on a different BizTalk Server. Multiple host instances are used to provide high availability of BizTalk Server. If one server fails, the load is taken up by the remaining servers. For high availability with the FTP adapter, you broadly have two choices. One is to use multiple host instances and implement any necessary custom logic to detect and eliminate duplicate messages. If the messages are idempotent, it might not be necessary to detect duplicates. The other approach is to configure a single host instance and to cluster the machine on which it runs to provide failover. This might require greater outlay on hardware and licenses.

Staging Files in Temporary Folders

The FTP adapter provides some built-in support for reliable messaging using temporary files in staging folders. This capability is supported by both receive and send handlers. It does not overcome the possible issues that can arise when using multiple host instances, but does allow a greater degree of reliability when using a single host instance to receive or send messages.

For receive handlers, staging folders are used to overcome issues that can arise due to connection timeouts. BizTalk Server polls the FTP server and retrieves files that are then submitted to BizTalk's messaging infrastructure. After messages have been published to the Message Box, the receive handler tells the FTP server to delete the received files. However, the connection to the FTP server might time out if any significant delay occurs in publishing messages to the Message Box. This might happen when processing large files, especially if there is any significant pipeline processing or mapping. In this scenario, configure a local temporary folder on the receive handler. The adapter retrieves files and saves them to disk before submitting them to BizTalk Server. This allows the adapter to tell the FTP server to delete the received files much earlier and breaks the dependency on keeping the connection open until messages have been published.

For send handlers, temporary folders are used to support recovery in the event of a transmission failure. You configure a temporary folder located on the target FTP server rather than the local BizTalk Server box. BizTalk Server sends each message to this temporary location. When the adapter completes the transfer, it sends raw FTP messages to the FTP server telling it to transfer the file from the staging folder to the configured FTP location. If the transmission fails, the behavior of the adapter depends on the setting of the Representation property. In Binary mode, the adapter restarts the message from the point of failure. In ASCII mode, the adapter resends the message in entirety. Support for recovery in ASCII mode is a newly introduced feature in BizTalk Server 2010.

You may be able to implement a similar approach outside of BizTalk Server to avoid partially written files being retrieved by the FTP adapter. The system that originally submits messages to the FTP server can use staging to ensure that complete files are transferred atomically to the FTP server before being retrieved by a BizTalk FTP receive handler.

Raw FTP Commands

The FTP adapter can issue raw FTP commands before or after each retrieval or transmission. FTP supports raw commands for a variety of purposes. You can configure the FTP adapter to perform additional actions such as creating, deleting, or changing to a given directory on a target server or appending data to an existing file.

Secure Messaging

BizTalk Server 2010 introduces secure messaging capabilities by supporting FTPS. Do not confuse FTPS with *SSH FTP* (SFTP), which, despite its name, is not associated with the FTP protocol.

FTP interchange involves the use of two channels. The control channel is used to communicate commands to the FTP server, and the data channel is used to transfer message content. The control channel transmits user account and password data to the server in plain text. Using SSL, you can ensure that this data is encrypted on the wire. In addition, you can optionally choose to protect message content in the data channel by encrypting it.

To establish a secure connection using SSL, the FTP adapter may need to present an X.509 client certificate to the FTP server. If this is required, set the **Use SSL** property to **Yes** and configure the **Client Certificate Hash** property. The certificate is stored in the local Windows certificate store and selected by configuring a hash of the certificate. Client certificates must be stored in the personal certificate store of the user account under which the adapter will run. The hash can be obtained by opening the certificate from the Certificates MMC console and copying the details of the Thumbprint property displayed in the Details tab.

The FTP adapter supports both Implicit and Explicit modes. In Implicit mode, the SSL protocol is used as soon as the adapter establishes a connection with the FTP server or firewall. Connections are made over port 990. In Explicit mode, the adapter establishes a connection and then issues a command to the FTP server to select the type of security required (SSL or *Transport Layer Security* [TLS]). The connection is generally made over port 21.

By default, the adapter encrypts both the control and the data channels. You can use the **Use Data Protection** property to configure the adapter to encrypt the control channel only.

HTTP Adapter

The HTTP adapter is illustrated in Figure 6.13. It supports both one- and two-way messaging. On the receive side, it supports HTTP GET and POST verbs. The adapter implements an *Internet Server Application Programming Interface* (ISAPI) extension that runs together with dynamically generated code under IIS. An IIS application must be created for each HTTP receive location. Running the adapter under IIS equates to using an isolated receive handler in BizTalk Server. On the send side, the adapter POSTs messages directly to an external HTTP server. The adapter supports HTTP and also secure interchange using HTTPS (SSL).

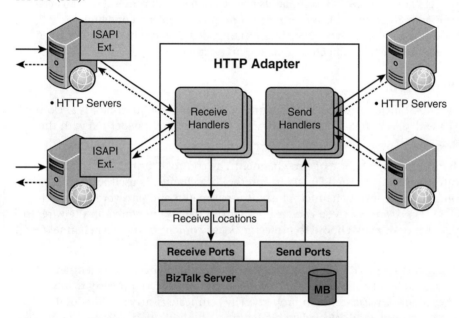

FIGURE 6.13   HTTP adapter.

The HTTP adapter plays an important role in enabling AS2 interchange over the Internet. BizTalk Server offers extensive out-of-the-box support for *electronic data interchange* (EDI), including direct support for AS2 interchange between different parties.

Using HTTP Receive Handlers

To use the HTTP adapter on the receive side, you must first configure IIS to use the ISAPI extension. Two versions of the extension are provided for 32-bit and 64-bit platforms. The exact approach to configuration differs depending on the versions of Windows and IIS you use to host BizTalk Server. See the article titled "How to Configure IIS for an HTTP Receive Location" in the product documentation for further details. Follow the instructions carefully. Incorrect configuration of IIS is often the cause of problems with this adapter.

The receive handler generates code dynamically to handle requests and submit them to BizTalk Server. Code is generated in a temporary directory. The account under which the isolated receive handler will run must be granted read/write access to this directory. You set the account when configuring the BizTalk Server host instance. Use the TMP or TEMP environment variables to determine the location of your temporary folder. These two variables normally point to the same location.

When a message is sent to the IIS application, the ISAPI extension (BtsHttpReceive.dll) looks for a receive location configured to match the path of the IIS virtual directory and the extension. For example, if the virtual directory path is /OrderProcessing, the extension searches for a BizTalk receive location whose virtual directory and ISAPI extension property is set to /OrderProcessing/BtsHppReceive.dll. Optionally, the receive location can specify an additional query string. In this case, only messages posted to BtsHtppReceive.dll in the OrderProcessing application where the first part of the query string matches the query string configured on the receive location are accepted. You can use query strings to enable a single IIS application to deliver messages to different receive locations.

When you POST messages to BizTalk Server, the body of the message is passed as the message content. When you perform a GET, the entire query string is passed as the message content. If the body is empty in a POST, or if no query string is passed in a GET, the request is rejected by the handler because there is no message content that can be passed to BizTalk Server.

The receive handler supports batching. This is configured at the level of a handler rather than on individual receive locations. By default, the batch size is set to 10. This can be an important setting to control in low-latency scenarios. It causes HTTP adapter to delay submission of messages to BizTalk Server until enough messages have been received to fill the batch or an internal timeout of one second occurs. The timeout is not configurable. In low latency scenarios, an additional second of latency may not be acceptable. In this case, reduce the batch size to 1 to ensure that all messages are submitted immediately.

By default, if a message fails, it is discarded rather than suspended. This is unusual in BizTalk Server where the normal behavior of adapters is to suspend failed messages. Use the **Suspend Failed Requests** option in the port-level configuration to configure the receive handler to suspend failed messages. This option includes the optional use of BizTalk Server's failed message routing facility.

For one-way receive ports, BizTalk Server returns a 202 Message Accepted response when a message is successfully persisted to the Message Box. It returns a 200 Message OK response on a two-way port. If a message fails, the adapter returns a 500 Internal Server Error response. On a one-way port you can configure the handler to return a message body, even though there is no response message. To do this, check the **Return Correlation Handle on Success** option in the port-level configuration. The message body will contain a correlation token generated automatically by BizTalk Server.

For two-way receive ports, you can configure the content type specifier for the response message. By default, this is set to text/xml. There is also an option for loopback. When this is selected, the inbound message is returned as the response message. This is sometimes useful for testing and prototyping, and also allows implementation of HTTP services using only BizTalk Server's messaging infrastructure. This, in turn, reduces latency because only a single traversal of the Message Box occurs.

Using HTTP Send Handlers

Like all send handlers, HTTP handlers run in the context of the BizTalk service (BTSNTSvc.exe) rather than IIS. They transmit message content to endpoints via HTTP and therefore function as a user agent in HTTP terms. To support HTTP 1.1, set the Connection header to Keep-Alive (this is strictly redundant, but common practice for legacy purposes), and set the user agent to a string starting with Microsoft BizTalk Server 2010.

At the handler level, you can configure the request timeout, the maximum number of redirects that the adapter will allow (to a maximum of 10), and the content type that the handler will transmit. These settings can each be overridden at the port level. You can also configure proxy settings at the handler level if you are using a proxy server to communicate with the outside world. Again, these can be overridden at the port level.

At the port level, you configure the URL of the site or service to which messages will be sent. There is also an option to control chunking of larger messages. By default, the handler uses HTTP chunked encoding. Larger messages are split into smaller sections and transmitted consecutively. Chunking allows the adapter to communicate larger messages more effectively over an open HTTP connection.

Send handlers support a range of authentication mechanisms including anonymous, basic, and digest authentication. They can also use Kerberos authentication. For basic and digest authentication, you can either configure the handler with a username and password or link it to BizTalk Server's SSO service to use the credentials for an affiliate application.

If the URL uses the HTTPS scheme, the handler may need to present an X.509 client certificate to the server to establish a secure SSL connection. This depends on the requirements of the external server. As with the FTP adapter, you must ensure that the correct certificate is stored in the personal certificate store of the user account under which the adapter will run. Enter the hash value in the SSL client certificate thumbprint box on the Authentication tab. The hash can be obtained by opening the certificate from the Certificates MMC console and copying the details of the Thumbprint property displayed in the Details tab.

Like receive handlers, send handlers support batching. This is configured via the Windows Registry. By default, the batch size is set to 5. This causes the handler to delay publishing responses to the Message Box until enough messages have been received to fill the batch or when an internal timeout of 1 second occurs. Again, the timeout is not configurable. As for receive handlers, batching introduces additional latency. Set the `HttpOutCompleteSize` Registry setting (see product documentation) to 1 in low-latency scenarios.

Additional Configuration

The HTTP adapter supports a number of additional options configured via the Windows Registry rather as part of handler configuration. The settings and locations in the Windows Registry are defined in the product documentation. These settings control various behaviors and settings, including support for HTTP chunked encoding in receive handlers, thread pools, number of concurrent requests and sends, and so on.

MQ Series Adapter

BizTalk Server provides two adapters to handle integration with MQ Series queues. This section describes the native adapter. The native adapter has a dependency on IBM WebSphere MQ Server for Windows versions 6 or 7. It can also work with older versions of MQ Server 5.3, CSD10 or later. BizTalk Server also provides the WebSphere MQ adapter as part of the BAHS, which can communicate directly with WebSphere MQ running on non-Windows platforms via the MQ client. In addition to these two adapters, BizTalk Host Integration Server provides a WCF channel for WebSphere MQ (IBM also supplies a WCF channel as part of WebSphere MQ Server) and an MSMQ-MQSeries bridge. Hence, there are several options available for integration with MQ Series.

The MQ Series native adapter is illustrated in Figure 6.14. BizTalk-hosted handlers manage the interchange of messages between MQ Series and BizTalk Server. On the receive side, the handler polls queues for messages, and on the send side it writes messages to queues. However, the adapter does not communicate directly with MQ Series queues. Instead, it relies on a COM+ component (MQSAgent) with which it communicates through DCOM remoting. The COM+ component is an agent that runs local to WebSphere MQ Server for Windows and manages the exchange of data directly with the WebSphere MQ queue manager. This agent is 32-bit only. It supports distributed (two-phase commit) transactions via Windows *Distributed Transaction Coordinator* (MS DTC) for both reads and writes.

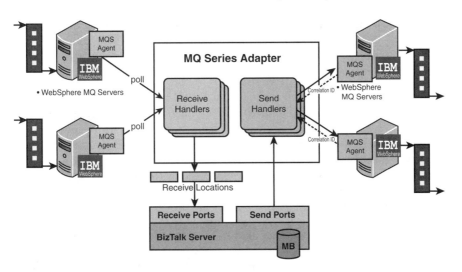

FIGURE 6.14   MQ Series adapter.

At the handler level, the adapter supports configuration of the name of the Windows server that hosts WebSphere MQ Server. These settings can be overridden at the port level. For send handlers, you can also configure the maximum number of messages that may be included in a batch.

Using MQ Series Receive Handlers

Receive handlers poll queues to retrieve messages and submit them to BizTalk Server. All configuration is provided through the handler, although polling is undertaken on the handler's behalf by the COM+ agent. The handler supports batched communication of dequeued messages. These batches are communicated to the handler by the COM+ agent. The handler specifies two limiting parameters on batch size. One limits the overall size of the batch in kilobytes, and the other limits the number of messages in a batch. By default, batches can be a maximum of 100KB and contain a maximum of 100 messages. The handler will wait up to 3 seconds to fill a batch before submitting it to BizTalk Server. This is not configurable but is reduced automatically when the polling interval is set to less than 3 seconds. Low latency is often not a major concern when passing messages via asynchronous queues, but if necessary, you can reduce the maximum batch size to reduce latency. Also, beware of using transactions with large batches as this can use significant resources. The handler supports chunked encoding of batched interchange. The chunk size is controlled using the Fragmentation Size property.

In addition to chunking, the handler also provides support for segmented messages. MQ Series uses segmentation to handle large messages that exceed a configured maximum length. Segments appear as separate messages on the queue and must be reassembled by the handler to build the complete message for submission to BizTalk Server. If segmentation support is not used, each segment is delivered to BizTalk Server as a separate message.

The receive handler supports transactional reads using an MS DTC distributed transaction. It coordinates the inner BizTalk Server transaction with this distributed transaction to ensure that each transaction is committed only after the batch has been persisted to the Message Box. Transactional control is optional.

Receive handlers support a multithreaded approach to handle multiple receive locations more efficiently. The size of the thread pool used to dequeue messages in configurable. Handlers also support ordered delivery. The threaded behavior of handlers for ordered delivery is undocumented, but the maintenance of order implies the serialization of dequeued messages and therefore is likely to impact performance. When configuring ordered delivery, you also select the handler's behavior for failed messages or other errors. The handler can either stop the receive location when an error is encountered or suspend the messages in the batch. This second option includes the optional use of BizTalk Server's failed message routing facility. The handler can be configured to suspend failed messages as either resumable or nonresumable.

When implementing ordered delivery, you must configure the MQ Series receive handler to run in a single host instance for each endpoint. Running the handler in multiple instances will result in out-of-order messages. To implement a resilient solution, consider clustering the BizTalk Server that runs the handler to provide failover. This may require greater outlay on hardware and licenses.

Receive handlers provide support for converting data to Unicode character sets (UTF8 and UTF 16). They also copy values from MQ Series transmission queue (MQXQH), IMS (MQIIH), and CICS (MQCIH) headers to properties in the inbound message context. Handlers parse the contents of these headers to populate a large number of defined message properties with rich information about the message interchange and host systems from which the messages originated. Handlers can be configured to optionally retain these property values in the message body, or to remove them automatically. There is no explicit mechanism for handling custom properties. These should be passed in the message body and handled using custom logic (for example, in a custom pipeline component).

Using MQ Series Send Handlers

Send handlers transmit messages to WebSphere MQ Series via the COM+ MQSAgent. As you saw earlier, send handlers supports message batching. The maximum number of messages in a batch can be configured at the handler level. In addition, send handlers can be configured to support ordered message delivery, message chunking, message segmentation (where large messages are segmented and enqueued as multiple messages) and distributed transactions. Handlers also support conversion of message content to ANSI.

Send handlers support both one- and two-way send ports. Use the adapter with a solicit-response send port to obtain a correlation ID from the MQ queue manager, passed via the MQMD_MSGId and MQMD_CorrelId identifiers. The correlation ID can be used by BizTalk Server to correlate later messages received from MQ Series.

Managing Queues

You saw earlier that you can configure the name of the Windows server that hosts WebSphere at the handler level. At the port level, you can use the Queue Definition dialog shown in Figure 6.15 to override this value and also set the WebSphere queue manager and queue names. These can be selected from drop-down boxes populated by connecting to WebSphere MQ server on the designated Windows server. Alternatively, you can type in the names of the Queue Manager and the Queue fields.

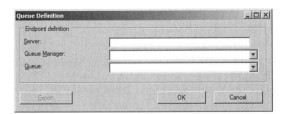

FIGURE 6.15   MQ Queue Definition dialog.

Having defined the queue endpoint, you can export the definition of the endpoint to a script. If you supply the name of a queue that does not exist, this script can be used to create the queue within WebSphere MQ Server. Click the **Export** button to reveal the Export dialog shown in Figure 6.16. You can optionally create transmission queues for transmission of messages to remote queue managers. You can save your script to file or you can create the queue on the designated server. Scripts can be run at a later time using IBM's runmqsc command-line utility.

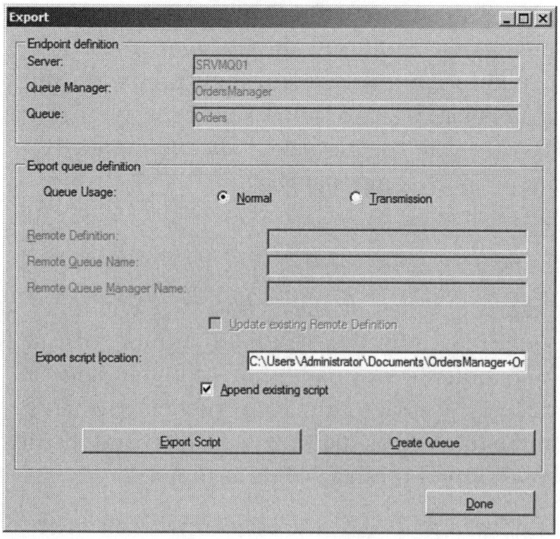

FIGURE 6.16   MQ export queue definition.

Configuring MQSAgent

The product documentation provides information on how to deploy and configure the MQSAgent. Ensure that you use the later version of this agent (MQSAgent2), and that you have correctly configured your environment to allow COM+ and DTC interaction. If WebSphere MQ Server is running on a clustered node, see http://support.microsoft.com/kb/893059 for information about handling failover with respect to the agent.

MSMQ Adapter

The MSMQ adapter supports Microsoft's message queuing technology. *Microsoft Messaging Queue* (MSMQ) is often used in conjunction with BizTalk Server as a convenient way to enable reliable messaging when integrating with external systems. Although MSMQ provides similar facilities to MQ Series, it is designed to handle small messages only. There is a maximum size limit of 4MB imposed by the file mapping approach implemented in MSMQ. If you must pass larger messages to BizTalk Server via MSMQ, BizTalk Server provides large message handling extensions for this purpose.

The MSMQ adapter is illustrated in Figure 6.17. It works directly with the local MSMQ service. MSMQ must be installed on the BizTalk Server box. This is true even if reading or writing to remote queues. If you are using MSMQ version 3 or earlier, transactional reads are limited to local queues only, but in MSMQ 4, you can perform transactional reads against a remote queue. The MSMQ service is used by both the receive and the send handlers.

MSMQ is also supported by the native WCF-NetMsmq BizTalk adapter. In this case, the adapter uses a predefined WCF binding to communicate with MSMQ. This is covered in greater detail later in this chapter.

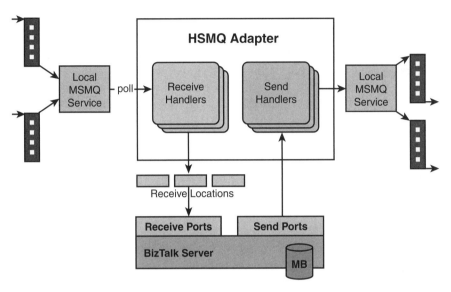

FIGURE 6.17   MSMQ adapter.

Using MSMQ Receive Handlers

Receive handlers poll local queues to retrieve messages and submit them to BizTalk Server. Each receive location uses a fixed poll interval of 0.5 second to read batches of messages from a given queue. By default, the batch size is set to 20 messages. Low latency is often not a major concern when passing messages via asynchronous queues, but if necessary, you can reduce the batch size to reduce latency. Beware of using transactions with large batches because this can consume significant resources.

If you must pass messages larger than 4MB to BizTalk Server via MSMQ, you can use the BizTalk Message Queuing Large Message Extension. This is part of the BizTalk Server SDK and consists of a DLL called mqrtlarge.dll located under the SDK folder in BizTalk Server's installation directory. The version of the library will be 32 bit or 64 bit, depending on which version of BizTalk Server 2010 you install. You can freely distribute this library to other non-BizTalk Server machines. The API provides the MQReceiveLargeMessage and MQSendLargeMessage functions, which mimic the MQReceiveMessage and MQSendMessage functions provided by MSMQ. The API supports only these two functions. Use the library in custom code to submit large messages to MSMQ. The messages are fragmented, and each chunk is passed as a separate message with additional metadata that the handler uses to reconstruct the message in its entirety.

Receive handlers support transactional reads using MS DTC distributed transactions. Internal BizTalk Server transactions are coordinated with the distributed transactions to ensure that each transaction is committed only after the batch has been persisted to the

Message Box. Transactional control is optional. MSMQ versions earlier than version 4.0 do not support remote transactional reads. Instead, you must run MSMQ locally to perform reads transactionally. This limits the receive handler to running in a single BizTalk Server host instance.

Receive handlers support a multithreaded approach to service multiple receive locations efficiently. They use the host's thread pool for this purpose. The number of threads is therefore configurable using the BizTalk Settings dashboard at the host instance level. The adapter also supports ordered delivery. When ordered delivery is selected, the adapter operates in a single-threaded fashion and passes each message to BizTalk Server in a separate batch.

When implementing ordered delivery, you must configure MSMQ receive handlers to run in a single host instance for each endpoint. Running a handler in multiple instances results in our-of-order messages. To implement a resilient solution, consider clustering the BizTalk Server that runs the receive handler to provide failover. This might require greater outlay on hardware and licenses.

The adapter can be configured with respect to its behavior for failed messages or other errors. The adapter can either stop the receive location when an error is encountered or suspend the messages in the batch. This second option implies the optional use of BizTalk's failed message routing facility. The adapter can be configured to suspend failed messages as either resumable or nonresumable.

Using MSMQ Send Handlers

Send handlers transmit messages to the local MSMQ service to be forwarded on to the destination queue. This may be a local or remote queue. Send handlers support message batching. The maximum number of messages in a batch can be configured at the handler level. By default, this is set to 100 messages. The maximum message size can be configured at the port level. When sending messages to a remote queue, the local queue manager must authenticate itself using the correct username and password. These can be configured on the adapter.

Each MSMQ message is structured as a collection of properties. For example, the PROPID_M_BODY property holds the contents of the message. Send handlers allow a number of addition property values to be configured at the port level. These include the Body Type (PROPID_M_BODY_TYPE), which is an integer value taken from the COM variant structure (see also the .NET VarEnum enumeration). The default value is 8209, representing a byte array. The values listed in Table 6.1 are allowed.

The Destination Queue property (PROPID_M_DEST_QUEUE) is used to specify the queue to which messages will be sent. Queues may be public (published within Active Directory) or private. Different paths are used depending on the type of queue. Private queues may be addressed using the DIRECT or PRIVATE formats. See product information for the adapter and MSMQ for further details.

Messages can be sent in one of two modes controlled by the Recoverable property. This sets the PROPID_M_DELIVERY property in the message. When Recoverable is set to False, the messages are passed in express mode without persistence. When set to True, each message is persisted to disk to support recoverability on failure.

The Message Priority property (PROPID_M_PRIORITY) controls the preference given to a message when routing it and its position when placed in a queue. A higher number indicates a higher priority.

TABLE 6.1   Body Type Values

Value	COM Alias	Description
0	VT_EMPTY	Treated as an array of bytes.
2	VT_I2	A short integer.
3	VT_I4	A long integer.
4	VT_R4	A float (4-byte floating point).
5	VT_R8	A double-float (8-byte floating point).
6	VT_CY	A CURRENCY type (8-byte).
7	VT_DATE	An OLE DATE (8-byte) type.
8	VT_BSTR	String data in Unicode (does not have to be NULL terminated).
9	VT_DISPATCH	A COM Automation object (IDispatch object).
11	VT_BOOL	A VARIANT_BOOL (2-byte) type, which takes the values of VARIANT_TRUE (-1) and VARIANT_FALSE (0).
13	VT_UNKNOWN	A COM object (IUnknown interface).
16	VT_I1	A Char (1-byte) type.
17	VT_UI1	A Char (1-byte) type. An array of bytes when joined by the OR operator with VT_ARRAY (VT_ARRAY ¦ VT_UI1).
18	VT_UI2	A short integer.
19	VT_UI4	A long integer.
30	VT_LPSTR	A variable-size, NULL-terminated ANSI string.
31	VT_LPWSTR	A variable-size, NULL-terminated Unicode string.
68	VT_STREAMED_OBJECT	A persistent, serialized object whose format is the output of a call to OleSaveToStream using IPersistStream.
69	VT_STORED_OBJECT	A persistent, serialized object whose format is the output of a call to OleSave using IPersistStorage.
8209	VT_ARRAY ¦ VT_UI1	An array of bytes.

The Timeout and Timeout Interval properties control the time limit allowed for messages to reach the destination queue when using transactions. They set the underlying

PROPID_M_TIME_TO_REACH_QUEUE property in the message. If the message fails to reach the queue in time, and the Use Destination Queue property is set to True, it is routed to the dead letter queue. This property, together with the Use Journal Queue property, sets the value of the PROPID_M_JOURNAL property as an array of flags. The Use Journal Queue property, when set to True, tells MSMQ to store a copy of each successfully delivered message in the Journal queue.

Set the Acknowledgement Type property (PROPID_M_ACKNOWLEDGE) and the Administration Queue property (PROPID_M_ADMIN_QUEUE) if you want MSMQ to return an ACK or NACK message. A number of options are available in the drop-down box in the property list. Acknowledgment messages are stored in the Administration queue, and can be retrieved by BizTalk Server using an MSMQ receive handler. Any nontransactional queue can be used as an Administration queue.

Use the Transactional property to specify that messages will be sent as part of a transaction. Send handlers will create MS DTC transactions for this purpose. In addition, you can use the Support Segmentation property to exploit the BizTalk Message Queuing Large Message Extension described earlier. In this case, messages larger than 4MB in size re chunked as individual messages. The message can be reconstructed in its entirety by reading it from the destination queue using the MQReceiveLargeMessage function exported by mqrtlarge.dll.

The use of transactions with recoverability, timeouts, and acknowledgments provides message reliability. However, by themselves, these properties do not provide full resilience. In accordance with Microsoft's guidance, the local MSMQ service should also be clustered to support failover. Because the MSMQ service runs locally to BizTalk Server, this implies that BizTalk Server must also be clustered. This might require greater outlay on hardware and licenses. See the product documentation for further information about configuring clustered solutions for MSMQ.

Authenticating and Securing Messages

When transmitting messages via a send handler, you can configure the handler to request that MSMQ provides integrity, nonrepudiation, and privacy for messages that are transmitted from the local MSMQ service to the destination queue. MSMQ provides the ability to digitally sign messages and to authenticate the digital signatures when they are received by the destination queue. Use the Use Authentication property to indicate authentication requirements. This is used to set the value of the PROPID_M_AUTH_LEVEL message property.

By default, the MSMQ service uses an internal certificate to sign outgoing messages. Internal certificates are generated automatically and designed for use within an Active Directory environment. If messages are delivered across organizational boundaries, then it may be necessary to use an external certificate. In this case, you must enter the hash value of the certificate in the Certificate Thumbprint property. The hash can be obtained by opening the certificate from the Certificates MMC console and copying the details of the Thumbprint property displayed in the Details tab. MSMQ passes certificates to the destination queue via the PROPID_M_SENDER_CERT message property.

In addition to digital signatures, you can also request MSMQ to use message-level encryption. Use the Encryption Level property to set the value of the PROPID_M_ENCRYPTION_ALG message property. Messages are encrypted in the channel between the local and remote queue manager using either RC2 or RC4 encryption. Although MSMQ 4 also supports *Advanced Encryption Standard* (AES), this is not supported by the MSMQ adapter.

POP3 Adapter

Post Office Protocol 3 defines a simple and widely supported Internet protocol for enabling store-and-forward message delivery via an email system. BizTalk Server provides a native POP3 adapter that polls a mailbox for messages and publishes new messages to the Message Box. After messages have been published, the POP3 adapter immediately deletes those messages from the mailbox.

The POP3 adapter is illustrated in Figure 6.18. Unlike previous adapters, the POP3 adapter supports receive handlers only. It cannot be used to send messages. Use the SMTP adapter to send email messages. Receive handlers support one-way messaging only. The adapter supports both plain text and MIME-encoded/encrypted message content. MIME encoding allows attachments to be passed with the main body of the message. Note that the POP3 adapter is 32 bit only, and must therefore be hosted in a 32-bit host instance.

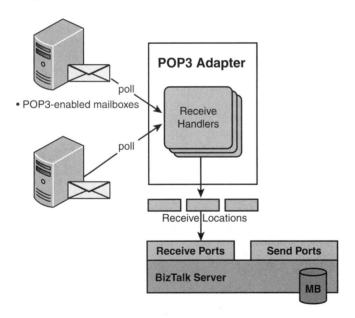

FIGURE 6.18   POP3 adapter.

Using POP3 Receive Handlers

All configuration of the POP3 adapter is handled at the port level. To connect to a mail server, set Mail Server to the name of the server that hosts the mailbox and, if necessary, assign a port number to the Port property. This property is set to 0 by default, which indicates use of the default POP3 port. This is either port 110 for nonsecure interchange or 995 for interchange over SSL. To authenticate the handler to the mailbox, set the User Name and Password properties as required. The handler supports standard Basic and Digest authentication together with Microsoft's proprietary *Secure Password Authentication* (SPA) protocol. SPA is a form of integrated Windows authentication that can be used when communicating with Microsoft Exchange mailboxes.

The POP3 adapter supports secure links using SSL. However, it provides no support for selection and presentation of client certificates to the server. It therefore supports only server authentication.

By default, POP3 handlers poll the mailbox every 5 minutes. You can configure a different interval using the Polling Interval and Polling Interval Unit properties. If errors occur during polling, the handler continues to poll a number of times, as defined by the Error Threshold property. If it is still unsuccessful, it closes down. The Error Threshold property is set to 10 by default.

POP3 handlers can process both plain text messages and MIME encoded messages. The MIME decoder is built in to the adapter and does not require additional pipeline processing. Use the Apply MIME Decoding property to switch the decoder on or off. MIME provides a standardized approach to framing messages and is widely used for formatting email content. It is a multipart message format. The POP3 adapter decoder maps MIME messages to BizTalk Server multipart messages. Specifically, it handles mail attachments as separate message parts. Each part of a MIME message has a content type specifier, such as text/xml, and an index specifier for its position within the message.

BizTalk Server multipart messages are useful constructs. They can be used to directly represent multipart messages such as MIME messages, SOAP RPC messages, and so on, and are often used as a way to decouple representation of actual content type from the .NET types of message objects. Each multipart message can optionally designate any part, regardless of its index, as the body part. If no body part is designated, BizTalk Server automatically assumes that the first part is the body part. BizTalk artifacts and components such as maps and disassemblers generally act only on the body part. When mapping a MIME message to a BizTalk multipart message, the POP3 handler allows the body part to be selected using two criteria. These are the Body Part Index property and the Body Part Context property. For example, to use the third text/plain part of the MIME message, set these properties to **3** and **text/plain**. Handlers always create the body part as the first part in the BizTalk multipart message. They also automatically populate various message context properties with data obtained from headers in the MIME encode message.

POP3 does not support transactions and cannot enforce reliable messaging constraints. If instances of the same handler run on multiple BizTalk Server boxes, they all poll the same mailbox. There is a danger that the same message may be delivered multiple times to BizTalk Server. One way to prevent this is to run a single instance of the handler in a single BizTalk host instance. In this case, you might need to cluster the BizTalk Server box to provide resilience. This may require greater outlay on hardware and licenses. Another option is to allow duplicate messages to be published to the BizTalk Server Message Box and then use custom logic to perform deduplication. This might not be necessary if the messages are idempotent.

Handling Encrypted Messages

MIME supports data encryption. POP3 handlers support encrypted MIME messages by automatically searching for a certificate in the personal certificate store of the user account under which the handler is running. This certificate must match the certificate included with the MIME message and provides the key value used to decrypt the message. Automatic decryption within the adapter can be a security risk because BizTalk Server will persist plaintext content to the Message Box. Decryption occurs only if the Apply MIME Decoding property is set to True. If it set to False, the encrypted content is persisted. In this case, the content can be accessed by writing custom code to decrypt the message and process its parts. Another approach is to decrypt the message in the adapter and then encrypt sensitive data in the receive pipeline before the message is persisted. Always take care to ensure that sensitive data is not inadvertently stored as plain text in the tracking database.

SMTP Adapter

Simple Mail Transfer Protocol (SMTP) defines a widely supported Internet protocol for routing email to destination email addresses via an SMTP server. BizTalk Server provides a native SMTP adapter that transmits messages to SMTP servers. The SMTP adapter is illustrated in Figure 6.19. It supports one-way send handlers only. Much like the POP3 adapter, it provides built-in MIME support for encoding. However, it does not support *Secure MIME* (S/MIME). If you need to encrypt message content, use the MIME/SMIME encoder. This is a native pipeline component provided as part of BizTalk Server. The adapter also supports options for defining and storing content within handler configuration.

Although the SMTP adapter will run in 64-bit hosts, the MIME/SMIME pipeline component is 32-bit only. Because pipelines run in the same process as adapters, this restriction means that, when using the MIME/SMIME encoder, you must run the adapter in a 32-bit host.

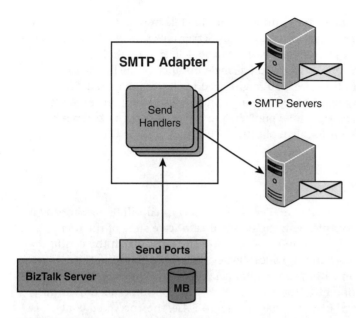

FIGURE 6.19   SMTP adapter.

Using SMTP Send Handlers

In a typical configuration, the SMTP server to which messages will be transmitted is configured at the handler level together with the any username and password needed for authentication of the adapter instance. Authentication is optional and may not always be required. The adapter supports Basic authentication and NTLM (integrated Windows) authentication. NTLM authentication is against the user account under which the host instance is running. In addition, the From email address can optionally be used as the return address for receipts requested by the handler. Receipt requirements are set at the port level using the Read Receipt and Delivery Receipt properties

Handler-level configuration can be overridden at the port level. All other configuration is managed at the port level. The adapter provides a custom tabbed property page for this purpose.

The General tab allows the To and CC email address to be defined, together with the Subject property. Most SMTP servers allow multiple addresses to be defined, generally using a separator character such as a semicolon (;). This tab also supports the delivery properties described earlier. Macros can be included in the To, CC, and Subject properties, and also in the From property. See the product documentation for further details.

The Compose tab controls the message content. By default, the adapter transmits the body part of the BizTalk message as the content. Alternatively, it can transmit text entered directly within the tab or the contents of a selected file. These options allow send ports to be configured to transmit standard email content. Ensure that you select the correct character set for either text or file content.

The Attachments tab controls the addition of additional attachment parts to the outgoing email message. The Remaining BizTalk Message Parts property enables you to control how the parts of a BizTalk multipart message are handled. If the body part was not specified under to Compose tab, this can be added as an attachment. Alternatively, you can add all remaining parts of the message as separate attachments to the outgoing email or choose to send no attachments. In addition, one or more files can be defined as attachments.

The Handler Override tab allows the handler-level configuration to be overridden at the port level.

Providing static configuration at the port level caters for many common scenarios. However, you might sometimes need to set certain properties dynamically at runtime in accordance with business logic within your application. The adapter defines a comprehensive set of message context properties that can be used for this purpose. Context properties can be set in an orchestration or pipeline. These properties are always used in conjunction with dynamic ports and may also be used in conjunction with static ports.

> **NOTE**
>
> The handling of message context properties in the SMTP adapter demonstrates some of the more subtle aspects of BizTalk send adapter behavior. Depending on how adapters are implemented they may pass a batch object back to the messaging engine, allowing the adapter to see each message as it is added to the batch, but before the batch is passed to the send pipeline. Each adapter is free to exploit this mechanism as it wants. The SMTP adapter uses this feature to override message context properties set further upstream in an orchestration or receive pipeline. If the adapter is running in the context of a static send port, it overrides a number of SMTP context properties with values held in the port-level configuration. If the port is dynamic, these context properties are not overridden. If a custom pipeline component in the send pipeline then creates or overrides any of these context properties, these new values are used by the adapter at the point the message is transmitted to the SMTP server.

Windows SharePoint Services Adapter

The WSS adapter allows interchange of documents between BizTalk Server and SharePoint. This includes SharePoint Foundation Server 2010 and the older Windows SharePoint Services (WSS 3.0 with SP2), and standard and enterprise editions of SharePoint Server 2010 and SharePoint Server 2007. It is used to retrieve documents from or send documents to SharePoint libraries, although it can also support interaction with SharePoint lists. The adapter handles translation between the different representations of properties in SharePoint and BizTalk Server and also provides built-in transformation services to handle InfoPath metadata.

The WSS adapter is illustrated in Figure 6.20. It supports one-way receive and send handlers. All communication with SharePoint is via an ASP.NET web service (BTSharePointAdapterWS.asmx) that runs locally on the same server as SharePoint. The web service handles direct interaction with SharePoint via the SharePoint Object Model. The web service can be installed separately onto each SharePoint server box without incurring additional licensing costs. Use the BizTalk Server Installation Wizard to install the service. Select the **Windows SharePoint Services Adapter Web Service** under Additional Software. Full installation details are included in the product documentation, including guidance on security considerations and permissions, configuration of the web service, load balancing, and so on.

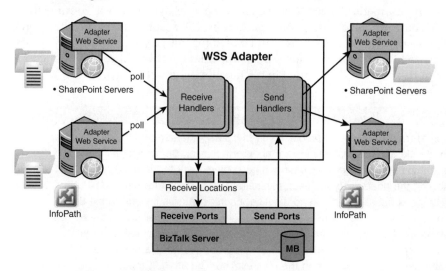

FIGURE 6.20   WSS adapter.

Using WSS Receive Handlers

Receive handlers are configured only at the port level. Enter the URL of the SharePoint site and the port number for the adapter web service running on the same machine to establish a connection. Enter a relative URL to connect to a specific document library together with an optional SharePoint view name. The adapter polls the library at regular intervals to download any documents from the library. You can configure the polling interval in seconds together with the maximum size of each batch of messages retrieved from SharePoint. There is also a timeout property to control how long the adapter waits for a response from the adapter web service.

As documents are downloaded from the SharePoint document library, they are deleted by the adapter web service. The web service checks out each document before returning it to the handler. When each document in a batch is safely persisted to the Message Box, the adapter web service deletes each of the checked-out documents. This mechanism is used to prevent duplicate delivery of documents to BizTalk Server but is not fully reliable. In the event of failure, it is possible for checked-out documents to remain undeleted within the SharePoint library.

Handlers support an alternative to document deletion. Configure the Archive Location URL property with a relative URL to another document library or library folder to archive downloaded files. Documents are moved to this location after successful delivery to BizTalk Server. Use the Archive Overwrite property to control how existing files of the same name are overwritten in the archive folder. If this property is set to No, and a file of the same name already exists in the archive folder, the web service retains the checked-out file in the source library.

By default, the web service archives files under the same name used in the source library. To change and control the names of archived files, use the Archive Filename property. If this is set to a simple filename, and Archive Overwrite is set to Yes, each file overwrites the last. Alternatively, a unique filename can be specified using macros. The WSS adapter supports a small number of macros for BizTalk message IDs, sending orchestrations, and source filenames/extensions. It also supports the %XPATH=<xpath>% macro. This is used to retrieve a node value from with the file content, assuming that the file contains XML content. If the XML content uses namespaces, XPaths can become long and unwieldy due to the need to select nodes using their fully qualified names. To combat this, the adapter supports a Namespaces Aliases property. This is used to define a comma- or semicolon-delimited list of prefix definitions for different namespace URIs. The defined prefixes can then be used by the %XPATH% macro.

Receive handlers support InfoPath documents. InfoPath captures form data as XML documents, and these documents are often stored within SharePoint document libraries. InfoPath documents contain the mso-infoPathSolution and mso-application XML processing instructions. These are used to identify InfoPath forms so that they open automatically within InfoPath using the correct InfoPath template. Use the Microsoft Office Integration property to control how these processing instructions are handled for received documents. By default, this property is set to Optional. In this case, the adapter removes the processing instructions if it finds them but otherwise submits documents to BizTalk Server as is. If the property is set to Yes, the adapter expects to find the processing instructions and will remove them. If they are not present, the document is ignored. If the property is set to No, the adapter always submits the document to BizTalk Server as is.

Using WSS Send Handlers

Send handlers transmit messages to the web service, which, in turn, uploads their contents to a SharePoint document library. By default, handlers transmit batches of up to 20 messages at a time. The batch size is configured at the handler level.

To connect to SharePoint, enter the URL of the SharePoint site together with the port number for the adapter web service running on the same machine. Enter an additional relative URL to deliver messages to a specific document library. There is also a Timeout property to control how long the handler waits for calls to the adapter web service to complete.

Use the Filename property to control the name under which the file is saved. If this is set to a simple filename, and assuming the Overwrite property (see below) is set to Yes, each file overwrites the previous one. Alternatively, as with receive handlers, the filename can be constructed using macros. This includes the `%XPATH=<xpath>%` macro described earlier. Again, use the Namespaces Aliases property to define a list of prefixes to simplify your XPath expressions. If no filename is set, the adapter uses the WSS adapter's Filename property contained in the message context. This is generally set in an orchestration. If the Filename property is not set, the filename is set to `Msg-%MessageID%.xml`.

Use the Overwrite property to control how existing files of the same name are overwritten in the destination folder. If this property is set to No, and a file of the same name already exists in the destination folder, the document is not written, and the message is suspended in the BizTalk Server Message Box. If set to Yes, the file is overwritten. If the value is set to Rename, the adapter web service appends a unique GUID token to the end of the filename to differentiate it from the existing file. Set it to Orchestration to indicate that the Overwrite property will be specified by the `ConfigOverwrite` property in the message context. `ConfigOverwrite` is typically set in an orchestration. If the property has not been set, the Overwrite property is set to Rename.

Send handlers provide direct support for uploading InfoPath documents to SharePoint document libraries. Use the Microsoft Office Integration property to control the required behavior. If this property is set to No, the document is uploaded as is. If it is set to Yes or Yes (InfoPath Form Library), and if the content of the documents is XML, the adapter amends the content by adding InfoPath processing instructions to link the document to an InfoPath solution represented by an XSN template file. The template is associated with either the destination folder or some other location.

The Yes option uses additional properties to specify which locations to search for the template. The adapter web service first searches the document library specified in the Templates Document Library location and then, if no template is found, it searches the Templates Fallback Document Library location. If it still cannot find a template, the message is suspended in the BizTalk Server Message Box. The specified libraries may contain multiple InfoPath templates. To select the required template, each library must define a column that specifies an XML namespace. For each template stored within the designated libraries, populate this column with the namespace of the document node of the XML messages you want to match to that template. Enter the column names into the Templates Namespace Column and Templates Fallback Namespace Column properties of the send handler.

The Yes (InfoPath Form Library) option avoids the need to specify template document libraries. Only use this option when documents will be uploaded to an InfoPath form library. Each form library should have an attached InfoPath template. The adapter web service checks for the existence of an InfoPath template and suspends the message if none is found. Ensure that you upload only documents to an InfoPath form library that match the attached template.

If you set the Microsoft Office Integration property to Optional, and the content of the document is XML, the adapter web service first searches for a template as if the property were set to Yes, assuming that search criteria have been configured. If no template is found, it searches as if the property were set to Yes (InfoPath Form Library). If the adapter web service still cannot find a template, or if the content is not XML, it saves the document as is.

If you prefer, you can set the Office integration approach through the `ConfigOfficeIntegration` message context property and other associated properties. (See the product documentation for further details.) You will generally set these context properties within an orchestration. Set the Microsoft Office Integration property to Orchestration.

Mapping SharePoint Columns

As well as document content, the adapter handles SharePoint document library columns and maps their values to and from BizTalk message content properties. Receive handlers automatically copy standard SharePoint column values to corresponding adapter-defined properties and promote a number of these properties for routing purposes. The name of each of these context properties is in the form `In<xxxx>`. See the product documentation for further information. Any custom SharePoint columns are copied into an XML document, which is then accessible via the `InPropertiesXml` context property in BizTalk Server.

Send handlers can control SharePoint property promotion for up to 16 custom properties. If you are sending documents to InfoPath form libraries, you can also use SharePoint's capabilities to promote values contained in the form content into columns in the form library. To promote values using the handler, use the 16 pairs of Column n and Column n Value properties. For Column n Value properties, you can use the same macro-based approach as for filenames, including the `%XPATH=<xpath>%` macro described earlier.

Instead of sending documents to document libraries or InfoPath form libraries, you can send them to SharePoint lists. In this case, the content of the document is not uploaded. However, the property promotion mechanism can still be used to assign values to list columns. Hence, the adapter can be used to populate SharePoint lists dynamically.

SOAP Adapter

The SOAP adapter is formally deprecated and is described only briefly here. It is largely superseded by the WCF-BasicHttp and WCF-WSHttp adapters. The SOAP adapter provides support for interchange using SOAP and *Web Service Definition Language* (WSDL). It implements receive handlers used to publish SOAP endpoints to which external systems can send messages and send handlers that transmit messages to external SOAP endpoints. The adapter supports both one- and two-way interaction.

The SOAP adapter predates the emergence of WCF and uses ASP.NET technologies. On the receive side, a wizard is used to manufacture ASP.NET web services that submit messages to BizTalk Server. These web services are hosted in the context of an IIS worker process. On the send side, the adapter uses a generated ASP.NET proxy to communicate with external SOAP services.

The SOAP adapter is unique among adapters in that it is explicitly supported by orchestrations. Using the Add Service Reference dialog, you can choose to add an ASP.NET web reference rather than a WCF service reference. The web reference generates web ports. These are specialized orchestration ports that configure outbound messages at runtime by adding a number of message context properties specific to the SOAP adapter. Using web ports, it is easy to consume external web services. However, this approach represents a degree of coupling between SOAP send handlers and orchestrations, which, in turn, can make it harder to maintain code.

The SOAP adapter is less performant than the newer WCF adapters and does not support WS-* specifications. In most scenarios, the WCF adapters can be used as a complete and more functional replacement for the SOAP adapter. However, in one respect, the SOAP adapter may still play an important role. Although WCF itself supports the full SOAP specification, the BizTalk WCF adapters do not fully support every aspect of SOAP. Specifically, they do not support the RPC-encoded SOAP style. This style has largely fallen out of favor in recent years. However, some older versions of web service frameworks, such as versions 1.*x* of Apache Axis, used RPC-encoded as the default style. When integrating with systems that use older versions of Axis, it is likely that you will need to support RPC-encoded interchange. To do this, you must use the deprecated SOAP adapter. The RPC-encoded style defines multipart messages. The SOAP adapter maps service interchange to BizTalk multipart messages to correctly represent the RPC style.

For further information on configuration, tooling and usage, see the product documentation.

WCF Adapters

BizTalk Server provides a library of seven WCF native adapters. These adapters are implemented using WCF's service model and allow interchange of SOAP messages via the WCF channel architecture. Five of the seven adapters use system-defined WCF bindings. These adapters are listed in Table 6.2.

In addition, BizTalk Server provides two custom WCF adapters. The WCF-Custom adapter is hosted in instances of BTSNTSvc.exe, and the WCF-CustomIsolated adapter is hosted under IIS. Both adapters support configuration using any suitable binding. This includes system-defined and custom bindings. The WCF-CustomIsolated adapter, however, is restricted to supporting only those transports that can be hosted in IIS. If you are using IIS7, this includes `net.tcp`, `net.pipe`, and `net.msmq` binding types.

The rest of this chapter describes the native WCF adapters in detail and introduces the SQL Server line-of-business WCF adapter.

TABLE 6.2   Adapters for System-Defined WCF Bindings

Adapter	WCF Binding	Description
WCF-BasicHttp	`BasicHttpBinding`	Supports SOAP-based interchange via HTTP with web services that conform to the WS-Basic Profile specification. This includes services built with most web service development frameworks, including ASP.NET.
WCF-NetMsmq	`NetMsmqBinding`	Supports the interchange of SOAP messages with other WCF-based services via MSMQ.
WCF-NetNamedPipe	`NetNamedPipeBinding`	Supports SOAP-based interchange using named pipes. This is an interprocess communication protocol supported on local Windows boxes.
WCF-NetTcp	`NetTcpBinding`	Supports SOAP-based interchange between different machines using TCP/IP sockets.
WCF-WSHttp	`WSHttpBinding`	Supports SOAP-based interchange with web services via HTTP. This binding supports a range of WS-* specifications that extend the SOAP envelope to provide secure and reliable messaging.

Windows Communication Foundation

Windows Communication Foundation is a class library included as part of the .NET Framework. It enables the construction of service-orientated endpoints and manages the exchange of messages between endpoints at runtime. Conceptually, an endpoint is one end of a communication link. A link has two ends, which we typically designate the consumer and the server. WCF is used to build both consumer and service endpoints. This does not imply, however, that WCF must be used at both endpoints. WCF enables loose coupling of consumers and services and comes with predefined support for a variety of common transports and encodings (for example, TCP/IP sockets, HTTP, and SOAP). It also supports development of custom approaches.

> **NOTE**
>
> The WCF-NetTcp, WCF-NetMsmq, and WCF-NetNamedPipe BizTalk adapters use the WCF Binary message encoder to handle encoded SOAP messages in an efficient manner. This encoding is WCF-specific and proprietary. Hence, to encode and decode messages, external endpoints must also use WCF. This restriction does not apply to the WCF-BasicHttp, WCF-WSHttp, or WCF-Custom/CustomIsolated adapters.

WCF service endpoints are defined by an address, a binding, and a contract (so-called ABC). An address provides the identity of the service and indicates its location. A binding comprises a number of channel components that are composed together at runtime to handle message transport and encoding and additional concerns such as transaction control, reliability, and security at both the message and transport levels. A contract defines the operations that a service supports, the message interchange patterns, and the message content schemas. WCF allows contracts to be defined programmatically using interfaces and annotations, and supports the generation and publishing of contract metadata in association with service endpoints. Endpoints are highly configurable and customizable. Indeed, it is common to compose endpoints through the use of XML configuration files that specify addresses and bindings.

WCF implements a highly symmetrical approach to handling consumer endpoints. For example, when consumers communicate with a service endpoint, WCF can be used to dynamically construct client-side message channels based on near-identical configuration to that used on the service side. These channels can be used in a simple and straightforward manner in client-side code. This symmetry is possible through the use of a common channel model that is exploited on both the consumer and the service side.

WCF provides an additional model which supports the implementation of both service and consumer functionality. This service model provides a framework for the implementation of behaviors. A behavior is a component that handles some aspect of service or consumer functionality at the service, operation, endpoint, or contract level. This might include message filtering and validation, enrichment, transformation, metadata publishing/consumption, or many other concerns. Behaviors are customizable, configurable, and reusable.

WCF is used to implement different message interchange patterns (one-way, request-response, and duplex) in a service-orientated fashion. It offers extensive support for SOAP-based messages and growing support for RESTful interchange. It provides a foundation on which to build services, including cloud services, service buses and adapters. BizTalk Server predates WCF, but increasingly offers support for, and integration with, the WCF model.

Comparing WCF to BizTalk Server

WCF is a programmatic and foundational class library for service-orientated communication. By contrast, BizTalk Server is a licensed, enterprise-level server product for integration and process automation, together with a number of additional companion technologies and capabilities. As such, any direct comparison with WCF is questionable. However, in one important respect, BizTalk Server and WCF both address common concerns in a similar fashion. Both technologies can be used to build and manage message channels for delivery and transmission of messages between endpoints. In BizTalk Server, a message channel consists of a hosted adapter handler, a pipeline, and an optional message transformation stage. These channels are associated with BizTalk ports and communicate message content and metadata to and from the BizTalk Message Box. WCF message channels are composed using bindings and behaviors, and deliver or transmit messages to and from service implementations.

To compare this commonality, consider Figure 6.21, which illustrates the logical construction of two-way (request/response) service endpoints in BizTalk Server and WCF.

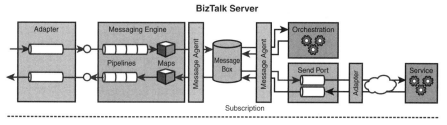

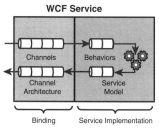

FIGURE 6.21   Comparing BizTalk Server and WCF channels and services.

Bindings built using the WCF channel architecture are broadly analogous to BizTalk adapters. They handle similar concerns such as transactions, reliability, security, encoding, and transport. Earlier in this chapter, you saw how these concerns are addressed by the various native BizTalk adapters. Similarly, behaviors, implemented using the WCF service model, are analogous to BizTalk pipeline components. However, their semantics correspond less closely. In BizTalk Server, pipeline components are used to mediate messages. For example, they may disassemble messages and then encode and process the inner messages for consumption by multiple services further downstream. A WCF behavior handles aspectual concerns of a specific service implementation.

In BizTalk Server, receive-side channels and ports always deliver messages to the BizTalk Message Box, where they are routed and submitted asynchronously to orchestrations or send ports or returned as response messages. Service implementation is fully decoupled from the transport and encoding mechanisms. Services can be implemented internally using BizTalk orchestrations or invoked by transmission of messages to external endpoints via send ports.

In WCF, service implementations bind their logic more closely to the message channel. Of course, any service implementation may, itself, be a consumer of additional services and may communicate with other services asynchronously via subscription services, queues, and so on. However, WCF does not provide any prebuilt equivalent to the BizTalk Message Box. The advent of Windows Server AppFabric, however, provides WCF-based services with platform-level hosting and recovery features that are similar to some of BizTalk Server's capabilities.

The Role of BizTalk Native WCF Adapters

The WCF native adapters provided with BizTalk Server use the WCF service model to bridge between BizTalk Server's messaging engine and WCF's channel architecture. This allows BizTalk Server to exploit WCF bindings in much the same way it uses adapters. Five of the native WCF adapters implement explicit bridging support for some of the system-defined WCF bindings. Two further custom adapters provide general-purpose facilities for exploiting WCF bindings, including custom bindings, within BizTalk Server environments.

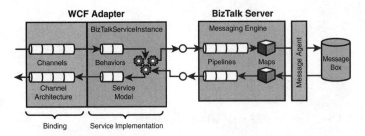

FIGURE 6.22   Using WCF adapters with BizTalk Server.

Each native WCF adapter uses the `BizTalkServiceInstance` class to implement receive handlers. This is a common service implementation that manages the exchange of messages between WCF channels and the BizTalk messaging engine. It implements a number of WCF contracts for different message exchange patterns. WCF adapters bind different transport channels to this common service.

`BizTalkServiceInstance` addresses an important difference between BizTalk Server and WCF. BizTalk Server implements a type-agnostic approach at the port level. Receive ports are not constrained by contracts and can potentially process message content of any type. WCF, by contrast, is service-orientated and manages message exchange through endpoints defined by contracts. `BizTalkServiceInstance` must support contracts, but internally manages the exchange of messages with BizTalk Server in a type-agnostic fashion. To meet this requirement `BizTalkServiceInstance` implements programmatic contracts that pass raw WCF messages, converting them to and from BizTalk Server messages without regard to their content. Like a receive port, `BizTalkServiceInstance` is also type agnostic, allowing this one class to be used as a common service implementation for all the WCF adapters.

By itself, this would be an inconvenient model in service-orientated architectures. When composing request messages and processing response messages, consumers benefit from strong contracts that provide a detailed description of content types. Developers need some additional mechanism to publish metadata to facilitate the generation of strongly typed consumer code. BizTalk Server supports this via the BizTalk WCF Service Publishing Wizard. The wizard manages the publishing of metadata for BizTalk orchestrations and schemas. It creates and configures metadata endpoints hosted in IIS. In addition, it also manages the publishing of `BizTalkServiceInstance` services via IIS, where this is required. Using the Publishing Wizard, developers can easily provide strongly typed contracts for use with the native WCF adapters.

Hosting Native WCF Adapters

Before describing the functionality of the BizTalk WCF Service Publishing Wizard, we must first consider the hosting options for native WCF adapters. Each adapter binds a common WCF service implementation, `BizTalkServiceInstance`, to a transport channel. At runtime, BizTalk Server hosts a singleton instance of this service for each receive location configured to use a WCF adapter. `BizTalkServiceInstance` can be hosted locally using BTSNTSvc.exe or it can be hosted by IIS as part of an isolated handler.

WCF is agnostic with regard to hosting. Services may be self-hosted or hosted by other applications, including IIS. However, BizTalk Server draws a sharp distinction between local and isolated hosts. The native WCF adapters are registered with BizTalk Server according to this model. Each adapter is constrained to run in one or other host type. The WCF-WsHttp and WCF-BasicHttp adapters always run as isolated handlers in the context of IIS. Other adapters run locally in instances of BTSNTSvc.exe. Two separate custom adapters are provided to support both host types. The WCF-Custom adapter runs locally while the WCF-CustomIsolated adapter runs under IIS.

In addition to their service endpoints, WCF services are often configured with additional *metadata exchange* (MEX) endpoints. A MEX endpoint provides information that describes the operations and message formats supported by a service endpoint. Typically, metadata is expressed using WSDL. MEX endpoints can be configured for a service endpoint in conjunction with the predefined `ServiceMetadataBehavior` behavior. These MEX endpoints run in the same host environment as the service endpoints they describe.

The WCF Service Publishing Wizard

The WCF Service Publishing Wizard publishes service endpoints for BizTalk receive locations. The endpoints are published via IIS. Specifically, the wizard publishes service endpoints for WCF-WsHttp, WCF-BasicHttp, and WCF-CustomIsolated handlers. To host these handlers and corresponding BizTalk receive locations, the wizard creates IIS web applications and WCF SVC files. The SVC files invoke a WCF service host factory that instantiates a singleton instance of `BizTalkServiceInstance`. BizTalk Server provides three service host factory classes: `BasicHttpWebServiceHostFactory`, `WSHttpWebServiceHostFactory`, and `CustomWebServiceHostFactory`. Listing 6.1 illustrates the contents of an SVC file for a WCF-WSHttp handler.

LISTING 6.1   Generated SVC File for WCF-WSHttp

```
<%@ ServiceHost Language="c#"
  Factory="Microsoft.BizTalk.Adapter.Wcf.Runtime.WSHttpWebServiceHostFactory,
    Microsoft.BizTalk.Adapter.Wcf.Runtime,
    Version=3.0.1.0,
    Culture=neutral,
    PublicKeyToken=31bf3856ad364e35" %>
```

As well as publishing service endpoints, the wizard publishes MEX endpoints. These can be published as additional endpoints of the BizTalkServiceInstance service. However, the wizard also supports publishing metadata-only endpoints. In this case, a MEX endpoint is published using an SVC file and MexServiceHostFactory class. Metadata-only endpoints are used as a convenient mechanism for publishing service contract information. They are chiefly created for local receive locations that use WCF-NetTcp, WCF-NetNamedPipes or WCF-MSMQ running under BTSNTSvc.exe.

The WCF Service Publishing Wizard is available from the Tools menu in Visual Studio, and also under Start, All Programs, Microsoft BizTalk Server 2010. Do not confuse this with the Web Services Publishing Wizard. This second wizard is used with the deprecated SOAP adapter to publish web services using ASP.NET (ASMX) rather than WCF.

On the first page of wizard, show in Figure 6.23, select the service type you want to create. For service endpoints, select one of the three isolated native WCF adapter types. The wizard optionally configures a MEX endpoint for the service to publish a WSDL definition of the service contract. It can also optionally create a BizTalk receive location within a selected BizTalk application.

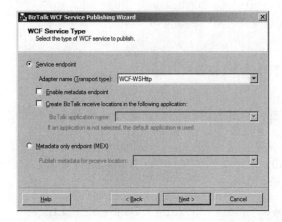

FIGURE 6.23   WCF Service Publishing Wizard: WCF Service Type.

NOTE

At runtime, the receive handler locates the correct receive location dynamically by matching the configured endpoint address of the receive location to the actual URL of the published service. These must match. The wizard can optionally create a new receive location and assign the correct endpoint address. The wizard creates a new receive port for each receive location. If you do not use this option, you must create and configure receive locations manually.

Instead of publishing service endpoints, you can elect to publish a metadata-only endpoint. In this case, you can optionally select a receive location with which the MEX endpoint will be associated. If you do not specify a receive location, this needs to be configured later in the web.config file of the IIS application.

On the Create WCF Service page, shown below in Figure 6.24, select between publishing an orchestration or publishing schemas. Publishing orchestrations will result in the creation of receive ports (sometimes termed physical ports) to which the specified orchestration ports (sometimes termed logical ports) will be bound. Generated WCF services will deliver messages to orchestrations via these bound ports. Note that the Type Modifier property of the orchestration port types must be Public to enable publishing.

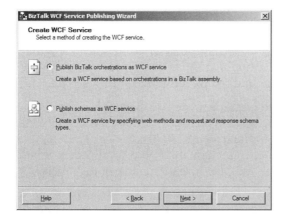

FIGURE 6.24   WCF Service Publishing Wizard: Create WCF Service.

Publishing schemas will result in the generation of receive ports, but no orchestration ports will be bound to these ports. Generated WCF services will deliver messages to the Message Box via the messaging ports. Orchestration can be manually bound to the receive ports, or messages can be directly routed by creating appropriate subscriptions.

Publishing Orchestrations

When publishing orchestrations, select the .NET assembly that contains the orchestrations. This is done using the BizTalk Assembly page shown below in Figure 6.25. Next, select the orchestrations and ports you want to publish.

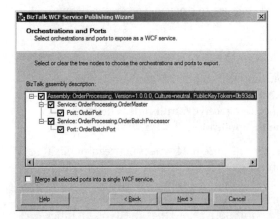

FIGURE 6.25   WCF Service Publishing Wizard: Orchestrations and Ports.

Each orchestration is identified as a separate service in the Orchestrations and Ports page. Uncheck any orchestration ports you do not want to publish.

You can optionally choose to merge the selected orchestration ports into a single WCF service. When unselected, this option generates a separate WCF service for each orchestration port. Each service is in the same IIS application that is named after the BizTalk assembly. The wizard generates separate receive ports and receive locations for each service.

When the Merge option is selected, the wizard creates a single WCF service containing multiple operations. It creates a corresponding single receive port and receive location. All messages submitted by the service are passed to the same BizTalk receive location. This imposes some limitations. For example, all selected orchestration ports must use the same message pattern (one-way or request-response). Also, the operation name of each orchestration port must be unique.

Publishing Schemas

If you choose to publish schemas, the wizard displays the WCF Service page shown in Figure 6.26. This is used to define the metadata that will be published.

To define metadata, right-click the root node and select **Rename**. Enter the name of the service description. This name is used as the IIS application name, and also as the service name in the WSDL definition of your service.

By default, the page displays a single service named Service 1 with a single operation named Operation 1. You can add additional services and operations. Operations may be one-way or request-response. Service names are used as the names of the generated SVC files and also as port type names in the WSDL definition. Operation names are published directly as WSDL operations.

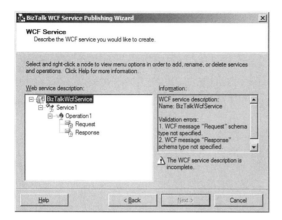

FIGURE 6.26   WCF Service Publishing Wizard: WCF Service.

For each operation, you must define one or two schemas for web messages, depending in the message exchange pattern. Right-click each web message, and click **Select Schema Type**. The wizard will display the RequestMessage Type dialog box shown below in Figure 6.27. Use the **Browse** button to select the .NET assembly of a deployed BizTalk application that contains the required schema. Then select the schema from the list and click **OK**.

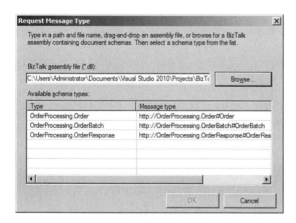

FIGURE 6.27   WCF Service Publishing Wizard: Selecting schema types.

The remaining pages of the wizard are displayed for both orchestration and schema publishing. On the WCF Service Properties page, enter the target namespace for the WCF service. Then, on the WCF Service Location page, shown below in Figure 6.28, enter the location to which the service will be published. This should be a URL path for an IIS application. If the application does not exist, it is created. If it does exist, you generally want to select the **Overwrite Existing Location** option to regenerate the service. You can also indicate whether the published service should allow anonymous access.

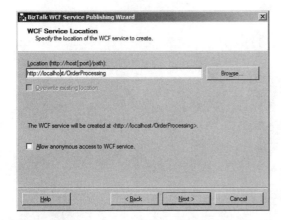

FIGURE 6.28   WCF Service Publishing Wizard: WCF Service Location.

The wizard displays the WCF Service Summary page for review. This contains an XML description of the WCF services that will be created. When satisfied that this is correct, click the **Create** button to generate receive ports, receive locations, WCF services, and the IIS application.

WCF Send Handlers

As well as receive handlers, the native WCF adapters support send handlers. All send handlers are hosted by BTSNTSvc.exe. A send handler is a WCF service consumer. WCF consumers and services are broadly symmetrical in the way they bind channel stacks to the service model. For consumers, the service model implements service proxies that manage interchange on behalf of applications. Like services, consumers can use behaviors to manage higher-level processing requirements. There are some minor differences in terms of extensibility points, but the model is similar on both the consumer and the server side.

BizTalk Server supports development-time generation of orchestrations, schemas, and bindings using the BizTalk WCF Service Consuming Wizard. This is a straightforward example of metadata harvesting in which WSDL and XSD schemas are used to generate various artifacts. To run the wizard, right-click a BizTalk project in the Visual Studio Solution Explorer and select **Add, Add Generated Items**. In the dialog box, select **Consume WCF Service** in the Installed Templates pane and then double-click the template or click **Add**.

The Metadata source page, shown below in Figure 6.29, supports two approaches for importing metadata. You can provide the URL for metadata published for a given service endpoint or import WSDL and XSD files directly.

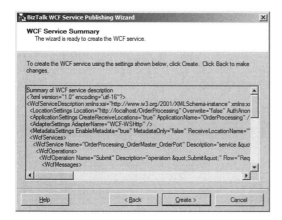

FIGURE 6.29   WCF Service Consuming Wizard: Metadata source.

Importing MEX Endpoints

When importing metadata from MEX endpoints, enter the endpoint URL in the Metadata Endpoint page, shown below in Figure 6.30, and click the **Get** button. If necessary, you can provide user credentials for authentication to secure endpoints. Click the **Edit** button and enter a username and password.

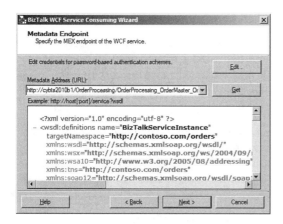

FIGURE 6.30   WCF Service Consuming Wizard: Metadata Endpoint.

If the metadata retrieved from the MEX endpoint is successfully retrieved and displayed, click the **Next** button.

Importing Metadata Files

The wizard supports the import of metadata files. In the Metadata Files page, shown in Figure 6.31, import WSDL files for target services, together with any additional XSD schemas.

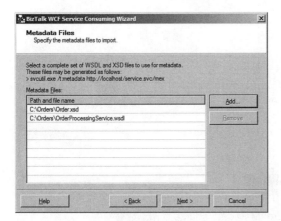

FIGURE 6.31   WCF Service Consuming Wizard: Metadata Files.

WARNING

The wizard cannot always import WSDL unchanged. For example, ASMX web services may generate WSDL that combines separate bindings for SOAP 1.1 and 1.2. This can lead to name clashes when the wizard attempts to create message types for both bindings. In this case, manually remove one of the bindings from the WSDL file or add a second WSDL message definition for one of the bindings.

The final page of the wizard, shown in Figure 6.32, displays the Import WCF Service Metadata Summary page for review. You can define the .NET namespace you want to use for the orchestrations and schemas that will be created and review the work that the wizard is about to carry out. When satisfied that this is correct, click the **Import** button to generate artifacts.

The wizard generates schemas, orchestrations, and binding files. Generated orchestrations contain port types and multipart message types for interchange with the external service. To support regeneration of artifacts at a later time, do not amend these orchestrations. Instead, create separate orchestrations for your business logic and use the types contained in the generated orchestrations.

Two BizTalk binding files are created. One is designed for use with the custom WCF adapters. The other is designed to be used with noncustom WCF adapters. Noncustom adapter bindings hold WCF configuration data as part of their transport type data. Custom adapters rely on WCF configuration files to provide this data.

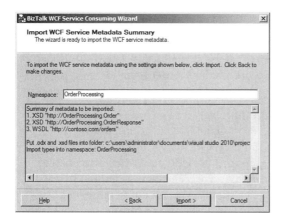

FIGURE 6.32   WCF Service Consuming Wizard: Summary.

Dynamic Ports

WCF adapters can be used with dynamic send ports. In orchestration code, set the
`Address` property to the required address and use the `TransportType` property to indicate
which WCF adapter should be used, as shown in Listing 6.2.

LISTING 6.2   Selecting a WCF Adapter for a Dynamic Send Port

```
OrderSendPort(Microsoft.XLANGs.BaseTypes.Address)=
    "http://contoso.com/orderprocessing.svc";
OrderSendPort(Microsoft.XLANGs.BaseTypes.TransportType)="WCF-WSHttp";
```

BizTalk Server defines a set of WCF message properties that can be further used to control
messaging via dynamic send ports. Use the `WCF.Action` property to control the SOAP
action. If using one of the custom WCF adapters, use the `WCF.BindingType` and
`WCF.BindingConfiguration` properties to control which system-defined binding to use and
how that binding is configured. See the product documentation for further details.

Configuring WCF Adapters

The native WCF adapters support a range of configuration options. In mainstream WCF
development, configuration data is managed through the use of configuration files.
However, in BizTalk Server, configuration data is stored securely in the SSO database. This
includes WCF configuration data and additional configuration specific to the BizTalk
Server environment.

Addresses and Identity

WCF endpoints define an address. This is specified as a URI on the General tab of the Transport Properties dialog. For receive handlers that are hosted in IIS, the URI must match the URL of the generated SVC file. For send handlers, enter the address of the endpoint to which messages will be sent.

The native WCF adapters support the WS-Addressing Identity extensions defined jointly by IBM and Microsoft and covered by the Microsoft Open Specification Promise (OSP). This specification has been incorporated into the OASIS Identity Metasystem Interoperability version 1.0 standard. These extensions provide mechanisms to enable clients to authenticate services before submitting messages. They are supported by WCF. At runtime, services can present identity claims to clients. The WS-Addressing Identity extensions specify the type of identity claim and control the use of certificates. For receive handlers, they also control the publishing of metadata, via WSDL, which specifies the claims that will be used at runtime.

WCF adapters support five identity claim types, as described in Table 6.3.

TABLE 6.3   Identity Claim Types

Claim Type	Description
DNS	Specifies a DNS-level identity check. The service must provide an X.509 certificate containing the given DNS name in the Subject or SubjectAltName fields.
Service Principal Name	Used in conjunction with Kerberos (see the "Security and Credentials" section). SPNs are Kerberos identifiers that are associated with Windows security principals in Active Directory. The SPN must be associated with the account under which the adapter is running.
User Principal Name	Used in conjunction with Windows authentication (see the "Security and Credentials" section). UPNs are Active Directory identifiers in the form of someone@somedomain (for example, johndoe@contoso.com). Use the UPN of the account under which the adapter is running.
RSA	Checks the RSA key value provided by an X.509 certificate.
Certificate	Checks the thumbprint of an X.509 certificate. This is typically a SH6 hash of the certificate.

Identity claims are set in the Identity Editor dialog shown below in Figure 6.33. The Certificate claim type is further qualified using a Certificate Reference. This reference provides additional information for locating and retrieving the correct certificates from a certificate store. Specify a search type and value (Find Type and Find Value), together with the certificate store location and name. You can also control validation of the X.509 certificate by switching certificate chaining on or off.

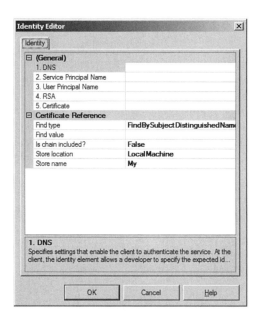

FIGURE 6.33   Identity Editor.

Bindings

The noncustom native adapters each use one of the system-defined WCF bindings. They support facilities for refining the binding. This includes standard binding elements used to control various timeouts (opening connections, sending messages and closing connections) and the maximum message size that can be received. In addition, each of the noncustom adapters supports binding elements that are specific to the system-defined binding.

The web adapters (WCF-BasicHttp and WCF-WSHttp) support the WCF text and MTOM message encoders. *Message Transmission Optimization Mechanism* (MTOM) is a W3C standard for encoding binary attachments for transmission to and from SOAP web services using MIME. For text encoding, the binding can be configured to support UTF-8 or UTF-16 (little-endian and big-endian) text encoding. The other noncustom adapters (WCF-NetTcp, WCF-NetMsmq, and WCF-NetNamedPipe) support the WCF Binary message encoder. Binary encoding is an efficient but noninteroperable mechanism for exchange of SOAP messages. Therefore, using these adapters implies that WCF will be used by external consumers and services to handle encoded binary data.

With the exception of the WCF-BasicHttp adapter, the noncustom native WCF adapters support transactions. As with other adapters, these transactions are synchronized with the internal transactions used to publish and route messages to and from the Message Box. The transaction mechanisms depend on the binding. For example, the WCF-WSHttp, WCF-NetTcp, and WCF-NetNamedPipe adapters support WS-AtomicTransaction. The WCF-NetTcp and WCF-NetNamedPipe also support distributed transactions via DTC (select **OleTransaction**). The WCF-NetMsmq transaction supports transactional queues. On the receive side, transactions are supported only on one-way receive ports.

The WCF-NetMsmq adapter can be used for reliable messaging purposes. Transactional control supports exactly once semantics. The adapter also supports ordered message delivery to the Message Box, ensuring that the message order within external queues is maintained as those messages pass through BizTalk Server. If a message expires or fails for any reason, it can be routed to a dead letter queue. This can be either the system-defined dead letter queue or, for MSMQ 4.0, a custom queue. The adapter also supports the optional retention of successfully processed messages on the system-defined source journal queue.

The WCF-NetTcp adapter supports IP layer load balancing. However, it also pools connections on specific machines. This causes per-machine affinity for specific connections. Use the Lease Timeout setting to control the lifetime of pooled connections.

Each of the noncustom adapters supports WCF throttling via the system-defined `ServiceThrottling` behavior. The adapters run as singleton services and allow only the maximum concurrent calls to be controlled by this behavior.

The Custom and Custom Isolated adapters are not associated with a specific binding. Instead, they can be configured with any registered WCF binding via the Binding tab of the Transport Properties dialog. Custom WCF bindings are generally configured in Machine.config. Select a binding from the drop-down Binding Type list. This displays a predefined set of bindings that includes the bindings used by noncustom adapters and additional bindings. The selected binding can then be configured appropriately using the Configuration Properties list. Note that this provides a mechanism in which bindings such as `basicHttp` and `wsHttp` can be used in-process with BTSNTTSvc.exe, rather than in an IIS worker process.

You can construct a custom binding by selecting **customBinding** from the drop-down list and then adding binding extension elements to the list. Extensions must be added in an appropriate order, depending on their function.

Behavior

WCF includes many extension points. Some of the most commonly used extension types are service and endpoint behaviors. These are pluggable components that run in the context of WCF's Service mode. For native WCF adapters, service and endpoint behaviors extend the functionality of BizTalk receive and send ports. They play a similar role to pipeline components, but are WCF artifacts. Consider the following:

▶ Pipelines are registered in the BizTalk management database and configured as part of receive locations and send ports. Behaviors are unknown to BizTalk, but can be configured through the Custom and Custom-Isolated WCF adapters.

▶ Behaviors work with the WCF message model. Pipeline components work with the BizTalk message model. This model includes explicit support for multipart messages and the ability to capture, process, distinguish, and promote contextual properties which flow with each message.

▶ Pipeline components are executed in the context of internal BizTalk transactions. Behaviors run in the context of a WCF service or proxy. Of course, as with other BizTalk adapters, WCF adapters can synchronize message handling with BizTalk Server's transactions.

The decision to implement custom logic as either a WCF behavior or a BizTalk pipeline component depends on several considerations that are discussed in greater detail later in this chapter.

To configure custom behaviors, use either the Custom or Custom Isolated WCF adapter. Behaviors are configured on the Behavior tab of the Transport Properties dialog. Right-click the desired behavior type and choose **Add Extension**. Select the required behavior from the Select Behavior Extension list and configure it is the Configuration Properties dialog.

Security and Credentials

WCF supports secure interchange of messages. Security can be configured at the transport and message levels. Transport-level security is specific to the protocols used to transmit messages and is therefore governed by the binding used by the adapter. Message-level security is independent of the transport and relies on the use of headers within the message to pass credentials. Message-level security is potentially more flexible than transport-level security and can be used to manage secure interchange across complex, highly distributed environments where messages may undergo multiple levels of protocol adaptation as they traverse networks and devices. Transport-level security generally provides a simpler, faster, and more convenient model.

Consider, for example, the WCF-BasicHttp adapter. This adapter supports SSL at the transport protocol level and SOAP-based security at the message level. SSL encrypts packets before sending them over the wire. When sending data to a service, SSL ensures that the service is authenticated based on an X.509 certificate. SSL uses encryption to protect data privacy and guards the integrity of the data. At the message level, SOAP provides similar facilities but applies encryption and digital signatures to the body of the message, rather than to packets. It supports user names as credentials, and certificates, and can exploit a wide range of different cryptography algorithms.

WCF supports hybrid models in which transport protocols are used in conjunction with credentials communicated via SOAP headers. This approach allows services to combine and exploit the strengths of both approaches. Another pattern, supported by several bindings, is to use transport-level security to communicate credentials only. This supports authentication but does not provide privacy or integrity.

For noncustom WCF adapters, set the security requirements using the Security tab of the Transport Properties dialog. The available settings depend on the WCF binding and vary from adapter to adapter. The general approach allows selection between different models of transport and message-level security and configuration of the selected level. This may involve selection of credential types or authentication modes and additional selection of cryptographic algorithms for encryption and signing. Where appropriate, adapters can be configured to use X.509 certificates (for example, to support SSL) by entering thumbprint values. On send ports, adapters that support SSL allow selection of client certificates and server certificates. This allows BizTalk Server to support client authentication when sending messages to SSL-enabled services.

The Custom and Custom Isolated WCF adapters do not provide a Security tab. Instead, equivalent settings are configured directly in the Binding tab. In addition, the custom adapters provide facilities for configuring credential information on the Other tab. All the WCF adapters support integration with Enterprise SSO to retrieve credentials from the secure SSO store.

Message Handling

The configuration options described so far have chiefly involved WCF-specific configuration captured and stored within the BizTalk SSO database. The purpose of the WCF adapters is to mediate message transfer to and from BizTalk Server by bridging between the BizTalk and WCF models. In addition to WCF-specific configuration, each adapter supports configuration that controls this exchange of messages between WCF and BizTalk Server. To understand the bridging approach, we need to understand various differences between he WCF and BizTalk models.

WCF and BizTalk Server both represent messages by objects that manage data streams. However, messages are structured in different ways. WCF messages communicate data between channel and service implementations in accordance with well-defined contracts associated with each endpoint. These contracts are defined in code and shape the implementation of services. WCF maps data directly to data contracts and uses these, together with service, operation, and message contracts to generate and publish metadata (for example, WSDL).

In BizTalk Server, message objects convey messages to and from the Message Box regardless of any contract supported by an adapter. BizTalk Server is a message-orientated integration server, and integration techniques do not always use published service and message contracts. For example, no contracts are required when pulling files from an FTP server. BizTalk Server, however, makes extensive use of message contracts internally. These contracts are generally defined using XSD. Code contracts are also supported at the orchestration level. These contracts define message content. They may also be used when generating public service contracts for specific adapters.

WCF adapters deliver messages to the BizTalk messaging engine and return response messages. Each adapter implements a predefined WCF contract that delivers and returns raw XML documents. Instead of defining code contracts for each service, developers use the WCF Service Publishing Wizard, described earlier in this chapter, to generate WSDL metadata describing service contracts for SOAP interchange. This metadata is generated from BizTalk schemas and can be published and consumed to shape requests and handle responses. However, the WCF adapters do not implement these contracts explicitly. They merely pass XML documents to and from BizTalk Server, regardless of their content.

Internally, BizTalk Server implements a WSDL-like approach to represent concepts such as ports, bindings, messages, and schemas. For example, BizTalk messages are defined as multipart structures with zero or more content parts. By contrast, WCF handles all messages as a single stream of data. BizTalk Server implements rich capabilities for associating and flowing metadata with messages. Metadata is stored as qualified name-value pairs and supports features such as array data, value caching and flags that mark properties for routing purposes.

HANDLING RPC-STYLE INTERCHANGE

You saw earlier that the WCF adapters do not support RPC-style SOAP interchange. The RPC style is represented using multipart messages in WSDL. RPC-Literal services can be consumed by using carefully crafted messages in the Document-Literal style. However, the WCF adapters cannot consume RPC-encoded services in a standards-compliant fashion because there is no mechanism for setting the `encodingStyle` attribute on the SOAP body element.

RPC styles are supported by the deprecated SOAP adapter. Although the WCF Service Consuming Wizard will create schemas for RPC-style services, it encourages the use of the SOAP adapter by generating a local ASMX web service that "wraps" the interaction with the external web service.

When handling inbound messages, WCF adapters pass the XML content of the SOAP body to the BizTalk messaging engine by default. However, other options are available. The Message tab of the Transport properties dialog allows developers to select the entire SOAP envelope or to specify an XPath for a given node. The XPath is evaluated against the contents of the SOAP body and must conform to the restricted XPath syntax supported by the `XPathReader` class in Microsoft.BizTalk.XPathReader.dll. This helper class is based on Microsoft's `XPathReader` described at http://msdn.microsoft.com/en-us/library/ ms950778.aspx. The adapter selects the first node found sequentially in accordance with the XPath and processes the node according to the selected node encoding. When the node encoding is XML, the adapter submits a message containing the outer XML of the selected node. When set to `String`, it outputs the text contents of the node. Select `Base64` to automatically convert Base64-encoded node contents to its original representation. Select `Hex` to handle binary data passed using MTOM.

For outbound messages, WCF adapters pass the content of the BizTalk message body part as the content of the SOAP body. Alternatively, the adapter can be configured with a template that defines a static envelope for the content. To control the location of the content within the envelope, use the `<bts-msg-body>` tag. The encoding attribute can be used to control the way data is encoded. As with node encodings for inbound messages, this can be set to `xml`, `string`, `base64`, or `hex`.

The WCF adapters support error handling. Each receive handler can be configured to suspend received messages in the Message Box or to discard them. In both cases, fault messages are returned to consumers, if supported. In addition, the custom adapters and the MSMQ adapter allow BizTalk receive locations to be suspended if an exception occurs.

This is sometimes useful for bindings that poll external sources for new messages and prevents further polling if an exception is encountered. It is generally good practice to avoid setting both the Suspend Request Message on Failure and Disable Location on Error Settings to False, because this can result in unexpected message loss. For bindings that return fault messages, adapters can be configured to optionally include details of the exception in the fault message. By default, details are not returned as this may represent a security risk.

Send handlers support optional propagation of fault messages when an outbound message fails. When the Propagate Fault Message setting is True, the handler delivers SOAP fault messages to the Message Box to be routed to an orchestration or a send port. When using the custom adapter, send handlers also support distributed transactions and isolation levels.

Using the SQL Server LoB Adapter

The custom WCF adapters provide an extension mechanism that allows the use of additional bindings and behaviors. As described earlier, each WCF binding provides adaptation and handles the concerns common to all adapters. Microsoft provides the WCF LoB framework and SDK for WCF-based adapter creation.

WCF LoB Framework and SDK

The WCF LoB framework supports development of custom and third-party adapters that are exposed as WCF bindings. The framework provides facilities for handling connections to LoB applications and dynamic representation of metadata. Custom LoB adapters are particularly useful when external applications change over time and must publish new or amended metadata to enable interaction. The framework is free of charge. It is included with BizTalk Server 2010, which also provides the BizTalk Adapter Pack. This is a collection of adapters built using the WCF LoB framework. The adapter pack is included, at no additional charge, with the BizTalk Server license. It contains adapters for SAP, Siebel, Oracle, and Microsoft SQL Server.

Each LoB adapter is exposed as a WCF binding and can be configured via the custom or custom isolated WCF native adapters. The adapter pack also installs each binding as a BizTalk adapter at machine level, allowing them to be registered with BizTalk groups using the Administration Console. When selected on a receive location or send port, registered LoB adapters can be configured in a similar way to the custom WCF adapter. However, the Transport Properties dialog may provide additional settings and does not allow the binding to be changed.

SQL Server Adapter

The old native adapter for SQL Server is no longer supported in BizTalk Server 2010, except when used to support EDI batched interchange via out-of-the-box pipelines. Instead, the WCF LoB adapter for SQL Server should be used to access SQL Server databases. The new adapter provides greater functionality and better tooling than the old adapter and can be used outside of BizTalk Server.

The adapter is registered with BizTalk Server under the alias WCF-SQL. The receive handler supports one-way message interchange and uses either polling or notification to pull messages into BizTalk Server. The send handler supports both one and two-way message interchange and supports selection, insertion, updating and deletion on tables and views and invocation of stored procedures and functions. The adapter supports integration with BizTalk Server development tooling to generate BizTalk artifacts directly over database metadata.

Receive and send handlers both specify URIs for the SQL Server database with which they will communicate. These URIs have the following format:

```
mssql://<server name>[:<port>]/[<instance name>]/<initial catalog>?
[FailoverPartner=<partner server name>]
```

If the instance name is blank, the default instance of SQL Server is used. The `FailoverPartner` parameter allows the adapter to connect to a mirror server if the primary server fails.

When using the SQL Server adapter within BizTalk Server, ensure that the `EnableBizTalkCompatibilityMode` binding property is set to `true`.

Polling and Notification

Receive handlers pull data from a SQL Server database using either polling or notification. Polling offers the simplest approach. Ensure that the `InboundOperationType` binding property is set to `Polling` and define a SQL statement for the `PolledDataAvailableStatement` binding property. This can be a `SELECT` or `EXEC` statement and must return a single numerical value. The adapter invokes this statement at regular intervals, defined by the `PollingIntervalInSeconds` property. If this returned value is greater than zero, the adapter automatically invokes a second SQL statement defined by the `PollingStatement` to obtain the required data. The `PollWhileDataFound` property can optionally be used to configure the adapter to repeatedly invoke the statement until no further data is returned, and then wait for the next polling interval to elapse.

The basic polling mechanism results in the adapter delivering polling messages to the Message Box. Each message contains an unbounded number of datasets, depending on the number of datasets returned by the `PollingStatement`. Each dataset contains an XSD schema and a diffgram containing the polled data.

In addition to the basic polling mechanism, the adapter supports two further polling approaches. Use `TypedPolling` to return polling messages that contain strongly typed XML payloads rather than a schema and diffgram pair. When using `TypedPolling`, the `Address` URI must be configured with an `InboundID` property value. This value is used as a query parameter to differentiate otherwise identical `Address` URIs. It can be used to configure multiple receive ports to poll the same SQL Server database for different data. The `InboundID` property can optionally be used with basic polling, but is mandatory for typed polling.

The adapter can be configured to use XML polling. In this case, the adapter runs a `for XML` polling statement to return XML generated directly by SQL Server. To obtain a schema for this XML, run a modified version of the same query in SQL Server Management Studio using XMLSCHEMA to generate the XSD. For example, if the polling statement is

```
SELECT * FROM dbo.People for XML AUTO
```

run the following SQL Statement to obtain the XSD schema:

```
SELECT * FROM dbo.People for XML AUTO, XMLSCHEMA
```

The schema must, however, be modified after importing it into BizTalk Server. Because a polling statement can return multiple datasets, the adapter always encloses returned XML in an outer node. Modify the schema to define this node, and configure the node and its namespaces using the XmlStoredProcedureRootNodeName and XmlStoredProcedureRootNodeNamespace binding properties. You must also add Microsoft's sqltypes.xsd schema for the version of SQL Server you are using, and import it into the main schema. You can download additional version-specific schemas from http://schemas.microsoft.com/sqlserver/2004/sqltypes/.

As an alternative to polling, the SQL Server adapter supports query notification. Query notification was introduced with SQL Server 2005, and is based on the SQL Server Service Broker, which must be installed on the SQL Server box. Set the InboundOperationType binding property to Notification to exploit this facility. When using query notification, the adapter registers a SQL statement (a SELECT or EXEC statement) with SQL Server. This statement is provided in the NotificationStatement binding property. SQL Server caches the results of this statement in an internal view. The notification statement is restricted in various ways. See http://msdn.microsoft.com/en-us/library/ms181122.aspx for more information about defining query notification statements. When a change occurs to the cached data, SQL Server automatically generates a notification that is routed to a listener hosted by the adapter. The adapter delivers the notification to the Message Box and registers for the next notification.

NOTE

Do not confuse SQL Server Query Notification with SQL Server Notification Services. Notification Services was removed from SQL Server 2008, although a version is available with BizTalk Server to enable BAM notification. The adapter uses SQL Server Query Notification, which is an entirely different technology.

Typically, developers create BizTalk orchestrations that subscribe to notification messages and query the SQL Server database for changes, either directly or via a send port. As well as change notifications, the receive handler can optionally submit a notification message each time the adapter listener is restarted (for example, when the receive location is started). These can be used to ensure that any relevant changes that occur within the database while a receive location is disabled are immediately retrieved. Test the value of the `Type` element of the notification message to distinguish between change and startup notifications.

Performing Operations via a Send Handler

Polling and notification are used by receive handlers. However, the adapter can also perform a range of operations on SQL Server via send handlers. To perform an operation, all that is required is to pass a correctly formed XML message to a send port properly configured to use the SQL adapter. The adapter can perform the following operations:

▶ Single SELECTs, INSERTs, UPDATEs and DELETEs on tables or views. Note that the adapter cannot handle SQL synonyms.

▶ Composite SELECTs, INSERTs, UPDATEs and DELETEs. In this case, an arbitrary number of individual operations can be passed to the send handler in a single XML message.

▶ Inserts or updates of unstructured FILESTREAM data using Set<column name> operations.

▶ Execution of stored procedures, scalar functions, and table-valued functions.

▶ Execution of one or more arbitrary SQL statements in a single message using ExecuteNonQuery, ExecuteReader, or ExecuteScalar operations.

The documentation provides examples of the XML formats required for each operation type, together with examples of XML responses returned to the Message Box. See http://msdn.microsoft.com/en-us/library/dd788515(v=BTS.70).aspx. Send handlers can be configured on either one-way or two-way send ports. In the case of a one-way port, no response message is returned by the adapter.

A single send handler can manage one or more individual operations. This is configured using the SOAP Action header in the General tab of the Transport Properties dialog. To perform the correct operation on the database, the Action header must be set correctly. For example, to invoke a stored procedure called dbo.InsertOrder in the database referenced by the Address URI, configure the following SOAP Action header:

```
Procedure/dbo/InsertOrder
```

The SOAP Action header should be set for all single SELECT, INSERT, UPDATE, and DELETE operations and all procedure and function invocations. For composite operations, set the header to CompositeOperation. For arbitrary execution of SQL statements, set the header to GenericOp/ExecuteNonQuery, GenericOp/ExecuteReader, or GenericOp/ExecuteScalar. Again, further information on Action headers is available in the documentation. Note that in some cases, the operation information provided by the header is also contained in the XML message passed to the send handler.

To configure a send handler for multiple operations, you must specify BtsActionMapping XML as the Action header. Listing 6.3 provides an example.

LISTING 6.3   BtsActionMapping Example

```
<BtsActionMapping xmlns:xsi=http://www.w3.org/2001/XMLSchema-instance
                  xmlns:xsd="http://www.w3.org/2001/XMLSchema">
  <Operation Name="InsertOrder" Action="Procedure/dbo/InsertOrder" />
  <Operation Name="UpdateOrder " Action="Procedure/dbo/UpdateOrder" />
  <Operation Name="DeleteOrder " Action="Procedure/dbo/DeleteOrder" />
</BtsActionMapping>
```

When using a BtsActionMapping, you must ensure that each message handled by the adapter has a BTS.Operation context value set to the same value as the Name attribute of on the Operation elements. If the handler cannot map the BTS.Operation value to an action, an UnsupportedOperation exception is thrown and the outgoing message is suspended. If the outbound message is sent by an orchestration, ensure that the Name attribute matches the operation name configured on the orchestration port. The port uses this name to set the BTS.Operation property.

When performing INSERTs, UPDATEs and DELETEs, you can define the batch size on the SQL binding. This controls how many records are passed to SQL Server in a single call. By default, the adapter passes 20 rows at a time. Increasing this value allows more data to be passed in a single call but increases the overhead of in-memory data buffering. When performing FILESTREAM operations, use the ChunkSize property to control buffering for Set<operation name> operations. For INSERTs and UPDATEs, use the AllowIdentityInsert property to allow or prevent the insertion of explicit values in identity columns.

When performing composite operations, you must ensure that the MaxConnectionPoolSize property is set to at least one more connection than the number of individual operations that return a result set. Avoid passing a large number of individual operations in a single composite operation, because this might require a high number of concurrent connections and result in possible failure.

When configuring the send adapter, set the Use Transaction and Isolation Level properties on the Messages tab of the Transport Properties dialog to appropriate settings. By default, the adapter uses serializable transactions. This is safe, but might not perform or scale well. In addition, use the UseAmbientTransaction property to control synchronization between SQL Server transactions and internal BizTalk transactions.

Additional Adapter Capabilities

The adapter supports SSL encryption of data over the network. SQL Server can be configured with a server certificate to support data encryption. Use the Encrypt property to control the use of SSL encryption for data interchange with SQL Server.

The adapter supports a range of configurable timeouts for opening and closing connections and sending and receiving messages. It also supports setting the WorkstationId property. This can be used to provide SQL Server with a connection-specific ID that represents the network client. The NetBIOS name of the BizTalk Server provides an appropriate ID value for tracing purposes.

The SQL adapter and WCF adapter SDK provide a range of performance counters to monitor connection requests and usage, outbound calls, latency and caching. Use the `EnablePerformanceCounters` property to enable or disable these performance counters.

Metadata Harvesting

The SQL adapter provides development tooling for creating BizTalk artifacts, including schemas and orchestration ports. The adapter can also generate binding files used to configure send handlers. Artifacts are generated from metadata retrieved from databases.

The Add Adapter Metadata Wizard

The SQL Server adapter supports the Add Adapter Metadata Wizard. This wizard provides a common starting place for metadata harvesting. To start the wizard, right-click a BizTalk project in Visual Studio, and select **Add**, **Add Generated Items**. Select **Add Adapter Metadata** in the Add Generated Items dialog, as shown in Figure 6.34.

FIGURE 6.34   The Add Generated Items dialog.

The Add Adapter Wizard dialog, shown in Figure 6.35, displays a list of adapters registered for metadata harvesting. Select the **WCF-SQL** adapter.

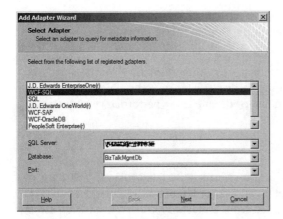

FIGURE 6.35   The Add Adapter Wizard.

Ensure that the SQL Server and Database properties are configured to connect to the BizTalk Server management database. Optionally, select a BizTalk messaging port from the Port drop-down list. The list is populated automatically with existing ports configured to use the selected adapter. If a port is selected, the wizard automatically uses its existing binding configuration by default. However, note that binding data is cached. If you run the wizard and then subsequently change binding properties on a port, you might need to restart Visual Studio to pick up changed binding properties the next time the wizard is run.

Click the **Next** button to display the Consume Adapter Service Wizard.

The Consume Adapter Service Wizard

Instead of using the Add Adapter Metadata Wizard, developers can start the Consume Adapter Service Wizard directly from the Add Generated Items dialog. The main difference concerns the generated artifacts. Both wizards generate schemas. The Add Adapter Wizard generates an empty orchestration containing orchestration ports that can be bound to receive locations and send ports. The Consume Adapter Service Wizard generates a binding file that can be used to add and configure messaging ports to a BizTalk application.

The Consume Adapter Service Wizard, shown in Figure 6.36, is used to generate artifacts for WCF bindings provided by the BizTalk Adapter Pack. Ensure that **sqlBinding** is selected and enter a URI. Click the **Configure** button to generate a URI and to configure binding and security properties. These settings are used to establish a connection to a SQL Server database at development time. In most scenarios, you want to use configuration settings that are equivalent to those used at runtime. However, you can use a different configuration if required. For example, you could harvest metadata from one database and use it to connect to a second database at runtime. When satisfied that the binding is configured correctly, click the **Connect** button to connect to the database.

Select either **Server (Inbound)** or **Client (Outbound)** operations. Server operations are supported via receive handlers, whereas client operations are handled via send handlers. Selecting the root node (/) displays three operations (Polling, Typed Polling, and Notification) for server operations and three generic SQL operations (ExecuteNonQuery,

`ExecuteReader`, and `ExecuteScalar`) for client operations. Additional client operations are listed under categories. Expand a category and select a database object to display a list of operations supported by the database. Use the **Add** and **Remove** buttons to build a list of selected operations.

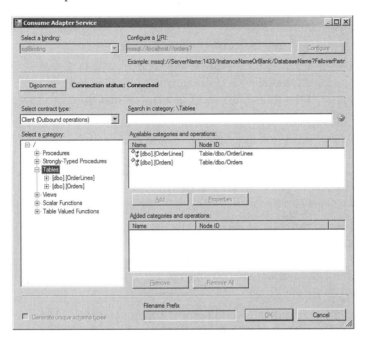

FIGURE 6.36   The Consume Adapter Service Wizard.

If the database returns a large list of items for any one category, use the Search box to filter by name. You may type in any one part of a multipart SQL identifier. The wizard supports wildcard characters. Use an underscore, _, to match a single character and a percentage sign, %, to match multiple characters. Use square brackets, [ ], to escape wild-card characters. You can also specify ranges of nonrequired characters using [^<*character list/range*>].

To generate artifacts, first build a list of all required operations using the **Add** and **Remove** buttons. You can select individual operations or entire categories. If you select a category, the wizard creates artifacts for all available operations within that category. Click **OK** to generate artifacts within the current BizTalk project.

You can run the wizard repeatedly to add additional artifacts to a project. However, there is a danger that subsequent invocations of the wizard may generate schema elements whose names clash with those generated in an earlier invocation. To prevent this, select the option to generate unique schema types. This ensures that each invocation generates schemas with unique namespaces. You can use the `UseDatabaseNameInXSDNamespace` binding property to control inclusion of the database name within generated XSD name-spaces. You can also specify a filename prefix on each invocation to avoid filename clashes.

Summary

This chapter described the role of adapters, the various categories and types of adapters that exist for BizTalk Server, and the characteristics that adapters exhibit. Adapters lie at the heart of enabling message-based interchange via BizTalk Server between different systems, services, and platforms. You learned how to register adapters with BizTalk Server, define adapter handlers, and bind those handlers to BizTalk messaging ports.

This chapter introduced the family of native adapters that ship as part of BizTalk Server and provided an overview of each native adapter and the functionality they provide. The native adapters are just one subset of the full complement of adapters that ship with the product, but are among the most commonly used adapters.

This chapter discussed the role and functionality of the WCF native adapters in BizTalk Server 2010. It compared the WCF channel and service models with BizTalk Server's messaging model and explained how WCF bindings broadly handle the same concerns as BizTalk adapters. The Web Service Publishing Wizard was described, together with the capabilities of WCF send and receive handlers.

As well as the native WCF adapters, the chapter described the use of the SQL adapter provided as part of the WCF-based BizTalk Adapter Pack. This adapter is used as a WCF binding via one of the WCF-Custom native BizTalk adapters. The capabilities of the adapter were described, together with metadata harvesting via the Consume Adapter Service Wizard.

BizTalk Server's support for WCF has rapidly grown to become a major feature of the product. It aligns BizTalk Server closely with the evolving .NET Framework and supports service-oriented design patterns alongside other messaging and integration approaches.

PART II

Advanced Topics

IN THIS PART

BizTalk 2010 and WCF: Extensibility

The integration between BizTalk adapters and *Windows Communication Foundation* (WCF) was inevitable. In many ways, WCF borrowed much from the architecture of BizTalk and brought a pluggable communication stack to the .NET developer.

BizTalk Server, at its heart, is a messaging engine. It has a rich set of capabilities for sending and receiving messages using a variety of different protocols (through its adapter framework) and message formats (for example, XML, EDI, flat file, binary) and capabilities for message transformation and decomposition. The underlying engine is a durable pub-sub messaging engine centered on a Microsoft SQL Server database known as the Message Box.

Staring with BizTalk Server 2006 R2, the messaging engine was extended into the world of services by the addition of an adapter for WCF. The WCF adapter enables BizTalk to expose its functionality as WCF endpoints. Because of its rich adapters and message-transformation capabilities, using BizTalk Server to create a service endpoint (using its messaging engine) can enable new and interesting scenarios where the service implementation is actually a non-service-enabled endpoint that is exposed through BizTalk Server. For example, imagine a back-end batch process that requires flat files to be placed into a directory on a server using File Transfer Protocol (FTP). A BizTalk Server receiving endpoint using the WCF adapter could make this process service enabled to consumers. BizTalk Server could take the incoming XML, transform it into the correct flat file format, and then use the FTP adapter to put the file onto the server.

A number of "strongly typed" adapters utilize particular WCF channel stack combinations (known as bindings). Of course, one of the powerful features of WCF is its extensibility. This extensibility can be taken advantage of in BizTalk using the WCF-Custom adapter. This chapter focuses on how using the WCF-Custom adapter with additional components can provide a vehicle for intense customization.

WCF Extensibility

To discuss how WCF provides extensibility inside of BizTalk Server, it is useful to examine how WCF extensibility works in WCF without considering BizTalk.

The WCF Channel Stack

WCF puts together a set of objects at runtime that provide a particular structure for communication. This set of objects is known generally as the channel stack (see Figure 7.1).

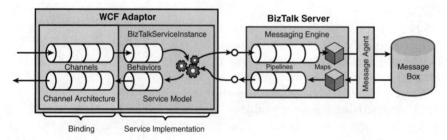

FIGURE 7.1   WCF channel architecture.

The channel stack is created by the particular binding configured on the endpoint. This configuration can come from code or from a configuration file. (Of course, in the BizTalk case, it always comes from a configuration file.)

There are a couple of important points about channels and endpoints in WCF. One point is that the architecture is symmetrical between client and server. That is, the same architecture (and often the same objects) is (are) used to create endpoints of communication that consume other endpoints (a client) or to create endpoints that expose functionality through communication (a service).

Another important point to note is that the out-of-the-box bindings such as the WsHttpBinding and the BasicHttpBinding are just prebuilt configurations of a channel stack. When WCF was created, they could have just provided the basic architecture without any of the out-of-the-box bindings. The out-of-the-box bindings do provide the configuration needed for a large majority of endpoints, but when a more custom configuration is needed, you can always drop down and create your own custom configuration (and potentially your own binding).

Similarly, if you go back to Chapter 6, "Adapters," and note the use of the native WCF adapters (the ones that mimic many of the out-of-the-box bindings of WCF), those will cover a large number of potential use cases within BizTalk Server 2010. On the other hand, you might sometimes need to go beyond those native WCF adapters and use the WCF-Custom or the WCF-CustomIsolated adapters. When you are using the custom adapters, you have more responsibility for making sure that the configuration of the WCF endpoint within the BizTalk adapter context will work successfully with BizTalk.

Another important thing to understand is which parts of the WCF extensibility architecture is open to you as a BizTalk developer.

ABCs Reviewed

Channels are, of course, just one part of the picture when it comes to WCF. WCF's overall endpoint architecture is based on something commonly known as the ABCs: address, binding, and contract.

- ▶ The *address* is the network address that the endpoint is either listening on (in the case of a service endpoint) or the address that the endpoint will communicate to (in the case of a client endpoint). The address will vary based on the transport channel used, which is the first channel in every channel stack. A typical endpoint uses HTTP or TCP/IP, but other forms of communication are possible, as well.

- ▶ The *binding* provides the configuration to build the channel stack. The binding also provides configuration for other objects that act as part of the endpoint, the most important being behaviors. Behaviors are objects that change the way an endpoint behaves internally, as opposed to bindings, which change the way an endpoint behaves externally.

- ▶ The *contract* is the definition of the communication stack. It is defined as a .NET type with a special well-known attribute (`ServiceContract`). When you are defining your own WCF services, you will generally also be defining the contract.

The code in Listing 7.1 is simple service contract example, but it is part of the makeup of a successful WCF endpoint to have a contract defined. One part of this contract definition to note is the `OperationBehavior` attribute applied to the `Send` method. The `OperationContract` attribute makes the `Send` method be part of the contract defined by this interface. The `OperationBehavior` attaches a specific behavior to this method and causes specific actions to be performed at runtime (in this case to call `Dispose` on parameters that implement `IDisposable`).

LISTING 7.1   A Typical Service Contract

```
[ServiceContract(Namespace="http://mycomp.com/schemas/Service")]
public interface IProcessSchedule
{
        [OperationContract(IsOneWay = false)]
        [OperationBehavior(AutoDisposeParameters=true)]
         void SetSchedule(ScheduleInfo info);
}
```

ServiceContract in BizTalk

One of the first things to learn when using the WCF adapters in BizTalk (whether they are the custom or the native adapters) is that you cannot change the contract. The contract is predefined by the WCF adapter.

This means that one of the basic building blocks of any WCF endpoint is unavailable for you to change in your BizTalk solution. This turns out to not be a big issue because the contract defined by the BizTalk WCF adapter is completely adequate to work with the architecture of most BizTalk solutions. There are, in fact, a number of different contracts defined for different scenarios. For example, there are different contracts for one-way versus request-response message-exchange patterns, which are dictated by BizTalk by the type of receive or send port created. There are also different contracts if you want transactions to flow with the message call.

For example, if I want to expose the previously defined contract through BizTalk, the BizTalk WCF adapter (assuming I am not using transactions) uses the following contract (shown in Listing 7.2)

LISTING 7.2   The BizTalk Service Contract

```
[ServiceContract(Namespace="http://www.microsoft.com/biztalk/2006/r2/
wcf-adapter")]
public interface ITwoWayAsyncVoid
{
    // Methods
    [OperationContract(AsyncPattern=true, IsOneWay=false, Action="*",
ReplyAction="*")]
    IAsyncResult BeginTwoWayMethod(Message message, AsyncCallback callback,
object state);
    [OperationContract(IsOneWay=false, Action="BizTalkSubmit")]
    void BizTalkSubmit(Message message);
    void EndTwoWayMethod(IAsyncResult result);
}
```

One interesting thing to note about this contract (other than it is using the WCF Async pattern to implement its functionality) is that the object that is being passed to the BizTalkSubmit operation (Message. Message) is a special type in the WCF world. It is actually the raw Message object that is passed up and down the WCF channel stack.

In a typical endpoint (a server-side endpoint in this example), the Message object is created by the transport channel and passed down through the rest of the channel stack. When the Message reaches the dispatching layer, which is the layer that actually calls the service, WCF typically deserializes the message into a .NET type (such as the ScheduleInfo type in the earlier contract example).

When a contract uses Message, the infrastructure just passes Message along to the service implementation. What the BizTalkServiceHost does is take this WCF Message, turn it into a BizTalk message, and publish that message to the Message Box. This is typically called a universal or generic contract. Using this type of contract is more work if you are implementing a service or client using WCF, but it is also more powerful and opens up a number of interesting possibilities, such as building a generic WCF message router, which the BizTalk WCF adapter is, to some extent.

This is totally consistent with all the other BizTalk adapters, which are generally message content type agnostic. The File adapter, for example, doesn't actually care what the content of a file it picks up is; it just picks up the files as specified by the receive location's configuration.

Similarly the BizTalk WCF adapter is message type agnostic and just passes a stream of bytes to the Message Box. As with any other adapter, to gain certain functionality (such as restricting messages to XML message or known XML message types or schemas) you still need to use the additional BizTalk artifacts (such as the XMLReceivePipline) to achieve your desired results. As explained in Chapter 6, this is how you can cause a particular "contract" to be published from a BizTalk WCF adapter receive location.

> **NOTE**
>
> Remember that even though you have "published" a schema or orchestration through the WCF Adapter Publishing Wizard, any message can still be sent through the WCF adapter endpoint because of the generic nature of the contract. Of course, if a message doesn't meet certain other BizTalk specific criteria (most important, if there are not subscribers listening for that message), the message is rejected by the BizTalk infrastructure.

As is the case with WCF in general, the BizTalk WCF adapter infrastructure is also symmetrical. The contracts that the BizTalk WCF receive adapters use are the same contracts that the BizTalk WCF send adapter will use. Which contract, of course, depends on the message-exchange pattern of the send port and whether the BizTalk WCF adapter send port configuration uses transactions.

> **NOTE**
>
> There is a different contract for transactional adapter configuration because that functionality in WCF is applied via a set of attributes that apply behaviors to the endpoint so that functionality has to be baked into the contract definition.

The BizTalk WCF send adapter builds up a channel stack dynamically using a special object in WCF called the ChannelFactory. This is a slightly unimportant technical detail of how the BizTalk WCF send adapter works, but it does make the lack of contract configuration in the BizTalk WCF adapter configuration dialog slightly less confusing.

Besides being a technical detail that you can pretty much forget after you've learned it, the lack of a contract configuration can sometimes become an issue when using the WCF adapter in BizTalk. One thing that does become a potential roadblock to using certain functionality is that some WCF functionality is provided only with behaviors, and some of the behaviors can be applied only to a particular endpoint configuration using attributes on the operations of the contract. Because that extensibility point is closed to you in BizTalk, you must come up with other ways to deal with those issues. (As discussed later in this chapter, it is often possible to solve such a problem in a different way.)

WCF Behaviors

Earlier in the chapter, it was mentioned that some functionality of WCF is provided by an object known as a behavior. Generally speaking, the way to know whether functionality is provided by a behavior or a binding (for example, a channel) is by looking at the scope of the functionality. If the functionality is outward-looking, it is provided by a binding. Such an example is the transport channel used. Whether an endpoint sends or listens over HTTP or TCP is determined by its binding.

Whether a particular operation impersonates an authenticated principal is a more internal-facing functionality. The client of such an endpoint is unaware that the WCF code in the dispatcher layer is impersonating its provided authentication information before the dispatcher calls into the method on the service. That kind of functionality is typically provided by a behavior.

A behavior is an extra object that gets configured as part of a WCF channel stack instance. The behavior's job is to modify or add something to the channel stack before the channel stack opens. In the impersonation example, the behavior modifies the behavior of the dispatcher by setting a property that tells the dispatcher to impersonate before calling into the service.

There are different types of behaviors that are used depending on the functionality needed. There are service behaviors, operation behaviors, endpoint behaviors, and contract behaviors.

The most commonly used are service behaviors and endpoint behaviors. Endpoint behaviors are the only type of behavior that is useful in BizTalk. Because of the closed nature of the service host and the contract, the other behavior types cannot generally be used. (Although service behaviors can be used, they generally are of limited functionality in BizTalk.)

Example of WCF Extensibility in BizTalk

As you can see from the flexibility of using the WCF custom adapters, there aren't likely to be many scenarios that cannot be covered by using a custom configuration of the different out-of-the-box components from WCF. However, you will sometimes need to create custom components or use third-party components to provide certain functionality.

For example, what if you want to use the BizTalk WCF send adapter to send HTTP messages to a simple HTTP endpoint (perhaps one that is exposing a RESTful endpoint for functionality). This is a fairly common situation today. Imagine if your application functionality requires that you do a search of current feeds (commonly known as tweets) on a site such as Twitter.com. This could be a common enterprise requirement, as many businesses are using Twitter for marketing and customer service purposes.

WCF 3.5 comes with a perfect set of functionality for calling Twitter from WCF in the form of something called the WebHttpBinding. The WebHttpBinding is a new binding introduced in WCF 3.5 that provides the capabilities to expose and consume RESTful endpoints from WCF.

Using this new binding from WCF outside of BizTalk requires use of two new attributes that apply extra metadata to a ServiceContract to enable the normally Simple Object Access Protocol (SOAP) action-driven WCF stack to use HTTP verbs instead. These attributes are placed on operations to specify which HTTP verbs each operation will use or expose and what URIs those operations will entertain.

As mentioned earlier in this chapter, because the BizTalk WCF adapter has its contracts preset, there is no direct way to use this new binding with BizTalk. So, even if you were to configure either of the WCF custom adapters with this new binding on either the receive or send side, this binding would have no extra metadata to execute on, and the usage of the binding would at best not work, and likely it would cause an error.

However, by using a little knowledge of WCF, another solution can be created. Imagine that Fine Foods wants to query Twitter during the execution of certain orchestrations and process the results into another internal system.

In this situation, you can take advantage that the WebHttpBinding actually uses many features that have been part of WCF since its inception. Specifically, you can take advantage that the transport channel can have its behavior modified by sending it special well-known message properties. As a BizTalk developer, this should be familiar to you because it is almost exactly the same as sending a BizTalk adapter a custom promoted property with a BizTalk message, which can cause a BizTalk adapter to change its execution behavior for a particular message.

This particular message property in WCF is known as the HttpRequestMessageProperty. When the HTTP transport channel sees this message property associated with a message it is going to send out as part of a client endpoint, the HTTP transport channel changes its execution path.

These message properties are associated with a WCF message through the use of the WCF Message object's Properties collection. See the code in Listing 7.3.

LISTING 7.3   Changing the **HttpRequestMessageProperty**

```
HttpRequestMessageProperty mp = null;
if (request.Properties.ContainsKey(HttpRequestMessageProperty.Name))
    mp = (HttpRequestMessageProperty)request.Properties[HttpRequestMessageProperty.
Name];
else
```

```
{
    mp = new HttpRequestMessageProperty();
    request.Properties.Add(HttpRequestMessageProperty.Name, mp);
}
mp.Method = "GET";
if (mp.Method == "GET")
{
    mp.SuppressEntityBody = true;
    Message msg =
        Message.CreateMessage(MessageVersion.None, "*");
    msg.Properties.Add(HttpRequestMessageProperty.Name, mp);

    request = msg;
}
```

In the preceding code snippet, the request variable is presumed to be of type Message. The code first checks to see whether the HttpRequestMessageProperty is already associated with this particular Message. If it isn't, a new HttpRequestMessageProperty object is created and added to the Message.Properties collection.

When this happens, the code sets the HTTP method (or verb) to GET. This causes the HTTP transport channel to send an HTTP GET request rather than the default (which is to send an HTTP POST). When calling a RESTful endpoint to gather information, an HTTP GET is generally required by most endpoints. The HTTP POST is generally sent when a new resource is being requested of the RESTful endpoint (such as creating a new entity, or in the case of Twitter, a new tweet). Because the goal here is to ask for certain resources, an HTTP GET request is necessary.

The code in Listing 7.3 does the job, but the question is how to get the BizTalk send adapter to incorporate it into its channel stack. The answer is to create a behavior.

In this case, an endpoint behavior can be created. The job of the endpoint behavior is to install a special object called a MessageInspector into the channel stack. The MessageInspector can then be programmed to manipulate the HttpRequestMessageProperty based on the properties of the behavior.

Creating a custom endpoint behavior is quite easy. All you need to do is implement a single interface: IEndpointBehavior. Listing 7.4 shows a sample implementation of an IEndpointBehavior.

LISTING 7.4 **HttpVerbBehavior**

```
public class HttpVerbBehavior : IEndpointBehavior
{
    public HttpVerbBehavior(string verb)
    {
        this._verb = verb;
```

```
    }
    string _verb;
    #region IEndpointBehavior Members

    public void AddBindingParameters(ServiceEndpoint endpoint,
System.ServiceModel.Channels.BindingParameterCollection bindingParameters)
    {
    }

    public void ApplyClientBehavior(ServiceEndpoint endpoint,
System.ServiceModel.Dispatcher.ClientRuntime clientRuntime)
    {
        clientRuntime.MessageInspectors.Add(new
VerbMessageInspector(this._verb));
    }

    public void ApplyDispatchBehavior(ServiceEndpoint endpoint,
System.ServiceModel.Dispatcher.EndpointDispatcher endpointDispatcher)
    {
    }

    public void Validate(ServiceEndpoint endpoint)
    {
    }

    #endregion
}
```

The implementation of this IEndpointBehavior (named HttpVerbBehavior) is fairly simple. All it does is add a new MessageInspector to the ClientRuntime object (which is part of the client channel stack) when the ApplyClientBehavior method is called. This method is called once, and then the channel stack is first created. Listing 7.5 shows the implementation of the MessageInspector.

LISTING 7.5 **VerbMessageInspector**

```
public class VerbMessageInspector : IClientMessageInspector
{
    public VerbMessageInspector(string verb)
    {
        this._verb = verb;
    }
    string _verb;
    public void AfterReceiveReply(ref System.ServiceModel.Channels.Message
reply, object correlationState)
```

```
    {


    }
    public object BeforeSendRequest(ref
        System.ServiceModel.Channels.Message request,
        IClientChannel channel)
    {
        HttpRequestMessageProperty mp = null;
        if (request.Properties.ContainsKey(HttpRequestMessageProperty.Name))
            mp =
(HttpRequestMessageProperty)request.Properties[HttpRequestMessageProperty.
Name];
        else
        {
            mp = new HttpRequestMessageProperty();
            request.Properties.Add(HttpRequestMessageProperty.Name, mp);
        }
        mp.Method = this._verb;
        if (mp.Method == "GET")
        {
            mp.SuppressEntityBody = true;
            Message msg =
                Message.CreateMessage(MessageVersion.None, "*");
            msg.Properties.Add(HttpRequestMessageProperty.Name, mp);

            request = msg;
        }
        return null;

    }

}
```

It's the VerbMessageInspector that does the real work (modifying the HttpRequestMessageProperty as necessary based on its verb property, which gets passed from the EndpointBehavior). This is the typical pattern where the behavior exposes properties that get set as part of the endpoint's configuration and then those properties are used to set the properties of the underlying object in the channel stack that performs the actual work. In this case, the work is done by the MessageInspector.

As of this point, this code will work in a code-based WCF system. When the ChannelFactory is created, the behavior can be added, and it will then add its functionality.

In BizTalk or any other WCF-based system that requires configuration, another step is required. This step is to create a `BehaviorExtensionElement` derived class that can be plugged into the WCF eXtensible Markup Language (XML) configuration system. Then this behavior can be configured in both the code and in the XML configuration for an endpoint. See Listing 7.6.

LISTING 7.6 **BehaviorExtensionElement**

```
public class HttpVerbElement : BehaviorExtensionElement
{
    public override Type BehaviorType
    {
        get { return typeof(HttpVerbBehavior); }
    }

    protected override object CreateBehavior()
    {
        return new HttpVerbBehavior(this.Verb);
    }
    ConfigurationPropertyCollection _properties;
    [ConfigurationProperty("verb")]
    public string Verb
    {
        get { return (string)base["verb"]; }
        set { base["verb"] = value; }
    }
    protected override ConfigurationPropertyCollection Properties
    {
        get
        {
            if (this._properties == null)
            {
                ConfigurationPropertyCollection propertys = new
ConfigurationPropertyCollection();
                propertys.Add(new ConfigurationProperty("verb",
typeof(string), null, null, null, ConfigurationPropertyOptions.None));
                this._properties = propertys;
            }
            return this._properties;
        }
    }
}
```

After the assembly that contains these types is signed and put into the *Global Assembly Cache* (GAC), the configuration shown in Listing 7.7 needs to be added to the `system.ServiceModel/extensions/behaviorExtensions` element in the `machine.config` that enables this behavior to be used from the BizTalk WCF adapter.

LISTING 7.7   Configuration Element

```
<add name="httpVerb" type="HttpVerbBehavior.HttpVerbElement,
HttpVerbBehavior, Version=1.0.0.0, Culture=neutral,
PublicKeyToken=7cb86bbf37ae0d00"/>
```

The first thing to do to use this inside of BizTalk is to create a new static solicit-response send port. After picking the WCF-Custom adapter as the transport, you can move into the adapter configuration. The address to configure is http://search.twitter.com/search.atom?q=FineFoods, which is the address that can do a simple Twitter search for the text "FineFoods."

On the Binding tab, pick a custom binding, but there is an important property that needs to be changed. The `messageVersion` property needs to be changed to None. See Figure 7.2. This makes the Message Encoder leave out the SOAP envelope (which isn't needed in this case because you are doing raw HTTP and not SOAP).

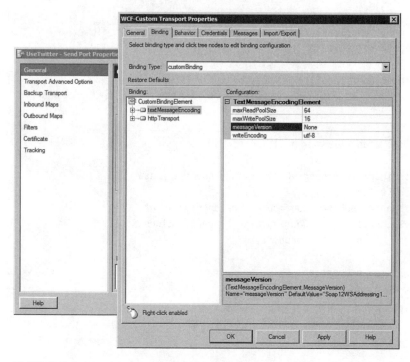

FIGURE 7.2   Changing the message version.

Next on the Behavior tab, you can right-click the **EndPointBehaviors** node in the pane on the left and select **Add Extension**. See Figure 7.3.

From the list, pick the **httpVerb** extension. See Figure 7.4.

Then you can set the `verb` property to **GET**, as shown in Figure 7.5.

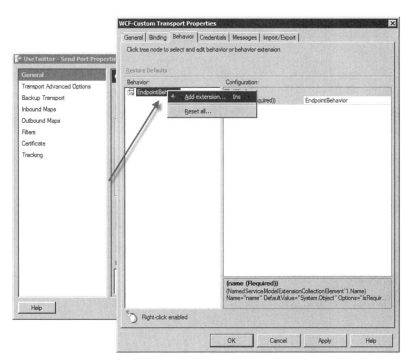

FIGURE 7.3   Adding an extension.

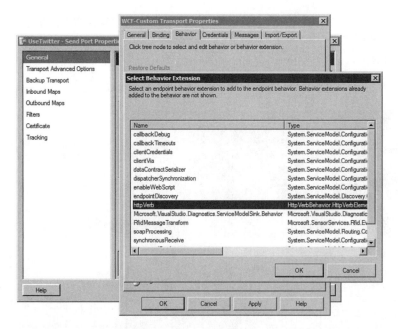

FIGURE 7.4   Choosing an extension.

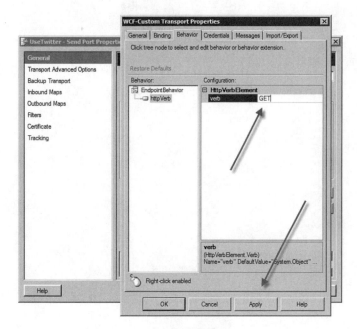

FIGURE 7.5   Setting the configuration.

After clicking **Apply** and then saving the send port configuration, you'll have a WCF-Custom send port that can do HTTP GET requests against the Twitter (or any other address) application programming interface (API).

Summary

The BizTalk WCF adapters provide strong integration between WCF and BizTalk. Sometimes, however, you must move out of the strong validation of the native WCF adapters and move into the realm of the custom adapters.

By using a custom configuration with the custom adapters, either in-process with the WCF-Custom adapter or inside of *Internet Information Services* (IIS) with the WCF-CustomIsolated adapter, you can provide additional functionality not exposed by the native WCF adapters.

When you need to move beyond the out-of-the-box functionality of WCF, the WCF custom adapters give you the power to modify the configuration by adding additional behaviors that can enable a multitude of scenarios and can solve most of the general problems you can throw at WCF.

CHAPTER 8

BizTalk and Windows Azure

Cloud computing is a powerful trend that is fundamentally transforming the information technology industry, changing the way you create, deploy, run, and manage applications. In this chapter, you look at the Windows Azure platform from a BizTalk perspective, and cover how BizTalk developers can leverage the services provided by the Windows Azure cloud platform.

NOTE

This chapter was written shortly after the initial Windows Azure platform went live. So, it is possible (and indeed likely) that there will be evolutionary changes in the platform itself that might in turn impact the techniques detailed in this chapter. However, the overall pattern will likely remain the same, although this too could potentially change over time.

Extending the Reach of BizTalk Applications

Inevitably, you will sometimes need to cross organizational boundaries to get trading partners, customers, or suppliers integrated into your business processes. Windows Azure AppFabric provides a mechanism to do so.

Windows Azure AppFabric (in the initial release of the platform) consists of two pieces: the Access Control Service and the Service Bus. These are the services you will use to extend the reach of your on-premise BizTalk applications to

Windows Azure. It is surprisingly simple thing to do, but opens up many powerful new architectural opportunities. Windows Azure AppFabric becomes a rendezvous point on the public Internet and facilitates the traversal of enterprise and network boundaries. Figure 8.1 shows a simplified example of one use case.

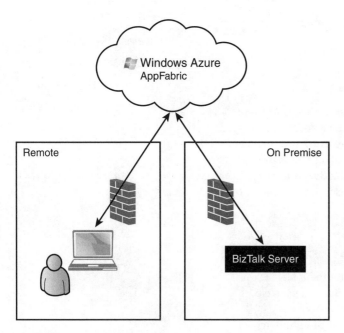

FIGURE 8.1   Windows Azure AppFabric as a rendezvous point on the Internet.

The AppFabric SDK

To interact with the Windows Azure AppFabric, you first install a *software development kit* (SDK), available from the Windows Azure site. That SDK provides several new *Windows Communication Foundation* (WCF) bindings that allow you to communicate with the Service Bus. There is nothing BizTalk-centric involved here; these are custom WCF bindings that we will use with the WCF-Custom adapter, but they could also be used from any other environment that supports WCF, such as a .NET application or an InfoPath form. (More on this later in the chapter.)

This chapter is not intended to be a tutorial on Azure AppFabric. It is intended to show how to leverage AppFabric Service Bus from BizTalk. For comprehensive information and documentation on Azure AppFabric, visit the Azure Developer Portal at https://windows.azure.com/.

Receiving Messages

Traditionally (and most of the time), if you wanted to extend an on-premise BizTalk solution, it would mean that you would have web services hosted in *Internet Information Services* (IIS) or in the BizTalk process on the BizTalk servers, and then you would reverse-proxy those services to make them available outside your firewall. You would also likely have a load balancer in play for either volume or high-availability reasons. You would also need to define a security strategy and negotiate this with the external participants. Crossing a security boundary like this was never easy and always entailed many moving parts and, potentially, some degree of risk if the environment was not set up and secured properly.

However, with Windows Azure AppFabric, instead of directly opening (and potentially exposing a vulnerable environment by increasing our attack surface) our infrastructure to the outside world, we instead use the relay capability of the Service Bus. Our trading partners publish their messages to the Service Bus, and we receive them because we are a subscriber. The fact that we have an "in the cloud" relay means we effectively have a rendezvous point where we can exchange messages indirectly.

BizTalk Server ships with a variety of WCF adapters, and there is excellent support for WCF from BizTalk. The most powerful of these adapters is the WCF-Custom adapter, which lets you select any bindings that are available on the machine. This approach also aligns neatly with the common *service-oriented architecture* (SOA) approach of loosely coupled and asynchronous communications.

From an implementation perspective, it is trivial to receive messages from the Service Bus. To begin with, you go to your Azure AppFabric portal and create the namespace (`finefoods` in our case). Next you create a new BizTalk receive location, choose one of the relay bindings, set the security credentials, and enable the receive location. After you have enabled the receive location, you have created an endpoint in the Service Bus (with an identifying namespace), and the Windows Azure Service Bus will send messages matching that endpoint to you. Figure 8.2 shows what the receive location would look like. Notice the WCF-Custom adapter, and the URI specified in it, which indicates a Service Bus endpoint address. At the time of this writing, there were two potential monikers: sb:// and https://, which respectively represent NetTCP and Ws2007Http transports.

Also, the receive pipeline being used here, `ItinerarySelectReceivePassthrough`, is one of the standard pipelines included with the *Enterprise Service Bus Toolkit* (ESB Toolkit, see Chapter 12), which means we could potentially implement something like passing a received message into the BizTalk rules engine, having a *Business Rules Engine* (BRE) evaluation determine which itinerary to use, retrieve that itinerary from the repository, and stamp it on the message, as was shown in the reference architecture presented in the ESB Toolkit chapter. This sequence is identical to the sort of sequence we may go through if we were picking up a message from a SharePoint document list or from a flat file, the only difference is we made a couple of minor configuration changes to the WCF-Custom adapter settings, and now we have extended our on-ramp to the cloud.

8

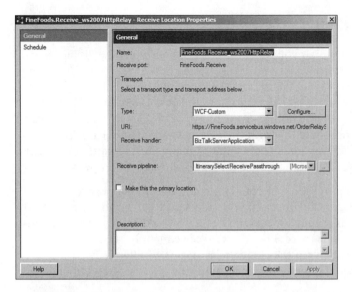

FIGURE 8.2   Receive Location Properties.

When the receive location is enabled, the custom binding uses the specified credentials to attempt to authenticate with the Access Control Service. If it succeeds, an endpoint is created in the Service Bus. We now have a pipe up to the Service Bus, because we are the ones who initiated the connection, and we have it secured, as well. (Standard WCF message/transport security options are available.) In addition to this, anyone publishing messages intended for our endpoint must be authorized by the Windows Azure platform Access Control Service before they can do so, which secures the link from the partner to the cloud.

This is an extremely powerful pattern, one that will likely become popular because it dramatically simplifies the steps required to securely open up your processes, BizTalk, and ESB messaging exchanges to the outside world.

Sending Messages

Sending messages to the Service Bus can be achieved just as easily as receiving messages, leveraging the same relay bindings provided by the AppFabric SDK.

You can send messages using the following:

▶ Static send port

▶ Dynamic send port

▶ ESB off-ramp

Static Send Port

Sending to the Service Bus is, as with all aspects of Azure AppFabric communication, a simple thing to do because the custom bindings from the SDK do all the hard work and integration for you.

Figure 8.3 shows an example of a static send port that sends a message to the Service Bus. This static send port uses the WCF-Custom adapter and the Ws2007HttpRelay binding, which means that it is the most current support of the WS* specifications, and it travels over *Hypertext Transfer Protocol* (HTTP) or *HTTP Secure* (HTTPS), making outbound communications possible from most networks. Also note the https:// moniker of the URI.

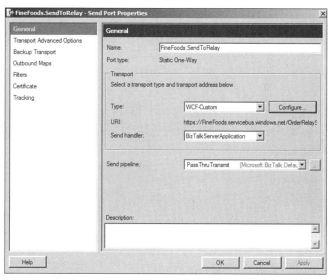

FIGURE 8.3   Send Port Properties.

For the bindings, on this tab I just needed to select the Ws2007HttpRelay binding, as shown in Figure 8.4.

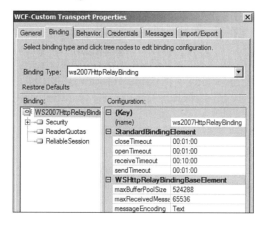

FIGURE 8.4   WCF-Custom Transport Properties.

To be able to send a message to the Azure AppFabric Service Bus, we need to be authenticated and authorized. For this particular example, a shared secret is used, as shown in Figure 8.5 (with the secret blurred).

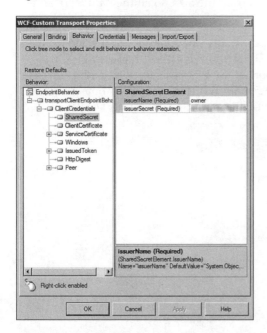

FIGURE 8.5   WCF-Custom Security Credentials.

Dynamic Send Port

Dynamic send ports are just what they sound like: Instead of specifying endpoint details by manual configuration or importing a binding, endpoint information can be set programmatically at runtime.

From a best practices standpoint, it can be advantageous to first create a static send port that does what you need it to do because that way you will be certain you know which properties need to be set and their values before using a dynamic send port. In addition, using a dynamic send port means that you will be using the default host binding for that transport, so for performance reasons, you might want to use a static send port to provide increased scalability. The ESB off-ramp, discussed next, uses a dynamic off-ramp, but you could also implement a dynamic send port directly (in a slightly less-generic manner).

ESB Off-Ramp

In addition to extending the ESB on-ramps to the cloud, we can take advantage of the Windows Azure Service Bus by sending messages to it from our on-premise ESB. Doing this is actually extremely simple, and we have all the building blocks we need. The ESB

Toolkit includes an adapter provider for BizTalk's WCF-Custom adapter, and as we saw the Windows Azure AppFabric SDK gives us the relay bindings, so it is just a matter of setting the appropriate adapter-provider properties.

Our itinerary is simple. We receive a message, resolve destination and adapter properties, and then relay the message on. Figure 8.6 shows this itinerary.

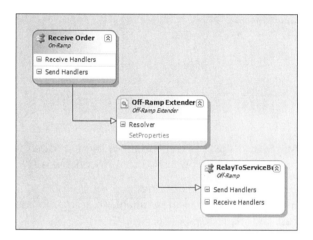

FIGURE 8.6   Sample ESB Toolkit Itinerary.

Figure 8.7 shows the properties of the Resolve Settings resolver. For the sake of simplicity, this example uses a STATIC resolver (which means that the statically defined settings are dynamically applied when the itinerary is executed).

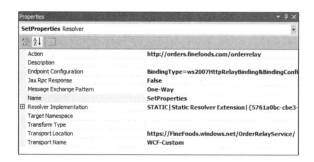

FIGURE 8.7   Resolver Properties.

For this to function properly, it is crucial that the Endpoint Configuration and Transport Location properties be set correctly.

The Endpoint Configuration properties are set in an editor dialog, as shown in Figure 8.8.

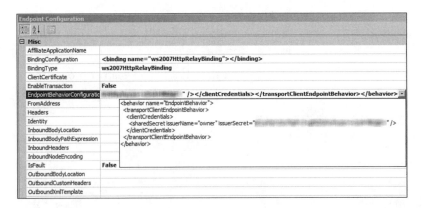

FIGURE 8.8   Endpoint Configuration.

When the message is sent to the AppFabric Service Bus, the credentials are authenticated by the Azure Access Control Service before the message is published to the Service Bus.

This example uses the `ws2007HttpRelayBinding` (one of the bindings you get from installing the Azure AppFabric SDK). However, other options are available to accommodate other messaging patterns, such as multicast and request/response.

Using InfoPath as a Client

You can use InfoPath as a client application to submit XML documents to the Azure Service Bus, for subsequent processing by BizTalk. This is a powerful pattern, particularly with a distributed workforce, and it is surprisingly simple to implement. Figure 8.9 shows the relevant part of the code behind the SendForm button on the InfoPath form to send a message to the Service Bus. The development environment doing the InfoPath portion does not need to know about BizTalk, but it does need the Azure AppFabric SDK installed so that you get access to the bindings required to communicate with the Azure AppFabric Service Bus.

Using the AppFabric cloud services between your clients using InfoPath and your BizTalk Server ESB guarantees worldwide scalability and many fewer worries about opening up your system to lots of outside users and the accompanying security challenges.

```
public void SendForm(string orderform)
{
    //ServiceBusEnvironment.SystemConnectivity.Mode = ConnectivityMode.Tcp;
    ServiceBusEnvironment.SystemConnectivity.Mode = ConnectivityMode.Http;

    My Secret Credentials

    // create the service URI based on the solution name
    //Uri serviceUri = ServiceBusEnvironment.CreateServiceUri("sb", serviceNamespaceDomain, "OrderRelayService");
    Uri serviceUri = ServiceBusEnvironment.CreateServiceUri("https", serviceNamespaceDomain, "OrderRelayService");

    // create the credentials object for the endpoint
    TransportClientEndpointBehavior sharedSecretServiceBusCredential = new TransportClientEndpointBehavior();
    sharedSecretServiceBusCredential.CredentialType = TransportClientCredentialType.SharedSecret;
    sharedSecretServiceBusCredential.Credentials.SharedSecret.IssuerName = issuerName;
    sharedSecretServiceBusCredential.Credentials.SharedSecret.IssuerSecret = issuerSecret;


    try
    {

        string dummyAction = "SendMessage";
        System.ServiceModel.Channels.Message msg = System.ServiceModel.Channels.Message.CreateMessage(
                                  MessageVersion.Soap12WSAddressing10, dummyAction,
                                  new System.Xml.XmlTextReader(orderform, XmlNodeType.Document, null));

        ChannelFactory<IOutputChannel> cf = new ChannelFactory<IOutputChannel>(new WS2007HttpRelayBinding(),
                                                      new EndpointAddress(serviceUri));

        cf.Endpoint.Behaviors.Add(sharedSecretServiceBusCredential);

        cf.Endpoint.Contract.SessionMode = SessionMode.Allowed;
        IOutputChannel channel = cf.CreateChannel();
        channel.Open();

        channel.Send(msg);
        channel.Close();
        cf.Close();

    }
    catch (Exception e)
```

FIGURE 8.9   Using InfoPath as a Client

Summary

In this chapter, you learned how to take on-premise BizTalk or ESB solutions and extend them to the outside world by using the Azure AppFabric Service Bus. The ability to create hybrid solutions that are partially on-premise and partially off-premise is compelling, and the techniques shown here enable BizTalk to be a first-class participant in these types of solutions.

8

CHAPTER 9

Business Activity Monitoring with BizTalk BAM

B*usiness activity monitoring* (BAM) plays an important role in modern service-oriented architectures.

Metrics collection in BizTalk solutions is often overlooked by many architects and developers who are more focused on designing and developing the services that will be composed to meet business needs. It often gets lost in the rush to get to code and deployment, and it is only later in the lifecycle of a project that questions start being asked about metrics.

BAM and Metrics

Metrics in a BizTalk solution, and service-oriented architecture in general, can occur at three levels:

▶ Infrastructure metrics

▶ Services metrics

▶ Business metrics

Infrastructure metrics are all about server health. Is the server functioning? Is the *central processing unit* (CPU) pegged? This is the kind of information that is of concern to IT professionals charged with maintaining the server environment, and it is typically provided by tools such as Microsoft's *System Center Operations Manager* (SCOM). SCOM enables monitoring of specific performance counters and, among other things, allows for previously scripted corrective actions to be invoked once certain events, such as a server outage, have occurred. However, it is not the purpose of this chapter to address this level of infrastructure metrics.

Service metrics are all about instrumenting the services in your solution. The types of metrics that may be gathered here could (for example) include items such as service latency, number of method invocations, number of exceptions, and so on. Depending on the toolset and the environment, there might be some crossover here with governance tools that require service metrics to determine *service level agreement* (SLA) compliance.

Business metrics enables you to gain visibility into the business processes themselves, which may include metrics from service composition or aggregation. Of lesser concern to the server administrators, the data collected at this level is typically of greater concern to the stakeholders or business owners. Just as infrastructure metrics enable identification of server issues, and service metrics may highlight service latency degradation, business metrics can provide powerful trend analysis and highlight business problems before they become a crisis. In addition, having deep business metrics could also lead to the discovery of new business opportunities that might otherwise go unnoticed. A well-planned business process metrics solution ensures that timely information is provided to business decision makers, which is a critical factor in the success of any business.

Now that we have identified the three types of metrics in an organization, try to look at them from a business executive's perspective. Generally, they are not concerned with server metrics. A CIO might be interested in both infrastructure and service metrics. Business metrics, on the other hand, are of interest to all executives. This is the portal into their business, the vista point from which they can see how their business is performing. Providing a world-class solution to a business problem is a laudable achievement, but providing business stakeholders with visibility into the process may have profound ramifications on the profitability and efficiency of the organization.

From a business stakeholder perspective, BizTalk and solutions developed with it provide the steak, BAM provides the sizzle.

In this chapter, we look at BizTalk Server's BAM capabilities, and we examine how they can be used for both service and business metrics.

What Is BizTalk BAM?

To define it in one sentence, BizTalk BAM is a mechanism to generically externalize the tracking of business process data and metrics, isolating tracking from process.

BizTalk BAM is part of BizTalk Server, but the licensing is such that it can also be used to instrument solutions beyond BizTalk, and can in fact be the foundation for BAM within an enterprise. In effect, it is a product in its own right, and could just have easily been a standalone product. However, Microsoft believed that it should be part of the BizTalk product. By contrast, many other vendors view BAM as a separate product.

It is BizTalk BAM's responsibility to capture data in either SQL Server or in SQL Analysis Services and make it available for rendering. BizTalk BAM is an open architecture whose sole responsibility is to capture data, and as you will see, there are several ways in which data can be captured. In addition, once captured, how you render or leverage that data is your decision, and you can use whichever solution makes sense for your organization and its needs.

In earlier times, a conventional approach to capturing data may have involved tracking data points in state tables associated with a solution. For example, a web service method may register the fact that it has been invoked, or from inside an orchestration you may update the state table to indicate the current process stage. If a credit check fails, perhaps a table outside of the process is updated. However, this approach is tightly bound to the implementation: Should you need to change the metrics you are tracking, it would entail a code change, which in large organizations can trigger multiple processes and be a somewhat less-than-agile process.

In contrast, BizTalk BAM uses an observation model, whereby events that occur are noticed by interceptors that track data points. The tracking of metrics is isolated from the application, and the tracking can (in most cases) be modified without any code changes to the existing application. In the case of a BizTalk solution, it is possible to deploy a solution and then some time later deploy BizTalk BAM metrics tracking, without redeploying or in any way changing the existing solution. It is a completely "touch-free" way to instrument BizTalk solutions. (It becomes less touch-free when you start instrumenting non-BizTalk solutions and/or use the BAM *application programming interfaces* [APIs].)

BizTalk BAM is all about data. It captures data, and ultimately, tracked data is available to be queried, either from SQL Server tables or from SQL Analysis Services *online analytical processing* (OLAP) cubes.

Two types of data are tracked:

▶ Business data, such as Order Amount and Customer Account

▶ Process milestone date and time, such as Order Received and Order Shipped

A single metrics monitoring application could include data from one or more of the following sources:

▶ BizTalk process automation solutions (orchestrations)

▶ BizTalk messaging-only integration solutions

▶ *Windows Communications Foundation* (WCF) interceptors

▶ *Windows Workflow* (WF) interceptors

▶ Calls into the BAM APIs

Figure 9.1 shows a logical model of the participants in a metrics tracking solution.

On the left side of Figure 9.1 are the metric sources. These are the BizTalk applications, BizTalk messaging, or other applications that are generating business data and process milestone events. The event observation layer (interceptors) captures data and stores it in SQL Server tables. The interceptors can be created programmatically or through the tools provided with BizTalk.

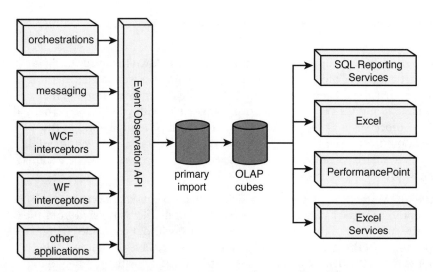

FIGURE 9.1   High-level Logical View of BAM Flow.

BizTalk Server 2010 runs on SQL Server 2008 and SQL Server 2008 R2. (Best practice is, of course, to use the latest to benefit from the inevitable performance improvements.) Unlike earlier versions of BizTalk that used earlier versions of SQL Server, *real-time aggregations* (RTAs) take advantage of real-time cube updates, where data will be kept in SQL Server Analysis Services and will be migrated there automatically. In addition to enabling enhanced querying mechanisms, this means that larger data sets can be retained before there are performance repercussions, although you should set the RTA time windows to retain only what you really need (to keep everything as lean and high performing as possible).

There is nothing proprietary about the data formats. When you are querying against the Analysis Services cubes, any of the standard approaches work, including Excel, PerformancePoint, a SharePoint Web Part, SQL Server Reporting Services, or any of your favorite OLAP tools.

Using BizTalk BAM

In the following section we will walk you through how to use BizTalk BAM, from end to end.

End-to-End, High-Level Walkthrough of the BAM Process

Figure 9.2 shows the various participants in a BAM solution.

The first step in the BAM tool chain entails defining the metrics capture model. Although this can be done programmatically through the BAM API, it is usually done in Excel (referred to the left in Figure 9.2 as BAM.XLSX). The vision is that this process could potentially be performed by a business analyst, perhaps someone who knows nothing about the technologies that will be used to solve a business problem but who has a deep knowledge of both the process and the metrics he wants to track. For more information about this step, see the section "Defining Activities and Views," later in this chapter.

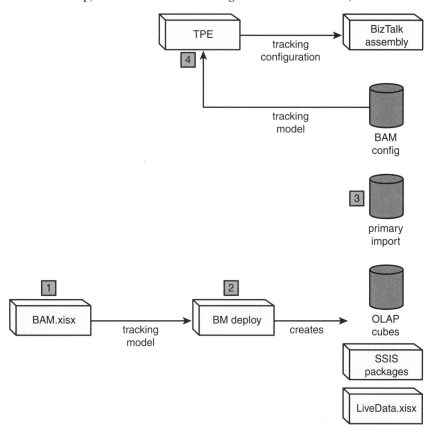

FIGURE 9.2   Tooling and artifact flow.

After the logical model has been completed, it is used as input to the BAM Management utility (BM.EXE) command-line tool. The BAM Management utility is a useful tool that does a lot of the "heavy lifting" required to create the following artifacts used in the tracking solution:

▶ It creates the primary import tables, the first stop for metrics data. (This includes the creation of triggers if RTAs are used.)

▶ It creates the *SQL Server Integration Services* (SSIS) packages required for scheduled aggregations, to move data from the primary import table to the OLAP cubes.

▶ If using scheduled aggregations, it creates the OLAP cubes.

▶ If using real-time aggregations, it creates the real-time cubes with default update settings (that you can adjust as required).

▶ If using real-time aggregations, it creates a LiveData spreadsheet to view the data. (The spreadsheet is stamped with a connection string to your primary import table.)

▶ It deploys information about the activity and views to the BAM configuration tables (which are also in the BAMPrimaryImport database).

As you can see, this one command-line utility performs numerous important tasks. In addition, as a command-line utility, it lends itself well to the creation of deployment scripts.

After the BAM utility has been used, the current state of our environment is that we have defined a logical model, and we have created the containers and transports for the data. If all metrics data will come from the WF or WCF interceptors or from API calls, we are done. If the metrics data will originate in a BizTalk process or messages flowing through BizTalk, we have an additional step, which is to map the logical model to the physical implementation in BizTalk.

The *Tracking Profile Editor* (TPE) is the tool that enables us to link the logical model to the physical implementation in BizTalk. It is a *graphical user interface* (GUI) tool that shows the logical model on the left and implementation on the right. The developer establishes the link by dragging a connecting line. (For further information, see the "Using the Tracking Profile Editor," section, later in this chapter.)

After the tracking profile has been defined, it is "applied" to an assembly. (Note that you can have only one tracking profile per assembly and it is tied to the version of the assembly.) In a development environment, this can be done directly from inside the TPE by choosing the **Apply** menu option. However, in a *quality assurance* (QA) or a production environment, the TPE is not available, because when BizTalk Server is installed, it detects whether Visual Studio is present, and if not, it does not install the TPE (which is a developer tool). To apply the tracking profile in a QA or production environment, you export a tracking profile from the TPE as a BTT file, and then use the BTTDeploy command-line utility to apply it. This, too, can be scripted.

It is important to note that although the SSIS packages for scheduled aggregations were created (Figure 9.2), they have not been scheduled to run. Scheduling them is the final step, and this is typically performed by the IT professional doing the deployment.

Now that you've seen an overview of the BizTalk BAM architecture, let's drill into some of the individual pieces in greater detail.

Real-Time Versus Scheduled Aggregations

As mentioned previously, BizTalk BAM includes two types of aggregations: scheduled aggregations and real-time aggregations. Both are great ways to aggregate metric data, but they have different intentions.

Real-time aggregations enable you to obtain real-time, up-to-the-minute metrics, which is an important requirement for some processes, but is less important for others. A business example of this is having a large shipment of perishable goods sitting on a loading dock and requiring process before the goods spoil.

Scheduled aggregations, by contrast, are intended to capture larger data sets. If your intention is to track metrics for the purpose of trend analysis over time, this is the technique to use. Although scheduled aggregations are not real time, they can be near real time, which for many purposes is good enough. As a business example, you might want to track activity in an order process over an extended period of time. In this case, if you're looking at a multimonth or multiyear data set, having 12-hour-old data might be perfectly acceptable. The data in a scheduled aggregation is as current as the last run of the SSIS package, so you can control the currency of the data by adjusting the frequency of package execution. If you have multiple scheduled aggregations, the update frequency can be defined by aggregation, so you could have some data sets more current than others. One final key benefit is that because all the data is being collected into OLAP cubes, it can be viewed in multiple ways, with a wide range of tools, so it is possible that you could create new views into this data months after collection was started.

Defining Activities and Views

The first step in creating a service or process instrumentation is to define the logical model that answers this question: What am I tracking? Excel is used as the modeling tool, which might seem an odd choice to many BizTalk developers. However, the reason for this is that this means a sufficiently trained business analyst, someone who is not a developer but is deeply familiar with the process and which metrics matter, could create the metrics tracking model.

Using Excel, you first model an activity, and then model views into that activity. An activity defines two types of entities:

▶ Business milestones (the date or time an event occurred, or a stage in a process was reached)

▶ Business data (extracted from a message in flight, or service data contract, or metadata associated with a message)

Figure 9.3 show a *service-oriented architecture* (SOA) monitoring activity modeled in an Excel spreadsheet using the BizTalk BAM add-on.

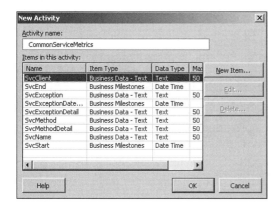

FIGURE 9.3   Defining an activity.

After you have an activity defined, the next step is to create one or more views into the activity.

There is no formal guidance as to how to structure views, but a good rule of thumb is to create a view for each role that needs visibility. For an order process, this may mean that you provide views for sales, manufacturing, and accounting. Taking a role-based approach like this also makes it easier to ultimately secure the views, and provides a more granular approach to scheduling the OLAP updates.

The view-creation process is wizard driven. The first step is selection of the activity items. We could, ultimately, in the same spreadsheet have multiple views into a single activity or have a view that includes items from multiple activities. In this particular case, we select everything from the CommonServiceMetrics activity, as shown in Figure 9.4.

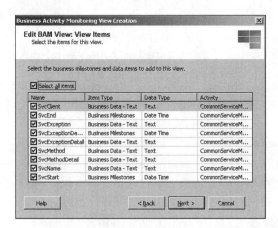

FIGURE 9.4   Creating a BAM View.

The next step is to specify which of the data items will be included in the view. Because the view is the basis for the physical infrastructure that will be generated further along in the BAM deployment process, carefully consider which items will be included. Any nonrequired data that you include will inefficiently propagate into the tracking tables, data migration, and data maintenance tasks.

Aliases in the view enable us to change the name that will be presented further downstream in the process. We also have the ability to create two virtual constructs: durations and groups. Both durations and groups are related to business milestones (the date/time that an event occurred, such as order placed or service invoked).

A duration is a calculated column that is the elapsed time between two existing milestones. In Figure 9.5, we are using a duration to represent the overall time elapsed between the SvcStart and SvcEnd milestones.

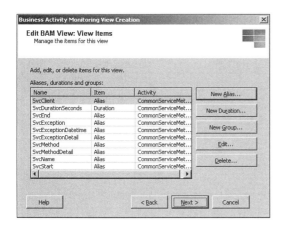

FIGURE 9.5   Editing a BAM View.

A group, by contrast, can be thought of as a "rollup" of multiple (one or more) milestones. This does not pertain to the example shown, but can be valuable in more-complex scenarios, such as an order process. Order fulfillment could consist of multiple milestones, and those could form a group. A group is a collection of multiple milestones where only one is expected to be reached. Therefore, in this example, you might have order fulfilled or order denied in the same group; that group in turn could be a milestone in the overall order process.

Now that we have defined the items we will be tracking, let's define how they are stored. Figure 9.6 shows how we define the measures and dimensions of our data. Ultimately, this stage determines the structure of the OLAP cubes in SQL Analysis Services, and any SQL Server tables.

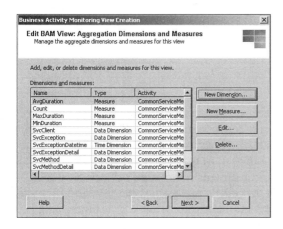

FIGURE 9.6   Defining Measures and Dimensions.

The New Dimension submenu presents a number of options, as shown in Figure 9.7.

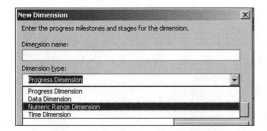

FIGURE 9.7   Creating a New Dimension.

Progress Dimension

A progress dimension is a virtual dimension. It allows you to create stages in a process (order preprocessing, order fulfillment, order invoicing), which means that you can divide your data into those groups. Ultimately, you could use a progress dimension to produce a pie chart showing relative percentages of orders at different defined stages, such as 25% of orders are in fulfillment.

Data Dimension

A data dimension retrieves business data as has been defined in the activity.

Numeric Range Dimension

A numeric range dimension groups data items into buckets. Although we do not have one in the profile shown, we could have specified service duration ranges such as fast (less than 1 second), medium (1–10 seconds), or slow (more than 10 seconds), which ultimately would allow for the creation of a pie chart showing the relative percentage of service duration ranges (for example, 50% of durations are fast).

Time Dimension

A time dimension is a time stamp for a milestone or a milestone group. It is at this stage that you specify the time resolution. It is a best practice to define only the granularity you require. For example, if you do not need to track the hour and minute a milestone occurred, do not select it here. During the data migration to the SQL Analysis Services process, there is a stage that prepopulates the time dimension for a year. If you have specified fine granularity down to the minute, this part of the process takes longer, and the cube structure is larger than it needs to be. Figure 9.8 shows how to define a time dimension.

Measures are the numeric values we track. When specifying measures, the options shown in Figure 9.9 are available.

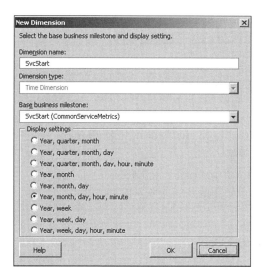

FIGURE 9.8   Defining a Time Dimension.

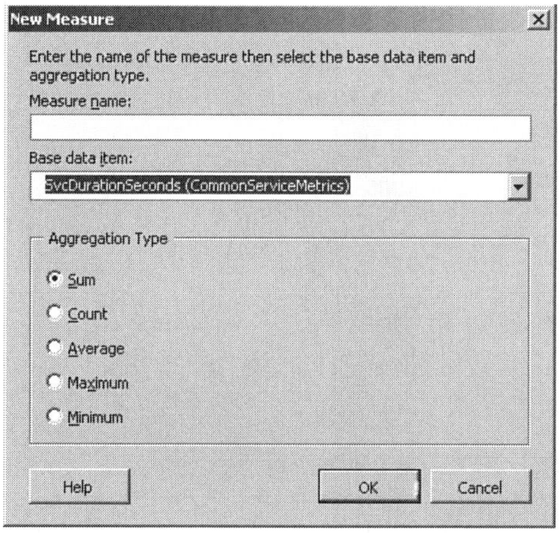

FIGURE 9.9   Creating a new Measure.

Note that the base data items available will change based on the aggregation type. For example, a sum of dates makes no sense, but a minimum and maximum may. Count is normally always present in a view, because this is the count of the instances of the activity. If you are using scheduled aggregations, you will ultimately have the ability to perform drill-through analysis such as minimum/maximum values over a month, average number of items per day, and so forth.

This is the last step in the view creation. After this, you are presented with a summary screen showing you the view you have just created. Accepting it invokes a macro that emits a tab in the spreadsheet for each view you have defined. At that point, you are presented with a pivot table. You can drag items into the pivot table, and you can also specify that the aggregation is a real-time aggregation by clicking the toolbar button. You can also associate a chart with the pivot table from the pivot table toolbar.

Using the Tracking Profile Editor

The *Tracking Profile Editor* (TPE) is the graphical tool that enables developers to create the link between the logical track profile and the actual implementation. It is a design-time tool and is used only in a development environment.

As shown in Figure 9.10, the pane on the left shows the logical activity. This is what would have initially been defined using either a BAM spreadsheet or using the Orchestration Designer for Business Analysts. When you select the activity in the TPE, you are browsing the activities that have been deployed to the local machine using the BM.EXE BAM Management utility. A check box allows you to retrieve any tracking profile that has been deployed for that activity.

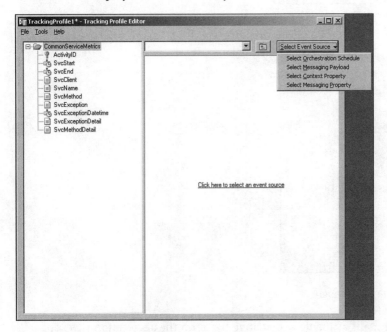

FIGURE 9.10   The Tracking Profile Editor.

The Select Event Source button allows you to choose the type of event source you want to use. These are as follows:

▶ **Orchestration Schedule:**A BizTalk orchestration (which includes access to active messages that flow through the orchestration).

▶ **Message Payload:**Contents of a message flowing through BizTalk (in a messaging-only solution, such as content-based routing).

▸ **Context Property:**Allows tracking of context properties of messages flowing through BizTalk. (This includes the default context properties every message in BizTalk has, and any that you may have defined through an associated property schema.)

▸ **Messaging Property:**Allows tracking of system-level messaging properties of messages flowing through BizTalk, such as `MessageId`, `InterchangeId`, and so on.

Note that in our example we are using the API and as such we are not using this tool (shown in Figure 9.10) to create the interceptors. If we were, we would load an event source in the pane on the right side, and we would link that physical implementation (perhaps an orchestration) to the logical model shown in pane on the left.

There are two final outputs of this tool, both of which lead to the creation of interceptors.

You could use this to directly "apply" the tracking profile, and this is what you may typically do if you are developing a BizTalk solution and are in a development environment.

The other alternative is to save a BTT file, which you subsequently use in conjunction with a command-line utility to apply the tracking profile (and create interceptors) in nondevelopment environments.

Note that if you are using API calls to populate tracking data, or if you are using the WCF or WF interceptors, you do not need to perform this step.

Using the BAM APIs

As is the case with most parts of BizTalk, an exposed API can be invoked to interact with the BAM tracking infrastructure. This enables you to extend a BizTalk BAM-based instrumentation process beyond BizTalk solutions.

Registering events with BAM involves the use of an `EventStream`. There are four types of `EventStream` APIs discussed in the following section. Regardless of which API is used, the ultimate result is the same: Data is captured (by default) in the BAMPrimaryImport database.

DirectEventStream (DES)

The `DirectEventStream` is a synchronous call. There is no latency; once you register an event, it is immediately available in the BAMPrimaryImport tables. However, being a synchronous operation, this is not a good choice if you are dealing with a system where there could be surges in message volumes, because this is a blocking operation that could become a bottleneck. This is the only API that writes directly to the BAMPrimaryImport database.

BufferedEventStream (BES)

In most cases, for an external application that needs to call into the BAM tracking infrastructure, this is usually the correct API to use. It is an asynchronous operation that writes data to a temporary spooling table, and in time, the *Tracking Data and Decoding Service* (TDDS) moves those into the BAMPrimaryImport table. When you use the TPE to link your activity model to an orchestration or message, it is creating interceptors that use the BufferedEventStream.

OrchestrationEventStream (OES)

The `OrchestrationEventStream` is similar to the `BufferedEventStream`, in that it is asynchronous and well suited to volatile event volumes. It is specifically intended to be used in those cases where you are calling the API from inside an orchestration, because events can participate in orchestration transactions. When an orchestration transaction commits, the BAM data is written out, and if a transaction is rolled back, so is the tracked data, ensuring synchronization between actions and tracked data. To minimize database latency, data is temporarily persisted in the Message Box database and is migrated into the BAMPrimaryImport database by the TDDS service.

IPipelineContext Interface

The `IPipelineContext` interface exposes a `GetEventStream` method that returns a `MessagingEventStream` object. This is an asynchronous API for use in pipeline components and participates in pipeline transactions. So when a pipeline transaction commits, the BAM data is persisted.

Creating a Higher-Level API Specifically for Service Metrics

You've seen that BizTalk BAM already includes APIs to allow you to programmatically participate in a BAM tracking strategy. However, these are generic APIs that require some knowledge of the underlying activity definition. It is better to shield the developer from that by creating a higher-level abstraction layer that makes it easier to use, by wrapping those lower-level APIs.

To illustrate this concept, we create an API for capturing service metrics. We wrap a class library around the BAM API as a layer of abstraction, and call into that to register events. Because this API will be for use on machines that do not have BizTalk installed, but they do want asynchronous operation, the API is based on the `BufferedEventStream` class.

The API for tracking service metrics essentially has to fulfill three tasks:

- ▶ Track service start
- ▶ Track service end
- ▶ Track exception information

To maintain continuity, we need some way to tie a service end or service exception back to its corresponding start. To do that, the service start method will return a *globally unique identifier* (GUID) that we will then present to the other two methods. Note that the maintenance tasks need to be configured in such a way that any incomplete instances (such a, a service start occurs but there is a failure that prevents the service end from running) are removed at some point.

LISTING 9.1   ServiceTracker Class, Recording a Service Start

The TrackServiceStart method is overloaded, for the convenience of the developer:

```
public class ServiceTracker
{
const string ACTIVITY_NAME = "CommonServiceMetrics";
const string CONNECTION_STRING = "Integrated
        Security=SSPI;Persist Security Info=False;
Initial Catalog=BizTalkMsgBoxDb";
public static Guid TrackServiceStart(string serviceName,
string methodName, string client)
{
return TrackServiceStart(serviceName, methodName,
client, "");
}
public static Guid TrackServiceStart(string serviceName,
            string methodName, string client,
string methodDetails)
{
Guid guid = Guid.NewGuid();
BufferedEventStream strm =
new BufferedEventStream();
strm.ConnectionString = CONNECTION_STRING;
strm.BeginActivity(ACTIVITY_NAME, guid.ToString());
strm.UpdateActivity(ACTIVITY_NAME, guid.ToString(),
"SvcStart", DateTime.Now,
"SvcName", serviceName,
"SvcMethod", methodName,
"SvcClient", client,
"SvcMethodDetail",
 methodDetails
);
strm.Flush();
return guid;
        }
}
```

Assuming no exception is thrown, the next call to the API is to TrackServiceEnd as shown in Listing 9.2.

LISTING 9.2   ServiceTracker Class, Recording a Service End

```
public static void TrackServiceEnd(Guid guid)
{
BufferedEventStream strm = new BufferedEventStream();
strm.ConnectionString = CONNECTION_STRING;
strm.UpdateActivity(ACTIVITY_NAME, guid.ToString(),
"SvcEnd", DateTime.Now);
strm.EndActivity(ACTIVITY_NAME, guid.ToString());
strm.Flush();
}
```

If an exception occurs, we log the exception shown in Listing 9.3:

LISTING 9.3   ServiceTracker Class, Recording an Exception

```
public static void TrackServiceException(Guid guid,
string exceptionType, string exceptionDetail)
{
BufferedEventStream strm = new BufferedEventStream();
strm.ConnectionString = CONNECTION_STRING;
strm.UpdateActivity(ACTIVITY_NAME, guid.ToString(),
"SvcExceptionDatetime", DateTime.Now,
"SvcException", exceptionType,
"SvcExceptionDetail", exceptionDetail
);
strm.Flush();
}
```

With these three simple methods, and the activity definition we created earlier, we now have a wide range of reports we can generate around service usage, including the following:

▶ Successful versus failed service invocations, over time, which can be useful for trend analysis to see increasing failure rates.

▶ Service latency over time could be useful to spot service degradation that might not otherwise be noticed before it becomes critical.

▶ Which methods inside a service are being called over time, which could help you decide which services and methods might be candidates for retirement.

▶ A percentage breakdown of exceptions being tracked.

This API is by no means presented as an alternative to more comprehensive service monitoring and governance products, which provide numerous desirable enterprise-grade capabilities such as SLA monitoring. However, sometimes simple metrics tracking is all that's required, and the API presented here is a perfectly viable choice. Data captured for service metrics can be surfaced through a "process portal" to the process owners, as part of their overall view into the process performance and health.

Working with the WCF and WF Interceptors

BizTalk 2006 R2 introduced the ability to use interceptors to track data flowing through Windows Workflow Foundation processes and through Windows Communications Foundation services. This allows solutions written using those technologies to leverage BizTalk's BAM infrastructure.

Before the interceptors, you could have done this by making calls to the BAM API, but that would have tightly coupled tracking to the solution. Alternatively, the API also provides the capability to create interceptors programmatically, which is less tightly coupled than direct API calls, but more tightly coupled than a runtime configuration change. With the new capabilities, you have a broader set of choices, you can put tracking into code, or you can use configuration to define tracking.

The workflow using the interceptors is the same as when you use the API. The biggest difference is that instead of using the TPE to map from the activity definition to the actual implementation, you use configuration to add behaviors.

There is no user interface for creation of the interceptors, but the documentation leads you through adding the interceptor configuration schemas (there are three: common, WCF, and WF) to Visual Studios schema folder, or via the Visual Studios Xml|Schema option, so you can at least get the benefit of IntelliSense when creating interceptor configuration files. This is a suggested best practice because the files can become somewhat complex and IntelliSense enables you to validate the document before you deploy it. The schemas are located under the SDK\Samples\BAM folder.

It is possible to have multiple activities in a single interceptor configuration file. In our example, Listing 9.4, we have only a single activity, the `"OrderActivity"`.

The first step in creating an interceptor configuration file is the definition of an `EventSource`. This assigns a symbolic name to it that you will use later in the definition, and specifies the fully qualified assembly that you will be tracking.

Next we define a `BamActivity`. This contains filter conditions, and logic defining what we want to track. It could also contain continuation information, which is used if tracking spans multiple systems (for example, if an activity starts in a web page, gets updated by BizTalk, and gets finished in a Windows Forms application).

The filter expression (Listing 9.4) specifies that we are looking for a WCF `OperationName` of `"SubmitOrder"`. The `GetServiceContractCallPoint` indicates when we want to capture data, in this case it is as the service receives the request, but it could have been when the service returns its response.

The operators (Listing 9.4) "Equals" and "And" show that operations in an interceptor configuration file are implemented using Reverse Polish Notation. In Reverse Polish Notation, operators follow all of the operands, meaning "2 + 2" is expressed as "2 2 +", "3 + 4 – 9" is expressed as "3 4 9 + -", and so forth.

Finally, the CorrelationID (Listing 9.4) is used as the activity ID in the BAM infrastructure. We are asking for a new key (a GUID) to be generated, but we could just as easily have used something in the message for this (such as an order number). However, this must be a unique identifier. If there is a duplicate, you get a database error. The failed data is persisted in the failed tracking table, but attention must be paid to the choice of identifiers because this could lead to incorrect or incomplete tracking data.

LISTING 9.4   Interceptor Definition

```xml
<?xml version="1.0" encoding="utf-8" ?>
<ic:InterceptorConfiguration
xmlns:ic="http://schemas.microsoft.com/BizTalkServer/2004/10/BAM/
InterceptorConfiguration"
xmlns:wcf="http://schemas.microsoft.com/BizTalkServer/2004/10/BAM/
WcfInterceptorConfiguration">
  <ic:EventSource Name="OrderEventSource"
         Technology="WCF"
 Manifest ="FineFoods.Orders.IOrderManager, ServiceContracts, Version=1.0.0.0,
Culture=neutral, PublicKeyToken=null ">
    <wcf:NamespaceMappings>
<wcf:Namespace Prefix="a"
 Uri="http://finefoods.com/orders/2010/10/1"/>
    </wcf:NamespaceMappings>
  </ic:EventSource>
  <ic:BamActivity Name="OrderActivity">
    <ic:OnEvent Name="SubmitOrder"
Source="OrderEventSource"
IsBegin="true" IsEnd="true">
<!-- Filter so only the SubmitOrder method is tracked -->
      <ic:Filter>
        <ic:Expression>
          <wcf:Operation Name="GetOperationName"/>
          <ic:Operation Name="Constant">
            <ic:Argument>SubmitOrder</ic:Argument>
          </ic:Operation>
          <ic:Operation Name="Equals"/>
          <wcf:Operation Name="GetServiceContractCallPoint"/>
          <ic:Operation Name="Constant">
            <ic:Argument>ServiceRequest</ic:Argument>
```

```
        </ic:Operation>
        <ic:Operation Name="Equals"/>
        <ic:Operation Name="And"/>
      </ic:Expression>
    </ic:Filter>
<!-- Assign activity ID -->
      <ic:CorrelationID>
        <ic:Expression>
          <wcf:Operation Name="AutoGenerateCorrelationToken"/>
        </ic:Expression>
      </ic:CorrelationID>
```

The final section in the interceptor configuration file specifies which fields we want to update. Usage here is self-evident. As shown in figure 9.5 we are using XPath expressions to reach into the message and retrieve specific values. (The namespace used was declared as part of the EventSource.)

LISTING 9.5   Define Fields to be Updated and Which Data to Use

```
    <!-- Tracked fields to update -->
    <ic:Update DataItemName="CustomerNumber" Type="NVARCHAR">
<ic:Expression>
<wcf:Operation Name ="XPath">
  <wcf:Argument>//a:CustomerNumber</wcf:Argument>
</wcf:Operation>
</ic:Expression>
</ic:Update>
      <ic:Update DataItemName="BuyerName" Type="NVARCHAR">
        <ic:Expression>
          <wcf:Operation Name ="XPath">
            <wcf:Argument>//a:BuyerName</wcf:Argument>
          </wcf:Operation>
        </ic:Expression>
      </ic:Update>
      <ic:Update DataItemName="OrderTotsl" Type="INT">
        <ic:Expression>
          <wcf:Operation Name ="XPath">
            <wcf:Argument>//a:OrderTotal</wcf:Argument>
          </wcf:Operation>
        </ic:Expression>
      </ic:Update>
    </ic:OnEvent>
  </ic:BamActivity>
</ic:InterceptorConfiguration>
```

Using Notifications

BizTalk BAM supports event notifications, which allows you to set alerts based on threshold values. For example, should service latency of a given service exceed a predefined value, you can have it issue an alert.

The BAM portal includes a mechanism to enable you to create alerts and manage alert subscribers. The alerting transport can be either an email or a file emitted into a folder. The folder option is an interesting one, because you could then have BizTalk listening to that folder location and perhaps launch a business process when an alert event occurs.

In BizTalk Server 2006 R2 and BizTalk Server 2009 using SQL 2005 as BizTalk's data store, the alerting mechanism is implemented using SQL Server 2005 Notification Services. With BizTalk Server 2010 and BizTalk Server 2009, if you are using SQL Server 2008 or SQL Server 2008 R2 as a data store, a separate download is required to obtain notification capabilities.

Rapid Prototyping

Sometimes it is advantageous to be able to start capturing metrics early in the development cycle, perhaps before services you want to monitor have been written. Some situations where advance-development makes sense are as follows:

▶ You want to develop your tracking metrics so that you can begin the portal construction process and show stakeholders what a final product might look like (for example, showing a functional portal, as opposed to mocking up screenshots).

▶ Your process relies on other services that have not yet been implemented, or for any other reason are not available.

▶ You need to work with creative personnel and give them examples of what you expect metrics presentation could be.

▶ You want to show stakeholders the high value that effective instrumentation provides. Service and process instrumentation ties directly back to business values, and as such is something readily grasped by management at all levels.

Using BizTalk BAM, it is possible, and in fact relatively easy, to take a "metrics-first" approach to process and service instrumentation.

Consider that everything in BAM begins with a logical model created in Excel. Once we have that logical model, we can use the BM.EXE tool to create the database artifacts required to track that activity. With a service or process to instrument, we do not have a physical representation to map to from our logical model, so we cannot at that point use the TPE to create that link.

However, after we've used the BM.EXE tool, the stored procedures that insert tracking data exist. Normally, in a fully constructed and deployed BAM tracking infrastructure, these stored procedures are called by the interceptors; however, there's nothing to stop us from calling them directly. This is an extremely effective way to approach rapid prototyping of BAM instrumentation.

REST and BAM

Although with the current release of BizTalk Server there is no native support for *Representational State Transfer (REST)*, REST provides a good model for implementing resource and entity-based services. As you learned earlier in this chapter, a comprehensive API is available for interacting with BAM, and it's not a lot of work to create a RESTful API in front of that so that BAM capabilities and resources could be exposed as REST services. In fact, there have been community efforts to create such RESTful APIs, and the results of these efforts are available on the Internet.

Managing BAM

There are several logistical details that need to be considered in order to effectively manage a BAM infrastructure, including data retention windows and archival strategies.

BAM Database Considerations

The TDDS service is responsible for moving data into the BAMPrimaryImport database. This runs as a subprocess of a BizTalk "host" and is enabled by specifying that a host is a "tracking host."

If you are using any of the asynchronous APIs, an outage of the BAMPrimaryImport database is noncritical, because data continues to be collected in the Message Box database. When the BAMPrimaryImport database becomes available again, data migrates into it. By contrast, an outage of the BAMPrimaryImport database when using the synchronous API is a critical failure and results in an exception being thrown.

Database configuration and distribution is an important aspect of the capacity and performance of a BizTalk infrastructure. A wealth of information is available in the form of white papers and best practices that will enable you to implement a BizTalk infrastructure that meets the high-availability, SLA, and disaster recovery requirements of your enterprise. This blanket statement about BizTalk Server applies equally to the BAM components.

Deployment and Management

The BM tool will create a lot of the requirement maintenance jobs for you, but you will need to complete configuration and schedule them to run at a frequency that makes sense for your business need.

Examples of configurable items are the archival jobs, which will archive old data, and if using scheduled aggregations, the SQL Server Integration Services job that migrates data from temporary tracking tables into the OLAP cubes.

Security

Security is best managed by using role-based security. If you want to secure views, restricting access to only certain groups, you can do this by grouping tracked data into one view per group and then restricting membership in that group.

Depending on how you render data for the users, you might have additional options. If you are using SQL Server Reporting Services hosted in a SharePoint site, for example, you could make use of those security mechanisms to restrict visibility.

It is important to remember that BAM is about tracking data, and that means you could potentially also track sensitive data. In those cases, appropriate security measures and precautions must be taken to ensure that the confidentiality of the data is maintained.

Scripting Deployment

Experienced BizTalk developers know that with a little up-front effort, the deployment of their solutions, which may encompass a variety of technologies, can be reduced to a simple installation process, as shown in Chapter 14, "Deployment Concepts." Investing this effort up front leads to highly repeatable installations and faster migration between environments. Deployment of BAM artifacts can also be scripted.

Often, developers new to BAM create tracking solutions, attempt to deploy them into a QA or production environment, and find out that the TPE is missing. The reason for this is the BizTalk installation process detects whether Visual Studio is installed, and based on that, decides whether to install the developer tools. (Note that you should *never* install Visual Studio on a QA or production server; there should be no need to do so.) The question then becomes "how do I apply the tracking profile?" And, the answer is to use another command line utility: BTTDEPLOY.

Seasoned BAM developers generally have batch files to deploy/undeploy the BAM infrastructure. The reason for this is twofold. First, developing the tracking infrastructure is generally an iterative process, with multiple iterations until the logical model aligns with the physical implementation to the point where you can extract the required meaningful metrics. Second, undeploying and redeploying the tracking profile is a great way to remove any collected data and "reset" the environment to a clean state.

Needs will vary, and syntax may vary with operating systems, but the script shown in figure 9.6 is an example of a typical development-time deployment script.

LISTING 9.6   Batch File to Development Environment Deployment

```
@ECHO OFF
color a0
ECHO Deploying Common Service Metrics Tracking
```

```
rem :: delims is a TAB followed by a space
FOR /F "tokens=2* delims=        " %%A IN ('REG QUERY
"HKEY_LOCAL_MACHINE\SOFTWARE\Microsoft\BizTalk Server\3.0" /v InstallPath') DO
SET InstPath=%%B
echo Using BAM Manager from BizTalk installation path '%InstPath%'
"%InstPath%\Tracking\bm" update-all -DefinitionFile:"CommonServiceMetrics.xls"
```

The script needs to call the BAM Manager tool (BM.EXE) located in the "tracking" folder where BizTalk was installed. Note that no tracking profile is applied here. In this development environment, that would either be done using the TPE or, if using API calls or the interceptors, it would not be required. The use of the color command changes the background of the command window, which can be a great way to visually indicate the type of task (deploy or undeploy) being performed.

By contrast, the script shown in figure 9.7 is an example of what a typical deployment script may look like for a QA or production environment:

LISTING 9.7   Batch File to QA/Production Environment Deployment

```
@ECHO OFF
mode con cols=120
color a0
cls
ECHO ** Please note that you must have BizTalk Administrator rights to run this
script.
:: delims is a TAB followed by a space
FOR /F "tokens=2* delims=        " %%A IN ('REG QUERY
"HKEY_LOCAL_MACHINE\SOFTWARE\Microsoft\BizTalk Server\3.0" /v InstallPath') DO
SET InstPath=%%B
echo Using BAM Manager from BizTalk installation path '%InstPath%'
echo [[ Deploying activities... ]]
"%InstPath%\Tracking\bm" update-all -DefinitionFile:"CommonServiceMetrics.xml"
echo.
echo [[ Deploying tracking profile... ]]
echo.
"%InstPath%\Tracking\bttdeploy" "CommonServiceMetrics.btt"
```

You'll notice a couple of key differences from the development script. In this script, we are giving the BM utility an XML file as an activity definition, rather than an Excel spreadsheet. This is because, as a QA or production machine, Excel will presumably (hopefully!) not be installed. This XML file was created from the BAM toolbar menu inside the spreadsheet. Second, we are using BTTDeploy to apply the tracking profile (create the interceptors), because the TPE is a developer tool and also should not be available to us as we migrate through environments.

The corresponding undeployment script for development is this is shown in figure 9.8.

LISTING 9.8   Undeployment Script for Development Environment

```
@ECHO OFF
color e0
ECHO Undeploying CommonServiceMetrics
rem :: delims is a TAB followed by a space
FOR /F "tokens=2* delims=        " %%A IN ('REG QUERY
"HKEY_LOCAL_MACHINE\SOFTWARE\Microsoft\BizTalk Server\3.0" /v InstallPath') DO
SET InstPath=%%B
echo Using BTTDeploy from BizTalk installation path '%InstPath%'
"%InstPath%\Tracking\bm.exe"  remove-all -
DefinitionFile:"CommonServiceMetrics.xls"
Pause
```

And, finally, the corresponding undeployment script for QA or production could be something along the lines of what is shown in figure 9.9.

LISTING 9.9   Undeployment Script for QA/Production Environment

```
@ECHO OFF
mode con cols=120
color e0
cls

ECHO ** Please note that you must have BizTalk Administrator rights to run this
script.
:: delims is a TAB followed by a space
FOR /F "tokens=2* delims=        " %%A IN ('REG QUERY
"HKEY_LOCAL_MACHINE\SOFTWARE\Microsoft\BizTalk Server\3.0" /v InstallPath') DO
SET InstPath=%%B
echo Using BAM Manager from BizTalk installation path '%InstPath%'
echo [[ Removing tracking profile... ]]
"%InstPath%\Tracking\bttdeploy.exe" /remove "CommonServiceMetrics.btt"
echo [[ Removing activities... ]]
"%InstPath%\Tracking\bm" remove-all -DefinitionFile:"CommonServiceMetrics.xml"
```

As was the case with the no-development undeployment, here, too, we use the *Extensible Markup Language* (XML) version of the activity definition file, and BTTDeploy.

The last mile: Tracking data about service invocation and business processes is a vital part of a comprehensive SOA strategy but is meaningless without an effective rendering mechanism.

BizTalk Server includes an optional BAM portal. This ASP.NET site provides a generic way for surfacing data that has been tracked by BizTalk BAM, allowing ad hoc queries, and rendering charts using the Office Web Controls. This BAM portal can be useful during the development cycle, and could be used beyond just the development environment.

However, it is important to remember that at the end of the BAM tracking process, data is stored in a SQL Server. The fact that a standard data store is used opens up a lot of customization opportunities for rendering the data to users. In addition, this data could also be used to drive a business intelligence application such as PerformancePoint.

From a charting perspective, numerous options are available, and this is an area that has evolved somewhat over the past few years. A good choice based on current technologies is to use a combination of SharePoint and SQL Server Reporting Services. Using SharePoint as a host for your reports allows you to leverage SharePoint's identity management, and present data at a departmental portal level, and to secure access to those departmental sites based on domain group membership. SQL Server Reporting Services allows you to create textual reports on data. The chart control for SQL Server Reporting Services is a versatile chart control that provides compelling 3D rendering capabilities and fine-grained control for developers, so they can implement capabilities such as "drill through." (Click a pie slice in a chart and step into the data that makes up that slice and so forth.) An additional point worth mentioning is that because the reports are done in SQL Server Reporting Services, you could leverage the native report subscription model, so reports could be generated at predefined intervals and emailed to subscribers.

Summary

BizTalk BAM is a powerful infrastructure for tracking either service or business metrics. It operates in a decoupled manner, using an observation model to listen in on events and messages, without the need to embed specific tracking information or calls to tracking infrastructure in code. BAM data can be aggregated either in SQL Server tables (for smaller real-time data sets) or in SQL Server Analysis Services (for large datasets, trend analysis, historical reporting, and so on). BizTalk BAM is all about capturing metrics. When captured, you can render and report on this data with your tools of choice, including common options such as SQL Reporting Services, PerformancePoint Services, Excel Services, and Excel.

Implementing an effective metrics monitoring solution is a key component of a successful SOA, and BizTalk BAM gives you all the pieces you need to achieve that goal.

The Business Rules Framework

by Charles Young

BizTalk Server offers developers a rich and diverse toolkit for integration and process management. As well as messaging and orchestration, it provides support for managing business rules. The *Business Rules Framework* (BRF) defines programmatic models and component interfaces for rules-based development together with tools, components, and a rule repository. Tools include the Rules Engine Deployment Wizard for creating, testing, publishing, and deploying rule sets. The BRF also implements the Rule Engine Update Service. This Windows service runs locally on each BizTalk box and manages dynamic deployment of rule sets across multiple machines. The BRF also provides the *Business Rules Engine* (BRE) for processing rules against XML, .NET objects, ADO.NET data tables, and external databases.

This chapter introduces the concepts of rule processing and builds the case for externalization of rules. It describes a scenario in which a developer works closely with an analyst to elaborate business rule statements and ensure close alignment of a solution to business goals and requirements. It describes the Microsoft Business Rules Framework and explains its architecture, components, and function. It discusses each of the rule-processing tools and components provided as part of the framework. It introduces the Rule Composer and the Rules Engine Deployment Wizard in detail and explains how to explore fact types, compose rules, test rule sets, and create vocabularies. It provides practical strategies for creating versioned rule sets and vocabularies and describes how to migrate and deploy these artifacts to different environments. The chapter explains how rule processing is integrated with BizTalk Server orchestrations and RFID Server pipelines. It describes how policies can be managed through the BizTalk Administration Console and outlines the use of rule processing in the *Enterprise Service Bus* (ESB) Toolkit.

The Importance of Rules

Development teams avoid using Microsoft's BRF for many reasons. Some are entirely legitimate, but too often objections are based on misunderstandings and incorrect assumptions. Solution architects and developers need to make informed choices based on a solid understanding of the technology. The most common objections include the following:

▶ **"Our rules are very simple. We don't need a rule engine."**

This misses the point. It's not about the complexity of your rules, or even the number of rules you are dealing with. It's about cleanly separating rules from processes so that you can manage business policies independently.

▶ **"Our business users and analysts don't understand the tools."**

BizTalk Server 2010 is primarily a developer's toolkit. If you need out-of-the-box support for analysts and business users, there are some excellent rule management products you can purchase and integrate with BizTalk Server. Be aware, though, that the entry-level costs for these tools will be significant.

▶ **"We tried using it on our last project, but we couldn't figure out how to get it to work."**

Like any other development technology, there is a learning curve. It can be steep at times and you can run into difficulties. The rewards, however, will be significant. The next chapter highlights some of the more common issues people encounter and provides guidance.

▶ **"Using a rule engine will kill performance."**

That's a myth. The overhead introduced by the rule engine itself is tiny (often only submillisecond latency). The engine can be memory-intensive, but only when necessary. Thanks to some clever optimizations, the BRE often proves more efficient than custom code. Don't forget, though, that performance is not just about the engine and will be influenced by any custom code, database lookups, and so on that your rules execute.

Processes and Policies

Most BizTalk developers spend a lot of time designing and implementing automated business processes using BizTalk Server's orchestration capability. BizTalk Server activates orchestration instances in response to the arrival of messages in the Message Box. An orchestration instance may create and submit new messages and receive additional correlated messages. As it proceeds, the orchestration follows well-defined paths defined by decision points, loops, parallel branches, and event listeners. The process may define "unhappy" paths dedicated to handling various exceptions.

Looking at orchestrations from the outside, they are event-driven and reactive. Looking at them from the inside, they are procedural and imperative. This strange contrast illuminates the true nature of automated business processes. They represent planned, codified, and repeatable responses to external, often nondeterministic, events. Each orchestration is actually a reactive rule, something like "if Message A is received, then do X followed by Y followed by Z." A complex orchestration may require further rules to manage state transitions, select between different pathways, and react appropriately to correlated events.

Business Policies

Developers use orchestrations to define business processes. There is surprisingly little difference between a process and a policy. A business policy also represents a codified plan of action that governs what to do when specific circumstances arise. Organizations dictate policies according to specific business goals and align them with defined business requirements. Policies combine sets of rules that collectively drive behavior and decision making.

Any significant difference between a process and a policy is chiefly in terms of emphasis and intent, rather than mechanics. An automated process describes the overall shape and structure of some logical and repeatable sequence of steps. It specifies a natural progression of state transitions that results from specific activities. It codifies the different branches that arise at decision points within a process. Policies operate at a higher level. They describe how decision making governs which branches are followed, which values are used as parameters, how different subsystems interact dynamically, how validity is determined, and so forth. Policies codify how organizations apply decision making and governance to process instances.

Some policies may be formulated without reference to specific processes. A single policy may apply across the whole organization and may affect several different processes. The explicit identification, expression, and management of discrete policy rules provide a powerful mechanism for ensuring consistency across different business activities. For example, a technical policy that specifies a uniform approach to error logging can prove invaluable in ensuring that many different systems can be monitored and managed in a coherent, effective, and centralized manner. A business policy that specifies clear responsibilities for certain types of decision making can be applied across system and organizational boundaries to ensure consistent management of complementary business activities.

Wherever we look, we see the same pattern of repeatable sequences of activities governed by higher-level decision making and direction. Cars need drivers, disks have controllers, projects require managers, and companies are led by directors. Policies are fundamental to processes. They support decision making and governance. They allow change to be managed effectively and efficiently. They enable agility and support continuous cycles of process improvement.

10

Policy Externalization

There are many different ways to combine policies and processes. It is often acceptable to couple them tightly. The expressions in an orchestration decision shape might state that "if the employee is male, follow path A, else if female, follow path B." Such simple policies may never change and can be hard-wired directly to the process. In other circumstances, we might parameterize a tightly coupled policy expression and perform a runtime lookup to get values from a configuration file or database. This is familiar territory to most developers. This externalization of parameter values allows us to alter decision making without changing the process flow.

Some policies involve more than expressions. They implement actions, as well. Consider a simple policy that states that a system must record all errors in the Windows event log. Later, the organization revises this policy. The system must now log certain business exceptions to a database. If we tightly coupled the error logging code to the process implementation, we are forced to reengineer and redeploy the process when the policy changes. This could be a slow, disruptive, and costly exercise.

To avoid this, BizTalk developers often use logging frameworks such as Microsoft Enterprise Library or log4net. These tools separate the logging code from the process and describe policy through configuration. They support inversion-of-control patterns. Code on which logging depends is injected dynamically according to policy rules. BizTalk developers often use this approach for policies that control logging, tracking, notification, and other aspects. Dependency injection decouples both policy and aspects from the process.

Policy externalization plays a central role in decoupling the various parts of an application. However, there are other motivations for externalization. Consider some common characteristics of policies:

▶ **Policies are more granular than processes:** A process describes an entire sequence of activities as a whole. Organizations often describe policies as collections of discrete rules.

▶ **Policies often change at a faster rate than process definitions:** This is why policy externalization is such a powerful way of decoupling the various parts of an application.

▶ **Policies reflect ongoing changes to decision making:** Because businesses often change rapidly, we need mechanisms that enable us to trace directly between executable rules and business policies, and to manage change effectively through versioning and deployment.

As well as decoupling, policy externalization allows us to tackle other requirements such as storage, management, analysis, improvement, versioning, archiving, and deployment of policies. In some scenarios, the only driver for externalization is decoupling. However, as a general rule, the more closely aligned our executable rules are to corporate or departmental decision making, the greater need to manage and control our policy definitions separately to our process definitions.

It is here that rule engines come to the foreground. The engine, however, is often the least significant consideration. Although rule engines may implement clever mechanisms for reasoning and inference, architects and developers sometimes overestimate the centrality of these capabilities. In many business scenarios, the most important consideration is the management of straightforward rules through external repositories and tooling, and the deployment of those rules dynamically across distributed environments.

We need more than a rule engine. We need an entire rule-processing framework designed to externalize, store, manage, deploy, and execute policies within the production environment. We also need tooling that allows us to define, modify, analyze, implement, test, and troubleshoot executable policy rules.

Policy Scenarios

Rule-based policy has many potential applications in process automation and message brokerage. Here are a few of the most common ones:

Data Manipulation

- **Filtering:** We may use rules to filter messages and data.

- **Validation:** We may use rules to validate message content and other data.

- **Derivation and enrichment:** We may use rules to derive new data from existing data and to enrich messages.

- **Transformation:** We may use rules to drive dynamic transformation of message content.

Message and Process Flow

- **Routing:** We may use rules to control dynamic routing of messages. For example, BizTalk Server's in-built subscription mechanism is rules-based.

- **Process flow:** We may evaluate rules within an orchestration or workflow to control decision points in the process flow. For example, we may select which branch of a decision point to execute, or dynamically select which child process to invoke.

- **Versioning:** We may use rules to select which specific version of a process or workflow to invoke within a long-lived business activity.

Tracking and Notification

- **Logging:** We may use rules to control logging of errors, exceptions, and states.

- **Tracking:** We may use rules to track activities and maintain audit trails.

- **Notification:** We may use rules to control notification messages sent to administrators, business users, or services.

Workflow

- **Task issuance:** We may use rules to control the creation and dispatch of a new task within a human workflow.

▶ **Step management:** We may use rules to provide step management of activities within a workflow.

Rules processing frameworks are just one way to handle these concerns. Developers may instead use frameworks, *business activity monitoring* (BAM), workflow tools, and so on. Rules occur everywhere in modern enterprise-level computing. They take many different forms and are handled by many different technologies. Developers have a wide choice of technologies at their disposal. In any given scenario, they should aim to make good implementation decisions based on a detailed understanding of requirements and candidate technologies.

Business Versus Executable Rules

A major motivation for using rule-processing technology is to handle *business rules*. However, architects and developers should treat the term with care. The scope of these tools extends beyond business rules to encompass a wider range of processing concerns. Rule engines provide technical runtime technologies designed to handle executable rules. Not all executable rules represent business rules. Consider the following:

▶ Different people within an organization own business and executable rules. A business rule is a statement that defines or constrains some aspect of the business. Each business rule is owned and maintained by the business, and is not, itself, a technical or IT-related artifact. Executable rules are technical artifacts owned by IT rather than the business, and are not, therefore, business rules. Confusion arises because executable rules often map directly to business rules. They become synonyms of corresponding business rules.

▶ Not all business rules are encoded directly as executable rules. Business rules are expressed in many ways at different levels of the organization. They govern different activities within an organization and do not apply solely to IT systems. A high-level policy may directly or indirectly affect many different processes and activities in different ways.

▶ Not all executable rules directly encode business rules. Developers address many technical issues when implementing systems. As well as business requirements, they must implement technical policy and decision making which are of no relevance or interest at the business level. Executable rules represent a technical elaboration of higher-level business rules. They address the specific needs of a given application.

Business users are rarely permitted to change executable rules freely in production environments. Organizations must test and validate their executable rules carefully before releasing them into production. In some scenarios it may be useful to allow business users to change certain parameters directly. For example, a rule may use some threshold value that changes from time to time. This value could be stored in a database and changed directly by a business user via some *user interface* (UI). Each time the rule is evaluated, it can retrieve and use the current threshold value. Another strategy is to provide business users with a UI for construction of business rules from predefined templates. If the templates are carefully constrained, it might be possible to automate the conversion of business rule definitions directly into executable rule sets without further development effort. The organization may still need to test and validate these rule sets before deployment.

Business Rule Management

Having carefully distinguished between business and executable rules, we will now consider *business rule management* (BRM). It its widest sense, this term refers to the full business rules lifecycle, from their initial identification through to their eventual retirement. Figure 10.1 illustrates this lifecycle.

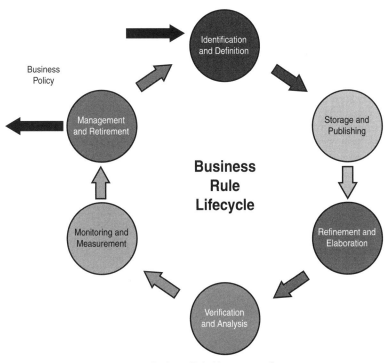

FIGURE 10.1   The business rule lifecycle.

Identification and Definition

Business analysts identify rules by interviewing users and managers, analyzing policy documents, inspecting existing processes, and so on. Business rules should be expressed formally and precisely using terms recognized by business users. This is often achieved through the use of natural language statements and defined vocabularies of business terms. These may be created in an ad hoc fashion by business analysts and captured in documents. Some organizations invest is specialized tools to define business rules in a more consistent fashion. The Object Management Group's (OMG) *Semantics of Business Vocabulary and Business Rules* (SBVR) specifies a formal standard for natural language modeling of business rules. SBVR is supported by several rule documentation tools and used to exchange business rules between different systems and repositories.

Storage and Publishing

Rule and vocabulary definitions are generally captured and stored so that they can be versioned and managed across their entire lifecycle. Versioned rule sets are published when deemed complete and correct. Organizations may store rule definition documents on a file system or document management system. They may invest in specialized business rule repositories and tooling. A business rule store constitutes a knowledgebase that plays a part in the wider knowledge management within the organization.

Refinement and Elaboration

Business rules encode aspects of knowledge within an organization. Knowledge continuously grows and changes. It undergoes refinement and elaboration. Business rule management supports iterative approaches to decomposition, extension and enhancement of existing rules and allows new rules to be added to the overall corpus. This capability plays an important role in enabling continuous cycles of process improvement.

Verification and Analysis

As a knowledgebase grows in size, it becomes harder to ensure that all the business rules and terms it contains exhibit consistency and accuracy. As business environments change over time, the knowledgebase may not be kept fully up-to-date. Refinement of existing rules and introduction of new rules can lead to inconsistencies and contradictions. Business terms may have different semantics depending on context. Various forms of redundancy may arise, including rule subsumption, in which the consequence of one rule is always implied by another rule. Business rule management involves ongoing analysis and verification of rules to detect and eliminate inconsistencies and redundancies.

Monitoring and Measurement

Policies reflect business strategy. They are applied to relevant business processes and activities. Organizations gather metrics and management information from these processes and activities to measure the effectiveness of their policies. This information drives change and refinement of business policy over time to meet goals and respond to changing circumstances.

Management and Retirement

The introduction of new and amended policies over time can lead to several problems. Long-lived business activities may need access to policies as they were at the time the activity started, rather than more recent changes. It is often necessary to retain a record of past policy to support auditing, historical analysis, and justification of past decisions. Organizations may implement retention policies to manage the retirement of old policies.

Some organizations make significant investment is tools and technologies to manage their business rules. They use commercial *business rule management systems* (BRMSs). Typically, a BRMS provides business rule repositories, rule authoring, verification, versioning, and many other features. These organizations implement processes around their BRMS to maintain sophisticated centralized knowledge bases. However, it is still common for organizations to adopt a more ad hoc, less-formal approach in which business rules are identified on a per-application or per-process basis as part of requirements gathering and managed through business documents.

BRMS and the BRF

The distinction between business rules and executable rules leads naturally to questions about the role and nature of the BRF. As you will see, the framework is designed to manage deployment and delivery of policies into runtime environments, and to execute rule sets within the context of automated business processes and activities. How does this framework relate to business rule management?

As well as the application of business policy, the BRF is often used to handle technical policies that are not of immediate relevance or interest at the business level. Even so, technical policies indirectly reflect aspects of business policy. For example, a technical routing policy reflects business decisions taken at the enterprise architecture level (for example, IT investments in given systems and platforms) and trading partnerships and other commercial and organizational relationships. Retry and exception-handling policies reflect service level agreements (SLAs) and quality requirements defined by the business.

From this perspective, executable rules can be understood as a technical elaboration and refinement of business policy, as illustrated in Figure 10.2. They define the way in which business rules are applied to business processes at runtime. They combine aspects of business policy with technical policy. They ensure alignment of applications to business goals and strategies. A deep correspondence exists, therefore, between business policy and executable rules. Sometimes this is reflected in direct equivalence. In other cases, the correspondence is indirect and less obvious.

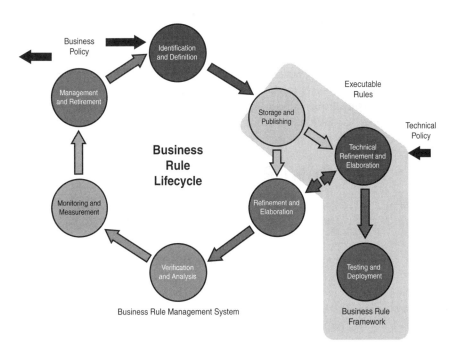

FIGURE 10.2   Executable rules and the business rule lifecycle.

Executable rules elaborate business policies in two ways. First, they specify how business policy is applied to runtime representations of business and application data and map business terms onto data models. Data representation is a technical matter, and business rules should be cleanly separated from such runtime concerns. A rule definition is independent of how data is represented in a given system. Second, executable rules specify how business policy is applied within composite applications. They bind business terms, conditional predicates, and actions to specific runtime functions and service calls. Executable rules are applied directly at the programmatic level.

Technical elaboration of business rules involves the extension of rule definitions and policies to include many different technical and programmatic concerns. This level of technical information distinguishes them from the business rules and policies on which they are based. This implies that executable rules should be cleanly separated from business rule definitions. They require parallel management to business rules and exhibit a coincident lifecycle. However, there needs to be a degree of indirection between business and executable rules.

The Microsoft BRF addresses the lifecycle management and application of executable rules. It provides mechanisms that allow BRMSs to be integrated with executable rule stores and runtime environments. However, Microsoft does not provide higher-level BRMS functionality with BizTalk Server. Several third-party vendors supply BRMS technologies and products together with integrated runtime engines. Some offer direct integration with BizTalk Server. Although vendors have generally chosen not to exploit Microsoft's BRF, it is exploited by the development and runtime tools supplied by Microsoft and is available to developers to enable custom integration with existing business policy stores and tools.

Rule developers often need to ensure good traceability between executable rules and higher-level business policies. Although this is a common feature of BRMS products, it is not directly supported through BizTalk Server tools. One aspect of customization may be to provide direct traceability from executable rules to business rule definitions in external documents or repositories. The simplest approach is to maintain documents that specify how business rules map to executable rules. More sophisticated approaches can be implemented if required.

Example Scenario: Order Processing

To illustrate the difference between business rules and executable rules, we consider a simple scenario in which a rule developer elaborates a simple business policy to create an executable rule set.

As part of its Order Processing policy, the business specifies the following rule:

```
When the total value of the order is greater than or equal to $1,000, the
organization performs straight-through processing of the Order if the customer's
credit score is greater than 730.
```

Admittedly, this rule is rather contrived for the purposes of illustration. In reality, the business policy would probably take into account several additional factors such as payment method, purchase history, and so on.

A developer analyses this single business rule and implements the following executable rule set. Listing 10.1 expresses the rules in pseudo code similar to rule representation in Microsoft's Business Rule Composer.

LISTING 10.1   Order-Processing Rule Set

```
// [1] Apply STP to all orders < $1K
If
  Order.OrderTotal is less than 1000
Then
  Order.UseSTP = true
  retract Order


// [2] Get current credit score for orders >= $1K
If
  Order.OrderTotal is greater than or equal to 1000
Then
  assert new CreditScore(Order.CustomerID)


// [3] Decide if STP can be applied to orders >= $1K
If
  And
    Order.OrderTotal is greater than or equal to 1000
    CreditScore.CustomerID is equal to Order.CustomerID
    CreditScore.Value is greater than or equal to 730
Then
  Order.UseSTP = true
  retract Order


// [4] Maintain audit trail for non-STP orders
[Priority(-10)]
If
  Not
     Order.UseSTP
Then
  AuditHelper.LogOrderRejectionToAuditDB(Order, "No STP. Credit score too low")
  retract Order
```

Incomplete and Implicit Business Rules

The preceding example illustrates that business rules are often specified in an incomplete form. In this example, the developer checks with a business analyst to confirm that the current credit rating must always be obtained dynamically for customers who place orders greater than $1,000. The business analyst states that it is not acceptable to use a cached record of a credit rating that may be out of date, and the developer explains that this implies additional logic. The business analyst now has a choice. He may decide to refine the single business rule so that it explicitly states that the current credit rating must be used, or he might create an additional business rule that states the following:

```
The organization always uses the customer's current credit score to decide if
straight-through processing can be used for orders with a total value greater than
$1,000.
```

The second approach is better. It represents a decomposition of the stated business policy to provide an additional atomic business rule that was not previously identified.

The rule developer checks with the business analyst to confirm that a further business rule is implied. This is stated as follows:

```
The organization always performs straight-through order processing when the total
value of the order is less than the current STP threshold.
```

The analyst confirms that this is the case and documents this additional rule for the sake of completeness and to avoid ambiguity.

Each additional business rule directly corresponds to an executable rule created by the developer. Because the developer elaborates and refines the original business rule, his feedback is invaluable in improving the higher-level definition of business policy. The knowledgebase maintained by the business analyst now provides a robust description of the current business policy for *straight-through processing* (STP).

Business policy statements often lack atomicity and should be decomposed as far as possible. Here is a single statement that decomposes into the three rules stated previously:

```
The organization always uses straight-through order processing unless the total
value of the order is greater than or equal to $1,000 and the customer's current
credit score is less than 730.
```

Indirect Policy Mapping

In addition to the two additional rules, the developer introduces a further rule to handle logging of order rejections to an audit database. This requirement was not identified as an explicit business rule in the order-processing policy. Instead, the developer notices that the nonfunctional application requirements state the following:

```
An auditable record will be maintained for every interaction or event in which
customer expectations are not met.
```

This additional rule reflects a general business requirement for the application and may affect several different business policies.

Technical Policy

The developer discusses the implementation of the rule set with the solution architect. The architect informs the developer that all auditing will be supported through a central audit database. This is not a business requirement, but a technical policy defined by the architect. Working in conjunction with a *database administrator* (DBA), the developer creates data access code to record auditable events to the audit database. `Rule [4]` directly invokes this code to implement the technical policy.

Data Models

The executable rule set applies rules to a data model. This model may already be defined as a database schema, *XML Schema* (XSD) file, or object model. Very often, however, the developer iteratively designs and implements the data model alongside rule definition. In this scenario, the rules are applied to data that represents `Order` and `CreditScore` entities. For simplicity, the example rule set uses dot syntax (for example, `Order.CustomerID`).

Programmatic Bindings

The developer binds an assignment action in `Rule [2]` to a constructor on the `CreditScore` class. The constructor ensures that the current credit score is obtained. In addition, he invokes a logging method on a helper object in `Rule [4]` to implement the technical auditing policy described earlier. The developer uses predefined `assert` and `retract` engine operations in each of the rules. The `retract` operation remove order data from the working memory of the rule engine.

Priority

The developer needs to ensure that rules are "fired" in the correct order. Specifically, the rule engine must detect and retract all STP orders from memory before instances of `Rule [4]` are fired. This is a purely technical concern that does not concern business users. It does not reflect any business or technical policy.

Traceability

The developer names each rule. Names are shown as comments in the example. To improve traceability, the rules developer may refine these names to provide references to documented business rules. Alternatively, the developer may deliver a document that specifies how business rules map to executable rules. In more advanced scenarios, the developer may update a database to record these mappings.

10

Refactoring

The developer considers a further aspect of the executable rule set. The technical auditing policy exhibited in `Rule [4]` (that is, logging to a common audit database) depends on a specific implementation of custom code and is not explicitly controlled by the rule. The developer decides to change the implementation. The rule is changed to invoke a general-purpose `Log()` method that internally calls into the Microsoft Enterprise Library to log to the audit database. This a much better design. The technical policy is now implemented using Enterprise Library configuration and is decoupled from the rule set whose primary purpose is to implement business policy. It also brings the rule set in-line with the approach taken in the rest of the application, which uses Enterprise Library extensively to manage various logging requirements.

Testing, Publishing, and Deployment

The developer saves the completed rule set to the SQL Server rule store and then performs unit testing using the supplied tooling. This involves asserting order and credit score data to the engine. Depending on how this data is represented, the developer may need to configure the test tools to obtain data from a database, an XML file, or via a Fact Creator helper object. Test tools and Fact Creators are described later in this chapter.

When unit testing is complete, the developer decides to test the rule set in the context of a BizTalk Server orchestration. The built-in support for invoking rule sets in orchestrations works only with published (and deployed) rule sets. The developer knows that published rule sets are immutable and is concerned that formal testing may highlight issues that require further changes. Hence, he renames the existing rule set to indicate that it is for development only. He then creates a copy of the rule set. He marks the copy as published and then deploys it so that it is available to BizTalk Server in the development environment.

Testing reveals that the rule set contains a bug. On occasion, a customer with a low credit rating places a high-value order that is incorrectly accepted for STP. The developer inspects the rule set and realizes that he has failed to retract old credit scores from the engine. The problem occurs because the Call Rules orchestration shape results in engine instances being cached for reuse in future orchestration invocations. Although the rule logic is correct for the first invocation, subsequent invocations evaluate rules over both current and historic credit scores. Objects such as credit scores are termed 'facts'. In the next chapter, you will see that developers must give careful attention to releasing facts from the engine's working memory.

To release credit score facts, the developer introduces an additional low-priority rule, as shown in Listing 10.2.

LISTING 10.2   Additional Rule

```
// [5] Clear the memory and agenda and end processing
[Priority(-20)]
If
```

```
  CreditScore is not equal to <null>
Then
  clear
```

When the developer is satisfied that the rule set is performing correctly, he uses a wizard to export the rule set version to an XML file. He hands this off to the test team. The tester uses the same wizard to import the rule set into the test environment, where it is automatically marked as published. The tester runs the wizard again to mark the rule set as deployed. Within a minute or so, the rule set is automatically picked up by each BizTalk Server box in the test environment. The tester is now ready to perform end-to-end testing of the BizTalk Server solution to ensure that the rule set provides the correct results.

If testing is successful, the rule set can be imported into the production environment and deployed to the BizTalk Server boxes. The BRF supports dynamic deployment of versioned rule sets without requiring BizTalk Server solutions to be restarted. Applications generally pick up the latest version of the rule set automatically. As in the test environment, it generally takes up to a minute for a new version of a rule set to be applied to each BizTalk Server box. We discuss deployment in greater detail later in this chapter.

Managing Change

At a future date, the business analyst informs the developer of a change to the order policy. Because of adverse economic conditions, several customers default on payment. The credit score of 730, which is approximately median, is judged to be too low. Having carefully analyzed historical data, it has been decided to retire an existing business rule and replace it with two new rules as follows:

```
When the total value of the order is greater than or equal to $2,000, the
organization only performs straight-through processing if the customer's credit
score is greater than 770.
When the total value of the order is between $1,000 and $1,999.99 (inclusive), the
organization only performs straight-through processing if the customer's credit
score is greater than 750.
```

The developer analyses these two rules and determines that the change can be directly reflected in the executable rule set by retiring Rule [3] and introducing two new rules. To do this, the developer makes the changes to his development version of the rule set and performs unit testing. He then copies the amended rule set as a new version, which he publishes and deploys to BizTalk Server in the development environment. He performs further testing, and when satisfied he exports and hands off the new version to the test team. It tests the new version and exports the rule set to the production environment. The new version is deployed and the amended policy is applied dynamically to the live BizTalk Server application.

10

Real-World Rule-Processing

It is a mistake to consider the BRF as a one-size-fits-all solution to policy application. For example, technical aspects of auditing and logging policy are generally better handled through a framework designed specifically to handle logging.

The policy adjustment described in the scenario required a restructuring of conditional logic. This is easily handled using versioned rule sets. However, many policies only ever vary parameterized values. In this case, it might be more appropriate to manage policy application through a configuration store, rather than through the rule engine.

An organization might have existing investments in rule-processing systems and conditional logic. For example, an application may integrate with an existing mainframe application that applies complex conditional logic to data. It is often necessary to integrate new applications with existing rule-based processing. This can be done in a variety of ways using BizTalk Server's integration capabilities. The BRF provides one possible approach, and may be useful in situations where new rule-processing capabilities must be introduced over existing functionality.

Executable rule sets are the primary unit of execution in the BRF. They represent custom code written in a domain-specific language. Writing custom conditional logic in a rules language can have advantages over using general programming languages such as C# or VB.NET:

- **Rule languages are specialized for policy representation:**They allow custom logic to be constructed in a highly correspondent format to the atomic rules contained in business or technical policy documents. This aids traceability and alignment of applications to business goals and strategies.

- **Rule languages are dynamic:**They are deployed as XML documents, converted to a runtime representation at the point of use and executed within a specialized runtime container (the rule engine). Versioned rule sets can therefore be deployed into production environments without requiring application restarts.

- **Rules can invoke custom code written in general-purpose languages:**This introduces dependencies on .NET assemblies that can compromise the dynamic nature of rules. If a change to a rule set requires a corresponding change in custom C# or VB.NET code, it will be necessary to deploy the new assemblies and restart BizTalk Server application in the production environment when the new rule set version is deployed.

- **Rule sets can be stored and managed through centralized repositories:**This aids clean separation of concerns. Policies are externalized and managed orthogonally to processes.

Executable rule sets and rule engines provide a powerful example of dependency injection and *inversion-of-control* (IoC). Indeed, the BRF can be thought of as an extended IoC technology for managing policy application in enterprise solutions. Other IoC frameworks exist and may be considered as alternatives in some scenarios. However, they do not generally provide equivalent tooling and repository support and normally use configuration and parameterization rather than the expression of conditional logic through domain-specific rule languages.

Using Vocabularies

Although Microsoft's rule language is domain-specific, it is not specific to any one business domain. In the rule set example provided earlier in this chapter, we used programmatic dot syntax to represent data entities and attributes and also method calls on helper objects. To convert the representation of rules to a form that is business domain specific, we need to replace these identifiers with synonyms that directly represent business terms and statements.

The BRF supports the optional use of custom vocabularies. A vocabulary is a dictionary of business-specific terms and statements and corresponding binding definitions to data models and programmatic functionality. Custom vocabularies provide a mechanism that allows rule developers to create business domain-specific rule languages. This is commonly used to provide near-natural language representations of executable rules. Using a vocabulary, the example rule set might be represented as shown in Listing 10.3.

LISTING 10.3   Order-processing Rule Set with Vocabulary

```
// [1] Apply STP to all orders < $1K
If
  the total value of the order is less than 1000
Then
  set the order to use straight-through processing = true
  retract the order


// [2] Get current credit score for orders >= $1K
If
  And
    the total value of the order is greater than or equal to 1000
Then
  assert the current credit score for the ordering customer


// [3] Decide if STP can be applied to orders >= $1K
If
  And
    the total value of the order is greater than or equal to 1000
    the credit-scored customer is equal to the ordering customer
    the credit score value is greater than or equal to 730
Then
  set the order to use straight-through processing = true
  retract the order
```

```
// [4] Maintain audit trail for non-STP orders
[Priority(-10)]
If
  Not
     the order will use straight-through processing
Then
  log the STP rejection to the audit database for the order
  retract the order

// [5] Clear the memory and agenda and end processing
[Priority(-20)]
If
  the credit score is not equal to <null>
Then
 clear
```

This is much closer to the representation of the underlying business rules. Vocabularies aid traceability and comprehension. However, they should be used with care. They add complexity to rule development and are difficult to evolve in conjunction with rule sets. Often, they add little value to the rule development process. Indeed, they serve to hide the underlying technical details of data and method binding from the developer. They can be very useful when rules will be maintained and changed by nondevelopers. For example, dynamic routing policies may be managed by system administrators who need to change endpoint specifications and message type identifiers from time to time. A custom vocabulary can help to make the routing rules far easier to understand for people who are not acquainted with the details of the underlying data and programmatic models. Vocabulary development is discussed in greater detail later in this chapter.

What About Performance?

One of the most common objections to rule-processing technologies concerns performance. It is often assumed that rule engines introduce unwelcome overhead and latency into performance-critical applications. At first sight, this assumption appears reasonable. Most developers know that generic systems are rarely as performant as custom-built code.

In reality, the issue of performance is more complex. It is certainly true that the rule engine introduces additional latencies due to the use of internal bindings to data and programmatic types. However, this is not necessarily a significant factor in assessing the suitability of the rule engine. There are two reasons for this:

▶ BizTalk Server applications typically exploit the rule engine within the context of an orchestration. Orchestrations are normally invoked asynchronously using BizTalk Server's pub-sub mechanism and Message Box. The latencies introduced by asynchronous queue-based message routing vastly exceed any overhead introduced by the rule engine. When optimizing a BizTalk Server application, rule engine latency is generally a low-priority issue. Using custom code instead of the rule engine does not normally make any significant difference to overall performance of an automated business process.

▶ Even in the rare case where rule-processing overhead is deemed significant, it is not necessarily true that custom code provides better performance. The opposite is often true. The rule engine exploits an approach that rigorously eliminates various types of runtime redundancy. Wherever the same condition appears in multiple rules, the engine ensures that this evaluation is performed just once for each relevant data item. When a rule changes state, the engine performs the minimum possible work by reevaluating change deltas only. It does not perform redundant reevaluation of all state. In addition, the engine uses data indexing, caching and other optimizations to minimize overhead.

The rule engine exhibits a degree of optimization that may not be emulated in custom code. For small, simple rule sets, it might be feasible to implement custom code that provides better performance. However, this is unlikely to yield any significant improvement to the performance of the business process as a whole. Hence, the decision to use a rule engine can generally be made on the basis of its utility, rather than performance.

Rule engines are sometimes rejected on the basis of being memory intensive. It is true that they can store significant amounts of in-memory state at runtime. This is done to enable joins between different data types. For example, Rules [2] and [3] both contain an identical condition that finds matching orders and credit scores based on a common customer ID. The engine optimizes this by performing joins just once for both rules but must materialize views of order and credit score data internally to allow those joins to be performed. A custom code approach over the same data model would likely store a similar amount of data for the same purpose. There is some truth in the assertion that rule engines tend to maximize in-memory data storage. However, this represents a simple trade-off between data storage and redundancy elimination. This is often the most effective trade-off, but might sometimes be undesirable, especially when processing large data sets with rules that perform a large number of different joins.

Inference and Reasoning

Inference refers to the capability of rule engines to derive new data (conclusions) by reasoning over existing data. A simple example is shown in Rule [1]. We can say that the value of the UseSTP flag is inferred from the evaluation of the total value of the order. If the total value is less than $1,000, we infer that the STP should be used.

Like similar rule engines, Microsoft's engine can undertake more sophisticated forms of reasoning. This capability sometimes leads to the suggestion that rule engines are too complex for simple rule requirements. Machine reasoning is linked to approaches that emerged from the world of artificial intelligence, and this is sometimes seen as a reason to discount rule engines.

In reality, although reasoning requirements can sometimes prove quite complex, the mechanisms provided by the rule engines are straightforward and often apply to simple

10

scenarios. Like many similar engines, Microsoft's rule engine implements a forward-chaining mechanism. Forward-chaining is a reasoning approach in which the engine draws intermediate conclusions that it then evaluates to find further conclusions. A forward-chaining engine continues this cycle until it cannot reason any further.

The example rule set used in this chapter provides a good example of reasoning based on forward-chaining. It starts by finding as many rule matches as it can. This includes matches for orders that need to be evaluated using current credit scores (Rule [2]) and orders under $1,000, which can undergo STP without further evaluation (Rule [1]). It also finds a preliminary set of orders whose UseSTP flag is false (Rule [4]).

To begin with, there are no matches for Rules [3] or [5]. No CreditScore facts have yet been asserted. Activations of Rules [1] and [2] begin to fire. Because they have the same priority (that is, 0), they fire in an arbitrary order. Rule [4] has a lower priority. No activations of Rule [4] fires until all instances of Rules [1] and [2] have fired.

Each time an activation of Rule [2] fires, it asserts a CreditScore fact. If the credit score value is greater than 730, a match for Rule [3] is found. Like Rules [1] and [2], Rule [3] has a priority of 0, and the engine now fires instances of all three rules in an arbitrary order. Each time an activation of Rule [1] or [3] fires, a flag is set on the order to indicate STP is allowed, and the Order fact is then retracted from the working memory of the engine. This results in a decrease in the number of activations of Rule [4].

Eventually, there are no further activations of Rules [1], [2], or [3]. At this stage, the only activations of Rule [4] remaining are those for orders with a total value over $1,000 where the credit score is too low for STP. There are also activations of Rule [5] for each CreditScore fact. Rule [4] has a higher priority than Rule [5], so its activations start to fire. The rule actions insert a record into the audit database and then retract the order.

Finally, the engine only has activations for Rule [5]. These activations begin to fire. However, the first activation to fire results in the clear engine operation being invoked. This clears the working memory of all remaining CreditScore facts, and hence all the remaining activations of Rule [5] are removed. The engine has now fully completed its work and processing stops. There are no more rule matches.

Rule [5] represents a degree of redundancy because it matches every CreditScore but only needs to fire once. The developer could consider changing the implementation so that Rule [5] matches a single instance of some "dummy" fact rather than each of the CreditScore facts. This is slightly more optimal.

It takes a little time to understand and become comfortable with forward-chaining mechanisms and reasoning cycles. This is partly because the rules are declarative, rather than procedural, and partly because the rule engine reasons over entire sets of data in a very cyclic fashion. If you find the preceding description confusing, be assured that a little effort in understanding the behavior of the engine will lead to significant rewards. Even in the simple scenario discussed in this chapter, the engine reasons over data using forward-chaining. This is not because the engine is unnecessarily complex but rather because forward-chaining is widely employed in human reasoning and is often implied in the way business rules and other types of policy are expressed. We explore the forward-chaining mechanism in more depth in the next chapter.

> **NOTE**
>
> At this point, you might prefer to skip forward to the "Components and Tools" section halfway through this chapter. It explains how to start working with the toolset to define rules. The following sections discuss the BRF as a whole and provide context for all that follows. However, they were also written for reference purposes. You might want to revisit the topic later, after you have learned more about rule composition.

The Business Rules Framework

Microsoft's rule-processing tools are built on the common foundation of the Business Rules Framework. The BRF provides class libraries, interface definitions for pluggable components, and a Windows service that manages deployment of rule set definitions to local boxes. A solid understanding of the framework helps developers to exploit the rule-processing technology effectively and understand how the various parts work together.

Introducing the BRF

The BRF provides a foundational technology for rule processing. It is a supported technology that ships with BizTalk Server 2010 together with various tools and components and a SQL Server rule store database. The BizTalk Server Installation Wizard supports optional standalone installation of the business rules components or installation alongside BizTalk Server. This is illustrated in Figure 10.3. The business rules components are listed as "additional software" in Microsoft's Product User Rights (PUR) document and can be installed and run on as many virtual or physical environments and devices as you want provided they are only used in conjunction with licensed nondevelopment editions of BizTalk Server software. Microsoft's FAQs for BizTalk Server licensing specifically lists one exception to this. The rule engine must run on a correctly licensed BizTalk Server box. Even though it is included in the installation of the business rules components, it cannot be exploited on unlicensed machines in production environments.

The BRF covers four distinct areas:

▶ **Rule storage and administration:** The framework provides interfaces and base classes for rule storage, deployment, and retrieval. These are used by rule composition and deployment tools and within other parts of the framework.

▶ **Rule deployment:** The framework implements a Windows service to manage rule deployment across a distributed environment. Each local instance of the service retrieves rule set definitions from a remote rule store and caches them for local use. The framework defines an interface for *publish and subscribe* (pub-sub) components used by the service.

10

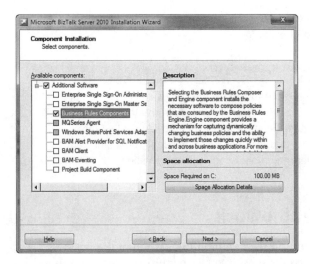

FIGURE 10.3   Standalone installation of business rule components.

▶ **Rule modeling:**The framework provides a class library for modeling rule sets and vocabularies. This allows programmatic definition and manipulation of rules.

▶ **Rule execution:**The framework provides interfaces and classes for rule engine components. These define pluggable components for rule set translation, fact retrieval, execution, and tracking.

Rule Storage and Administration

The framework defines interfaces and base classes for rule store interaction. Two component types are defined: rule store components and rule set deployment driver components.

Rule Store Components

Rule store components provide design-time data access to database repositories, file stores, runtime resources, or any other source of rule definitions. They are used by development and testing tools to save, publish, load, and delete rule sets and vocabularies. They provide dependency analysis between rule sets and vocabularies. For rule stores that support secure access, they are also used to manage authorization settings on individual rule sets.

Rule Set Deployment Driver Components

Rule set deployment driver components support deployment/undeployment of rule sets within live environments. They enable retrieval of deployed and undeployed rule sets together with histories of recent status changes. They support the transfer of rule sets and vocabularies between different environments via file exports and imports. They also handle management of centralized tracking configuration.

Figure 10.4 illustrates the use of rule store and rule set deployment driver components.

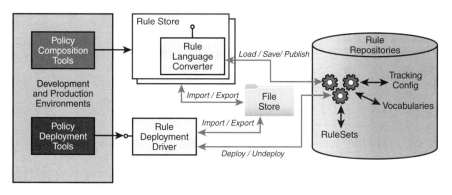

FIGURE 10.4   Rule storage and administration components.

Rule store components are derived from the `RuleStore` base class. They use rule language converter components to convert between store-specific and framework-specific representations of rule sets and vocabularies. The framework provides `RuleSet` and `Vocabulary` classes for this representation. These top-level objects manage collections of rule and vocabulary definitions defined as object graphs.

Rule language converter components implement the `IRuleLanguageConverter` interface. Rule set deployment drivers implement the `IRuleSetDeploymentDriver` interface.

Storage and deployment components define states for rule sets and vocabularies. These states have the following semantics:

▶ **Saved:**Indicates that rule sets and vocabularies are not complete or ready for use. They are mutable and can be changed as required. This state is used during development.

▶ **Published:**Marks a rule set or vocabulary as complete and ready for use within live environments. Published rule sets and vocabularies should be treated as immutable. Tools should not allow them to be changed; although they can be deleted.

▶ **Deployed:**Used for rule sets only. Vocabularies are not deployed. A deployed rule set is a published rule set marked as available to run in live environments. Deployed rule sets can be undeployed and redeployed at a later time. Rule stores may raise deployment events to notify remote agents of deployment status changes.

Rule Deployment

The *Rule Engine Update* (REU) service is a Windows service that runs locally on each BizTalk Server. It acts as a local source of deployed rule sets stored centrally in a rule store or repository. It manages a local cache of rule set information and subscribes to deployment events raised by the repository. Figure 10.5 illustrates the architecture of the REU service and associated components.

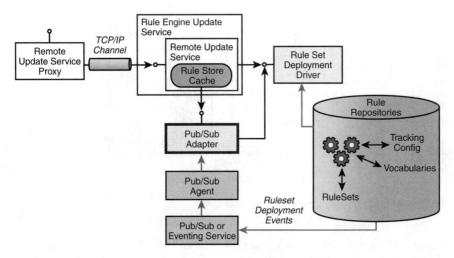

FIGURE 10.5   Rule deployment components.

The REU service hosts a singleton service called the *Remote Update* (RU) service. The RU service listens for local requests on a TCP/IP port. It refuses any remote requests and responds only to service consumers running on the same box. The RU service manages the cache of rule set information obtained from a remote rule store.

The RU service implements the IRuleEngineUpdateServiceInterface interface. It provides functionality for registering and unregistering remoted objects used to call back to clients when rule sets or authorization settings are updated. Clients can check whether rule sets are currently available and if authorization is supported. They can request information about the latest deployed version of a rule set and retrieve the rule set definition as a byte array.

To support client implementation, the framework provides the Remote Update Service Proxy. This proxy class exposes the IRuleEngineUpdateServiceInterface interface locally and remotes all interaction to the RU service through the TCP/IP channel.

The RU service registers a callback method with an external agent or event service via a configured Pub-Sub Adapter. The framework defines the IPubSubAdapter interface used to implement these adapters. Pub-sub agents and event services can publish events via the adapter and notify the RU service of deployment or security changes to rule sets. The framework does not define any interfaces for agents and event services. These are specific to given rule stores.

Microsoft provides a prebuilt adapter for the SQL Server rules repository. This adapter does not use an event service directly, but instead polls Microsoft's SQL Server rule database at regular intervals to obtain event history. It uses the configured Rule Set Deployment Driver provided for the SQL Server repository to obtain a list of recent changes at regular intervals and notifies subscribers accordingly. It also obtains tracking configuration for the rule set, if available.

When the RU service is notified of a change, it uses the configured Rule Set Deployment Driver to obtain all deployed versions of the relevant rule sets. It caches these and drops old entries from the cache. It also notifies all registered clients. Clients may respond to notifications by requesting the latest deployed version of the rule set.

Registry Settings

The REU service is configured using Windows Registry settings. These are located at the following Registry paths:

▶ **32-bit systems:**HKEY_LOCAL_MACHINE\SOFTWARE\Microsoft\BusinessRules\3.0

▶ **64-bit systems:**HKEY_LOCAL_MACHINE\SOFTWARE\Wow6432Node\Microsoft\BusinessRules\3.0

Table 10.1 lists the relevant Registry settings for the REU service.

TABLE 10.1   REU Service Settings

Value	Description
CacheEntries	Recommended number of items in the remote update cache. Default is 0x20.
CachePruneInterval	Interval at which cache entries are pruned (in seconds). Default is 60.
CacheTimeout	Time-To-Live of objects in the cache (in seconds). Default is 0xe10.
DeploymentDriverAssembly	Fully qualified name of .NET assembly that contains the deployment driver. Default is Microsoft.RuleEngine.
DeploymentDriverClass	Class name of the deployment driver. Default is Microsoft.RuleEngine.RuleSetDeploymentDriver.
PubSubAdapterAssembly	Fully qualified name of .NET assembly that contains the Pub-Sub Adapter. Default is Microsoft.RuleEngine.

10

Value	Description
PubSubAdapterClass	Class name of Pub-Sub Adapter. Default is `Microsoft.RuleEngine.PubSubAdapter`.
UpdateServiceHost	Machine name of location of remote update service. Default is `localhost`.
UpdateServiceName	Remote update service name. Default is `RemoteUpdateService`.
UpdateServicePort	Port number used to communicate with the remote update service. Default is `0xc3c`.
UpdateServiceImpersonationLevel	Impersonation level to use for communication with REU service. Valid entries are `impersonate`, `identify`, `delegate`, and `none`. Default is `impersonate`.
UpdateServiceAuthenticationLevel	Authentication level to use for communication with REU service. Valid entries are `call`, `packetintegrity`, and `packetprivacy`. Default is `call`.
UpdateServiceSecurityPackage	Security package to use for communication with REU service security. Valid entries are `ntlm`, `Kerberos`, and `negotiate`. Default is `ntlm`.

Pub-Sub Adapter Settings   These values, listed in Table 10.2, are used by Microsoft's Pub-Sub Adapter. The Registry values are also used by the RU Service and may be exploited by deployment tools. It is, therefore, good practice to set these values for custom Pub-Sub Adapters, even if they do not perform polling or use a deployment driver. The REU service uses the values internally to control error message construction and other secondary issues, and has a dependency on a Rule Set Deployment Driver which must be configured.

TABLE 10.2   Pub-Sub Adapter Settings

Value	Description
PollingInterval	Interval at which SQL Server database is polled for event history changes (in seconds). Default is `60`.
DeploymentDriverAssembly	Fully qualified name of .NET assembly that contains the deployment driver. Default is `Microsoft.RuleEngine`.
DeploymentDriverClass	Class name of the deployment driver. Default is `Microsoft.RuleEngine.RuleSetDeploymentDriver`.

Rule Set Deployment Driver settings   These values, listed in Table 10.3, are used by Microsoft's Rule Set Deployment Driver for their SQL Server rule database. The Rule Set Deployment Driver is used by Microsoft's Pub-Sub Adapter to obtain a `RuleStore` object for the SQL Server repository and tracking configuration and deployment history data.

TABLE 10.3   Rule Set Deployment Driver Settings

Value	Description
DatabaseName	The SQL Rule Store database name
DatabaseServer	The SQL Rule Store database server.

Application Configuration

The rule engine supports application-level configuration for all Registry settings, including those previously listed. To use application-level configuration, create or edit a .NET .config file for your application with the appropriate entries. For BizTalk Server, edit the BTSNTSvc.exe.config file. Listing 10.4 shows an example.

LISTING 10.4   Rule Engine Application-Level Configuration

```
<configuration>
  <configSections>
    <section name="Microsoft.RuleEngine"
             type="System.Configuration.SingleTagSectionHandler" />
  </configSections>
  <Microsoft.RuleEngine
    CacheEntries="32"
    CachePruneInterval="60"
    CacheTimeout="3600"
    DatabaseName="BizTalkRuleEngineDb"
    DatabaseServer="(localhost)"
    DeploymentDriverAssembly="Microsoft.RuleEngine"
    DeploymentDriverClass="Microsoft.RuleEngine.RuleSetDeploymentDriver"
    PollingInterval="60"
    PubSubAdapterAssembly="Microsoft.RuleEngine"
    PubSubAdapterClass="Microsoft.RuleEngine.PubSubAdapter"
    UpdateServiceAuthenticationLevel="call"
    UpdateServiceHost="localhost"
    UpdateServiceImpersonationLevel="impersonate"
    UpdateServiceName="RemoteUpdateService"
    UpdateServicePort="3132"
    UpdateServiceSecurityPackage="ntlm"
  />
</configuration>
```

For any additional Registry settings under the same key, it can be assumed that attributes of the same name are supported in application-level configuration.

Troubleshooting the REU Service

If you need to troubleshoot the REU service, you can use a couple of useful features. The first is to start it from a command line rather than as a Windows service. This enables you to view trace output generated by the service. To start from a console command line, follow these steps:

1. Stop the REU Windows service. Only one instance of this service can run on a machine:

   ```
   net stop RuleEngineUpdateService
   ```

2. Locate the RuleEngineUpdateService.exe file. This is generally installed in the \Common Files\Microsoft BizTalk directory under Program Files.

3. From a command line, run the `RuleEngineUpdateService` as follows:

   ```
   RuleEngineUpdateService -a
   ```

You can use the `-c` flag instead of `-a`. This has identical semantics. Note that `/a` and `/c` are not recognized.

The service runs at the command line and displays all trace output, as illustrated in Figure 10.6. You can see which security principal the service runs under (normally be the user who is currently logged on) and which port the RU service is listening on.

FIGURE 10.6   REU service trace.

Another option is to log all trace output to a file. This is controlled using the `-d` flag on the command line together with additional configuration. To configure the Windows service for file logging, locate the `ImagePath` name at the following Registry key and add the `-d` parameter:

```
HKEY_LOCAL_MACHINE\SYSTEM\CurrentControlSet\services\RuleEngineUpdateService
```

To configure the service with a log file path, create a .NET configuration file called RuleEngineUpdateService.exe.config and save it to the same directory as RuleEngineUpdateService.exe. Enter the following in the configuration file. You can set the `logfilename` attribute to an appropriate file path.

```
<configuration xmlns="http://schemas.microsoft.com/.NetConfiguration/v2.0">
  <system.diagnostics>
    <assert logfilename="C:\Temp\RuleEngineUpdateService.log" />
  </system.diagnostics>
</configuration>
```

Rule Modeling

The framework defines object models for rule sets and vocabularies. These models support programmatic creation and manipulation of rules and vocabulary definitions. Figure 10.7 illustrates the meta-model.

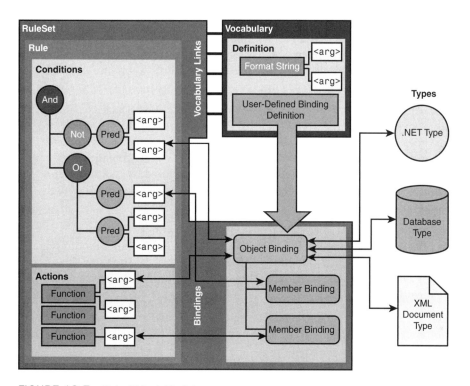

FIGURE 10.7   Rule Object Model.

Rule Set Model

A rule set is a collection of rules. Rule sets are modeled using the following entities:

► **Rule:**Each rule contains a collection of conditions and actions. This approach models production rules.

► **Logical expressions:**The condition collection is a tree of logical expressions. A rule engine evaluates the expressions at run time to determine an overall truth value. The model defines three types of logical connectives (AND, OR, and NOT). AND and OR connectives nest multiple logical expressions. All other logical expressions are predicates.

- **Predicates:**Predicates are logical expressions that evaluate arguments to determine truth values. The model defines a number of relational, temporal (point in time) and regular expression predicates and an XPath-based `exists` predicate and a `range` predicate. Developers supplement these as required by creating user-defined predicates. Most public .NET methods or property `getters` that return a Boolean value can be bound as user-defined predicates.

- **Terms:**Terms are used to model functions. In addition, they are used to model constants (literals) and object references. Object references can refer to .NET, database, or XML document objects. Terms are used as arguments to predicates and functions.

- **Functions:**Functions are terms used to access attributes of .NET, Database, and XML facts and to invoke helper methods. They are used as arguments to predicates and functions. Rule actions are functions. The model defines a number of arithmetic, temporal, and regular expression functions together with engine functions (`assert`, `retract`, and so on.). Developers supplement these as required by creating user-defined functions. Most public .NET methods or properties can be bound as user-defined functions.

- **Bindings:**Bindings provide references to .NET, Database, and XML types, or members of those types. Member bindings also control value caching. Bindings are associated with user predicates, functions and object references. They specify concrete implementations for each term. They allow rule models to be "situated" within real-world systems.

- **Vocabulary links:**Each term and predicate can be associated with a specific vocabulary definition using vocabulary links. Links can be established to definitions drawn from many different vocabularies.

When binding to .NET members, the model supports public methods and properties of classes, interfaces, value types, and delegates. Static and virtual methods are supported. Enumerations and nullable types can be used as arguments. Database bindings are defined in terms of tables and columns. XML Document bindings are defined using XPaths. XPath selectors define object bindings, while XPath fields define member bindings.

The Rule Set Model provides additional facilities for defining execution configuration. This includes the rule set translator and fact retriever components to be used by the rule engine together with upper limits for working memory size, rule set translation duration, and execution loop depth. Rule sets define version information. The model does not support versioning at the rule level.

Vocabulary Model

A vocabulary is a dictionary of definitions keyed by name and GUID.

- **Vocabulary definitions:**Each vocabulary definition maps a format string to a type. The model defines specialized vocabulary definitions for literal values, sets, and ranges, and engine operations. It also supports user-defined type bindings.

▶ **Format strings:**Format strings contain literal text and positional arguments. Each argument can be assigned a literal value or a reference to another vocabulary definition, possibly from a different vocabulary.

▶ **User-defined binding definitions:**User defined binding definitions are used to map vocabulary definitions to .NET, Database, or XML Document types. User-defined binding definitions are also created for members of these types. Binding definitions for members are associated with format string arguments.

Vocabulary items are linked to predicates, functions, and other terms in the Rule Set Model. Format strings define domain-specific languages for rule expression. They are often used to represent natural language statements. User-defined binding definitions drive the creation of bindings in the Rule Set Model.

Vocabularies define version information. The model does not support versioning at the definition level.

Rule Execution

The BRF supports model-driven development. Rule developers model their rule sets programmatically as rule set object graphs. Alternatively, they use a high-level rule language to express rules. These rules are then passed to a rule language converter component at runtime for conversion into a rule set object graph. Rule sets are handed off to a rule engine object, which translates the model directly into an executable format. Figure 10.8 illustrates the various components that constitute a rule engine.

The framework provides a `RuleEngine` class. Instances of this class use a rule set translator to manufacture a rule set executor. The engine may optionally use a fact retriever. These components are pluggable and are defined using the `IRuleSetTranslator`, `IRuleSetExecutor`, and `IFactRetriever` interfaces. The `RuleEngine` object instantiates instances of these components in accordance with configuration information included as part of the rule set. The engine may also instantiate a rule set tracking interceptor for tracking, testing, troubleshooting, or debugging purposes. Interceptors are defined using the `IRuleSetTrackingInterceptor` interface.

When `RuleEngine` objects are first instantiated by an application, they invoke the configured rule set translator, which manufactures a `Rule Set Executor` object. Subsequently, the application calls `Execute()` on the `RuleEngine` and asserts facts. Each fact is an instance of a .NET type, Database type, or XML Document and represents the data input to the engine. The `Rule Set Executor` object evaluates each rule against the facts. For each complete match found, the executor can choose to `fire` the rule actions against the matching facts.

Each rule set can optionally define a custom fact retriever. Fact retriever classes must implement the `IFactRetriever` interface and may optionally implement the `IFactRemover` interface. The rule engine instantiates the fact retriever and uses it to retrieve and assert facts at runtime. This mechanism can be used alongside or in place of direct fact assertion. Rule-based applications access fact retrievers from the rule engine and ask them to update facts at appropriate points in the application code. An additional data object is round-tripped between the applications and the fact retriever each time the application calls its `UpdateFacts()` method.

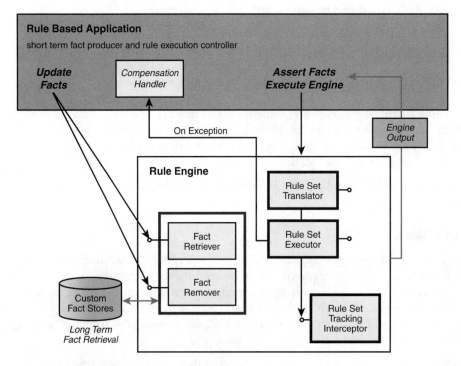

Rule Based Application
short term fact producer and rule execution controller

Update Facts

Compensation Handler

Assert Facts Execute Engine

On Exception

Engine Output

Rule Engine

Rule Set Translator

Rule Set Executor

Fact Retriever

Fact Remover

Custom Fact Stores

Long Term Fact Retrieval

Rule Set Tracking Interceptor

FIGURE 10.8   Rule execution components.

Fact retrievers provide a flexible mechanism for management of fact assertion. A fact retriever may poll a data store for changes or respond to event notification to determine which facts need updating. The application may even send facts directly to the fact retriever via the data object. Fact retrievers are generally used to handle retrieval of facts that change slowly and which are valid across multiple rule set executions. The optional `IFactRemover` interface can be used to maintain clean semantics for fact retraction and other cleanup operations.

Rule-based applications can optionally register a compensation handler with each instance of a rule engine. A compensation handler is a callback method invoked via a delegate. The rule set executor uses it to call back into application code when an error occurs. It passes the exception back to the application code together with a round-tripped data object. This callback mechanism allows rule-based applications to implement appropriate logic for each exception type. The application indicates success or failure to the rule set executor that will generally halt any further processing if the application indicates failure.

Rule set tracking interceptors are used to track and monitor engine activities such as fact assertion/retraction, condition evaluation, agenda updates, and rule firing. An interceptor can optionally be handed off to the rule engine during execution and used by the rule set executor to track progress.

Components and Tools

Microsoft supplies a number of rule-processing components and tools with BizTalk Server 2010. These build on the foundation of the BRF.

Microsoft Business Rule Language

The Microsoft *Business Rules Language* (BRL) is defined using an XML schema. The schema describes rule sets and vocabularies. A single BRL document can define multiple rule sets and vocabularies. BRL is based on the rule set and vocabulary models described earlier.

The framework is strictly agnostic with regard to rule languages. However, BRL is used by Microsoft Rule Composer tool and is strongly aligned with the framework. The schema for Microsoft BRL is included as a resource called businessruleslanguage.xsd in the Microsoft.RulesEngine.dll assembly, which includes the framework implementation. You can extract it using Red Gate's Reflector or some similar tool.

BRL is not a scripting language, and few rule developers will need to write BRL directly. Instead, they use the Business Rule Composer UI provided by Microsoft. This UI provides a friendlier interface for constructing BRL and displays rules in human-readable format. It also enables developers to create, manage, and apply vocabulary definitions. Occasionally, however, rule developers will need to edit BRL XML directly. For example, some advanced optimization facilities cannot be accessed through the UI and require direct editing of the XML.

Business Rules Database

Microsoft provides a SQL Server database for storing and managing rule sets and vocabulary definitions. Databases are normally provisioned using the BizTalk Server 2010 Configuration Wizard. They can also be created manually using the BTS_RulesEngine_Logic.sql and BTS_RulesEngine_Schema.sql scripts located at <Program Files>\Common Files\Microsoft BizTalk\Schema.

The database stores rule sets and vocabularies as binary images. These are generally images of Microsoft BRL XML documents. However, other representations can be used. Rule sets and vocabularies are versioned and published. In addition, the database tracks deployment of rule sets, maintains dependency information for rule sets and vocabularies, and manages a number of additional concerns.

Authorization
The database provides authorization mechanisms to control execution of stored procedures and access to artifacts. Authorization is controlled at two levels. Database roles are used to control execution rights on stored procedures. Individual stored procedures use additional fine-grained authorization to control access to each rule set and vocabulary artifact.

The database defines various database roles, as described in Table 10.4.

TABLE 10.4   SQL Server Rule Store Database Roles

Engine Role	Permissions
BTS_ADMIN_USERS	May execute all stored procedures and access all artifacts. Admin users can control authorization at the database level, adding and removing users to database roles, creating logins, and so on.
BTS_HOST_USERS	Can save, update, publish, and delete rule sets; secure individual artifacts; interrogate the rule store; and so on.
BTS_BACKUP_USERS	Perform backup and restore operations only.
BTS_OPERATORS	Can interrogate the rule store to obtain information, only.
RE_ADMIN_USERS	Save privileges as a BTS_HOST_USER with additional rights on individual artifacts. May deploy/undeploy rule sets, change authorization configuration, rename artifacts, configure the store, and update tracking information.
RE_HOST_USERS	Can save, update, publish, and delete rule sets; secure individual artifacts; interrogate the rule store; and so on.
RE_OPERATORS	Can interrogate the rule store to obtain information, only.

Role membership is set appropriately. For example, the RE_ADMIN_USERS, BTS_ADMIN_USERS, and BTS_HOST_USERS roles, together with the Windows user account under which the REU service runs, are all members of the RE_HOST_USERS role.

In a full BizTalk installation, members of the BizTalk Server Administrators, BizTalk Application Users, and BizTalk Server Operators Windows groups are added to the corresponding BizTalk database roles. For standalone installations of rule-processing components, it might be necessary to add Windows users and groups manually as members of each role.

Table 10.5 describes the stored procedures provided for managing authorization at the database role level.

TABLE 10.5   SQL Server Rule Store Role Authorization Stored Procedures

Stored Procedure	Description
adm_AddDbUserToRole	Adds a Windows user or group to a database role
adm_AddLoginUser	Adds a Windows user or group as a SQL login and adds them to a database role
adm_ChangeRolePrivForUser	Applies GRANT/DENY/REVOKE privileges to a user in a given role
adm_CreateBTSAdminLogin	Adds a Windows user or group as a SQL login and adds them to the BTS_ADMIN_USERS database role
adm_CreateBTSHostLogin	Adds a Windows user or group as a SQL login and adds them to the BTS_HOST_USERS database role

TABLE 10.5   SQL Server Rule Store Role Authorization Stored Procedures

Stored Procedure	Description
`adm_CreateBTSOperatorLogin`	Adds a Windows user or group as a SQL login and adds them to the `BTS_OPERATORS` database role
`adm_DropDbUserFromRole`	Drops a Windows user or group from database role membership
`adm_IsMemberOfRole`	Checks to see whether a Windows user or group is a member of a database role
`adm_RemoveBTSHostLogin`	Removes a Windows user or group from the `BTS_HOST_USERS` database role
`adm_RemoveLoginUser`	Removes a Windows user or group from a database role
`adm_RemoveRole`	Drops a database role from the rule database

By default, fine-grained authorization on individual artifacts is switched off and authorization is handled at the database role level only. Members of the `BTS_ADMIN_USERS` or `RE_ADMIN_USERS` roles can toggle artifact authorization using the `re_setconfig` stored procedure as follows:

```
EXEC re_setconfig 'authorization', 1  -- 0 = OFF; 1 = ON
```

To manage artifact authorization, administrators create named authorization groups with specific privileges and associate them with individual rule sets and vocabularies. They then add users to authorization groups. Users can be Windows users /groups or SQL Server users/roles. Each authorization group specifies one of the privileges listed in Table 10.6.

TABLE 10.6   SQL Server Rule Store Authorization Group Privileges

	Privilege
0	Users denied access to associated artifacts
1	Users granted read/execute privileges on associated artifacts
2	Users granted modify/delete privileges on associated artifacts
3	Users granted full privileges on associated artifacts

Table 10.7 describes the stored procedures provided for managing authorization on artifacts.

TABLE 10.7   SQL Server Rule Store Authorization Group Stored Procedures

Stored Procedure	Description
`re_addauthgroupforartifact`	Adds authorization group for artifact
`re_addauthgroupuser`	Adds authorization group user

10

TABLE 10.7   SQL Server Rule Store Authorization Group Stored Procedures

Stored Procedure	Description
re_check_artifact_access	Checks whether current user has read/execute privileges on an artifact
re_deleteauthgroup	Deletes individual authorization group
re_deleteauthgroupsforartifact	Deletes authorization groups for artifact
re_getallauthgroups	Gets all authorization groups
re_getauthgroup	Gets individual authorization group
re_getauthgroupsforartifact	Gets authorization groups for artifact
re_getauthgroupusers	Gets authorization group users
re_saveauthgroup	Creates of update authorization group

Auditing

By default, the rules database maintains an audit trail of actions performed on rule set and vocabulary artifacts. Actions includes saving, deleting, renaming and publishing of artifacts. Administrators can toggle auditing using the re_setconfig stored procedure as follows:

```
EXEC re_setconfig 'audittrail', 0  -- 0 = OFF; 1 = ON
```

In addition, administrators can configure the number of days of audit history they want to maintain. This setting is used by the re_cleanup_database stored procedure to prune the audit trail table. By default, the rule database is configured to maintain 90 days of history:

```
EXEC re_setconfig 'audithistory', 90   -- No. days data to retain
```

Deployment History

As well as audit history, the rules database maintains a separate history of rule set deployment events. This history plays a central role in enabling the REU service to maintain its rule set cache via Microsoft's Pub-Sub Adapter for the rules database. Its chief importance, therefore, is to provide information about recent deployment changes. The deployment history table records deployment and undeployment of rule sets and updates to tracking information. It is not possible to switch off the recording of deployment history.

Administrators can configure the number of hours of deployment history they want to maintain. This setting is used by the re_cleanup_database stored procedure to prune the deployment history table. By default, the rule database is configured to maintain 48 hours of history:

```
EXEC re_setconfig 'deploymenthistory', 48   -- No. hours data to retain
```

Tracking Configuration

The rule database optionally stores tracking configuration. Like rule sets, tracking configuration can be deployed across a distributed environment via the REU service and used to control tracking of rule execution on each local machine at run time. This allows administrators to inspect and troubleshoot rule execution at the application level.

Administrators use the re_updaterulesettc stored procedure to add tracking configuration for a specific version of a rule set.

```
EXEC re_updaterulesettc 'Rule Set',        -- Rule Set name
                        1,                 -- Major version number
                        0,                 -- Major version number
                        15,                -- Tracking configuration
                        'DOMAIN\user',  -- User
                        'DOMAIN\user',  -- Credentials
                        'RULESERVER'       -- Machine name
```

The last three parameters are for auditing purposes. By convention, the username is substituted in place of credentials. The tracking configuration value represents a set of the flags listed in Table 10.8.

TABLE 10.8   SQL Server Rule Store Tracking Configuration Values

Flag	Tracking
0	Tracking disabled
1	Fact activities (assert, retract, update)
2	Rule firings
4	Condition evaluation
8	Agenda updates

An alternative mechanism for setting tracking configuration is to write custom code to invoke the SetTrackingConfigForRuleSet() method of the Microsoft.RuleEngine.RuleSetDeploymentDriver class. This method takes two informational objects. A RuleSetInfo object provides the rule set name and version information. Use an instance of RuleSetTrackingConfiguration to set the tracking configuration flags. Audit information is added automatically.

For advanced scenarios, the rule database also supports storage and retrieval of tracking configuration documents. However, this feature is not exploited by any tools provided by Microsoft and is not supported via the REU service.

10

Rule Database Maintenance

Audit and deployment history builds up over time. Retention of large volumes of historical data could have a detrimental effect on performance. Hence, it is good practice to ensure that historical data is pruned on a regular basis. The rule database provides the re_cleanup_database stored procedure for this purpose. Audit and deployment history is pruned in accordance with the audithistory and deploymenthistory configuration settings described earlier.

BizTalk Server automatically installs the following SQL Agent job to invoke re_cleanup_database at regular intervals:

```
Rules_Database_Cleanup_BizTalkRuleEngineDb
```

By default, this is set to run each hour. The SQL Server Agent needs to be started on the database machine to ensure that this job runs.

As well as data pruning, the rule database provides support for backup. This includes a log marking mechanism in line with databases created by BizTalk Server 2010. Log marking is used to back up data to a state that is consistent across a group of databases and should be used where the rule database is exploited in conjunction with BizTalk Server. BizTalk Server 2010 provides the Backup BizTalk Server SQL Agent job to manage backups across multiple databases, including the rules database. You can find additional information about backing up BizTalk Server databases in the product documentation and on Microsoft's MSDN website.

The Backup BizTalk Server job is not created for standalone installations of the rule-processing components. It is the responsibility of system administrators to implement and configure a backup regime. The sp_BackupBizTalkFull stored procedure can be used for this purpose.

Pub-Sub Adapter

Microsoft provides a Pub-Sub Adapter for use with the REU service. This adapter supports the SQL Server rule database. The database does not implement a deployment event notification mechanism. Hence, the adapter is implemented to poll the database at regular intervals and retrieve recent deployment history.

The Pub-Sub Adapter is configured using Registry settings. These are located at the following Registry paths:

- **32-bit systems:**HKEY_LOCAL_MACHINE\SOFTWARE\Microsoft\BusinessRules\3.0

- **64-bit systems:**HKEY_LOCAL_MACHINE\SOFTWARE\Wow6432Node\Microsoft\ BusinessRules\3.0

The Registry values, listed in Table 10.9, are also used by the REU service and may be exploited by deployment tools. It is, therefore, good practice to set these values for custom Pub-Sub Adapter, even if they do not perform polling or use a deployment driver.

The REU service uses the values internally to control error message construction and other secondary issues, and has a dependency on a deployment driver, which must be configured.

TABLE 10.9   SQL Rule Store Pub-Sub Adapter Settings

Value	Description
PollingInterval	Interval at which SQL Server database is polled for changes (in seconds). Default is 60.
DeploymentDriverAssembly	Fully qualified name of .NET assembly that contains the deployment driver. Default is Microsoft.RuleEngine.
DeploymentDriverClass	Class name of the deployment driver. Default is Microsoft.RuleEngine.RuleSetDeploymentDriver.

Rule Store Components

Microsoft provides three rule store components. Each one is derived from the abstract RuleStore class.

SqlRuleStore

SqlRuleStore supports the SQL Server rule database provided by Microsoft. It provides a full rule store implementation, including dependency analysis between rule sets and vocabularies and authorization management.

OleDbRuleStore

OleDbRuleStore supports access to custom SQL rule stores. The component uses simple SQL statements to add, save, retrieve, delete, and publish rule sets and should work with most SQL-based OLE DB providers. It has some limitations with regard to analyzing dependencies between rule sets and vocabularies and does not support authorization management.

The custom rule store must contain two tables with specific schemas. The first table stores rule sets. Its schema is described in Table 10.10.

TABLE 10.10   OLE DB Table Name: **re_RuleSet**

Column Name	Column Type	Description
nRuleSetID	BIGINT / INT8	Unique – Use as primary key
strName	NVARCHAR(256)	Rule set name
nMajor	BIGINT / INT8	Major version number
nMinor	BIGINT / INT8	Minor version number
strDescription	NVARCHAR(2048)	Optional description of rule set

10

TABLE 10.10   OLE DB Table Name: **re_RuleSet**

Column Name	Column Type	Description
strModifiedBy	NVARCHAR(256)	Identity of user who made last modification
dtModifiedTime	DATETIME, DATE	Date and time of last modification
nStatus	TINYINT / BYTE / INT1 / BOOL	Status of rule set. 0 – Not published, 1 – Published
imBRML	IMAGE / TEXT / LONG RAW	Raw contents of rule set. Typically, this is a BRL (XML) document.

The second table stores vocabularies. Its schema is described in Table 10.11.

TABLE 10.11   OLE DB Table Name: **re_Vocabulary**

Columns Name	Column Type	Values
nVocabularyID	BIGINT / INT8	Unique – Use as primary key
strName	NVARCHAR(256)	Vocabulary name
strID	NVARCHAR(256)	GUID identifier for vocabulary
nMajor	BIGINT / INT8	Major version number
nMinor	BIGINT / INT8	Minor version number
strDescription	NVARCHAR(2048)	Optional description of vocabulary
strModifiedBy	NVARCHAR(256)	Identity of user who made last modification
dtModifiedTime	DATETIME, DATE	Date and time of last modification
nStatus	TINYINT / BYTE / INT1 / BOOL	Status of vocabulary. 0 – Not published, 1 – Published
imBRML	IMAGE / TEXT / LONG RAW	Raw contents of vocabulary. Typically, this is a BRL (XML) document.

FileRuleStore

This component supports files as rule stores. It supports dependency analysis between rule sets and vocabularies but does not support authorization management.

Rule Set Deployment Driver

Microsoft provides a rule set deployment driver component for importing and exporting rule sets and vocabularies and deploying/undeploy rule sets to and from the SQL Server rule database. The component also supports retrieval of rule sets and management of tracking information.

Business Rules Language Converter

The BRL Converter implements the `IRuleLanguageConverter` interface. It converts Microsoft BRL content into rule set and vocabulary object graphs. BRL has such a close correspondence to the framework object models that this component could be considered to be a framework serializer/deserializer for BRL.

Business Rules Engine

Microsoft's BRE is implemented using a rule set translator component and a corresponding `Rule Executor` class. For each rule set, the rule set translator manufactures an instance of the rule executor.

The BRE is a set-based, forward-chaining engine that implements the Rete algorithm. These terms are explained in further detail in the next chapter. The rule set translator class is named `RuleSetToReteTranslator`. The rule set executor class in named `Rete`. `RuleSetToReteTranslator` is used as the default rule set translator by the `Rule Engine` class.

Policy Class

The `Policy` class is a helper component designed to simplify integration of rule engines with rule-based applications. Although developers can interact with `Rule Engine` objects directly and write their own code to obtain rule sets via the REU service, it is generally easier and more convenient to use the `Policy` class to manage this interaction. Figure 10.9 illustrates the `Policy` class and its association with rule engines and the REU service.

Each policy is configured to execute a single rule set. When the policy is instantiated, it checks a cache of rule engine instances to find a free instance. If no rule engine instance is found, a new one is created and initialized with a `RuleSet`. If the `RuleSet` object has not yet been created, the cache retrieves the rule set via the remote update service proxy. It assumes the use of MS BRL, which it converts in to a `RuleSet` object using the BRL Converter. The `RuleSet` is cached and the `Policy` object instantiates and caches an instance of the rule engine. The rule engine cache stores multiple instances of the rule engine depending on load. Caches are shared by all instances of `Policy` at the application domain level. The rule engine cache registers itself with the remote update service proxy to receive update notifications and drops existing engine instances when they become out of date.

10

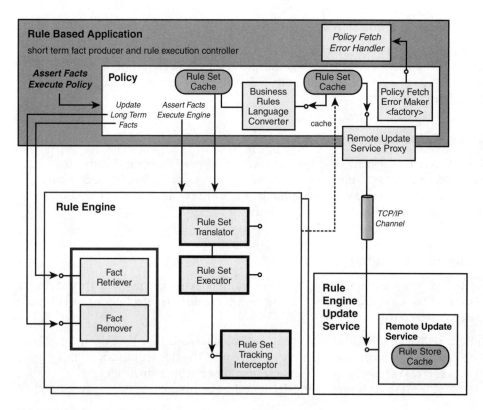

FIGURE 10.9   The **Policy** helper class.

Application code calls the Execute() method on the Policy object and passes a collection of facts. Policy then executes the instance of the rule engine returned from the cache. The sequence of processing is as follows:

1. If a Rule Set Tracking Interceptor is specified, the Policy initializes it with tracking configuration. The Policy object uses Registry settings to select a default rule set tracking interceptor. Alternatively, a rule set tracking interceptor can be provided by the application code. The tracking configuration is retrieved from the rule database via the remote update service proxy.

   The TrackingInterceptorAssembly and TrackingInterceptorClass Registry values for the default tracking interceptor are located at the following Registry paths:

   ▶ **32-bit systems:**HKEY_LOCAL_MACHINE\ SOFTWARE \Microsoft \BusinessRules\3.0

   ▶ **64-bit systems:**HKEY_LOCAL_MACHINE\SOFTWARE\Wow6432Node\Microsoft \BusinessRules\3.0

2. If the rule set specifies an optional fact retriever, the `Policy` calls its `UpdateFacts()` method. The fact retriever retrieves and asserts facts to the engine. These are considered to be long-term facts.

3. The `Policy` calls `Execute()` on the rule set executor, passing an array of facts to it for assertion. These are considered to be short-term facts.

4. After execution is complete, the `Policy` retracts all short-term facts from the engine.

5. If the optional fact retriever implements an `IFactRemover` interface, the `Policy` calls the its `UpdateFactsAfterExecution()` method. This allows the fact retriever to retract long-term facts if it wants.

6. The `Policy` drops any rule set tracking interceptor it used to ensure that resources are released.

The notions of short-term and long-term facts are specific to the `Policy` class. `Policy` always retracts short-term facts from the engine when execution is complete. Long-term facts are not retracted unless the fact retriever implements an `IFactRemover` interface to handle this. Hence, long-term facts remain in the rule engine when it is returned to the rule engine cache and are available the next time it is retrieved and executed. A fact retriever implements custom logic to manage the lifetime of long-term facts independently. This feature allows developers to avoid unnecessary and costly lookups for slowly changing data each time the rule engine is executed.

`Policy` objects support an optional policy-fetch error handler. This is a delegate for a callback method implemented in a custom component. The `Policy` invokes this handler when exceptions occur while retrieving rule sets via the remote update service proxy. By default, the `Policy` class uses the `PolicyFetchErrorHandlerAssembly` and `PolicyFetchErrorHandlerClass` Registry values to locate a configured policy-fetch error handler. Alternatively, the application can pass a policy-fetch error handler delegate directly to the `Policy`.

Note that the `Policy` class does not support the registration of compensation handler callback delegates. As you saw earlier, compensation handlers are invoked directly by the rule set executor when exceptions occur during rule processing. When you are using `Policy`, any exceptions are thrown back to the application code, and there is no mechanism to inform the rule set executor of successful compensation.

Policy Tester Class

The Policy Tester class is a helper component designed to simplify testing of rule sets when developing rule-based applications. It emulates the `Policy` class when executing rule engines and follows precisely the same pattern of execution outlined earlier. However, unlike the `Policy` class, it does not use the remote update service proxy and does not cache rule sets and rule engines. Also, it ignores the default rule set tracking interceptor configured via the Registry. Figure 10.10 illustrates the use of the policy tester.

The policy tester is designed to be used by policy testing tools and test harnesses. A policy testing tool typically uses a rule store component to retrieve a rule set from a store.

10

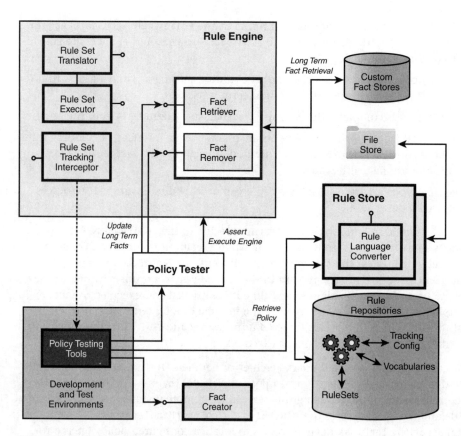

FIGURE 10.10   The **Policy Tester** class.

In addition, the framework defines an `IFactCreator` interface to aid implementation of fact creation components for testing purposes. Microsoft supports fact creators in their own policy testing tooling. A policy testing tool or test harness then instantiates a policy tester for a given rule set and calls its `Execute()` method, asserting facts in the same way as for `Policy`.

`Policy` testing tools can optionally provide a custom rule set tracking interceptor that implements the `IRuleSetTrackingInterceptor` interface. Microsoft provides the `DebugTrackingInterceptor` class as a simple ready-to-use interceptor for testing. Tracking interceptors will generally provide feedback on rule execution to policy testing tools and test harnesses.

Imported rule sets and vocabularies are marked as published in the target rule database and cannot be amended. Once rule sets have been imported, they can be deployed or undeployed using the wizard.

BizTalk Server 2010 Rule Engine Extensions

Microsoft provides a library of additional components for use in conjunction with BizTalk Server 2010. These include the following framework-based components.

Rule Set Deployment Driver

The BizTalk Server rule set deployment driver is similar to the rule set deployment driver described earlier. It operates against the SQL Server rule repository. However, it supports additional facilities such as tracking deployment with the BizTalk Server tracking database and the use of *Windows Management Instrumentation* (WMI).

Rule Set Tracking Interceptor

This component is a specialized tracking interceptor that logs engine activities directly within the BizTalk Server tracking database.

Subscription Rule Store

This is a rule store component for accessing subscription rules held in the BizTalk Server Message Box database. This component supports read-only access and cannot be used to change subscription rules. It is used to support programmatic representation of subscription rules for reporting purposes only. BizTalk Server 2010 does not use the Microsoft BRE internally to process subscription rules.

> **NOTE**
>
> Although these components are designed for use with BizTalk Server, they are also included in standalone installations of the business rule components. Default Registry settings for various components are configured to use them. Because BizTalk Server is not installed, this leads to problems. For example, when you attempt to deploy a rule set using the Rules Engine Deployment Wizard, an error will be encountered:
>
> ```
> The database "MyServer:BizTalkRuleEngineDb" associated with the deployment
> driver does not match the database ":" specified during product configuration.
> ```
>
> Amend the Registry settings to reference components in the `Microsoft.RuleEngine` assembly.

Rule Definition and Deployment

Microsoft built the rule processing tools supplied with BizTalk Server on the foundation of the BRF. These tools exploit Microsoft's SQL Server rule database and provide mechanisms for defining, testing, managing and deploying rules within a distributed BizTalk Server environment. They are central to rule development and management in most BizTalk scenarios.

The Rule Composer

The Microsoft Business Rule Composer is a graphical UI for developing and testing rule sets. It is a development tool and is not intended for direct use by business analysts or end users.Unlike most BizTalk development tools, it is a standalone application and is not integrated into Visual Studio. It is installed as part of BizTalk Server's business rules components. However, it can be freely distributed to non-BizTalk Server client boxes for the purposes of development and testing. It supports creation of rule sets and vocabularies and stores artifacts in the SQL Server rule database. It does not support alternative rule stores. Developers can publish and deploy rule sets directly from the UI. The UI also provides an environment for testing policies.

The Rule Composer is organized as a set of resizable panes. These are illustrated in Figure 10.11. They are not dockable windows and cannot be rearranged in different positions. The window also displays a toolbar and menu.

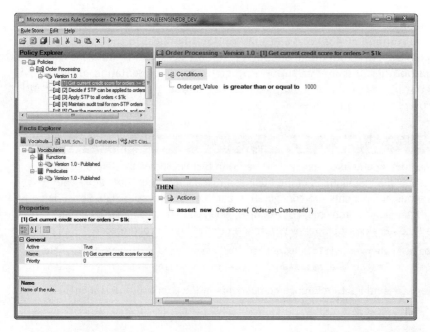

FIGURE 10.11   The Rule Composer UI.

Policy Explorer

The Policy Explorer provides a tree view of policies stored in the SQL Server rule database. Each policy is a collection of one or more versioned rule sets. The Policy Explorer supports the creation, amendment, and deletion of policies, rule sets, and rules.

Facts Explorer

The Facts Explorer is a tabbed pane used to explore fact types and vocabulary definitions. It supports three kinds of fact schema:

- ▶ **XML schemas:**XSD schemas used to describe XML document types.

- ▶ **Database schemas:**The Rule Composer supports SQL Server database schemas only.

- ▶ **.NET types:**Any public, nongeneric class or value type.

The Vocabulary pane provides a tree view of vocabularies stored in the SQL Server rule database. Each vocabulary is a collection of one or more vocabulary versions. Each vocabulary version contains a set of vocabulary definitions. The Facts Explorer supports the creation, amendment, and deletion of vocabularies, vocabulary versions, and vocabulary definitions.

The Facts Explorer is used in conjunction with the Properties pane to define rules and bindings.

Properties

The Properties pane is a context-sensitive property list of property values. Many properties are read-only. Others can be edited as required.

Policy Instructions

An initial screen of instructions displayed each time the Rule Composer is first opened or reloaded.

Condition Editor

One of two panes used for defining a production rule, the Condition Editor is used to define rule conditions. Conditions are structured as a tree of logical expressions using connectives (AND, OR, NOT), predicates, functions, object references, and literal values.

Action Editor

One of two panes used for defining a production rule, the Action Editor is used to define a list of rule actions. Each action is a function or engine operation. Arguments can be functions, object references, or literals.

Output

This pane is displayed during rule set testing. It displays output from the default Debug Tracking Interceptor.

10

Loading Rule Stores

Each time the Rule Composer is opened, it loads policies and vocabularies from a SQL Server rule database. The Rule Composer can work only with instances of Microsoft's SQL Server rule store and does not support custom stores. When the business rule components are first installed, use the Microsoft BizTalk Server 2010 Configuration Wizard, shown in Figure 10.12, to create an initial rule database.

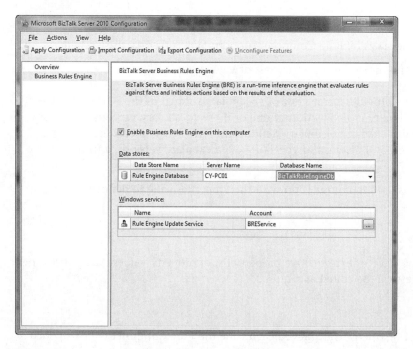

FIGURE 10.12   Configuring the Business Rules Engine feature.

The wizard is used to configure both the data store and the REU service. Select **Business Rules Engine** from the left pane, and click **Enable Business Rules Engine on This Computer**. Then enter the server name and database name for the new rule store. By default, the database will be called BizTalkRuleEngineDb and be created on a local instance of SQL Server. If the rule database already exists, enter its server and database names to configure use of this database. You must also configure an account for the local REU service. Click **Apply Configuration** to create the new rule database and configure the Registry settings on the local machine.

Configuring Multiple Rule Stores
You might want to create multiple rule stores. For example, during development you may want to maintain separate development and test rule stores. You can perform unit testing of rule sets without marking them as published, but must mark them as published (and deployed) to test them in the context of your BizTalk application using the Call Rules shape in an orchestration. When a rule set is marked as published, it becomes immutable and cannot be altered.

In the scenario described earlier in this chapter, the developer handled rule set immutability by creating a copy of his rule set (probably under a different policy) within the same rule database. One copy was designated for development and unit testing and was never published. The other copy was published for system testing.

A variation of this approach is to create two distinct rule databases, as illustrated in Figure 10.13. This allows the developer to maintain a clean separation between unpublished development and unit-test rule sets and published system test rule sets. To perform system testing in the context of a BizTalk application, deploy the rule set to the second database using the Rules Engine Deployment Wizard.

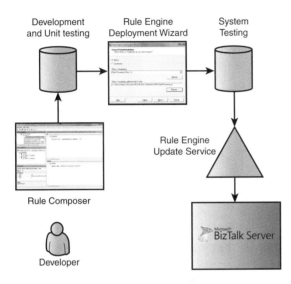

FIGURE 10.13   Separating development and system testing rule databases.

Use the BizTalk Server 2010 Configuration Wizard to create multiple rule databases on a single machine or on different machines. The wizard is designed to configure the use of rules processing on a single machine and therefore recognizes only a single configured rule store. To create a second or subsequent rule database, first run the wizard and unconfigure the BRE feature. Then rerun the wizard and configure this feature with a new database. When all databases have been created, unconfigure the feature one last time. Then reconfigure it to use the rule database designated for deployment of rule sets. Doing so configures the REU service to use this rule database.

When working with multiple rule databases, you can switch between databases at any time in the Rule Composer using the **Rule Store**, **Load** menu option. Select the required rule database in the Open Rule Store dialog box, as shown in Figure 10.14.

You can use the **Rule Store**, **Reload** menu option or **F5** to reload the current rule database at any time.

10

FIGURE 10.14   The Open Rule Store dialog box.

Using the Policy Explorer

The Policy Explorer enables developers to interact with policies, rule sets, and rules. A policy represents the higher-level concept of a business or technical policy. It is represented as a collection of executable rule sets. Each rule set is distinguished by a unique version number. Policies and rules are identified using free-form names. There are no constraints on the rules any one versioned rule set can contain, but it is usual for multiple versions within a single policy to share a great deal of commonality.

Naming Policies and Rules

The Policy Explorer displays policies and rules in the lexical order of their names. Versioned rule sets are displayed in version order. For policies, lexical order is often ideal. However, this can be problematic for rule names. For example, developers often want to group rules logically within a single rule set. Also, there is often a need to support traceability between executable rule sets and external definitions of policies and rules. Careful attention should be given to naming of policies and rules to support these requirements. For example, rules may be named in accordance with some defined format, such as this:

```
[<ruleGroup>:<ruleNumber] <businessRuleId>: <free form name>
```

For example:

```
[005:0107] OP3.7: Assign discount to Gold Club member
```

Ensure that you provision sufficient leading zeros for numeric components of a name. In the preceding example, a single rule set can contain up to 999 logical rule groups and each group can contain up to 9,999 rules. This more than suffices for most scenarios.

Earlier in the chapter, the scenario provided an example of poor naming practice. The developer included literal values as part of the rule names. For example, one rule is named as follows:

```
[2] Get current credit score for orders >= $1K
```

A future version of this rule set may introduce a different threshold value for STP. It is good practice to avoid using literal values in rule names, and instead use some defined business term. For example, this rule could be renamed as this:

```
[2] Get current credit score for orders >= STP threshold
```

This principal applies to business rule specification and executable rule sets. The developer could work with the business analyst to improve the specification of the underlying business rules. In this case, the business rule could be rewritten to use the term *STP threshold*:

```
The organization always uses the customer's current credit score to decide if
straight-through processing can be used for orders with a total value greater than
the current STP threshold.
```

This new term can be defined as part a business vocabulary and may reference some authoritative source of information that provides its current value.

Another questionable aspect of the rule name is that it represents the runtime behavior of the executable rule rather than the semantics of the underlying business rule. For traceability, the rule developer might want to ensure that the name reflects the semantics of the stated business rule and includes some agreed identifier. The same name and identifier can be used by the business analyst in their documentation. The rule might be renamed as follows:

```
[001:002] OP1.2: Use current credit score to determine STP applicability
```

It is important to give careful attention to the naming of policies and rule sets. As rule sets grow in size and complexity, good naming strategies help to ensure manageability, traceability, and accuracy.

Policies

To create a new policy, right-click the **Policies** root folder and select **Add New Policy**. A new policy is created with a default name and an unsaved rule set. Rename the policy. You cannot save your changes until the rule set contains a completed rule. See the Rules section below for information on creating rules.

Existing policies can be renamed using the Name property in the Properties pane, or by clicking twice on the policy name and editing in-situ. They can be deleted by right-clicking the policy name and selecting **Delete**.

Rule Sets

To create a new empty rule set, right-click the policy name and select **Add New Version**. By default, the version number is a minor increment of the latest existing version. You cannot change the version number until you have saved the rule set, which, in turn, cannot be done until you have created at least one rule. You can save a rule set by right-clicking it and selecting **Save**. Change the version number using the **Current Version** property in the Properties pane. You can also enter an optional description for the version using the **Version Description** property.

When creating a new rule set, you will often want to start with a copy of the existing version to avoid having to re-create the rules it contains. Right-click an existing saved rule set and select **Copy**. Then right-click the name of the destination policy and select **Paste Policy Version**. You can copy rule sets from one policy to another. You can also cut and paste to move rule sets between policies. You cannot, however, cut, copy, or paste between different instances of the Rule Composer.

You can reload the current `Policy`. This can be useful when you need to abandon unsaved changes to a rule set. Right-click the rule set and select **Reload**.

Rule sets can be published by right-clicking the rule set and selecting **Publish**. A published rule set is immutable. No changes can be made to the rules it contains or to its properties. There is no facility for unpublishing a published rule set.

> **TIP**
>
> If you publish a rule set prematurely and want to return to an unpublished state, first copy the rule set as a new version. Save your new rule set. You can then delete the old version and decrement the minor version number of the new version.

Rules

To create a new rule, right-click an unpublished rule set and select **Add New Rule**. Name the rule. You can rename the rule at any time using its **Name** property in the Properties pane or by clicking the rule name twice and editing in-situ.

Rule sets cannot be saved until each rule contains at least one condition. Creating conditions and actions is discussed in detail later in this chapter. Sometimes you might want to save a rule set with "placeholder" rules that have been created but not yet specified. You can create a dummy condition to do this. Select each empty rule and right-clicking **Conditions** in the Condition Editor and selecting **Predicates/Equal**. The following condition template is displayed:

`argument1` **is equal to** `argument2`

Click each of the arguments in turn and enter **1**. The condition now reads as follows:

`1` **is equal to** `1`

This allows the rule set to be saved. However, the rule set throws an exception at runtime because the condition does not reference any fact. Note that this condition is not, in itself, invalid. If a rule contains this condition, and also references a fact in its action list, it does not throw a runtime exception.

Individual rules can be cut, copied, and pasted between different rule sets. To copy an individual rule, right-click the rule name and select **Copy**. Right-click the target rule set and select **Paste**. The target rule set can be in a different policy. To delete a rule, right-click the rule name and select **Delete**.

By default, all rules are marked as active when first created. Individual rules can be deactivated by setting their Active property to False in the Properties pane. A deactivated rule is retained in the rule set, but is not represented in the engine at runtime. This feature is often useful when testing and debugging rule sets during development.

Example Business Rules Mappings

At this point, let's review the business rule documentation for the scenario described earlier in this chapter and the way it maps to the executable rule set. The documentation has been elaborated and refined iteratively by the developer and business analyst.

The business analyst maintains the "Order Processing Requirements" document. This contains a section titled "Order Processing [OP] Business Vocabulary," which lists and defines the following vocabulary terms. The definitions are not shown here. The vocabulary may also reference authoritative sources for current STP and credit score warning values:

```
OP_Term001: Credit score
OP_Term002: Credit score warning value
OP_Term003: Current credit score
OP_Term004: Order
OP_Term005: Total order value
OP_Term006: Organization
OP_Term007: STP threshold value
OP_Term008: Straight-through processing (STP)
```

The document also contains another section titled "Order Processing [OP] Business Rules." This defines the following three business rules:

▶ **OP1.1: Allow STP without further checks:**The organization always performs STP when the total value of the order is less than the current STP threshold value.

▶ **OP1.2: Use current credit score to determine STP applicability:**The organization always uses the customer's current credit score to decide whether STP can be used for orders with a total value greater than the current STP threshold value.

▶ **OP1.3: Determine STP applicability:**When the total value of the order is greater than or equal to the current STP threshold value, the organization performs STP only if the customer's current credit score is greater than the current credit score warning value.

10

This document now provides a complete and unambiguous description of the order-processing business rules as part of the overall description of requirements for the order-processing process.

The solution architect owns the "Technical Architecture" document. Under its "Solution Requirements" section, it defines the following requirement:

▶ **TR5.7: Maintain audit trail for unfulfilled customer expectations:**An auditable record will be maintained for every interaction or event in which customer expectations are not met.

The developer maintains an executable policy called `Order Processing`. This contains a rule set that defines the following five rules:

```
[001:0001] OP1.1: Allow STP without further checks
[001:0002] OP1.2: Use current credit score to determine STP applicability
[001:0003] OP1.3: Determine STP applicability
[002:0001] TR5.7: Maintain audit trail for unfulfilled customer expectations
[003:0001] Clear the memory and agenda and end processing
```

Using the Facts Explorer

The Facts Explorer enables developers to inspect schemas for different data models and to use those schemas to create bindings to data models as part of rule definition. It also allows developers to define and use vocabularies for their executable rule sets. Vocabulary definition is explained in greater detail later in this chapter. The Facts Explorer supports XSD schemas for XML documents, SQL Server database schemas, and .NET types. Each schema type has its own distinctive characteristics. In the case of .NET types, developers can also create programmatic bindings to methods and properties.

Although schemas provide the foundation for defining bindings, the generation of each binding is controlled using property values in the Properties pane. Bindings are generated by dragging and dropping schema items from the Facts Explorer onto the Condition Editor or Action Editor panes. However, default bindings generated in this way are not always what the developer requires. Developers must learn the discipline of checking property values first before dragging and dropping schema items. This provides fine-grained control over binding definition.

XSD Schemas for XML Documents

XML is the most frequently used fact format in BizTalk applications. Messages are the primary unit of data interchange in BizTalk Server. Although BizTalk Server can handle any type of message payload, it provides strong support and tooling for XML. Messages are often represented internally using canonical XML formats regardless of their external representation. In turn, business rules are often applied directly to message payloads.

TABLE 10.12 XML Schema Binding Generation Properties

Property	Description
Document Type	A type identifier of the XML document. This is used programmatically to identify the type of XML documents asserted to the engine. By default, the Rule Composer defines this property as the filename of the XSD file without its extension. When passing XML messages to the rule engine in a BizTalk Server orchestration, the Call Rules shape uses the fully qualified programmatic name of the BizTalk schema type. (`<namespace>.<class name>`). This can be obtained by inspecting the properties of the XSD schema contained in a BizTalk Server project in Visual Studio. In this scenario, you must change this property to reflect the document type specified by the Call Rules shape.
Type	By default, the Rule Composer assigns the `Microsoft.RuleEngine.TypedXmlDocument` type to each record and an inferred .NET type for each field based on the optional type attribute of an element or attribute definition. `System.String` is used by default. The use of `TypedXmlDocument` indicates that the generated binding will be used to select zero or more XML nodes as individual facts. Other types indicate that the binding will be used to access an attribute of a fact. The default Type property value might not be appropriate in all cases and should be manually adjusted as required.
XPath Selector	An XPath used to select an XML node set using the XML DOM `SelectNodes()` method. Each node is asserted to the engine internally as an individual fact.
XPath Field	An XPath used to select a single node using the XML DOM `SelectSingleNode()` method. The node is selected relative to a node returned using the XPath Selector property. This XPath is used to select individual attribute values from XML facts. It is not available for schema items whose Type property is set to `Microsoft.RuleEngine.TypedXmlDocument`.

The XML Schemas pane of the Facts Explorer allows developers to load, inspect, and use XSD schemas. XSD schemas are used only to represent XML documents. Unlike BizTalk Server, the rule engine provides no explicit support for parsing flat file formats using grammar metadata contained in XSD annotations.

To load an XSD schema, select the **XML Schema** pane, shown in Figure 10.15, and right-click the **Schemas** folder. Select **Browse** and navigate to a folder containing the required XSD. Select the **.xsd** file and click **Open**. You can select multiple files at one time. Schemas are displayed as a tree of nested records and fields in a similar way to the BizTalk Server Schema Editor.

XSD schemas support the properties described in Table 10.12 for binding generation.

These four properties allow developers to map XML data models precisely onto the internal relational approach used by the rule engine. We explore using these properties in greater depth in the next chapter.

10

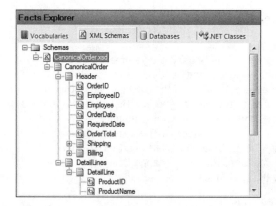

FIGURE 10.15   The XML Schema pane.

SQL Server Database Schemas

Facts are often obtained from existing database stores and represented as rows of data within tables. Microsoft Business Rule Language supports bindings to ADO.NET DataTable and DataRow objects. In addition, it supports data connection bindings to databases. These bindings specify a SQL Server or OLE DB data connection string and a table name. Data connection bindings are used by the rule engine to retrieve data tables from databases at runtime and populate ADO.NET DataSets with DataTable objects. The DataRows contained by the DataTable are then asserted internally as individual facts.

The Rule Composer uses SQL Server as a mechanism for defining database schemas. However, database bindings do not specify connection strings and are not tied in any way to SQL Server. Connection strings are defined programmatically at runtime. Hence, although database bindings are generated using SQL Server schemas, they can be used to bind to ADO.NET DataTable/DataRow and OLE DB bindings. The developer must create dummy databases in SQL Server to define schemas for these non-SQL Server data sources. The schemas can then be accessed via the Databases pane of the Facts Explorer, as shown in Figure 10.16. Dummy databases can be populated with data for test purposes.

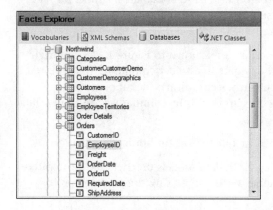

FIGURE 10.16   The Databases pane.

TIP

It is possible to use data connection bindings to access views. However, this can be done safely in only very limited circumstances, which are not necessarily obvious to the developer. It is not a supported approach and should not be attempted. Using views is likely to lead to runtime exceptions. The Rule Composer does not display SQL Server views in the Databases pane. To assert view data, load the `View` data into an ADO.NET `DataTable` and assert as a `TypedDataTable` fact.

TIP

Stored procedures can be used to return data sets. Microsoft *Business Rule Language* (BRL) and the rule engine provide no support for binding to stored procedures. However, stored procedures can be exploited through custom code. One approach is to invoke a stored procedure before invoking the engine, populate an ADO.NET `DataSet` with the results, and then assert the `DataTables` is contains to the engine. A more advanced technique uses the built-in `executor` function to assert facts during rule execution.

Database schemas support the properties described in Table 10.13 for binding generation.

TABLE 10.13   Database Binding Generation Properties

Property	Description
Database Binding Type	Specifies if the database binding is direct over ADO.NET `DataTable`/`DataRow` objects or via a data connection to an external data-base. The Rule Composer defaults to data connection bindings.
Dataset	An identifier used to qualify database binding fact names. The Rule Composer uses the name of the SQL Server table from which the database binding is generated as the fact name. By default, it sets the Dataset prop-erty to the name of the SQL Server database that contains that table. If a rule set obtains data from different tables that share the same name, use the Dataset property to differentiate between those tables.

.NET Types

.NET type definitions differ from other schemas in that they define programmatic functionality and data. The two notions are interwoven. For example, a method call invokes code to return data. .NET type bindings provide predicates and functions and object references.

The Rule Composer supports most .NET types. These include reference types (classes and delegates) and value types, including enumerations. The Rule Composer supports public methods and properties but provides no support for direct field access. It can handle both static and instance reference types. There is no direct support for enumerable objects (for example, collections), although it is possible to write rules to invoke enumeration methods directly. An example of this is provided in an MSDN library page titled "How to Iterate ArrayList in Business Rules." Arrays are supported as arguments, but there is no support for directly indexing an array.

The Rule Composer imposes additional limitations. Generic types, generic members and nullable types are unsupported. It is not possible to access nested members (that is, `objA.SomeMethod().SomeProperty`). These features are supported programmatically but cannot be exploited within the Rule Composer.

To load a .NET type definition, first select the **.NET Classes** pane, illustrated in Figure 10.17.

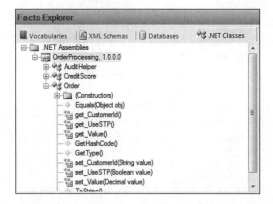

FIGURE 10.17   The .NET Classes pane.

Right-click the **.NET Assemblies** folder. Select **Browse** to open the .NET Assemblies browser, illustrated in Figure 10.18.

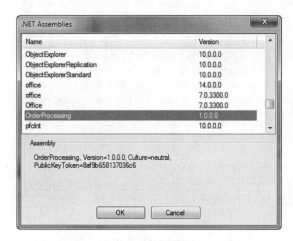

FIGURE 10.18   The .NET Assemblies browser.

The .NET Assemblies browser lists strong-named assemblies in the *Global Assembly Cache* (GAC). You must place custom assemblies in the GAC to access them via the Rule Composer. To quickly locate a given assembly, type the first few letters of its name. The browser jumps to the first match for the typed letters. Select the required assembly and click **OK**.

There are no additional binding generation properties for .NET types.

Composing Rule Conditions

The Rule Composer is used to define production rules using Microsoft Business Rule Language. BRL is an XML rule modeling language. Developers do not generally edit BRL directly. Instead, they use the Rule Composer, which provides a user interface for constructing rules.

Developers define rules by dragging and dropping items from the Facts Explorer to the Condition Editor or Action Editor panes on the right side of the Rule Composer screen. Items are used to create predicates, functions, object references, and literals. They are used to define the runtime bindings used by the engine. The developer can type literal values directly as arguments to predicates and functions. For arguments that are typed using enumerations, or that are based on vocabulary sets, the developer can select a value from drop-down lists.

Understanding BRL

BRL is distinct from the *Rule Object Model* (ROM) defined by the BRF. BRL must first be converted into a ROM graph before the rule set can be translated into an executable format. However, BRL uses an almost identical meta-model to the ROM. It is the default rule language for the BRF and can be converted directly into a ROM graph. The ROM was described earlier in this chapter.

BRL is a rule modeling language. It defines primitives for modeling the abstract structure of rules (rule sets, rules, conditions, actions, logical expressions, and terms), together with libraries of built-in predicates (for example, relational operators) and functions (for example, `assert`, `update` and `retract` engine commands, arithmetic operators). BRL also defines bindings to attach external procedural code to individual model items. BRL binds items to .NET methods and properties. This includes methods of `TypedFact` classes provided by the engine for handling XML nodes and ADO.NET data rows. At runtime, procedural attachments can be used to situate the engine within an external environment. The structure of BRL is illustrated in Figure 10.19.

BRL provides vocabularies as a simple mechanism for associating custom strings with binding definitions. Vocabularies allow developers to create domain-specific rule languages for building BRL models. Microsoft provides pre-defined vocabularies for built-in predicates, functions, object references, and literals. Developers can create additional custom vocabularies for procedural attachments.

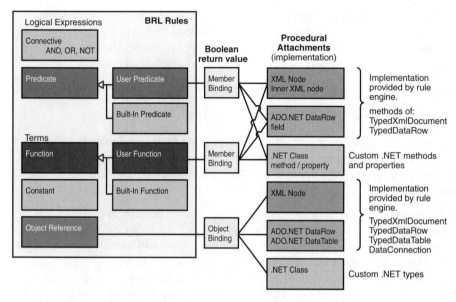

FIGURE 10.19   BRL model items and bound attachments.

Creating Conditions

The Condition Editor is used to create rule conditions. A rule may contain one or more conditions within a tree structure. The tree is composed of logical expressions that yield truth values. Logical expressions can optionally define arguments.

BRL defines three connectives. These are logical expressions whose arguments must, themselves, be logical expressions. Connectives represent non-leaf nodes. They provide the mechanism for structuring logical expressions as a tree. The three connectives are described in Table 10.14.

TABLE 10.14   BRL Connectives

Connective	Description
AND	Logical AND. Takes two or more logical expressions as arguments. Each argument must yield true for the entire AND expression to yield true. Will exhibit imperative-style short-circuiting in specific circumstances. Do not depend on this behavior.
OR	Logical OR. Takes two or more logical expressions as arguments. At least one argument must yield true for the entire OR expression to yield true. Does not support imperative-style short-circuiting.
NOT	Logical NOT. Takes a single logical expression as an argument and yields the opposite truth value to that expression. Note that this is not an existential quantifier. It does not test for the absence of any match.

To add connectives, right-click the **Conditions** root or an existing connective, and select **Add Logical AND**, **Add Logical OR**, or **Add Logical NOT**. The connective is displayed with a red squiggly to indicate that it does not yet contain the minimum required number of logical expressions as arguments. You can also right-click an existing predicate and add a connective. In this case, the connective replaces the predicate in its current position within the tree, and the predicate is demoted to become a child of the connective.

The short-circuiting behavior of the AND and OR connectives is different from that commonly used in imperative programming languages and is discussed in detail in the next chapter.

All non-connective logical expressions are termed predicates. They can only appear as leaf nodes is the logical expression tree. BRL defines a number of built-in predicates. These include relational operators listed in Table 10.15, temporal operators listed in Table 10.16, and various miscellaneous operators listed in Table 10.17.

TABLE 10.15   BRL Built-In Predicates: Relational Operators

Predicate	Description
Equal	Test equality of two arguments.
NotEqual	Tests inequality of two arguments. Logically equivalent to using the NOT connective with the Equal predicate.
GreaterThan	Compares the first argument with the second. Returns true if the first is greater than the second.
GreaterThanEqual	Compares the first argument with the second. Returns true if the first is greater than or equal to the second.
LessThan	Compares the first argument with the second. Returns true if the first is less than the second.
LessThanEqual	Compares the first argument with the second. Returns true if the first is less than or equal to the second.
Range	A ternary relational operator. Tests that the first argument is greater than or equal to the second argument and less than or equal to the third argument.

TABLE 10.16   BRL Built-In Predicates: Temporal (Point-in-Time) Operators

Predicate	Description
After	Tests that the first DateTime argument is later than the second DateTime argument
Before	Tests that the first DateTime argument is earlier than the second DateTime argument
Between	Tests that the first DateTime argument is later than the second DateTime argument and earlier than the third DateTime argument

TABLE 10.17   BRL Built-In Predicates: Miscellaneous

Predicate	Description
Match	Part of BRL's support for regular expressions. Matches the first (string) argument against a RegEx pattern and returns true if a match is found. Uses the RegEx.Match() method.
Exists	Used only with XML Document facts. Matches the second (XML node) argument against an XPath using an XPathNavigator and returns true if at least one match is found.

To add built-in predicates, right-click the **Conditions** root or on an existing connective and select **Predicates**. Select the required predicate from the pop-up menu.

As well as the built-in predicates, developers can use XML nodes, data row fields, and .NET methods or properties as user predicates. The selected item must return a Boolean value. .NET methods and properties must be public and the assembly in which the code resides must be placed in the GAC. The Rule Composer imposes additional restrictions on .NET types which will be discussed in the next chapter. For example, it disallows generic members or the use of nullable data types as arguments. User predicates greatly extend the possibilities when creating rule-based logic.

When a predicate is added to a rule, its parameters are displayed in blue text. The developer must assign arguments to each of these parameters. Parameters are typed. Arguments can be literal and enumerated values, object references or functions dragged and dropped from the Facts Explorer or functions. BRL defines a number of built-in functions. These include arithmetic operators listed in Table 10.18, temporal operators listed in Table 10.19, and regular expression operators listed in Table 10.20.

TABLE 10.18   BRL Built-In Functions: Arithmetic Operators

Function	Description
Add (+)	Adds two numbers
Subtract (-)	Subtracts the second number from the first
Multiply (*)	Multiplies two numbers
Divide (/)	Divides the first number by the second
Remainder (%)	Modulo. Divides the first number by the second and returns the remainder
Power (^)	Raises the first number to the power of the second

TABLE 10.19   BRL Built-In Functions: Temporal

Function	Description
Year	Returns the year (integer between 1 and 9999) from a DateTime value. The year is in the Gregorian calendar.
Month	Returns the month (integer between 1 and 12) from a DateTime value.
Day	Returns the day (integer between 1 and 31) from a DateTime value. The day is in the Gregorian calendar.
Hour	Returns the hour (integer between 0 and 23) from a DateTime value. Uses a 24-hour clock.
Minute	Returns the minute (integer between 0 and 59) from a DateTime value.
Second	Returns the second (integer between 0 and 59) from a DateTime value.
DayOfWeek	Returns the day of week (integer between 0 and 6) from a DateTime value. 0 indicates Sunday. 6 indicates Saturday.
TimeOfDay	Returns a TimeSpan that represents the fraction of the day that has elapsed since midnight

TABLE 10.20   BRL Built-In Functions: Regular Expressions

Function	Description
FindFirst	Returns a string containing the first match found in the second argument for a regular expression provided as the first argument.
FindAll	Returns an array of strings containing all matches found in the second argument for a regular expression provided as the first argument.
Executor	Returns a reference to the current IRuleSetExecutor. This can be passed to custom predicates and functions. They can then deliver directive events (assert, update, retract, clear, and so on) to the engine to inform it of changes in the external world. Custom predicates can therefore be used as sensors, and custom functions can be used as effectors.
CreateObject	Represented as new in the Rule Composer. Calls a specified instance constructor and returns a new instance of a type. For value types, can be used only if the value type explicitly declares a constructor.

With the exception of the CreateObject function, all other functions can be added by right-clicking an appropriately typed argument and selecting **Functions**. Select the required function from the pop-up menu.

As well as the built-in functions, developers can use XML nodes, data row fields, and .NET methods or properties as user functions. For XML nodes and data row fields, the user function acts as a setter. A .NET method or property must be public, and the assembly in which it resides must be placed in the GAC. The Rule Composer disallows generic members and nullable data types as arguments, together with some further restrictions discussed in the next chapter.

10

User functions can be used as arguments to functions and predicates. This allows the developers to invoke custom business logic to supply values. To assign a custom function as an argument, drag and drop the method or property from the .NET Classes or Vocabulary pane of the Facts Explorer. If you drag and drop a public instance constructor, the Rule Composer automatically uses the built-in `CreateObject` function to instantiate the class using the selected constructor. The `CreateObject` function is represented by the new keyword in the rule condition.

To remove an argument and reset the parameter to its unbound state, right-click the argument and select **Reset Argument**. Depending on the type of the parameter, you might also be able to set the argument to **Null** or an empty string.

Deleting and Moving Logical Expressions

To delete a connective, right-click it and select **Delete Logical Operator**. For predicates, select **Delete Predicate**. Deletion of a connective does not delete its child expressions. Instead, each child expression moves up the tree and is reparented using the parent of the deleted connective. This may invalidate the rule and require further editing.

To adjust the position of logical expressions, click the connective or predicate to highlight it. Hold down the **Shift** and **Ctrl** keys and use the **Up/Down-Arrow** keys to move the expression. Each time an arrow key is pressed, the expression is moved up or down one row in the screen and may be reparented according to its new position. In some situations, the highlighted expression will simply be reparented. Each expression must be moved individually to its correct position in the tree. You cannot highlight and move multiple expressions at one time.

As an alternative to using the keyboard, you can move an expression by right-clicking the connective or predicate and selection **Move Up** or **Move Down**.

Creating Rule Actions

Rule actions are created using the Action Editor. Each rule contains a list of zero or more actions. Each action is an engine operation or a function. Developers can use the built-in functions or user functions.

Engine operations are a special set of built-in functions. They directly change the state of the rule engine and are handled differently to other functions. Table 10.21 describes the engine operations defined by BRL.

TABLE 10.21   BRL Engine Operations

Operation	Description
Assert	Asserts a fact to the engine. If the fact has previously been asserted, the `Assert` operation reasserts the fact. Reassertion is logically equivalent to retracting the fact and then asserting it.
Clear	Retracts all facts from the working memory and removes all rule activations from the agenda.
Halt	Halts all further processing until the next call to the `Execute()` method of the rule engine. The `Halt` operation accepts an argument indicating if all rule activations should be removed from the agenda. Facts are not retracted. Used when control must be passed back temporarily to the calling program.
Retract	Removes a fact from the engine. Any rule activations that match the fact will be removed from the agenda.
RetractByType	Removes all facts of a given type from the engine. Any rule activations that match the facts will be removed from the agenda.
Update	Reasserts a fact to the engine. This operation differs from `Assert`. If a fact is used only in the rule's actions and does not appear in its conditions, the engine does not reevaluate the rule against the updated fact. The `Assert` operation reevaluates the rule. `Update` is used as a convenient way to prevent unwanted "loops" of reevaluation and reactivation of rules. It implements an extended form of "refraction" that extends across match-resolve-act cycles. Refraction refers to the ability of an engine to fire a rule just once for any specific match. Refraction has the sense of breaking off or curbing an activity.

Handling Multiple Fact Instances

Rule conditions must sometimes match multiple instances of the same fact type. For example, consider the following rule:

```
If
  Order(1).get_Total is less than Order(2).get_Total
Then
  retract Order(1)
```

When the rule engine evaluates this rule, it finds every possible match between two orders and retracts each order whose value is less than another order. Assuming each order has a unique value, when the engine has completed its work, a single order remains in the working memory of the rule engine. This is the order with the highest value.

The numbers in parenthesis are used as instance identifiers within the context of the rule. The rule engine evaluates every possible combination of two orders, including a comparison of each order with itself. The only requirement for instance identifiers is that they differ for each instance. They may be positive or negative integers and do not need to be assigned consecutively. They merely qualify the fact name. To set an instance identifier, select the fact definition in the Facts Explorer and set its Instance ID property to the required value. Then drag and drop the fact onto the Conditions Editor or Actions Editor. Repeat for each instance.

Rule Priority

Rule prioritization results in rule activations being ordered before being fired. Rule activations for rules with a higher priority will always fire before rules with a lower priority. Ordering rule activations is often important. Consider the following rules:

```
If
  Order(1).get_Total is less than Order(2).get_Total
Then
  retract Order(1)
If
  Order is not equal to <null>
Then
  Helper.TraceOrder(Order)
```

Without prioritization, the rule activations for these two rules have equal salience and will fire in an arbitrary order. Some orders will be retracted by the first rule before they can be traced by the second, whereas others will be traced before being retracted.

If the second rule is set to a lower priority than the first rule, all activations of the first rule will fire before any activations of the second rule. Assuming that all orders have unique total values, by the time all activations of the first rule have fired, there will be one remaining activation of the second rule for the order with the highest total value. Hence, the rule set traces this single order.

To set rule priority, select the rule in the Policy Explorer and set its Priority property to the required value. The value can be a positive or negative integer value. Priority values do not need assigned consecutively.

Rule Engine Component Configuration

BRL supports four additional properties for controlling various miscellaneous aspects of rule engine behavior at runtime.

Fact Retriever

The Fact Retriever property specifies the assembly and class names for a class that implements the `IFactRetriever` interface. The assembly must be placed in the GAC. Fact retriever components are optional. They provide a mechanism for retrieving facts, asserting them to the engine, and updating them through their lifecycle. This mechanism is abstracted from the host application, but can be controlled by that application.

Fact retrievers are generally used to assert long-term facts to the engine in conjunction with the `Policy` helper class. The `Policy` class automatically retracts all facts asserted via its `Execute()` method but leaves facts asserted by a fact retriever in working memory. The `Policy` class caches rule engine instances between invocations. Each subsequent time a rule engine instance in executed, the long-term facts are already in memory. The `Policy` class calls the `UpdateFacts()` method of the fact retriever, allowing the fact retriever to `assert`, `update`, or `retract` long-term facts, and also calls the `UpdateFactsAfterExecution()` on the optional `IFactRemover` interface after execution.

To specify a fact retriever, click the ellipsis button at the right side of the Fact Retriever property of a versioned rule set. Use the **Browse** button to find an assembly in the GAC and select its **IFactRetriever** class.

Maximum Execution Loop Depth

Microsoft's rule engine implements a match-resolve-act cycle. This recursive mechanism is used when evaluating facts. During development, it is quite common for the engine to cycle endlessly as a result of some logic error. To break these loops, the rule engine supports a maximum number match-resolve-act cycles, after which it automatically throws an exception. By default, this maximum value is set to 65,536. The value can be changed by editing the Maximum Execution Loop Depth property of a versioned rule set.

The Rule Composer allows the value to be set between 1 and 65,536. However, the value can be set to 0 or to values greater 65,536 programmatically or by editing the BRL directly. Setting the property to 0 switches off the feature. The value can be set to a maximum value of 2,147,483,647. It is rare, however, to need to increase this value above 65,536. You might want to reduce this value to detect endless loops more quickly. Note that for some rule sets, the number of match-resolve-act cycles depend on the number of facts asserted and the data they contain and therefore cannot be determined at design time.

Translator

By default, the BRF uses the `RuleSetToReteTranslator` component to translate rule sets, represented as a Rule Object Model, into an executable form called a Rete. The Translator property of a versioned rule set can be used to select a custom `IRuleSetTranslator` component. Microsoft does not provide any alternative translators with BizTalk Server 2010, and this property is rarely used. It could be used to integrate third-party rule engines with the Microsoft BRF.

Translation Duration

This property specifies a maximum number of milliseconds for the `IRuleSetTranslator` component to complete its work. If it fails to return an `IRuleSetExecutor` within that time, further processing is halted and an exception is thrown. Although BRL supports this property, it is read-only in the Rule Composer. You can edit the BRL directly to set this property. If the rule set does not specify a value, the engine will use the `TranslationTimeout` value configured at following Registry location:

- ▶ **32-bit systems:**HKEY_LOCAL_MACHINE\SOFTWARE\Microsoft\BusinessRules\3.0

- ▶ **64-bit systems:**HKEY_LOCAL_MACHINE\SOFTWARE\Wow6432Node\Microsoft\BusinessRules\3.0

To edit rule engine component configuration properties directly in BRL, export the BRL to a file using the Rules Engine Deployment Wizard and open in a text or XML editor.

10

Listing 10.5 illustrates how configuration is specified. Save your changes and then import the amended rule set using the Rules Engine Deployment Wizard.

LISTING 10.5   Rule Engine Component Configuration in BRL

```
<brl ...>
  <ruleset ...>
    ...
    <configuration>
      <translator>
        <assembly>CustomTranslator, Version=1.0.0.0, Culture=neutral,
                            PublicKeyToken=9b0ac769248147d7</assembly>
        <class>SomeNamespace.SomeTranslator</class>
      </translator>
      <factretriever>
        <assembly>CustomFactrRetriever, Version=1.0.0.0, Culture=neutral,
                            PublicKeyToken=9b0ac769248147d7</assembly>
        <class>SomeNamespace.SomeFactRetriever</class>
      </factretriever>
      <loopdepth>3000</loopdepth>
      <translatortimeout>5000</translatortimeout>
    </configuration>
    ...
  </ruleset>
</brl>
```

> **NOTE**
>
> The framework also defines a Maximum Working Memory Size configuration property. This can be set programmatically. However, it is not used in the current version of the rule engine and is not supported in BRL.

Testing Rule Sets

The Rule Composer supports unit testing of versioned rule sets. Unit testing is performed in the context of the Rule Composer rather than a host application such as BizTalk Server. The Rule Composer uses the `PolicyTester` helper class internally and therefore emulates the use of the `Policy` helper class in the live environment.

To test a saved rule set, right-click the rule set, and select **Test Policy** or click the **Test Policy** button on the toolbar.

The Select Facts dialog box is displayed. This dialog box, illustrated in Figure 10.20, is used to select facts and fact creator components to assert facts to the engine for testing purposes.

FIGURE 10.20   The Select Facts dialog box.

The upper list displays three folders for XML, Database, and .NET types. Each folder is prepopulated with the schemas and types used by the current rule set. You cannot add or remove schemas and types.

Click an XML or Database schema to highlight it, and then click the **Add Instance** button. If you select a .NET type and click **Add Instance**, the Policy Tester displays a message stating that you must use a Fact Creator or Fact Retriever object. If you selected an XML schema, you can select an XML file from the Open dialog box. The Policy Tester does not validate this XML file. It is the developer's responsibility to ensure that it corresponds to the selected schema.

If you selected a Database schema, the Policy Tester opens the Connect to SQL Server dialog box. You saw earlier that the Rule Composer uses SQL Server as a schema designer for data table/row and data connection bindings. The SQL Server table defined by a schema can be used by the Policy Tester as a source of facts. You can therefore maintain your test data for Database bindings in SQL Server. To exploit this feature, select the required database in the Connect to SQL Server dialog box and click **OK**. The Select Bindings dialog box is displayed. This is illustrated in Figure 10.21. Select a table from a database and click **OK**.

You can remove instances by selecting the instance and clicking the **Remove Instance** button.

10

FIGURE 10.21   The Select Binding dialog box for database bindings.

Fact Creators

Developers use fact creator components to assert facts to the `PolicyTester` helper class during testing. Fact creators are typically used to assert objects as .NET facts, but can also be used to assert XML and Database facts. They are distinct to fact retriever components and are used only for testing purposes.

Fact creator classes implement the `IFactCreator` interface. To add fact creators in the Select Facts dialog box, these classes must be defined in strong-named assemblies that are placed in the GAC. The `IFactCreator` interface defines two methods. The `CreateFacts()` method returns a collection of .NET objects that the tester then asserts to the engine. The `GetFactTypes()` method returns a collection of types for the objects that are returned by the `CreateFacts()` method. This second method is not used in the current version of the policy tester.

Developers are free to implement the `CreateFacts` methods as they want. The method takes a `RuleSetInfo` object that specifies the version information for the rule set being tested. For XML and Database facts, add instances of `TypedXmlDocument`, `TypesDataTable`, `TypedDataRow`, and `DataConnection` classes to the collection of fact objects returned by the `CreateFacts` method.

To add a fact creator, click the **Add** button and select an assembly with a `FactCreator` class from the .NET Assemblies dialog box. Then, select the fact creator from the Select Bindings dialog box. You can add multiple fact creator instances for different classes and remove instances using the **Remove** button

Fact creators are not listed in the .NET Classes pane of the Facts Explorer. The Rule Composer does not allow bindings to be created to these types as facts in their own right.

Tracking Output

The Rule Composer policy tester uses an instance of the DebugTrackingInterceptor to track engine activity during testing. This class implements the IRuleSetTrackingInterceptor interface, which is provided with Microsoft's rule engine. The policy tester uses it to save all tracking output to a temporary file during execution of the rule set. After the rule set has been executed, the contents of the file are displayed in the Output pane of the Rule Composer, and the temporary file is removed. The Output pane is illustrated in Figure 10.22.

FIGURE 10.22   The Output pane.

The Tracking Output pane displays fact activities (asserts, retracts, and so on), conditional evaluations, agenda updates, and rule firings. It also displays any error messages that occur when releasing facts after processing. Releasing facts is done automatically and includes saving changes to XML documents and performing updates on databases.

> **NOTE**
>
> Because of a long-standing issue, tracking information for condition evaluation tests sometimes reports incorrect values for operand values. This affects XML Document facts. This is a problem with tracking information only and does not affect the correct operation of the engine.

10

Vocabularies

Vocabularies provide a mechanism for defining bindings and associating them with format strings. The format strings can be used directly to create conditions and actions in the Rule Composer. Vocabularies provide a mechanism for layering domain-specific languages over rule definitions to align rule expressions more closely with the language used to express business and technical policies.

Like rule sets, vocabularies are defined using BRL. They are stored separately to rule sets in the SQL Server rule database. The Rule Composer allows developers to create and use vocabularies through the Facts Explorer. This is logical. Developers use the Facts Explorer to create bindings within their rule sets. A vocabulary allows developers to predefine bindings separately to any rule set, and use those definitions to create rule set bindings at a later time. To create bindings from vocabulary definitions, the developer drags and drops items from the Vocabularies tab of the Facts Explorer in much the same way as for schema items. However, they cannot change vocabulary properties to control the bindings. Instead, they must set properties correctly at the time they create each vocabulary definition.

Vocabularies are often used to associate natural English terms with binding definitions. This allows rules to be expressed in a language that nontechnical users can more readily understand. However, although the rules might appear to be expressed in near-natural language, they remain precise and unambiguous. Care needs to be taken in selecting unique natural language terms that effectively capture the semantics of the binding in a way that nontechnical users can readily understand.

Vocabulary definition is orthogonal to rule set definition. A single rule may reference terms from multiple vocabularies. A single vocabulary may be used across multiple rules, rule sets, and policies. Where the binding definition defines arguments, one vocabulary can reference terms from another. Developers can create multiple vocabulary definitions with identical binding definitions.

The Vocabulary pane of the Facts Explorer lists vocabularies in a tree structure similar to policies and rule sets. Abstract vocabularies are created with a given name. Each vocabulary defines one or more versioned sets of vocabulary definitions. Each definition maps a binding definition to a format string.

To create a new vocabulary, right-click the **Vocabularies** root folder, and select **Add New Vocabulary**. A new vocabulary is created with a default name and an unsaved definition set. Rename the vocabulary. You cannot save your changes until the definition set contains a completed definition. See the Vocabulary Definitions section for information on creating definitions.

Existing vocabularies can be renamed using the Name property in the Properties pane or by clicking twice on the vocabulary name and editing in-situ. They can be deleted by right-clicking the vocabulary name and selecting **Delete**

Definition Sets

To create a new empty definition set, right-click the vocabulary name and select **Add New Version**. By default, the version number is a minor increment of the latest existing version. You cannot change the version number until you have saved the definition set, which, in turn, cannot be done until you have created at least one definition. You can save a definition set by right-clicking it and selecting **Save**. Change the version number using the Current Version property in the Properties pane. You can also enter an optional description for the version using the Version Description property

When creating a new definition set, you will often want to start with a copy of the existing version to avoid having to re-create the definitions in the current version. Right-click an existing saved definition set, and select **Copy**. Then right-click the name of the destination vocabulary and select **Paste Vocabulary Version**. You can copy definition sets from one vocabulary to another. You can also cut and paste to move vocabulary sets between vocabularies. You cannot, however, cut, copy, or paste between different instances of the Rule Composer.

You can reload the current vocabulary. This can prove useful when you need to abandon unsaved changes to a definition set. Right-click the definition set and select **Reload**.

Definition sets can be published by right-clicking the definition set and selecting **Publish**. A published definition set is immutable. No changes can be made to the definitions it contains or to its properties. There is no facility for unpublishing a published definition set.

TIP

If you publish a definition set prematurely and want to return to an unpublished state, first copy the definition set as a new version. Save your new definition set. You can then delete the old version and decrement the minor version number of the new version. Note, however, that this will be possible only if no rule set or other vocabulary is currently referencing any of the definitions in the published definition set.

Vocabulary Definitions

To create a new definition, right-click an unpublished definition set, and select **Add New Definition**. The Vocabulary Definition Wizard is displayed, as shown in Figure 10.23.

The wizard lists four types of vocabulary definition.

10

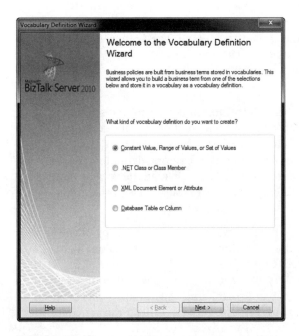

FIGURE 10.23   The Vocabulary Definition Wizard.

Constant Value, Range of Values, or Set of Values   This definition type limits arguments to literal values. When you select this option, you are prompted to select one of the three subtypes of definition.

If you select **Constant Value**, you can define a single value of a selected type.

If you select **Range of Values**, you can enter values for the low and high bounds of the range. You may only use numeric, DateTime, and Char types. When using a range definition as a predicate or function argument, the Rule Composer displays the range as a parameter in blue type. When you then enter a value, the Rule Composer checks to ensure that the value you enter is within the defined range.

If you select **Set of Values**, you can define multiple values of the same type and add them to the Values list. When you are using a set definition as a predicate or function argument, the Rule Composer displays a drop-down box containing the values in the set. Select one of the values.

.NET Class or Class Member   This definition type allows definitions to be created over .NET types such as classes, delegates, and value types.

Xml Document Element or Attribute   This definition type allows definitions to be created over XML Document elements and attributes defined in an XSD schema.

Database Table or Column   This definition type allows definitions to be created over a database schema defined in a SQL Server database. Definitions can be created for data table/row or data connection bindings.

Each option provides a different set of dialog boxes for specifying the vocabulary definition. For .NET, XML, and Database definitions, you can set the same properties listed earlier for binding generation from schemas. In addition, you can set an instance ID. This can prove useful when you want to use different terms to refer to two instances of the same fact type (for example, first order and second order).

Each definition has two of the following three standard properties:

▶ **Definition name:**A free-form name used for the definition and displayed in the Vocabularies pane of the Facts Explorer. This property must be set for all definitions.

▶ **Display name:**A free-form name used for bindings that take no arguments. This is really a format string, but without any parameters. The display name is used in the Conditions and Actions editors when defining rules

▶ **Display format string:**A .NET format string used for bindings that take arguments. Each parameter is specified by a number in braces. The format string is used in the Conditions and Actions editors when defining rules. For example, a format string might be defined as follows:

```
Set the order value to {0} for currency {1}.
```

In addition to these properties, you can use the Definition Description property to provide a definition for .NET, XML, and Database definitions.

You can rename definitions at any time using the Name property in the Properties pane or by clicking the definition name twice and editing in-situ.

Individual definition can be cut, copied, and pasted between different definition sets. To copy an individual definition, right-click the rule name and select **Copy**. Right-click the target definition set and select **Paste**. The target definition set can be in a different vocabulary. To delete a definition, right-click the definition name and select **Delete**.

Defining Format Strings

For .NET types, the Vocabulary Definition Wizard chooses the Display Name or Display Format String property depending on the number of arguments defined for the selected member. For property members, Display Name is always used for getter methods and Display Format String is always used for setter methods.

XML and Database types do not define programmatic behavior. Instead, the Vocabulary Definition Wizard allows the developer to select either a `Get` or `Set` operation for bindings to fields. Display Name is always used for `Get` operations, and Display Format String is always used for `Set` operations.

10

When defining format strings, the Vocabulary Definition Wizard displays a table of parameters listing the position, field specifier, type, and default value. To edit a parameter, highlight it, and click the **Edit** button. The Rule Composer displays the Parameter Definition dialog box, as shown in Figure 10.24.

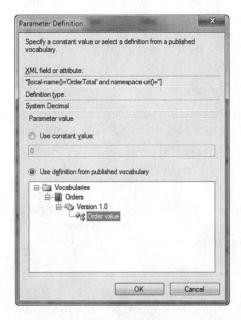

FIGURE 10.24   The Parameter Definition dialog box.

Parameters can be defined with a default constant value. Alternatively, they can be defined to use a published vocabulary definition. The tree view displays all vocabulary definitions that are published and that have a compatible type. This includes definitions in published definition sets for the same vocabulary.

The ability to link vocabulary parameter definitions to published vocabulary definitions enables developers to create macros for rule definition. Parameter values can be constrained to predefined ranges and sets or populated from specific data and programmatic sources. A single vocabulary definition can reference multiple additional definitions to obtain argument values. This implies that careful attention should be given to the structure of vocabularies. Terms that can apply more generally across many policies should be separated from terms that are specific to a given policy to facilitate reuse.

As for any language definition, attention should be given to the syntax provided by vocabularies. The syntax is defined using Display Name and Display Format String properties and maps to the underlying data and programmatic models via binding definitions. In most scenarios, the emphasis is on ensuring that terms can be combined and composed to yield natural language statements.

Display format strings must contain a single placeholder for each of the defined parameters. You can reset the format string to its default value at any time by clicking the

Default button. The Vocabulary Definition Wizard displays how the format string will appear in the Condition and Action editors.

Parameter definitions are defaults rather than constraints. When creating rules, the developer can always replace default arguments with alternative definitions. However, a parameter definition that references a vocabulary definition can only accept vocabulary definitions as arguments. You cannot pass a literal value. You can pass literal values to parameters defined using a constant value.

Strategies for Vocabulary Versioning

Vocabulary definitions are simple, flexible, and powerful. However, they can be difficult to develop. The central issue is that they must be published before they can be referenced from a rule or another vocabulary definition. Like rule sets, once published they become immutable. Hence, they cannot naturally be developed side-by-side with rule sets.

Each vocabulary definition set and definition is identified using a *globally unique identifier* (GUID). If you copy and paste a vocabulary definition or definition set, the copy is created with different GUIDs and will therefore have a unique identity. The GUIDs are used as references within rule sets. Therefore, a rule condition or action that references a given vocabulary definition must be dropped and re-created to use another vocabulary definition. This includes copies of the original vocabulary definition.

The immutability of published vocabularies is often perceived as a major constraint on their use. Developers attempt to develop vocabularies iteratively at the same time they develop rule sets. In effect, they try to drive the elaboration of the syntax of an emerging domain-specific language from their experience of writing executable rules in that language. This is unsupported in the tooling. However, developers may need to create vocabularies without any clear and unambiguous set of predefined business terms.

Developers can adopt a number of strategies when defining vocabularies:

- ▶ **Do not define vocabularies:**This is the simplest strategy. Vocabularies can be useful when rules must be maintained by nondevelopers (for example, administrative staff or power users). If executable rule sets will only ever be maintained by developers, consider avoiding the use of vocabularies. Indeed, vocabularies serve to obscure the technical bindings used within rule definitions and might therefore prove a hindrance to developers.

- ▶ **Define and publish vocabularies before designing rules:**This approach corresponds to an understanding of vocabularies as definitions of *Domain Specific Languages* (DSL) grammar. It implies careful language design at an early stage. Languages should be prototyped and tested before being released for general use to ensure that they are complete and unambiguous.

- ▶ **Define and publish vocabularies after designing rules:**This approach involves the design and retrofitting of vocabularies to existing rule definitions. Because vocabularies must map onto the underlying syntax of rule definitions, this can be a useful approach for defining small, well-defined languages for constrained use. However, it requires recreation of existing rule sets to use the vocabulary definitions.

When an existing vocabulary must be extended or changed, there are two broad of approaches that may be taken:

▶ **Copy definition sets:** Copy an existing definition set and paste it as a new version. Then amend the version as required. To switch to the new definitions, you might need to extensively re-create existing rule sets to use the new definitions. This can be a costly and time-consuming exercise. Alternatively, use the new definition set for new rule development only. However, this might lead to ambiguity and incorrect rule definition.

▶ **Create supplemental definition sets:** Create an empty definition set and add new definitions to it. Amend existing rules to use new definitions where appropriate. A weakness of this approach is that conflicts with the semantics of versioning. A version of a definition set exists only to redefine some existing terms and introduce new terms. Also, vocabularies may become unmanageable. Rule sets may use definitions across several different versions of a given vocabulary.

When vocabularies must be developed iteratively alongside rule sets, the following techniques may be used:

▶ **Export - Edit - Import:** Create and publish a new version of a vocabulary. Identify each rule set and vocabulary that has a dependency on the old version. This can be done using the `re_check_vocabulary_in_use` stored procedure in the SQL Server rule database. Then, use the Rules Engine Deployment Wizard to export each of the dependent rule sets and vocabularies. Manually perform search and replace and other editing to upgrade the rule sets and vocabularies to use the new version. Then import each of the amended artifacts as a new version. This can be a costly and time-consuming exercise and is error-prone.

▶ **Unpublish a vocabulary:** This approach is entirely unsupported but is widely used. Developers use this technique at their own risk. Open the `re_vocabulary` table in the SQL Server rule database. Locate the required vocabulary and manually adjust the value of its `nStatus` field, setting the value back to 0. This will mark the vocabulary as unpublished. In the Rule Composers, reload the definition set. You can now amend and change the vocabulary. However, great care must be taken. For example, if you remove a vocabulary definition on which existing rules are dependent, those rule sets will be invalidated and will no longer load. For safety, leave existing definitions in place and create new definitions. Change your rule sets to use these new definitions and only delete the old definitions when you are sure that no dependencies remain. Another safety mechanism is to export your existing vocabulary definition to file before unpublishing it so that that it can be re-created from this backup if necessary.

▶ **Create custom code/scripts to automate updates:**On larger projects you may want to consider creating custom logic to automate the update of rule set and vocabulary dependencies.

In summary, vocabularies define domain-specific languages. These languages should, wherever possible and appropriate, be fully defined and specified before using them to create rule sets. This is logical but can require extensive up-front design. Only use vocabularies where there is a clear requirement and benefit.

Publishing and Deployment

To publish a rule set or a vocabulary definition set from the Rule Composer, right-click the item and select **Publish**. After an item is published, it cannot be changed in any way. This includes its properties. It can, however, be cut, copied, and deleted. Publishing marks an item as complete and ready for use.

Rule sets can be deployed. When a rule set is marked as deployed, its change in status is detected by instances of the REU service. Each instance retrieves the deployed version of the rule set and caches it locally for use on a given machine. Deployment does not apply to vocabularies.

Deployed rule sets can be undeployed. When a rule set is marked as undeployed, this change in status is detected by each instance of the REU service, which drops its local copy from the cache. This withdraws the rule set from service.

To deploy and undeploy rule sets from the Rule Composer, right-click the rule set, and select **Deploy** or **Undeploy**. You must first publish a rule set before you can deploy it. A deployed rule set cannot be cut or deleted. You must first undeploy a rule set before removing it.

NOTE

When using standalone installations of the business rule components, you might encounter the following error:

```
The database "<MyServer:BizTalkRuleEngineDb>" associated with the deployment
driver does not match the database ":" specified during product configuration.
```

This error is caused by incorrect Registry settings. You must manually change the following Registry settings:

32-bit systems: HKEY_LOCAL_MACHINE\SOFTWARE\Microsoft\BusinessRules\3.0

64-bit systems:
HKEY_LOCAL_MACHINE\SOFTWARE\Wow6432Node\Microsoft\BusinessRules\3.0

Change the DeploymentDriverAssembly value to the following:

```
Microsoft.RuleEngine, Version=3.0.1.0, Culture=neutral,
PublicKeyToken=31bf3856ad364e35
```

Change the `DeploymentDriverClass` to the following:

```
Microsoft.RuleEngine.RuleSetDeploymentDriver
```

Reload the Rule Composer. You should now be able to deploy rule sets without errors.

The Rules Engine Deployment Wizard

The Rules Engine Deployment Wizard, illustrated in Figure 10.25, supports publishing and deployment of rule sets and vocabularies. It handles migration of rule sets and vocabularies from one environment to another and administrative deployment and undeployment of rule sets in the live environment. The wizard is a standalone tool launched from the Start menus. It works directly with the SQL Server rule database and is not intended for use with custom rule stores.

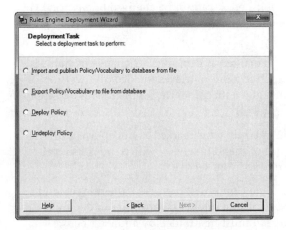

FIGURE 10.25   The Rules Engine Deployment Wizard.

The Rules Engine Deployment Wizard allows rule sets and vocabulary definition sets to be exported from the SQL Server rules database as BRL files. BRL is an XML-based rule language. These files can be copied to the target environment and imported into another SQL Server rules database using the same wizard. Each time a rule set or vocabulary definition set is imported it is automatically marked as published. The source artifact does not need to be published before exporting.

The Rules Engine Deployment Wizard saves each rule set and vocabulary definition set to a separate file specified in the wizard page shown in Figure 10.26. However, a BRL file may legitimately define multiple rule sets a vocabulary definition sets. The contents of multiple BRL files can be manually merged before being imported via the wizard.

As well as importing and exporting, the Rules Engine Deployment Wizard can be used to deploy and undeploy rule sets. Each time the wizard is run, it allows the user to select a target SQL Server instances and rule database. The wizard can therefore be used to import, export, deploy, and undeploy remotely across a network.

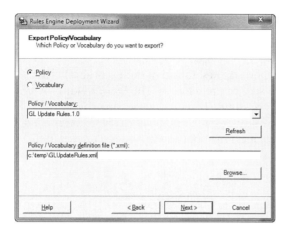

FIGURE 10.26   Exporting policies and vocabularies.

Depending on the task being performed, the user selects a rule set, vocabulary definition set, or BRL file. When exporting, the user also provides a path and filename for the BRL file. The wizard then carries out the required task.

Using Rules with BizTalk Server

BizTalk Server 2010 provides a rich environment for integrating systems, processing message interchanges, and implementing automated business processes. It offers many opportunities for exploiting policy-driven decision making. Perhaps the most common use of the rule engine is to apply policy directly within orchestrations. Policy is used to control the flow of processes, message routing, message validation, and derivation of inter-change data. Policy is a central component in the design of dynamic solutions that change and adapt over time in response to evolving business requirements.

As well as orchestrations, there are situations where it is desirable to apply policy to indi-vidual messages within pipelines. These policies may govern validation, transformation, and routing of messages. BizTalk Server pipelines do not support general-purpose out-of-the-box integration with the rule engine. Instead, developers must write custom pipeline components to invoke the rule engine within custom pipelines.

ESB Toolkit

Service-oriented architectures often use service bus patterns to connect and mediate between services. BizTalk Server 2010 plays a central role in implementing service buses on the Microsoft platform. It provides a suite of capabilities for bus implementation including persisted, recoverable message brokerage, service orchestration, publish and subscribe message routing, transformation single-point administration, adapter-based integration, service mediation, and much more. The BizTalk *Enterprise Service Bus* (ESB) Toolkit provides a programmatic framework, prewritten components, tooling, and architectural guidance

10

for implementing service buses. It extends the core capabilities of BizTalk to provide on-ramp and off-ramp capabilities, itinerary-based routing, endpoint resolution, transformation services, and centralized error handling.

The ESB Toolkit implements a resolution framework. Resolution of endpoints and other data is central to itinerary-based routing and service interchange. The ESB Toolkit provides out-of-the-box support for driving resolution from rule-based policies using the rule engine. Instead of implementing a full-blown service directory using *Universal Description, Discovery and Integration* (UDDI), BizTalk developers may opt to implement a policy directory using the business rules repository and framework to enforce routing and governance policies across the service bus.

RFID Server

BizTalk Server 2010 incorporates the BizTalk RFID Server. RFID Server supports distributed sensor and device management with single-point administration through the Device Service Provider Interface. In addition, it provides an event-processing engine that passes events through pipelines. Pipelines are defined as part of RFID processes. They can be structured as a simple sequence of event handlers or as trees where each node represents a logical event source. BizTalk RFID Server integrates the rule engine into pipelines via the Rule Engine Policy Executor event handler component.

Using Rules in Custom Code

Using custom code, there are many additional ways to exploit the rule engine within BizTalk Server applications. Developers are not limited to the built-in integration points. The rule engine can be exploited within custom pipeline components, helper libraries or web services designed for use by the application. The only restriction on usage is the BizTalk Server license. The rule engine must run on a correctly licensed server.

Policy Management in the Administration Console

The BizTalk Server 2010 Administration Console provides single-point administration for BizTalk Server groups. It is used to configure, manage, and deploy the various artifacts that constitute a BizTalk application. This includes versioned policies stored in the SQL Server rule store.

The Administration Console provides each BizTalk Server application with a Policy folder. This includes the special <All Artifacts> pseudo-application. The Policy folder in <All Artifacts> supports import and export of rule sets as policy versions. The Policy folder in each BizTalk application supports publishing, deployment, and various other actions. The one exception is the BizTalk.Server application. This is a special application referenced by all other applications. Its use is reserved by Microsoft. Administrators are not allowed to add new artifacts, and therefore policies cannot be added to the Policy folder. BizTalk Server 2010 does not implement any system policies.

To import a rule set as a policy version, right-click the Policies folder under <All Artifacts> and select **Import**. Browse to a BRL file and select it. The rule set is imported into the SQL Server rule store. The Administration Console only displays policies. Vocabularies are not displayed. However, vocabularies can still be imported through the Administration Console. Use the Rule Composer to verify that they have been imported correctly. Unlike the Rules Engine Deployment Wizard, the Administration Console does not automatically publish imported policies and vocabularies.

To export policies and vocabularies, right-click the Policies folder under <All Artifacts> and select **Export**. The Export Policies dialog box is displayed, as illustrated in Figure 10.27. Alternatively, right-click a policy version in the Policies pane of the Administration Console.

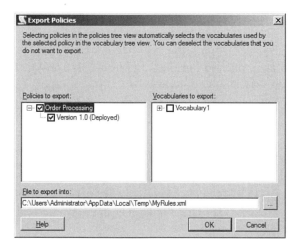

FIGURE 10.27   The Export Policies dialog box.

Select the policy and vocabulary versions you want to export. If you select a policy or vocabulary at the top level, all versions are selected. For each selected policy version, the dialog box automatically selects any vocabulary versions used by that policy. However, selecting a vocabulary version does not automatically select corresponding policies. The Export Policies dialog exports all selected policy and vocabulary versions to a single BRL file. Unlike the Rule Composer, the Export Policies dialog does not display vocabularies for built-in predicates and functions.

To publish, deploy, and undeploy a policy version, right-click the policy version in the Policies pane of the Administration Console and select the appropriate command. You may also view the properties of the policy version.

Policies can be associated with individual BizTalk applications. This aids operational management and allows policies and vocabularies to be exported to Windows Installation packages for deployment onto other environments. To add policies to a BizTalk application, right-click the Policies folder and select **Add/Policy**. The Add Policies dialog box is displayed, as illustrated in Figure 10.28. It displays a list of all published and deployed policies. Select the required policy versions and click **OK**.

10

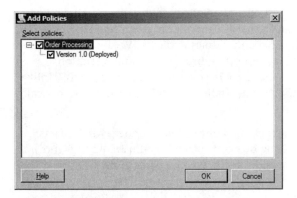

FIGURE 10.28   The Add Policies dialog box.

Each policy can be associated with just one BizTalk application. Note, however, that a policy does not have to be associated with an application in the Administration Console to be executed from within that application. Association of policies with BizTalk applications is for management and deployment reasons only.

Policies added to BizTalk applications can be deployed or undeployed. Undeployed policies can be removed from the application. Right-click the policy version in the Policies pane of the Administration Console and select the appropriate command. You can also move policies to another BizTalk application and export policies to disk.

Policies added to BizTalk applications support tracking. Policy execution is tracked whenever the `Policy` helper class is used within the context of a BizTalk orchestration. The Call Rules orchestration shape uses the `Policy` class internally. The `Policy` class uses the tracking interceptor registered at the following locations:

▸ **32-bit systems:**HKEY_LOCAL_MACHINE\SOFTWARE\Microsoft\BusinessRules\3.0

▸ **64-bit systems:**HKEY_LOCAL_MACHINE\SOFTWARE\Wow6432Node\Microsoft\BusinessRules\3.0

By default, BizTalk Server registers the `RuleSetTrackingInterceptor` provided as part of the BizTalk rule engine extensions. This interceptor inspects the call context to determine whether the policy is being invoked within the context of an orchestration. If so, it tracks policy execution according to the tracking configuration specified through the Administration Console. To specify tracking configuration, right-click the policy version in the Policies pane and select **Tracking**. Select the required tracking options. Tracking information is collected internally through BAM event observation and imported into the BizTalk tracking database.

To view policy tracking information, select the **BizTalk Group** node and then select **Tracked Service Instances** in the Group Hub. Right-click the orchestration instance and select **Message Flow**. The message flow displays this link: Follow This Link to View the

Policy Execution Details for This Orchestration Instance. Use this link to navigate to tracking reports for different aspects of policy execution. These include fact activities (`asserts`, `updates`, and `retracts`), rules that fired, rules that did not fire, condition evaluation, and agenda updates. A tracking report is illustrated in Figure 10.29.

Policy Execution Details

Service Name	OrderProcessingBts.ProcessOrders
Orchestration ID	ec68d78f-3cca-47d8-928b-f6e9de44b41f
Time	22/01/2010 10:36:54
Policy ID	Order Processing.1.0

Rules that Fired

Rule ID	Rule Name
0	[1] Get current credit score for orders >= $1k
1	[2] Decide if STP can be applied to orders >= $1k
2	[5] Clear the memory and agenda, and end processing

FIGURE 10.29   Tracking report for policy execution.

The Administration Console allows policies to be exported at the application level. Right-click the application name and select **Export**. Polices can be exported as part of a Windows Installer package (MSI file) or directly as a BRL file using the Export Policies dialog box. When you export policies as part of an MSI file, BizTalk Server exports all policies selected in the Export MSI File Wizard. The wizard includes any associated vocabularies and also exports SQL Server rule store authorization groups.

The Call Rules Orchestration Shape

Policies are most often used within the context of processes. To support this, BizTalk Server provides the Call Rules orchestration shape. Internally, the Call Rules generates XLANG/s script to invoke the rule engine via the `Policy` class. It also handles various additional housekeeping tasks such as creating `TypedXmlDocument` objects over the XML content of messages and reconstructing BizTalk messages over XML after rule processing has completed. An example of the script code generated for a configured Call Rule shape in an orchestration file (ODX file) is provided later in Listing 10.6.

To use the shape, drag it from the Toolbox onto the orchestration designer canvas and name it appropriately. Double-click the shape to display the CallRules Policy Configuration dialog illustrated in Figure 10.30.

Use the drop-down box to select the policy that will be executed. The shape automatically lists all saved policies in the rule repository. However, one restriction of the Call Rules shape is that it always invokes the latest version of a given policy. There is no support for selecting a specific version of a given policy. This restriction must be borne in mind when deploying policies to production environments. In most cases, an orchestration should always invoke the latest version of a published and deployed policy, but occasionally it might be necessary to invoke a specific version. In this case, you must use an alternative approach to the Call Rules shape. We discuss alternative approaches later.

10

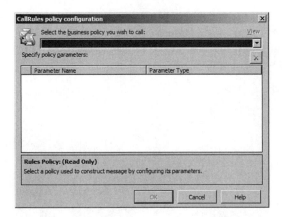

FIGURE 10.30   The CallRules Policy Configuration dialog.

The CallRules Policy Configuration dialog often causes confusion to developers when first encountered. It is natural to expect that, once a policy has been selected, the dialog box will display a prepopulated list of parameter types. However, the list often remains empty, and the dialog box contains no mechanism to add items to the list.

This behavior is entirely logical, but a little counterintuitive. The policy parameter list is, in reality, the list of facts that will be asserted to the rule engine at runtime. The Call Rules shape can inspect the policy definition to discover the various fact types that the policy handles. However, this is not enough information to create a prepopulated list. You might need to assert multiple facts of the same type. Instead of asserting some facts via the Call Rule shape, your policy may use fact retrievers, rule actions, or even custom predicates to assert those facts. The Call Rules shape only knows about fact types. It does not know what facts are to be asserted by the orchestration.

To set parameters, you must first define facts. Each fact is defined as an orchestration variable or message. This includes variable and message orchestration parameters. When using the Call Rules shape, you often need to postpone parameter configuration, close the dialog box, and then use the orchestration designer to define facts. When you next open the CallRules Policy Configuration dialog box, the parameter list is enabled as illustrated in Figure 10.31. You can then create as many rows as required. In each row, you can select one of the facts you have defined. The dialog box lists only variables and messages whose type corresponds to a fact type defined in the policy.

If you are not sure of the policy types supported by the selected policy, click the **View** link in the upper-right corner of the dialog box. This displays the policy definition as a BRL document, as illustrated in Figure 10.32. You can inspect the <bindings> element near the top of the document to discover the fact types that the policy defines.

XLANG/s does not directly support arrays. Therefore, there is no way to assert an array of facts to the engine via the Call Rules shape. Each fact must be defined as a separate variable or message.

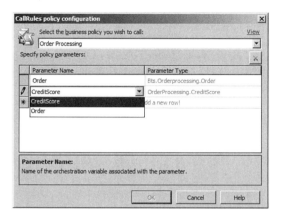

FIGURE 10.31   Selecting CallRules parameters.

FIGURE 10.32   Viewing BRL policy bindings.

BizTalk Server provides rich support for handling message parts of different types, and the Call Rules shape benefits from these features, allowing the generated XLANG/s script to automatically deserialize message part content to an appropriate type when asserting the message to the engine, and to reserialize facts as messages after the policy has been executed. The Call Rules shape handles message deserialization and reserialization automatically. For example, it generates a message construct block in the generated XLANG/s script to assign facts back to messages after the policy has been executed. In addition, the

Call Rule shape automatically assigns message content for messages types using XSD schemas to an instance of TypedXmlDocument.

Listing 10.6 demonstrates a simple example of a generated XLANG/s script for assertion of two BizTalk orchestration messages via the Call Rules shape. The orderMsg message is types using an XSD schema. The creditScoreMsg is typed using a serializable .NET class.

LISTING 10.6   XLANG/s Script Generated by Call Rule Shape

```
scope
{
    Microsoft.RuleEngine.Policy policy_1__;
    System.Xml.XmlDocument policyParam_1_1__;
    Microsoft.RuleEngine.TypedXmlDocument policyParamAsTXD_1_1__;
    OrderProcessing.CreditScore policyParam_1_2__;

    body
    {
        policyParam_1_1__ = orderMsg;
        policyParamAsTXD_1_1__ =
            new Microsoft.RuleEngine.TypedXmlDocument(
                                        "B10U.OrderProcessing.Order",
                                        policyParam_1_1__);
        policyParam_1_2__ = creditScoreMsg;

        policy_1__ = new Microsoft.RuleEngine.Policy("Order Processing");
        policy_1__.Execute(
            policyParamAsTXD_1_1__,
            policyParam_1_2__
        );

        construct orderMsg, creditScoreMsg
        {
            orderMsg = policyParamAsTXD_1_1__.Document;
            creditScoreMsg = policyParam_1_2__;
        }

        policy_1__.Dispose();
    }
}
```

The orderMsg and creditScoreMsg orchestration messages are used to assert two facts to the engine. After the policy has been executed, these two messages are reconstructed so that they represent the post-execution state of the facts. Hence, if the policy changes fact data in any way, these changes are reflected in the content of the two messages.

Note that the code assigns the orderMsg message to an XmlDocument variable and then uses this to construct an instance of TypedXmlDocument. The Call Shape generates this code because it is able to match the orchestration message type to an xmldocument binding in the policy. The match is based on the BizTalk (.NET) type name of the schema (B10U.OrderProcessing.Order). When creating a policy for use via the Call Rule shape, you must ensure that the Document Type property of the schema is set to the correct type name value in the XML Schemas tab of the Facts Explorer in the Rule Composer. If this property is not set correctly, the Call Rules shape cannot generate the script to manufacture instances of TypedXmlDocument.

TIP

By setting the Document Type property to Microsoft.XLANGs.BaseTypes.Any, you can build generic policies that can process any BizTalk orchestration message with XML content. This can be useful, for example, in situations where the same policy applies to different versions or variations of a common schema. Use the Microsoft.XLANGs.BaseTypes.Any schema in your orchestrations as the message type. If necessary, you can assign a strongly typed message to an Any message in a Message Assignment shape using code similar to anyMsg = (System.Xml.XmlDocument)orderMsg;. The Call Rules shape will match the Any type to the Document Type used in the policy and wrap the message in an instance of TypedXmlDocument.

When using TypedDataTable, TypedDataRow, or DataConnection facts, you must first create variables of those types and then write the code to instantiate the wrapper objects. For other .NET types, just create appropriately typed variables, initialize them, and pass them as parameters to the Call Rules shape.

Alternative Approaches

The Call Rules shape provides a convenient mechanism for executing policies and can be used in most orchestration-based scenarios. However, it does suffer from some limitations. As you saw earlier, it does not support invocation of specific policy versions. It does not support assertion of arrays of facts, and it does not allow the use of custom tracking interceptors. More generally, it uses the Policy helper class, and can therefore only be used with BRL rule sets delivered via the REU service.

It might sometimes be necessary to overcome one or more of these limitations. BizTalk developers can write custom code to execute policies. One approach is to create helper code in C#, VB.NET or F# and invoke custom methods within an Expression or Message Assignment shape, or within a rule in a Decide shape.

Another approach is to execute the rule engine directly via XLANG/s code. You can use the generated script in Listing 10.6 as a starting point. Reproduce the script in an Expression shape and amend it as required. You could use this approach, for example, to invoke a specific policy version or use a custom tracking interceptor. Replace variable names with more friendly names.

10

Policy-Driven Features of the ESB Toolkit

BizTalk Server provides a messaging infrastructure built around the Message Box and subscription engine. To this, it adds an orchestration engine based on a superset of the BPEL 1.1 specification. With the introduction of the Message Box in 2004, BizTalk Server provides a rich framework for dynamic message routing. It also supports an extensible framework for custom message processing within pipelines.

The ESB Toolkit builds on the existing features of BizTalk Server and extends them with additional features for configuring and managing dynamic message routing and mediation. Itineraries are central to its approach. An itinerary (sometimes called a routing slip) is used to model a specific interchange pattern in an abstract fashion. Itineraries are created using a DSL to define interchange between services. Itineraries explicitly model on-ramp and off-ramp services. They also model additional itinerary services. These are generally implemented as messaging services invoked within a BizTalk Server pipeline or as BizTalk orchestrations. The toolkit provides mediation services for routing and transformation, and supplies these as both messaging-based and orchestration-based itinerary services. It also provides an additional service for brokerage between other itinerary services.

Microsoft describes itinerary-based processing as a form of policy-driven mediation and service composition. Policies are defined using a graphical DSL designer in Visual Studio. They can be exported to XML files or published to an itinerary store in a SQL Server database. The ESB Toolkit provides a command-line tool for publishing and deploying itinerary XML to database stores. Like business rule policies, itineraries can be versioned, published, deployed and undeployed. However, The ESB Toolkit offers no equivalent to the REU service and does not support dynamic deployment within runtime environments. The itinerary store does not provide any additional auditing or security features.

The toolkit provides an extensible Resolver and Adapter Provider framework. Resolvers are used within itineraries to dynamically determine endpoints and maps. Adapter providers are used to assign properties to messages to route them successfully via specific BizTalk Server adapters. Several predefined resolver components are provided with the toolkit, including a BRE-based resolver. In addition, the toolkit provides a specialized BRE-based resolver for dynamic selection of itineraries. This resolver is used in conjunction with the ESB Itinerary Selector pipeline component that is included in a number of predefined on-ramp pipelines.

As well as the ESB Itinerary Selector pipeline component, resolvers are used by Itinerary Services to resolve endpoints and maps. The ESB Toolkit passes message context to the BRE resolver using a `Resolution` helper object as a fact. The properties of the `Resolution` object, listed in Table 10.22, are populated from BizTalk message context for evaluation by BRE.

To obtain the schema strong name in a messaging pipeline, you must set the Recognize Message Format property to True for the Itinerary Service resolver. However, this only works when using the Message Extender. If this property is set to True when using the Orchestration Extender, the resolver framework throws an exception.

TABLE 10.22 BizTalk Message Context Properties Passed to the BRE Resolver

Property	Type	Notes
`DocumentSpecName`		Derived from `SchemaStrongName` or document type specifier. Named Doc Spec Name in `ESB.ContextInfo` vocabulary.
`SchemaStrongName`	BTS	Named Doc Spec Strong Name in `ESB.ContextInfo` vocabulary.
`EpmRRCorrelationToken`	BTS	
`InboundTransportLocation`	BTS	
`InboundTransportType`	BTS	
`InterchangeID`	BTS	
`IsRequstResponse`	BTS	
`MessageType`	BTS	
`ReceiveLocationName`	BTS	Messaging only - not passed within orchestrations
`ReceivePortName`	BTS	
`Methodname`	SOAP	Named SOAP Method in `ESB.ContextInfo` vocabulary
`Action`	WCF	Named WCF Action in `ESB.ContextInfo` vocabulary
`WindowsUser`	BTS	Named Windows User'in `ESB.ContextInfo` vocabulary

You can optionally configure Itinerary Services to pass BizTalk message content to the BRE resolver as an additional fact. The content must be XML and is passed as a `TypedXmlDocument`. Set the `UseMsg` property to `True` to pass the message.

To resolve endpoints and maps, rule actions in the BRE policy are used to assign values to properties of the `Resolution` fact object. The ESB Toolkit provides the `ESB.EndPointInfo` and `ESB.TransformInfo` vocabularies for this purpose. The properties listed in Table 10.23 can be set using these vocabularies and are used at assign corresponding context values to outbound BizTalk messages.

All these properties are supported by the `ESB.EndPointInfo` vocabulary with the exception of the `TransformType` property, which is supported by the `ESB.TransformInfo` vocabulary.

The `TransportType` property is used to select an adapter when sending messages via a dynamic BizTalk send port. Use the `EndpointConfig` property to assign values to the context properties of the selected adapter. Use an & delimited string of name/value pairs, such as the following:

```
AlgorithmSuite=TripleDes&MessageEncoding=MTOM
```

10

TABLE 10.23   Resolution Properties Used to Assign Message Context
Properties

Property	Vocabulary Display Name
Action	End Point WCF Action
EndpointConfig	Set End Point Config
FixJaxRpc	Set End Point Fix JAX RPC
MessageExchangePattern	Set End Point Message Exchange Pattern
TargetNamespace	Set End Point Target Namespace
TransformType	Set Transform Type to {0}
TransportLocation	Set End Point Outbound Transport Location
TransportNamespace	Set End Point Transport Namespace
TransportType	Set End Point Outbound Transport Type

The BRI resolver is used to dynamically select itineraries using the BRE. This specialized
resolver is similar to the BRE resolver. Rules can evaluate message context properties and
content in the same way. However, the BRI resolver also asserts an additional
ItineraryFact object to the rule engine. An ESB.Itinerary vocabulary is provided which
supports the Name property and one of the overloaded SetVersion methods of this class.
Use these members in rule actions to select itineraries.

The RFID Server BRE Event Handler

RFID Server is a companion product that ships with BizTalk Server 2010. It is an edge
server that manages sensor and other devices and provides a framework for processing
event streams. It provides specific support for RFID devices and standards; although, it is
capable of more general application in event-driven scenarios. For example, it may also be
used to manage barcode scanners and other sensor types.

Event streams are processed using event pipelines. An event pipeline comprises a series of
event handler components. RFID server supports the configuration of tree-structured
pipeline processing in which events pass from multiple sensors to different branches of
event handlers. Events are passed from handler to handler. The branches converge toward
a single root defined by a common last event handler in each branch. In effect, RFID
Server pipelines provide a framework for creating a kind of event-processing network in
which raw event streams emitted by sensors are filtered and refined by successive event
handlers before being delivered, typically, to some external endpoint (for example, a
BizTalk Server receive location or a SQL Server database). RFID Server 2010 provides a
number of prebuilt event handlers out of the box, including new filtering, deduplication,
and delivery handlers. One of the event handlers, included in earlier versions of the
product, is the RuleEnginePolicyExecutor component. This handler asserts events and
other facts to the BRE and executes policies to handle event pattern matching.

The `RuleEnginePolicyExecutor` component asserts an instance of the `RfidRuleEngineContext` object as a fact each time a policy is executed. The `RfidRuleEngineContext` is a rich .NET fact type which represents the current event being processed by the rule engine and provides additional helper functionality for inspecting event data, generating output events, logging errors and information, reading and editing vendor-specific data provided by the sensor and managing additional data connections asserted to the rule engine. A full list of the properties and methods supported by this fact type are documented in the RFID Server help pages.

Persistent Facts

RFID Server provides support for asserting additional facts to the rule engine. One approach is to define so-called persistent facts when configuring an instance of the `RuleEnginePolicyExecutor` component. The Properties dialog box used for configuration provides facilities for specifying database and XML facts. Database facts are asserted as `DataConnections`. For each fact, the administrator configures a connection string, table name and dataset name, and can select between using a SQL Server or OLE DB data connection. Persistent XML facts can be defined as XML strings or paths to XML files. In either case, the administrator also configures a corresponding XSD schema. The administrator can define multiple XML facts. Persistent facts are passed to the `RuleEnginePolicyExecutor` component at runtime and automatically asserted.

A similar approach to asserting facts is to use a `FactRetriever`, as described in the next chapter. `FactRetriever` components implement the `IFactRetriever` interface defined by the BRF and must be placed in the GAC. Each policy can be configured with a single `FactRetriever` type. At policy execution time, the `FactRetriever` is instantiated and used to assert facts to the engine. The `Policy` helper object, used internally by `RuleEnginePolicyExecutor`, retracts facts it asserted directly. However, facts asserted via a `FactRetriever` component are not retracted by `Policy` and typically remain cached in working memory between multiple executions of the rule set. The `Policy` object passes control to the `FactRetriever` before and after each execution to allow it to manage the facts for which it is responsible.

Transient Facts

RFID Server provides additional support for asserting transient facts. Custom upstream event handler components can generate facts and add them to an Event Data dictionary programmatically. The `RfidRuleEngineContext` component provides functionality to allow facts to be retrieved using a key value to select a given Event Data dictionary. If an upstream event handler uses the string `BREFacts` as the key name for a given Event Data dictionary, the collection of facts within this dictionary is automatically asserted by the `RuleEnginePolicyExecutor`. For other dictionaries, you need to write custom code to assert the facts. This can be done by wrapping the `RuleEnginePolicyExecutor` in a custom event handler class or by using a rule action to pass the `RfidRuleEngineContext` fact, the `Executor` object, and, optionally, the key value to a custom `method`. The method can then assert the facts for the given dictionary.

Tracking Interception

The `RuleEnginePolicyExecutor` event handler supports tracking interception. In the RFID Manager management console, expand **Processes** and right-click the RFID process for a given `RuleEnginePolicyExecutor` component binding. Select **Properties**. If the Inherit Log Level box is checked, uncheck it. Then set the log level to **Verbose**. Doing so causes tracking information to be written to the RFIDServices.log file each time a policy is executed.

Limitations of RuleEnginePolicyExecutor

The `RuleEnginePolicyExecutor` event handler supports the assertion of individual event representations to the BRE, together with assertion of additional facts. The event handler executes the rule set over a single instance of `RfidRuleEngineContext` and then automatically retracts this and other facts before returning the rule engine instance to the internal cache. `RfidRuleEngineContext` provides rich data and support for interaction with event context and state and allows rules to create multiple output events that are then passed to the next downstream event handler, if any.

This approach is extremely flexible when processing single events within the event stream. However, the `RfidRuleEngineContext` event handler has significant limitations. Specifically, it does not support pattern matching over multiple events. We can consider that `RuleEnginePolicyExecutor` supports *event-condition-action* (ECA) rules for single events represented by instances of `RfidRuleEngineContext`.

When processing event streams generated by sensors, it is often useful to search for patterns of multiple events within single event streams or across multiple event streams. This is especially true for RFID tag-read events, where it is often necessary to infer information or system state from the detection of multiple events. For example, when a pallet of goods is detected at a dock door in a warehouse, it might be necessary to infer whether this represents a goods-in or goods-out movement. As well as the tag-reads at the dock door, there may be additional tag-read events that were generated earlier when stock was picked or events that indicate changes to the state of a traffic lights system. By analyzing and searching for patterns across different event types, the system can correctly infer the movement of stock.

To handle these types of requirement, event handlers need to be able to process multiple event representations across time. The RFID pipeline framework can deliver multiple events of different types to a single event handler instance. However, the `RuleEnginePolicyExecutor` event handler processes each event separately. In addition, the rule engine offers only rudimentary support for temporal processing and supports point-in-time semantics only.

RFID Server 2010 helps to mitigate these limitations by adding new event filter components. The `DuplicateEliminationFilter` event handler can be used to deduplicate event streams within a configurable sliding time window. The `VisibilityFilter` event handler outputs a `TagArrived` event when the first occurrence of an event is detected, and then automatically discards additional occurrences. It raises a `TagDeparted` event if no subsequent occurrence is detected within a given period. Both these filters support a set of simple rules for matching events. RFID Server 2010 also offers an `EpcFilter` event handler to filter events in accordance with various *Electronic Product Code* (EPC) schemas. Custom filters can be created to implement filtering, pattern matching and different types of temporal logic.

Upstream event handlers can be constructed to detect patterns within time windows and to output complex events. A complex event is a single event that denotes or signifies an aggregation of other events. Generally, it is best to use filters to process the raw event streams and to output a much smaller number of complex events, which can then be processed singly by the `RuleEnginePolicyExecutor` in conjunction with additional facts. `RuleEnginePolicyExecutor` is often best used close to event forwarding components that deliver events to external endpoints.

It is possible to construct a custom event handler that exploits the rule engine for complex event detection. However, this is an advanced topic beyond the scope of this book. Using the situated agent features of the engine described in the next chapter, it is possible to situate the rule engine in a custom handler that manages temporal logic and that exploits the engine to perform continuous queries over multiple event streams. This is a powerful approach that allows RFID Server to perform complex event processing using the pattern matching and inferencing features of the BRE.

With the advent of SQL Server 2008 R2, an alternative approach is to construct custom event handlers that exploit Microsoft StreamInsight. StreamInsight is an event stream processing engine with explicit support for different types of temporal logic and complex event detection. It is designed as a scalable engine for this purpose and offers an ultra-low-latency approach and features for handling out-of-order event delivery. StreamInsight shares some similarity with rule-processing technologies such as BRE. Both technologies support pattern-matching approaches using internal dataflow networks. However, StreamInsight is designed explicitly for continuous query and temporal processing over event streams, rather than inferencing over events and other facts. Instead of rule-based policies, StreamInsight uses continuous query definitions defined using LINQ.

Summary

This chapter introduced the concept of separation of business policies and processes, and described the benefits of policy externalization. It described common rule-processing scenarios and drew a distinction between business and executable rules. It discussed the business rule lifecycle and its relationship to the lifecycle of executable rules. We investigated a scenario in which a developer works with a business analyst to elaborate a simple business rule and implement an executable rule set. The rule set maps directly to the stated business policy together with aspects of technical policy and other runtime concerns. Over time, the rule set is amended to reflect changes in business policy. Other issues were discussed together with some of the common objections to using rule technologies.

The chapter provided an introduction to the Microsoft Business Rule Framework and identified its four main areas of rule storage and administration, rule deployment, rule modeling, and rule execution. It described the purpose of various component classes and

10

interfaces defined by the framework. Microsoft provides a number of prebuilt framework components together with a SQL Server rule database and tools for development, testing, and deployment. These were briefly defined, together with BizTalk Server extensions.

Rule developers use the Microsoft's Rule Composer and Rules Engine Deployment Wizard to create and deploy rules. The chapter explained the function of these tools and explained how to work with schemas, create rules and vocabulary definitions, and publish and deploy rule sets. These tools enable developers to work with the SQL Server rule database to create, store, manage, and apply rule sets across a distributed environment and to migrate rule sets and vocabularies between different environments.

The Business Rule Engine provides integration with BizTalk Server and companion technologies. The BRE is most commonly used in the context of BizTalk orchestrations through the Call Rules shape. The BizTalk Administration Console provides support for deployment and management of policies. In addition, the BRE can be used to resolve endpoints and maps in the ESB Toolkit, and to select itineraries in on-ramp pipelines. The BRE is also supported for use in RFID Server, where it can be combined effectively with other prebuilt and custom event handler components.

CHAPTER 11

Rule-Based Programming

by Charles Young

The structure and definition of production rules is deceptively simple. In reality, rule development can be challenging. This chapter explores the foundations of the technology and its processing model. It equips developers with the knowledge needed to understand how to exploit the rule engine. It investigates the strengths and weaknesses of the rule-processing approach and explains various behaviors of the engine.

Microsoft's engine supports facts encoded as *Extensible Markup Language* (XML) nodes, ADO.NET data tables and data rows, and .NET objects. Developers need to understand how to handle these three fact representations effectively within their rules. The chapter describes each of the fact representations in detail together with mechanisms for manipulating those representations within the engine. In addition, the chapter describes features for caching facts and optimizing fact evaluation.

The Business Rule Framework provides an extensive .NET *application programming interface* (API) for creating, managing, deploying, and executing business rules. The chapter explores some of the programmatic techniques that developers can use to exploit the framework, build custom components, and execute rule sets.

The Roots of Confusion

The rule-processing model is built on a solid foundation of more than three decades of theory and practice. However, this model is unfamiliar to many developers. Although the

Rule Composer invites developers to think of rules as "If...Then" constructs, there is only a superficial correspondence to the conditional logic constructs found in most procedural and object-orientated programming languages. There are three main areas of unfamiliarity, as discussed in the following subsections.

Declarativity

Rules are declarative, rather than procedural. The flow of execution is inferred rather than coded explicitly by the developer. A rule set is an executable program, but without the control features and direct memory manipulation familiar to most developers. There are no variables, subroutines, or branching and looping constructs.

The declarative programming model corresponds closely with the way business and technical policies are expressed. The scenario introduced in the preceding chapter provides examples of business rule statements expressed in natural language. Policy statements are declarative in nature. They specify constraints and outcomes but do not define the procedural mechanics of policy implementation. Contrast the structure of the rules in that scenario with the procedural code shown in Listing 11.1.

LISTING 11.1   Procedural Logic

```
foreach (Order order in facts)
{
    order.UseSTP = true;

    if (order.Total >= 1000)
    {
        order.UseSTP = (new CreditScore(order.EmployeeId).Value > 730);
    }

    if (!order.UseSTP) AuditHelper.LogOrderRejectionToAuditDB(Order,
                            "No STP. Credit score too low");
}
```

The code expresses the same business logic and, in this simple example, is less verbose. However, it does not align so closely to the business rule expressions. The code is concerned with additional aspects of control of execution. It implements a loop to iterate through a collection of facts. It defines conditional branching to handle certain conditions. It explicitly orders statements to provide the correct outcome.

In this simple example, proceduralism does little to obscure the underlying business logic. It is easy to see how the logic relates to higher-level business rules. However, as requirements become more complex, procedural code becomes harder to maintain, validate, and trace against business rules. For example, where business logic compares attributes of different facts, procedural code requires nested loops to handle these comparisons in a set-based fashion. Of course, we could use LINQ expressions to join and compare data.

However, this serves only to illustrate the point. LINQ's strength is its capability to support a declarative style of coding based on a functional model rather than a procedural one.

The declarative approach supports a number of automatic optimizations. Experienced developers know that if or switch statements with many conditions can quickly become inefficient. Modern compilers help by using smart compilation of these constructs. Nevertheless, the declarative approach enables rule engines to provide a consistent level of high optimization without additional development effort. By contrast, writing well-optimized procedural code often serves to obscure the underlying business logic even further.

Set-Based Programming

The use of the foreach loop in the preceding example illustrates another important characteristic of rule processing. The rule engine is set-based. It processes unordered collections of distinct facts. Set-based processing avoids explicit procedural iteration of collections. Instead, it supports declarative comparison of sets to find Cartesian products, intersections, and unions.

Many developers are familiar with set-based programming. SQL is a widely used set-based language for data definition, control, and manipulation. There is a profound similarity between the conditions of a given rule and a SQL SELECT statement. Rule conditions are expressed similarly to the WHERE clause of a SELECT statement. Rule conditions often imply joins between different sets of facts.

Some developers find it useful to visualize a rule as equivalent to a combination of a WHERE clause, within an implied SELECT * statement, and an action list. However, the rule-processing model is different to SQL in two important respects. First, the basic unit of execution is the rule set, rather than individual rules. Execution of a rule set is rather like executing multiple SELECT statements simultaneously and then processing a single collection containing all the results. Second, rule actions define behavior that is applied directly to each match found by that rule. This is reminiscent of object orientation, which binds behavior, defined at the class level, to data in individual objects. There is no direct equivalent in SQL, although cursors can be used to emulate aspects of the rule-processing approach. Although rule processing shares many similarities to SQL, significant differences exist, as well.

Recursive Processing

The rule engine implements a recursive approach to conditional pattern matching and action processing. We explore this "match-resolve-act" mechanism later in this chapter. Recursion is central to the engine's design and extends the engine's set-based processing capabilities. It supports the ability of individual rule actions to change state. Rule actions can modify or remove the matched facts that caused those actions to fire. They can also add new facts. Whenever a single rule action changes the state of the engine, the change may invalidate the current set of matches. The engine uses recursion to immediately recalculate this set.

We can illustrate this using a simple analogy. Consider a SQL SELECT statement that joins order lines with stock items. This is illustrated in Listing 11.2.

LISTING 11.2   Conditional SQL Join

```
SELECT ol.OrderId, ol.Quantity, si.Id
FROM OrderLine AS ol, StockItem AS si
WHERE ol.ItemId = si.Id
AND ol.Quantity < si.QtyOnHand — enough stock on hand to fulfill this order
line
```

We declare a cursor over the results of this query and fetch each row in turn. For each row, we assign stock from the warehouse to fulfill the order. The query initially eliminates any order lines that we know we cannot fulfill. However, there is an obvious problem. As we work through each order line and assign stock, we deplete the stock available for fulfill-ment of other order lines. Hence, each iteration of the cursor can invalidate the current result set being processed by that cursor.

SQL cursors handle this problem by adjusting the result set in each iteration. The ISO SQL standard defines the INSENSITIVE option to control this aspect of cursor behavior. If INSENSITIVE is omitted from its declaration, the cursor recursively removes rows from the result set wherever they no longer match the second condition of the WHERE clause. As our code progressively fetches data from the cursor and depletes stock levels, it reasons that certain order lines can no longer be fulfilled and eliminates them from further consideration.

The rule engine uses recursion to handle this kind of behavior in a natural and efficient way. It implements a sophisticated approach in which the collection of all results is dynamically recalculated across many different rules. This recursive model lies at the heart of the rule engine's ability to reason over data. New information inferred during process-ing is fed back to the engine and directly affects its progress through repeated recalcula-tion of the set of valid and logically consistent rule matches.

Contrast the recursive approach with processing of collections in languages such as C# where collections are immutable during iteration. For many developers, the recursive behavior of the rule engine is unfamiliar. Its implications can be difficult to grasp at first, but with practice, developers will soon begin to understand how to exploit it to build reasoning capabilities directly into their rule sets.

Blended Paradigms

Microsoft's engine blends different computing paradigms and models. The rule engine evaluates data and executes actions over matches. The various models supported within the engine can therefore be categorized into data models and programmatic models.

Data Models

The rule engine implements an approach to rule processing called the Rete algorithm. Conceptually, this algorithm operates on relational data. However, facts are asserted to the engine as .NET objects. Internally, the engine implements an object-orientated implemen-tation of the Rete algorithm, which inevitably exhibits a degree of impedance mismatch with the relational model. This mismatch is exhibited in various ways, including restrictions on the use of objects, especially when using the Rule Composer, issues concerning object identity, and so on.

The engine can process relational data asserted as ADO.NET data tables and rows. It also supports hierarchical XML data. The XML model exhibits significant impedance mismatch with both the relational and object-oriented models. The rule engine supports an XPath-based approach for XML processing that enables developers to map XML data to a relational view.

Programmatic Models

.NET objects provide programmatic behavior and data. Consider the use of the AuditHelper class in the scenario described in the preceding chapter. The LogOrderRejectionToAuditDB() method of this class is invoked as a rule action. Note that this method could be implemented as a static member of the class.

By default, we need to assert an instance of the AuditHelper class to the engine. Even when we invoke only static class members, and do not naturally think of the object as a fact, we must still assert an instance to the engine. This is a direct consequence of the impedance mismatch between the object-oriented model implemented by the engine and the underlying relational model of the Rete algorithm. Later in this chapter, you will see that the engine supports an alternative mode that allows direct invocation of static methods without object assertion.

In the previous chapter, we saw that the rule engine maps methods and properties of .NET objects to predicates and functions defined in BRL. .NET code is procedural and object-oriented. Predicates and functions combine two additional programming paradigms. Predicates represent a form of logical programming. Rule processing draws extensively from predicate logic; although it does not strictly implement a formal logical system. Functions represent a type of functional programming. Again, the rule engine implements an impure functional model with semi-procedural aspects and some direct control over side effects.

The combination of object-oriented, relational, and hierarchical data models with procedural, logical, and functional processing within a single specialized runtime environment might seem challenging. Consider, however, that a similar blending of paradigms is increasingly seen in mainstream programming languages. C#, VB.NET, and F# all provide extensive support for functional constructs alongside procedural and object-orientated approaches. VB.NET allows XML literals to be embedded directly into procedural code. The .NET class library implements extensive support for hierarchical and relational data processing and declarative approaches to querying data. Developers are increasingly expected to handle multiple paradigms simultaneously and side by side. In this respect, rule processing is different only in the details of how this blending is implemented.

Limits of Expressivity

Microsoft Business Rule Language (BRL) enables executable rules to be aligned closely with the declarative statements contained in business and technical policy definitions. However, all rule engines exhibit limits to their expressivity. Natural languages enable greater expressivity than formal executable languages. This is another type of impedance mismatch that can cause confusion and difficulty.

Developers often encounter a lack of expressivity when implementing rules. For example, the current version of the rule engine provides limited support for quantification. Quantification evaluates entire sets to find "at least one" or "all" matches. Consider the following business rule:

```
Loyalty discounts will only be given to customers who have placed at least one
order worth $150 or more in the past 6 months.
```

BRL provides some built-in support for explicit representation of this rule when handling XML data. It relies on the use of an XPath expression exploited via the `exists` predicate. For other fact types, there is no built-in support for quantifying a set of facts. BRL's limited expressivity reflects an absence of corresponding functionality within the rule engine itself. Developers should expect to encounter scenarios that require custom logic to supplement the built-in facilities of the rule language.

Understanding the Rule Engine

At first, most developers find the Business Rules Engine hard to understand. Specialized terminology is used to describe an unfamiliar model. Rule logic often exhibits behavior which is different to what procedural programmers expect. In this section we will explore some of the core concepts and behaviors of the engine.

Understanding Production Systems

Microsoft's rule engine is a Production System. Production systems have a long history in computer science. Their theoretical foundations predate the emergence of modern computing. They were defined in the early 1920s by Emil Post as a computational method based on recursive "rewrite" rules that match sequential patterns of symbols and output new sequences. Modern Production Systems have broader applicability and are more elaborate than Post's system but retain the essential characteristics he described.

> **NOTE**
>
> In general computing, the term *production system* is widely used to designate software applications that are complete, tested, and deployed to a production environment. In this chapter, we use the same term in an entirely different sense; the term has been capitalized to remind readers of this distinction.

A Production System evaluates facts about some "universe of discourse." It uses productions (rules) to match patterns and to act on the matches it finds. It maintains an internal representation of the "world" by storing facts and matched aggregations of facts within its working memory. It implements some mechanism for ordering and prioritizing the conflict set of matches before performing actions. It allows actions to change the state of its internal representation of the world and recursively recalculates the conflict set each time such a change is made.

Some terms in the preceding paragraph will be unfamiliar to most readers. The following sections explain the concepts and terminology in greater detail.

The Universe of Discourse

The universe of discourse comprises all the things (entities) we are interested in when performing logical reasoning. In the example in the preceding chapter, the universe of discourse includes orders, customers, and credit scores. The universe of discourse is often referred to loosely as the world.

Production Systems naturally handle a closed world. This assumes that every relevant fact about the world is made available to the Production System. By contrast, an open world implies that there may be relevant facts which are not known to the system. In the "open world" approach, the Production System maintains only a partial representation of the universe of discourse. This introduces uncertainty. Production Systems are capable of reasoning under uncertainty. However, Microsoft's engine does not implement any explicit support for this.

Facts

A fact is an assertion about an entity within the universe of discourse. It is a data item asserted to the rule engine. Conceptually, Production Systems model facts as relational tuples. In a database system, a relational tuple is represented and stored as a row in a table. It maps a set of attribute names to a set of values

```
{ OrderID=1234, CustomerID='ABC9876', Date='20100101', Total=756 }
```

Most Production Systems extend this representation by defining a type specifier for each tuple. The example tuple represents an order. We can modify the representation as follows:

```
Order { OrderID=1234, CustomerID='ABC9876', Date='20100101', Total=756 }
```

Unlike a relational database, a Production System does not provide persisted storage for facts and has no equivalent to tables. A database table defines a schema for tuples and persists a set of tuples that correspond to the schema. The schema and tuple set, taken together, constitute a relation. Although Production Systems do not provide tables, they generally handle tuple sets according to their schemas.

At runtime, Microsoft's engine always represents facts physically as .NET objects. It supports logical bindings for XML, Database, and .NET types. Each binding specifies either a type or an attribute. Each type specifier is qualified using two parts. These specifiers are shown in Table 11.1.

TABLE 11.1   Binding Specifiers for Fact Types and Attributes

Bindings	Type Specifier	Attribute Specifier
XML	[Document Type] : [XPath Selector]	[XPath Field]
Database	[Dataset] : [Table]	[Column]
.NET	[Assembly] : [Class]	[Method] [Property]

At runtime, facts can be asserted to the engine using the.NET types or their subtypes listed in Table 11.2. In addition, the engine allows entire collections of XML and Database facts to be asserted as a single object. The rule engine provides special wrapper classes for handling XML and Database data and distinguishing these facts from other .NET objects.

TABLE 11.2   Runtime Representation of Facts

Type	Tuple	Tuple Collection	Type Wrapper
XML (XML DOM)	XmlNode	XmlDocument	TypedXmlDocument
Database (ADO.NET)	DataRow	DataTable	DataConnection TypedDataTable TypedDataRow
.NET	Object	N/A	N/A

Productions

A production is a rule in an If...Then form. They are often termed production rules. We can specify a production as follows:

```
<conditions> → <actions>
```

A production matches a pattern of facts and specifies a list of actions to undertake for each match. The left side of the production defines the match criteria as a set of conditions. The right side of the production defines the list of actions.

Productions are informal. They do not correspond precisely to any recognized construct in any formal system of logic. They are computational, rather than logical.

Consider this well-known logical argument (a syllogism):

```
All men are mortal
Socrates is a man
Therefore, Socrates is mortal
```

This is an example of a type of reasoning called *modus ponens*. The first line implies a rule in the form of

```
<conditions> → <consequence>
```

For example

```
If being is a human then being is mortal
```

This rule is different to a production. A production does not yield a logical consequence directly. Instead, it suggests a set of actions to the engine that may be undertaken for each specific match. The engine decides when and how to undertake those actions at runtime. Of course, the actions may represent or encode logical consequences. For example, they may derive or assert new information about an entity. Production rules are flexible constructs that can be used to model many different rule types and reasoning strategies. In this case, we might construct a production rule as shown in Listing 11.3.

LISTING 11.3   Modeling *Modus Ponens* with a Production Rule

```
IF
  Being.Species is equal to human
THEN ...
  Being.IsMortal = true
  update Being
```

Production actions can "rewrite" the state of the Production System. This is one of the central features of Production Systems and, together with recursive evaluation, is the foundation for rule-based reasoning. Actions can be used to assert new facts and to modify or delete existing facts.

Conditions

Microsoft's rule engine models rule conditions as a tree of logical expressions. The three connectives (AND, OR, and NOT) each take logical expressions as their arguments. All other logical expressions are predicates. The rule engine defines a small library of built-in predicates and allows any .NET method or property getter that returns a Boolean value to be used as a custom predicate.

Functions, object references, and constants are used as arguments to predicates and functions. The engine evaluates the condition tree against all possible combinations of facts to find every possible match. When the root logical expression evaluates to true, this indicates that all its nested logical expressions also evaluate to true. For the *not* connective, its immediate child must evaluate to false.

Understanding Short-Circuiting

Developers often encounter difficulties that arise due to incorrect expectations about short-circuiting. Most developers are familiar with short-circuiting in imperative programming languages such as C#. Short-circuiting is a procedural optimization that reduces the amount of evaluation work done by the code. In C# the && and || operators specify the use of short-circuiting. Consider the following conditional expression:

```
if (objA.Property1 > 5 && objA.Property2 < 9){ ... }
```

If evaluation of the first condition (`objA.Property1 > 5`) yields `false`, the code avoids the unnecessary overhead of evaluating the second condition (`objA.Property2 < 9`). This is optimal, but can lead to problems due to side effects. Both conditions invoke property getter methods when evaluated. Short-circuiting the second condition can lead to unexpected results if there is an assumption that the code in `Property2` is always invoked. Developers use the & and ¦ operators to avoid short-circuiting:

```
if (objA.Property1 > 5 & objA.Property2 < 9){ ... }
```

Short-circuiting makes a great deal of sense in procedural code. Developers understand and control short-circuiting behavior as a natural consequence of the imperative style. This is not the case in declarative coding. The developer works at a higher level without consideration of detailed procedural execution. Developers often try to understand rules as if they were equivalent to procedural statements. They are not.

Short-circuiting behavior is used internally by the rule engine. It happens as a natural consequence of the way the engine filters facts. However, inferring the exact runtime behavior from the rules expressed in BRL is difficult and requires a deep knowledge of the implementation of the rule engine. For example, the rule set translator normalizes each rule set before translating it into an executable form. The normalized rule set is logically equivalent to the rules expressed by the developer, but may be structured differently. The normalizer removes redundant connectives, applies Disjunctive Normal Form and enforces De Morgan's laws. By this stage, the developer has lost sight of the exact structure of rule conditions at runtime. Short-circuiting behavior is also affected by the use of caching optimizations, which you will encounter later in this chapter.

Rules are declarative, not procedural. A significant difference exists between the declarative nature of rules and the procedural nature of custom .NET predicates and functions written in languages such as C# and VB.NET. Problems also arise when using built-in predicates and functions to process XML and ADO.NET data. Incorrect beliefs about short-circuiting behavior can lead to bugs that are hard to diagnose.

To avoid problems related to short-circuiting, learn to apply two simple constraints when designing rules and writing custom .NET code:

▶ **Always define rules as if short-circuiting is not supported:** At the BRL level, always assume that the engine will operate without short-circuiting. Consider short-circuiting to be an unexpected runtime bonus.

▶ **Always write custom .NET code to support short-circuiting:** This applies to custom .NET predicates and functions. Eliminate any side effects that would require short-circuiting to be avoided. You never know when short-circuiting may be applied.

Later in this chapter, you will see a common problem that arises when processing XML data where incorrect expectations about short-circuiting behavior lead to runtime exceptions.

Using OR Connectives

The OR connective is provided for convenience and expressivity. At runtime the engine evaluates a condition tree containing OR connectives in the same way it would evaluate multiple rules for each variation specified by the OR. Consider the rule in Listing 11.4.

LISTING 11.4   Rule with OR Connective

```
IF
  OR
    Order.Total is greater than or equal to GoldMemberDiscountThreshold.Value
    Order.Total is greater than or equal to LoyaltyDiscountThreshold.Value
THEN ...
```

The evaluation work undertaken by the engine is always logically and often physically equivalent to the evaluation work it would undertake for multiple rules that express the equivalent logic. Listing 11.5 shows the decomposition of the single rule into two rules.

LISTING 11.5   **OR** Decomposed to Two Rules

```
IF
    Order.Total is greater than or equal to GoldMemberDiscountThreshold.Value
THEN ...
IF
    Order.Total is greater than or equal to LoyaltyDiscountThreshold.Value
THEN ...
```

Consider the situation where the total value of an order is greater than or equal to both of the threshold values in the preceding example. When using separate rules, the engine finds distinct matches for each rule. Both rules are activated. What happens, though, for the single rule that uses the OR connective? Just as for two rules, the engine produces two distinct activations of the same rule. The first is for the match between the Order and the GoldMemberDiscountThreshold facts. The second is for the match between the same Order and the LoyaltyDiscountThreshold fact. Both rule activations share a common list of actions.

This behavior is deeply unfamiliar to developers used to short-circuiting in imperative code. However, it is entirely logical and consistent in declarative rule processing. The engine evaluates rules to find every possible match for each rule from the set of facts currently asserted to the engine. Internal runtime support for short-circuiting is allowed only wherever it does not violate this fundamental behavior. When using the OR connective, the engine logically finds every possible match for the disjoint conditions and may therefore produce multiple activations of the same rule.

The behavior of the rule engine is different to that of a simple SELECT statement in SQL. Consider the apparently "equivalent" SQL statement in Listing 11.6.

LISTING 11.6   SQL **SELECT** Statement with **OR**

```
SELECT *
FROM Orders, GoldMemberDiscountThreshold, LoyaltyDiscountThreshold
WHERE Orders.Total >= GoldMemberDiscountThreshold.Value
OR Orders.Total >= LoyaltyDiscountThreshold.Value
```

For simplicity, assume each of the three tables contains a single record. When the query is run, the SELECT statement returns a single row. This is analogous to a single activation of the rule and is quite different to the behavior of the rule engine. In SQL, the closest equivalent to the example rule is shown in Listing 11.7.

LISTING 11.7   SQL **UNION ALL**

```
SELECT *
FROM Orders, GoldMemberDiscountThreshold
WHERE Orders.Total >= GoldMemberDiscountThreshold.Value

UNION ALL

SELECT *
FROM Orders, LoyaltyDiscountThreshold
WHERE Orders.Total >= LoyaltyDiscountThreshold.Value
```

Mastering these subtle differences between the rule engine and other evaluation models is vital to use the rule engine effectively. The unfamiliarity of the rule engine model implies a steep learning curve for most developers. If you are new to rule processing, you may want to avoid using the OR connective until you are more familiar with the engine. Instead of using OR, create multiple rules. The engine eliminates any redundancies at runtime, so your rule set will generally be just as efficient.

There is an additional issue when using OR connectives. Consider the rule in Listing 11.8.

LISTING 11.8   No Duplicate Matches

```
IF
  AND
    Order.CustomerID = Customer.Id
  OR
      Order.Total is greater than or equal to 1000
      Customer.GoldMembershipStartDate is before 01/01/2000 00:00:00
THEN ...
```

This rule differs from the first example. It tests two different facts against literal values. Consider the scenario where a given order has a total value greater than 1000 and a corresponding customer has been a gold member since before the beginning of the millennium. Both disjoint conditions evaluate to true.

Based on the previous discussion, we might expect the engine to produce two activations of this rule. Indeed, this happens internally. However, in this case, there is an extra consideration. Each activation contains an aggregation of the matching facts. In the earlier example, the activations contained different aggregations:

```
Activation 1:    { order, goldMemberDiscountThreshold }
Activation 2:    { order, loyaltyDiscountThreshold }
```

In this example, however, both activations contain an identical set of facts:

```
Activation 1:    { order, customer }
Activation 2:    { order, customer }
```

The rule engine detects this duplication. When a single rule produces multiple activations that contain identical sets of facts, the engine performs automatic de-duplication and retains a single activation only. Again, this is entirely logical. The engine evaluates the rule to find every possible match from the set of facts currently asserted to the engine. It automatically removes any duplicate matches.

In rare circumstances you might want to retain all the duplicate activations. You can achieve this by explicitly rewriting the single rule as multiple rules and eliminating the OR connective, as shown in Listing 11.9.

LISTING 11.9   Allow "Duplicate" Matches

```
IF
  AND
    Order.CustomerID = Customer.Id
    Order.Total is greater than or equal to 1000
THEN ...

IF
  AND
    Order.CustomerID = Customer.Id
    Customer.GoldMembershipStartDate is before 01/01/2000 00:00:00
THEN ...
```

Understanding Implicit Conditions

BRL allows developers to define rules at a high level to maximize fidelity to business policy statements expressed in natural language. The language has a simple syntax when viewed in the Rule Composer. However, this simplicity comes at a cost. One of the more opaque issues that developers face is the presence of additional implicit conditions which are not expressed explicitly in the *left-hand side* (LHS) (that is, the IF section) of a rule. Consider the example in Listing 11.10.

LISTING 11.10   Implicit Condition: Example 1

```
IF
  SpecialDiscount is not equal to <null>
THEN
  Order.Discount = SpecialDiscount.Value
```

The intent of this rule can be expressed as follows:

```
If a special discount is available, apply it to every unfulfilled order.
```

We will assume that a single SpecialDiscount fact is asserted alongside multiple Order facts.

The action list of the rule contains a single action that assigns the special discount value to an order. This implies that each rule activation must have access to the following aggregation of facts:

```
{ order, specialDiscount }
```

This, in turn, implies that the rule must match Order facts and the SpecialDiscount fact. However, there is no explicit condition in the LHS of the rule for matching Orders. Instead, there is an implicit condition that the developer must infer from studying the action list on the *right-hand side* (RHS) (that is, the THEN section) of the rule. We can visualize the underlying rule as logically equivalent to Listing 11.11.

LISTING 11.11   Explicit Condition Representation

```
IF
  AND
    Order is not equal to <null>
    SpecialDiscount is not equal to <null>
THEN
  Order.Discount = SpecialDiscount.Value
```

In natural language, we can state this rule as follows:

```
If a special discount is available, and there are any unfulfilled orders, apply
the special discount to each order.
```

The use of implicit conditions can help to make the intention of the rule clearer by hiding logical implications that can be inferred from the context (in this case, the actions we intend to undertake). This approach is common in natural language where it is used to ensure that the emphasis and intent of a statement is clearly understood. However, when conditions are implicit, it can be harder to troubleshoot issues and spot the cause of problems. Consider the variation of the rule shown in Listing 11.12.

LISTING 11.12   Implicit Condition: Example 2

```
IF
  Order is not equal to <null>
THEN
  Order.Discount = SpecialDiscount.Value
```

In this case, we have changed the emphasis of the rule:

```
If there are any unfulfilled orders, apply a special discount to each one.
```

This statement assumes is that there is a special discount. If there is no special discount, the rule will not fire. Imagine that, at runtime, the rule fails to fire when expected because the developer has forgotten to assert an instance of `SpecialDiscount`. An inspection of the single condition of this rule will not suggest the nature of the problem to the developer. They may fail to infer the implicit condition from the action list.

Explicit definition of all conditions can have a detrimental effect. The `update` engine operation is similar to `assert`, but reevaluates rules that only explicitly reference the updated object on the LHS. If you make all conditions explicit, the behavior of the rule set changes if any of the rules use the `update` operation. The `update` operation, used with implicit conditions, helps to reduce the amount of reevaluation work and avoid unintentional loops.

Common Rule Patterns

Rule developers repeatedly encounter common requirements when designing and implementing rule set logic. This section explores design patterns for handling different types of quantification and negation. It introduces the concept of modeling state transitions and explores the use of the engine as a situated reasoning agent.

Implementing Quantification

You saw earlier that the rule engine offers no support for quantification except for the built-in `exists` predicate, which uses an XPath to test for node sets within XML data. A quantifier is an operator that ranges over all available facts that meet some given condition. The quantifier can be used to test some assertion about the entire range of facts. Quantifiers add significant expressivity to rules. For example, Listing 11.13 provides an example of universal quantification.

LISTING 11.13   Universal Quantifier

```
IF
  FORALL Order, Customer
    WHERE
      Order.CustomerID is equal to Customer.Id
    Order.Total is greater than or equal to 1000
THEN
  Customer.GoldMember = True
```

This rule assigns gold membership to any customer for whom all the orders currently asserted to the engine have a value of greater than or equal to $1,000. This is an example of universal quantification. There is no FORALL...WHERE quantifier construct in BRL.

Listing 11.14 provides an example of existential quantification.

LISTING 11.14   Existential Quantifier

```
IF
  FORANY Order, Customer
    WHERE
      Order.CustomerID is equal to Customer.Id
    Order.Total is greater than or equal to 1000
THEN
  Customer.GoldMember = True
```

This rule assigns gold membership to any customer for whom there is at least one order currently asserted to the engine that has a total value of greater than or equal to $1,000. This is an example of existential quantification. Again, there is no FORANY..WHERE quantifier construct in BRL.

> **NOTE**
>
> In formal logic, support for quantification is the main differentiator between propositional logic and first-order logic. BRL approximates to a propositional logic language. The engine has no built-in mechanism for performing a forall or forany. It does, however, implement the equivalent of a foreach mechanism.

In BRL, quantification requirements can be handled in several ways. For example, Listing 11.15 contains two rules that can be used to achieve the same result as the example in Listing 11.13.

LISTING 11.15   Encoded Universal Quantification: Example 1

```
// [1] Tentatively set candidate customers as Gold members
Priority(10)
IF
  AND
    Order.CustomerID is equal to Customer.Id
    Order.Total is greater than or equal 1000
THEN
  Customer.GoldMember = True

// [2] Remove gold membership if any orders are less than $1,000
IF
  AND
    Order.CustomerID is equal to Customer.Id
    Order.Total is less than 1000
THEN
  Customer.GoldMember = False
```

Rule [1] has a higher priority than Rule [2]. Rule [1] ensures that initially, any customer for whom there is at least one order worth $1,000 or more is designated as having gold membership. This single rule could be used by itself to implement an alternative to the FORANY example.

Once all Rule [1] activations have fired, Rule [2] activations fire. These ensure that, for any customer for whom at least one order is less than $1,000, his or her gold membership is revoked.

There are two problems with this rule set. First, it is inefficient. If multiple orders exist for a given customer, either of the rules may fire several times, redundantly resetting the GoldMember flag. Second, the semantics of this rule set is different to the example in Listing 11.13. If a customer is already a gold member, his or her membership may be revoked. In Listing 11.13, their gold membership is not revoked. To achieve the same effect as Listing 11.13, it is possible to elaborate the model. Listing 11.16 does this by using an additional IdentifiedAsGoldMembershipCandidate attribute to record the preliminary assessment for gold membership for customers who are not currently gold members.

LISTING 11.16   Encoded Universal Quantification: Example 2

```
// [1] Tentatively set candidate customers as Gold members
IF
  AND
    NOT
      Customer.GoldMember
    NOT
      Customer.IdentifiedAsGoldMembershipCandidate
    Order.CustomerID is equal to Customer.Id
```

```
    Order.Total is greater than or equal 1000
THEN
  Customer.GoldMember = True
  Customer.IdentifiedAsGoldMembershipCandidate= True
  update Customer

// [2] Remove gold membership if any orders less than $1,000
IF
  AND
    Customer.GoldMember
    Customer.IdentifiedAsGoldMembershipCandidate
    Order.CustomerID is equal to Customer.Id
    Order.Total is less than 1000
THEN
  Customer.GoldMember = False
  update Customer
```

The rule set assumes that the IdentifiedAsGoldMembershipCandidate attribute is initialized to False before each Customer is asserted. A high-priority rule could be used to initialize this attribute to False. Initially, a Customer who is already a gold member will not match rule 1 and will not match rule 2 either because IdentifiedAsGoldMembershipCandidate is False. There is no need to use priority in this example because Rule [2] will only match Customer facts updated by Rule [1]. Each time Rule [1] updates a Customer fact, any remaining activations of Rule [1] for that customer will be invalidated and will not fire. The engine reevaluates the updated Customer fact and may match it against Rule [2]. When an activation of Rule [2] fires, it updates the Customer fact. However, the IdentifiedAsGoldMembershipCandidate attribute is still True, and therefore the updated Customer fact does not match Rule [1]. It also no longer matches Rule [2]. Any remaining activations of Rule [2] for that Customer fact will therefore be invalidated and will not fire.

Listing 11.17 states the logic of the two rules in natural language.

LISTING 11.17   Encoded Universal Quantification: Natural Language

```
// [1] Tentatively set candidate customers as Gold members
If the customer is not currently a Gold member and we haven't yet identified
the customer as a candidate for Gold membership, then if any order exists for
that customer whose total value is greater than or equal to $1,000, tentatively
mark the customer as a Gold member and record that we have identified them as a
candidate for Gold membership.

// [2] Remove gold membership if any orders less than $1,000
If the customer is marked as a Gold member but is also identified as a candidate for
Gold membership, then if any order exists for that customer whose total value is less
than $1,000, mark the customer as a non-Gold member.
```

The lack of support for quantification reduces the expressivity of BRL. However, developers can write rules to apply equivalent logic using the available features of the engine. An alternative approach is to delegate quantification to external code. For example, a custom predicate could be created that queries a `DataTable`, `XMLDocument` or .NET collection fact using quantification. The `exists` predicate provides a built-in example of this approach. It uses an XPath to define the query criteria.

Handling Negation-as-Failure

One of the most common difficulties experienced by rule engine developers concerns the need to express negated existential quantifications. We often need to express the concept of an absence of any match in our rules. Consider the following business rule:

If a gold membership customer has not placed any order worth $1,000 or more in the past 6 months, their gold membership is automatically revoked.

With no support for quantification, there is no direct way to express this rule in BRL. We would like to define a rule, as shown in Listing 11.18.

LISTING 11.18   Negated Existential Quantification

```
IF
  AND
    Customer.GoldMember
    NOT
      FORANY Order
        AND
          Order.CustomerID is equal to Customer.Id
          Order.Total is greater than or equal to 1000
          Order.Date is after DateHelper.SixMonthsAgo
THEN
  Customer.GoldMember = False
```

The rule revokes gold membership for any customer for whom no orders currently asserted to the engine have a total value of greater than or equal to $1,000. However, without a FORANY quantifier, we cannot express the rule as shown. Instead, Listing 11.19 shows how to use a combination of flag attributes and priority to encode the necessary logic.

LISTING 11.19   Negation-as-Failure: Example 1

```
// [1] Set candidate customers for revocation consideration
IF
  AND
```

```
      Customer.GoldMember
      NOT
         Customer.ConsiderForRevocation
      NOT
         Customer.RevocationDecisionMade
THEN
   Customer.ConsiderForRevocation = True
   update Customer


// [2] Do not revoke gold membership if order >= $1,000 and in last 6 months
[Priority(10)]
IF
  AND
      Customer.ConsiderForRevocation
      NOT
         Customer.RevocationDecisionMade
      Order.CustomerID is equal to Customer.Id
      Order.Total is greater than or equal to 1000
      Order.Date is after DateHelper.SixMonthsAgo
THEN
   Customer.ConsiderForRevocation = False
   Customer.RevocationDecisionMade = True
   update Customer


// [3] Revoke gold membership
IF
  AND
      Customer.ConsiderForRevocation
      NOT
         Customer.RevocationDecisionMade
THEN
   Customer.GoldMember = False
   Customer.ConsiderForRevocation = False
   Customer.RevocationDecisionMade = True
   update Customer
```

This approach works but is verbose and difficult to understand. Later in this chapter, you will see ways to improve the code.

Negation of existential quantification is used to implement *negation-as-failure* (NaF). You saw earlier in this chapter that Production Systems generally handle a "closed world" where every relevant fact about the "world" is made available to the Production System. NaF is a direct application of the *closed-world assumption* (CWA). The CWA is a well-known approach in logic that states that if something cannot be proven to be true, it is assumed to be false. Compare this to the *open-word assumption* (OWA) that states that if something cannot be proven to be true, it is assumed that it could be true.

NaF is a form of "weak" negation based on assumption. The negation is assumed on the basis of the *failure* to prove whether a condition is true. In the preceding example, a customer's gold membership is revoked if we fail to prove that the customer has placed an order for more than $1,000 in the past 6 months. The failure to prove that the customer is eligible for gold membership is treated as an assertion that the customer is not eligible. This depends on having a closed world. We must ensure that all relevant orders for the past 6 months have been asserted to the engine. If any orders are omitted, a customer's gold membership might be incorrectly revoked.

> **NOTE**
>
> Production systems generally support *inflationary negation* rather than true NaF. This is a technical distinction in logic based on the possibility that, where no proof exists for a given predicate (i.e., no matches currently exist), the engine may fire rules based on assumed negation and then subsequently fire a rule that provides the missing proof. Logically, the engine can assume negation on the basis of nonground atoms. We follow the common practice of using the term *NaF* loosely to include inflationary negation.

Using Strong Negation

The previous section illustrated the limits of expressivity in BRL. BRL offers no support for NaF and, as a result, encoding NaF can be difficult. One answer to this is to recast the problem using "strong" negation. A strong negation asserts the negation of a proposition as an explicit fact or attribute, rather than assuming it from the absence of matches.

In the example used in the previous section, we could redesign the Customer fact so that it provides a new attribute called EligibleForGoldMembership. If Customer is a .NET type, this might be implemented as a property that runs a SELECT COUNT(*) query against a database for all orders in the past 6 months that have a total value greater than $1,000 and returns true if the count is greater than 0. For XML facts, we could run this same query and prepopulate an element or attribute with a Boolean value before asserting the XML document to the engine. Alternatively, we might use a helper object directly within our rule set to obtain the Boolean value. Having converted a weak negation into a strong negation, our rule might now be as defined as in Listing 11.20.

LISTING 11.20   Strong Negation: Example 1

```
IF
  AND
    Customer.GoldMember
    NOT
      Customer.EligibleForGoldMembership
THEN
  Customer.GoldMember = False
```

Converting NaF to strong negation has some drawbacks. It might require costly redesign of object models, XML schemas, or databases. It might obscure the semantics of the business rule by requiring some of the logic to be implemented externally to the engine. The preceding example is problematic because it no longer conveys the basis on which eligibility is assessed. Listing 11.21 shows different design that makes the intention of the rule a little clearer.

LISTING 11.21   Strong Negation: Example 2

```
IF
  AND
    Customer.GoldMember
    NOT
      Customer.HasPlacedEligibleOrder(1000, 6)
THEN
  Customer.GoldMember = False
```

If vocabularies are used, this rule could be rendered more clearly still, as shown in Listing 11.22.

LISTING 11.22   Strong Negation with Vocabulary

```
IF
  AND
    the customer has gold membership status
    NOT
      the customer has placed an order for $ 1000 or more in the last 6 months
THEN
  set customer's gold membership = False
```

Conversion from weak to strong negation should be employed as a common strategy when designing rules. Rules allow business semantics to be expressed clearly in a declarative fashion. This benefit is undermined by writing complex and verbose code to work around the limits of expressivity in BRL. The rule engine works directly with XML nodes, ADO.NET DataRows and .NET objects. Developers should exploit the power and expressivity of the .NET Framework, XPath, SQL, and other technologies wherever appropriate to maintain clarity and declarativity.

Designing Rule Sets as State Machines

Sometimes, we cannot avoid encoding a degree of complexity directly into our rules. We have seen that rules can all too quickly become heavily polluted with additional process-flow code that obscures the higher-level intent. The rule language is declarative. It does not support procedural constructs (branching, looping, and so on). Proceduralism requires convoluted approaches that obscure the code.

One of the most powerful ways of taming this complexity is to implement rule sets explicitly as state machines. Listing 11.23 provides a version of the NaF example described in Listing 11.19 where the `ConsiderForRevocation` and `RevocationDecisionMade` attributes have been replaced with a single `ReviewState` attribute. By testing and varying the value of this single attribute, we add state transition semantics to the rule set.

LISTING 11.23   NaF Using State Machine

```
// [1] Initially set candidate customers for revocation consideration
IF
  AND
    Customer.ReviewState is equal to CutomerNotReviewed
    Customer.GoldMember
THEN
  Customer.ReviewState = ReviewCustomer
  update Customer


// [2] Do not revoke gold membership if order >= $1,000 and in last 6 months
[Priority(10)]
IF
  AND
    Customer.ReviewState is equal to ReviewCustomer
    Order.CustomerID is equal to Customer.Id
    Order.Total is greater than or equal to 1000
    Order.Date is after DateHelper.SixMonthsAgo
THEN
  Customer.ReviewState = CustomerReviewComplete
  update Customer


// [3] Revoke gold membership
IF
  Customer.ReviewState is equal to ReviewCustomer
THEN
  Customer.ReviewState = CustomerReviewComplete
  Customer.GoldMember = False
  update Customer
```

Although this is still verbose, and although it still depends on the careful use of priority, the intent of the rule set is clearer. The state transition semantics control which rules are "switched on" for a given `Customer` fact each time we update that fact. The updating of the `Customer` fact triggers a state transition for that fact.

With state transition semantics, we can now visualize our rule set as a workflow. The Figure 11.1 diagram superimposes the state transitions over a corresponding workflow.

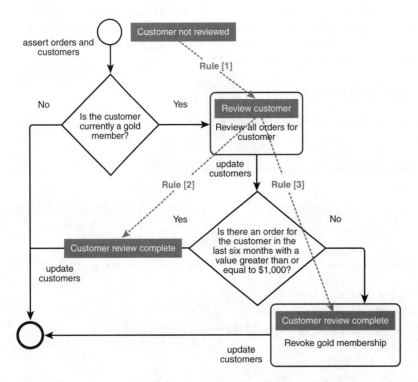

FIGURE 11.1   Visualizing state machine rule sets as workflows.

Rule sets share a deep correspondence to state machines used in workflows and automated business processes. In theory, any state machine can be modeled as a rule set. In the preceding chapter, you saw that there is little difference conceptually between a policy and a process. A BizTalk orchestration could therefore be considered to be a kind of rule set.

The preceding example applied state transitions to individual Customer facts. Sometimes, however, it is useful to model state transitions at the rule set level. Doing so enables developers to modularize their rule sets by grouping multiple rules under different states. Within any given state a group of rules is switched on and used to evaluate facts. After all processing is complete within that state, the rule set transitions to another state.

BRE provides no built-in support for this common pattern. However, it is easy to implement. First, create a fact type to represent the current state. You normally assert a single instance of this fact at runtime. The state fact will typically represent the current state using a single attribute.

When implementing your rules, follow a common pattern for each state, as illustrated in Listing 11.24.

LISTING 11.24   State Machine Pattern

```
// [00x:0001] A rule in state A
IF
  AND
    State.Current is equal to State A
    ...
THEN
  ...


// [00x:0002] Another rule in state A
IF
  AND
    State.Current is equal to State A
    ...
THEN
  ...


// [00x] Low-priority rule to transition to state B
[Priority -100]
IF
  State.Current is equal to State A
THEN
  State.Current = State B
  update State
```

For each state except the last, create a low-priority rule to transition to the next state. You should assign a preliminary state specifier to the State fact before it is first asserted.

This pattern can be elaborated in several ways. A single state may contain multiple low-priority state-transitioning rules that conditionally branch the workflow or "pick" a path. A higher-priority rule within a given state may contain logic to force a state transition when it detects a given condition.

Exploiting Situated Reasoning

Microsoft's rule engine supports the concept of "situated reasoning." A "situated" system is connected to the external world through sensors and effectors. Sensors detect the current state of the world. Effectors change the state of the world. Sensors and effectors both report back to the situated system so that it can keep its internal representation of the world up to date.

The engine uses member bindings to associate procedural attachments to predicates and functions described in BRL and the Rule Object Model. Procedural attachments are external to the engine. They are implemented as methods and properties of custom .NET types. As well as custom methods and properties, this includes the `Get` and `Set` methods of the `TypedXmlDocument` and `TypedDataRow` classes. These are described later in this chapter.

Whether we regard a .NET method or property as a sensor or an effector depends on the semantics of that method or property. Predicates are typically bound to sensors, as are functions used as predicate arguments. Functions used as rule actions are typically bound to effector code. However, it is entirely possible for an action to invoke sensor code or a condition to invoke effector code.

When matching a given rule, we can use return values of bound methods and properties to report the state of the world to the rule engine. For Boolean return values, we can use the bound member as a predicate. However, using return values is limited. Sensors and effectors may also need to issue directives to the rule engine to request that it changes the state of it working memory to match the state of the external world. To facilitate this, developers can pass the `IRuleSetExecutor` to custom .NET methods and properties. The engine provides a built-in `executor` function for this purpose. .NET members can then raise "directive events" by invoking `Assert()`, `Update()`, `Retract()`, `Clear()`, and other methods directly on the `IRuleSetExecutor`. These directives are enqueued internally and processed as engine operations in synchronization with the match-resolve-act cycle. Using `IRuleSetExecutor`, sensors and effectors can act as facts about a given situation and can notify the engine when they change.

The broad aim of situated reasoning is to take the rule engine to the world, rather than bring the world to the rule engine. This is illustrated in Figure 11.2. Sensors and effectors are driven by reasoning logic to observe and act on the real world. Microsoft situates the rule engine so that it can interact directly with external XML documents, ADO.NET data tables, and databases. The engine can also exploit custom .NET code to extend its reach across the enterprise and into the cloud.

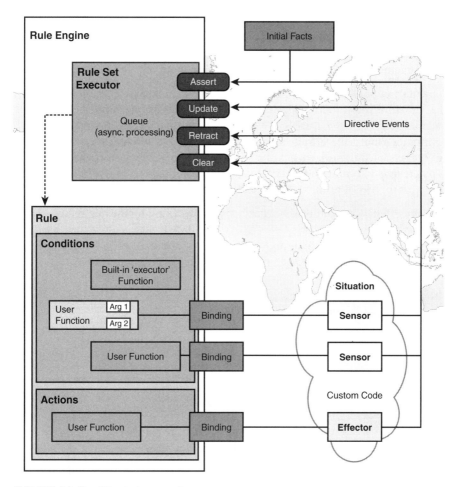

FIGURE 11.2   Situated reasoning.

Rule Engine Mechanisms

Although rule development is broadly declarative, rule developers need to have a clear understanding of the basic mechanisms of the rule engine in order to understand its behavior, troubleshoot issues and tackle more complex problems.

Understanding Working Memory

Conceptually, Production Systems are relational query engines. They implement an approach that is sometimes characterized as a database-in-reverse, in which rules are long-lived and data is transient. This implies that in relational database systems, it is the data that is long-lived and queries that are transient. While this is broadly true, some relational databases provide mechanisms for defining long-lived queries as part of extended event-handling and rule-based features.

Production Systems implement an internal database for storing facts. However, because facts are generally transient, most rule engines, including Microsoft's engine, implement this database as an in-memory data store. The store does not persist fact data during execution. The in-memory data store is called the working memory.

A naïve implementation might store each fact within a list or dictionary and query these collections directly. However, the Rete algorithm defines a more complex approach that captures partial matches. Consider a single rule that tests multiple facts. It filters facts by testing their attributes against literal values and performs joins on different facts types. The Rete algorithm breaks down the evaluation of rules into discrete steps. It stores lists of filtered facts. Wherever a join on two fact types is performed, it stores the results in the working memory. These partial results are retained in-memory while the engine is executing.

The rule engine provides no mechanism for querying the working memory directly. Internally, each fact is stored as a *working memory element* (WME). It is customary to call these elements *wimees*. Each partial match yields an aggregation of WMEs. These aggregations are progressively built until they become full matches for individual rules.

The Match-Resolve-Act Cycle

Production Systems are recursive engines. The recursive mechanism is often called the match-resolve-act, or recognize-act, cycle. It is illustrated in Figure 11.3.

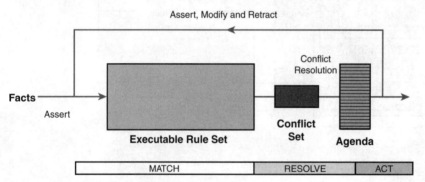

FIGURE 11.3   The match-resolve-act cycle.

The Match Phase
The cycle starts with the assertion of facts to the rule engine. Each fact enters an executable representation of a rule set. The executable rule set evaluates each fact against rule conditions to detect every possible match for each rule. This is the match-phase of the cycle. Matching is highly combinatorial. The engine tests every permissible combination of facts to find all possible matches.

The Resolve Phase
In a Production System, the unit of execution is an entire rule set rather than an individual rule. By contrast, a relational database system executes individual queries and has no equivalent concept to a rule set. The result of executing a set of declarative rules is a single set of all current matches for all the rules in the rule set. This set is called the conflict set.

This somewhat alarming name highlights a fundamental challenge of declarative computing. The matching process is not procedural, and each match is an equal member of a single unordered set. This is all very well, but a rule defines actions and conditions. Individual actions may rewrite the state of the working memory by modifying and deleting existing facts or asserting new facts. All rules in a rule set share a common working memory. Like any other software system in which shared memory can be altered by many different parts of the code, care must be taken to perform changes in an acceptable order. This challenges the fundamental concept of declarativity and requires a degree of procedural processing.

The resolution step of the processing cycle is concerned with resolving the conflict between individual matches in the conflict set. The engine must decide how to order the matches before firing any rules. Microsoft's rule engine implements a specific philosophy with regard to conflict resolution, as discussed later in this chapter.

The Act Phase

The action step of the processing cycle involves "firing" the actions of the appropriate rule over each individual match. The conflict resolution stage produces an ordered, or partially ordered, collection of matches from the unordered conflict set. This collection is called the agenda. During the action phase, the engine works through each match in strict order, executing the actions of the appropriate rule for each one. Each time a match is fired, it is removed from the agenda.

If none of the rules performs any rewriting of the working memory, the engine continues to fire rules for each match in turn until the agenda is empty. It then stops. However, if any rule actions assert, update, or retract facts, the engine completes any other actions in the same rule and then immediately enters a new match-resolve-act cycle. This is the point at which it exhibits recursion. The aim of each recursive cycle is to recompute the conflict set in accordance with the changes made to the working memory and adjust the agenda accordingly. After this has been done for each rewrite performed by the activated rule, the engine starts to process the ordered matches on the recomputed agenda.

This cycle may continue many times during rule set execution depending on how the rules have been written. It is not unknown for rule sets to perform many millions of cycles during a single rule set execution; although, this is rare in automated business processing scenarios. At the other extreme, it is quite common for simple rule sets to perform no recursion at all. Everything depends on the way the rules are written and the amount of rewriting they perform.

Action Order

In Microsoft's rule engine, a single rule contains zero or more actions. Each action is either an engine operation or a function. The term *function* is used because action lists are conceived as a form of functional programming. In a pure functional language, no function exhibits visible side effects, and hence the order of function execution can be inferred by the compiler from dependencies. The rule engine, however, allows .NET methods and properties to be invoked as functions within the action list. The .NET code may exhibit side effects.

The rule engine handles this impedance mismatch in a very simple fashion. Each function is invoked in strict order of declaration within the action list. When designing .NET methods and properties to be used as rule actions, ensure that, as far as a possible, each member performs a discrete unit of work with minimal side effects. However, side effects may be unavoidable. For example, an action might change the value of a fact attribute, and a subsequent action might pass the fact to some helper code to be logged. The attribute value is stored as a shared value that can be read in different places within the code. It may be important to ensure that the value is changed before the fact is logged.

Engine operations (assert, update, retract, and so on) are treated as functional. Although they change the state of the working memory, the underlying implementation ensures that these side effects are not visible to other actions within the list. You can therefore add engine operations in any order you want. At runtime, each engine operation is temporarily enqueued until all functions have been invoked. Only then does the engine perform assertions, updates, and retractions.

You might sometimes want to perform engine operations within custom code rather than directly within the action list. This might be convenient if, for example, you want to assert facts from some external data source and drive the look-up of this data through rules. The rule engine defines the built-in executor function for this purpose. You can use it to pass the IRuleSetExecutor as an argument to a custom function. The custom code can then perform engine operations directly. Again, all engine operations will be enqueued until other functions have completed their work. You may be tempted to use this facility to perform conditional assertions, updates and retractions. In most scenarios, this should be avoided. Conditional changes to the working memory should generally be encoded at the rule level and not embedded in opaque custom code. Consider the following nonatomic business statement:

If an order has been fulfilled from available stock, then if the order specifies a ship address, dispatch the order to the ship address; otherwise dispatch it to the customer address.

This is a poorly defined business rule. It should be decomposed into atomic business rules before being encoded in the rule engine. However, it could be encoded using a single rule and conditional assertions in custom code, as illustrated in Listing 11.25. However, this is poor practice.

LISTING 11.25   Conditional Engine Operation Antipattern

```
IF
  Order.IsFulfilled
THEN
  Order.Dispatch ( executor, Order, State )

public void Dispatch(IRuleSetExecutor executor, Order order, State state)
{
    if (order.ShipAddress != null)
```

```
    {
        executor.Assert(order.ShipAddress);
    }
    else if (order.CustomerAddress != null)
    {
        executor.Assert(order.CustomerAddress);
    }
    else
    {
        throw new ApplicationException("No valid order address");
    }

    state.Current = "OrderFulfilled";
    executor.Update(state);
}
```

Introducing the Rete Algorithm

Most modern Production Systems implement a common, well-defined approach to pattern matching called the Rete algorithm. By long tradition, the word *Rete* is pronounced "ree-tee" within the rules community, although a more correct pronunciation is "ray-tee." Rete is a Latin word for "net" or "snare." In modern Italian, it also means "network."

> **NOTE**
>
> The term *Rete* was originally chosen by way of analogy between the network of pattern-matching nodes defined by the algorithm to a fine-grained network of veins or arteries termed a rete in biology and medicine.

The Rete algorithm was originally formulated in the mid-1970s by Dr. Charles L. Forgy and described in his Ph.D. thesis at Carnegie-Mellon University. Dr. Forgy's thesis was supervised by the late Dr. Allen Newell, who is widely regarded as one of the most significant pioneers of artificial intelligence. Charles Forgy continues to develop advanced variations of the Rete algorithm and maintains a Java-based rule engine called OPSJ.

Microsoft's engine provides an object-orientated implementation of the Rete algorithm. Fortunately, there is no need for developers to learn the intricacies of the Rete algorithm to exploit the rule engine, and a detailed description is beyond the scope of this book. You can find further information about the Rete algorithm on the Internet.

The Rete algorithm optimizes Production Systems by eliminating a number of redundancies:

▶ **Selection redundancies:** If two or more rules share an identical condition that filters individual facts, these conditions are represented by a single selection node.

▶ **Join redundancies:** If two or more rules perform the same join or produce the same Cartesian product, these conditions are represented by a single join node.

▶ **Reevaluation of change deltas:** By maintaining partial matches across recursive cycles, the engine minimizes reevaluation work ensuring that it only ever reevaluates the latest changes to the working memory. The engine avoids complete recalculation of the agenda.

The Rete algorithm optimizes recursion on the assumption that the engine will perform only a small number of changes to the working memory in any one cycle. A naïve implementation of a Production System would reevaluate all asserted data on each cycle. The Rete algorithm constrains reevaluation to changed data only.

The Microsoft rule engine uses indexing to optimize joins. The engine stores indexed data sets within the working memory. The Rete algorithm trades memory use against performance by materializing partial matches at each point a join is performed. This allows it to minimize reevaluation work wherever possible. The Rete algorithm is sometimes criticized for being memory-intensive. However, in most scenarios, memory usage is unlikely to prove a significant concern. If a large number of complex joins are performed on a large volume of asserted facts, attention may be needed with regard to memory use.

Microsoft's rule engine performs all matching on a single thread during any one execution. Although the Rete algorithm can be multithreaded, obtaining significant performance benefit through multithreading is hard to achieve. In most BizTalk scenarios, multithreading is of little benefit. BizTalk Server already executes multiple concurrent orchestrations on different threads and will therefore execute multiple instance of a rule set in parallel within different orchestration instances.

Managing Conflict Resolution

The engine's match phase produces an unordered conflict set of matches that must be ordered appropriately on the agenda before rules are fired. Conflict resolution is one of the most problematic aspects of Production System use. Unlike many Production Systems, Microsoft's engine offers no support for declarative conflict resolution strategies; although, it does support rule priority. Rule activations are grouped by priority, and activations of rules with higher priority always fire before those with lower priority.

Declarative conflict resolution strategies define a context in which a given rule set is used to perform reasoning. They control the order of facts on the agenda. They control the direction of search through the problem space (the conceptual "space" that contains all candidate solutions) across multiple match-resolve-act cycles. The most common strategies are termed depth-first, breadth-first, *means-ends analysis* (MEA) and *lexicographic* (LEX). Strategies may order matches by time stamp so that the most recently detected matches, or those with the most recently asserted facts, are fired earlier, or later, than older matches. Another approach uses some measure of match complexity (for example, how many facts are aggregated within the match) or rule complexity (for example, the number of conditions within a rule).

Conflict resolution strategies are useful in certain scenarios. However, BizTalk developers encounter these scenarios infrequently. In any case, the consequences of a given strategy are not always obvious to the developer. Learning to use different strategies effectively is difficult and often requires considerable insight into the underlying mechanisms of the engine.

The absence of support for conflict resolution strategies represents a deliberate design philosophy that is reinforced by ensuring that all activations within any one priority group are ordered is a truly arbitrary, pseudo-random, fashion. The rule engine carefully avoids any undocumented side effects due to rule ordering. Without this approach, rule sets could unintentionally depend on opaque and arbitrary ordering characteristics to provide the correct results.

By avoiding conflict-resolution strategies, Microsoft's rule engine simplifies the learning curve and avoids additional complexity. By eliminating opaque and undocumented ordering issues, it ensures that developers cannot inadvertently depend on arbitrary characteristics of the engine. This helps developers to create higher-quality rule sets that express their logic more completely and correctly. The trade-off is that Microsoft's rule engine is not well suited for solving certain types of more advanced logical inference. In some cases, developers may need to implement greater complexity within their rule sets. This design philosophy is well aligned to the requirements of a business rule engine. It would not be the best choice in certain areas of research or *artificial intelligence* (AI).

Forward- and Backward-Chaining

Reasoning can proceed in two different directions. Consider the following business rule:

```
A discount of 10% is applied to every order whose total value is greater than or
equal to $1,000.
```

In this case, forward-reasoning is used by the business to implement an order processing system. In forward-reasoning, the executable rule might be expressed with the following semantics:

```
If the total value of the order is greater than or equal to $1,000 then apply a
10% discount to it.
```

Now consider the same business rule from the perspective of a customer. The customer is aware that he can obtain a 10% discount for any order he places that is more than $1,000. He might want to implement an automated order placement system that, wherever possible, delays order placement until his requirements are large enough to attract the 10% discount. From this perspective, the customer might encode the same business rule with the following backward-reasoning semantics:

```
To obtain a 10% discount, place an order worth $1,000 or more.
```

Backward-reasoning starts with a desired goal (obtain a 10% discount) and works out how to achieve that goal. This is, of course, a trivial example. In more complex scenarios, we may need to perform several recursive cycles to satisfy subgoals before we can satisfy the main goal.

In rule engines, we encode these different forms of reasoning using forward-chaining and backward-chaining. The word *chaining* distinguishes between rule engine mechanisms and abstract logic. The engine executes actions for each match that may, or may not, encode logical consequences. We can use the engine's chaining capabilities to encode both forward-and backward-reasoning.

Forward-chaining is often used as a synonym for the match-resolve-act cycle. However, this is inaccurate. The same match-resolve-act cycle is also used for backward-chaining. The real difference is in terms of the representation and assertion of goals. Microsoft's rule engine does not provide any first-class support for goal representation and does not implement any explicit support for backward chaining. However, it is possible to write goal-orientated rules. One technique involves the use of the built-in executor function to pass the IRuleSetExecutor to a custom predicate in the LHS of a rule. The predicate asserts subgoals. Listing 11.26 shows a simple example.

LISTING 11.26   Basic Backward-Chaining

```
IF
  AND
    Goal.Name is equal to GetTenPCDiscount
    Goal.AssertSubGoal(executor, CreateOrderGTEQ1000)
    Order.Total is greater than or equal to 1000
THEN
    Order.Dispatch  // Satisfy the main goal

IF
  AND
    Goal.Name is equal to CreateOrderGTEQ1000
    CurrentStockRequirments.SumValue is greater than or equal to 1000
THEN
    assert new Order(CurrentStockRequirments)  // Satisfy the subgoal
```

We create a .NET class (Goal) to represent goals and subgoals. The first rule matches the main goal. The second condition of this rule uses a custom predicate to assert a subgoal, which matches the second rule. The second rule also tests to see whether the current stock requirements are greater than or equal to $1,000. If they are, the second rule asserts a new order for the stock. The order matches the first rule and the order is dispatched.

This is a simplistic implementation of backward-chaining. One problem is that, in certain circumstances, we could end up asserting many subgoal facts where only one is required. The custom predicate could implement additional logic to maintain an internal collection of active goals and use it to ensure that each subgoal is asserted just once. Another problem is that the developer has to manually instrument each rule to support this pattern. This can prove tedious and error-prone when using backward-chaining extensively in larger rule sets. More sophisticated approaches can be implemented to handle backward chaining efficiently.

Working with Facts

Facts are assertions about entities. Rule engines perform conditional evaluation of facts to reason over the entities, make decisions, and perform actions. The rule engine provides support for handling facts encoded as XML nodes, ADO.NET data tables and data rows, and .NET objects. Developers need to understand how to handle these three fact representations effectively within their rules.

Using Typed Fact Classes

At runtime, all facts are asserted to the rule engine as .NET objects. The engine applies different processing to different fact types. This poses a potential problem. Consider a scenario where an `XmlDocument` object is asserted as a fact. The engine can potentially handle this fact in two different ways. It could automatically process the fact as XML data, applying binding XPaths to extract node sets and reference node content. Alternatively, it could recognize the `XmlDocument` fact as a .NET object, allowing the developer to exploit XML DOM methods and properties directly as functions and predicates within the rule set.

The engine adopts the second of these approaches. If an `XmlDocument` is asserted, it is treated as any other .NET object. To handle the object as an XML fact, we must explicitly represent it as such to the engine. This is done through a wrapper class. The rule engine defines wrapper classes for XML data, ADO.NET data tables and data rows, and data connections.

- ▶ `TypedXmlDocument`: Wraps an `XmlNode` object. This can be any class derived from `XmlNode`, including `XmlDocument`, `XmlDocumentFragment`, `XmlElement`, or `XmlAttribute`. The wrapper can also be populated using an `XmlReader` object. The class specifies a document type name and optional XPath selector. These are matched to type identifiers in BRL bindings. In addition, the class can optionally specify a parent `TypedXmlDocument` and an `XmlNamespaceManager` for managing namespace prefixes in XPaths. The class also implements a number of helper properties and methods used internally by the engine.

- ▶ `TypedDataTable`: Wraps an ADO.NET `DataTable` object. This class is used as a convenient way to assert a collection of `TypedDataRow` objects.

- ▶ `TypedDataRow`: Wraps an ADO.NET `DataRow` object. The class also implements a number of helper properties and methods used internally by the engine.

- ▶ `DataConnection`: Wraps a `SQLConnection` or `OleDbConnection` object. The class specifies a data set name and table name. These are matched to type identifiers in BRL bindings. The engine creates a SQL query to populate ADO.NET `DataSet` and `DataTable` objects and asserts `TypedDataRow` objects to the engine. The `DataConnection` class can also wrap an optional `SqlTransaction` or

OleDbTransaction object for updates. It implements a number of helper properties and methods used internally by the engine. An Update() method is provided for performing updates on the underlying data store, but this method is not called automatically by the engine.

TypedXmlDocument, TypedDataTable and DataConnection facts each support functionality for asserting inner facts to the engine. They are asserted as single facts but represent a source of multiple facts. Assertion of these inner facts is handled automatically be the engine.

Much of the functionality of these types is intended primarily to support the internal workings of the engine, but public members are available to be used in custom code. For example, developers may assert a DataConnection fact and then invoke its Update() method after rule execution has been completed.

Handling XML Documents

Handling XML data in the rule engine poses some interesting challenges. Hierarchical XML data is structured differently than relational data and does not fit neatly into the model employed by Production Systems. The issues faced by rule developers, however, are no different from those encountered elsewhere when mapping between relational and XML data. Some of the main differences between the two models are summarized in Table 11.3.

TABLE 11.3   XML Versus Relational Data Models

XML Model	Relational (SQL) Model
Hierarchical/nested structure	Tabular/flat structure
Elements and attributes	Records and fields
Localized parent/child relationships	Nonlocalized data related through primary/foreign keys
Facets and derivation	Constraints
Optional nodes	Unpopulated fields / null values
Ordered sequences of elements	Named columns
Repeating elements allowed	Singleton field values
Permissive schemas (for example, <xs:any>)	Strict schemas (*Binary Large Objects*, BLOBS, supported)

When a TypedXmlDocument is asserted to the engine, it represents a source of hierarchical data from which inner facts can be harvested. This is done automatically within the engine. However, this requires a mapping layer that specifies how to construct flat data tuples from nested hierarchical data. Everything depends on this mapping layer. The engine uses XPath 1.0 within XML bindings to implement mapping. XPath is a standardized addressing language for XML. It has many features of a query language.

XML data must be mapped to facts (tuples) and attributes. The rule engine uses two separate XPaths for this purpose:

- **XPath selector:**This XPath is used to select a node set from an XML document. Each node in the node set represents a distinct fact. It is valid for an XPath selector to return an empty node set. This represents an empty set of facts.

- **XPath field:**This XPath is used to access a node on each fact returned by the XPath selector. It is specified relative to each of the fact nodes. Because XPath supports location paths and axes, an XPath field can address nodes to an arbitrary nested depth below the fact node or even address ancestor and sibling nodes. If an XPath field addresses a nonexistent node, an exception is raised at runtime.

The full flexibility of XPath 1.0 is available. For example, XPath defines filters. These can be used in an XPath selector to extract only those nodes that meet the filter condition. Developers should use filters with care because they can obscure the logic of the rule set by performing conditional selection that is not expressed directly at the rule level. However, filters are often a vital tool for managing the impedance mismatch between XML and relational models.

Consider the following XPath pair:

- **XPath selector:**`/Orders/Order[Discount]`
- **XPath field:**`Discount`

The XPath selector returns a node set containing `Order` elements. However, it selects only `Orders` if they contain a `Discount` element. The XPath field addresses the `Discount` element. If the `Discount` element is optional, the filter ensures that the XPath field will always succeed and that no runtime exceptions will be thrown.

The rule engine automatically harvests facts from the asserted `TypedXmlDocument` by applying XPath selectors and fields. Each node in the returned node set is wrapped in an instance of `TypedXmlDocument` and asserted to the engine. The `TypedXmlDocument` is therefore used to represent XML nodes and entire documents.

Setting XPath Properties in the Rule Composer

The Rule Composer displays XPath selector and XPath field properties in the Properties pane when you are browsing an XML schema, or in the Vocabulary Definition Wizard you are in when creating a vocabulary definition for an XML document, element, or attribute. The XPath field property is displayed only when a field is chosen from the schema tree view. XPath selector properties are always displayed.

The Rule Composer generates default values for XPath properties. The default XPath field property addresses the selected field in the schema tree view. The default XPath selector property returns a node set for the parent record. These default values can often be used as-is. However, the developer must learn to review the XPaths and ensure that they provide the correct set of facts and attributes. The XPaths may need to be edited or completely rewritten.

When the developer drags and drops an item from an XML schema to the Condition or Action editors, the Rule Composer creates a term and a corresponding binding in the rule set. The binding is defined by the settings in the Property pane at the time the item is dragged and dropped from the Fact Explorer. Note that XPath properties are fully editable. It is possible that they might not exhibit any obvious correspondence to the schema node that is dragged and dropped.

The developer might need to create different XPath pairs for the same XML schema item for use in different conditions. Edit the XPath properties appropriately before dragging and dropping. Each time the XPath properties are edited, the changes are stored in memory for the currently selected schema item. However, these changes are not persisted. If the schema is removed and then reloaded, all changes are lost.

The Rule Composer creates bindings each time a schema item is dragged and dropped. It does not support in-place editing of bindings after they have been created. If you need to change the XPath properties for an existing binding, edit the XPath properties and then re-create the binding by dragging and dropping.

The Condition and Action editors display XPaths in an abbreviated format. This reduces the length of condition and action lines. There is a limit to the visible length of lines. This limit may be reached if, for example, deeply nested schema items are selected. The abbreviated format makes this problem a rare occurrence. Even if the limit is reached, the Rule Composer still creates the condition or action.

XML Type Specifiers

The abbreviated XPaths shown in the Condition and Action editors represent a concatenation of the XPath selector and XPath field property values. The XPath selector is also used to define the type specifier for an XML item. It is used together with the value of the Document Type property that is appended to the front of the XPath representation. A typical abbreviated XPath might be represented as follows:

```
BatchedOrders:/Orders/Order[Discount]/Discount
```

As for XPath selectors and fields, the Rule Editor generates a value for the Document Type property that can then be edited by the developer. The value of this property is used with the XPath selector to define a type specifier for the facts selected by the XPath selector.

It is natural to assume that each physical XML node object represents a distinct, unambiguous fact at runtime. However, the engine's concept of a fact is conveyed through bindings to the XML node. This is often a cause of confusion. The same XML node can be selected by different XPath selectors. Consider the following XPath selectors:

▶ **XPath Selector 1:**/Orders/Order

▶ **XPath Selector 2:**/Orders/Order[Discount]

The second selector yields a node set containing a subset of the nodes yielded by the first. Developers may expect that a specific node yielded by both XPath selectors represents the same fact. This is not the case. Even though there is only one physical XML node object, the engine has two different bindings to it and therefore sees it as two distinct facts. Internally, the engine automatically wraps the same XML Node object in two distinct instances of the TypedXmlDocument class before asserting the facts. The type specifiers for each fact include the Document Type property value:

- ▸ **Type Specifier 1:**BatchedOrders:/Orders/Order

- ▸ **Type Specifier 2:**BatchedOrders:/Orders/Order[Discount]

When editing XPath selectors and the Document Type property, take great care to ensure that type specifiers are identical for conditions that test the same type. Consider the rule in Listing 11.27.

LISTING 11.27   Incorrect XML Type Specifiers

```
IF
  AND
    BatchedOrders:/Orders/Order/OrderTotal is greater than or equal to 1000
    BatchedOrders:/Orders/Order[Discount]/Discount is less than 0.1
  THEN
    BatchedOrders:/Orders/Order[Discount]/Discount = 0.1
```

The developer's intention was to construct a rule that states that if the total value of the order is greater than or equal to $1,000, and the order is being discounted, the minimum discount is 10%. Discount is an optional field. For simplicity, the rule assumes that if no discount is applicable, the order has no Discount field, regardless of its total value. The developer has added a filter to an XPath selector to select only orders that have a Discount field. However, the same filter has not been specified for the first condition.

The rule does not express the intended semantics. Instead, it creates a Cartesian product over two distinct fact types. This leads to two problems. If there is just one order whose total value is more than $1,000, every order with a Discount element is set to a minimum discount of 10% regardless of its total value. Also, the rule causes the engine to do more evaluation work and use more memory than is necessary. The problem is easily fixed by changing the first condition, as shown in Listing 11.28.

LISTING 11.28   Corrected XML Type Specifiers

```
IF
  AND
    BatchedOrders:/Orders/Order[Discount]/OrderTotal _
                                is greater than or equal to 1000
    BatchedOrders:/Orders/Order[Discount]/Discount is less than 0.1
```

THEN

```
BatchedOrders:/Orders/Order[Discount]/Discount = 0.1
```

Type specifiers are constructed from strings in BRL bindings. If two strings differ, even by just a single whitespace character, they represent different type specifiers. The strings are specified in the Properties pane of the Rule Composer. The preceding listing illustrates how type and attribute specifiers may be displayed in the Condition and Action editors as abbreviated versions of the true binding strings.

Handling XML Namespaces

By default, the Rule Composer creates XPaths using the local-name() and namespace-uri() XPath functions as filters. This is a verbose format that makes XPaths difficult to edit within the Properties pane. The abbreviated forms of XPaths used in the Conditions and Actions editors are displayed without these filters.

The Rule Composer generates verbose XPaths to identify nodes correctly by their fully qualified identifiers. There is no mechanism in the Rule Composer for defining and managing dictionaries of namespace prefixes that can be used by the XPaths at runtime. However, it is possible to create and provide dictionaries within custom code. The .NET Framework already provides a type for this purpose. The XmlNamespaceManager class allows developers to build a collection of namespace definitions. Each definition defines a namespace URI and a prefix.

The TypedXmlDocument provides several overloaded constructors. Some of these accept an instance of the XmlNamespaceManager class. The developer must take responsibility for writing code to create the XmlNamespaceManager, instantiate the TypedXmlDocument and assert it to the engine. The namespace prefixes passed via the XmlNamespaceManager class at runtime can be used in XPath selector and XPath field properties when defining rules in the Rule Composer. The Rule Composer does not validate XPaths and enables prefixes to be used freely. Using prefixes greatly improves the readability and maintainability of XPaths but requires manual editing of the default XPaths generated by the Rule Composer.

Reading and Writing XML Data

The TypedXmlDocument wraps an instance of an XmlDocument or some other XmlNode class. It can use an XmlReader to load this internal XmlDocument. A common design pattern is to hand off an existing XmlDocument to the engine using the TypedXmlDocument wrapper and use rules to change values within the XML. The XMLDocument can then be inspected after the rule engine has completed its work. A variation of this pattern uses rules to add and remove nodes within the XML.

To support these patterns, the engine uses prebuilt helper code. Internally, it uses Get and Set methods implemented on the TypedXmlDocument class to read and write XML values.

TypedXmlDocument implements a large number of these methods to support casts to different data types. Each method accepts an XPath to address the required node. The Rule Composer generates these from the XPath selector and XPath field properties. The generated XPaths are displayed in abbreviated form. They can be used as functions and object references within rule definitions. Elements and attributes that return a Boolean value can be used as predicates.

Developers can set the Type property on an XML binding to ensure that the correct method is selected at runtime to cast data appropriately. This property specifies a .NET type. The Rule Composer initially sets this property according to the type definitions used in the XSD schema, if any. It defaults to System.String. Developers can change the property to cast the XML data to another type at runtime. If the data is incompatible with the selected .NET type, the engine throws an exception.

The Get and Set methods are public and may be used in custom code. Developers may prefer to use these methods rather than perform direct access on the wrapped XmlDocument.

Rules may need to add or remove nodes from XML. This can be done through custom functions. Developers can create custom methods that accept an instance of TypedXmlDocument. The TypedXmlDocument class allows the wrapped XmlNode to be accessed via the Document property.

The rule engine provides a class called XmlHelper. This class provides static methods that can be invoked as functions. Each method adds a new element or attribute. XmlHelper supports functionality to conditionally add nodes only to empty node sets. It also supports initialization of new nodes with values. By default, you must assert an instance of XmlHelper to the engine to call the helper methods, even though the methods are marked as static. XmlHelp is used like any other helper code.

Be careful when adding and removing nodes from XML. Changing the wrapped XMLDocument does not automatically notify the engine of changes to individual facts within the working memory. You must update, assert, or retract the facts to reflect your changes. Fortunately, the rule engine can handle this in an elegant fashion. You can make multiple changes and then reassert or update the TypedXmlDocument just once. To do this, use a binding to the XML schema node. This is displayed as the root node of the schema in the Fact Explorer. The engine automatically determines which facts must be retracted and which ones must be asserted.

Managing Optional XML Nodes

Handling XML introduces complexity due to the need to map the XML data model onto the internal relational model used by the rule engine. The impedance mismatch between these two models may cause problems. We have seen that one common issue is the need to match optional elements or attributes within an XML document. The relational model has no corresponding concept of *optionality*.

Consider a schema for orders that defines an optional ShippingAddress element in the header. This element contains further elements for the various parts of the address. The developer creates a rule as shown in Listing 11.29.

LISTING 11.29   Corrected XML Type Specifiers

```
IF
    BatchedOrders:/Orders/Order/Header/ShippingAddress/State is equal to WA
THEN
    ...
```

If the State element is mandatory, this rule functions without error at runtime using the default XPath selector property. The XPath selector selects all ShippingAddress elements. If the node set is empty, no fact is asserted. However, if the State element is also optional, problems can arise. If a document has a ShippingAddress element but no State element, a runtime exception occurs. This is because the engine will attempt to use the XPath field to address a nonexistent node relative to the ShippingAddress.

Faced with this scenario, many developers attempt to resolve the issue by using the built-in exists predicate. They change the rule, as shown in Listing 11.30.

LISTING 11.30   Corrected XML Type Specifiers

```
IF
    AND
    BatchedOrders:/Orders/Order/Header/ShippingAddress/State _
                                            exists in BatchedOrders
    BatchedOrders:/Orders/Order/Header/ShippingAddress/State is equal to WA
THEN
    ...
```

This approach does not work. The rule set continues to throw exceptions at runtime for XML documents that contain no State element. The reason was discussed earlier in the chapter. You should always assume that rules do not use short-circuiting. In this case, the exists predicate does not short-circuit the second condition. The second condition is still evaluated at runtime and continues to throw an exception.

> **NOTE**
>
> The preceding listing does not quite reflect what is seen in the Rule Composer. The left argument of the exists predicate specifies a full XPath, rather than the abbreviated form shown here. The XPath is generated as a string when you drag and drop from an XML schema. It is not a binding. However, the right argument of the exists predicate does specify a binding. This is automatically set when you drag and drop a schema item to the left argument. By default, the Rule Composer configures the right argument as a binding to the XML document.

One way to eliminate the runtime exception is to take advantage of short-circuiting by editing the arguments of the exists predicate. In the preceding rule, if the right argument of the exists predicate is identical to the XPath selector passed as the left argument of the equals predicate, short-circuiting will be used. If we change the right argument of the exists predicate, its left argument must be changed accordingly. You can reset the left argument of the exists predicate and then type an XPath in directly if you want. The rule will now be as shown in Listing 11.31.

LISTING 11.31   Corrected XML Type Specifiers

```
IF
  AND
    /State exists in BatchedOrders:/Orders/Order/Header/ShippingAddress
    BatchedOrders:/Orders/Order/Header/ShippingAddress/State is equal to WA
THEN
  ...
```

Earlier in this chapter, you saw that this is a dangerous approach. Rules should never assume short-circuiting behavior. Although the preceding rule always exhibits short-circuiting as written, it is difficult to infer when short-circuiting will occur for more complex rules. This approach is therefore poor practice.

The exists predicate exhibits another problem. It operates without any knowledge of the internal state of the working memory. It merely calls SelectNodes() on the right argument using the XPath defined as the left argument and returns a truth value stating if any nodes were returned. It is an example of converting a weak negation to a strong negation but operates separately to the engine itself. It returns true when one or more nodes are found even if those nodes are not represented as asserted facts within the engine. The exists predicate can be useful in certain scenarios but should be used with care. It is not a true equivalent to an engine-level quantifier.

You saw a better approach to handling this problem earlier in this chapter. Instead of using the exists predicate, define your rule with a single condition using a filter in the XPath selector, as shown in Listing 11.32.

LISTING 11.32   Corrected XML Type Specifiers

```
IF
  BatchedOrders:/Orders/Order/Header/ShippingAddress[State]/State is equal to
WA
THEN
  ...
```

Handling ADO.NET `DataTable` and `DataRow` Objects

Compared to XML data, writing rules to evaluate ADO.NET data is much simpler. `DataTable` and `DataRow` objects represent data in a relational format and do not require additional mapping layers. They provide a natural way to assert data to the engine.

The rule engine defines `TypedDataTable` and `TypedDataRow` classes for wrapping instances of ADO.NET `DataTable` and `DataRow` objects. If a `TypedDataTable` is asserted, the engine asserts each row as a `TypedDataRow` fact internally. Alternatively, the developer can assert individual `TypedDataRow` directly.

In the preceding chapter, you saw that the Rule Composer depends on SQL Server to provide schema definitions for ADO.NET data. The data does not have to be stored in SQL Server. Developers can create ADO.NET `DataSets` by any means they want and use them to assert `TypedDataTable` or `TypedDataRow` facts. The schema of the `DataTables` must, however, conform to the SQL Server tables used as schemas in the Rule Composer. The SQL Server tables can be used to store test data, if desired.

When writing custom code to create ADO.NET `DataTables` and `DataRows`, always ensure that `DataTables` are added to a `DataSet`. A runtime exception is thrown by `TypedDataRow` if this is not done.

BRL uses a two-part identifier as the type specifier for ADO data. The specifier is composed of a data set name and a table name. When asserting `TypedDataTable` or `TypedDataRow` facts in custom code, ensure that ADO.NET `DataSet` and `DataTable` are named in accordance with dataset and table names used in the BRL bindings.

Reading and Writing `DataRow` Data

As for XML data, a common design pattern is to assert a wrapped `DataTable` to the engine using `TypedDataTable` and use rules to change field values. The `DataTable` can then be inspected after the rule engine has completed its work. When asserting individual rows using `TypedDataRow`, the rows can be inspected individually after processing or by enumerating the Rows collection of the underlying `DataTable`.

Internally, the engine uses `Get` and `Set` methods implemented on the `TypedDataRow` class to read and write values. There are several different methods for different data types. Each method accepts a column name as an argument. `TypedDataRow` bindings can be used as functions and object references within rule definitions. Boolean fields can be used as predicates. Unlike XML data, the developer cannot change the value of the `Type` property for a `TypedDataRow` binding. This property specifies the .NET type of the `DataColumn` for a given field and is used internally to select the appropriate `Get` or `Set` method.

The `Get` and `Set` methods are public and available for use in custom code. Developers may prefer to use these methods rather than perform direct access on the wrapped `DataRow`.

Rules may need to add or remove rows on the `DataTable`. This can be done through custom code. Developers can create custom methods that accept an instance of `TypedDataTable` or `TypedDataRow` and use them as custom functions. Both type wrapper classes allow access to the wrapped ADO.NET objects. Unlike XML data, the rule engine does not provide a helper class for this purpose.

Be careful when adding and removing rows in a `DataTable`. Changing the `DataTable` does not automatically notify the engine of changes to individual `TypedDataRow` facts within the working memory. You can update, assert, or retract the facts within the working memory to reflect your changes. If you make multiple changes, simply reassert or update the `TypedDataTable` to which you made changes. The engine will automatically determine which facts must be retracted and which ones must be asserted.

Handling Data Connections

The `DataConnection` class is an ADO.NET `TypedFact` wrapper that works in conjunction with specialized handling within the rule engine. The rule engine uses specialized Rete nodes to create and execute SQL queries against an external data store represented by this fact. The results of each query are used to create and assert `TypedDataRow` facts automatically. The `DataConnection` allows rules to run directly over data in an external database.

The `DataConnection` class wraps an instance of a `SqlConnection` or an `OleDbConnection`, and maps it to a table name. Queries are generated directly over this table. The engine never performs updates on external data directly. Instead, updates are performed in custom code once the rule set has been executed. SQL views cannot be accessed safely and should not be used.

The engine implements a trade-off when using `DataConnection` facts. Instead of fetching all records from the designated table in a single query and asserting them as facts, the engine performs multiple queries at runtime to fetch only those records that are required. In effect, the engine converts the relevant rule conditions into parameterized SQL `WHERE` clauses. For example, when another fact is joined on a `DataConnection`, the generated SQL is parameterized using that fact to dynamically assert only the matching rows from the database.

The database table should always specify a primary key. This can be a single field or a compound key. If no primary key is specified, the `DataConnection` may raise an exception at runtime. Primary keys are used by the `DataConnection` to determine row identity. When the normalized rule conditions contain an `OR` connective, the same row may be fetched twice. In this case the engine enforces the requirement for a primary key and uses it to de-duplicate fetched rows. This requirement for a primary key is the reason why the `DataConnection` does not support SQL views.

A `DataConnection` can be given a transaction. This is recommended practice. Transactions are created in custom code and passed to an appropriate `DataConnection` constructor. The engine does not begin, rollback or commit transactions internally. This must be done within custom code.

All internal queries are enlisted into the one transaction, if present. If you need to ensure that the rule engine processes database data on a true point-in-time basis, use Snapshot or Serializable isolation, if supported. Begin the transaction before asserting the

DataConnection and commit the transaction after rule set execution is complete. If a transaction is not used, or if the isolation level is low, you may get inconsistent or unexpected results when executing rule sets. The rule set may run multiple queries over data without isolation from changes to that data.

In almost all cases, transactions should be used when updating data. The DataConnection provides an Update() method for updating changes. Always use this method to perform updates. As the rule set executes, the engine builds a list of SqlUpdateCommandEntry or OleDbUpdateCommandEntry objects for all changes. Invoke the Update() command in custom code once rule set execution is complete. This performs updates for each of the UpdateCommandEntry objects. If you do not call Update(), no changes are made to the underlying data in the database. The update engine operation cannot be used. It will throw an exception for DataConnections.

The decision to use a DataConnection should be taken with care. DataConnections can be useful when running rules over large tables. If the rules filter the data to a significant degree, the DataConnection provides a mechanism for minimizing the amount of data pulled back from the database. DataConnections, however, have a number of constraints:

▶ **Multiple queries:** The DataConnection will perform multiple queries to control the data that is pulled back through parameterization. The number of queries performed depends on the number of additional facts to which the DataConnection facts are compared. For rule sets that are highly combinatorial, it may be better to avoid using DataConnection.

▶ **Table based:** The DataConnection is restricted to querying single tables. Tables should always have a primary key. Views should not be used. There is no support for stored procedures. If relevant facts are produced by performing joins across multiple tables, DataConnection is of limited use.

▶ **SQL translation:** The engine supports DataConnections by translating rule conditions into SQL WHERE clauses. In some cases, conditions cannot be fully translated into equivalent SQL. These are documented in an MSDN article titled "Considerations When Using DataConnection." For example, the Power, FindFirst, and FindAll functions have no SQL equivalents. In these cases, the rule set will execute. However, the engine must pull back all data from the database and process it internally inside the rule engine. This may be costly for large tables.

Configuration
When you are using DataConnections, the engine supports a DataConnectionMaximumRows configuration setting. This is located at one of the following Registry paths:

▶ **32-bit systems:** HKEY_LOCAL_MACHINE\SOFTWARE\Microsoft\BusinessRules\3.0

▶ **64-bit systems:** HKEY_LOCAL_MACHINE\SOFTWARE\Wow6432Node\Microsoft\BusinessRules\3.0

The `DataConnectionMaximumRows` setting controls the maximum number of fetched rows allowed. If the `DataConnection` fetches a larger number of rows, an exception is raised at runtime. The default value is `100000`. Set the value to `0` or less to switch off this feature.

Handling .NET Types

.NET types provide a natural form in which to assert facts to the rule engine. All facts are asserted as .NET types. Special wrapper classes are used when asserting other fact types such as XML or Database facts. The engine does not provide any special handling for facts asserted directly as `XmlDocument`, `DataTable`, or `DataRow` objects. It treats them like any other .NET object.

The rule engine provides an object-oriented implementation of the Rete algorithm but is a relational query engine. .NET types must be mapped internally to a relational model. This happens as a natural consequence of using BRL bindings. There is no requirement for any additional mapping layer. There is, however, a degree of impedance mismatch between the .NET object-oriented model and the relational model used by the engine. This gives rise to a few restrictions on the use of .NET types, as described in Table 11.4.

TABLE 11.4   .NET Type Restrictions

Feature	Description
Nonpublic types and members	Private, internal, and protected types are not visible to the rule engine.
Noninstantiable types	Types that cannot be instantiated cannot be used to create facts. This may be due to a lack of a public constructor or the use of the static qualifier or nonpublic scope. Facts are always asserted as instantiated objects.
out Parameters	The rule engine does not support out parameters.
Parameter arrays	The rule engine does not support parameter arrays.
Arrays and collections	The rule engine does not provide mechanisms for indexing or enumerating arrays and collections. However, these objects can be passed as arguments.

The Rule Composer imposes further restrictions, as described in Table 11.5. These restrictions are specific to the Rule Composer and do not apply when creating rule sets programmatically.

The rule engine handles static and instance members. Types include classes, interfaces, delegates, and values, including enumerations.

TABLE 11.5   Rule Composer Restrictions on .NET types

Feature	Description
Generic types	The Rule Composer does not support generic types or members.
Nullable types	The Rule Composer does not support nullable types.
Nested type members	The Rule Composer does not allow access to nested members using dot syntax. It can invoke only direct members of a given type.

NOTE

The Rule Composer loads assemblies from the *Global Assembly Cache* (GAC) when creating rules or performing testing. Unfortunately, it does not release loaded assemblies. During development, each time you change an assembly, you must re-import it into the GAC and then close and reopen the Rule Composer.

The rule engine honors .NET type inheritance. For example, consider the inheritance hierarchy shown in Figure 11.4.

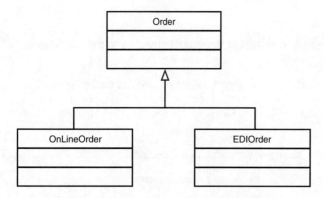

FIGURE 11.4   .NET fact inheritance hierarchy.

In the rule set in Listing 11.33, the first rule is evaluated against all instances of Order, OnLineOrder, and EDIOrder. The second rule will be evaluated against instances of EDIOrder only.

LISTING 11.33   Corrected XML Type Specifiers

```
IF
    Order.Total is greater than or equal to 1000
THEN
    ...
```

```
IF
    EDIOrder.Customer is equal to Northwind
THEN
    ...
```

Rules can bind to interfaces to match any .NET fact that implements the interface. Interface inheritance (derivation) is honored.

Fact Identity and Hash Codes

When a .NET fact is reasserted or updated, and at least one rule refers to the fact in its conditions, the engine first retracts the fact from the working memory before asserting it again. To find the correct fact to retract, the engine looks up the fact in a Hashtable. Internally, the Hashtable uses the inherited `GetHashCode()` method to find candidate objects and then performs an `Equals` comparison, if required, to determine the correct fact unambiguously. The additional step is required because hash codes are not guaranteed to be unique.

Unfortunately, this mechanism works correctly only if `GetHashCode()` returns the same hash code across the entire lifetime of the object. The default implementation of `GetHashCode()` always returns the same hash code regardless of object state. However, some classes override `GetHashCode()` and may return a value based on the object state. In this case, each time a fact is modified, the returned hash code may be different. The engine will fail to find the existing fact and will assert the modified object as a new fact. There will now be two facts in the working memory, one for the original state and one for the modified state. This compromises the logical integrity of the rule set and causes a memory leak. Under no circumstances assert facts for a .NET type that returns hash codes based on current state. When defining custom fact types, do not override `GetHashCode()` to return hash values based on current state.

Thread Safety

The rule engine does not provide any mechanism for notifying .NET facts when their state changes within the engine. In addition, the rule engine does not support any observer patterns for .NET facts (for example, the `INotifyPropertyChanged` interface). Care must be taken if the state of a .NET fact can be changed by an external thread. The engine will be unaware of any changes.

Asserting multithreaded objects should generally be avoided. A better approach is to "snapshot" the state of a .NET object by serializing state to XML or populating an ADO.NET `DataRow`. The XML or Database fact can then be asserted to the engine. When rule processing is complete, any changes made to the snapshot fact can be applied to the .NET object in a thread-safe fashion in custom code.

If there is truly a need to assert mutable multithreaded objects to the rule engine, consider locking each fact before assertion and releasing locks once the rule set has been executed. A number of patterns support this. For example, the .NET class could implement a lock on a static object. The lock could be acquired before invoking the rule engine. Each fact instance would then use the common lock to serialize state changes. No other thread could update any fact of the given type until the lock is released after rule execution is complete.

In the extremely rare situation where external threads must be allowed to change object state during rule execution, the built-in executor function can be used to implement thread-safety. Create a rule that initializes each fact by injecting the executor via a custom method. This could be done using a predicate method, but in most scenarios a better approach is to use a high priority rule and perform initialization as a rule action.

Each thread-safe fact object can now direct the engine to perform update operations via the executor each time the state of the object is changed. Engine operations (asserts, updates, and retracts) are implemented in a thread-safe fashion. The rules can simply update values and rely on the facts to request asserts and updates, rather than specify these directly as actions. Alternatively, the fact class could be implemented to determine whether state changes are made on the engine thread, and only assert or update on nonengine threads.

The Policy helper class pools and recycles rule engine objects. Short-lived thread-safe facts should be de-initialized cleanly once rule processing is complete. The internal reference to the rule engine executor should be dropped. This can be done using a low-priority rule. Alternatively, facts can be de-initialized, disposed, or destroyed in custom code. Be careful to avoid asserting the same fact to multiple instances of the rule engine concurrently, because each one uses a different instance of an executor. If you have to support this, the fact must maintain references to multiple executors and update each one whenever a change is made.

Asserting Delegates

Delegates can be asserted as facts, and their Invoke() method can be used as a function in rules. This provides a powerful mechanism for calling back to external code from within an executing rule set. This approach may be useful in scenarios where specific rule firings represent events that will be handled by the calling application. The multicast features of .NET delegates can be used to notify multiple listeners, each of which remains decoupled from the executable rule set.

Using Helper Code

Identification of object references as facts and its members as attributes is useful, but is merely a matter of semantics. BRL provides no first-class representation of these terms. It deals with the notions of object references and member bindings that define predicates and functions. Bindings map these notions to concrete implementations regardless of semantics.

For XML and Database types, member bindings map to the Get and Set methods of the TypedXmlDocument and TypedDataRow classes. However, for .NET types, member bindings map to methods and properties. They can therefore represent behavior and data. This applies to BRL predicates and functions. Predicates can be mapped to Boolean XML nodes or data row fields. For .NET objects, they can be mapped to any method or property that returns a Boolean value. The method or property can exhibit behavior.

It is often natural to think of predicates and functions as helpers rather than facts or attributes. For example, we might bind a function to a custom logging method or to code that performs database lookups or web service calls. We may implement a helper class to manage state transitions and bind its methods to predicates and functions

To use a helper method or property, we must assert an instance of the class that defines that member, even if we consider this to be a "helper" object rather than a fact. Microsoft's rule engine evaluates object members. We may think of some objects as facts, some as helpers, and others as predicate libraries. A single .NET type may combine all these notions.

In an earlier chapter, you saw that BRL rules may contain implicit conditions for object references where the objects are used in rule actions but are not referenced in rule conditions. This is true regardless of semantics. The rule in Listing 11.34 contains an implicit condition matching the `AuditHelper` object.

LISTING 11.34   Implicit Match for Helper Object

```
IF
  NOT
     Order.UseSTP
THEN
  AuditHelper.LogOrderRejectionToAuditDB(Order, "No STP. Credit score too low")
     retract Order
```

We could make the extra condition explicit, as shown in Listing 11.35.

LISTING 11.35   Explicit Match for Helper Object

```
IF
  NOT
    AND
     AuditHelper is equal to <null>
     Order.UseSTP
THEN
  AuditHelper.LogOrderRejectionToAuditDB(Order, "No STP. Credit score too low")
  retract Order
```

This might detrimentally affect our rules. If we use the `update` engine operation to update the `AuditHelper` object anywhere else in the rule set, this version of the rule may fire again.

Invoking Static Type Members

Developers are often surprised to discover that, to call static members of a .NET type, they must first assert an object of that type to the engine. The reason, however, should now be obvious. By default, the engine must always match an asserted object to an object reference in the rules to invoke custom code via a member binding. Hence, we must instantiate and assert at least one object of a given .NET type, even if we invoke only its static members.

Helper code is often implemented using static type members only. The rule engine provides alternative modes in which static methods and properties are invoked directly without the need to assert objects. The engine no longer matches objects for the purpose of invoking their static members.

BRL does not allow these modes to be specified at the level of individual rule sets. Instead, they are configured at machine or application level. Create and use the StaticSupport DWORD value in the Windows Registry to change the engine's behavior at the machine level. This is located at the following registry paths:

▶ **32-bit systems:** HKEY_LOCAL_MACHINE\SOFTWARE\Microsoft\BusinessRules\3.0

▶ **64-bit systems:** HKEY_LOCAL_MACHINE\SOFTWARE\Wow6432Node\Microsoft\BusinessRules\3.0

The modes are defined in Table 11.6.

TABLE 11.6   Static Support Registry Settings

Value	Description
0	Default. An object must be asserted to invoke static type members.
1	Static type members are invoked without the need to assert an object.
2	As for 1, but with additional optimization. Where all parameters of the static type member are constants, or no parameters are passed, the member is invoked once prior to rule set execution at translation time, and its result value, if any, is then used during execution.

As for other Registry settings, static support can be configured at the application level using the Microsoft.RuleEngine section in the .NET .config file. See the preceding chapter for further details.

Before deciding to use modes 1 or 2, consider that static support introduces new semantics. Static class members that return values can no longer be thought of as fact attributes. The developer may need to take this into account when designing object models and rules. Static support may break existing rule sets. Any rule that evaluates only static members in its conditions will cause a runtime exception stating "No user object is associated with Rule <some rule>." Because static support can be configured only at the machine or application level, using this feature may cause existing applications to break. Another consideration is that some helper methods and properties may be implemented as instance members. Static support does not necessarily lead to cleaner semantic distinction between facts, predicates, and helpers.

Optimizing Rule Sets

In BizTalk Server applications, rule sets are often straightforward and will perform sufficiently well without further effort. However, in some cases, it may be necessary to optimize rule sets in order to maximize throughout or reduce latencies. This section describes built-in mechanisms for rule set optimization.

Controlling Side Effects

BRL maps functions to .NET type members to support actions, fact attributes, and helper methods. In a pure functional model, functions always return the same value given the same arguments and do not affect the return value of any other function. These are important requirements for referential transparency. They allow a function to be evaluated just once. Its return value can then be substituted directly for each subsequent function call made with the same arguments. Functions that do not adhere to the pure model are said to exhibit side effects.

BRL provides a mechanism that allows developers to enforce a more functional model by reducing the visibility of side effects. The mechanism, however, only approximates to true functionalism and is based on caching.

When an object is asserted to the rule engine, it is represented internally as a WME. WMEs allow access to the attributes of the object. WMEs implement an optional caching mechanism for attribute values. Each attribute is accessed using a function in the Rule Object Model, and its corresponding member binding to an XML node, Database field, or .NET method or property.

Caching can be controlled via BRL. Each member binding specifies a Boolean `sideeffects` attribute. If the `sideeffects` attribute is `True`, no caching is used. If it is `False`, the attribute value is cached the first time it is accessed at runtime.

The rule engine, itself, produces side effects. Asserts, updates, and retracts indicate that the state of a specific WME has changed and that the agenda must be recomputed accordingly. WME state is changed using rule actions. Rule actions ignore caching and always allow the state of underlying objects to be changed, regardless of the `sideeffects` flag. If the WME is asserted or updated, its entire cache is invalidated. The WME is reevaluated in the next match-resolve-act cycle and rebuilds its internal cache based on the new values of the underlying object.

The `sideeffect` flag controls side effects during the match phase of any one match-resolve-act cycle. With `sideeffects` set to `False`, the WME's attributes are generally guaranteed to yield a single value no matter how many times they are accessed. However, there are exceptions. The `sideeffects` flag is applied to individual member bindings but is controlled at the WME level. If just a binding for just one member is marked to allow `sideeffects`, and that member is accessed during the match phase, the entire WME cache will be invalidated at that point. This is logical. The side effect may be visible through some other member, rather than the member that is being accessed. By invalidating the cache, any side effects within the scope of the single WME become visible.

It is possible that a binding for a member of one object may cause a side effect that is visible via a member of some other object referenced by another WME. In this case, the side effect will be visible only if the binding for the attribute of the second WME is marked to allow side effects. The second WME's cache is not invalidated when the attribute of the first WME is accessed.

Regardless of the value of the `sideeffects` attribute, XML and Database fields are always treated as if their `sideeffects` flag is `False` for getters and `True` for setters. WMEs always cache XML and Database attributes. This is an optimization. By default, the Rule Composer always sets the `sideeffects` flag to `True` for .NET type members. Because of the default settings, it is often more optimal to process XML and Database facts than .NET facts. The performance difference is often insignificant but can be important for some rule sets. If performance is an issue, consider preventing side effects (that is, using caching) on .NET facts. The diagram shown as Figure 11.5 illustrates an extreme case for a benchmark test. This is not necessarily indicative of the degree of performance difference that will be encountered in real-world scenarios.

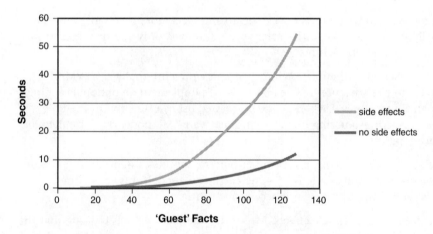

FIGURE 11.5   Performance benefits of caching.

If you set `sideeffects` to `True`, the Rule Composer ensures that custom predicates and functions behave as .NET developers expect. They exhibit side effects. Developers must be careful to ensure that side effects do not compromise rule logic by changing values of .NET objects unexpected during the match phase.

The Rule Composer does not support direct editing of the `sideeffects` flag on member bindings. To change these flags, you must first export your rule set from the SQL rule database using the Rule Engine Deployment Wizard, edit the BRL directly, and then import it back to the database. This compromises the maintainability of the rule set and is a strong incentive to use the default settings. Only amend `sideeffects` flags if there is a strong case to do so. This will generally be for reasons of performance. BRL member bindings are defined at the level of individual predicates and functions. This allows fine-grained control of side effects. Change the `sideeffects` flag only on `classmember` bindings for predicates and function on the LHS of rules. Any other changes will be ignored.

Optimizing the Rete Network

The Rete algorithm is optimized for performing joins within recursive match-resolve-act cycles. Unlike a SQL database system, rule engines do not store data in tables and cannot calculate optimal action plans for performing joins based on the size of tables and index statistics. The rule engine uses indexing at runtime, but these indexes must be manufactured on-the-fly as facts are asserted. The engine has no way of knowing, in advance, how many facts of different types will be asserted for any given execution.

To improve join performance, the rule engine allows developers to provide statistical hints within BRL. These hints are used internally to alter the structure of the Rete node network. Specifically, they alter the order of join nodes so that joins over multiple fact types are structure optimally. The logic of the rule set is not affected by these changes, but performance can be significantly improved for highly combinatorial rules sets that perform a large number of conditional joins.

Unfortunately, the Rule Composer does not support this optimization feature. The only way of optimizing a rule set created using the Rule Composer is to export it from the SQL Server rule database using the Rule Engine Update Wizard, manually edit the object bindings at the top of the file, and then import the rule set back to the database.

For any given rule set, BRL contains a bindings section that lists bindings for object references. This section may contain a mixture of `xmldocument`, `datarow`, and `class` bindings. Each binding contains two optional attributes called `instances` and `selectivity`. These have the following semantics:

- ▶ `instances` **attribute**: A hint as to the number of instances of this binding that are expected to be asserted at runtime. For any one binding, this value is relative to the instances attributes of other bindings. The attribute holds an integer value. Setting this value on bindings is effective in scenarios where the relative quantity of facts of specific types asserted at runtime does not vary too significantly across multiple executions of the rule set. For example, if 20% of asserted facts are type A, 30% are type B, and 50% are type C, you could set these values to `20`, `30`, and `50`, respectively on each binding. Equally, you could set the values to 2, 3, and 5 or 40, 60, and 100, and so on.

- ▶ `selectivity` **attribute**: A hint as to the percentage of instances of this binding that are expected be selected during rule execution. This value is somewhat problematic. Each rule in a rule set may exhibit different selectivity characteristics for a given fact type. However, multiple rules may share common join nodes. The `selectivity` attribute is merely a hint. It can usually be estimated based on the total expected selections of a give fact type across all the rules. However, in some situations it might be worthwhile undertaking performance testing using different values to determine the most optimal settings. The `selectivity` attribute is set as a floating value between `0.0` and `1.0`, inclusive.

When the rule set is translated into executable form, the rule set translator uses these two values to decide on node ordering. It multiplies the `instances` and `selectivity` values for each binding to create a `capacity` value. It then sorts the bindings in ascending order of capacity. It uses this to influence the order of join nodes so that joins on lower `capacity` fact types are performed first. This minimizes the evaluation work when performing joins and optimizes the rule set.

In many scenarios, any performance improvement will be insignificant. However, for rule sets that perform a large number of joins over many different types of data, optimization may be significant.

Programming with the Rule API

The following sections introduce programmatic use of the rule API provided by the Business Rule Framework. The most common way to execute rules is using the `Policy` helper class. However, in more advanced scenarios, it is sometime necessary to interact with rule engine instances directly. Fact retriever components can be used to automate management of facts in rule engine instances. Compensation handlers can be registered to handle faults.

We will discuss the implementation of a custom rule store component and explain how the `RuleSetDeploymentDriver` class can be used to import, export, and deploy rule sets via the SQL Server rule store. We also investigate the basics of creating rules programmatically and provide an example of construction of a simple rule set.

To access the Business Rule Framework API, you must first provide an application with a reference to the `Microsoft.RuleEngine` assembly. This is generally located in the <Program Files>\Common Files\Microsoft BizTalk folder. On 64-bit machines, the assembly is located under Program Files (x86) but is compiled to run on both 32-bit and 64-bit platforms. To make it easier to use the API, import the `Microsoft.RuleEngine` namespace into the appropriate code files.

Using the Policy Class

The `Policy` class provides helper code designed to take much of the hard work out of executing rule sets programmatically. As well as retrieving, converting, and executing rule sets from the *Rule Engine Update* (REU) service, it handles local caching of rule sets and rule engine instances and the use of fact retriever components.

The `Policy` class is designed primarily for use in enterprise-level applications where rule sets are deployed dynamically across a distributed environment from a central rules store and where the same rule set is executed repeatedly during the lifetime of an application. These conditions hold true when invoking rules within BizTalk orchestrations or pipelines or within RFID Server event pipelines. Microsoft's Call Rules orchestration shape, ESB BRE Resolver, and RFID Server `RuleEnginePolicyExecutor` component all use the `Policy` class internally.

You might sometimes want to write custom code to invoke a rule set. For example, you might want to create a rule-driven pipeline component or custom functoid. To execute the latest published and deployed version of a given rule set, you need only to instantiate the `Policy` class over the name of the rule set, execute it over an array of facts, and then dispose of the policy object. We will assume an existing method called `GetFacts()` that returns an array of fact objects. The code in Listing 11.36 illustrates how a policy called `Orders` can be executed.

LISTING 11.36   Executing the Latest Deployed Policy Version

```
var facts = GetFacts();

using (var orderPolicy = new Policy("Orders"))
{
    orderPolicy.Execute(facts);
}
```

The code exploits C#'s using statement to ensure that the `Dispose()` method is always called after execution, even if an exception occurs. If you do not call `Dispose()`, you may seriously compromise the performance of your application. Disposing the `Policy` object allows it to deterministically return the instance of the rule engine to a cache. The cache recycles rule engine instances. Each time a rule engine instance is instantiated, it is populated with an inner node network (object graph) representing an executable rule set. This is a very costly operation. By caching and reusing rule engine instances, the `Policy` class eliminates this overhead, except on the first execution. The cache is held at the application domain level, and is not tied to the lifetime of individual `Policy` objects. If you do not dispose the `Policy` object after use, the rule engine instance will not be returned to the cache and will die with the `Policy` object.

WARNING

Do not rely on finalization to return the rule engine instance to the cache. The `Policy` class does not implement a finalizer and will only recache rule engine instances when the `Dispose()` method is called.

In most scenarios, you will always execute the latest version of a rule set. However, you can also select a specific version. The `Policy` class has an overloaded constructor to facilitate this. The code in Listing 11.37 executes version 1.0 of the `Orders` rule set.

LISTING 11.37   Executing a Specific Deployed Policy Version

```
var facts = GetFacts();

using (var orderPolicy = new Policy("Orders", 1, 0))
{
    orderPolicy.Execute(facts);
}
```

Using a Tracking Interceptor

During development, you might want to capture a trace of the engine behavior in a text file. When you use the built-in unit testing facilities of the Rules Composer, you can view a trace immediately after execution. To capture an equivalent trace to a file, you can use the DebugTrackingInterceptor class provided as part of the framework.

The code in Listing 11.38 executes the current version of the Orders rule set with tracking using DebugTrackingInterceptor. The interceptor is passed as an additional argument to an overload of the Execute() method.

LISTING 11.38   Executing a Policy with the Debug Tracking Interceptor

```
var facts = GetFacts();
var debugTi = new DebugTrackingInterceptor();

using (var orderPolicy = new Policy("Orders"))
{
    orderPolicy.Execute(facts, debugTi);
}
```

In the preceding code, the tracking interceptor saves a trace file to one of the following locations, depending on the environment variables currently set on your machine.

► The path specified by the TMP environment variable. Otherwise

► The path specified by the TEMP environment variable. Otherwise

► The path specified by the USERPROFILE environment variable. Otherwise

► The Windows directory.

The filename is manufactured from the directory name, the rule set name, the time and date at which the file was created, and the extension .trace.

Alternatively, you can specify a path and file name as an additional parameter to an overload of the DebugTrackingInterceptor constructor.

You can create your own custom tracking interceptors by implementing the IRuleSetTrackingInterceptor interface on a custom class. The interface defines a number of callback methods that the rule engine will invoke at runtime to notify your interceptor of various activities. These include assertions, retractions, and updates of facts, condition evaluations, agenda updates, and rule firings. Interceptors are also notified at the point where the interceptor is first associated with an instance of the rule engine.

Custom tracking interceptors can be configurable. Implement the SetTrackingConfig() method to configure your interceptor. For example, you might want to be able to configure and control which activities are tracked. The Policy class invokes this method before rule set invocation and also just before the interceptor is associated with a rule engine instance. Note that the DebugTrackingInterceptor class does not support any form of configuration.

The Policy class always obtains rule sets from the REU service. This service allows rule sets to be deployed dynamically across a distributed environment. As well as rule sets, you can store configuration data in the rule store and distribute it dynamically with each rule set. The Policy class fetches configuration data distributed via the REU service, rather than using some local configuration file. Hence, when using a custom configurable interceptor, you need to populate the rule store with additional configuration data. Configuration data distributed by the REU service always consists of as integer value interpreted as a bit field. Each bit represents a flag used to switch different tracking capabilities on or off. The flags are listed in Table 11.7.

TABLE 11.7   SQL Server Rule Store Tracking Configuration Values

Flag	Tracking
0	Tracking disabled
1	Fact activities (assert, retract, update)
2	Rule firings
4	Condition evaluation
8	Agenda updates

The preceding chapter described how tracking configuration can be captured in the SQL Server rule store using the re_updaterulesettc procedure to update the flags for each individual rule set version. It can also be set using the SetTrackingConfigForRuleSet() method of the RuleSetDeploymentDriver class.

Tracking interceptors represent additional overhead and are generally best avoided in production environments. If you do want to use a custom tracking interceptor, ensure that it offers reasonable performance, and consider making it configurable so that you can de-select it dynamically or minimize the amount of tracing it undertakes.

Handling Exceptions

In previous code examples, any exception raised when instantiating the Policy class or executing a rule set has been unhandled. The Policy class may throw RuleEngineExceptions during instantiation and PolicyExecutionExceptions during execution. Figure 11.6 illustrates the hierarchy of exceptions derived from RuleEngineException that may be thrown by the Policy class and describes their meaning.

Exception Hierarchy	Description

System.Exception
  ↳RuleEngineException
    ↳RuleEngineArgumentException
      ↳RuleEngineArgumentNullException
      ↳RuleEngineArgumentInvalidValueException
    ↳RuleStoreException
      ↳RuleStoreConnectionException
    ↳RuleStoreCompatibilityCheckException
 	
  ↳RuleEngineDeploymentException
    ↳RuleEngineDeploymentDatabaseConnectionException
	
	Policy name is null
	Major or minor version number is invalid
	
	Could not connect to rule store
	The version of the rule engine is incompatible with the SQL Server rule store version
	
	An existing connection to the rule store failed

FIGURE 11.6   Rule engine exception hierarchy.

During execution, any exception that is thrown by the rule engine is caught and wrapped in an instance of the `PolicyExecutionException` class. When logging errors, be careful to capture the details of any inner exception. Because the rule engine can invoke custom code during execution, an unbounded set of errors may be wrapped by `PolicyExecutionException`. A suggested pattern for exception handling is shown in Listing 11.9.

LISTING 11.39   Executing Policy with Exception Handling

```
var facts = GetFacts();


try
{
    using (var orderPolicy = new Policy("Orders"))
    {
    orderPolicy.Execute(facts);
    }
}
catch (PolicyExecutionException polEx)
{
    // Log the inner exception.
    Trace.WriteLine(polEx.InnerException.ToString());
}
catch (RuleEngineException)
{
    Trace.WriteLine("Rule Engine exception: Policy could not be instantiated.");
}
```

Handling Long-Term Facts

The preceding chapter described how each instance of the rule engine can instantiate a fact retriever component. Fact retrievers implement the `IFactRetriever` interface. They are configured within the rule set. Fact retrievers are custom components that support a declarative approach to instantiating custom fact retrieval code. Fact retrievers are invoked just prior to execution of the rule set. They are generally implemented as stateless components, but can use the rule engine to round-trip a data object described as a handle. Handles are generally created by fact retrievers the first time a rule set is instantiated and then handed on to the rule engine instance. When you are using the `Policy` class, handles are cached with the rule engine instance. The next time the rule engine instance is retrieved from the cache and reexecuted, the handle is passed to a new instance of the fact retriever. In this way, fact retrievers can, if necessary, persist state over a long period of time and communicate state across multiple executions of the same rule set.

Each time a rule engine executes a rule set that declares a fact retriever, the rule engine instantiates the fact retriever and calls its `UpdateFacts()` method. It passes itself to the fact retriever together with current rule set information and any previously cached handle. If no handle is passed, the fact retriever can create a new handle and pass it back as the return value of the `UpdateFacts()` method. A handle can be any .NET type, including a custom class or struct. When the rule engine passes a handle to the fact retriever, there is nothing to prevent the component from creating a new handle for future round-tripping. It can return a `null` value to the engine to stop round-tripping of handles.

The fact retriever can use the information stored within the handle in any way it sees fit. Generally, the task of the fact retriever on each invocation of `UpdateFacts()` is to make decisions about any changes that should be made to the working memory of the rule engine instance. Using the executor passed to the fact retriever, the component can assert additional facts, retract existing facts, or modify them. Fact retriever components often retrieve data from specific data stores according to some given business logic.

By themselves, fact retrievers provide a declarative mechanism for managing facts. However, when invoked in the context of a `Policy` object, they can be used to distinguish between short-term and long-term facts. This is because the `Policy` class retains a reference to the original array of facts passed to its `Execute()` method and uses this to automatically retract any of those original facts from working memory if they still exist after execution of the rule set. Facts asserted directly via the `Execute()` method are therefore short term. They are never retained by the rule engine instance when it is returned to the `Policy` cache. All other facts, however, are retained unless explicitly retracted. This includes any new facts asserted by rule actions and any facts asserted by a fact retriever. Hence, when using the `Policy` class, facts asserted by a fact retriever are generally considered to be long term.

Consider a scenario where rules evaluate reference data stored in a database. This data changes only occasionally and is used repeatedly over many invocations of the same rule set. Retrieving the reference data from the database on every invocation is inefficient and unnecessary. However, if we retrieve the data just once and then cache it, our rule set will not pick up subsequent changes to the reference data. By caching the reference data as facts in each instance of the rule engine and implementing a custom fact retriever, we can manage the cached data over time. We might choose to refresh the cached facts once a day or after every 1,000 invocations of the rule set. In a more sophisticated implementation, we might implement a Windows service to monitor the database for changes and expose a custom fact retriever to communicate detected changes to the rule engine.

Fact retriever components can optionally implement an IFactRemover interface. This interface defines a single UpdateFactsAfterExecution() method. If a fact retriever implements IFactRemover, the UpdateFactsAfterExecution() method is invoked automatically immediately after execution of the rule set. Like the UpdateFacts() method, it receives an instance of the executor together with current rule set information and any previously cached handle. The IFactRemover interface can be implemented to tidy up rule engine instances before fact retrievers are returned to the Policy cache. For example, they may retract short-term facts asserted in the UpdateFacts() method.

We have seen that fact retrievers do not necessarily have the semantics of long-term fact providers. Although they are most commonly used for this purpose, they can be implemented to manage short-term facts, as well. They provide a flexible mechanism for automated assertion, retraction, and updating of facts per instance of the rule engine.

Implementing Compensation Handlers

The BRE supports a callback mechanism that allows it to notify custom code whenever an exception occurs within the engine. The rule engine performs the callbacks by invoking registered multicast delegates. It passes the exception to the custom code together with any arbitrary data object registered with the delegate. This error-handling mechanism is referred to as compensation because it allows custom code to perform compensatory actions when an error occurs.

To enable this mechanism, the Business Rules Framework defines the RuleEngineCompensationHandler delegate type. Unfortunately, compensation handlers cannot be registered with the rule engine via the Policy class. To use this mechanism, you must either write code to invoke the rule engine directly or write a rule that fires early and registers your compensation handlers with the executor. We discuss invoking the rule engine directly in the next section. In this section, we illustrate the second technique.

To demonstrate the use of compensation handling, consider a custom fault logger class called CentralLogger that provides two public methods and a read-only property, as shown in Table 11.8.

The LogException() method has a signature compatible with the RuleEngineCompensationHandler delegate. It is implemented to log the exception to a central exception store. The Initialize method is implemented to register the delegate with the IRuleSetExecutor instances passed to it. The IsInitialized property returns a Boolean value indicating whether the custom logger has been initialized.

The CentralLogger class defines an inner LogData class. This class defines a single EventType integer property.

TABLE 11.8   Public Members of the Custom **CentralLogger** Class

Member Name	Return Type	Arguments	
		Name	Type
Initialize	void	executor	IRuleSetExecutor
LogException	bool	ex	Exception
		userData	object
IsInitialized	bool		

Listing 11.40 shows the implementation of the Initialize method.

LISTING 11.40   Initializing a Custom Logger for Compensation

```
public void Initialize(IRuleSetExecutor executor)
{
    if (executor != null)
    {
    var logData = new LogData();
    logData.EventType = 2500;

    var reLogger = new RuleEngineCompensationHandler(LogException);
    var compHandlerInfo = new CompensationHandlerInfo(reLogger, logData);
    executor.SetCompensationHandler(compHandlerInfo);
    this.IsInitialized = true;
  }
}
```

The code creates a user data object and assigns an event type to it for use in the central exception store. It then creates a RuleEngineCompensationHandler delegate over the LogException() method and also creates an instance of the CompensationHandlerInfo class provided as part of the Business Rules Framework. The CompensationHandlerInfo object wraps the delegate and the user data. Finally, the code registers the compensation handler with the rule engine by calling the SetCompensationHandler method of the executor and passing it the CompensationHandlerInfo object. It also sets a local field to true to indicate that the custom logger has been initialized.

Microsoft's design of multicast delegates makes it easy to assign additional delegates to the invocation list of the first delegate created, and to assign all these at one time to the executor. Each time you call SetCompensationHandler(), the existing multicast delegate will be replaced by a new one, or by null if you want to end compensation handling.

Listing 11.41 demonstrates one way of initializing the CentralLogger within a rule set. Each rule checks to see whether the CentralLogger has been initialized. The first rule fires if this is not the case and initializes the `CentralLogger` in the action list, passing the current executor to it. After the first rule has fired, any subsequent exception thrown by the rule engine is logged to the central exception store.

LISTING 11.41   Initializing Compensation in a Rule Set

```
[01]: Initialize error logging
IF
  NOT
    CentralLogger.IsInitialized
THEN
  CentralLogger.Initialize(Executor)
  Assert CentralLogger

[02]: Assign discount for gold customers
IF
  AND
    CentralLogger.IsInitialized
    Order.IsGoldCustomer
  THEN
    Order.SetDiscount = 10%

[03]: Assign high value transfer discount for non-gold customers
IF
  AND
    CentralLogger.IsInitialized
    Order.Value greater than or equal to 5000
    NOT
      Order.IsGoldCustomer
THEN
  Order.SetDiscount = 2.5%
```

By extending this pattern demonstrated, you can apply different compensation handlers to different subsets of rules. In effect, this enables you to supplement your rule sets with additional business rule logic that is invoked when an error occurs. For example, you could use compensation to implement logic for the following business rule:

```
If the value of an order is greater than $10,000, and an unanticipated error
occurs during rule processing for that transfer, immediately escalate the problem
to the senior account manager.
```

Using the `RuleEngine` Class

In most BizTalk-related scenarios, the `Policy` class provides an appropriate and convenient mechanism for executing rule sets. However, you might encounter situations where you want to invoke rule sets in a more direct fashion using instance of the rule engine. Listing 11.42 illustrates the steps required to execute a rule set directly using the `RuleEngine` class.

LISTING 11.42   Executing **RuleEngine** for a Specific Policy Version

```
var facts = GetFacts();
var sqlRuleStore = new SqlRuleStore("Data Source=SERV01;" +
                                    "Initial Catalog=BizTalkRuleEngineDb;" +
                                    "Integrated Security=True");
var ruleSet = sqlRuleStore.GetRuleSet(new RuleSetInfo("Orders", 1, 0));
var re = new RuleEngine(ruleSet);
re.Execute(facts);
```

Because the `Policy` class is not being used, we need to write code to retrieve the rule set. In this case, the rule set is retrieved directly from a SQL Server rule store using the `SqlRuleStore` class. The REU is not used. The code obtains a rule set using an instance of the `RuleSetInfo` class to communicate the name and version number. Instances of the `RuleEngine` class are instantiated directly over rule sets.

The `RuleEngine` class instantiates a given executor internally. The only executor currently supplied by Microsoft is the built-in Rete class, but custom executors can be created. Rule sets specify the executor they require as part of their metadata.

> **NOTE**
>
> One of the overloaded `RuleEngine` class constructors takes an additional `doOptimizations` argument. However, this is ignored in the current implementation.

Compared to the `Policy` class, the preceding code is missing a great deal of functionality. It retrieves rule sets direct from a rule store rather than via the REU service and does not implement any form of caching. It is potentially inefficient in scenarios where the same rule set will be invoked many times.

You should consider implementing exception-handling code when using `RuleEngine` directly. The Business Rules Framework defines a wide variety of `RuleEngine` exceptions to provide fine-grained control over exception handling. All these exception types are derived from the `RuleEngineException` class.

This sample code invoked a specific version of the `Orders` rule set. You can invoke the latest published rule set by using a filter value when obtaining rule sets from the rule store. An example is shown in Listing 11.43.

```
var facts = GetFacts();
var sqlRuleStore = new SqlRuleStore("Data Source=SERV01;" +
                                    "Initial Catalog=BizTalkRuleEngineDb;" +
                                    "Integrated Security=True");
var ruleSetInfos = sqlRuleStore.GetRuleSets("Orders",
                                    RuleStore.Filter.LatestPublished);
var re = new RuleEngine(sqlRuleStore.GetRuleSet(ruleSetInfos[0]));
re.Execute(facts);
```

For production purposes, this code should be improved with checks to ensure that a single rule set is returned in the RuleSetInfoCollection.

You can assign tracking interceptors and compensation handlers directly to a RuleEngine instance and can retrieve any configured fact retriever. The RuleEngine also provides wrapper functions for several engine operations, including Assert, Retract, RetractByType, Update, Halt, ClearAgenda and Clear. These calls are passed through to the underlying executor.

Implementing Custom Rule Store Components

In the previous examples, rule sets are retrieved directly or indirectly from the SQL Server rule store. The code in Listing 11.44 implements a custom rule store component to retrieve rule sets from managed resources contained in the executing assembly.

```
public class ResourceRuleStore : RuleStore
{
    private BusinessRulesLanguageConverter converter;
    private VocabularyDictionary vocabDic = new VocabularyDictionary();
    private RuleSetDictionary ruleSetDic = new RuleSetDictionary();

    public ResourceRuleStore(string resourceName)
        : base(resourceName)
    {
        // Get this type's assembly - assumes resource is in same assembly
        var assem = this.GetType().Assembly;

        // Get the stream that holds the BRL resource
        var stream = assem.GetManifestResourceStream(resourceName);

        VocabularyDictionary vocabDic = null;
        RuleSetDictionary ruleSetDic = null;
```

```
        var brlLangConv = new BusinessRulesLanguageConverter();
        brlLangConv.Load(stream, out vocabDic, out ruleSetDic);

        this.vocabDic = vocabDic;
        this.ruleSetDic = ruleSetDic;
        this.converter = brlLangConv;
    }

    protected new IRuleLanguageConverter Converter
    {
        get
        {
            return this.converter;
        }
    }

    public override RuleSet GetRuleSet(RuleSetInfo ruleSet)
    {
        if (ruleSet == null)
        {
            var resString = "Parameter \"{0}\" must be specified for " +
                                            "call to \"{1}\"";
            throw new RuleEngineArgumentNullException(
                                            resString,
                                            "GetRuleSet",
                                            "ruleSet");
        }

        var resRuleSet = this.ruleSetDic[ruleSet.Name];

        if (resRuleSet != null)
        {
            var verInf = resRuleSet.CurrentVersion;
            var majNum = 0;
            var minNum = 0;

            if (verInf != null)
            {
                majNum = verInf.MajorRevision;
                minNum = verInf.MinorRevision;
            }

            if ((majNum != ruleSet.MajorRevision) ||
```

```
                minNum != ruleSet.MinorRevision)
        {
            var resString = "Unable to get rule set \"{0}\" due to " +
                            "version mismatch.  Asked for {1}.{2} " +
                            "but assembly contains {3}.{4})";
            throw new RuleStoreRuleSetVersionIncompatibilityException(
                                            resString,
                                            ruleSet.Name,
                                            ruleSet.MajorRevision,
                                            ruleSet.MinorRevision,
                                            majNum,
                                            minNum);
        }
    }
    else
    {
        var resString = "Unable to get rule set \"{0}\" due to version " +
                        "mismatch.  Assembly does not contain this " +
                        "rule set.";
        throw new RuleStoreRuleSetNotAvailableException(
                                            resString,
                                            ruleSet.Name,
                                            0,
                                            0);
    }

    return resRuleSet;
}
// All other interface members can be implemented to throw a
// System.NotImplemented exception
}
```

Managing Deployment Programmatically

Rule set deployment drivers are components that implement the
IRuleSetDeploymentDriver interface. They work closely with a given rule store and are
responsible for

▶ Exporting rule sets and vocabularies to file

▶ Importing rule sets and vocabularies from file

▶ Deploying and undeploying rule sets

▶ Testing the deployment status of rule sets

- ▶ Getting rule store components

- ▶ Retrieving information about deployed and undeployed rule sets

- ▶ Retrieving deployment history

- ▶ Getting or setting tracking configuration for rule sets

The Business Rules Framework implements a single driver for the SQL Server database store. The class is named `RuleSetDeploymentDriver`.

To export an existing rule set to file, use the `ExportRuleSetToFileStore()` method, as shown in Listing 11.45.

LISTING 11.45   Exporting a Rule Set to File

```
var ruleSetDeploymentDriver = new RuleSetDeploymentDriver();
ruleSetDeploymentDriver.ExportRuleSetToFileRuleStore(
                                new RuleSetInfo("Orders", 1, 0),
                                @"C:\Temp\orders.brl");
```

To import a rule set from file and mark it as published (immutable), use the `ImportAndPublishFileRuleStore()` method, as shown in Listing 11.46.

LISTING 11.46   Importing a Rule Set from File

```
var ruleSetDeploymentDriver = new RuleSetDeploymentDriver();
ruleSetDeploymentDriver.ImportAndPublishFileRuleStore(@"C:\Temp\orders.brl");
```

To deploy a published rule set, use the `Deploy()` method. The example in Listing 11.47 traps the `RuleEngineDeploymentAlreadyDeployedException` exception if the rule set is already deployed.

LISTING 11.47   Deploying a Rule Set

```
var ruleSetDeploymentDriver = new RuleSetDeploymentDriver();
var ruleSetInfo = new RuleSetInfo("Orders", 1, 0);
try
{
    ruleSetDeploymentDriver.Deploy(ruleSetInfo);
    Console.WriteLine(
                    "Rule set '{0}', version {1}.{2} deployed",
                    RuleSetInfo.Name,
                    ruleSetInfo.MajorRevision,
                    ruleSetInfo.MinorRevision);
}
catch (RuleEngineDeploymentAlreadyDeployedException)
{
```

```
Console.WriteLine(
                "Rule set '{0}', version {1}.{2} is already deployed",
                ruleSetInfo.Name,
                ruleSetInfo.MajorRevision,
                ruleSetInfo.MinorRevision);
}
```

To undeploy a deployed rule set, use the Undeploy() method. The example in Listing 11.48 traps the RuleEngineDeploymentNotDeployedException exception if the rule set is currently undeployed.

LISTING 11.48   Undeploying a Rule Set

```
var ruleSetDeploymentDriver = new RuleSetDeploymentDriver();
var ruleSetInfo = new RuleSetInfo("Orders", 1, 0);
try
{
    ruleSetDeploymentDriver.Undeploy(ruleSetInfo);
    Console.WriteLine(
                "Rule set '{0}', version {1}.{2} undeployed",
                ruleSetInfo.Name,
                ruleSetInfo.MajorRevision,
                ruleSetInfo.MinorRevision);
}
catch (RuleEngineDeploymentNotDeployedException)
{
    Console.WriteLine(
                "Rule set '{0}', version {1}.{2} is not currently deployed",
                ruleSetInfo.Name,
                ruleSetInfo.MajorRevision,
                ruleSetInfo.MinorRevision);
}
```

To set tracking configuration, you need to obtain a GUID value for the rule set. To do this, first call GetTrackingConfigForRuleSet() to get the current tracking configuration data, and then call SetTrackingConfigForRuleSet() with new tracking configuration data using the same GUID. This is illustrated in Listing 11.49.

LISTING 11.49   Setting Tracking Configuration

```
var ruleSetDeploymentDriver = new RuleSetDeploymentDriver();
var ruleSetInfo = new RuleSetInfo("Orders", 1, 0);

var trackingConfigCurrent = ruleSetDeploymentDriver.GetTrackingConfigForRuleSet(
```

```
                            ruleSetInfo);

var trackingConfigNew = new RuleSetTrackingConfiguration(
                        trackingConfigCurrent.RuleSetGuid,
                        RuleSetTrackingConfiguration.TrackingOption.All);

ruleSetDeploymentDriver.SetTrackingConfigForRuleSet(
                                        ruleSetInfo,
                                        trackingConfigNew);
```

Creating Rules Programmatically

The Business Rule Framework provides a comprehensive object model for constructing
rule sets programmatically. The topic is too large to be addressed fully in this book. An
introduction to the structure of the object model was provided in the preceding chapter.
This chapter provides a simple worked example in which a rule set is constructed containing a single rule as follows:

If the order value is greater than or equal to $1,000, set the order discount to 10%.

To facilitate this example, Listing 11.50 shows a simple .NET type that will represent
Order facts.

LISTING 11.50   A Simple Fact Type

```
public class Order
{
    public Order()
    {
    }

    public Order(Decimal value)
    {
        this.Value = value;
    }

    public Decimal Value { get; set; }
    public Double Discount { get; set; }
}
```

The code in Listing 11.51 constructs the rule set programmatically. It creates the rule set
and rule and then creates a number of bindings to access the Value and Discount
members of the Order class. When constructing bindings, the object model dynamically
locates class members by name.

LISTING 11.51   Creating and Testing a Simple Rule Set

```
/*** Create rule set and rule ***/


var testRuleSet = new RuleSet("Test order discount rule");
var offerDiscountRule = new Rule("Offer discount");


/*** Create all required bindings ***/

var orderBinding = new ClassBinding(typeof(Order));
var orderValueBinding = new ClassMemberBinding("Value", orderBinding);
var argc = new ArgumentCollection() { new Constant(0.1) };
var orderDiscountBinding =
                   new ClassMemberBinding("Discount", orderBinding, argc);


/*** Create LHS of rule ***/

// Create a user function bound to the Value property of the Order class
var orderValue = new UserFunction(orderValueBinding);

// Create a constant term for 10,000
var threshold = new Constant(typeof(Decimal), 1000M);

// Create a logical expression for the condition
var conditionOrderGTE10K = new GreaterThanEqual(orderValue, threshold);


/*** Create RHS of rule ***/

// Create a user function to set the discount
var setDiscount = new UserFunction(orderDiscountBinding);


/*** Assemble the rule ***/

// Add the condition to the rule;
offerDiscountRule.Conditions = conditionOrderGTE10K;

// Add the action to the rule
offerDiscountRule.Actions.Add(setDiscount);
```

```
// Add the rule to the rule set
testRuleSet.Rules.Add(offerDiscountRule);

/*** Test the rule ***/

// Create policy tester and facts
var policyTester = new PolicyTester(testRuleSet);
var discountedOrder = new Order(2000);
var nondiscountedOrder = new Order(500);
var facts = new object[] { discountedOrder, nondiscountedOrder };

// Execute the test rule set
policyTester.Execute(facts);

// Check the results
foreach (Order order in facts)
{
    Console.WriteLine(
    "Order with value of ${0} is offered a discount of {1}%.",
    order.Value,
    order.Discount * 100);
}
```

The code constructs a logical expression for use as a single condition on the LHS of the rule. Every rule contains a single top-level logical expression that may nest a collection of additional logical expressions (that is, LogicalAnd and LogicalOr expressions). In this case, the single logical expression uses the GreaterThanEqual predicate and contains no nested expressions.

The code constructs a single action. Actions are functions. In this case we create a user function to assign the value of 0.1 (10%) to the Discount property of the Order. The assignment of a constant value is defined in the binding created earlier.

After the condition and action have been created, the rule and rule set are constructed. The rule set is then passed to an instance of the PolicyTester class. PolicyTester is a helper class that is used to test rule sets directly. It is constructed to offer a similar programmatic interface to the Policy class. After the rule set has been executed over two facts, the code displays the results in terms of the discounts set on the Order objects.

NOTE

In many rule-processing technologies, creating rule sets programmatically is a verbose and detailed process. Microsoft's Business Rules Framework is no exception. Examples like the one here often attract criticism. Why, people ask, should a developer write so much code when all they want to do is test the value of one property and set the value of another accordingly? The basic logic of the simple rule could be implemented in a few lines of simple procedural code. This argument, however, entirely misses the point. The preceding example is not about creating executable logic, despite executing the rule set using the `PolicyTester` class. It is about constructing a detailed document object model that captures conditional business logic in a robust and abstract form. Having done so, the rule set can easily be serialized and converted into different forms, stored in rule repositories, versioned, published, and deployed dynamically across distributed environments. The same object model can be used to represent existing rules currently stored in a variety of different repositories to extend their reach across the enterprise.

In any case, developers mostly use the Rule Composer provided with BizTalk Server to define rules in a far less verbose fashion. The rule object model is used less frequently to enable custom rule generation.

To save the rule set to file in the form of Microsoft BRL, use the `BusinessRulesLanguageConverter` class. This class implements the `IRuleLanguageConverter` interface and converts between rule set object graphs and BRL. Listing 11.52 writes the BRL to a `FileStream` and then saves the contents of the stream to disk. Note that the rule set must be added to a rule set dictionary. The `BusinessRulesLanguageConverter` is designed to convert entire collections of rule sets and vocabularies in a single operation.

LISTING 11.52   Saving the Rule Set to File

```
var ruleSetDictionary = new RuleSetDictionary();
ruleSetDictionary.Add(testRuleSet);

var brlConverter = new BusinessRulesLanguageConverter();
var fileStream = new FileStream(
                    @"C:/Temp/Test_order_discount_rule.brl",
                    FileMode.Create);
brlConverter.Save(fileStream, default(VocabularyDictionary), ruleSetDictionary);
fileStream.Close();
```

Summary

Production rules are represented using a simple form. However, when properly understood, rules can express many sophisticated concepts. Several of the concepts and mechanisms used by the rule engine are unfamiliar to many developers. The learning curve can be high. This chapter illustrated some of the sources of confusion and explained the core concepts behind the rule engine. It also described some of the common design patterns and techniques used in effective rule writing. Armed with a solid understanding of the rule processing approach, developers can exploit the engine to represent a range of business and technical policies in executable form.

This chapter described the handling of XML, Database, and .NET objects by the rule engine. Different considerations apply to each type, and developers need to understand these considerations to design object and data models for use with the engine. In a complex rule set, developers may freely mix all three types to exploit their different characteristics effectively. Although it is often necessary to design XML, Database, and .NET types explicitly for use in the rule engine, the support for different object types makes it easier to situate the rule engine within real-world enterprise applications. Rules can be bought to bear directly on existing data objects such as BizTalk Server messages and can exploit existing helper functionality.

The chapter introduced various aspects of using the .NET API provided by the Business Rule Framework. Programmatic access to the components and object models provided by the framework gives developers a powerful and flexible platform for defining, managing, and executing rule sets. Developers can extend the framework with a variety of custom components to integrate rules processing with existing rule stores, manage facts for efficient and fast processing, build comprehensive exception handling and logging features around rule sets, and construct rules dynamically.

CHAPTER 12

ESB with BizTalk Server

For BizTalk developers and architects, this chapter explains what an *enterprise service bus* (ESB) is, why it matters, and how, at a high level, it is implemented using BizTalk Server as the core messaging infrastructure. This chapter also explains the key role that ESBs have as part of a *service-oriented architecture* (SOA).

What Is an ESB?

Although definitions can vary, for the purpose of this book we will settle on a definition that an enterprise service bus is a design pattern that builds on the principles of SOA and can play a key role in an SOA. This chapter provides you with an architectural overview of the functional capabilities generally considered to be part of an ESB and, where appropriate, discusses design considerations primarily from a BizTalk Server-centric point of view.

Introducing the Enterprise Service Bus

The ESB concept took hold in the early 2000s, growing out of the integration middleware space, merging in SOA principles along with the increasing popularity of web services and the emergence and maturation of the WS-* specifications.

The term was a source of significant confusion as vendors clamored to claim that their products were "ESB products." ESB definitions differed widely among both vendors and analysts, and marketplace confusion was rampant.

In the Microsoft camp, in those early days, an ESB was not viewed as being a product, which was a stark contrast from other vendors who claimed that it was a product. Microsoft's view was that an ESB was an architectural pattern; it offered a certain set of capabilities, and those capabilities could be provided by the Microsoft technology stack, including *Windows Communications Foundation* (WCF) and BizTalk Server. To help clarify this position, in late 2006 Microsoft released the first version of ESB Guidance, a set of prebuilt components and architectural guidance that showed architects and developers how to implement an ESB on the Microsoft platform. This has evolved over time, providing richer functionality with each release, and is now known as the *Enterprise Service Bus Toolkit* (ESB Toolkit). We examine the ESB Toolkit in detail in this chapter.

Simply put, an ESB is a core set of capabilities that can be combined in a way that solves a problem. It is a way to achieve application and process integration in, and beyond, an enterprise. It can be a cornerstone of an SOA, providing certain base sets of functionality that facilitate integration and interactions between applications. It provides a messaging fabric, and a common set of services, upon which developers can build their own services and that applications can use to intercommunicate. An ESB provides a runtime environment for services.

The confusion that initially existed when ESBs were just emerging has been mitigated, as over time similar requirements have led to similarities in the thinking behind various implementations, and a consensus agreement of what core functionality an ESB should provide has been reached.

What Problems Does an ESB Solve?

Developing contemporary applications increasingly means bolting together pre-existing blocks of functionality, and relying on platform services. An ESB provides messaging capabilities that are available to use out-of-the-box.

Messaging Backbone

An ESB is a messaging backbone. It is foundational infrastructure available to applications throughout an enterprise.

A good analogy is the power grid, and the electrical wiring in your house. If you purchase an electrical appliance, say a toaster, you do not have to worry about whether it is compatible with the wiring in your house. You expect the power plug to fit into your electrical outlets and the voltage to be the same as what you have at home. Adding a new appliance in your kitchen is as simple as buying it, installing it, plugging it in; it just works.

Traditionally, application integration has been somewhat more complex than this analogy. Integrating applications would mean that architects or developers would need to talk and exchange message protocols and contracts, perhaps code would need to be written or middleware would need to be configured, and then you would need to test thoroughly as you had no guarantees that everything was done correctly. There would be many moving parts, and they would be tightly coupled together.

An ESB tries to bring the world of distributed applications exchanging data closer to the new toaster analogy. The panacea of fully automated, seamless plug and play may be unattainable, but by providing common services and an operating environment for services, we can reduce the effort required for communication between services and applications.

Centralized Management

We saw that with a proliferation of point-to-point integrations, management quickly becomes a problem. An ESB may not directly transport all messages (because in some use cases there is no need for a message to flow through the bus), but it will include functionality for endpoint provisioning or monitoring, and as such can provide centralized management over the provisioning of those endpoints.

Enhances SOA

The services provided by an ESB are readily usable by other services in an SOA. By leveraging these core services, new services can be developed more rapidly.

Runtime Environment for Services

Services can be created and run on distributed nodes in the ESB. From a Microsoft stack perspective, this could be orchestrations that are surfaced as services, or WCF services.

What Are the Components of an ESB?

As previously stated, the list of services provided by an ESB will vary widely depending on which vendor you speak with, but over time the discrepancies have grown fewer.

Most vendors agree that an ESB should provide the core services listed in Table 12.1.

TABLE 12.1   ESB Core Services

Capability	Description
Dynamic routing	The ability to send a message to a dynamically selected endpoint. (Resolution of the endpoint address is performed at runtime either based on message content or by querying an external system, typically a service registry, Business Rules Engine, custom assembly, and so on.)
Dynamic transformation	The ability to transform a message from one type to another. (The transformation used is determined at runtime either based on message content or by querying an external system, typically a Business Rules Engine, custom assembly, and so on.)
Message validation	Verification that a message conforms to a specified schema or contract.
Message-oriented middleware	Software supporting communications between applications (This is the hub in a pub-sub messaging model.)
Protocol and security mediation	The ability to bridge between different protocols and security models.

Supplemental, or extended, ESB capabilities could include any of the items listed in Table 12.2.

TABLE 12.2   Extended ESB Capabilities

Capability	Description
Service orchestration	The mechanism to compose and coordinate services or processes. (There is usually more than one way, depending on the requirements of the composition.)
Rules engine	The mechanism to decouple business rules from business process or service implementation.
Service level agreement (SLA) support	Management and compliance checking for SLAs.
Lifecycle management	Tools for managing ESB communications from inception and modeling through to versioning and ultimate retirement.
Policy-driven security	The mechanism to use policies across an ESB to define and enforce security constraints.
Registry	Centralized registry for services that facilitates self-service discovery of available services.
Repository	Often related to both lifecycle management and registry, a repository contains metadata and metrics (potentially), models, and additional artifacts related to a service.
Application adapters	Used by the message-oriented middleware to communicate with various line-of-business applications.
Fault management	The mechanism for monitoring and resolving system and business process faults.
Monitoring	Ongoing monitoring of service operations and message flow. (This can include operational monitoring [how many calls, latency of each call, and so on] and process monitoring [how many orders from each region, dollar amount of orders, and so forth]).

If you look down those two lists, you'll see that most map directly to capabilities provided by the Microsoft technology stack. Some capabilities even have more than one implementation option available, such as service orchestration that could be implemented with either BizTalk orchestration or Windows Workflow Foundation, and routing, which could be performed by BizTalk or WCF.

Figure 12.1 depicts, at a high level, how an ESB may be integrated into a fully featured SOA.

For the purpose of this chapter, we assume that BizTalk is providing most of the capabilities listed in Figure 12.1, either natively or in conjunction with the ESB Toolkit. In that context, we take a deeper look at each of these capabilities later in this chapter. First, however, we examine the core services.

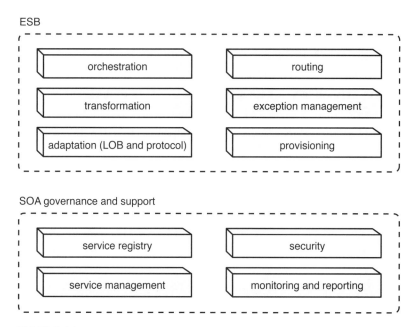

FIGURE 12.1   ESB as it relates to SOA.

Dynamic Routing

Out-of-the-box, BizTalk provides dynamic routing capabilities. Generally, this is used in a content-based routing scenario, where a message endpoint (such as a ConfirmationReturnURI, or from WS-Addressing, ReplyTo address) is provided in either the message itself or in the metadata associated with the message (message context properties). To implement this, you create a dynamic send port and set its address, likely by assigning the address as a property of the corresponding logical send port in an orchestration. Alternatively, this can be achieved by having a filter condition on the send port that is routing based on a promoted value in the message (that the filter and routing engine have visibility into).

To effectively implement dynamic routing in an ESB scenario, you could build on that capability. The out-of-the-box capability enables you to incorporate dynamic routing into a business process but gives you only the capability to specify a known endpoint. Determination of what that endpoint is will still need to be implemented (as well as potential other factors around delivery, such as SLA, compliance, and auditing).

To provide a truly flexible and manageable solution, endpoint resolution should be done against a data store that can be managed outside of code. This could be in the form of a services registry, such as *Universal Description, Discovery and Integration* (UDDI), or some type of services repository. This would allow for endpoints to be defined, and changed, without affecting deployed code.

Using our agent model, this is a key consideration. We could implement a delivery agent whose role it is to pick up any ESB messages that require delivery, perform an endpoint lookup, and then dynamically deliver the message to that endpoint.

Although all the capabilities are provided natively by BizTalk Server, the ESB Toolkit adds a higher level of abstraction that implements the glue that developers would otherwise need to write.

How and when dynamic resolution occurs is a discussion that transcends dynamic routing and is listed in the ESB Toolkit section of this chapter.

Dynamic Transformation

In a perfect world, there would be only one universal transport protocol and only one canonical schema for a given type of message. In the real world, this does not happen, and we usually need to transform messages between types as we integrate across application and organizational boundaries.

BizTalk Server includes a high-performance transformation mechanism, one that accommodates real-world requirements for enterprise-grade transformations, such as mapping large messages by streaming them. Developers can include BizTalk maps either as part of receive and send port processing or in orchestrations. If the maps are specified at a port level, map specification is configured by the system administrator using the BizTalk administration tools (or it could be imported from a binding file). If a mapping operation is specified by the developer in an orchestration, the normal approach is to include a Transform shape and specify the map and input message types. In this case, any change to the map requires developer involvement and code redeployments. (More-advanced techniques allow programmatic application of maps, so potentially this could invoke a dynamic resolution mechanism.)

With the BizTalk ESB Toolkit, transformations can occur as part of a messaging flow or through a transformation agent that could transform the message and then redeposit it on the ESB for further processing. The transformation type can either be specified through configuration or can be resolved dynamically at runtime.

In a non-BizTalk implementation, transformation (of *Extensible Markup Language* [XML] messages) could be performed using *Extensible Stylesheet Language Transformations* (XSLT). In addition, transformation could be provided by a web service that would implement either XSLT transformation or directly leverage BizTalk's transformation engine.

Message Validation

Message validation is a process to ensure that a message conforms to an established contract (for example, confirming that an XML document complies with a schema).

In BizTalk, validation can be performed as part of the message receipt process through a receive pipeline with a validation component. In pure .NET, validation against a schema can easily be performed, as well.

A validation service could be created as part of the ESB infrastructure that takes a message and compares it against a schema, returning the result of that comparison operation. Invoking services or processes would use the validation result to determine their next steps (for example, publishing an exception message). A validation service could perform validations beyond just ensuring structural conformity; it could use the Business Rules Engine to ensure that a message also conforms to business rules (as is often the case with some protocols, such as SWIFT messaging used by the financial services industry).

Message-Oriented Middleware

Message-oriented middleware (MOM) forms the engine of our ESB. In the Microsoft technology stack, BizTalk provides the middleware to flow messages between endpoints in a highly scalable and extensible manner. (Message flow in BizTalk is determined by subscriptions.) Alternatively, it is possible to create a messaging infrastructure based on WCF (potentially incorporating Windows Server AppFabric workflow hosting capabilities, or the routing capabilities in WCF 4.0), although the magnitude of this task should not be underestimated. Look at the administrative tools in BizTalk and the scalability, high availability, traceability, state management, and so on, and then consider how much effort it would require to create the same.

Is BizTalk a Fully Functional ESB?

If you look through the list of core components of an ESB just enumerated, and you are familiar with the capabilities of BizTalk Server, you'll note that all those capabilities are indeed something BizTalk can do. So, is BizTalk a fully functional ESB?

The answer to this depends on your definition of *fully functional*, and this question can be somewhat controversial. To qualify as a fully functional ESB, BizTalk would need some higher-level functionality specifically required for what we have defined as core ESB capabilities. Although some of those dynamic runtime capabilities might not be there out of the box, the building blocks are there, and when coupled with some understanding and diligent design work and other offerings in the Microsoft technology stack, you can indeed build a fully featured ESB. When implemented properly, a BizTalk-based ESB can be a highly available, highly scalable, and very flexible solution.

Fortunately, much of the work you need to do to implement these capabilities has already been done for you and is available in the form of the ESB Toolkit. This chapter highlights the capabilities of the toolkit and explains some of the architectural reasoning behind decisions made in its implementation.

What Is the ESB Toolkit?

Using BizTalk Server, ESB functionality is implemented by the ESB Toolkit. It provides the core ESB capabilities required by BizTalk developers.

History of the ESB Toolkit

The history of the ESB Toolkit goes back to circa 2005, when there was a realization that several high-level BizTalk consultants were implementing solutions using similar architectural styles, and that we were re-inventing these as we moved between projects. The first release grew out of a project to package up this commonality and make it available to the public.

Since that time, there has been a steady evolution, and at the time of this writing it is owned by the BizTalk product team. The code is now being treated as product grade, which means formal development processes, testing, and so on. When BizTalk Server 2009 was released, a new version of the ESB Toolkit also became available, which was by far the most feature rich and rigorously tested. It provides all the capabilities needed to put BizTalk at the center of a modern ESB. In fact, in many ways the ESB Toolkit for BizTalk Server 2009 was the best new feature of BizTalk Server 2009, even though it was not part of the product. It is available for free to any licensed BizTalk users (and, because it is built on top of BizTalk Server, is of little use to people who have not licensed BizTalk Server, although as you'll see it exposes web services for users of other technology stacks in heterogeneous environments).

What Is in the ESB Toolkit?

The ESB Toolkit is a set of prewritten components and architectural guidance that extends the capabilities of BizTalk by providing the functionality needed to implement an ESB pattern. It embodies best practices and leads BizTalk developers down a path of creating applications using broadly accepted best practices.

BizTalk is built on and takes advantage of the .NET framework and the rest of the Microsoft stack. It does not, for example, introduce a new way to do web service calls; instead, it leverages WCF by implementing a set of adapters built on that foundation. In the same vein, it is important to note that the ESB Toolkit does not in any way change the way that BizTalk works. It does not, for example, introduce a new pub-sub mechanism; it leverages and builds on the capabilities BizTalk provides.

What's the Difference Between Native BizTalk Server and BizTalk Server with the ESB Toolkit?

A lot of the parts of a BizTalk integration are all about configuration. Configuration happens at development time, or post deployment. As previously mentioned, with a little extra work, you can add some dynamic behavior to the project, but this requires additional effort.

The ESB Toolkit adds the runtime resolution capabilities required for truly dynamic mediation and operation.

The Magic Behind an ESB

In an ideal world, an ESB is something that you can fire a message at, and magic happens. If the message needs to be transformed, an appropriate transformation occurs. The message's passing registers in an audit trail and perhaps some other form of metrics tracking system. The message is delivered (optionally using a reliable messaging mechanism for guaranteed delivery) to the ultimate endpoint, perhaps undergoing a protocol hop such as being received as *Simple Object Access Protocol* (SOAP) and delivered to an IBM MQ Series queue. If the message needs to be delivered to multiple recipients, that somehow gets taken care of for you by the ESB.

However, this is software, and there is no magic. Somehow, those capabilities need to be implemented, and it is our role as architects and developers to make that happen.

Whether you purchase a set of technologies that together constitute an ESB or build your own that is specifically tailored to your requirements, the need is the same. If you have to perform operations on a message, and the details of those operations are not part of the message itself, that operational metadata needs to exist somewhere. A common approach is to utilize a centralized repository. For example, when the time comes to deliver a message, the ESB could perform a runtime lookup into a UDDI services registry directly to perform endpoint resolution and determine where to send the message. Likewise, you could store transformation and validation requirements in a centralized repository.

Regardless of the data store or resolution mechanisms, metadata needs to be associated with a message travelling through an ESB, and most likely will stay with the message throughout its lifetime inside the ESB.

With BizTalk, this can be implemented in two practical ways:

- As an envelope around the message, where the message itself becomes payload in an envelope message that also contains the metadata

- As BizTalk context properties

The envelope approach is perfectly valid and is easy to grasp. However, it requires that a transformation occurs every time a message is received by the ESB to insert the message into an envelope, and most likely another transformation prior to message delivery to remove the envelope (unless the message is being delivered to a service or process that understands or requires the envelope). This imposes an overhead on every message flowing through the system and has performance implications. In addition, it is a structural change to the message itself; the original message becomes a payload inside the envelope.

BizTalk context properties are properties associated with a message for the duration of its lifetime inside BizTalk. Context properties are created and added to messages as they are received, or at any point in their lifecycle inside BizTalk. Because they are not physically part of the message itself, context properties are by definition lost when a message leaves BizTalk (although you can demote values from message context into message content by

use of a property schema and the XML Assembler pipeline component). Context properties are a key part of BizTalk's architecture and can be leveraged in many ways, including
loosely coupling applications and communicating with adapters.

Many global context properties are created for you when a message is constructed or
received, but in addition, BizTalk developers can create their own context properties.

The ESB Toolkit uses BizTalk's context properties to house the metadata it needs to operate
on a message as it goes through its lifecycle in the ESB.

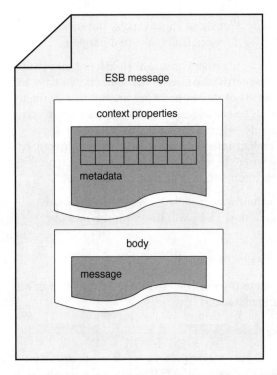

FIGURE 12.2   Metadata used by the ESB toolkit is kept in message context properties.

It is important to note that regardless of which approach you opt for (context properties
or an envelope) the downstream operations are the same. The only difference is the source
of the message metadata. In addition, you may opt to host some of the metadata in external stores, such as a registry.

For people new to the concept of ESBs, it is convenient to think about what happens by
considering an agent model: Messages arrive in the ESB, and agents handle their processing. Agents are an implementation (but not the only one) of core services. They pick up
messages that require their service, perform the service, and then redeposit the message
into the ESB. For example, we have a transformation agent that picks up a message and
performs a transformation. This is not to say that all services are performed by agents; in

some cases, it might be more appropriate to take a more direct-bound approach; however, these agents exist in our infrastructure can provide core services in an asynchronous manner.

In addition, for BizTalk developers and architects that are new to the concept of service orientation, you can consider that an orchestration can be an agent (or service) that is deployed to the fabric of your bus and can be called (reused) by multiple processes.

Now that you have a basic understanding of the glue that holds the services together, we will walk through the core and extended functionalities discussed earlier and examine them in greater detail.

The ESB Toolkit Stack

Just as BizTalk builds on the functionality of the .NET framework and leverages capabilities such as WCF, the ESB Toolkit builds on top of BizTalk. It does not change the way BizTalk works. It doesn't add a new messaging engine. The ESB Toolkit builds on and extends existing capabilities. As mentioned earlier, it adds to BizTalk a lot of runtime resolution and dynamic capabilities that are not natively present.

At the highest level, the stack looks as shown in Figure 12.3.

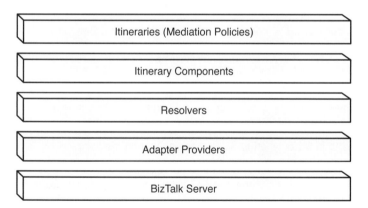

FIGURE 12.3   ESB Toolkit stack.

The two topmost elements, the itineraries and the itinerary components, work hand in hand. The itineraries (also called routing slips) describe a message flow, and the itinerary components make it happen. The resolvers are where the dynamic runtime lookup magic happens. The adapter providers are the bridge between the world of .NET (most of the ESB Toolkit components are .NET code) and the world of BizTalk adapters, allowing us to take settings that were dynamically determined and apply those in a way that works with the BizTalk adapters.

Let's now look at each of these in detail.

Itineraries

Message lifecycle inside the ESB is controlled by itineraries. At the simplest level, an itinerary can be thought of as the series of steps that a message will go through. For example:

1. Receive message.
2. Apply map.
3. Send message.

However, itineraries can be much more than that; they can also be used as a lightweight service composition model. (In some other platforms, this notion is called a microflow.) The idea here is not to include a lot of business logic, compensation, and complex branching control. For that, we have service composition capabilities using BizTalk orchestrations. The goal and appropriate use for an itinerary is a simpler series of steps, not a complete process.

The metadata envelope
(`Microsoft.Practices.ESB.Itinerary.Schemas.System_Properties`) contains properties that are related to flow control of messages through our ESB, as described in Table 12.3.

TABLE 12.3   Metadata Envelope Properties

Property	Description
ServiceName	The name of the service to be invoked. (This usually forms part of a message subscription.)
ServiceState	Current message state typically used as part of a message subscription. (Examples are pending, in process, and complete.)
CurrentServicePosition	An index indicating which step we are currently on. (An itinerary can contain many steps.)
IsRequestResponse	Used to indicate whether a response should be returned.
ServiceType	Execution context. (Should this step be executed as part of pipeline processing or by an orchestration? Valid values are MESSAGING and ORCHESTRATION.)
ItineraryHeader	Contains the entire itinerary.
ItineraryName	Name of this itinerary.
ItineraryVersion	Version of this itinerary.
ItineraryGuid	Unique identifier for this itinerary.

The `ServiceName` and `ServiceState` are generally used to define a subscription. For example, to pseudo code, a subscription may conceptually be something like "send me all messages that are of type `Order` that have a `ServiceName` of `OrderProcess` and a `ServiceState` of `pending`." Message publishers (either the application sending messages to the bus or the proxy that receives a message and puts it on the bus or the receive pipeline through which the message flows) set these properties, and filters on subscribers use them to determine whether a message should be picked up. With this technique, publishers and subscribers are completely autonomous. If you want to introduce a new subscriber to an existing message flow, it could be deployed and could start processing the messages without any need to modify the publishing application, or even notify them.

An itinerary is essentially a set of services to be invoked. These services can happen in one of two execution contexts, either in the messaging layer or in orchestration. In either case, when the service is complete, it should then advance the itinerary to the next step (that is, remove the current step and make the next step the current step). It is essentially a stack, with a linear flow of states.

This technique might seem like a sequential flow, but it doesn't need to be. For example, nothing prevents multiple agents from listening for the same subscription properties, which would effectively be a parallel branch in the message flow.

In addition, the starting itinerary might not be the same itinerary that exists with a message throughout the message's lifecycle. It might be perfectly valid for an agent performing an operation on a message to completely replace the itinerary with a new itinerary. This could be the case if an error condition is encountered, or a business exception occurs such as a customer failing a credit check (in which case you would not complete the order processing flow).

In Microsoft's ESB Toolkit, a message's entire itinerary is serialized and stored in the `ItineraryHeader` context property of that message. For BizTalk's routing engine to have visibility and be able to fulfill subscriptions, parts of the current itinerary step are denormalized and kept in context properties.

Specifying Itineraries

As discussed, itineraries control the flow of messages through the system, There are three ways to specify itineraries:

- ▶ **Server side:** This is the preferred approach from an architectural standpoint. Itineraries can be stored in a centralized repository and be retrieved from there. There are several ways in which this can be done, as you will see later in this chapter.

- ▶ **Client-side hybrid:** In this scenario, the client makes some calls into the ESB infrastructure (for example resolving an endpoint address) and then constructs an itinerary. The itinerary is then stored in SOAP headers, and the message is sent to the on-ramp.

- ▶ **Client side:** In this scenario, the client constructs an itinerary. The itinerary is then stored in SOAP headers and the message is sent to the on-ramp.

Note that the client-side and client-side hybrid options are somewhat less desirable because they put a lot of responsibility on the client to specify what will happen to the message as it is being processed. Although in some situations this might be acceptable if you are in a large enterprise and are leveraging services within the same enterprise, it is still a fairly brittle approach, and you would have to consider factors such as updates and versioning.

The server-side option is by far the most desirable because it provides a single source of truth for itineraries (the repository), and relieves the client of any responsibility around message processing; they just send in a message. In addition, this approach can be used with any transport because there is no reliance on SOAP headers.

The Itinerary Lifecycle

Figure 12.4 shows the itinerary lifecycle.

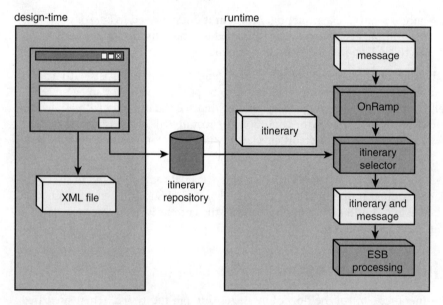

FIGURE 12.4   Applying an itinerary to a message.

At development time, the following occurs:

1. Itineraries are created using a visual design surface inside Visual Studio; however, because itineraries are just XML, you could in theory create them in code.

2. Itineraries are exported either as XML (possibly for migration to other environments) or to the itinerary repository (SQL Server).

At runtime, the following occurs:

1. A message is received at an ESB on-ramp, and an itinerary is selected. (We explore how this can happen soon.)

2. The itinerary is applied to the message, meaning the details of the itinerary are added to the message context properties associated with that message.

3. The message continues on into the ESB for processing.

We continue with the construct that the preferable design pattern is to have itinerary selection occur server side. For the actual selection, we use an itinerary selector pipeline in the receive location, which is to say a pipeline that includes an itinerary selector pipeline component (included with the ESB Toolkit), and look up the itinerary in the itinerary repository. In the properties of that component, you specify a resolver string. Typically, you would do one of two things:

▶ Hard code the value to be looked up using a STATIC:// resolver string that specifies which itinerary to use. (Note, though, that this is just putting in a static reference to the itinerary to use; you could change the flow by updating the itinerary without needing to change the receive location properties.)

▶ Use a BRI:// resolver string to query the Business Rules Engine. (From an architectural perspective, this is an attractive option because it allows you to change which itinerary is selected by changing a business rule; no code changes, no itinerary changes.)

Figure 12.5 shows the message receipt flow.

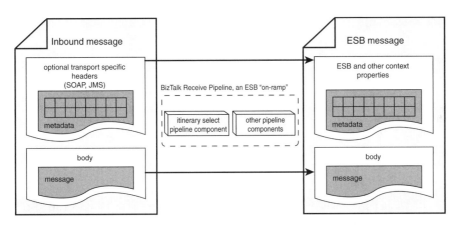

FIGURE 12.5   Receiving a message through an on-ramp.

Dynamic Resolution: The Resolvers

You have seen that some parts of our ESB infrastructure, especially dynamic routing and dynamic transformation, require dynamic runtime resolution of values. This functionality has been abstracted into a series of prebuilt components called resolvers that are called at defined points in a message lifecycle to do this resolution.

It is the responsibility of the resolver to know how to query some sort of metadata store, and a set of values that fill the needs of the query. One of the most commonly used examples of this is the UDDI resolver, which is used to query a UDDI registry and return an endpoint location. However, resolvers are not just about endpoints; they can be used to resolve other artifacts (such as maps or itineraries), as well.

Resolvers that are included in the box with the ESB Toolkit 2.1 are as follows.

For endpoint resolution

▶ UDDI 2.0

▶ UDDI 3.0

▶ WS-MEX

▶ Static

▶ BRE

▶ XPath

For artifact resolution

▶ Static

▶ Static (for itineraries)

▶ SQL Server

▶ Composite

▶ BRE (for maps)

▶ BRE (for itineraries)

There are many extensibility points in the ESB Toolkit, and this is one of them. Should you require, for example, endpoint resolution to occur against a custom registry, you could create and register a new resolver.

Resolution can occur as part of the execution of an itinerary, or the components can also be invoked programmatically.

Typically, resolution will occur at one of two points:

▶ When a message is received, if it has some properties that we know will lead to a resolution requirement (for example, messages will be routed, but the endpoint address is not defined yet)

▶ At the last possible moment (*just-in-time*, or JIT, resolution) before a specified operation is performed (for example, if a message is about to be transformed but we don't know the map type yet)

It is possible that resolution could fail when a message is first received, perhaps because a process has not yet run that would provide that information. However, a resolution failure at this stage would be nonfatal because the operation that requires the information is not about to be performed. In addition, as is the case with long-running processes, the location of an endpoint could change from the time the process starts and the time we invoke the service. By using JIT resolution, we are not affected by changes in endpoint location during process execution.

If the JIT resolution of an endpoint fails, it is a fatal error because the operation in question is the next thing that needs to occur, and the failure means that we are missing a required piece of information.

In our scenario, items that require resolution are as follows:

- Endpoint addresses
- Endpoint configuration information
- Map types

Resolution could be performed by querying a variety of sources. In our scenario, we have provided for the following sources (as you can see by examining the metadata schema):

- Hard coding (specified through post-deployment configuration, not in code)
- UDDI
- BizTalk Rules Engine
- XPath into the message itself
- Custom assembly that implements the `IResolver` interface

This last option allows developers to effectively extend the resolution mechanism by creating custom assemblies that perform custom actions, perhaps invoking a web service or querying a database to perform resolution.

The resolution mechanism itself is also exposed as a web service, although for performance reasons the internal ESB components make direct calls to it. However, the fact that the resolver mechanism is exposed as a web service allows other parties to call into the resolution mechanism.

Adapter Providers

The itinerary (mediation) components included in the ESB Toolkit are .NET components. When resolution is performed by a resolver component, a .NET dictionary object is returned. However, when we go to set adapter properties that will be required for messaging, we're working in terms of the BizTalk adapters, and we cannot just hand them a dictionary object. The adapter providers form a bridge, taking the appropriate values from the dictionary object and setting the corresponding adapter property.

The adapter providers included with the ESB Toolkit 2.1 are as follows:

- WCF-BasicHttp
- WCF-WsHttp
- WCF-Custom

- ▶ FTP

- ▶ File

- ▶ SMTP

- ▶ MQSeries

Those of you familiar with BizTalk Server will notice that there are fewer adapter providers than there are adapters provided with BizTalk. This does not mean that the other adapters cannot participate in ESB-based messaging exchanges. To use the other adapters, you could either use a hybrid solution (such as using a static send port, ideally subscribing to a specific `ServiceName`/`ServiceState` combination), or you could extend the ESB Toolkit by creating a new adapter provider. The latter is actually quite easy to do (in the order of an hour of effort, not days), and there are several examples and new adapter providers available from the community for some of the other adapters.

It is important to note that there is an adapter provider for WCF-Custom. This opens the key to being able to use it with the adapters that are provided as part of the BizTalk Adapter Pack, and with any other WCF bindings that might be available. We look at an example of this later in this chapter when we extend the ESB to the Azure cloud.

You do not invoke the adapter providers explicitly; they are invoked as part of the resolution process. If the resolver connection string contains an `EndPointConfiguration` attribute, this is populated by the resolution component with a dictionary of name/value pairs. When the resolution process ends, if this attribute is present and populated, the adapter manager instantiates the appropriate adapter provider. The adapter provider then iterates through the dictionary object setting appropriate properties in message context that is ultimately used by the dynamic off-ramp when the message is transmitted.

Service Composition

Composition of services is a key feature of a SOA. On the .NET platform, there are several ways to compose services: in code, Windows Workflow Foundation, BizTalk orchestration. But how does service composition look in the context of a BizTalk-based ESB? The architecture outlined in this chapter relies on loose coupling, using message metadata to route messages to services. The services are autonomous, self-contained units that are not aware of each other. To tie these services together, we need some form of coordinator service, which is something BizTalk orchestration is well suited for.

However, this chapter has also introduced a fourth mechanism for implementing service composition: itineraries. Although sometimes having a lot of options can result in confusion, in this case the various capabilities of each composition mechanism dictate when to use which capability.

Windows Workflow Foundation enables you to compose services outside of the context of the ESB. Use cases where this may be appropriate are in low-latency situations, or where there is just no need to flow messages through the ESB because there will never be additional subscribers (acknowledgment messages for noncritical transmissions, for example). Because this will all occur outside the ESB, we do not discuss it further here.

Itineraries, which you can also call microflows, are intended to be used for very simple short-running service compositions and message flows. Itineraries include a broker capability that enables you to perform conditional branching from inside an itinerary. However, this should be used only sparingly and when required, because it is yet another point in which you could embed business logic. Itineraries allow you to do something like call a service, transform the response, call a second service, and finally a third. However, there are no transactional or compensation semantics in an itinerary, because capabilities like that are beyond the lightweight service composition role they are intended to play.

Of the three options, BizTalk orchestrations provide the richest model for service composition.

You can use an orchestration to act as a coordinator for any invoked services and maintain state information for the overall process. Orchestrations contain the constructs required for transactional semantics and compensation, and they use the BizTalk host model to provide a wealth of other services, such as persistence, failover, and tracking.

Orchestrations could be constructed for either synchronous or asynchronous invocation. From an orchestration design and implementation perspective, the specifics of how the process are invoked at runtime are not relevant at design time because we are concerned only with the calling pattern (one way, request/response), which is done through logical ports. In traditional BizTalk development without using the ESB Toolkit, these logical ports are bound after deployment to physical ports, such as a web service, and it is that binding that establishes the link between the logical design and the physical transport layer. In addition, it is possible to bind more than one physical receive location to a single physical receive port, which enables service invocation in more than one way.

Orchestrations can be registered with the ESB as an orchestration service, and it then becomes available in the itinerary designer and part of an itinerary.

Messaging-Only Implementations

Experienced BizTalk developers know that they have the option of creating messaging-only solutions, which are appropriate for simple message flows that do not require the more complex capabilities that could be implemented in an orchestration (and so avoid the overhead of invoking an orchestration).

Microsoft's ESB Toolkit supports this, as well. For example, runtime resolution of an endpoint could be performed in a receive pipeline as a message is being received, and that message can subsequently be published to the Message Box as being ready for delivery.

From an implementation standpoint, the way this works is that once itinerary resolution has occurred. The itinerary processing components starts walking through the itinerary, performing steps that are specified as having a `ServiceType` (execution context) of `Messaging`. Once a step is encountered with a `ServiceType` of `Orchestration`, pipeline processing ends, and the message is handed to the next component in the pipeline.

Unified Exception Management

When faced with new BizTalk requirements, developers often ask themselves the same set of project start-up questions. Inevitably, one of those questions is this: How are we going to handle exceptions? This question is often complicated by the fact that the solution could span multiple technologies.

In an ESB environment, effective exception management takes on increased importance because debugging failures in a loosely coupled solution can at times be challenging. By using a well-planned exception management strategy, it is possible to construct solutions that can not only record failures but also potentially invoke compensation processes or services in response to exception conditions.

Exceptions fall into one of two categories: business exceptions (for example, credit check failed) and system exceptions (for example, could not load assembly). BizTalk solutions, such as the BizTalk-based ESB in our case study, can span multiple technologies, including orchestrations, pipeline components, web services (internal and external), custom assemblies, and more, often crossing security and organizational boundaries. A unified exception handling mechanism would be able to provide exception handling capabilities for all of those disparate participants and technologies.

Typically, developers who are new to BizTalk gravitate toward the same exception management strategies they may have used in a code-centric development environment, possibly logging failures to the event log for *System Center Operations Manager* (SCOM) to handle, or perhaps writing out to a logging service. However, with BizTalk Server, we are working in a message-oriented paradigm. Why then should we not embrace that paradigm for our exception management strategy?

BizTalk Server 2006 introduced the notion of failed message routing, which for the first time allowed BizTalk developers to create subscribers for messages that failed during receipt (for example, messages that did not conform to an expected schema). If we take that technique and apply it to exception management, we can create a mechanism that allow processes encountering failures to publish an exception message and handlers that subscribe to those exception messages.

This loosely coupled approach to exception management offers many benefits. By decoupling exception handling from the process itself, we have the opportunity to stratify assemblies so that exception management for a given process becomes a separate assembly that can be versioned and deployed without affecting the currently deployed and running process. In addition, multiple handlers could potentially respond to a given type of exception, as may be the case if you want to track metrics of all exceptions flowing through the ESB.

A message-oriented exception management system allows creation of both generic handlers (for example, record all exceptions) and highly targeted handlers (for example, to handle failure in the `PrintCheck` process of the `Payroll` solution).

In a fully functional message-based exception management strategy, you also have the ability to include, as payload in an exception message, any messages that might have been in-flight at the time the exception condition was encountered. If you have the exception management strategy capability, you have the capacity to reconstruct those messages in an exception handler, enabling a repair and resubmit scenario.

> **NOTE**
>
> A great way to incorporate human interaction into a BizTalk-controlled process is by the use of Microsoft's InfoPath and SharePoint technologies. InfoPath forms are XML documents that have two additional XML processing instructions, indicating that it is an InfoPath form and the name of the InfoPath template to use in rendering the XML document. SharePoint form libraries are a great place to store InfoPath forms. By using the SharePoint adapter, BizTalk can write messages out to a SharePoint site as InfoPath forms. Users can then interact with the forms, and they can be constructed so they have a submit process that can reenter an appropriately designed running business process or trigger a new one. This submit process usually entails writing the document back to a SharePoint library with a given state (for example, a state column at the SharePoint level with a value of APPROVED) and then having BizTalk poll the library using a SharePoint view (configured to filter by that state). As an added bonus, by adopting this approach we have decoupled the act of human intervention from the processing by BizTalk, making human intervention an asynchronous operation that can occur even if the BizTalk environment is not currently available, or is set to retrieve only intervened messages on a scheduled basis.

In a repair and resubmit scenario, users could access InfoPath forms on a SharePoint site, perhaps edit data in the form, or approve it, and submit it. This pattern is effective in situations where a message could be repaired by changing a value (for example, shipping address is invalid) or where a human-intervention approval step might be required (for example, credit limit exceed, process anyhow?).

To implement a unified exception management system, you first need to create a schema that defines what an exception message looks like. A well-defined schema includes enough information that both generic and targeted handlers will be able to, either generically or selectively, subscribe to. This may include such items those listed in Table 12.4.

TABLE 12.4   Exception Message Properties

Property	Description
Application	Application name (for example, Payroll).
Process	A specific process that encountered the exception condition (for example, PrintCheck).
Exception message	Human-meaningful description of the failure (for example, could not contact printer).

TABLE 12.4   Exception Message Properties

Property	Description
Fault code	Standardized code that can be used as a filter condition by subscribers (Codes are usually governed and allocated by a centralized group to ensure that no overlap occurs.)
Severity	Allows creation of varying priority handlers (For example, a handler may listen for critical severity exceptions and invoke a human-notification process.)

Exposing Core Services

The ESB Toolkit has some core services available, as BizTalk orchestrations and helper classes, which are also exposed as web services, as described in Table 12.5.

TABLE 12.5   ESB Web Services

Capability	Purpose
Resolver service	Allow external applications to leverage the resolution mechanism. (This could be a good way to abstract service registry access and make it broadly available in a heterogeneous environment.)
On-ramp services	Allow web service clients to send messages to the ESB. (Web service SOAP headers become message context properties as the message passes through a context setting component in a receive pipeline.)
Transformation services	Allow non-BizTalk applications to access and leverage the BizTalk transformation engine. (Allows access to all web service clients, including those not running on the Microsoft platform.)
Exception management service	By publishing the fault schema using the default BizTalk schema publishing mechanism, web service clients can submit messages and non-BizTalk or non-.NET applications can participate in the ESB exception management scheme.
BizTalk operations web service	Web service that returns information about BizTalk artifacts.

Distributed ESBs

No discussion of ESBs is complete without touching on the topic of distributed (or federated) ESBs. The notion here is that although you already have distributed services within your ESB, you might also have additional ESBs within your enterprise, or perhaps have some agreements with trading partners. Distributed ESBs within an enterprise could be at a business unit level (the HR ESB, the Accounting ESB, and so on) or stratified at a geographic level (the NorAm ESB, the EU ESB, and so forth).

Regardless of the stratification reason, there is now a need to flow messages between the distributed islands. Fortunately, the ESB Toolkit provides the building blocks we need to implement this functionality. If they are in direct communication, an off-ramp on one ESB sends a message to an on-ramp of another ESB. In other cases, you might opt to relay through an intermediary. So a message is sent from one ESB to the Windows Azure AppFabric Service Bus, and from there is relayed to the other ESBs.

In addition, you could consider various strategies that involve using SQL Server's replication capabilities to replicate the itinerary repository, and using UDDI 3.0's syndication capabilities to federate distributed UDDI directories.

The correct patterns to use depends on the specific requirements. This is very much an emerging frontier, as many enterprises are currently only thinking of implementing their first ESB. However, when you get to this stage, you will find the building blocks already in place and ready for you to use.

REST and BizTalk ESB

Increasingly, communications between distributed parts of applications and message exchanges takes place over REST. This raises some interesting questions, as we see next.

A Stylistic Comparison

Representational State Transfer (REST) and ESB architectures have fundamental philosophical differences in their underlying principles.

REST is a programming model used to create resource/entity services. There are many fundamental principles behind REST, but two of the core principles are that everything is stateless and that all resources are URI addressable. For example, in the case of an order, these principles mandate that the order itself is passed from one service to another, and the one sending it off does not retain any state information for that order. Everything about the order travels as a comprehensive and complete entity. Status of the order could potentially be retrieved through an RSS feed or by entering an appropriate URI into a web browser.

However, ESB exchanges often involve long-running transactional processes where it is essential to maintain state information. In this scenario, if I send order information to a supplier, that order information is retained in a stateful store, and subsequent messages that are part of that business transaction can be correlated back to it. The notion of URI addressable resources is also somewhat foreign to flow in an ESB. Because a client does not know (and should not know) who the subscribers are, after a client has published a message to the bus, that client has no inherent notion of how to find it.

Both models have a time and place where it is appropriate to use them; it is not a question of using one or the other. Rather, it is a question of using the model that is the best fit for a given need. And, although the two models are so fundamentally and philosophically different, there are certainly valid use cases for using them together. For example, although an order processing system may be implemented by composing services available on the ESB, and all message traffic related to it flows through the ESB, you could as an example expose a RESTful (perhaps RDF or Atom) service to track order status.

Incorporating REST into the BizTalk ESB

Although there is no support in the ESB Toolkit for REST, this does not preclude the use of REST, although it means that some development is effort required.

From the receiving side, you could expose a RESTful service that uses the PUT verb to submit data to the service. The service would then act as a relay, and submit that data into BizTalk as a message. You could do so by potentially interacting with the helper components or core services and directly submitting the message using the direct submit approach (see the BizTalk Server *software development kit* [SDK]) or by invoking a WCF on-ramp service.

From the sending side (invoking a RESTful service), you have several options. You could, of course, programmatically call a RESTful service from a helper class and invoke that from an expression shape in an orchestration, but this goes around the pub-sub mechanism and means any changes you make are code changes. A better approach is to use the WCF-Custom adapter, just as we did when communicating with Windows Azure, only this time it is in conjunction with the WebHttpBinding. If you were using the GET verb, you would need to implement a custom behavior to do so, and there are examples from the community that show how this can be done.

So, although there is no native support for REST in BizTalk or in the ESB Toolkit, with not too much effort, the two fundamentally different worlds can be brought together so that you can leverage the benefits each approach offers.

Management

Deploying ESB solutions is more than just thinking about a solution as a message-based asynchronous exchange. It touches on management aspects as well.

Provisioning and Runtime Governance

Runtime governance is a multifaceted issue, and can become complex depending on your specific requirements. Early in the SOA adoption lifecycle, not much attention is usually paid to governance and provisioning because there are not many services yet and it starts as a nonissue. However, as services proliferate, endpoints multiply, and new applications get on the bus, a lack of a cohesive and well-planned approach can result in greater administrative burden and costs.

What provisioning new services entails will vary by enterprise, but typical requirements include the following:

- ▶ Advertising service availability (service registry or repository)
- ▶ Implementing monitoring of messages based on type or services
- ▶ Creation of custom on-ramps
- ▶ Definition of security policies

The ESB Toolkit does not add a governance layer onto BizTalk or the .NET framework. It does, however, have hooks into some of the industry's best-of-breed governance solution providers to integrate their governance capabilities into a BizTalk-based ESB.

In addition, service virtualization solutions such as the Managed Services Engine (available on Codeplex) can be used as containers for on- and off-ramps, allowing policy-driven enforcement of SLAs or tracking at the container level.

SLA Enforcement

SLA enforcement means confirming that an agreed-upon service level, perhaps response time, is being met.

If you are going to monitor service metrics, there are two common models used: the observation model or the container model.

In a Microsoft context, the observation model could mean instrumenting the service using BizTalk's BAM capabilities. (For a full discussion of BizTalk BAM, see Chapter 9, "Business Activity Monitoring with BizTalk BAM.") Essentially, tracking of events (for example, service start) is monitored and subsequently reported on. This model could easily be applied over various transport protocols. Note that this will capture only data; you would need to execute the logic to respond to conditions outside of the SLAs.

Using the container model is similar but takes a slightly different approach. The proxy is invoked at the client side of a web service call. It registers metrics, but can also perform other capabilities, such as usage metering, service virtualization, and so on.

Monitoring

Monitoring of an ESB breaks down into three distinct areas:

- ▶ Infrastructure monitoring (machine health)
- ▶ ESB component monitoring (ESB health)
- ▶ Custom application and service monitoring (solution/service health)

The first level of monitoring is the server health type of monitoring that is provided by tools such as Microsoft SCOM and IBM's Tivoli. This is the lowest level of monitoring, from confirmation that the server is running and specific services are operational through to *central processing unit* (CPU) and memory utilization. In a well-planned environment, these tools enable you to not only monitor changing server conditions but to also perhaps react to them and reassign resources as required.

The next level of monitoring is concerned with the monitoring of ESB core services and components. At this level, you could leverage BizTalk's BAM capabilities to track service metrics. (For a full discussion of BizTalk BAM, see Chapter 9.) Metrics gathered could include historical trend data, allowing server administrators to spot service latency degradations and other trends that might not be readily apparent from a tabular listing.

Furthermore, if you are using *business activity monitoring* (BAM) scheduled aggregations, the data is collected in SQL Server Analysis Services *online analytical processing* (OLAP) cubes, which allow for new views into service metrics to be created long after the metric data has been collected. Both the ESB Toolkit and the Managed Services Engine leverage BizTalk BAM for this type of monitoring. In the case of the ESB Toolkit, tracking activity for part of an itinerary is as simple as enabling tracking on that step and then reporting on it.

Other applications and services created in your enterprise but outside of the realm of the ESB core services can also take advantage of the metrics tracking infrastructure provided by BizTalk BAM. Developer documentation, samples, and training ensure this is done in a reasonable manner that does not adversely affect the other services.

Organizational Considerations

Deploying an ESB and ESB-solutions may also mean some "soft" or organizational changes. Thinking this part through will increase adoption, and simplify the rollout process.

Ensuring a Smooth Transition

Developers new to BizTalk usually have a learning curve to scale because they are not used to thinking in terms of message-oriented solutions (although generally once the transition is made there is no going back). Moving to an ESB topology marks a fundamental change for most enterprises; a completely new infrastructure is being deployed, and along with it, a new development paradigm. This is a foundational upheaval and entails significant change.

To ensure a smooth transition that reaps the most benefits of the new environment, it is essential that care and consideration be paid to the soft aspects of this transition. In most large enterprises, it will not be a case of "if you build it they will come." Developers have varying learning curves they need to move through, infrastructure administrators require training, and architects need to understand the range of new capabilities they have available to them.

Your transition plan should include, at least, the following:

- Training
- Consulting
- Developer SDK
- Development environments

Training can take many forms. Formal training for BizTalk developers is strongly encouraged, given the breadth of the product's capabilities, and many companies now offer this. Training for infrastructure personnel is now readily available, as well, and will instruct your infrastructure personnel on the installation, administration, and tuning of BizTalk Server.

If you do not have experienced BizTalk developers on your team, consider working with a consulting firm that has extensive experience in the deployment of BizTalk and how to develop ESB-based solutions. The additional cost incurred will be well worth the time saved, by applying broadly accepted best practices and experiences. Your transition will be smoother, and your time-to-value will be reduced.

A developer SDK can be a powerful tool to help people ramp up quickly on how to use your ESB infrastructure. The target audience here should be developers who understand how to develop BizTalk solutions, because this will show them how their solutions can integrate into the ESB environment and take advantage of the services and capabilities it offers. An SDK should include documentation on the core services targeted at service consumers, documenting how to use them. (A separate document, not part of the SDK, would be for developers who may modify or extend these services in the future.) The SDK should also provide examples that are very approachable and easy to understand that show usage of ESB capabilities. The developer SDK should also include any naming conventions you want to implement.

Finally, you should make ready-to-use development environments available. Ideally, this should be a fully self-contained and fully functional environment running inside a virtual machine. Having the environment preinstalled, with the SDK installed as well, will allow developers to immediately begin learning their new toolset, as opposed to spending a lot of time installing and configuring software.

Gatekeeper Process

Typically, and ideally, BizTalk solutions are developed in isolation and then deployed into shared staging (or developer integration), validation, and production environments. How an application is initially constructed in a self-contained development environment isn't crucial, but it becomes extremely important as solutions migrate through the various shared environments on their way to production.

Many corporations that have successfully deployed ESBs ensure that application administration is simplified by implementing a gatekeeper process. From an ESB perspective, the gatekeeper process ensures application consistency by examining the following:

  ▶ **Exception handling:** Was the unified mechanism employed?

  ▶ **Naming conventions:** Were they followed?

  ▶ **Unit and functional testing:** Was coverage adequate?

  ▶ **Versioning:** Has this been addressed?

Additional considerations may include examining other nonproduction factors such as documentation, build process, and metrics.

Adherence to a formalized solution migration process such as this is crucial for effective management and administration of the shared BizTalk environment and is a good software engineering practice.

Summary

This chapter has shown how you can use the ESB Toolkit to provide ESB capabilities, building on top of the capabilities already provided by BizTalk Server. You have seen how the ESB Toolkit adds runtime resolution capabilities and a lightweight service composition model. This chapter also addressed some of the softer issues surrounding ESB deployment that are key to a successful deployment.

As you have seen, an ESB plays a key role in a service-oriented architecture.

PART III

Deployment and Administration

IN THIS PART

Administration Console Concepts

The BizTalk Administration Console is one of three methods of administering BizTalk Server, the others being the BTSTask command-line tool and various scripting/programmability *application programming interfaces* (APIs). Ideally, many routine/repeatable tasks are driven through command line and scripts when administering BizTalk, but the Administration Console remains the primary tool for troubleshooting and ad hoc configuration tasks.

Introducing the Administration Console

The BizTalk Administration Console is launched from within the Microsoft BizTalk Server 2010 program group and is titled simply BizTalk Server Administration. When you first open it, you usually see that the console is already connected to a BizTalk group (see Figure 13.1)—at least if the machine you are using is itself a member of a BizTalk group (perhaps just a single server group, as on a developer workstation). You can right-click the **BizTalk Server Administration** node in the tree (or use links provided in the center pane) to connect to any BizTalk group in your environment; you just need to know the SQL Server and database name that contain the corresponding management database (typically called BizTalkMgmtDb).

FIGURE 13.1   BizTalk Server Administration Console, showing highest-level view.

BizTalk Group Properties

After you connect to a BizTalk group, you can review properties of a group (in right-click menu **Properties** within *Microsoft Management Console* [MMC]) to see the databases, security groups, and *Single Sign-On* (SSO) details for the group. This can be particularly helpful when you have several groups within an environment (where the various security groups and databases are different per group by necessity and a quick authoritative reference is useful). See Figures 13.2 and 13.3 and note the additional tabs available for viewing.

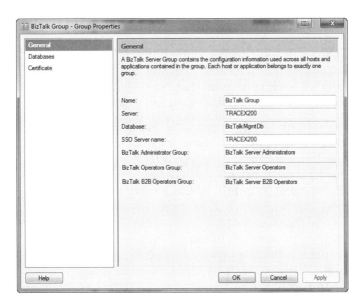

FIGURE 13.2   General BizTalk group properties.

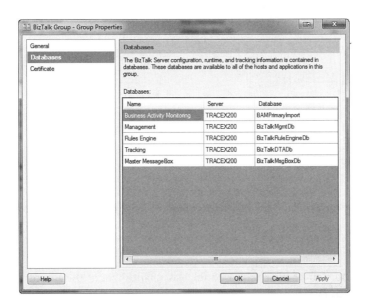

FIGURE 13.3   BizTalk group properties, databases.

BizTalk Settings Dashboard

In addition to the properties of a group, you can review settings (in right-click menu). This is referred to as the Settings Dashboard, and most of what you find here is new to BizTalk 2010, representing a significant improvement in what can be configured via user interface (rather than various Registry keys, configuration files, and database table values).

Figure 13.4 shows the portion of the dashboard that governs the group as a whole. The Configuration Refresh Interval refers to how often the messaging configuration (port configurations and such) is reloaded from the database by the BizTalk infrastructure to absorb changes that have been made. Message Batch Threshold refers to a maximum size beyond which BizTalk splits an incoming message into smaller batches for processing. Large Message Size refers to the size limit after which disk-backed streaming for batches and transformations will be used. The Message Box Performance Counter Sampling Interval helps you trade off pressure on the database (because these counter values are populated by queries) against freshness in the data presented. Finally, Enable Group-Level Tracking allows you to have a master switch for tracking across the entire group (whereas this is normally a fine-grained per-artifact decision).

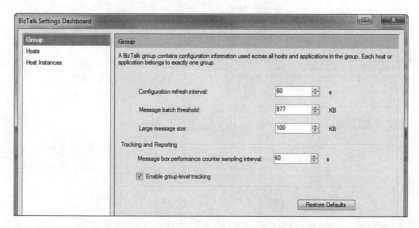

FIGURE 13.4   BizTalk Settings Dashboard, Group level.

Figure 13.5 shows the General portion of the dashboard for hosts. Note that at the top of this dialog, you can choose which host you are currently modifying. Settings you apply across all tabs (General plus the three throttling tabs) apply to all instances of the host appearing in this drop-down.

Move Tracking Data to DTA DB refers to whether this host will use the tracking database (and tracking tables in the Message Box), and as a consequence, indicates whether this host (and all objects running in it) has read/write permissions to these locations. You may decide it is appropriate to disable this for host instances running in particular portions of your network infrastructure.

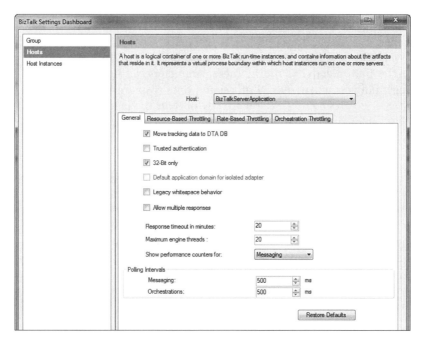

FIGURE 13.5   BizTalk Settings Dashboard, Hosts (General) level.

Trusted Authentication refers to whether a particular host is allowed to collect authentication information (via digital signature, Windows authentication, and so on), and subsequently stamp a message with a party ID and a Windows Security ID. If the host is not configured with Trusted Authentication, the Message Box just overwrites the party ID with the guest ID, and the SSID with that of the host instance's service account.

32-Bit Only forces 32-bit host instances on 64-bit servers, typically used when you have legacy native components involved (perhaps COM-based.). Also, certain adapters are 32-bit only.

Default Application Domain for Isolated Adapter causes messaging engine objects to be loaded in the default appdomain (typically of a web worker process) rather than in the first appdomain of the isolated host instance. The latter behavior can create an error condition if that first appdomain unloads before others.

Legacy Whitespace Behavior allows you to indicate that you want to preserve whitespace when creating maps.

Response Timeout in Minutes indicates the default timeout for request-response messages (such as those originating from a *Hypertext Transfer Protocol* [HTTP] transport and configured as two way).

Maximum Engine Threads refers to the maximum number of threads used by the *End Point Manager* (EPM) within instances of the host. The actual number of threads varies depending on activity level.

Show Performance Counters allows you to set whether the Message Agent counters are showing activity for orchestrations or messaging activity.

Finally, Polling Intervals allows you to configure how often BizTalk will look for new messages and new orchestration activity. Tuning these parameters can help in low-latency scenarios, depending on where overall processing time is spent. In earlier versions of BizTalk, these settings could be done directly only in the management database (adm_ServiceClass table) and they applied to all hosts. Now these can be configured here and specifically per host, enabling you to create low-latency hosts versus high-throughput hosts.

Resource-Based Throttling (Figure 13.6) allows you to configure resource-related criteria for when the host will go into a throttled mode, limiting new activity in various ways. Threads refers simply to the threshold thread count per *central processing unit* (CPU). Database Connections is the threshold count of database connections per CPU. In-Process Messages refers to messages delivered to the EPM or XLANG (orchestrations) that have not yet been processed. Especially when using orchestrations that apply the sequential convoy pattern (or any other aggregator pattern) that processes lots of messages (which are all "in-process" as long as they are not released), it can be necessary to increase the In-Process Messages threshold to avoid zombie messages.

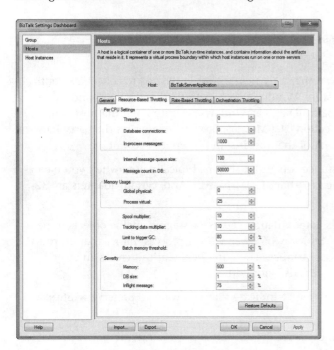

FIGURE 13.6   BizTalk Settings Dashboard, Hosts (Resource-Based Throttling) level.

Internal Message Queue Size refers to the size on the in-memory queue that acts as a placeholder for delivering messages. For low-latency scenarios, this can be increased, but at the expense of available memory when messages are large.

Message Count in DB refers to a total of count work, state, and suspended queues in hosts that are subscribed to the messages published by *this* host. In addition, if messages in the spool or tracking tables exceed a value of 10 times this value, a throttling condition is also triggered.

Memory Usage allows you to set throttle triggers based both on a percentage of available physical memory and percentage of virtual memory for the process. If you use a value greater than 100 here, the units become megabytes rather than percent.

Spool Multiplier is a value that will be multiplied by Message Count in DB and then compared against the size of the spool table. A growing spool table can be caused by multiple factors (growing application queues, purge jobs that are not keeping up, and so forth), and so throttling based on the size of this table is appropriate. Tracking Data Multiplier is identical but pertains to the size of the tracking table. Zero in both cases causes this throttling criteria to not be used.

Limit to Trigger GC allows you to configure the percentage of memory consumption prior to a .NET garbage collection bring triggered.

Batch Memory Threshold refers to a behavior whereby a publishing batch is actually exempt from the Process Virtual limit referred to earlier. This value is multiplied by the Process Virtual threshold to compute a limit applied to the batch. Zero indicates no special treatment for batches.

Finally, the Severity settings refer to what severity will be assigned for memory-triggered, database size-triggered, or in-flight message count-triggered throttling conditions. These values come into play when BizTalk is deciding what type of throttling instruction to issue because this is based on the condition with highest severity. In addition, delay periods in publishing/processing are proportional to severity.

Rate-Based Throttling (Figure 13.7) allows you to configure rate-based criteria for when the host will go into a throttled mode. The Publishing portion refers to the rate at which messages are published from this host (to downstream hosts). The Delivery portion refers to the rate at which messages are delivered to the orchestration or messaging engine (within this host). This set of controls lets you determine what will be the definition of too great a mismatch between inflow and outflow and what will be the resulting action. Specifically, Minimum Number of Samples and Sampling Window Duration work together to define how much traffic will be observed to determine real operational rates. Rate Overdrive Factor refers to the allowable mismatch in the producer/consumer relationship. Maximum Throttling Delay is the maximum delay BizTalk will impose (at highest severity throttling). Throttling Override allows you to manually introduce throttling, or disable it altogether. If you manually introduce it, Throttling Override Severity allows you to control the severity level for that case.

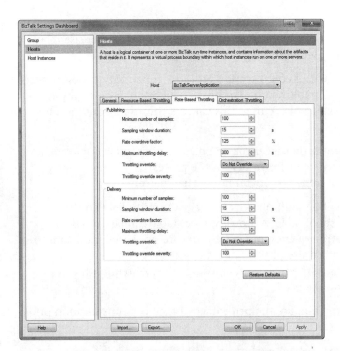

FIGURE 13.7   BizTalk Settings Dashboard, Hosts (Rate-Based Throttling) level.

Orchestration Throttling (Figure 13.8) allows for fine-grained control over dehydration/rehydration. When Dehydration Behavior is set to Custom, the Maximum Threshold is used to determine the maximum idle time (blocked and waiting for a message) before dehydration, and Minimum Threshold sets the minimum idle time. You can see by default the minimum is 1 second and the maximum is half an hour. If you check the Subscriptions check box, you are overriding the behavior of when the Message Box will decide to pause/resume moving messages to the subscription instance based on the number waiting to be consumed.

Figure 13.9 shows the .NET CLR tab of the dashboard for host instances. Note that at the top of this dialog you can choose which host instance you are currently modifying. Settings you apply across this tab and the Orchestration Memory Throttling tab apply to a particular host instance. On the .NET CLR tab, you can configure thread settings that in other kinds of applications you apply using the processModel configuration element. Depending on what kinds of longer-running work you do on particular threads, you might find tuning these numbers useful.

Figure 13.10 shows throttling settings for orchestrations based on memory usage. It makes sense for these to be per host instance (rather than host) because different instances may have different physical memory usage patterns. When memory use (either physical or virtual) reaches the optimal usage level, dehydration throttling begins in an effort to preserve available memory at the set level. When memory reaches the maximal usage, dehydration throttling is at its most aggressive (highest severity).

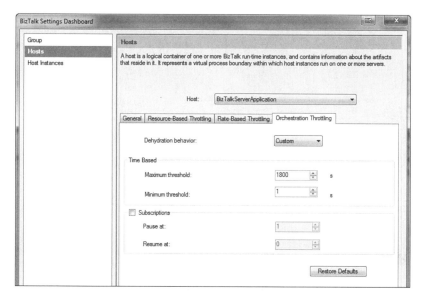

FIGURE 13.8   BizTalk Settings Dashboard, Hosts (Orchestration Throttling) level.

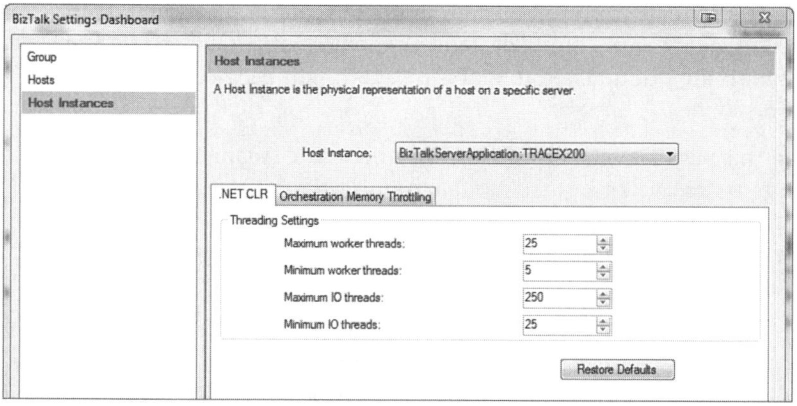

FIGURE 13.9   BizTalk Settings Dashboard, Host Instances (.NET CLR) level.

A final topic regarding the Settings Dashboard is the ability to import and export all the settings discussed to a single *Extensible Markup Language* (XML) file. Note the Import and Export buttons at the bottom of the dialog. You can use these for backup purposes, or (if the file is edited to account for differences in host/host-instance names) to duplicate settings for another BizTalk group.

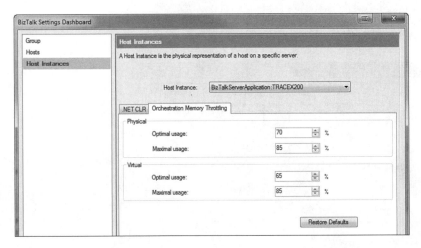

FIGURE 13.10   BizTalk Settings Dashboard, Host Instances (Orchestration Memory Throttling) level.

Group Hub and Query View

When you click a BizTalk group within the BizTalk Administration Console, you are presented (in the center pane) with the Group Hub view, with the ability to switch to the New Query view.

The Group Hub view is essentially a convenient grouping of typical operational queries you will be interested in, along with counts of items that match a particular state (such as Resumable). These counts are not updated in real time and might be stale. (You can force a refresh by pressing F5.)

A few of the links on this page (Applications, Host Instances, and Adapter Handlers) simply navigate you to other portions of the BizTalk Administration tree. However, the rest of the links are to preformulated queries—queries that you could have written manually on the New Query tab but will find useful to navigate to quickly (especially as you learn how to write custom queries).

The preformulated queries slice things in several different ways, such as work that is in progress versus work that is suspended. For work that is suspended, you can group further by application, service name, error code, or *Uniform Resource Identifier* (URI). In the bottom portion of the *user interface* (UI), you can initiate queries around items/work that have tracking enabled (replacing the *Health and Activity Tracking* [HAT] tool in earlier versions of BizTalk).

Often, after you have chosen a query from the Group Hub page, the resulting query that is displayed will be close to what you want, but you will add additional criteria (or modify existing criteria) to suit your needs. You can do so directly in the query editor provided. (Each line in the grid acts as another criteria or grouping option.) After you have queries customized to a certain degree, you will find it quite helpful to use the Save As option to save query files for later use (using the Open Query option).

FIGURE 13.11   Group Hub view.

Figures 13.12 and 13.13 show the ability to write queries manually. Initially, you choose what you want to search for in the system and then add criteria that constrain the results. Note that both the old HAT tool (for tracking queries) and the BTS Subscription Viewer tool (for subscription queries) from earlier versions of BizTalk are subsumed by what is shown in Figure 13.12.

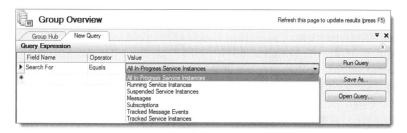

FIGURE 13.12   New Query view.

Figure 13.13 shows how one or more criteria or grouping can be added to your query. Note that the operators and values applied are generally just from a drop-down, unless a specific ID is required.

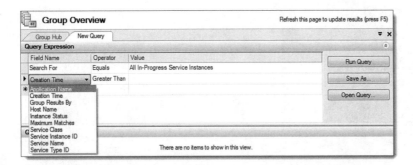

FIGURE 13.13   New Query view, additional criteria.

You can interact with the results of a query to achieve a variety of goals (through right-click actions). The options available to you depend on which types of entities appear in the results list. Through the right-click menu, orchestrations can be suspended, resumed, or terminated (individually or in bulk). Ports can also be suspended. You can view the message flow or the messages for a given service instance. You can also initiate orchestration debugging. In this way, a good portion of all BizTalk troubleshooting and investigation of work in flight begins with a query, the results of which can then be manipulated in various ways.

Applications Node

The Applications portion of the BizTalk Administration Console is covered in detail in Chapter 14, "Deployment Concepts." This is the area of the console where you can view deployed applications, import and export applications, and create or modify artifacts within applications.

Whether an administrator spends significant time in this portion of the console depends on to what degree applications are viewed in a given shop as self-contained and hands-off, and on whether significant aspects of configuration are left to the administrator after an application has been deployed. In addition, within some shops it might be standard practice to create applications purely through the console—using preexisting pipelines and maps—because significant functionality can be achieved with that model apart from the normal Visual Studio process. Orchestrations, maps, pipelines, and pipeline components require Visual Studio, of course, but if a toolkit of such artifacts is made available to savvy BizTalk administrators, they can create at least messaging-only solutions purely by using the console.

It is also worth noting that the tracking settings of every deployed artifact can be modified in a fine-grained way by visiting the artifact within its containing application. Tracking settings, as a general rule, should be delivered via binding files, but an administrator can modify them in this way, potentially for short-term troubleshooting.

Platform Settings

The Platform Settings portion of the BizTalk Administration Console is the area where administrators deal most closely with the physical implementation of a BizTalk group. The tree is broken into five sections: Hosts, Host Instances, Servers, Message Boxes, and Adapters.

Hosts

When you click the **Hosts** node (Figure 13.14), you see a list of defined hosts (that may or may not have any instances associated with them). For each host, you see whether it is In-Process (meaning an instance of the BizTalk service) or Isolated (typically running within *Internet Information Services* [IIS]). You also see the associated Windows security group that is used in granting access to database resources, whether the host has tracking enabled, whether it is trusted, and whether it is acting as a BizTalk cluster resource.

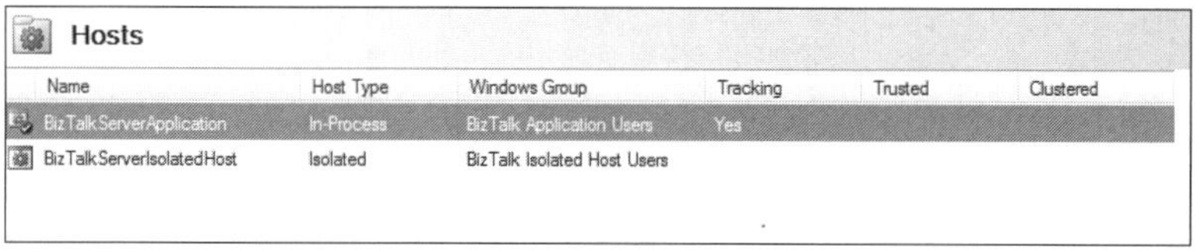

FIGURE 13.14   List of defined hosts, appearing under Platform Settings / Hosts in MMC.

Right-click options within this view enable you to visit the relevant portion of the Settings Dashboard (discussed earlier) or to view properties of the host defined when it was created. In addition, you can choose to enable clustering for the host, which provides for high availability around transports such as *Microsoft Message Queuing* (MSMQ), *File Transfer Protocol* (FTP), or *Post Office Protocol 3* (POP3). Specifically, because transports such as these cannot have multiple host instances servicing the same URI, clustering ensures that at least one of the host instances is always running. A cluster resource group must exist already prior to enabling clustering here for a host.

When you create a new host (Figure 13.15) by right-clicking the Hosts node, many of the options presented (Allow Host Tracking, Authentication Trusted, and 32-bit Only) are the same as presented on the BizTalk Settings Dashboard (discussed earlier). The notion of a default host (that is, the default host in the group) causes ports and orchestrations that do not specify a host to appear in this host (be careful with that). The Certificates tab allows for specification of a certificate that will be used to decrypt inbound messages.

Host Instances

When you click the **Host Instances** node, you see a list of all host instances (Figure 13.16), with their type, server name, current running status, and service account, and whether they are disabled. Right-clicking any entry enables you to start/stop/restart the host instance (if it is an in-process host) or bring up the corresponding settings on the Settings Dashboard discussed earlier. In addition, you can display general properties, and thus change the service account identity if you want.

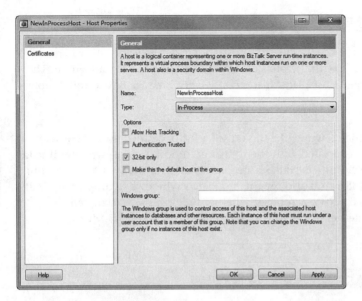

FIGURE 13.15   New Host dialog.

FIGURE 13.16   Platform Settings / Host Instances.

When you right-click **Host Instances** to create a new host instance (Figure 13.17), you will find the options fairly brief. A hostname can be identified, along with a server (that has already been configured and joined to the BizTalk group previously) and account identity. Always ensure that service account identities are members of the Windows group defined with the associated host. You can disable the host instance from starting, which might be appropriate for creating a warm standby.

Servers

This node doesn't allow for doing anything other than viewing a list of existing servers within the BizTalk group. To add additional servers to the group, you need to run BizTalk Server Configuration on a server (and join it to the BizTalk group). At that point, it will be available to create host instances on.

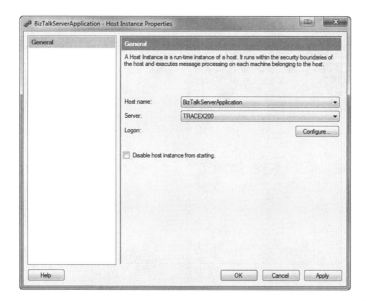

FIGURE 13.17   Platform Settings / New Host Instance.

Message Boxes

When you initially configure BizTalk, a Message Box database is created that will be your Master Message Box by default. There is always only a single master, as the name suggests. It is possible to create additional Message Box databases for scalability; in this case, the master contains subscription information and is in charge of routing messages to the appropriate Message Boxes. Activation messages are distributed among Message Boxes in a round-robin fashion. Dehydration of business processes (that is, orchestrations) that occurs sometime after activation will take place in the Message Box that received the initial activation message. The master will ensure future messages that are correlated to a dehydrated orchestration are routed to the correct Message Box so that rehydration can occur.

The Message Box node in the BizTalk Administration console allows you to create additional Message Boxes (see Figure 13.18) and to disable message publication for particular Message Boxes. The latter is usually done only for the master to have it focus on routing only.

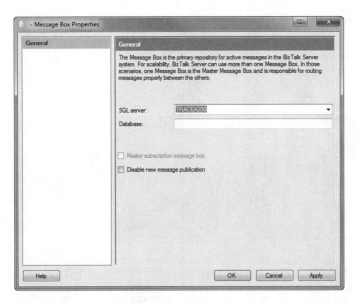

FIGURE 13.18   New Message Box.

Adapters

When you click the **Adapters** node, you are presented with a list of all adapters that have been installed for the BizTalk group, and you can see whether they are currently config-ured to run within a particular host. You can right-click the **Adapters** node to add new adapters. In practice, this doesn't happen very often unless you install adapters from a third party or have previously removed an existing adapter.

Each adapter appears underneath the Adapters node, and clicking any adapter allows you to view the handlers associated with it. A send handler is just a host that is designated to handle the send portion of a transport, and a receive handler handles the receive portion. For some transports (not FTP, MSMQ, or *Simple Mail Transfer Protocol* [SMTP]), it is some-times appropriate to have multiple handlers for scalability, depending on your scenario and throughput requirements.

Note that some transports have properties surfaced within the handler property dialog that act as defaults and that can be overridden with specific ports using that adapter.

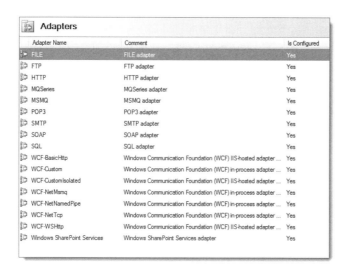

FIGURE 13.19   Adapters list.

Summary

In summary, the BizTalk Administration Console (particularly in BizTalk 2010) is the central location whereby the majority of configuration, troubleshooting, and management tasks take place. As you tune your BizTalk group, query for current operational state, debug various issues with orchestrations, modify application configuration, or evolve the physical topology of your BizTalk group, you will be using this tool.

CHAPTER 14

Deployment Concepts

The process of deploying BizTalk applications is an extensive topic, driven by the combination of inherent complexity in integration solutions and the typical physical topology of a BizTalk installation. In this chapter, we cover both the concepts behind deployment and some specifics that you need to focus on in designing this aspect of your solution.

The Work to Be Done

When you deploy a BizTalk application, four jobs have to be accomplished:

▸ Metadata about the application itself (bindings, subscriptions implied by both bindings and orchestrations, schemas, assembly information, and so on) needs to make its way into the BizTalk management database. When you deploy, you are bringing a large quantity of metadata to the table that needs to be "imported" into BizTalk's preferred structure for that metadata so that the runtime can operate on your behalf.

▸ The .NET assemblies that comprise your application need to be deployed to all (or most) servers that comprise your BizTalk group. Specifically, they need to be delivered to the *Global Assembly Cache* (GAC). All members of the BizTalk group that will execute any logic that relies on your assembly content (schemas, maps, pipelines, pipeline components, orchestrations, and so on) need to be a deployment target.

▶ All physical endpoint creation and configuration needs to be accomplished. This may refer to file shares and associated permissions, *Internet Information Services* (IIS) virtual directories and application pools, `File Transfer Protocol` (FTP) sites, `Microsoft Messaging Queue` (MSMQ) queue creation, or other adapter-specific infrastructure. BizTalk offers some automation here for virtual directories, but for the most part, this is a manual piece. You must decide where the line should be between prerequisite setup versus what should be incorporated into your deployment via scripts. (For instance, some environments might choose to require a particular named application pool in IIS to already exist, versus scripting the creation of that application pool.)

▶ Related to the third point, all physical endpoints in the solution need to have any necessary modifications made that are appropriate for the particular physical environment you are deploying to. That is, production send ports send to production URIs, whereas development send ports send to development URIs (and so forth throughout your application).

Figure 14.1 illustrates this.

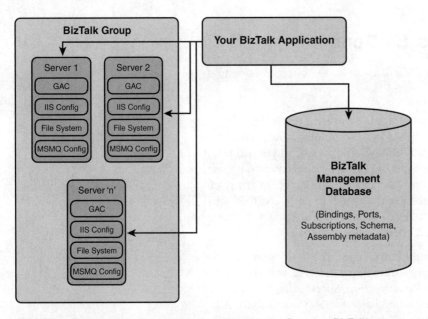

FIGURE 14.1   How BizTalk application components flow to a BizTalk group.

As you go about design work for a BizTalk application, think about the mechanics of deploying as a first-class design and development activity in its own right. You will deploy your application many times per day, per developer to local environments, multiple times per day to your shared development environment, and of course, (aligned with your ship rhythm) to multiple higher environments such as Test, Acceptance, and Production (where the stakes for getting it right continue to go up).

Your goal for local a development environment should be to reach a state for your deployment where new developers (or developers with new workstations) can be productive immediately, without having to tap "tribal knowledge" (or out-of-date documents) from the team. The process should simply be "retrieve from source control, build, one-step deploy" (instead of requiring a tedious sequence of manual steps).

Your goal for your higher environments should be a robust, minimum-intervention transition from one state to another (that is, from an older version of your application to a newer one). Depending on your environment, part of reaching this goal might involve figuring out lines of responsibility within your organization. Who has rights to deploy new stored procedures required for an adapter you are using? Who owns the MQ infrastructure? Who owns the account and password information for the production IIS application pools? All these issues have to be sorted out specific to your organization, and then captured in a deployment process that obtains the right information (and people) at the right time.

Of course, a lot of what we have just said applies to any deployment process, not just BizTalk. What makes BizTalk deserve special attention in this regard? Simply this: Most BizTalk applications are integration solutions, and integration solutions by their nature require more tentacles to external systems than the average app. Moreover, the nature of the BizTalk runtime makes deployment an explicit step. Nothing "runs" from where the compiler happens to deposit your assemblies. Everything "runs" only from inside a specialized (potentially multiserver) container that is offering a sophisticated set of runtime services. The price you pay to play in that environment is more attention to deployment.

"Application" as a Formal Concept

Starting back in BizTalk 2006, BizTalk embraced the notion of an "application" as a formal concept to act as a container for various application artifacts. The application notion features prominently in management tools, binding files, Visual Studio property pages, and so on.

Under most circumstances, you should consider a 1:1 relationship between your BizTalk application (as you think of it) and a BizTalk application in BizTalk's terminology. (Moreover, you should consider housing this application in a single Visual Studio solution for simplicity's sake.) The only time you might want to consider multiple "physical" BizTalk applications for a single "logical" application is for the case where you have a sharp delineation in deployment lifecycle; that is, a particular piece may need to deploy on a different schedule than the rest. (However, at that point, you are probably already starting to think of these as distinct applications in your own efforts, and if a separate solution is introduced, we are back into the normal case.)

So, what is found within an application? The answer is simply "every BizTalk resource" that is required by an application, divided by type (plus a catchall category termed *resources*). You can see this illustrated in the BizTalk Management Console screenshot (see Figure 14.2) and the (logical) class diagram for BizTalk applications (see Figure 14.3).

FIGURE 14.2   View of an application within the BizTalk Management Console.

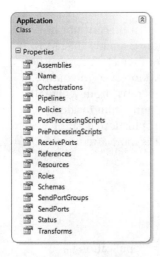

FIGURE 14.3   Logical view of a BizTalk application entity.

An application represents more, both a unit of deployment and a unit of management. Not only are applications imported, exported, and configured within a BizTalk environment, but also an application can be started and stopped as a whole, and many operational queries can be scoped to a particular application.

Note that BizTalk offers the concept of application references to formalize dependencies that one application might have on another. Typical use cases for this functionality include the situation where a shared set of enterprise-level schemas, maps, pipelines, policies, certificates, and so on are made available as part of a (potentially shared) environment, ready for consumption by other BizTalk apps. The application reference formalizes the dependency and allows for sharing of resources such as schemas, as shown in the following illustration.

Application references also enforce deploy/undeploy order. Specifically, BizTalk prevents the removal of an application that has references from other applications. In addition, upon deployment, applications that are referenced by the application being deployed are checked for existence. (Although the specific artifacts being used are not verified.) For this reason, artifacts that are shared by multiple applications should themselves be in a separate application (distinct from any consuming application).

Where Does It All Begin? (Inside Visual Studio)

Planning your deployment strategy begins, in some measure, with the initial decisions regarding folder/file organization and Visual Studio solution/project layout. There is no single "correct" answer for how this should be undertaken, but a good guideline is to aim for as much consistency (and least surprise) as possible.

Folder and Project Structure

At the highest level, consider having your Visual Studio solution name and the folder in which it is placed be named identically (excluding the file extension). Each project that is contained by your solution should be in a subfolder, with the .CSPROJ or .BTPROJ in that folder and named the same as the folder itself.

Further, consider prefixing your project files (and their containing folders) with the name of the solution. See the following example, where square brackets denote folders:

```
[BTDeploySample]
 BTDeploySample.sln
 [BTDeploySample.Transforms]
   BTDeploySample.Transforms.btproj
 [BTDeploySample.Schemas]
   BTDeploySample.Schemas.btproj
 [BTDeploySample.Orchestrations]
   BTDeploySample.Orchestrations.btproj
 [BTDeploySample.Components]
   BTDeploySample.Components.csproj
```

See also Figure 14.4 for a view of what this solution looks like in the Solution Explorer.

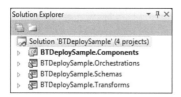

FIGURE 14.4   A structured BizTalk solution within the Solution Explorer.

Note that in this sample structure, we're also proposing a division of your BizTalk artifacts. For the *simplest* of BizTalk solutions, you might find it sufficient to put all assets into a single BizTalk assembly (orchestrations, maps, schemas, and even C# files in the most recent release of BizTalk). There is definitely a simplicity offered by this approach. However, as a solution gains complexity, it is useful to divide a solution by file type (C# classes, orchestrations, schemas, transforms, pipelines, pipeline components, and so on) as an initial factoring. The goal is to group the elements of your application into assemblies that have a similar deployment rhythm, and it just happens that dividing by file type is a good initial choice for this purpose. This division also tends to steer your solution into a spectrum of assemblies that are "most dependent" (like orchestrations) to "least dependent" (like schemas and components), which is quite helpful. As your solution gains more complexity, you will likely have multiple schema projects, orchestration projects, and so on that are grouped by purpose and (more important) deployment rhythm.

Namespaces and Assembly Names

Beyond the naming of folder and project (BTPROJ/CSPROJ) files, there is the issue of .net namespaces and assembly names. Although you might have reason (or corporate standard) to deviate, the simplest approach here is to align these with our previous convention. Thus

Folder Name = Project File Name = Assembly Name = Namespace

So, BTDeploySample.Components[.csproj] would use that same name as a namespace for all classes, and the assembly name that is set within project properties would also match and likewise for BTDeploySample.Orchestrations. Note that namespaces for orchestrations are set by opening the designer, clicking the orchestration background, and then using the Properties window (see Figure 14.5).

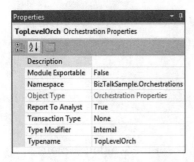

FIGURE 14.5   Orchestration Properties window. (Namespaces can be set here.)

For many .net projects, assembly names and namespace names are just implementation details that developers deal with, with attention necessary only to ease developer understanding and maintenance. However, in a BizTalk solution, assembly names (and type namespaces) wind up being visible throughout the BizTalk Management Console. The team responsible for managing a BizTalk application in production needs to be able to rapidly associate the names they encounter (in dealing with suspended messages, running orchestrations, exceptions, and so on) with the corresponding set of application assets. Poor attention to naming will make this task much more difficult. Moreover, if you plan on modifications to your BizTalk environment that will be managed administratively rather than through formal application deployments (like the introduction of new ports with corresponding pipeline or schema references), self-documenting names for your BizTalk assets become even more important so that correct choices can easily be made.

If you know your project will be of reasonable size, it will be useful to go ahead and create a skeleton of the entire solution with all of the desired projects (even if initially empty) right away. After you have created the solution and the projects with the recommended folder and project-file names, visit each of the project's property pages to set the assembly name and default namespace (on the Application tab; see Figure 14.6) to the values we've discussed.

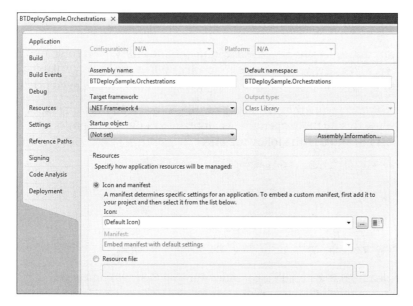

FIGURE 14.6   View of orchestration project properties (assembly name and default namespace set here).

Applying Strong Names

After you have completed this step, you want to establish a strong name for all assemblies. Because assemblies used in a BizTalk application are deployed into the GAC, they require signing. For many environments, a newly created (and non-password-protected) key suffices. You also want to consider using the same key for all projects in your solution simply so that all assemblies share the same public key token, which will sometimes appear in configuration files and the like. To proceed down this path, create a key in the same directory as your solution (SLN) file, as shown in Figure 14.7.

```
Visual Studio Command Prompt (2010)

C:\c\devproj\BTDeploySample>dir
 Volume in drive C has no label.
 Volume Serial Number is 827B-C0AA

 Directory of C:\c\devproj\BTDeploySample

06/04/2010  10:56 AM    <DIR>          .
06/04/2010  10:56 AM    <DIR>          ..
05/25/2010  04:41 PM    <DIR>          BTDeploySample.Components
06/04/2010  10:55 AM    <DIR>          BTDeploySample.Orchestrations
05/27/2010  03:49 PM    <DIR>          BTDeploySample.Schemas
05/25/2010  04:45 PM             3,053 BTDeploySample.sln
05/27/2010  03:50 PM    <DIR>          BTDeploySample.Transforms
               1 File(s)          3,053 bytes
               6 Dir(s)  53,477,867,520 bytes free

C:\c\devproj\BTDeploySample>sn -k sn.snk

Microsoft (R) .NET Framework Strong Name Utility  Version 4.0.30319.1
Copyright (c) Microsoft Corporation. All rights reserved.

Key pair written to sn.snk

C:\c\devproj\BTDeploySample>
```

FIGURE 14.7   Creating a strong name key from command-line window.

Here, a key is created called sn.snk using the sn.exe command-line utility. (You could instead choose to name the key after your solution for clarity.) When the key is available at a directory location sitting directly above the various projects, each project can reference it.

There are two methods of referencing the (common) key file. The first allows for reuse of the sn.snk file itself. To use this method, open the AssemblyInfo.cs file for all projects in the solution (see Figure 14.8) and add the following line:

```
[assembly: AssemblyKeyFile(@"..\..\..\sn.snk")]
```

FIGURE 14.8   Navigating to AssemblyInfo.cs inside of the Solution Explorer.

This method is convenient, but it generates a compiler warning (CS1699) unless you suppress that warning using the Build tab in project properties (Suppress Warnings field). You can read about the reasons for the warning by searching C# help for CS1699 and decide whether you are still comfortable with this method.

Alternatively, you can open the project properties for all solutions in the project and use the Signing tab, checking **Sign the Assembly** and browsing for the sn.snk file. This method, unfortunately, duplicates the sn.snk file in each project's directory but is more compliant with how Visual Studio likes to operate. This latter approach is used by the FineFoods solution used throughout this book.

Setting Deployment Properties

A final step that is useful is to visit the properties of each BizTalk project file and set the application name (typically to a value that matches your solution name; see Figure 14.9). Without this step, your application deploys to an application named BizTalk Application 1. This can be confusing (and difficult) if developers have multiple BizTalk applications they are working on at once. Unfortunately, although it would be desirable to be able to set the

BizTalk application name at the solution level, this isn't possible with the current version of the tooling.

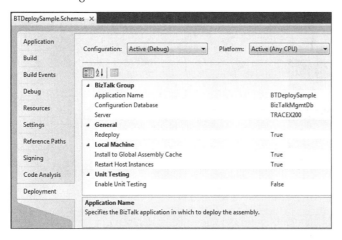

FIGURE 14.9   Configure the application name from within the project deployment properties.

While in this dialog, ensure **Redeploy**, **Install to Global Assembly Cache**, and **Restart Host Instances** are all set to **True**.

As an alternative to the method of opening each project individually, an MSBuild PropertyGroup similar to the following can be added to the top of each btproj.user file. (Note that projects have to be reloaded for this to take effect.)

```
<PropertyGroup Condition="'$(Configuration)¦$(Platform)' ==
'Debug¦AnyCPU'">
  <Server>YOURMACHINE</Server>
  <ConfigurationDatabase>BizTalkMgmtDb</ConfigurationDatabase>
  <ApplicationName>BTDeploySample</ApplicationName>
  <Redeploy>True</Redeploy>
  <Register>True</Register>
  <RestartHostInstances>True</RestartHostInstances>
</PropertyGroup>
```

With either technique, these settings (related to application name, database name, and so on) have to be applied *per developer* working with the BizTalk solution because they reside in the .user file.

Another step required here is to configure non-BizTalk projects (standard .net assembly library projects) to deploy to the GAC after building, which will be required if they are to be used by other BizTalk artifacts such as orchestrations or maps. To accomplish this, open the project properties, and select the Build Events tab. Set the post-build event command line to the following (see also Figure 14.10):

```
"%programfiles%\Microsoft SDKs\Windows\v7.0A\Bin\NETFX 4.0
Tools\gacutil.exe" /if $(TargetPath)
```

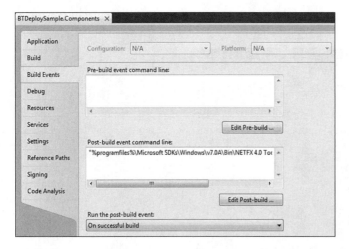

FIGURE 14.10   Setting the post-build event command line for GAC deployment.

Fine Foods Solution

We have discussed folder and project structure, solution and project names, namespaces and assembly names, and so on in the context of a simplified solution (BTDeploySample) in the interest of letting the conventions come through clearly. Throughout this chapter, we rely on BTDeploySample in figures and listings. However, it is important to note that the Fine Food solution used in other chapters conforms to these exact same guidelines (see Figure 14.11). The set of guidelines discussed can therefore scale to much more complex solutions; although, you might add additional information into the naming conventions as you move beyond more than one assembly for each type of artifact (and begin to group based on deployment rhythm).

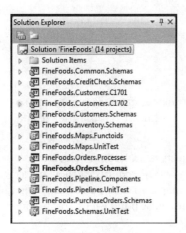

FIGURE 14.11   Fine Foods solution.

Deploying from Visual Studio

As a practical matter, deploying from within Visual Studio requires that you run Visual Studio as an administrator. If you see the following error, you know that you have attempted to deploy while running without elevation.

```
error DEPLOY:  at
Microsoft.BizTalk.Gac.Fusion.IAssemblyCache.InstallAssembly(AssemblyCacheIn
stallFlag flags, String manifestFilePath, IntPtr referenceData)
 at Microsoft.BizTalk.Gac.Gac.InstallAssembly(String assemblyPathname,
Boolean force)
...
```

```
error DEPLOY: Unspecified exception: "
Access is denied. (Exception from HRESULT: 0x80070005 (E_ACCESSDENIED))"
```

If you have started Visual Studio as an administrator, and you have prepared a solution in the ways we have discussed, you can simply right-click the (topmost) solution node within the Solution Explorer and select **Deploy**. Note that although it is possible to deploy individual projects within a solution, it is more error prone because it is only at the solution level that project-to-project dependencies are fully understood by the deployment engine. Moreover, you will often wind up with only a portion of the solution deployed because items that are dependent on the project you are deploying will only be undeployed (not redeployed). For this reason, the full solution should usually be deployed.

Within the Output window (showing output from Build), note that the full solution (all contained projects) compiles and then begins the deployment process. The projects deploy in the order defined by the build, which itself flows (by default) from the dependencies implied by project references within the solution.

For any given assembly that is deployed, the first step completed by the deployment process is to add the assembly as a resource for the BizTalk application. The next step is to determine whether the assembly is already being used by artifacts still deployed within BizTalk. If it is, those dependent artifacts are undeployed automatically so that the new version can be deployed (as long as the Redeploy flag has been set to True in the project's deployment properties). Next, binding information that is derived from the assembly (concerning ports, orchestrations, and so on) is extracted from the assembly and imported into the BizTalk management database. Finally, the assembly is placed in the GAC.

Note that the Restart Host Instances flag in the deployment properties should be set to True so that the runtime picks up the changed assembly from the GAC (and does not continue to run with the previous version).

14

After the deployment process completes for all assemblies in the solution, you should see something similar to the following:

```
: Restarting in-process host instances...
========== Build: 4 succeeded or up-to-date, 0 failed, 0 skipped ==========
========== Deploy: 3 succeeded, 0 failed, 0 skipped ==========
```

Your `Build` succeeded count will be bigger than your `Deploy` succeeded count if you have non-BizTalk projects in your solution, such as standard .net libraries.

At this point, all of your assemblies are in the GAC, and the BizTalk management database has all the metadata offered by the various artifacts in your solution. BizTalk has been restarted, so the "current" copy of your assemblies will be used when next used. However, if this is the first time you have deployed, you need to bind the solution to physical hosts, ports, and so on.

Binding and Starting the Application

The BizTalk Server Administration Management Console is used for the next step. If it is already running during your deploy, you need to right-click the **Group** or **Applications** node and select **Refresh**. To bind the application, right-click the application's node in the Administration Console and select **Configure**.

The dialog that is presented next (see Figure 14.12) enables you to make selections for everything in your solution that has so far been left unsaid. This process is known as binding, and it essentially refers to the process of choosing physical implementations for the logical constructs in your application. This process can be done in this dialog; although, it can also be done by importing a *binding file*, which is simply an *Extensible Markup Language* (XML) file that defines these associations in a reusable (and version controllable) way. As a practical matter, you will frequently start by binding manually through the user interface (UI) and then exporting the resulting bindings to a file that will be stored in a version control system and used for future deployments.

Each orchestration in your application requires setting a host that it will run under. For development purposes, it is often sufficient to simply use the default BizTalkServerApplication host; although, in some circumstances you might want the development workstation host layout to match what you intend for your downstream environments (where the host layout can be quite complex). To allocate hosts to orchestrations, select each orchestration listed in turn, and choose an appropriate host from the drop-down presented.

After doing this (and applying changes), the yellow warning triangles (as shown in Figure 14.12) will likely still remain because there are most often logical ports defined in orchestrations that must be mapped to physical ports. Within the configuration for each orchestration, you will have an Inbound Logical Ports list and an Outbound Logical Ports list that can be mapped to physical receive ports and send ports, respectively. If your BizTalk configuration does not yet contain any physical ports, you can create these directly using the **New** options in the physical port drop-downs.

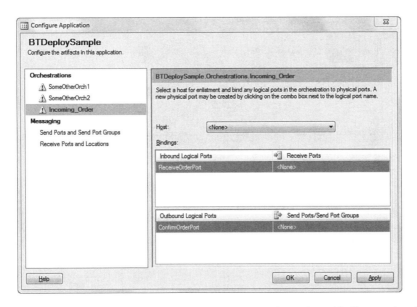

FIGURE 14.12   The Application Configuration dialog, where binding can be done manually.

Physical receive and send ports can be named using plainly worded phrases that will be clear to your operations staff as to the function they serve. There is no need to use underscores or Pascal-cased dense names. An example might be Sales Orders From CRM For Great Plains or Credit Check Requests To Credit Partners. The receive locations can use the same name as their ports, with a dotted suffix indicating the transport (for example, Sales Orders From CRM For Great Plains.MSMQ).

Figure 14.13 shows all orchestrations, hosts, and physical ports fully configured, as indicated by the green checkmarks. We can now right-click the application in the Management Console and choose **Start**. The default behavior is to enlist and start all orchestrations and send ports, enable all receive locations, start all needed hosts, and resume any suspended instances. For a developer scenario, this is usually the right behavior. After starting the application, interacting with it (by feeding appropriate messages to receive locations, and so on) should produce the intended results.

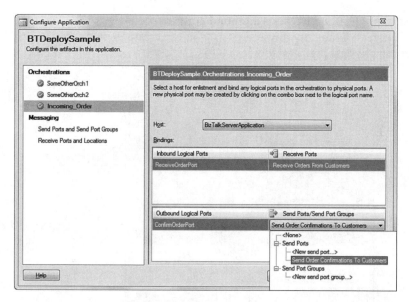

FIGURE 14.13   All orchestrations, hosts, and physical ports configured.

Edit/Debug Cycle

You have structured your solution correctly, you have built and deployed, and you have bound and started your application. You now have an "edit/debug/deploy/run" cycle ahead of you as you fix problems and add functionality. How does this work in practice?

At its simplest, you can simply make any desired change within any of your Visual Studio projects and then right-click the (topmost) solution node within the Solution Explorer and select **Deploy**. This causes all projects to recompile (in dependent order), and a full undeploy/redeploy cycle to occur.

For a certain class of changes, this process can be shortened somewhat. Depending on your solution, a full redeploy can be quite lengthy (especially if you are in the midst of testing changes where a rapid turnaround can help you converge on an answer). As it happens, if the activity you are engaged in fits in the following list, a shorter path is available:

- ▶ Modifying links and functoids in a map (but *not* changing schemas)

- ▶ Working with shapes in an orchestration (but not the logical ports)

- ▶ Changing basic .NET library components that are not actual BizTalk projects

- ▶ Changing elements or attributes in a schema (but *not* adding a root record, or distinguished fields/promoted properties)

The shorter path is to simply put the rebuilt assembly in the GAC and then restart BizTalk. This works because in the previously mentioned activities you have not changed any of the metadata in your projects that BizTalk normally needs to extract and store in the management database. Of course, this technique requires a bit more thought and is more error prone, so use with caution. But as you gain an intuitive sense for when you can simply "re-gac" an assembly, restart BizTalk, and then rerun your scenario, you will find it is much more efficient.

Note that changing pipelines, assembly versions, or the .NET type names of any artifact prevents you from using this method.

To automate this technique, create new external tools within Visual Studio by choosing **Tools**, **External Tools**, **Add**.

The first external tool you add should be named ReGac, with a command of `%programfiles%\Microsoft SDKs\Windows\v7.0A\Bin\NETFX 4.0 Tools\gacutil.exe` and arguments of `/if $(TargetPath)`. Select the **Use Output Window** option. When configured, this external command just takes the output of the selected Visual Studio project and places it in the GAC.

The second external tool you add should be named Restart BizTalk with a command of `powershell.exe` and arguments of `-command {restart-service "BizTalk Service BizTalk Group : BizTalkServerApplication"}`. Select the **Use Output Window** option. When configured, this external command restarts BizTalk. Modify as needed if you are using an alternative host.

Figures 14.14 and 14.15 show the configured external tools.

14

FIGURE 14.14   Configuring an external tool in Visual Studio to GAC an assembly.

FIGURE 14.15   Configuring an external tool in Visual Studio to restart BizTalk.

Handling Binding Files During Development

As your solution grows in size and complexity, it will be desirable to avoid having each developer go through the process of binding the application (as described earlier). The definition of physical ports and the logical-to-physical association should itself be a version-controlled asset just like other source code, maps, orchestrations, and so on. This asset comes in the form of an XML file typically referred to as a *bindings file.* There is a cycle to be followed here that looks as follows:

1. For a new solution or an existing solution where new logical ports have been added, the Configure Application dialog in the Management Console should be used (following a full deployment from Visual Studio) to provide appropriate logical-to-physical mappings. Note that in the case of an existing solution, all previous bindings will still be present (only the new logical ports will be missing a logical-to-physical association). Once the new associations have been made, the application must be restarted because corresponding orchestrations are in the unenlisted state.

2. Once the application has been configured as in a "known good" state from a bindings standpoint, right-click the application in the Management Console and select **Export Bindings** with the option **Export All Bindings from the Current Application** (see Figure 14.16). Place the file in the same directory as your solution, and version control it with all other source.

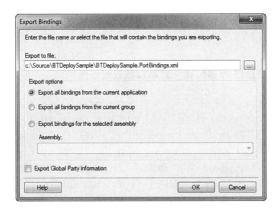

FIGURE 14.16   Exporting bindings for a BizTalk solution.

3. When the solution is next deployed on a workstation where not all bindings are present in the management database (such as by another developer on the team), these bindings can be *imported* rather than going through the manual "configure application" process. This is done by right-clicking the application in the Management Console, selecting **Import Bindings**, and then choosing the appropriate binding file.

Figure 14.17 shows the entire cycle.

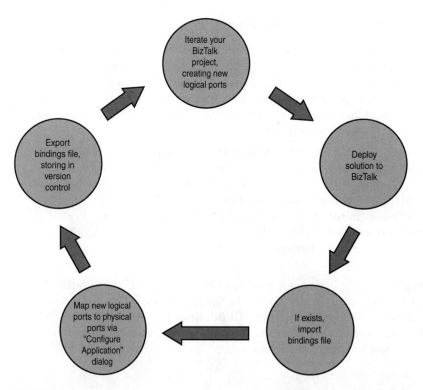

FIGURE 14.17   The cycle of iterating projects, mapping ports, and binding file import/export.

Creating and Managing Deployable Packages

Fairly early in the development of a Biztalk solution, it is necessary to deploy your application to a shared development environment (or a test environment) and begin preparing for further downstream environments (such as "staging" and production). Visual Studio is no longer be originating the deployments in those environments, and a standalone mechanism is needed. The BizTalk Administration Console (and command-line utilities) enables you to export an application to an MSI, which can then be used to deploy to a downstream environment.

Prior to being in a position to export an MSI, you want to have a functioning application that you have deployed either via Visual Studio (as just discussed) or via BTSTask.exe, a command-line tool that you can use from a build server to deploy a just-compiled BizTalk solution. The application should be ready to run, with all bindings in place. (Environment-specific bindings are discussed later.)

Beyond the application being ready to run, it is often necessary to add additional artifacts that allow the resulting MSI to represent as much of the application deployment process as possible. Notice in Figure 14.18 that we have the ability to add items to an application directly from the Administration Console.

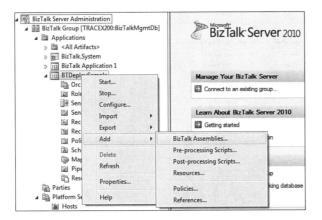

FIGURE 14.18   Adding artifacts to an application.

If you have been using Visual Studio to deploy, the BizTalk assemblies you require are already part of your application. However, there will be other parts of your application that need to be represented as "resources" prior to MSI export. These resources can be added manually (as shown in Figure 14.18) or through a BTSTask.exe (scripted) process. BTSTask can be used for a large number of administrative tasks, but for purposes of dealing with resources, the command-line syntax looks like this:

```
BTSTask AddResource [-ApplicationName:value] -Type:value [-Overwrite] [-
Server:value] [-Database:value]
```

To see what might be missing in terms of application resources, you can visit the Resources node within your application. If you right-click a particular BizTalk assembly and choose **Modify**, you can then visit the Dependencies tab. In the example shown in Figure 14.19, you can see that an orchestration assembly is missing a .net library component that it depends on, as denoted by the Status indicating Not Found. The schema and transform assemblies, by contrast, are already present as resources.

If you have .net library components that your solution relies on, your BizTalk application up until now has been using these components but without representation inside the application definition. To add the component, you can right-click the application and choose **Add Resources**. (*Resources* is used as a generic term to refer to an item that is not a BizTalk assembly, script, application reference, or BizTalk rules policy.) When you click the **Add** button and select a .net assembly, it automatically populates the dialog as shown in Figure 14.19. Note that the fact that you are adding a standard .net assembly (not a BizTalk assembly) has been inferred already. A "destination location" has been defaulted; this simply refers to where the assembly will be placed when an MSI that is generated from this application is installed. The Dependencies tab can show whether further references exist that need to be included for completeness. Finally, an option to place the assembly in the GAC upon installation is already checked.

FIGURE 14.19   Examining the dependencies of a resource.

This can also all be done from the command line instead, of course, via BTSTask.exe. In fact, one could make the case that instead of using gacutil in our component post-build step, as discussed earlier, you might choose to do this instead:

```
BTSTask.exe AddResource /ApplicationName:BTDeploySample
/Type:System.BizTalk:Assembly /Overwrite Source:$(TargetPath)
/Destination:%BTAD_InstallDir%\BTDeploySample.Components.dll
Options:GacOnAdd,GacOnInstall
```

This would ensure the component is always present as a resource in the application, and therefore always ready to be included in an MSI export. This can certainly be done, but it adds to the Visual Studio deployment time because BTSTask takes longer to execute than a simple gacutil.exe. Still, you might consider this in the name of further automation if many people will need to produce MSIs from developer workstations after completing a Visual Studio-based deployment. Frequently, the task of generating MSIs is delegated to a build server.

Note that the option to Add to the Global Assembly Cache on Add Resource is generally used only if you are scripting the operation. The options to make COM visible and to register serviced components are used only rarely and will be clear if their need is required.

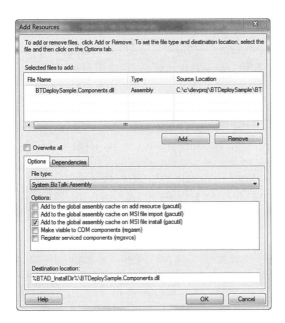

FIGURE 14.20   Adding an assembly resource to an application.

Other Types of Resources

Other types of resources can be added to a BizTalk application in a similar fashion. You can begin to think about the tooling provided as a very lightweight "setup" designer. Arbitrary files can be added as type `System.BizTalk:File`. *Business Activity Monitoring* (BAM)artifacts can be added with type `System.BizTalk:BAM`, and they will be deployed when an MSI is *imported* (not installed; a distinction discussed later). Certificates (type `System.BizTalk:Certificate`) can be added, but only via the BTSTask command line.

It is also possible to add a virtual directory as a resource. This operation also can only be done via the BTSTask command line but is really only required if you have a custom web service or ASP.NET application that needs to accompany your BizTalk application. If you are creating *Simple Object Access Protocol* (SOAP), *Hypertext Transfer Protocol* (HTTP), or *Windows Communication Foundation* (WCF) receive locations, the presence of those IIS-hosted endpoints in the management database causes an MSI export to include them in the MSI. When you then import this MSI into another BizTalk group, the virtual directory appears as a resource. Installation of the MSI causes the appropriate virtual directory and support files to be installed (*.svc, *.asmx, and so on). If you want to add your virtual directory as a resource explicitly via BTSTask, you use type `System.BizTalk:WebDirectory`. The `/Source` and `/Destination` parameters are interpreted as URIs in this case, rather than file system locations.

Note that with all resources, the "copy" that resides in the BizTalk management database (that will be used when exporting an MSI) can be updated or refreshed by visiting the Resources node of the application, right-clicking, selecting **Modify**, and then clicking the **Refresh** button.

Binding Files as Resources

A particularly important type of resource is a binding file. Now, as you configure an application after an initial deployment, you are creating bindings that are part of the application already. However, to make your application ready to deploy to multiple physical environments (and be self-contained in that regard), it is helpful to export your bindings, as shown in Figure 14.16, and then "rebind" the application to match the endpoint infrastructure of the "other" BizTalk groups that your application will be deployed to (for example, Test and Production). In other words, your bindings may start by reflecting what is necessary to run on a developer workstation or shared development environment, but you will want to create an *additional* set of bindings that reflect differences in your Test and Production environments. Those differences may be destination URLs, file paths, FTP sites, queue names, hosts chosen for orchestrations and ports, and so on. These alternative bindings should also be version controlled and managed according to the cycle depicted in Figure 14.16; though you will probably wait to augment some of your downstream-environment binding files until you have stabilized the set of ports you are dealing with in development. The key difference with the alternative (environment-specific) binding files is that you will want to add them to your application as resources of type `System.BizTalk:BizTalkBinding`. Note that the Add Resources dialog shown in Figure 14.21 recognizes when you have selected a binding file, and it offers a Target Environment field at the bottom. As you add each environment-specific binding file as a resource, you can give it a friendly name such as Test or Production, and upon import of the generated MSI later on, the administrator can select what environment the MSI is arriving in (see Figure 14.22).

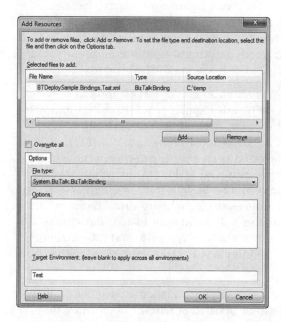

FIGURE 14.21   Adding environment-specific binding files.

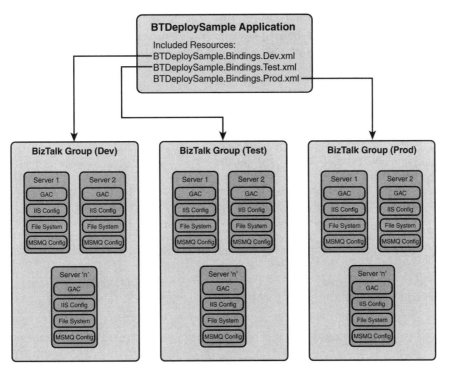

FIGURE 14.22   Environment-specific bindings.

Note that some aspects of downstream environment bindings (such as production pass-words) wouldn't be appropriate to store in binding files and version control and will have to be manually entered after the application has been deployed. If such items are left as manual steps, they need to be carefully documented as to which ports, which receive loca-tions, and so on require hand-editing after the automated portion is complete.

Deployment Scripts as Resources

It was stated earlier that you can begin to think about the tooling provided within BizTalk as a very lightweight "setup" designer. This extends a bit further with the notion of pre- and post-processing scripts. Notice in Figure 14.18 that it is possible to add such scripts as resources to your application. Preprocessing scripts are used before an application is imported or installed, and after un-installation completes. (So they can "undo" their action if desired.) Post-processing scripts run after import or installation completes, and before un-installation starts.

Think of these scripts as a way to package and automate any out-of-band tasks that need to accompany your application deployment. Consider tasks such as managing certificates, creating queues, fine-grained control over IIS configuration, and so on. The more these kinds of tasks are automated, the more reliable your deployment process is. Pre- and post-processing scripts are the place to make this automation happen. The scripts can be BAT/CMD files, VBScript/Jscript, or even EXE files.

Because your scripts typically must handle install (file delivery), import (metadata delivery), uninstall, and roll back cases, they need a way of distinguishing what the current operating mode is. This is communicated with environment variables, as shown in Table 14.1.

TABLE 14.1   Determining Pre-/Post-Processing Script Operating Mode

Deployment Operation	BTAD_Change RequestAction	BTAD_InstallMode	BTAD_HostClas
Importing to management database *without* overwrite	Create	Import	ConfigurationDb
Importing to management database with overwrite	Update	Import	ConfigurationDb
Install (delivery of files in MSI to BizTalk hosts)	Update	Install	BizTalkHostInstance
Uninstall (removal of files in MSI)	Delete	Uninstall	BizTalkHostInstance
Import rollback	Delete	Import	ConfigurationDb
Install rollback	Delete	Install	BizTalkHostInstance

Table 14.2 shows additional environment variables that you can reference in your deployment scripts.

TABLE 14.2   Additional Environment Variables for Pre-/Post-Processing Scripts

Name	Purpose
BTAD_InstallDir	Communicate the installation path of the MSI. Matches the TARGETDIR of the installation package.
BTAD_ApplicationName	The name of the BizTalk application. Use this to make your scripts reusable across applications.
BTAD_SilentMode	Value of 2 for a silent installation, which is the default. Scripts should avoid displaying UI in this case.
BTAD_Server	Name of the SQL Server instance running the management database.
BTAD_Database	Name of the database on the server (for example, BiztalkMgmtDb).

A simple example of pre-/post-processing is a script that changes the "idle timeout" of an IIS application pool to match your requirements. The default timeout for an IIS application pool is 20 minutes, but suppose we want to change this to 1 hour when we install, and reset it to the default upon uninstall. A script that could be added to a BizTalk application (as a pre- or post-processing script) is shown in Listing 14.1.

Upon import of the package (where metadata is brought into the management database), the script would execute but not do any work because of the value of %BTAD_HostClass%. Upon installation of the MSI, the default application pool will be modified to 1 hour idle timeout, whereas for uninstall or rollback it will be set to the default of 20 minutes.

LISTING 14.1   Pre-Processing Script for Modifying IIS Application Pool

```
Set LogFile=%temp%\BTDeploySampleScript.txt


REM Log what has been fed to this script in environment variables
echo %DATE% %TIME% >> %LogFile%
echo BTAD_HostClass %BTAD_HostClass% >> %LogFile%
echo BTAD_ChangeRequestAction %BTAD_ChangeRequestAction% >> %LogFile%
echo BTAD_InstallMode %BTAD_InstallMode% >> %LogFile%

REM Only deal with installations to BizTalk host instances
if /I %BTAD_HostClass% NEQ BizTalkHostInstance goto :EOF

REM Do our uninstall logic for uninstall and rollback cases
if /I %BTAD_ChangeRequestAction% EQU Delete goto :Uninstall

REM Proceed with install logic only for install cases
if /I %BTAD_ChangeRequestAction% NEQ Update goto :EOF
if /I %BTAD_InstallMode% NEQ Install goto :EOF

:Install
echo Attempting to set app pool to one hour idle timeout >> %LogFile%
%windir%\system32\inetsrv\appcmd set config /section:applicationPools
/[name='DefaultAppPool'].processModel.idleTimeout:0.01:00:00 >> %LogFile%
goto :EOF

:Uninstall
echo Attempting to set app pool to default of 20 minutes timeout >>
%LogFile%
%windir%\system32\inetsrv\appcmd set config /section:applicationPools
/[name='DefaultAppPool'].processModel.idleTimeout:0.00:20:00 >> %LogFile%
```

Exporting MSI Files

MSI files can be generated from a BizTalk application by right-clicking the application and selecting **Export MSI File**. The MSI file produced is a standard installation package that can be used to deploy your application in downstream environments.

The first step in the export process presents a dialog where you can choose which elements should be included in the MSI (see Figure 14.23). Typically, you will be including all resources presented here unless you are preparing a "patch" deployment. The list includes anything that you have deployed (via Visual Studio, command line, or manual additions to resources in the Administration Console). As discussed previously, virtual directories associated with IIS-hosted receive locations appear in this list automatically. Note that if you have included environment-specific binding files as resources, you see those as type System.BizTalk:BizTalkBinding. The bindings for the application as it is configured at the time you initiate the export are represented in the tree in Figure 14.23 as simply Bindings (with an option for any global parties you depend on). Be aware that existing bindings in a destination BizTalk group are overwritten by what is imported. So for that reason, if you are preparing an upgrade to an existing application, you might choose to *not* include bindings, or only include bindings for newly added ports, to avoid overwriting a downstream environment's configuration that was done post-deploy. (Consider the case where send ports in production have been configured with passwords as a manual step.)

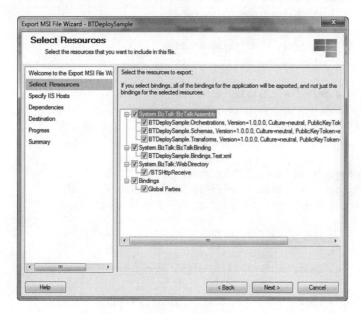

FIGURE 14.23   Select resources for export.

The next step (shown in the left of Figure 14.23 as Specify IIS Hosts) does not refer to BizTalk hosts, as you might expect, but rather to the servers where your IIS virtual directories reside. The export process needs to know this so it can "harvest" all the files needed by this virtual directory into the MSI. Next, the Dependencies step alerts you to any other BizTalk applications you have created references to (such as with the shared enterprise schema example discussed earlier). Applications that you are dependent upon need to arrive at a destination BizTalk group first; and when you import the dependent application, you are prompted to reestablish the reference. Finally, the Destination step allows you to choose the application name (should you want to change it) and the location where the MSI will be placed on the file system.

Handling MSI Export on a Build Server

The entire process that you perform via the Export MSI File Wizard can also be done via command line, using BTSTask.exe. Why might this be interesting? Primarily for use on a build server. Since BizTalk 2009, there has been a component within the BizTalk installation referred to as Project Build Component, which enables building BizTalk solutions without Visual Studio, such as with Team Foundation Server Team Build. After a project has been compiled by your build server, it is logical to think about how you can extend this automation to the creation of deployment packages as is often done with other kinds of projects. To do this, you want a BizTalk group available to your build server, perhaps just the shared development environment. After the compile portion of your build is complete, you augment your build script with a series of steps, as follows:

1. Stop the application. This can be done having your build script call out to a PowerShell script, such as shown in Listing 14.2.

2. Undeploy previously deployed bindings and artifacts. You can do this by having your build script call out to BTSTask.exe, either with a sequence of BTSTask `/RemoveResource` commands if you are going to "reuse" the application definition itself, or via BTSTask.exe `RemoveApp -ApplicationName:YourAppName` to remove the entire application definition. The latter is a cleaner option.

3. If you have removed the application, re-create the container by using BTSTask.exe `AddApp -ApplicationName:YourAppName`.

4. Deploy freshly compiled BizTalk artifacts and any other required resources via BTSTask.exe `/AddResource`. You just sequence these calls from least dependent to most dependent.

5. Deploy your intended bindings via BTSTask.exe `/ImportBindings`.

6. Export an MSI via BTSTask.exe `ExportApp -ApplicationName:BTDeploySample -Package:BTDeploySample.msi`. Note that if you need to selectively export resources into an MSI, you can use the `/ResourceSpec` parameter along with an XML file that conforms to what is generated with BTSTask.exe `ListApp`.

Listing 14.3 shows a script that encompasses all these steps. You might want additional error handling and reporting to be able to report a failed status for a build if the script is unable to generate an MSI.

LISTING 14.2   Stopping a BizTalk Application with PowerShell

```
#=== Stop-BizTalkApp.ps1 ===#
#=== Make sure the ExplorerOM assembly is loaded ===#
[void] [System.reflection.Assembly]::LoadWithPartialName("Microsoft.BizTalk.Explo
erOM")

#=== Connect the BizTalk Management database ===#
$Catalog = New-Object Microsoft.BizTalk.ExplorerOM.BtsCatalogExplorer
$Catalog.ConnectionString = "SERVER=.;DATABASE=BizTalkMgmtDb;Integrated
Security=SSPI"

#=== Loop through applications in the catalog trying to find a name match
===#
foreach($app in $Catalog.Applications)
{
    if ($($app.Name) -ieq $args[0])
    {
      Write-Host `r`nIssuing stop command to $app.Name ...`r`n
      $app.Stop([Microsoft.BizTalk.ExplorerOM.ApplicationStopOption] "StopAll")
      $Catalog.SaveChanges()
    }
}
```

LISTING 14.3   Script for Use by Build Server

```
REM Stop the application so it can be removed
powershell.exe .\Stop-BizTalkApp.ps1 BTDeploySample

REM Remove the old app, create a new empty one
BTSTask.exe RemoveApp -ApplicationName:BTDeploySample
BTSTask.exe AddApp -ApplicationName:BTDeploySample

REM Deploy all resources in least dependent to most dependent order
BTSTask.exe AddResource -ApplicationName:BTDeploySample -Overwrite -
Type:System.BizTalk:BizTalkAssembly -
Source:C:\BTDeploySample\BTDeploySample.Schemas\bin\Debug\BTDeploySample.Sc
hemas.dll -Destination:%BTAD_InstallDir%\BTDeploySample.Schemas.dll
/Options:GacOnInstall

BTSTask.exe AddResource -ApplicationName:BTDeploySample -Overwrite -
Type:System.BizTalk:BizTalkAssembly -
Source:C:\BTDeploySample\BTDeploySample.Transforms\bin\Debug\BTDeploySample
.Transforms.dll -Destination:%BTAD_InstallDir%\BTDeploySample.Transforms.dll
/Options:GacOnInstall
```

```
BTSTask.exe AddResource -ApplicationName:BTDeploySample -Overwrite -
Type:System.BizTalk:Assembly -
Source:C:\BTDeploySample\BTDeploySample.Components\bin\Debug\BTDeploySample
.Components.dll -Destination:%BTAD_InstallDir%\BTDeploySample.Components.dll
/Options:GacOnInstall


BTSTask.exe AddResource -ApplicationName:BTDeploySample -Overwrite -
Type:System.BizTalk:BizTalkAssembly -
Source:C:\BTDeploySample\BTDeploySample.Orchestrations\bin\Debug\BTDeploySa
mple.Orchestrations.dll -
Destination:%BTAD_InstallDir%\BTDeploySample.Orchestrations.dll
 /Options:GacOnInstall


BTSTask.exe AddResource -ApplicationName:BTDeploySample -Overwrite -
Type:System.BizTalk:BizTalkBinding -
Source:C:\BTDeploySample\BTDeploySample.Bindings.xml


REM Import our bindings
BTSTask.exe ImportBindings -
Source:C:\BTDeploySample\BTDeploySample.Bindings.xml -
ApplicationName:BTDeploySample


REM Generate an MSI file
BTSTask.exe ExportApp -ApplicationName:BTDeploySample -Package:BTDeploySample.msi
```

14

Deploying MSI Packages to a BizTalk Group

In the beginning of the chapter, we described the need for metadata about a BizTalk application to make its way into the BizTalk management database. This process is known as importing an application, and it is a group-level deployment task because there is one management database per BizTalk group.

We also described the need for the .NET assemblies that comprise your application to be deployed to the servers within your BizTalk group. This process is known as *installing* the application, and it is a server-level task that you will repeat (per physical BizTalk server).

Having followed naming conventions, built up a deployable application, and automated your build and packaging process, it is now time to actually deploy.

From within the BizTalk Administration Console, you can initiate the import process by right-clicking the **Applications** node (beneath the BizTalk group) and selecting **Import MSI File**. A wizard is then presented where you can select an MSI file from the file system.

In the Application Settings step (Figure 14.24), you can review what resources will be imported and select whether you will overwrite resources. Note that regardless of what you select here, application bindings that were selected for export overwrite bindings of the same name. If this behavior is undesirable, do not select bindings in the export process. Overwriting resources (BizTalk assemblies and other) is typically the correct choice; although, side-by-side versioning scenarios are discussed later.

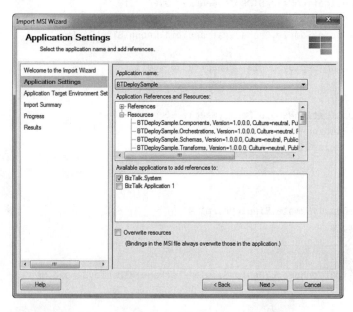

FIGURE 14.24   Importing a BizTalk application MSI.

The Application Target Environment Settings step allows you to select the name of the environment that you importing into. You are presented with a drop-down of choices that represent all the environment names you chose when adding binding files explicitly as resources. Note that when you import an application, bindings are applied in the following order:

1. Bindings that weren't added as resources explicitly but were included for export in the application export as bindings (see Figure 14.23)

2. Binding files that were added explicitly without a target deployment environment

3. Binding files that were added explicitly and match the deployment environment selected in the Application Target Environment Settings step of the Import Wizard

After you step past the informational Import Summary step, the import begins. When it completes, you have the option to now install the MSI on the server where you are running the import process. This is mostly a convenience; you could also simply run the MSI directly from the file system. For a single-node BizTalk group, though, this is your last step in the import/install deployment sequence.

Reversing the import process is as simple as stopping the application (terminating all instances) and using the right-click delete operation. Operationally, this usually requires careful planning to ensure all in-flight activity comes to a clean conclusion before removing the application and associated metadata.

Running the MSI (whether as the last step in the Import Wizard, or by running from the file system on each server in your BizTalk group) is a straightforward process. There are really no options presented except for an installation path. Be sure that you indeed run the MSI for each server in your BizTalk group, or at least each server that houses host instances for the hosts you reference in your binding files (or rely on inherently due to default adapter handlers). You might want to deploy to all servers in the group (regardless of where host instances currently reside) simply to make host reallocation a simpler operation should you need to.

Uninstalling the MSI through a user interface is done using the standard Windows Add/Remove Programs Wizard and must be done on each server where the MSI was installed.

Import/Install via Command Line

Both import and installation can be driven by a command-line operation instead of through the BizTalk Administration Console. You might do this with a build server or other automated deployment mechanism, particularly for environments that update frequently.

The import operation can be performed via BTSTask.exe:

```
BTSTask.exe ImportApp -Package:YourApplicationMSI [-ApplicationName:value]
 [-Overwrite] [-Server:value] [-Database:value] [-Environment:value]
For example: BTSTask.exe ImportApp -Package:BTDeploySample.msi –
ApplicationName:BTDeploySample -Overwrite
```

You will see output to the console indicating each step of the import process. This output can be redirected to a file just by adding something like >> BTDeploySampleImportLog.txt to the command line, which can be helpful for use from a build server or when deployments are done by a different team.

Remember that the import operation need only be performed once for the BizTalk group. You can pick one server in the group to do this, or do it on a server not in the group if you specify server and database parameters. Removing the application via a command line can be done with BTSTask and the RemoveApp parameter, as shown in Listing 14.3.

On each server in the BizTalk group where your assemblies are required, you can install the MSI from the command line using a syntax such as this:

```
msiexec.exe /i BTDeploySample.msi /quiet
```

The /quiet switch prevents the UI from displaying during the install process. You can also uninstall the application with a command line such as this:

```
msiexec /x BTDeploySample.msi /quiet
```

However, as a practical matter, you might not have the MSI (or product ID) conveniently available, so BTSTask can assist with this instead, requiring only the application name:

```
BTSTask.exe UninstallApp -ApplicationName:BTDeploySample
```

Handling Other Deployables

We've covered a number of the scenarios associated with deployment, but a few others are worth mentioning in brief.

Business Activity Monitoring

Business activity monitoring (BAM) deployment can conceptually be divided into two pieces. The first is the deployment of required infrastructure, such as SQL Server databases, Analysis Services cubes, SSIS tasks, and so on. This process is driven by a BAM definition or design time Excel workbook. There are two options for accomplishing this piece.

The first option is to add a BAM definition as a resource (of type System.BizTalk:Bam) directly to your BizTalk application. This is a good choice if your BAM definition is quite specific to your application (as opposed to multiple applications) or if you are calling BAM APIs as part of your solution and are coupled to a particular BAM definition as a result. With this technique, the BAM definition is deployed when the MSI is imported into a BizTalk group.

The second way to deploy BAM definitions is with the BAM Management Utility (BM.exe), which has command-line arguments such as deploy-all, update-all, and remove-all that can be used with a definition file. This is the best choice when handling BAM deployments out of band from application deployments, which is often the case.

The second conceptual piece associated with BAM deployment is the deployment of a mapping between a BAM definition and various BizTalk artifacts such as schemas and orchestrations. This mapping is known as a tracking profile, and it can be deployed either via the Tracking Profile Editor UI or via the command line by using the BizTalk Tracking Deployment (bttdeploy.exe) tool. The latter consumes a BTT file produced by the Tracking Profile Editor. The rhythm of deploying tracking profiles can be more frequent than deploying BizTalk applications (or BAM definitions), so treating this task as a separate and distinct deployment activity can make sense.

Rule Vocabularies and Policies

There are three ways to handle rule vocabularies and policies used by the Microsoft Business Rule Engine (BRE):

▶ The technique that fits most closely with what has already been described in this chapter is to just allow your rule artifacts to be packaged as resources deployed with your MSI. Upon import of the MSI, the vocabularies are available and the policies are associated with your BizTalk application. This model might not be a good fit if you deploy policies with a different rhythm than the rest of the application, or if your policies are used across multiple applications.

▶ If you want to treat your rule artifacts distinct from your BizTalk application, you can use the Rule Engine Deployment Wizard UI to manage imports and exports. The tool enables you to select a database of choice, meaning it can work across multiple environments.

▶ Finally, you can deal with rule deployment directly within the BizTalk Administration Console. Within the Policies node of a particular application, you can right-click and export a particular policy (and associated vocabulary). You can also export the entire set of policies for an application by choosing **Export Policies** at the application level (right-click). Importing within the BizTalk Administration Console is slightly different; you begin by right-clicking the **Applications** node (directly under the Group) and choosing Import Policies. Under <All Artifacts>, Policies, you will see your imported policy and can choose to publish that policy with a right-click. This makes the policy available to deployed applications. Within a particular application, you can now go to the Policy node and add a particular version of a policy.

Of the three options, only the first lends itself to automation and scripting. However, you will find third-party and open source tools that tackle command-line deployments of rules.

Handling Upgrade and Versioning Scenarios

Often, the desired behavior during an upgrade is to run the old version of your application's assemblies side by side with the new versions, on the same BizTalk group. This is particularly the case in the presence of longer-running orchestrations that will not arrive at a natural termination at the time of deployment.

New receive locations and send ports (with alternative URIs, file shares, FTP sites, queues, and so on) are often needed in an upgrade deployment if you have long-running orchestrations with outstanding correlated receives that still need to be processed.

To prepare for a side-by-side deployment, you need to increment assembly version numbers on all assemblies required to run side by side to allow for multiple versions within the GAC. After your version-incremented assemblies have been deployed to a given BizTalk group (workstation or Dev/Test), you can export an MSI using the techniques described earlier, optionally choosing to include only resources that are being upgraded (including relevant bindings).

If you are upgrading an orchestration for which there are long-running instances from previous deployments, and your intent is "retire" the old orchestration when in-flight work completes, you first bind the orchestration to the relevant ports and then unenlist the old orchestration before starting the new one. The "unenlist-old - start-new" sequence can be performed in a script (using Microsoft.BizTalk.ExplorerOM classes) to ensure the operation happens in a transaction, such that no messages are suspended because of missing subscriptions.

Keep in mind that upgrading assemblies in an application will almost always require a host instance restart for that change to take effect. Also, if you desire to undeploy the previous version of an assembly, consider what artifacts are dependent on that assembly (because those must be undeployed first).

For production environments where long-running work is the norm and deployment windows are short, careful planning and testing will be required for any upgrade and versioning strategy. Rehearse the precise sequence of deployment events in a test environment where you can create a set of in-flight work items that resembles production as closely as possible.

Summary

In this chapter, we discussed the architecture of BizTalk deployments, including how BizTalk organizes your artifacts and how that organization plays into the deployment process itself. We discussed how a deployment strategy begins with the organization of solutions, projects, folders, and naming conventions within Visual Studio. We also covered the automation of various tasks within Visual Studio to assist developer productivity. From there, we moved on to discuss the mechanics of deployment to BizTalk and what is required to build up a complete definition of an application through the definition and management of resources. Finally, we covered the lifecycle of application export and import, including special concerns for dealing with multiple physical environments, scripting, and build automation. We wrapped up with a short treatment of other types of BizTalk assets that require deployment handling such as BAM and rules and versioning and upgrade scenarios.

PART IV

RFID

IN THIS PART

CHAPTER 15

BizTalk RFID

R*adio frequency identification* (RFID) technology support is one of the best-kept secrets of BizTalk Server. In this chapter, you tour the key elements of RFID support, from installation notes to development tips and tricks. Like many of the other chapters in this book, this chapter could be the subject of its own mini-book, and so you must cover a lot of ground quickly. The goal is to introduce you to the capabilities present and to prepare you for the common developer tasks in RFID applications.

Starting with BizTalk Server 2006 R2 and continuing with 2009 and now the 2010 edition, BizTalk Server has extensive support for creating and deploying RFID-aware applications through the BizTalk RFID component.

RFID-aware applications can take two forms:

▶ Simple .NET applications that need access to RFID functionality through *application programming interfaces* (APIs) for performing tasks such as printing labels that contain RFID tags and reading and writing information to a tag's data segment

▶ Complete applications (called RFID processes) that handle the processing of RFID events using a hosted application model.

BizTalk RFID has a well-defined model for abstracting out the differences between the RFID device types and provides a uniform, consistent programming model across these device types, and even the specific kind of RFID technology in use (more on this topic later in this chapter). This lets you, the developer, create powerful reusable solutions that can be easily adapted and deployed against a wide variety of hardware configurations with minimal change.

This chapter presents an overview of the RFID capabilities of BizTalk Server from a developer viewpoint. You continue with the same application scenario of Food Inc.'s supply chain, specifically the receipt of physical goods in a distribution center. Given the early adopter stage of the RFID industry and the relatively small amount of information about creating RFID applications using BizTalk RFID, you take a step-by-step approach to illustrate concepts throughout this chapter (with extensive use of real devices in code examples).

RFID Overview

The technology for identifying objects in the real world by interrogating them with a *radio frequency* (RF) probe and reacting to the response received has been around for a long time, with many of the core interaction patterns being defined as part of the radar technology from more than 50 years ago.

The promise of this perpetually overhyped technology is to provide automatic identification that is significantly better than the ubiquitous barcode, with widespread applicability in a whole slew of applications, including retail, manufacturing, logistics, and healthcare automation, in addition to core asset-tracking scenarios.

One point of confusion regarding RFID stems from the wide variety of technologies that come under the umbrella of this abbreviation. The term *RFID* is used to imply automatic identification across the RF spectrum, including *low frequency* (LF), *high frequency* (HF), *ultra high frequency* (UHF), microwave, ultra wide band, and so on. And then there are differences based on whether the tag involved has a battery (active RFID) or is a pure transponder that is powered by an interrogating RF field from a reader (passive RFID).

Each such "flavor" of RFID has a completely different set of operational characteristics and constraints, including the size, dimensionality, and appearance of the tag; the capabilities of the tag such as whether it has a writable ID on it; the size of user memory on the tag;, the security mechanisms supported;, the kinds of substrate that the tag can be applied to; and the effective read range of the tag.

To compound this, even within a particular technology family, say passive UHF RFID, readers and tags come with a range of options, with vastly different form factors and capabilities. The tags are also getting more and more specialized as the technology becomes mainstream, with the tags suitable for application on laptops and IT assets, for example, being completely inappropriate for tagging pallets in a warehouse or apparel items in a retail scenario.

A full description of the physics of RFID and a scientific way to choose the right RF technology for a given application scenario is well beyond the scope of this chapter, but some questions that you should expect to have answered early on in any RFID project include the following:

- What is being tagged? What's its size and shape, what quantities are involved, are there any properties that are RF sensitive such as metallic substrate or RF absorbent material, and does it contain moisture or liquids?

- Where does it need to be read? That is, what is the operational environment (distance, number of tag read events or observations needed, whether human involvement occurs during the read process, and the physical proximity between the reader and the tagged item)?

- From an application processing perspective, what would you like to do with the observations?

The BizTalk RFID Framework

The last bulleted question is where BizTalk RFID comes in. Given the rich diversity of RFID devices and the potentially broad applicability of the technology, Microsoft has taken a platform approach to its RFID functionality. The feature set is aimed at addressing two significant development scenarios:

- Enable the developers to write device-agnostic applications. Most RFID (if not all) projects start with one device and tag and evolve to supporting multiple devices and tag form factors, in many cases even before the pilot stage is done. Given this, BizTalk RFID, with a robust layer that enables support for devices in a plug-and-play fashion, enables applications to scale easily from single-device environments to multi-device, heterogeneous-environment environments.

- Minimize the number of lines of code for common RFID scenarios, including event filtering, aggregation, processing, and delivery.

From a technology perspective, BizTalk RFID should have come with a disclaimer: Please leave your BizTalk Server at the door. (Because the base application model for BizTalk RFID is completely different from BizTalk Server.) It has its own installers, its own NT service host for hosting the RFID processes, its own object model and API, and its own event-processing model.

Architecturally, BizTalk Server is an *Extensible Markup Language* (XML)-centric orchestration and business process execution engine; BizTalk RFID is a .NET-centric event-processing engine.

BizTalk RFID applications come in two typical flavors: synchronous applications (those that interact with devices on demand) and asynchronous applications (those that respond to events instead of directly interacting with devices). In addition, you need to be aware of two fundamental abstractions: devices and events.

Devices are software abstractions for the physical RFID readers that your applications interact with. Underneath the covers, devices connect via web service calls to the remote

BizTalk RFID Device Manager API. The Device Manager, in turn, manages the physical connection to the device and performs the task of sending commands to the devices and processing responses from devices.

Events are the observations that are surfaced to the application when an RFID tag is detected. Each event is modeled as its own .NET class and is considered to be a light-weight abstraction. BizTalk RFID events are usually on the order of a few hundred bytes and are designed to be passed by value, if you will, from the device to the application.

Given the rich diversity of RFID devices, Microsoft has defined an interface that RFID device vendors can implement to plug into the Microsoft RFID hardware ecosystem, very much along the lines of the Windows driver model enabling PC peripherals to work with the operating system. This interface is called the *Device Service Provider Interface* (DSPI). The actual plug-in that translates the DSPI objects into the device-specific protocol messages is called the *device provider*.

A device provider is very much like a Windows device driver. It is a system-level compo-nent that abstracts away all the interaction specifics for a particular device and presents a uniform, consistent interface that users can program to. Just as you do not program to the device driver for a hard disk anymore for reading and writing files (thankfully!), the device-neutral RFID APIs in the System.IO.SensorServices.Rfid.Client namespace, the BizTalk RFID APIs, and the underlying device providers are responsible for interactions with the heterogeneous RFID devices.

So, what's the big deal with device providers?

First, RFID devices are considerably more feature rich than an abstract Windows device driver model. Microsoft has attempted to specify a lot of functionality at the DSPI layer, including the following:

- Connection management and support for multiple transports
- Authentication
- Tag inventory operations
- Tag operations, including reading/writing the tag ID and read, write, lock, unlock, permalock
- Tag-level security and support for killing RFID tags
- *General Purpose Input Output* (GPIO) functionality
- Device (and tag-level) filtering and duplicate elimination
- Device diagnostics
- Extensive support for device and antennae configuration.

All the these result in a rich interface that enables "best of breed" RFID applications, instead of the usual least common denominator approach to interacting with devices, but it does add complexity to both the implementation of the provider and its proper usage.

> **NOTE**
>
> Before deciding on the hardware, ensure that there is a BizTalk provider for it and that the interface is functional enough for your application. A great strategy is to create a functionality checklist for your application and walk through the device provider surface area to ensure that it is rich enough for your purposes. Having incomplete (or worse, unstable) device providers considerably increases the risk to your project.

Further, to enable BizTalk to support devices that come out after the actual product is released, there is a set of "future-proof" extensions for all the features just listed. This is especially important from an API longevity perspective. (Do you remember CreateFileEx2?). One piece of good news on this front: The DSPI has seen a small set of enhancements, but no major breaking changes from BizTalk Server 2006 R2 to BizTalk 2009 and now BizTalk Server 2010.

This means all providers that were created for the previous versions of BizTalk continue to work in the latest version with no modifications. This strong notion of compatibility bodes well for the continued adoption of BizTalk RFID and the DSPI.

Installation Notes for BizTalk RFID

The most important thing to keep in mind is that you do not need to install the full BizTalk Server components if you are going to be developing only RFID applications. You should pick only the BizTalk RFID and BizTalk RFID Mobile components from the first splash screen (see Figure 15.1).

FIGURE 15.1   Installing the RFID components.

> **NOTE**
>
> BizTalk RFID 2010 requires the Full profile of the 4.0 version of the .NET Framework, SQL Server 2008 SP1 or higher, and MSMQ Core as some of the key prerequisites when running on Windows Vista SP2 or Windows 7. On the server side, the minimum OS version supported is now Windows Server 2008 SP2, and *Internet Information Services* (IIS) 7.x is a required component. For the complete walkthrough on the installation process and troubleshooting, especially IIS configuration issues, go through the "Installing BizTalk Server RFID on Windows Server 2008 and 2008 R2.htm" and the "Installing BizTalk Server RFID on Windows Vista and Windows 7.htm" guides that are part of the product installation media. From a development perspective, BizTalk RFID 2010 supports projects created in both Visual Studio 2008 and Visual Studio 2010.

For the product flavor to install, in a developer environment, be sure to pick the **Complete** option (see Figure 15.2). This installs the examples and the device simulator, which could be of use in development scenarios where you want to test your applications without a physical device being present.

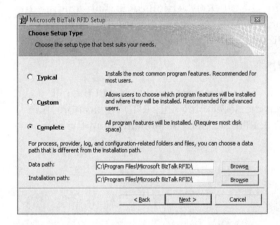

FIGURE 15.2   Pick the Complete install option if you are in Development mode.

After you install the prerequisites, you can breeze through the installation steps with the default options proposed and ignore the error that you might get about not being able to register the server in an Active Directory registry. The sequence of screens that you can safely ignore is shown in Figures 15.3 and 15.4.

FIGURE 15.3   Recording the AD marker during installation.

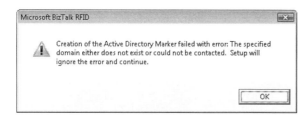

FIGURE 15.4   Ignorable error from the AD marker creation process.

At the end of the installation sequence, after you click the **Finish** button, you are prompted with this dialog, which has a penchant to hide in the background. This is the installation sequence for the BizTalk Server *Business Rule Engine* (BRE) component. If you are not going to be using the BRE, you can safely skip this step by clicking **Cancel**. If you are using the BRE, enter the information that will be used to configure the NT Services used by the BRE (highlighted in Figure 15.5).

Clicking **Next** takes you to screen shown as Figure 15.6, where you should pick the Business **Rules Engine** component and finish the installation step (shown in Figure 15.7).

FIGURE 15.5   Configuring the BRE Service credential.

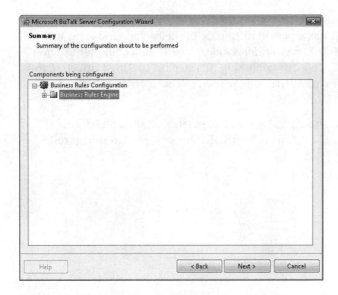

FIGURE 15.6   Selecting the Rule Engine component.

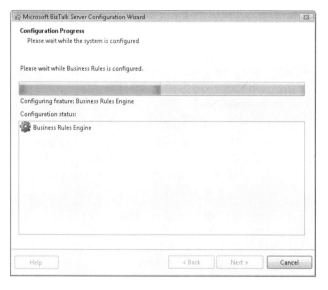

FIGURE 15.7   Completing BRE configuration for RFID.

Device Applications

Now that you are done with the installation part, roll up your sleeves and write your first RFID application. You can write an application that opens a connection to a device, reads some tags that are in the field of the device, and reports the tags back to the application. This simple functionality shows up in a variety of application scenarios, including on-demand reads for point-of-sale systems or tag commissioning applications. The second part of this chapter creates an extension to the Food Inc. scenario that shows how automatic warehouse receiving can be implemented using RFID technology.

Here is the code snippet for an application to read tags on-demand from a device:

```
using (var dc = new DeviceConnection("MyFirstDevice"))
        {
            dc.Open();
            ICollection<TagReadEvent> tags =
dc.GetTags(TagDataSelector.All);
            foreach (TagReadEvent tag in tags)
            {
                Console.WriteLine("Found Tag {0}",
tag);
            }
            dc.Close();
        }
```

The first line tells BizTalk RFID the name of the device that you are working with. Note that there is no mention of transport protocols, port numbers, and so on; all of that is abstracted away.

The Open() line opens the device specifically for your program and returns a GUID that represents your connection ID. At any time, only one application can have a connection to a device; the exception to this rule being administrative connections: Any number of administrative connections can be opened to a device at one time.

The next line makes the actual GetTags request. The quirky TagDataSelector argument is the BizTalk RFID equivalent of a SQL project list; it tells the underlying system the fields of the tag that the application is actually interested in. In this example, you want all the fields, so you can use the shorthand of TagDataSelector.All.

The return type from this method is a collection of TagReadEvent objects. The TagReadEvent is one of the primary objects that you will be working with; it is a specialization of the "Observation" class in the DSPI SDK. It brings together the tag ID, tag data, the device that observed the tag, and the time at which the observation was made. To accommodate returning information that is beyond this basic set of things, the TagReadEvent has a dictionary in it called VendorSpecificInformation.

And finally, when you are done with it, you must close the device connection. To repeat, you must close the device connection when you have finished working with it, to avoid locking it up. On the remote chance that you forget to do so, you can use the KillConnection API in the DeviceManagerProxy class to kill an existing connection to the device. But use that API sparingly; it will probably cause your application to error out if used indiscriminately.

Running Your First RFID Application

To make this scenario work, you need to have a device, called MyFirstDevice, that you are going to read the tags from. For this example, we use the FX7400 reader from Motorola. You can, of course, use any reader for which a device provider exists. The steps usually involve installing a device provider, discovering or adding the device to the system, and then powering up the device and interacting with it. In the next section, we go through the setup and operation of the FX7400.

Installing the FX7400 Device Provider

The FX7400 comes with a setup file and an installer; you can use it to install the provider (shown in Figure 15.8). The installer registers the provider with BizTalk RFID and starts the provider.

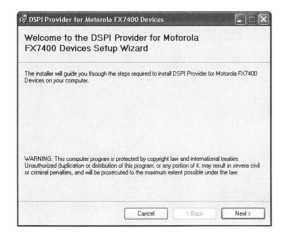

FIGURE 15.8   Installing the FX7400 provider.

After you have run the installer, if you go into RFID Manager, you should see the information shown in Figures 15.9 and 15.10 under the Providers node.

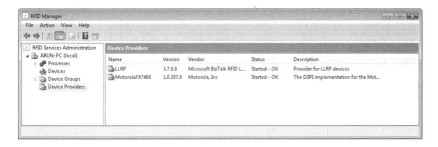

FIGURE 15.9   Viewing installed providers.

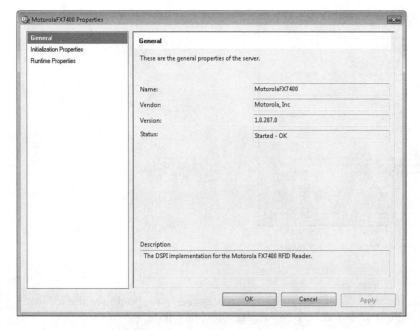

FIGURE 15.10   Viewing the FX7400 provider details.

Discovering the Device

When you have a provider running, you need to add definitions for the devices that will be accessed through the provider. You have two ways of doing this:

▶ **Autodiscovery:** Plug-and-play-like process of discovering devices through the provider

▶ **Manual addition of devices:** Through the AddDevice Wizard in the RFID Manager

For enterprise rollouts where *Dynamic Host Configuration Protocol* (DHCP) is involved and where devices do not typically have static IPs, autodiscovery is a good option.

BizTalk RFID abstracts out all the ways of discovering devices (for example, WS-discovery, UPnP, PnP, ZeroConf, to name a few) into one consistent model using the discovery APIs on the provider. There are two models for discovery:

▶ **Continuous discovery:** Continuous discovery implies that the process of discovering new devices is started when the provider starts and is shut down as part of the provider shutdown process. This is a great implementation of discovery for lightweight discovery mechanisms that can be running all the time, such as PnP.

▶ **Triggered discovery:** Triggered discovery requires administrator intervention. If the discovery mechanism is expensive or time-consuming (such as a WS-discovery probe and match sequence), an administrator might want to do this on-demand. The RFID Manager supports a Discover Now option in the right-click menu for the provider, which you can use to trigger the discovery process (shown in Figure 15.11)

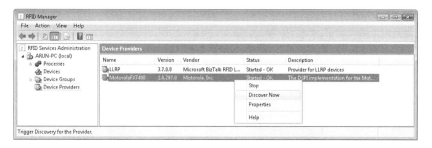

FIGURE 15.11   Triggered discovery from BizTalk RFID.

> **NOTE**
>
> Most network devices use some form of *User Datagram Protocol* (UDP) broadcast, typi-
> cally for device discovery. This implies firewall configuration in most cases, and the
> correct configuration of the subnet mask settings. Refer to your provider documenta-
> tion for the steps that you need to take to get discovery working within your network
> configuration.

The device discovery process reports devices in the BizTalk RFID store that are in the
Unconfigured state as shown in Figure 15.12 (that is, discovered but not configured). This
implies that the server does not yet know whether the device must be owned by this
server instance. This manual step helps avoid situations where a network-attached device
is discovered by multiple servers on the network but is intended to be used by one of
those servers only.

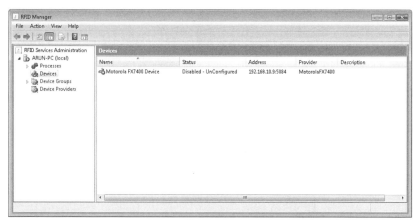

FIGURE 15.12   Device discovery: unconfigured devices.

You can right-click the device and enable it (as shown in Figure 15.13), which causes it to
get configured.

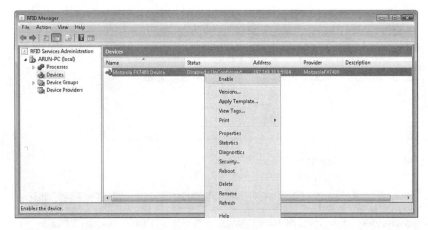

FIGURE 15.13   Configuring discovered devices.

In this step, you must provide device authentication information if required by the device manufacturer (shown in Figure 15.14). You should use the documentation that came with the device to get the default username and password for your device.

Finally, the device is in the Closed state (shown in Figure 15.15), indicating that it is configured and available for applications to use it.

FIGURE 15.14   Configuring device authentication information.

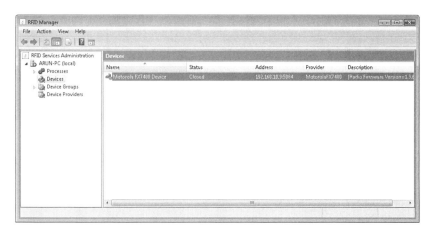

FIGURE 15.15   Device available for operation.

Manual Device Addition
Some providers do not support autodiscovery, neither continuous nor triggered. In that case, you can add the device manually, by specifying the transport parameters through the New Device Wizard. We repeat the same steps as for discovery to add the device manually, and the sequence is illustrated step-by-step in Figures 15.16 through 15.22:

  1. Launch the New Device Wizard.

FIGURE 15.16   The New Device Wizard.

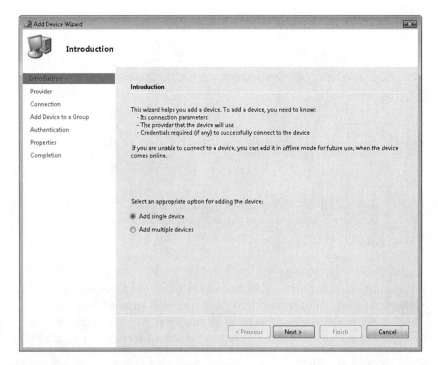

FIGURE 15.17   The Add Single Device option.

2. Choose the **Add Single Device** option.

3. Specify the provider that you will use to connect to the device; in this case, it is the Motorola FX7400 provider.

4. Enter the IP address and port for the device.

5. Use the default device group into which the device should be added. Device groups are folder-like containers that can contain devices. If you have a number of devices in your application, device groups are a convenient way to manage common settings such as device security settings and configuration properties.

6. Specify the authentication credentials, if needed.

7. The system connects to the device and reports back on the name and connection information. You can edit the name in this step and then click **Next** to finish the wizard.

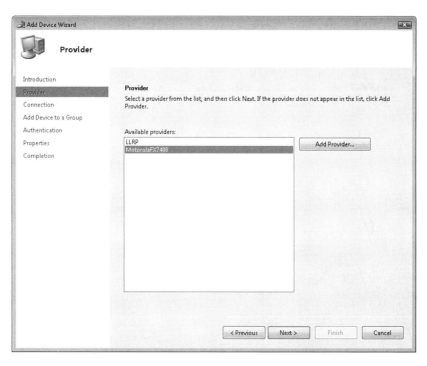

FIGURE 15.18   Pick the device provider.

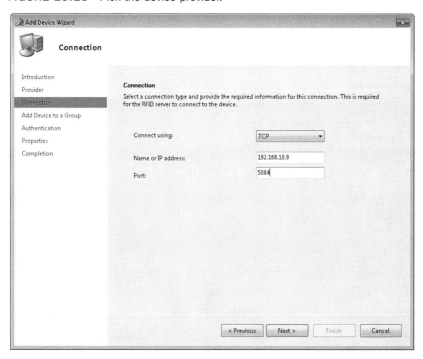

FIGURE 15.19   Device available for operation.

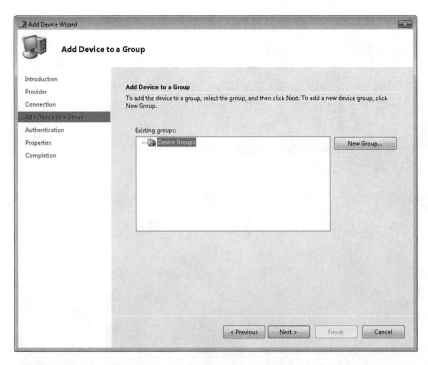

FIGURE 15.20   Specify the device group for the new device.

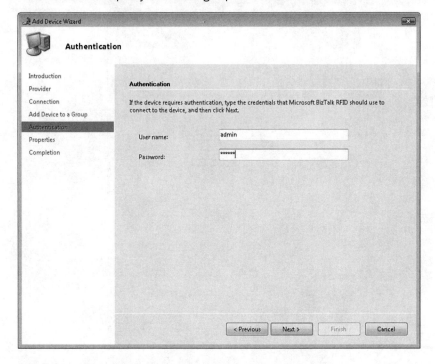

FIGURE 15.21   Specify the credentials to connect to the device.

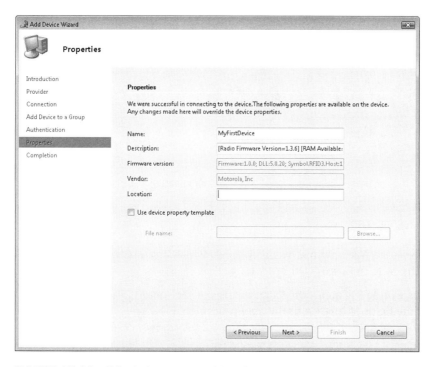

FIGURE 15.22   Edit device name and location.

Device Names
Devices are assumed to have three identifying characteristics: a friendly name that can typically be changed by an administrator; a device ID, which is an immutable thing like a MAC for a network card, which typically would never change for a device; and the transport settings, which would not change if static IPs were used but would change periodically if DHCP IPs were used.

Optionally, device discovery can report the friendly name of the device, in which case the same is reported to the application. If no friendly name is present, the device shows up as <provider name><device number>, and the administrator can rename the device subsequently.

You can change the name of the device from the RFID Manager or by programmatically using the SetProperty API.

Running the Program
Now that you have a device discovered and configured with BizTalk RFID with the correct name, you can execute the program that you created earlier, and if there is a tag in front of the reader, you should see the output from the program in the form of an XML string. Viewing the XML in say, Internet Explorer, produces the output as shown in Figure 15.23.

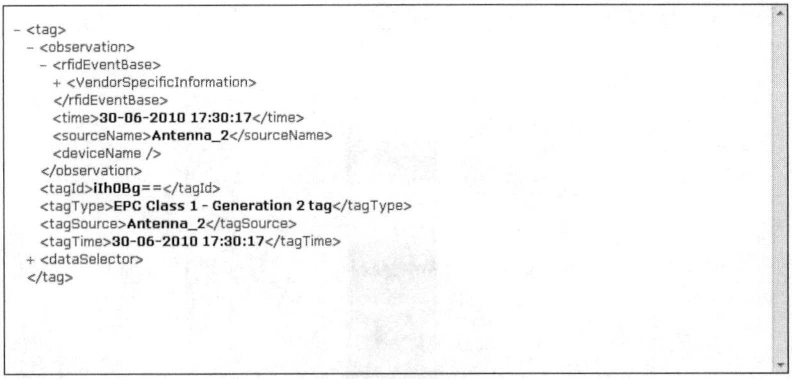

```
- <tag>
  - <observation>
    - <rfidEventBase>
      + <VendorSpecificInformation>
      </rfidEventBase>
      <time>30-06-2010 17:30:17</time>
      <sourceName>Antenna_2</sourceName>
      <deviceName />
    </observation>
    <tagId>iIhOBg==</tagId>
    <tagType>EPC Class 1 - Generation 2 tag</tagType>
    <tagSource>Antenna_2</tagSource>
    <tagTime>30-06-2010 17:30:17</tagTime>
  + <dataSelector>
  </tag>
```

FIGURE 15.23   Program output as XML.

If a device has more than one antenna, you can decide which antenna you want to read
tags from, using the code shown in Listing 15.1:

Also, you might be wondering about the TagDataSelector argument. This is a hint that
tells the provider the fields of interest to the application.

LISTING 15.1   Reading tags from a specific Antenna

```
        private static void
ShowTagsFromAntenna(DeviceConnection dc)
        {
            ICollection<TagReadEvent> tags =
                dc.GetTags(
                    "Antenna_2",
                    TagDataSelector.All,
                    null /*passcode*/,
                    null /*vendor specific
parameters*/);

            foreach (TagReadEvent tag in tags)
            {
                Console.WriteLine("Found Tag ID {0} At
Source {1}",
                    HexUtilities.HexEncode(tag.GetId()),
tag.Source);
            }


        }
```

Running this code against the FX7400 with tags in the field of antenna 2 produces the output shown in Figure 15.24.

FIGURE 15.24   Read tags from specific antenna.

Vendor Extensions and Extensibility

You might notice that the method GetTags takes about 3 seconds to run. From the provider documentation, it turns out that the FX7400 provider by default collects tags for a period of 3 seconds and returns the results to the caller. This behavior of blocking, batching, and returning a set of events is fairly typical in many RFID applications. The trade-off is between responsiveness and utility: If the reader inventories tags just once and returns the tags to the caller, one or more of the tags in the field of the reader might not have had a chance to respond in that inventory round, which would show up as a missed read in the application. However, waiting 3 seconds might not always be the right answer and could cause the application to be perceived as sluggish. To allow control of this behavior to the application, the FX7400 provider exposes a vendor extension to GetTags that tells the provider how long it should wait for tags. The code shown in Listing 15.2 illustrates how to call this overload with a wait of 500 milliseconds instead of the default behavior.

LISTING 15.2   Utilizing Vendor Extensions

```
        private static void
ShowTagsImmediate(DeviceConnection dc)
      {
          VendorDefinedParameters parameters = new
VendorDefinedParameters();
          parameters.InputParameters = new
VendorSpecificInformation();
          parameters.InputParameters["WaitTimeMillis"]
= 500;
          ICollection<TagReadEvent> tags =
              dc.GetTags(
                  "Antenna_2",
```

```
                    TagDataSelector.All,
                    null /*passcode*/,
                    parameters);

             foreach (TagReadEvent tag in tags)
             {
                  Console.WriteLine("Found Tag ID {0} At
Source {1}",
                       HexUtilities.HexEncode(tag.GetId()),
tag.Source);
             }


         }
```

Running this code fragment has the behavior that the GetTags command returns immediately, as shown in Figure 15.25, but you can see that three invocations of the program produce different results because of the short duration of the inventory, even though the set of tags in front of the reader did not change. In general, we find that inventory times below a second are not reliable from an application perspective.

FIGURE 15.25   Read tags from specific antenna for a short duration.

Given the rich variety of devices, and the "optional" support for various commands, here is a code snippet that shows you how to check whether a particular device supports a particular command:

```
             foreach (var capability in
dc.GetDeviceCapabilities())
             {
                  if (capability ==
DeviceCapability.GetTags)
                  {
```

```
                    return true;
            }
    }
    return false;
```

On a similar note, if you are wondering how you would know what antennas are available to program against on a particular device, you can use the `GetSources()` command on the `DeviceConnection` to get this information.

Here is code that shows you how to enumerate the sources on a device. The sources on a device can be of two types: antennas or GPIO ports. Antennas are typically read points that you can read/write tags through. Optionally, some devices also let you set properties on antennas, including the transmit power and the receive sensitivity. GPIO ports are extended functionality for getting input from digital sources such as motion sensors or photo eyes and for controlling the output to a stack-light, buzzer, magnetic door latch, or boom barrier.

The first step is to enumerate the sources on the device and identify the sources of type `Antenna` as illustrated in Listing 15.3; In addition to the antenna information, two flags called `System Enabled` and `User Enabled` are also obtained.

LISTING 15.3   Enumerating Device Sources

```
        private static void
PrintAntennas(DeviceConnection dc)
        {
            foreach (var sourceProfile in
dc.GetSources())
            {
                //get the source type from the property
profile dictionary
                PropertyKey pk = new PropertyKey(
                    StandardDevicePropertyGroups.Source,
                    SourcePropertyGroup.SourceType);
                object obj;
                if (sourceProfile.Value.TryGetValue(pk,
out obj))
                {
                    SourceType theSourceType =
(SourceType) obj;
                    if (theSourceType ==
SourceType.Antenna)
                    {
                        var antennaName =
sourceProfile.Key;
                        var systemEnabled =
dc.GetProperty(antennaName,
```

```
StandardDevicePropertyGroups.Source,

SourcePropertyGroup.SystemEnabled, null);
                        var userEnabled =
dc.GetProperty(antennaName,
StandardDevicePropertyGroups.Source,

SourcePropertyGroup.Enabled, null);
                    Console.WriteLine("Found Antenna
{0} System Enabled {1} User Enabled {2}",
                        antennaName, systemEnabled,
userEnabled);
                }
            }
        }
    }
```

The most common reason why you might not be able to read tags from a particular antenna on a device is because the device might not have a real antenna attached to the specified port. In BizTalk RFID parlance, such an antenna port is called a system-disabled port.

There is a companion property called `Enabled`, which is intended for applications that disable particular antennas to prevent stray reads, even if the port has an antenna attached to it.

Figure 15.26 shows the output from running the preceding code snippet.

FIGURE 15.26   View antenna information.

BizTalk RFID uses instances of type `PropertyProfile` in most places where named
key-value pairs are returned to the application, such as in the preceding example.
`PropertyProfiles` are named dictionaries where the key is of type `PropertyKey`,
which is a composite key of property group name and property name, and the value is
of type `Object`. In reality, `PropertyProfile` instances can hold instances of a small
set of types, including the primitive types, the DSPI types strings, and certain arrays of
these types. The restriction comes in part from the fact that these objects are serializable across the client/server and server/provider process boundaries.

A final note about antennas: They represent one of the physical points of failure in an
RFID application. If an antenna cable were to break or come loose, your application will
likely stop working. To deal with this situation correctly, providers can surface up a
management event, which can then be used by *Windows Management Infrastructure* (WMI)
and other scripting clients to report the issue.

Device Configuration

`Source:SystemEnabled` and `Source:Enabled` are just two examples of properties that are
available on a particular device or source. You can enumerate the available properties on a
device, and their associated metadata, using the GetDevicePropertyMetadata API on the
`DeviceManagerProxy` class. The metadata returned describes a number of facets of each
property, including the default value if any, validation rules such as min-max, and other
information such as whether the property is read-only, persistent, and so on.

BizTalk RFID keeps track of all changes to device configurations in a version store, which
comes in handy when troubleshooting readability issues.

To access device versions and associated details, bring up the Versions property on the
RFID Manager (see Figures 15.27, 15.28, and 15.29).

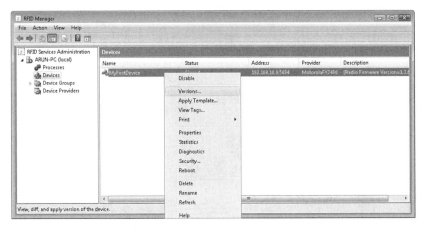

FIGURE 15.27   View device versions.

FIGURE 15.28   View change history.

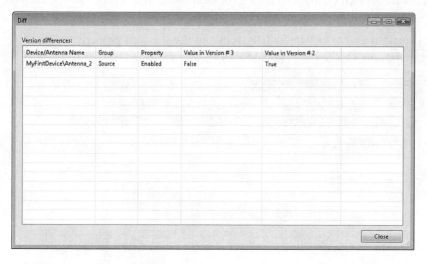

FIGURE 15.29   View individual changes.

Tag Operations

Next look at the mechanisms for performing operations on individual tags, such as reading or writing user memory. For consistency, we are going to stay with UHF Gen2 tags, but similar descriptions also apply for HF tags.

Most tag operations require you to singulate specific tags and then perform the operation on the tag. The model is similar to how you might operate on a file stream: You use the name of the file, or in this case the tag ID, to singulate the specific tag that you are looking for, and then specify the byte offset at which you would like to start reading. BizTalk RFID supports the concept of a SeekOrigin similar to file streams, but this is a bit aspirational. Current generations of readers and tags (and consequently providers) usually support only absolute seek offsets. For example, to read the first 4 bytes of user data from a tag with ID 0xAABBCCDD, Listing 15.4 shows you how to do this.

LISTING 15.4   Reading Tag Ids

```
        private static void
ReadAndWriteTagData(DeviceConnection dc)
        {
            string tagIdHex =
"08D895240000000000000000";
            byte[] tagId =
HexUtilities.HexDecode(tagIdHex);
            byte[] data =
HexUtilities.HexDecode("0xAABBCCDD");

            dc.WritePartialTagData(tagId, data,
SeekOrigin.Begin, 0);
            Console.WriteLine("Wrote tag data {0}",
HexUtilities.HexEncode(data));

            byte[] output = dc.GetPartialTagData(tagId,
SeekOrigin.Begin, 0, 4);
            Console.WriteLine("Read tag data {0}",
HexUtilities.HexEncode(output));
        }
```

The EPCGlobal Class1 Generation 2 Tag Programming Model
This section presents a brief overview of the EPCGlobal Class 1 Generation 2 (typically shortened to Gen2) standard. This standard has been around for a few years now and has seen widespread adoption both from a vendor support standpoint and geographic coverage. You can find the entire standard for the curios at http://www.epcglobalinc.org/standards/uhfc1g2/uhfc1g2_1_2_0-standard-20080511.pdf.

Features in the protocol directly address some of the limitations in previous iterations around tag readability and high-speed, reliable operation in real-world environments that have multiple readers operating concurrently and multiple tags that might be read simultaneously. The Gen2 protocol does this while still presenting a uniform and simple programming model to the application developer, which takes out a lot of the complexity around low-level reader synchronization that used to be typical of early RFID deployments. The combination of a reliable operation and simple model was one of the main reasons that Wal-Mart, the U.S. Department of Defense, and Metro chose Gen2 as the technology they would standardize on for their rollouts.

Enough theory, now look at what the Gen2 tag typically looks like.

From an application perspective, the most popular and distinctive feature of the tag is its *Electronic Product Code* (EPC). This is typically a user-programmable memory area, referred to as the EPC bank, and contains a fixed number of bits that you can encode to contain application-specific information. Early implementations of Gen2 had 64-bit EPC banks. Today, the commercial sweet spot is 96-bit EPC banks, and most tag manufacturers have already announced products that will support 128-, 256-, and 512-bit EPC banks. In addition, all Gen2 tags have a memory bank reserved for system operations such as passcode management, called the reserved bank, another dedicated to tag information, called the TID bank, and an optional memory bank called the user memory bank for additional data. Within the EPC bank, the Gen2 model specifies a checksum area, protocol control bits, a numbering system identifier that defines the tag family, and the actual tag itself.

Assuming the tag is read successfully, the checksum (CRC) and the PC (Protocol Control Bits) are stripped off at the protocol layer, and the provider surfaces up a `TagReadEvent` to the application. The attributes in a `TagReadEvent` map fairly directly, as depicted in Figure 15.30.

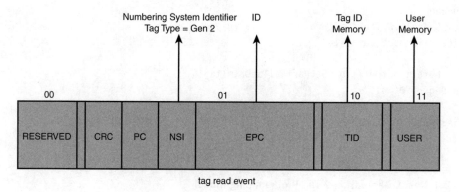

FIGURE 15.30   Attributes of Tag Read Event.

A common application dilemma at the start of an RFID application design cycle is to pick the tag layout (that is, how to make use of the EPC and user data areas of the tag). Like any complex design discussion, there are multiple considerations here, and your decision to go with a particular approach will depend on your use case scenarios. With that in mind, here are some rules of thumb:

- First, you have to decide up front whether the tag memory is going to be used just to store a unique immutable key, like a license plate, or a small database. The license plate approach has the implication that all points that need to process the tag must have access to a back-end system of record that has the other information related to the item. This connection to the back-end system is problematic, especially when the asset might cross company boundaries, as is common in many supply chain track and trace scenarios. However, an online or cloud-based solution to this problem using (for example) the EPC-IS service can be a very scalable application architecture.

- The small database approach has a number of pitfalls, such as the size of the information, the time for tag operations, reliability of operations and dealing with partial success, control over updates, synchronization of this database with the system of record, and so on. However, you should be aware that there are scenarios where the "writable data store" concept dramatically simplifies the application design. In fact, this is one of the core Auto ID scenarios that are just not possible using barcodes, which are read-only by definition. We have seen specific pieces of information such as expiry dates and critical service history markers being stored directly on the tag. A significant advantage in this approach is that the asset and its data are available simultaneously, and you can actually do a physical search for assets that match particular criteria (such as an expiry date) by doing an RFID scan of an area.

15

NOTE

Writing data to the tag is a slower and more cumbersome operation than reading the data. For most applications, programming the tag ID (or EPC) (either as a license plate or as a byte encoding of a standard tag data format such as an SSCC or a SGTIN for example) is the recommended option. Use the data bank only in data-logger type applications or if some special amount of information is stored with the tag. Watch out for operational patterns that require you to read or write the tag data with each operation; this can significantly affect both functionality and performance.

In addition, use a standard tag encoding wherever possible. You rarely want to program to a binary representation of a tag directly from an application. Designing a binary format that is correct, efficient, and version-tolerant is a significant activity. Also, the binary representation of the tag is usually hard to evolve once the application is deployed. Remember that the tags might no longer even be in your organization any more; at the same time, your application might come across tags that were not even issued by it.

Working with Standard Tag Encodings

One of the useful pieces of functionality within BizTalk RFID is the support for the EPC Global *tag data standards* (TDS). Almost all the standard encodings using SGTIN, GRAI, GIAI, SSCC, and the DoD formats are supported out-of-the-box. Each of these formats has a substructure, a serialization or projection to a tag byte array, and a range of available numbers that can be supported. Using these, you get pretty good interoperability with tags from other applications by using one of these standard encodings.

Creating a SGTIN RFID Tag

The *Serialized Global Trade Identification Number* (SGTIN) format is a format that you are likely to encounter in retail supply chain or point-of-sale applications. Here is an example code snippet for creating a SGTIN and serializing it to a tag and then reading the tag back:

```
        private static void WriteSgtin(DeviceConnection
dc)
        {
            var tagId =
HexUtilities.HexDecode("08D89524000000000000000");
            var sgtin =
IdentityEncoding.Parse(epc:tag:sgtin-
96:1.1234567.876543.1234");
            var newTagId = sgtin.GetByteArray();

            var parameters = new
VendorDefinedParameters();
            parameters.InputParameters = new
VendorSpecificInformation();
            parameters.InputParameters["Motorola.TargetTag"] =
tagId;
            dc.WriteTagId(null, newTagId, null, null,
null, parameters);
            Console.WriteLine("Wrote new tag id {0}",
HexUtilities.HexEncode(newTagId));
        }
```

NOTE

In the preceding listing, we use a vendor extension to limit the write to the "target tag" (or the tag explicitly selected). By default, BizTalk RFID attempts to write to all the tags in the field of the reader, which is problematic in deployments where more than one tag can be in the field of the reader at the same time.

```
        private static void
ReadAndParse(DeviceConnection dc)
        {
            foreach (var tag in
dc.GetTags(TagDataSelector.All))
            {
                IdentityEncoding value;
                if (IdentityEncoding.TryParse(tag.GetId(), out value))
                {
                    Console.WriteLine("Decoded tag {0}",
value.ToXml);
                }
            }
        }
```

Filtering on Tags

One of the common operations that you should expect to perform is filtering tag popula-
tions to eliminate tags that are not of interest. BizTalk RFID supports two ways of filtering
tags at the device level: through the `SetReadFilter` command and through an optional tag
ID match pattern. Listing 15.5 shows you how to set up filtering to only look at SGTINs:

LISTING 15.5   Filtering Tags

```
        private void FilterOnSgtinTags(DeviceConnection
dc)
        {
            //filter method 1: by using the
SetReadFilter command
            byte value = 0x30; //the SGTIN prefix of
0011 0000
            byte mask = 0xff;   //consider all the bits
in the first byte
            ByteArrayValueComparisonPattern pattern =
new ByteArrayValueComparisonPattern(
                new[]{value}, new[]{mask}, 0);
            FilterDataSelector selector = new
FilterDataSelector();
            selector.IsId = true;
            ReadFilter filter = new ReadFilter(pattern,
selector, false/*invert*/);
            FilterExpressionTree tree = new
FilterExpressionTree(filter);
            dc.SetReadFilter(tree);
```

```
        //filter method 2: by using a property
supported by the Motorola FX7400 and some other devices
            dc.SetProperty("Event Processing Service",
"Tag ID Match Pattern", "0x30:0xff:0");
        }
```

GPIO Functionality in BizTalk RFID

A common application of RFID is to observe an event from the physical world and take some action in response to it. The form of this action many times is in software, such as triggering an *Electronic Data Interchange* (EDI) message, or a web service call, or a database lookup, or even send an email informing interested parties of the occurrence of the event. Another form of response is hardware integration to provide some direct feedback to the operator on the ground. This could be a light stack or a buzzer or some other kind of alarm.

Most modern RFID readers support this hardware integration through a GPIO bus interface. GPIO stands for *General Purpose Input Output* and is a set of digital lines that are addressable directly by a program. Usually, the lines drive a relay or some other switch, and that in turn powers the equipment to be controlled. Most commonly, the input lines, (that is, the lines that are being watched for state transitions) and the output lines (or the lines that can be set by the reader) are completely separate, and readers come with four to eight input lines and four to eight output lines typically. On most reader platforms, input lines are pure read-only, and output lines are pure write-only.

BizTalk RFID uses the source model to expose the GPIOs on the device as another type of source. Here is a code snippet to view the GPIOs on a device:

LISTING 15.6   Viewing gpio Ports on a Device

```
        private static void
PrintIOPorts(DeviceConnection dc)
        {
            foreach (var sourceProfile in
dc.GetSources())
            {
                //get the source type from the property
profile dictionary
                PropertyKey pk = new PropertyKey(
                    StandardDevicePropertyGroups.Source,
                    SourcePropertyGroup.SourceType);
                object obj;
                if (sourceProfile.Value.TryGetValue(pk,
out obj))
                {
                    SourceType theSourceType =
```

```
(SourceType)obj;
                    if (theSourceType ==
SourceType.IOPort)
                    {
                        Console.WriteLine("Found IOPort
{0}", sourceProfile.Key);
                    }
                }
            }
        }
```

When the IOPort is available, the BizTalk RFID model is to set properties on the source to change the status of the port, as shown in the following code snippet:

```
        private void SetGpio(DeviceConnection dc, bool
enable)
        {
            dc.SetProperty("GPIO",
                StandardDevicePropertyGroups.Source,
                SourcePropertyGroup.PortOutputValue,
                new[] { (byte)(enable?1:0) }, null);
        }
```

NOTE

If you are using GPIOs, it is a good idea to initialize the state of the lines that you are interested in to Off when the device connection is opened. Remember, Off could be Hi or Low state, depending on the device that you are working with. Not doing this could have unintended consequences, such as setting off a buzzer when the device connection is opened because the port is in an unknown state, which could cause a lot of panic in a real deployment.

To work with GPIO functionality, you need to get the pin diagram for the relevant device that you are working with and wire up the appropriate hardware connector from the pin outputs to the sensors that are being actuated by the GPIO lines. Use caution in selecting the sensors and their power supplies to ensure that you do not overload the output power capabilities of the reader.

So far, we have been using the DeviceConnection class to directly interact with RFID devices. This approach is ideally suited if you need to augment an existing application with RF functionality. The DeviceConnection API is hostable in any .NET client, including Windows Forms and Windows Presentation Foundation applications and web applications, in addition to the command-line examples shown earlier. Under the covers, the calls to the DeviceConnection API are sent to the server using *Windows Communication*

Foundation (WCF) calls. So, you can use these APIs to interact with devices that are connected to RFID servers anywhere on your intranet, as long as you can connect to the server over WCF.

Introducing RFID Processes

To support asynchronous scenarios where the application needs to respond to events from devices, BizTalk RFID introduces a new asynchronous application programming model called an RFID process. The RFID process is much like a BizTalk orchestration, in that it is a declarative pipeline definition for event processing. Each pipeline, called a logical source, has a list of event handlers (thankfully called event handlers), and the output from one event handler is chained to the input of the second event handler. Events are assumed to be raised by logical devices and are routed automatically to the first event handler of the pipelines that are interested in that event. If any event handler decides to filter the event by returning a null value, the event is dropped on the floor and processing stops. Given the .NET-centric architecture, the type system that is used to connect event handlers is fully C# based, so the output type of one event handler has to be type compatible with the input type of the next event handler, or a validation error is thrown.

At runtime, the logical devices have to be bound to physical devices, which are real devices that have been discovered and registered with BizTalk RFID. When the process starts, BizTalk RFID automatically opens all the necessary physical devices, and for the lifetime of the process it monitors the health of the associated device connections. If connections go down, the server automatically reconnects. All the events that are delivered by the devices are stored in a per-RFID-process *Microsoft Messaging Queue* (MSMQ).

From a transactionality perspective, the RFID process can be set up in one of three modes:

- ▶ Express
- ▶ Reliable
- ▶ Transactional

These translate roughly to the similar modes available on MSMQ queues. Express mode is the most performant and least reliable; it is appropriate for applications that process a large number of events and throw most of them away. Transactional is the most durable and the most resource intensive; applications that perform a good amount of filtering at the device layer can use Transactional mode to get consistent application semantics with reasonable performance. The Reliable mode is a hybrid of the other two modes.

Scenario Description

In this section, we write an RFID process that extends the Food Inc. scenario in the following way: As goods enter the Food Inc. warehouse (shown in Figure 15.31), they are read at the loading dock logical reader (shown in Figure 15.32). Each read triggers a lookup against an *advance shipment notice* (ASN) in the back-end system, which in turn kicks off the business transaction: Expected items are received automatically; unexpected items are flagged as exceptions.

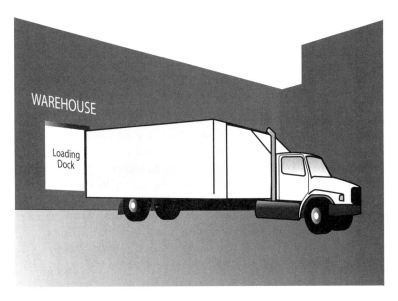

FIGURE 15.31   Receive at loading dock.

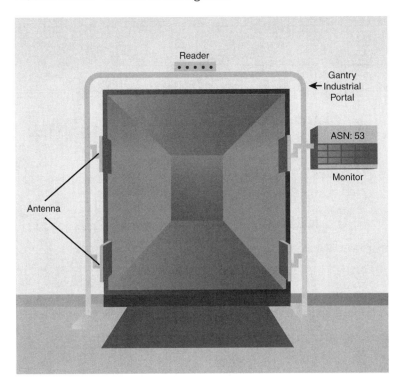

FIGURE 15.32   Receive gantry setup.

15

To provide a real-time view of what is happening, a client application running on a monitor is used to present the information to the loading zone operator. In keeping with the high standards of UI development espoused so far in this chapter, this application is a text-based console application. On a serious note, the choice of the console application is driven by the desire to keep the number of lines of code to a minimum, so you can focus on just the RFID aspects of the application instead of having to wade through pages of UI related code. Finally, a *goods received note* (GRN) is generated and posted to the back-end BizTalk Server for further processing by downstream line-of-business systems such as material management or procurement.

This scenario shown in Figure 15.33 is commonly referred to as *receive against ASN* and is one of the popular reasons to deploy RFID in receiving and shipping zones. Many companies today still do not receive against ASNs but have to back off to secondary mechanisms such as receive against purchase order, receive against dispatch order, or the dreaded blind receive or open receive, where goods are basically just accepted into the warehouse. Using RFID for this task enables automatic visibility of a critical warehouse process with granular information on when the item was received, when it was handled, what the chain of custody was, how damage inspections were done, and so on, resulting in reduced errors and improved labor productivity.

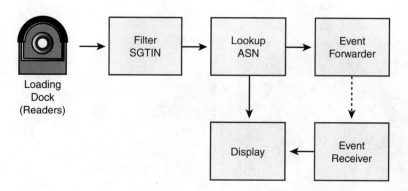

FIGURE 15.33   Application overview.

The heart of this process definition is two event handlers, one that translates RFID tags to SGTINs and the other that looks up the ASN. First, we define these two event handlers.

1. Create a new Visual Studio Class Library project called **ReceiveEventHandlers**.

2. Add references to the following assemblies: `Microsoft.Rfid.SpiSdk`, `Microsoft.Rfid.Design`, `Microsoft.Rfid.Util`, and `Microsoft.Rfid.ObjectModelExtensions`.

3. Create a new class called `TranslateTagToSgtin` that inherits from `RfidEventHandlerBase`.

4. This new event handler takes no parameters for simplicity, and has no initialization that needs to happen, so paste in the following boilerplate:

```
public class TranslateTagToSgtin : RfidEventHandlerBase
{
    #region boilerplate

    public override void Init(Dictionary<string,
object> parameters, RfidProcessContext container)
    {
    }

    public static RfidEventHandlerMetadata
GetEventHandlerMetadata(bool includeVendorExtensions)
    {
        var parameters = new Dictionary<string,
RfidEventHandlerParameterMetadata>();
        var md = new RfidEventHandlerMetadata(
            "Translate TagReadEvents to SGTINs",
            parameters);
        return md;
    }

    #endregion
}
```

5. Write the actual event handler method, using the encoding library, and annotate it with the `RfidEventHandlerMethod` custom attribute:

```
[RfidEventHandlerMethod]
public Sgtin96Encoding
ConvertTagToSgtinOrFilter(TagReadEvent tre)
{
    IdentityEncoding baseEncoding;
    if (IdentityEncoding.TryParse(tre.GetId(),
out baseEncoding)
            && baseEncoding == Sgtin96Encoding)
    {
        return (Sgtin96Encoding) baseEncoding;
    }
    //else filter the event
    return null;
}
```

6. Now do the same thing for the `LookupAsn` event handler. The boilerplate code of populating the `CurrentAsn` with the right tag information to compare against has been omitted for brevity but is available in the full listing of the code.

```
        [RfidEventHandlerMethod]
        public Sgtin96Encoding
ConvertTagToSgtinOrFilter(Sgtin96Encoding sgtin)
        {
            if
(CurrentAsn.Items.ContainsKey(sgtin.ToXml))
            {
                sgtin.VendorSpecificData["Status"] =
"Expected";
            }
            else
            {
                sgtin.VendorSpecificData["Status"] =
"Missing";
            }
            return sgtin;
        }
```

Now for the fun part of creating the RFID process definition.

There are two ways to do it: either through the RFID Process Wizard, or through the design-time APIs. We show you how to do both.

Creating a New RFID Process Definition Using the RFID Process Wizard

1. Choose **New Process** from the Processes node.

2. Fill out the name and description, and make sure that you have the **Start Bind Wizard** option checked, as shown in Figure 15.34.

3. Click past the Introduction screen by clicking **Next**.

4. On the Bind Processes to Logical Devices screen, click **New** to create a new logical device, and name it **Loading Dock Reader**. When you are done, the screen should look like Figure 15.35.

5. Skip past the binding step. (Do not select any physical readers, and click **OK** when the warning shows up that you have an empty binding. Do not worry; we do this later, after our process definition is completed.)

6. Click the **Add Component** option. You will see a list of preregistered event handlers. These are the out-of-box event handlers that ship with BizTalk RFID. Click **Register** to register a new private component. The private part is important. Make sure the radio box is checked correctly (see Figure 15.36).

FIGURE 15.34   The Bind Wizard .for a RFID process

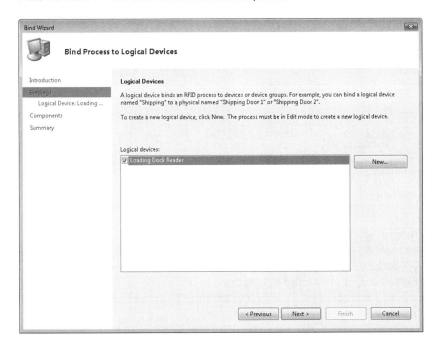

FIGURE 15.35   Create Loading Dock Reader.

NOTE

Private event handlers are defined in assemblies that are private to this RFID process. They are located from the bin directory of the RFID process.

Shared event handlers are defined in assemblies intended to be used by multiple RFID processes. Per Microsoft's recommendation, such shared .NET assemblies should be placed in the machine's *Global Assembly Cache* (GAC).

If the check box is set to Private (while adding an event handler from a private assembly as illustrated earlier), RFID Manager copies the files over to the bin directory; otherwise, it assumes that the DLL is already in the GAC.

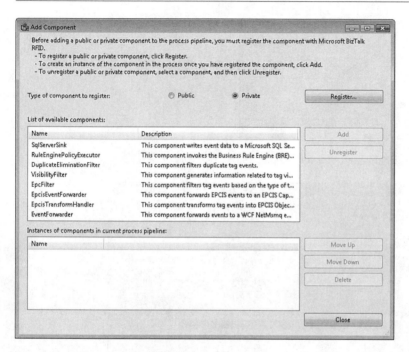

FIGURE 15.36   Register component.

7. Click **Add Files**, browse to the location of the DLL that you created from the event handlers' project, and select the file. All the event handlers defined in that DLL are registered with BizTalk RFID. If you scroll down, you will see the two event handlers that you just created, along with the descriptions that you put in. BizTalk RFID calls the GetEventhandlerMetadata method that you defined in your class to extract the design time metadata for your event handler.

8. Add the TranslateTagToSgtin event handler to the current pipeline by selecting it and clicking the **Add** button, as shown in Figure 15.37.

9. Provide a name for the event handler (shown in Figure 15.38) and click **Accept**. If your event handler has parameters, you fill them out in this Properties box.

10. Repeat the same process for the LookupAsn event handler. The order in which you add event handlers is important because it is a pipeline of event handlers, so you should make sure it is added after the previous event handler.

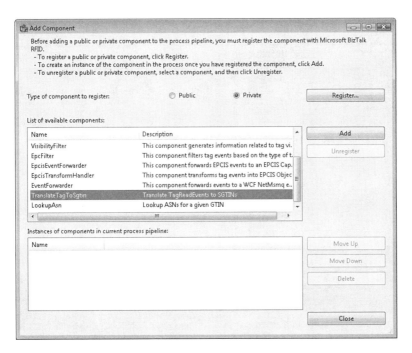

FIGURE 15.37   Add the newly registered event handler.

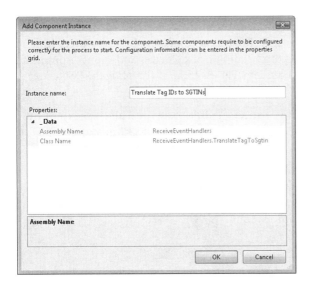

FIGURE 15.38   Naming the newly registered event handler.

11. Add the EventForwarder component to the process pipeline. We use this compo-
    nent, which is new in BizTalk RFID 2010, to support event delivery to the client
    application. It has one mandatory property, the endpoint name. Make sure it is set
    to **SendToMsmq**; as shown in Figure 15.39, this will be important later!

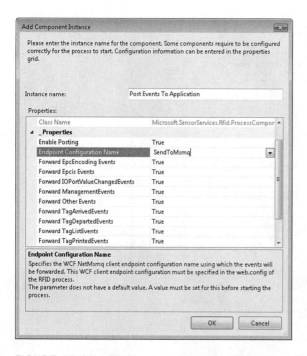

FIGURE 15.39   Add the **EventForwarder** event handler.

12. Click **Close** to exit out of the Add Component step, and click **Next** to finish the wizard. The summary screen for the process shows that it has one logical source, which in turn has one logical device called the Loading Dock Device, and events from that device are delivered to three event handlers. Figure 15.40 is the obligatory screenshot of the process summary.

To confirm that there is indeed a declarative process definition behind all this, export the process definition to a flat file from the **Processes**, **Export** menu selection, and browse the XML file produced.

The XML in all its glory is reproduced in Figure 15.41. You can see it contains all aspects of the process that was just defined. This gives you a definition that you can edit in a pinch if required, but more important, it is a really convenient way to define and distribute process definition with your application package.

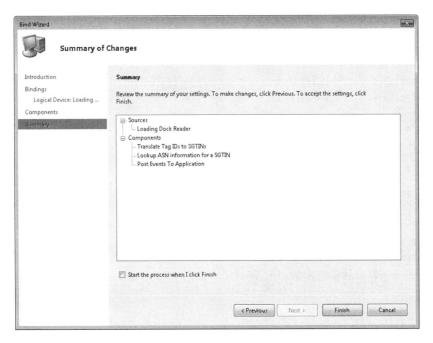

FIGURE 15.40   The summary of the newly created process.

```
- <rm_rfidProcess xmlns:d3p1="http://schemas.datacontract.org/2004/07/Microsoft.SensorServices.Rfid.Design">
    <d3p1:description>Receive-against-ASN</d3p1:description>
  - <d3p1:logicalSource>
    - <d3p1:componentList>
      - <d3p1:EventHandlerDefinition>
          <d3p1:componentName>Translate Tag IDs to SGTINs</d3p1:componentName>
        - <d3p1:eventHandlerInfo>
            <d3p1:assembly>ReceiveEventHandlers</d3p1:assembly>
            <d3p1:className>ReceiveEventHandlers.TranslateTagToSgtin</d3p1:className>
            <d3p1:description>Translate TagReadEvents to SGTINs</d3p1:description>
          </d3p1:eventHandlerInfo>
        </d3p1:EventHandlerDefinition>
      - <d3p1:EventHandlerDefinition>
          <d3p1:componentName>Lookup ASN information for a SGTIN</d3p1:componentName>
        - <d3p1:eventHandlerInfo>
            <d3p1:assembly>ReceiveEventHandlers</d3p1:assembly>
            <d3p1:className>ReceiveEventHandlers.LookupAsn</d3p1:className>
            <d3p1:description>Lookup ASNs for a given GTIN</d3p1:description>
          </d3p1:eventHandlerInfo>
        </d3p1:EventHandlerDefinition>
      - <d3p1:EventHandlerDefinition>
          <d3p1:componentName>Post Events To Application</d3p1:componentName>
        - <d3p1:eventHandlerInfo>
            <d3p1:assembly>Microsoft.Rfid.OobComponents, Version=3.7.0.0, Culture=neutral,
              PublicKeyToken=31bf3856ad364e35</d3p1:assembly>
            <d3p1:className>Microsoft.SensorServices.Rfid.ProcessComponents.EventForwarder</d3p1:className>
            <d3p1:description>This component forwards events to a WCF NetMsmq endpoint. The WCF endpoint is specified by adding a client
              endpoint configuration in the web.config of the process. This client endpoint configuration name should be provided as an event
              handler parameter.</d3p1:description>
          </d3p1:eventHandlerInfo>
        </d3p1:EventHandlerDefinition>
      </d3p1:componentList>
    - <d3p1:logicalDeviceList>
      - <d3p1:LogicalDevice>
          <d3p1:description />
          <d3p1:name>Loading Dock Reader</d3p1:name>
        </d3p1:LogicalDevice>
      </d3p1:logicalDeviceList>
      <d3p1:logicalSourceList />
    </d3p1:logicalSource>
    <d3p1:messageHandlingReliability>Transactional</d3p1:messageHandlingReliability>
    <d3p1:name>MyFirstRFIDProcess</d3p1:name>
```

FIGURE 15.41   The generated process definition XML.

Creating a New RFID Process Definition Programmatically

A more practical way to create processes programmatically is to use the process design APIs. Listing 15.7 shows how to create a process definition.

LISTING 15.7   Process Definition

```
class ProcessHelper
{
    private static EventHandlerInfo
GetEventHandlerInfo(Type t)
    {
        return new
EventHandlerInfo(t.Assembly.FullName, t.FullName);
    }

    public static void CreateProcessDefinition()
    {
        RfidProcess process = new RfidProcess();
        process.Name = "MyFirstRFIDProcess";
        process.LogicalSource.LogicalDeviceList.Add(
            new LogicalDevice("Loading Dock Reader",
null));

        var translateTagToGtin =
GetEventHandlerInfo(typeof (TranslateTagToSgtin));
        var lookupAsn = GetEventHandlerInfo(typeof
(LookupAsn));
        process.LogicalSource.ComponentList.Add(
            new EventHandlerDefinition("Translate
Tag", translateTagToGtin));
        process.LogicalSource.ComponentList.Add(
            new EventHandlerDefinition("Lookup ASN",
lookupAsn));
        //add other event handlers here as needed
    }
}
```

The client part of this application is simple. We have a WCF host that implements
IEventDelivery and writes the event to the console.

The service that implements this contract is shown in Listing 15.8:

LISTING 15.8   Client Application to Write Events to Console

```
public class ShowEvents : IEventDelivery
{
    #region Implementation of IEventDelivery
```

```
    public void OnEvent(object receivedEvent)
    {
        var ev = receivedEvent as RfidEventBase;
        string status = "Unknown";
        object obj;
        if (ev != null && ev.VendorSpecificData.TryGetValue("Status", out obj))
        {
            status = (string) obj;
        }
        Console.WriteLine("Event {0} status {1}",
receivedEvent, status);
    }

    #endregion
}
```

Here is the code snippet for the client program:

```
    private static void Main(string[] args)
    {
        string address =
"net.msmq://localhost/private/MyFirstRFIDProcessForwarde
rQueue";
        var binding = new NetMsmqBinding();
        binding.Security.Mode =
NetMsmqSecurityMode.None;
        binding.ExactlyOnce = false;

        CreateQueueIfNeeded();
        var host = new ServiceHost(typeof
(ShowEvents));
        host.AddServiceEndpoint(typeof
(IEventDelivery), binding, new Uri(address));
        //add Sgln96Encoding to the list of known
types
        foreach (OperationDescription desc in
host.Description.Endpoints[0].Contract.Operations)
        {
            desc.KnownTypes.Add(typeof
(Sgtin96Encoding));
        }
        host.Open();
        Console.WriteLine("Event Receiver is
```

```
running, Hit any key to exit");
        Console.ReadLine();
        host.Close();
    }
```

The preceding lines for adding the Sgtin96Encoding class to the KnownTypes are needed because BizTalk RFID in the beta did not know about this type.

Use the following steps to configure the process to forward events:

1. Find the web.config file for the RFID process. You can find it in the following location: C:\Program Files\Microsoft BizTalk RFID\Processes\MyFirstRFIDProcess\web.config.

2. Edit it to add the SendToMsmq endpoint configuration under the system.ServiceModel configuration section:

```
    <client>
            <endpoint name="SendToMsmq"
                address="net.msmq://localhost/private/MyFirstRFIDProcess
ForwarderQueue"
                binding="netMsmqBinding"
                contract="System.IO.SensorServices.Rfid.Client
                .IEventDelivery"
                bindingConfiguration="eventForwarderBindingConfiguration
"/>
    </client>
```

3. Edit the bindings section of the same configuration file to add the eventForwarderBindingConfiguration:

```
<netMsmqBinding>
    <binding name="eventForwarderBindingConfiguration"
            useActiveDirectory="false"
            exactlyOnce="false">
        <security mode="None"/>
    </binding>
</netMsmqBinding>
```

4. Bind the physical device to the logical device. You can do this through RFID Manager using the **Bind** option on the Process menu, as shown in Figure 15.42.

5. Select the device that you want to bind to the logical device. You will notice that you can select groups of devices or you can even select just an antenna of a particular device. This granularity of binding is the main benefit that you get from the logical to physical device binding step. You can write the code such that the logic is the same regardless of whether you use 1 antenna and 2, 3, or even 10 devices in the real deployment.

6. Start the process. Notice that the device is now in the opened state automatically (shown in Figure 15.43). BizTalk RFID supports a device being opened simultaneously for event delivery and for use by synchronous command applications at the same time.

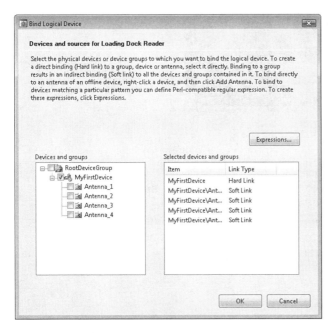

FIGURE 15.42   The device binding step.

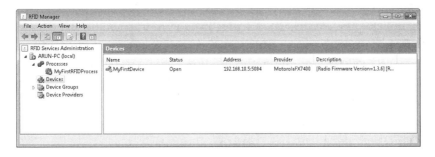

FIGURE 15.43   Automatically opened devices.

At this point, you should be all set. You can run the client and then post events to the process. Running the client produces the output shown in Figure 15.44, assuming you have the appropriate tag in front of the reader.

FIGURE 15.44   Event delivery client output

Modifying an Existing Process Definition

Assume that you would like to extend the preceding scenario in the following way: You can see that the same tag is being observed every 5 seconds in the UI if it happens to be stationary in front of the reader. If you want to change this operation and filter out the same tag if it is seen over a time interval, you can do this using another out-of-the-box event handler called the `DuplicateEliminationFilter`. To add this event handler to your process definition, follow these steps:

1. Stop the process.
2. Right-click the Process menu and pick **Edit**.
3. Identify the logical source and select the **Add New Component** option.
4. Pick the **DuplicateEliminationFilter** component and click **Add**.
5. Enter the appropriate value for the time for which you want it to eliminate duplicates (in this case, 30 seconds).

   The component gets added to the end of this pipeline, but you really need it as the first step in the pipeline for it to perform the role of a filter.
6. Use the **Move Up** option to move it to be the first component.

   When you have finished, the screen must look like Figure 15.45.
7. Use the **Validate** option on the Process menu to validate the change.
8. Start the RFID process.

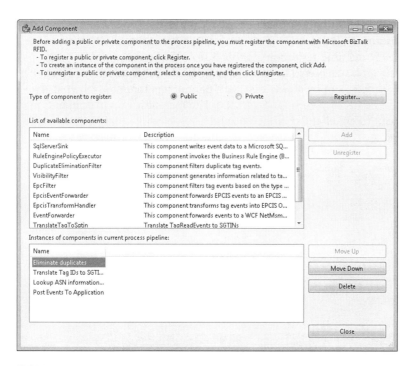

FIGURE 15.45   The modified process definition.

> **NOTE**
>
> You can post events to an RFID process from real devices, but you can also do this from within the RFID Manager using the **Process**, **View Tags**, **Send Tags** option. Another variant is to use the `rfidclientconsole` with the `AddEventToProcessPipeline` option.

Exception Handling

No discussion of programming models is complete without exception handling. In this section, look at how RFID process exceptions are handled.

Whenever an event handler method (that is, a method annotated with the `[RfidEventHandler]` custom attribute) is invoked, the process engine host keeps watch of two conditions:

▶ If any exception is thrown by the code itself, the exception is recorded and surfaced up in RFID Manager.

▶ If the code takes a long time to execute, the event handler invocation is deemed to have "hung," and evasive action is taken.

This evasive action involves aborting the current transaction (if the process is in Transactional mode) and moving the event from the current process queue to the suspended event queue. In queuing terminology, this is *unordered-exactly once-no-retries* semantics. Further, these errors are saved as part of the general health information for the process. Separately, the process can be configured with parameters that control what it means for the process to be healthy with knobs such as the maximum number of exceptions that the process can tolerate, and the maximum amount of time that an event handler can take to execute. Figure 15.46 is the configuration screen for RFID processes.

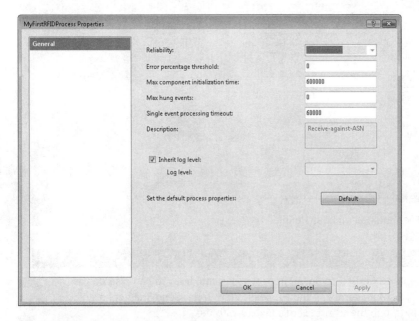

FIGURE 15.46   Error handling configuration

All this flexibility enables the administrator to set the error handling policy to compute the health of the process. When the process is deemed unhealthy, it is restarted automatically.

> **NOTE**
>
> If you notice that your process does not seem to be working correctly, but there is no information in the log files, check the most recent logs. The automatic restart has the unfortunate side effect that the log file that contains the exception is no longer the current log file.

For device operations, the model is similar to how Windows deals with driver calls. Each call to the device happens through a web service call, and when the invocation reaches the server, it is scheduled to be executed in its own thread. This thread is allowed a configurable amount of time within which it has to complete. Calls that don't complete in this time are presumed to have failed, and action is automatically taken. A provider that has too many such calls that failed is also deemed to be unhealthy and is recycled.

Debugging (Process Hosting Model)

Hand in hand with exception handling is debugging. To effectively debug the RFID process, you need to be aware of the hosting model. BizTalk RFID is designed to operate in two modes: in Desktop mode and in Server mode. On Windows Vista and Windows 7, it is in Desktop mode; and on Windows Server 2008 and Windows Server 2008 R2, it is in Server mode.

In Desktop mode, all providers and processes are hosted within the MSRFIDServices NT Service. Each process and each provider is hosted in its own application domain, with its own application configuration file. The application configuration file is called web.config, for reasons that will become obvious when we describe the server hosting policy. In Desktop mode, when a process or provider is deemed unhealthy, it is shut down, the application domain is shut down, but the NT service keeps running. Unhealthy processes and providers that leak unmanaged resources, for example, can thus affect their neighbors, because they all run in the same sandbox, so to speak.

In contrast, the server version of BizTalk RFID isolates each provider and each RFID process into its own Win32 process. To do this, it utilizes IIS as the application host along with the controls exposed by IIS for application pool management. To debug processes on Windows Server, you need to first find the w3svc.exe process that is hosting your code and then attach to it.

Other than the debugging experience, there should be no difference in the model between desktop and server, but in practice, the use of IIS comes with its own set of peculiarities to be aware of, such as the need to configure IIS correctly with the right version of ASP.NET, the need to correctly configure WCF services for hosting in IIS, the interaction with other system components such as antivirus scanners or instances of SharePoint Server. We do not go into these issues in any depth here, but suffice to say, if your RFID application encounters an HTTP 500 Service Unavailable error, IIS configuration might be the source of the problem. The BizTalk RFID documentation has a number of useful suggestions on how to troubleshoot faulty IIS installations and rectify them.

Integration and Deployment Considerations

As you have seen in this chapter, BizTalk RFID offers a very .NET-centric event-based programming model. The resultant application runs on the edge of the enterprise (that is, in the actual warehouse where the goods are being received) or in the factory floor that you are trying to monitor from a work-in-process perspective or within the retail store in which the RFID-based inventory tracking is happening. To be fair, multiple deployment architectures are possible, including a hub-and-spoke architecture (as illustrated in Figure 15.47) where the spoke includes an instance of BizTalk RFID that controls the devices locally, or a central hub instance with just the RFID readers at the edge. This flexibility in the architecture is powerful but is also one of the sources of confusion when you are designing a BizTalk-based RFID application.

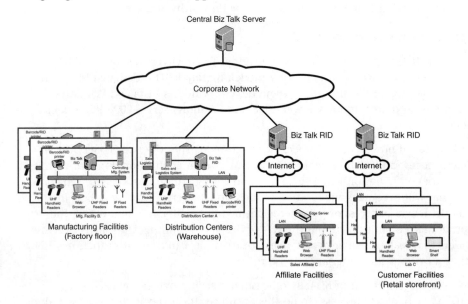

Deployment Topologies Overview

FIGURE 15.47   Deployment Topologies Overview

The central model has the advantage of running all the pieces of software within a centrally administered data center type of environment and also lets you make use of a central SQL server instance that you might already have setup with high availability, disaster recovery, and automated administration, which are all huge assets to leverage. The trade-offs typically come down to three things: the reliability of the network between the warehouse and the central server, the latency of operations, and the trust relationship, if you will, between the warehouse and the central operations.

In most modern logistics operations, Internet connectivity between edge and server can usually be assumed, but in many instances, the links are being used currently for operations such as email and batch transfers of orders and fulfillment responses. Using this network connection for your RFID application running centrally means that each relevant tag read has to be surfaced up to the central application and the response from the application has to be sent back to the UI. When the network is down, the RFID-enabled operations are not available. From a latency perspective, if you are planning to show the results of an RFID tag read on a display, a round trip of more than a second is usually considered unacceptable by your users. Achieving this level of responsiveness from a central deployment requires a fast network, and also a finely tuned RF deployment where tag reads are filtered on the reader appropriately.

To elaborate a bit on the trust relationship issues between the central server and the warehouse, if your scenario involves 3PLs (*third-party logistics companies*) or vendor-managed inventory, the warehouse automation system might be running on a computer network that is actually not part of your corporate network at all. Granting devices on that network access to your central corporate IT managed assets might be a nonstarter from a practical perspective.

For all these reasons, the edge deployment architecture has some natural advantages over the central model, but it does come with its own set of design considerations. In the edge architecture, the BizTalk RFID instance is running on a computer that is physically in the warehouse, and has access to a SQL Server instance typically running on the same box, or within the warehouse also (assuming they have an existing instance). So, if you have four warehouses, for example, you would have four edge instances of BizTalk RFID all talking to a central server. There are two considerations that you need to think about upfront in this architecture:

- ▶ The integration architecture
- ▶ The deployment architecture

Both of these topics are deep subjects that deserve their own chapter and are more of an administrative nature. In the interest of brevity and sticking to the development scenarios, we provide only brief overviews of the approach rather than deep-dive walkthroughs.

Integration considerations for the edge server deployment involve the following:

- ▶ How much business logic is actually implemented within the edge server as opposed to the central server. For example, in our automatic inventory receipt scenario, the edge server could be a relatively simple system that observes tag reads and triggers central processing using a BizTalk server orchestration, or it could be a more complicated scenario where the tag read is interpreted locally with or without local user intervention. In our experience, it is almost always the latter: Deploying RFID within your receive operations lets you react to physical goods movement in a real-time fashion as opposed to a batch-oriented scheme. The benefit of the RFID system is not limited to just automated data entry (which is really important for scenarios such as automatic billing, or automatic available-to-promise inventory systems), but also control. The control typically takes the form of a stack-light or a buzzer or a direct visual feedback to the warehouse operator on a computer display. This lets them catch problems such as incomplete receive, wrong receive, expired product, damaged product, and other exception conditions at the point where they occur. For such real-time applications, we recommend packaging up the logic for local execution, rather than a central round trip for each relevant tag read considering the added latency. To implement this functionality, you need to think about the business context that will have to be available on the edge to make the determination of the exception condition. This business context has to flow down from the central hub to the spoke server. Usually we see a combination of database replication, message queues, and flat files to accomplish this download flow of information.

▶ The upload of information back to the central server usually is performed in near real time, using web services or equivalent remote procedure calls. The out-of-the-box functionality for persistence of events as rows in database tables (using the SQL sink component) and as messages posted to MSMQ are two ways of exporting data out of the BizTalk RFID server. You also always have the option of making a call to a BizTalk Server WCF endpoint. All three of these mechanisms are essentially native BizTalk Server integration mechanisms, which mean no new adapters, connectors, or components have to be learned to integrate messages from the RFID server. Which mechanism is best for you really depends on both the degree of loose coupling desired and the acceptable latency. If near real-time response is required (say on the order of a few seconds) for an action in BizTalk Server in response to an RFID event, the WCF route is the best option. MSMQ gives you the benefits of loose coupling and delivery even if the server is temporarily unreachable, while not significantly changing the latency. The database integration is ideal for situations where the controlling application might want to query over the RFID event stream instead of processing each event sequentially that the message queue model would enable.

▶ Security. If the hub and spoke are not located within the same enterprise, we see that flat file exchange via FTP or similar mechanisms, and web service invocations are the most appropriate mechanisms to streamline the communication. In such cross-enterprise scenarios, there are usually less-stringent assumptions regarding latency, but there is a lot more emphasis on the security of information exchanged. It is also fairly common for the hub in the cross-enterprise scenario to be a SharePoint-based portal application rather than a central instance of BizTalk Server.

In the following paragraphs, you will look at the deployment considerations for RFID applications. To start with, the bad news is that RFID applications are not covered by the BizTalk Server deployment architecture. You cannot leverage the deployment tools that you use for other BizTalk Server applications. Instead, with a good understanding of the application artifacts involved, you need to craft up a deployment strategy for your application and implement it using standalone scripts and Microsoft Systems Center (SCOM and SCCM), assuming the customer is already running Systems Center, or the deployment is large enough to warrant them moving to Systems Center for this application.

The main artifacts in an RFID deployment consist of the following:

▶ **Device providers:** Each type of device that you are planning to use will come with a device provider that will have to be installed on each edge server. Device providers are like device drivers, so like device drivers you will get periodic updates from your device vendor that you will have to distribute and apply on all the spoke servers in your enterprise.

▶ **Device provider settings:** Each device provider will come with a set of settings for configuring things such as the port to use for device discovery, the frequency of discovery, and so on. You should manage these settings centrally, and again distribute them to each spoke server.

▶ **Device profiles:** Each device that is part of your application scenario will be operating in a particular role, such as a portal reader, a desktop pad, and so on. Each such role requires setting the device configuration including power and other parameters that control readability. BizTalk RFID has a concept of named device profiles that let a device be initialized with a known set of properties that can be administered centrally.

▶ **Device firmware:** Sometimes you will have to perform a firmware update of the device itself. This will usually be to resolve a problem condition or to add support for a new tag feature. Ensuring that all your devices are running the correct version of firmware, and updating the devices in an automated fashion when a new firmware update is available, is critical to a successful RFID deployment.

▶ **Application components:** These are the DLLs that you develop to implement the custom event handlers and RFID business processes. They are no different than distributing any other piece of software within your corporate network. You should follow standard .NET conventions for versioning, strong name signing, and deployment through a package such as an MSI.

▶ **Application settings:** The event handlers have custom knobs that you implement to control aspects such as the specific database instance you want the event handlers to use, for example. You can store and distribute these settings (called process bindings in BizTalk RFID vernacular) centrally.

All the management tasks, including the configuration of device settings and process bindings, can be done using the rfidclient console command-line utility. By using the client console, and XML-based application files that contain the stored settings, you can perform automated installation in a centralized fashion. BizTalk RFID comes with three samples that will you'll find very useful to delve deeper into the topics discussed in this section: one that shows you how to implement a BizTalk orchestration with a WCF adapter endpoint that you can call from within an RFID event handler, an event handler that lets you post an event to an MSMQ queue, and a sample that shows you how to use the SQL Server sink to persist events to a local SQL Server database.

15

Summary

In this chapter, we have covered the basic steps of creating RFID aware applications. We explored both kinds of application models, standalone applications and hosted RFID business processes. We saw how standalone applications use the DeviceConnection API and the synchronous command programming model to accomplish common tasks such as opening and closing connections to devices and reading / writing tag ids. We created a hosted RFID business process for receiving items at a warehouse loading dock against an ASN. Through this we explored the declarative nature of RFID processes including the design time support in the RFID Manager, and developed a custom event handler for processing events raised by RFID devices through a series of pipelined event handler components. We also saw the separation between logical and physical devices, and discussed integration and deployment considerations for RFID scenarios. In the next chapter, we will explore how the BizTalk RFID Mobile platform allows you to write applications on mobile devices and work in concert with applications on the server.

CHAPTER 16

BizTalk RFID Mobile

The preceding chapter covered the desktop *radio frequency ID* (RFID) functionality. This chapter drills into the development of mobile RFID applications.

You continue with the Food Inc. scenario and write a cycle-counting application using BizTalk RFID Mobile. Along the way, you look at the many similarities in the architecture between the desktop and mobile platforms, contrasted with some of the key differences that you need to be aware of.

Given the emphasis on passive *Ultra High Frequency* (UHF) technologies in the preceding chapter, this chapter focuses on passive HF technology on the handheld reader.

Again, you should have access to a real handheld reader to walk through the examples in this book; the examples work best with the Motorola 3090Z UHF and Unitech PA600 HF readers because these are the mobile devices used to create the examples. It is an interesting testament to the uniform device abstraction capabilities of BizTalk RFID Mobile that the application will run essentially unchanged with a Motorola UHF RFID Scanner, as well as on a Unitech HF RFID scanner.

Mobile RFID Overview

Most of the first wave of RFID technologies focused on fixed reader technology, such as long-range scanners and portal readers. As the scenarios evolved, particularly in logistics, healthcare, and retail, hardware providers realized that long-range RFID is often used in conjunction with human data entry and decision making. Often, this is in the context of exception handling or problem solving, where wirelessly connected barcode scanners have gained ubiquitous adoption. For RFID tagged items, a similar capability was found to be almost mandatory in most production deployments.

Similarly, in many field service scenarios, such as maintenance, inspection, or mobile servicing, a mobile RFID solution offers significant advantages over fixed readers from a practical deployment perspective. The combination of low cost, rugged scanners with long battery life, and a number of connectivity options, including Bluetooth, WiFi, GPRS, and 3G, makes it attractive for any number of applications. Sample scenarios include stock taking and inventory verification, parking enforcement, and yard management, to mention a few.

The holy grail of mobile RFID is consumer scenarios that involve smart phones and similar high-end cell phones and PDAs for applications such as consumer interactivity or product advertisement. Even the most ardent proponents agree, however, that the killer app for consumer RFID is yet to be discovered.

The BizTalk RFID Mobile Framework

BizTalk RFID Mobile carries forward many of the core concepts of the desktop product, including the core mission of enabling applications that can work with a rich set of devices. The key here is not to make applications "device agnostic" with some least common denominator interface, but to make sure that rich applications can take care of all the capabilities of a device, while retaining a single consistent model for the things that do not have to change, like connection management.

In practice, the desktop *device service provider interface* (DSPI) specification and interface is part of BizTalk RFID Mobile in a 100% compatible manner. This compatibility enables some interesting scenarios; for example, providers can be developed that share a single code base across BizTalk RFID desktop and mobile and are supported on both platforms with minimal code changes. This, of course, requires the underlying device protocols to be similar on both desktop and mobile platforms.

However, some key differences exist between the desktop and mobile products, both architecturally and from a functionality perspective. Architecturally, the desktop product supports the client *application programming interface* (API) over web services, and the providers are hosted by BizTalk RFID in a separate Win32 process. The mobile product does not have this separation; the client API is a thin wrapper over the BizTalk RFID functionality that is directly hosted within the client application. This in-proc model has a number of benefits, including smaller memory footprint, lower resource utilization, lower latency, and faster speed of operations, but it comes with a huge implication: At any time, only one application can work with a device. For a mobile platform, this is not actually a serious limitation, but it is one that you need to be aware of. The other major implication is that an error in the provider can cause your application to be affected, and vice versa.

Functionally, here is the bad news first: There is no hosted RFID process + event handler programming model on the mobile platform. The reasons are similar to what is listed previously: The lightweight nature of the CE platform precludes any server-like functionality and promotes an API approach instead of adding services. This means the mobile application model is strictly restricted to what you can do with the DeviceConnection API. On the positive side, a number of enhancements are directly targeted at mobile application development, including the following:

- Asynchronous event delivery through the `DeviceConnection` class

- Support for barcode scanners

- Support for triggers

- Services for store and forward of tag events to a desktop BizTalk RFID server

- Services for local storage of tag events in a SQL CE database.

- Services for remote manageability of the RFID device through a desktop RFID manager

---

NOTE

Mobile hardware selection is a tricky topic; you have to consider the hardware technical feature set, *user interface* (UI) ergonomics, and the weight and balance of the device. UI ergonomics will depend a lot on how the device is going to be used, the items that are going to be scanned, how far away the person who is scanning has to be, and so on.

Unlike the fixed reader selection, RF performance is many times not the dominant criterion for the choice, with additional factors such as connectivity options and battery life playing a significant part. Often, all these variables are not understood at the start of the project, which is an excellent reason to ensure you have the flexible application architecture to accommodate changes in hardware even late in the cycle. On the good-news front, the choice of available mobile hardware is only increasing, with devices from more than 20 vendors commercially available at the time of this writing.

Installation Notes

There is a desktop setup file and *Microsoft Installer file* (.MSI) for the mobile product, which installs the *software development kit* (SDK) and documentation on the local machine, along with the *cabinet* (.CAB) files required for device installation. The SDK files are installed at C:\Program Files\Microsoft BizTalk RFID\SDK\Mobile\v1.1\bin.

BizTalk RFID Mobile comes packaged as a .CAB file that can be downloaded and installed onto the device. It has two different flavors, the WM or Windows Mobile 6 option and the WCE or Windows CE 5.0 option; you can find these at C:\Program Files\Microsoft BizTalk RFID\SDK\Mobile\v1.1\bin\wce500\armv4i directory.

Some of the major prerequisites include .NET Compact Framework (version 2.0 SP2 or 3.5), and SQL Server CE 3.5. The best way to install the mobile product in Development mode

is to have a directory handy on the server with all the CABs available for the right platform and just copy over and install the CABs interactively. Especially during Development
mode, where you might be uninstalling and installing different versions of software, you
should be prepared to do a fresh install onto a device that has been cold booted.

> **NOTE**
>
> A number of features in BizTalk RFID Mobile have companion features on the desktop,
> so Microsoft has decided that the desktop and mobile products must have the same
> version to interoperate. This does require more planning during the provisioning phase
> but eliminates a number of interesting test configurations related to mismatched
> mobile and desktop versions.

Device Applications

The DeviceConnection API and the synchronous command invocation model are identical between desktop and mobile, so this should be a short section. The exact same code
that was written in the preceding chapter to read tags from a device should compile with
mobile, too.

> **NOTE**
>
> One source of terminology confusion introduced by the uniform desktop programming
> model is the word *device*. In the mobile vernacular, device usually refers to the mobile
> device itself. In the RFID APIs, the term device is intended to describe the RFID func-
> tionality, so you should map this term to the RF module.

This chapter focuses on an application scenario that builds on the Food Inc. supply chain
theme. Consider that you have a warehouse aisle with racks and shelves that have product
stocked on them. Your goal is to inventory the products on the shelves to determine the
actual quantity on hand, as shown in Figures 16.1 and 16.2. You can easily extend this
scenario to other interesting variations, such as searching for a particular product or identifying groups of items that match some criteria, which are both real-world warehouse
execution scenarios.

To keep the focus on the part of the code that needs to interact with the RFID Mobile
APIs, a minimal UI concept is presented.

Here is the code snippet for an application to read tags on demand from a device.

The first snippet of code shown is to find the radio module on the handheld reader and
use it. Because most handhelds will have just one module, there is no need to discover
and embed its name in the code.

```
        var deviceManager = new
DeviceManagerProxy();
        var devices = deviceManager.GetAllDevices();
        if (devices.Length < 1)
```

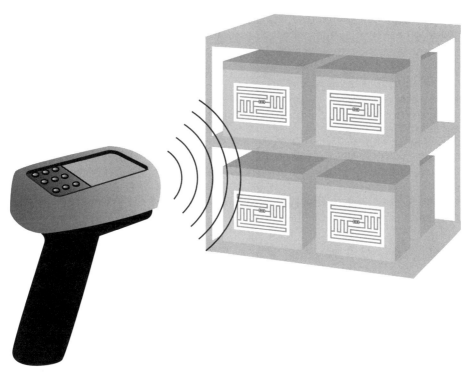

FIGURE 16.1   Stocktaking.

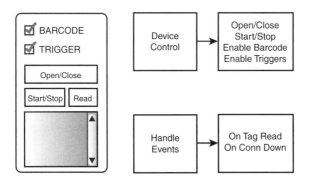

FIGURE 16.2   Application overview.

```
{
    MessageBox.Show("No RFID module found");
    return;
}
string deviceName = devices[0].Name;
```

When the device name is known, opening a connection to the device is the same process as on the desktop. However, after the device is opened, you can register for notifications from the device by just using a C# event handler for it, as shown in the following code snippet:

```
        MyDeviceConnection = new
DeviceConnection(deviceName);
        MyDeviceConnection.NotificationEvent += HandleEvent;
        MyDeviceConnection.Open();
```

The next snippet of code is to identify the RFID antenna of the RFID module (as opposed to the barcode module):

```
        var sources = MyDeviceConnection.GetSources();
        foreach (var pair in sources)
        {
            //no better way to distinguish barcode
sources
            if (pair.Key.ToLower().Contains("barcode"))
            {
                continue;
            }
            var profile = pair.Value;
            object obj;
            if (profile.TryGetValue(
                new

PropertyKey(

StandardDevicePropertyGroups.Source,




SourcePropertyGroup.SourceType), out obj))

                {
                    if ((
SourceType)obj ==




SourceType.Antenna)

                    {
                        RfidSourceName = pair.Key;
```

```
                    break;
                }
            }
        }
```

Again, you can see the similarity between the desktop code and the mobile code.

Finally, you can see that the device connection supports duplicate elimination directly, through the following property:

```
MyDeviceConnection.DuplicateEliminationInterval = 1000;
```

At this point, the device connection is open for business.

The following code snippet shows the user how to enable a device to read tags continuously after it's open.

```
        private void SetEnableContinuousRead(bool
enable)
        {
            if (EnsureOpen())
            {
                MyDeviceConnection.SetProperty(
                    RfidSourceName,

StandardDevicePropertyGroups.Source,


SourcePropertyGroup.ContinuousRead,

                    enable,
                    false /*applyOnReopen*/,
                    null);
            }
        }
```

When you are done, you must close the device connection, just like you would have to do on the desktop. In this case, you have one additional step of unregistering the C# event handler as follows.

```
        MyDeviceConnection.NotificationEvent -=
HandleEvent;
        MyDeviceConnection.Close();
        MyDeviceConnection = null;
```

By default, the device connection does not continuously perform tag inventory operations. There are two reasons for this: One is power management; the other is performance. Most RFID devices on the market are efficient at managing power consumption, specifically when the RF is off. For example, the Motorola MC9090 easily lasts a full shift of

16

8 hours on one battery. If the RF is on continuously, however, the battery must be changed after 2.5 hours or so. The preferred way to manage the RF module is by use of the trigger functionality described in the following code snippet

```
private void SetTriggerAction(string action)
{
    if (EnsureOpen())
    {
        MyDeviceConnection.SetProperty(

StandardDevicePropertyGroups.Notification,


NotificationPropertyGroup.OnTriggerPull,

            action);
    }
}
```

The OnTriggerPull property is a new addition to BizTalk RFID Mobile. It determines the action that the provider should take when the user pulls the trigger. It can have one of the following values, as defined by the TriggerAction property:

▶ ScanRfid

▶ ScanBarcode

▶ ScanBoth

▶ ScanNone

The meanings are self-explanatory.

This paradigm is new to BizTalk RFID Mobile. In the desktop, there is no notion of asynchronous event delivery through the device connection API. However, on CE, because the provider is in-proc with the client API, the convenient way to subscribe to events from the device is through the C# event handler mechanism. In this application, the event in the text box displays. Because the text box is a Windows Forms control, it can be accessed only on the UI thread. The HandleEvent method (shown in the following code snippet) is invoked directly by BizTalk RFID Mobile, so it needs to use the BeginInvoke mechanism on the TextBox control to post the update.

```
private void HandleEvent(object sender,


NotificationEventArgs args)

    {
```

```
        var theEvent = args.Notification.Event;

Action toBeInvoked = () => UpdateTextBox(theEvent.ToString());

        tbStatus.BeginInvoke(toBeInvoked);
    }

    private void UpdateTextBox(string message)
    {
        tbStatus.Text += (
Environment.NewLine + message);

        tbStatus.Refresh();
    }
```

The following code snippet performs the action of reading tags on demand; the exact code as the desktop version will work on the handheld.

```
        var tags =
MyDeviceConnection.GetTags(
TagDataSelector.All);

        foreach (
TagReadEvent tre in tags)

        {
            //handle the tag event in the usual way
            HandleEvent(this, new
NotificationEventArgs(new

Notification(tre)));

        }
```

Running Your First Mobile Application

This example uses the MC 3090Z handheld reader from Motorola. You can, of course, use any handheld for which a device provider exists. The steps involve installing a device provider, discovering or adding the device to the system and then interacting with the RF module. The next section goes through the setup and operation of the MC 3090Z.

Installing the Device Provider on the MC 3090Z

Use the mobile version of the RFID Manager, called the RFID Manager Mobile for this operation. The steps are as follows:

1. Click **Add** on the Providers tab (shown in Figure 16.3).

FIGURE 16.3   Installing the MC3090Z provider.

2. Browse to the provider DLL (called Motorolala3090ProviderCe for this device).

3. Click **OK** to register the provider. You should see a confirmation dialog that the provider was registered and started successfully, as shown in Figures 16.4 and 16.5.

FIGURE 16.4   Load the provider DLL.

FIGURE 16.5   Confirmation screen for loading the provider.

Discovering the Device

The same discovery model holds for the mobile platform. You can initiate a `TriggerDiscovery` operation by switching to the Devices tab and clicking the **Discover** menu option. After the device is discovered and added successfully, you should see the status shown in Figure 16.6 on the Devices tab. Unlike the desktop version, no additional step is required to configure the discovered device; it is automatically added in the Enabled state.

FIGURE 16.6   Device discovery.

> **NOTE**
>
> The RFID Manager Mobile does not support manually adding devices. If your scenario requires manual addition, you can do it programmatically using the DeviceManagerProxy API.

Running the Program

Now that you have a device discovered and configured with BizTalk RFID Mobile, you can execute the program that you created earlier. And if there is a tag in front of the reader, you should see the output from the program (see Figure 16.7).

FIGURE 16.7   Program output.

Advanced Device Programming

At this point, you have seen how to perform basic operations with the RF module such as opening the module, setting up inventory, and reading tags either continuously or based on a trigger pull. You could also choose to execute a variety of device commands, such as a "synchronous" `GetTagsCommand`, or the lower-level operations for reading and writing user data on the tag, or protecting the memory area for appropriate use through the commands to lock and unlock regions on the tag.

You generally have to take some application-level action in response to the tag read, and in many mobile scenarios, that involves storing the tag for transmission either to a central database or to an application component. Both of these are supported by BizTalk RFID Mobile out-of-the-box.

Barcode Support

One of the enhancements in BizTalk RFID Mobile is the support for barcodes. On the desktop, barcodes are typically handled through keyboard wedges or other programs that make barcodes identical to input from a keyboard. On the handheld, with BizTalk RFID Mobile, you have the same object model and consistent set of APIs for both RFID tags and barcodes. This mainstream support from Microsoft has been a long time coming, considering how long Windows CE-based handheld devices have been around, but it is welcome nonetheless.

To configure the device to read barcodes, you can use the `TriggerAction` property and set it to `Barcode` (or to `Both`, if you want to scan for both tag types simultaneously).

Here is a code snippet to process a tag read event and return the barcode representation for it.

```
    private string GetKey(
TagReadEvent tre)

    {
        if (tre.Type ==
TagType.Barcode)

        {
            object obj;
            if
(tre.VendorSpecificData.TryGetValue(
BarcodeConstants.Sca

nDataLabel, out obj))
            {
                return (string) obj;
            }
        }
        return
HexUtilities.HexEncode(tre.GetId());

    }
```

Note that in general you should not make any assumptions about the barcode scan label; it could be any number of alphanumeric characters, and some symbols as seen in Figure 16.8. To interpret the barcode, you can also use the BarcodeType vendor extension, which is expected to return the symbology, if present.

There are a couple advantages to using the Triggered mode for reading tags rather than Continuous mode: In Triggered mode, the RF module can efficiently manage the amount of power consumed by turning on the RF only when the trigger is pressed and shutting it off as soon as it is released. More important, application users can control when they want to actually read tags by just using the trigger on the device.

FIGURE 16.8   Reading barcodes from BizTalk RFID Mobile.

The alternative is to have a button in the application that users can push whenever they need to read a tag. The button approach is a two-handed operation: one to hold the unit, and the other to push the button and release it. The trigger pull is easily accomplished as a one-handed operation, however. Note that if the use case is laid out slightly differently, and the application user is expected to scan a large number of units, such as during an audit of a store, you might want to consider a different design. Keeping the trigger pressed continuously for long periods of time (typically more than just a few seconds) could also have ergonomic implications, and here the preferred approach might be a button push to start inventory (after which the RF operation is essentially hands free).

The preceding paragraph is just intended to illustrate that a large part of the application design for a handheld RFID application must involve a good understanding of the physical environment in which the device is going to be used.

BizTalk RFID Mobile Connector Architecture (Store and Forward)

Microsoft has decided to use the DSPI provider model as the way to integrate mobile RFID devices with the server architecture. This makes for a consistent end-to-end story, which also leverages a number of existing moving parts, such as RFID Manager for device administration. However, it can be confusing until you get your head around it. In this section, you look at how the components are designed to fit together; now begin by working your way up from the "Mobile" block in Figure 16.9.

Assume that you are running on the Unitech PA600 handheld reader that has a HF RFID module in it. The Unitech provider is the component that implements the DSPI and talks to the radio module underneath directly. Above the DSPI, the mobile APIs are responsible for implementing the DeviceConnection object model for application usage. The RFIDServerConnector is a component that is part of the mobile installation, and it talks to the radio module using the DeviceConnection API. The *Low Level Reader Protocol* (LLRP) server component is the key piece that enables the device to communicate with clients that implement LLRP. Not coincidentally, the desktop product includes an LLRP device provider (that is, a provider that can communicate with any LLRP-compliant device and surface it up to the rest of BizTalk RFID as a regular device). Way up top, RFID Manager interacts with the device, being completely provider agnostic.

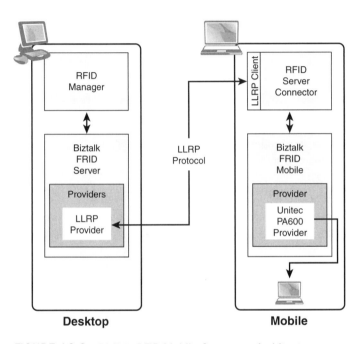

FIGURE 16.9   BizTalk RFID Mobile Connector Architecture

Phew, that was a lot of plumbing, so what does this architecture really enable?

▶ It enables a "remote management" experience, where you can use RFID Manager on the desktop to manage your handheld device.

You can treat your mobile device as yet another reader within BizTalk RFID and consume the events from the reader using desktop event handler components. This is powerful because it enables your components to work seamlessly with mobile devices without writing any code that runs on the device. That's right, you heard it first here: If you want to use your mobile device just as a data collection terminal and pass on RFID tag reads to your server application, you can do this with no code.

▶ Building on this concept, you can even post this event directly to an *Electronic Product Code Information Service* (EPCIS)-compliant service running in the cloud. In reality, if you need to annotate the event with some additional business context, you can do so using a custom component and then post the event. However, it is nice to have this "device to cloud" capability out-of-the-box.

Store-and-Forward Connectivity

The `RFIDServerConnector` object model enables persistence of events into a local SQL database on the device, and then sending the events to the server when network connectivity is established. You now have yet another option to implement store and forward in addition to flat file transfer, SQL replication, and *Microsoft Message Queuing* (MSMQ). You can use the `RFIDServerConnector` and LLRP to inject messages directly into your BizTalk RFID server-side process. The key benefit of using this mechanism is that it enables the events to be automatically processed by the same code that you already have on the server for processing events from fixed RFID readers. The downside is that if you have no BizTalk RFID process running and you connect to the device (say from RFID Manager for browsing properties), events that were stored on the device are not delivered to your process.

NOTE

If you are going to use BizTalk RFID store and forward, ensure that your BizTalk RFID process is running before you connect to the device.

You can use the Read Tags application to post tags from the device to the server using this new store-and-forward mechanism.

1. Create a simple RFID process, add a SQL Server sink event handler to it, and bind it to the Pocket_PC device that was discovered previously. When you have finished, the process definition should look like what you see in Figure 16.10.

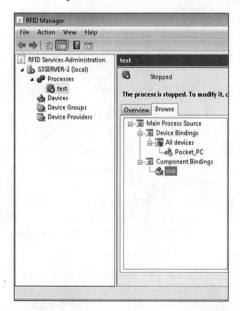

FIGURE 16.10   Create a new RFID process.

2. Start the Read Tags application on the handheld device (see Figure 16.11) and enable events to be posted from it.

3. Verify that the tags have reached the process, as shown in Figure 16.12.

That's it! You've now gone from reading a tag via the mobile hand-held and posted this successfully to the a server or desktop application to process further—the most basic and common mobile application for RFID tag processing.

FIGURE 16.11   Start the Read Tags application.

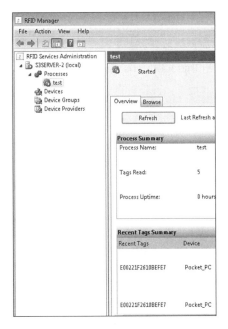

FIGURE 16.12   Refresh the process status to view tags.

Remote Device Management

This section looks at the remote device management functionality in BizTalk RFID Mobile 2010. You can use the Unitech PA 600 HF handheld terminal (shown in Figure 16.13) for illustrative purposes.

FIGURE 16.13   The Unitech PA600 HF handheld terminal.

1. Launch the RFID Manager Mobile tool on the handheld and enable remote management, as shown in Figure 16.14.

FIGURE 16.14   Enable remote management.

2. Ensure that the LLRP provider is running on the desktop and that port 5084 allows inbound access at the firewall. (5084 is the IANA-reserved port for LLRP.) If all goes well, you should see an entry for your mobile device, as shown in Figure 16.15.

3. Pick the device in RFID Manager and enable it. (You can leave the username and password blank.)

FIGURE 16.15   Discover mobile device.

4. Right-click the device and browse Properties (shown in Figure 16.16). You can see that there are three sets of properties: one from the LLRP provider, which views the device as an LLRP device (you can safely ignore this set of properties); standard BizTalk RFID Mobile settings; and finally, the actual properties exposed by the radio module. The last two sets are typically the ones you administer.

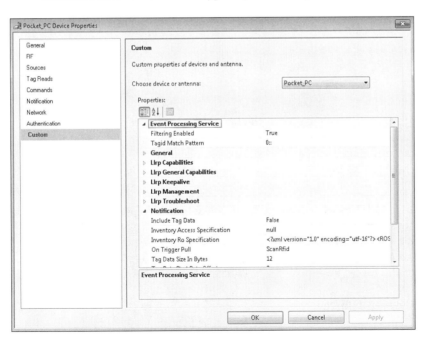

FIGURE 16.16   View device properties.

5. Pick the antenna and examine its properties, as shown in Figure 16.17. Note that the name of the antenna is massaged by the LLRP subsystem. In this case, the antenna on the device was called RFID, but when viewed through RFID Manager, it is called Antenna_0.

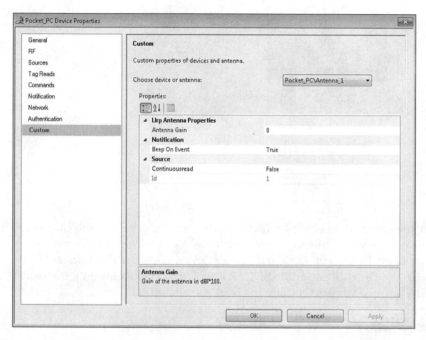

FIGURE 16.17   View source properties.

Summary

You have taken a tour of the key features of the BizTalk RFID Mobile platform, including the concepts that are common between the desktop and mobile editions. You created a small application to introduce the object model and available APIs. Finally, you looked at the connector architecture to build applications that span the mobile device and the server/desktop.

Between this chapter and the one preceding it, you have gotten an admittedly whirlwind tour of the RFID functionality that is in BizTalk Server 2010. Building successful RFID applications is a play in many acts, with tags and hardware and device connectivity and application integration all contributing to the mix. BizTalk, with its platform plug-and-play approach, enables robust enterprise-ready RFID applications, and we are excited about the prospects of "physical-world service-oriented architecture" and the "Internet of things" that this new capability enables.

Closing Notes

by Gijs in 't Veld

BizTalk Server is a great product; isn't it? Having worked with the product since its inception, I came to love it with the 2004 version, when the architecture and tooling was changed significantly and the product became mature enough to serve enterprises in their quest to deploy one integration product for both *application-to-application* (A2A) and *business-to-business* (B2B) integration. Since the 2004 version, BizTalk has been deployed more than 10,000 times, and it has become a serious competitor and even trendsetter in the *service-oriented architecture* (SOA) and *enterprise service bus* (ESB) world. Some of the world's largest companies use it as their mission-critical integration environment and have built successful, extremely scalable global integration services on it.

In the early days, it was hard to find information related to BizTalk. Back then, it was often the case that you were the first one to encounter an issue. Nowadays, there are BizTalk books, courses, white papers, and blogs galore, and the chance that you are the first one having a specific issue is becoming smaller and smaller. Bing "BizTalk" and you will be impressed with the sheer number of detailed results. The BizTalk community is an active community, and people all over the world working with it are sharing their experiences, and together they are responsible for building best practices.

During presentations and demos, I often tell people that BizTalk is the most complex product Microsoft has ever built (from scratch), because it involves so many moving parts and so many ways to integrate with so many different technologies. Integration is not something you'll learn overnight, and that's what makes our jobs so interesting: Not a day is the same when you work with BizTalk!

Summary and Conclusions

There is something special about this book: It has been written by an impressive group of authors from all over the world, and they all are BizTalk veterans and real authorities on their specific subjects. Real-world experience and blood, sweat, and tears have led to the creation of this book. For me, it was an honor to be the technical editor of this book (and I actually learned a thing or two, as well).

This book was written with the developer (you) in mind, and we are well aware that we have not covered every topic related to BizTalk. The idea was to create a "BizTalk Server 2010 developer reference", and it's up to you to decide whether we succeeded.

This book commenced by covering BizTalk Server's architecture and integration concepts. In-depth coverage of the foundation of the product followed (that is, schemas, maps, orchestrations, and pipelines). Lots of real-life experience went into these chapters, resulting in many tips and tricks on how to develop and test these artifacts effectively.

Then, the adapter framework and standard adapters were discussed. You learned how to build your own custom adapters and where and how to use the standard ones. *Windows Communication Foundation*'s (WCF) many uses and its extensibility came next, and the integration with Windows Azure through AppFabric was a current and interesting topic as well, describing how to involve "the cloud" in your integration architecture.

We then discussed *business activity monitoring* (BAM), a topic, together with the following chapter on the Business Rules Engine (BRE), that is often underestimated/undervalued. BAM is critical for both monitoring operations of your integration services and providing the means to implement operational *business intelligence* (BI). And I'm absolutely confident that there is no book on earth (or for that matter anywhere in our universe) that describes business rules in a depth even close to the level of this book.

BizTalk is used more and more as the core piece in the ESB in larger enterprises. Chapter 12, "ESB with BizTalk Server," described what an ESB actually is and how BizTalk can become an ESB (together with the other technologies that are part of the Microsoft Application Platform).

Chapter 13, "Administration Console Concepts," briefly introduced the concept of the Administration Console, introducing you to the new Settings Dashboard and describing how you can use it to configure, tune, and monitor your BizTalk applications and platform.

Chapter 14, "Deployment Concepts," provided good insight into how to design and manage deployments in your development, testing, acceptance and production (DTAP) environments, and more important, how to automate them.

Chapter 15, "BizTalk RFID," and Chapter 16, "BizTalk RFID Mobile," showed how you can use BizTalk RFID Server and BizTalk RFID Mobile to implement radio frequency solutions using BizTalk as the central (hub), edge, or mobile solution to read, scan, and handle physical events and how to integrate them within your "regular" BizTalk solutions.

As previously mentioned, all the chapters have a developer-centric focus and contain many real-life examples and tips and tricks.

This book is not exhaustive, however. By design, the following topics were not covered in this book:

- ▶ Infrastructure considerations

- ▶ How to implement integration patterns

- ▶ Configuration and administration

- ▶ Performance tuning

- ▶ Operations and monitoring

These are important topics, too, but just not the focus of this book. Many of these topics are discussed in various white papers and books (published recently) but do not underestimate the documentation that comes with the product, including the famous BizTalk posters.

Recommended Next Steps

After having read this book, you're probably ready to delve deeper into integration patterns. *Enterprise Integration Patterns* (Addison-Wesley Professional, 2003) is a must read before you start any integration project, and you can apply many of the patterns described directly in BizTalk Server. There are also several good books on SOA patterns that can be used to architect, design, and develop BizTalk solutions for service-oriented architectures.

Practical books have been written with "recipes" as the paradigm (problem-solution approaches), and there are also a number of specific books on detailed areas of BizTalk Server, such as mapping, RFID, and BAM.

Books on infrastructure, configuration, and administration, performance tuning, and operations and monitoring simply do not exist at the time of this writing, but there are numerous well-written and valuable white papers on these topics.

Here are a couple of trustworthy technical white papers on infrastructure, performance, and tuning:

- ▶ The "BizTalk Server Database Optimization" white paper is still the reference resource with regard to database, platform, and infrastructure tuning for high performance and throughput in BizTalk environments.

- ▶ The "BizTalk Server Performance Optimization Guide" is another good resource.

With regard to configuration, operations, and monitoring, the following publications are great resources:

▶ "The BizTalk Server Operations Guide"

▶ "BizTalk Server RFID Operations Guide"

However, no comprehensive guides are available for monitoring complete integration environments that include BizTalk Server, SQL Server, SharePoint, and other related integration technologies that are part of the Microsoft Application Platform. You can, for instance, deploy *System Center Operations Manager* (SCOM) and the various management packs, such as the BizTalk Management Pack, to monitor the health of all the different Microsoft servers in your IT landscape, but work will be needed to optimize this for your particular solution and requirements.

Another good resource for interesting, up-to-date articles about specific BizTalk topics is the *BizTalk Hotrod*. The articles in this online magazine are written by various BizTalkers from all around the world, and the magazine has a fast-growing list of subscribers.

Besides all this, it is always a good idea to subscribe to the RSS feeds of the blogs maintained by your favorite BizTalk MVPs and other BizTalk veterans, starting with the folks who created this book for you.We hope you enjoyed the book. Any feedback is welcome.

Happy BizTalking!

Index

A

How can we make this index more useful? Email us at indexes@samspublishing.com

database functoids, 118

   cross referencing, 119-120

   databases, 118-119

date/time functoids, 115

debugging, 161

   DebugView, 162-163

   inline and referenced functoids, 161

   inline functoid, 163

   runtime debugging, 161-162

deployment of custom functoids, 157-160

inline functoid, 148-151

logical functoids, 113-115

maps, 99, 102

mathematical functoids, 112-113

normal functoid, 146

properties, 109

scientific functoids, 116-117

string functoids, 111-112

Table Looping, 132-135

third-party functoids, 122

with variable number of inputs, 155-157

XSLT scripting functoids, 130

FX7400 device provider, installing BizTalk RFID, 732-734

G

Generate Delivery Receipt Request property, 278

generating

   instances, 74-75

   XSDs (XML Schema Definitions), 21

GetHashCode(), 611

governance, ESB (enterprise service bus), 662-663

GPIO functionality, BizTalk RFID, 754-756

GreaterThan, 527

GreaterThanEqual, 527

grids, maps, 96-97

Group Hub view, 678

group properties, 670-671

Group shape, orchestrations, 198

H

Halt, 531

hash codes, 611

Header Schema property, 271

helper code, 614

   .NET types, 612-613

hiding, properties, custom pipeline components, 321-322

history, of ESB Toolkit, 646

host adapters, BizTalk Server, 339

host instances, Platform Settings, 681-683

hosting

   BizTalk adapters, 342

   native WCF adapters, 389

hosts, Platform Settings, 681-682

Hour, 529

HTTP adapters, 364

   configurations, 366

   receive handlers, 364-365

   send handlers, 366

HttpRequestMessageProperty, 421-422

HttpVerbBehavior, 422-423

hub-and-spoke integration, 4-5

hub-bus integration, 6

I-J

N

O

OleDbRuleStore, 505

one-way receive, 341

one-way send, 341

on-ramp services, 660

OnTriggerPull property, 786

operations, performing via send handlers, SQL Server LoB adapter, 407-408

optimizing rule sets, 615

    controlling side effects, 615-617

    Rete algorithm, 617-618

OR, 526

OR connectives, 573-575

orchestration, BizTalk Server, 9

Orchestration Debugger, 250-255

Orchestration Designer, 175

    expression editors, 180-181

Orchestration Throttling, 676

Orchestration View, 175-176

OrchestrationEventStream, 454

orchestrations, 173-174, 657

    adding, 174

    building, 178

        BPEL, building and exporting to, 178

        BPEL compliancy, 178

        callable orchestrations, 179-180

        expression editors, 180-181

        flow, 179

        large orchestrations, 180

        xpath functions, 181-182

    calling pipelines, 218-219

    convoys. See convoys

    correlations, 229-233

    debugging, 250

        breakpoints, 250-255

        Debug and Trace, 250

        send out messages, 250

    defining, 177-178

dehydration, 228-229

delivery notification, 217-218

exception handling, 247-249

messages, 182

    creating new, 185

    defining, 182-183

    maps, 186

    multipart, 184-185

    .NET helper class, 186

    resources, 186

    restrictions on message types, 183-184

persistence points, 246-247

properties, 176-177

receive pipelines, 219-220

rehydration, 228-229

retries, 217-218

send pipelines, 220-221

shapes, 188

    Call Orchestration shape, 191-192

    Call Rules shape, 192-193

    Compensation shape, 193-194

    Construct Message shape, 194-195

    Decide shape, 195-196

    Delay shape, 196-197

    Expression shape, 197

    Group shape, 198

    Listen shape, 199-200

    Loop shape, 200-201

    Message Assignment shape, 201-203

    Parallel Actions shape, 198-199

    Port shape, 203-207

    Receive shape, 209-210

    role links, 210-211

    Scope shape, 189-191

    Send shape, 212

    Start Orchestration shape, 207-209

    Suspend shape, 212-213

data manipulation, 471

identification and definition, 473

management and retirement, 474

message and process flow, 471

monitoring and measurement, 474

policy externalization, 469-471

policy scenarios, 471

processes and policies, 468-469

refinement and elaboration, 474

storage and publishing, 474

tracking and notification, 471

verification and analysis, 474

workflow, 471-472

limits of expressivity, 567-568

recursive processing, 565-566

set-based programming, 565

Rules Engine Deployment Wizard, 511, 546-471

rules engine, ESB (enterprise service bus), 642

RuleSetInfoCollection, 628

runtime debugging, functoids, 161-162

runtime environment for services, ESB (enterprise service bus), 641

runtime governance, ESB (enterprise service bus), 662-663

S

Save method, 300

SBVR (Semantics of Business Vocabulary and Business Rules, 473

scalability, 9-10

scheduled aggregations, versus real-time, BizTalk BAM, 446-447

Schema Editor, creating XSDs (XML Schema Definitions), 22

schema elements, XSDs (XML Schema Definitions), 23

schemas, 15-16

EDI schemas, 60

FineFoods.Common.Schemas, 81-82

FineFoods.CreditCheck.Schemas, 82

FineFoods.Customers.C1701, 82-83

FineFoods.Customers.C1702, 83-84

FineFoods.Customers.Schemas, 84

FineFoods.Inventory.Schemas, 84

FineFoods.Orders.Schemas, 84-87

FineFoods.PurchaseOrders.Schema, 87

flat file schemas. *See* flat file schemas

internal schemas, 18-19

maps, 94-95

properties, 17-18

publishing, WCF Service Publishing Wizard, 392-394

SQL Server database schemas, 522-523

unit testing, 75-80

validating, 71-72

versioning, 69

transactions and downtime, 69-71

XML schemas. *See* XML schemas

existing XSDs, 20-21

generating XSDs, 21

XSD schemas, 520-521

XSDs (XML Schema Definitions), 16-17

scientific functoids, 116-117

Scope shape, orchestrations, 189-191

scripting deployment, BizTalk BAM, 462-465

Scripting functoid, 122

maps, 129-130

SDK

SQL Server LoB adapter, 404

Windows Azure AppFabric, 432

search feature, maps, 97-98

Second, 529

secure messaging, FTP adapter, 363

W

Y

Z

UNLEASHED

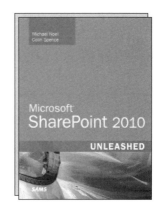

Microsoft SharePoint 2010 Unleashed
ISBN-13: 9780672333255

Microsoft Lync Server 2010 Unleashed
ISBN-13: 9780672330346

Microsoft SQL Server 2008 R2 Unleashed
ISBN-13: 9780672330568

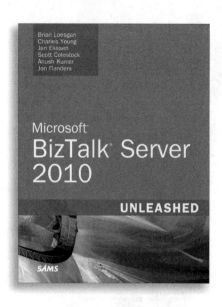